Linux®
Command Line
and Shell Scripting
Bible

Third Edition

Linux®
Command Line
and Shell Scripting
BIBLE

Third Edition

Richard Blum

Christine Bresnahan

WILEY

Linux® Command Line and Shell Scripting Bible, Third Edition

Published by
John Wiley & Sons, Inc.
10475 Crosspoint Boulevard
Indianapolis, IN 46256
www.wiley.com

Copyright © 2015 by John Wiley & Sons, Inc., Indianapolis, Indiana

Published simultaneously in Canada

ISBN: 978-1-118-98384-3
ISBN: 978-1-118-98385-0 (ebk)
ISBN: 978-1-118-98419-2 (ebk)

Manufactured in the United States of America

C10005759_110218

For general information on our other products and services please contact our Customer Care Department within the United States at (877) 762-2974, outside the United States at (317) 572-3993 or fax (317) 572-4002.

Wiley publishes in a variety of print and electronic formats and by print-on-demand. Some material included with standard print versions of this book may not be included in e-books or in print-on-demand. If this book refers to media such as a CD or DVD that is not included in the version you purchased, you may download this material at http://booksupport.wiley.com. For more information about Wiley products, visit www.wiley.com.

Library of Congress Control Number: 2014954688

About the Authors

Richard Blum has worked in the IT industry for more than 20 years as both a systems and network administrator and has published numerous Linux and open-source books. He has administered UNIX, Linux, Novell, and Microsoft servers, as well as helped design and maintain a 3,500-user network utilizing Cisco switches and routers. He has used Linux servers and shell scripts to perform automated network monitoring and has written shell scripts in most of the common Linux shell environments. Rich is an online instructor for an Introduction to Linux course that is used by colleges and universities across the United States. When he isn't being a computer nerd, Rich plays electric bass in a couple of different church worship bands, and enjoys spending time with his wife, Barbara, and two daughters, Katie Jane and Jessica.

Christine Bresnahan starting working with computers more than 25 years ago in the IT industry as a system administrator. Christine is currently an Adjunct Professor at Ivy Tech Community College in Indianapolis, Indiana. She teaches classes on Linux system administration, Linux security, and Windows security.

About the Technical Editor

Kevin E. Ryan holds a bachelor's degree in electrical engineering technology from Purdue University and has served as system administrator for a number of computing platforms including HP-UX, Solaris, and Red Hat Linux. He's also been involved with system planning, database management and application programming. When not pursuing his technical endeavors, Kevin enjoys reading, baseball, and camping with his wife and their fearless Papillon.

Credits

Associate Publisher
Jim Minatel

Project Editor
Martin V. Minner

Technical Editor
Kevin E. Ryan

Production Manager
Kathleen Wisor

Copy Editor
Gwenette Gaddis

Manager of Content Development and Assembly
Mary Beth Wakefield

Marketing Director
David Mayhew

Marketing Manager
Carrie Sherrill

Professional Technology and Strategy Director
Barry Pruett

Business Manager
Amy Knies

Project Coordinator, Cover
Patrick Redmond

Proofreader
Nancy Carrasco

Indexer
Robert Swanson

Cover Designer
Wiley

Cover Image
iStockphoto.com / Aleksandar Velasevic

Acknowledgments

First, all glory and praise go to God, Who through His Son, Jesus Christ, makes all things possible, and gives us the gift of eternal life.

Many thanks go to the fantastic team of people at John Wiley & Sons for their outstanding work on this project. Thanks to Mary James, the former acquisitions editor, for offering us the opportunity to work on this book. Also thanks to Marty Minner, the project editor, for keeping things on track and making this book more presentable. Thanks, Marty, for all your hard work and diligence. The technical editor, Kevin E. Ryan, did a wonderful job of double-checking all the work in the book, plus making suggestions to improve the content. Thanks to Gwenette Gaddis, the copy editor, for her endless patience and diligence to make our work readable. We would also like to thank Carole McClendon at Waterside Productions, Inc., for arranging this opportunity for us, and for helping us out in our writing careers. In addition, we would like to give a special thank you to H.L. Craft, who produced several diagrams for our chapters.

Christine would like to thank her husband, Timothy, for his encouragement, patience, and willingness to listen, even when he has no idea what she is talking about.

Contents at a Glance

Contents at a Glance

Contents

Contents

Contents

Contents

Contents

Contents

Contents

Contents

Contents

Introduction

Welcome to the third edition of *Linux Command Line and Shell Scripting Bible*. Like all books in the *Bible* series, you can expect to find both hands-on tutorials and real-world information, as well as reference and background information that provide a context for what you are learning. This book is a fairly comprehensive resource on the Linux command line and shell commands. By the time you have completed *Linux Command Line and Shell Scripting Bible*, you will be well prepared to write your own shell scripts that can automate practically any task on your Linux system.

Who Should Read This Book

If you're a system administrator in a Linux environment, you'll benefit greatly by knowing how to write shell scripts. The book doesn't walk you through the process of setting up a Linux system, but after you have it running, you'll want to start automating some of the routine administrative tasks. That's where shell scripting comes in, and that's where this book helps you out. This book demonstrates how to automate any administrative task using shell scripts, from monitoring system statistics and data files to generating reports for your boss.

If you're a home Linux enthusiast, you'll also benefit from *Linux Command Line and Shell Scripting Bible*. Nowadays, it's easy to get lost in the graphical world of pre-built widgets. Most desktop Linux distributions try their best to hide the Linux system from the typical user. However, sometimes you must know what's going on under the hood. This book shows you how to access the Linux command line prompt and what to do when you get there. Often, performing simple tasks, such as file management, can be done more quickly from the command line than from a fancy graphical interface. You can use a wealth of commands from the command line, and this book shows you how to use them.

How This Book Is Organized

This book leads you through the basics of the Linux command line and into more complicated topics, such as creating your own shell scripts. The book is divided into four parts, each one building on the previous parts.

Part I assumes that you either have a Linux system running or are looking into getting a Linux system. Chapter 1, "Starting with Linux Shells," describes the parts of a total Linux system and shows how the shell fits in. After describing the basics of the Linux system, this part continues with the following:

- Using a terminal emulation package to access the shell (Chapter 2)
- Introducing the basic shell commands (Chapter 3)
- Using more advanced shell commands to peek at system information (Chapter 4)
- Understanding what the shell is used for (Chapter 5)
- Working with shell variables to manipulate data (Chapter 6)
- Understanding the Linux filesystem and security (Chapter 7)
- Working with Linux filesystems from the command line (Chapter 8)
- Installing and updating software from the command line (Chapter 9)
- Using the Linux editors to start writing shell scripts (Chapter 10)

In Part II, you begin writing shell scripts. As you go through the chapters, you'll do the following:

- Learn how to create and run shell scripts (Chapter 11)
- Alter the program flow in a shell script (Chapter 12)
- Iterate through code sections (Chapter 13)
- Handle data from the user in your scripts (Chapter 14)
- See different methods for storing and displaying data from your Script (Chapter 15)
- Control how and when your shell scripts run on the system (Chapter 16)

Part III dives into more advanced areas of shell script programming, including these things:

- Creating your own functions to use in all your scripts (Chapter 17)
- Utilizing the Linux graphical desktop for interacting with your script users (Chapter 18)
- Using advanced Linux commands to filter and parse data files (Chapter 19)
- Using regular expressions to define data (Chapter 20)
- Learning advanced methods of manipulating data in your scripts (Chapter 21)
- Generating reports from raw data (Chapter 22)
- Modifying your shell scripts to run in other Linux shells (Chapter 23)

The last section of the book, Part IV, demonstrates how to use shell scripts in real-world environments. In this part, you will learn these things:

- How to put all the scripting features together to write your own scripts (Chapter 24)

- How to store and retrieve data using databases, access data on the Internet, and send e-mail messages (Chapter 25)
- Write more advanced shell scripts to interact on your Linux system (Chapter 26)

Cautions, Tips, and Notes

You will find many different organizational and typographical features throughout this book designed to help you get the most of the information.

CAUTION

This information is important and is set off in a separate paragraph with a special icon. Cautions provide information about things to watch out for, whether simply inconvenient or potentially hazardous to your data or systems.

TIP

Tips provide helpful advice to make your work easier and more effective. Tips may suggest a solution to a problem or a better way to accomplish a task.

NOTE

Notes provide additional, ancillary information that is helpful, but somewhat outside of the current presentation of information.

Downloadable code

You can obtain the book's code files at www.wiley.com/go/linuxcommandline.

Minimum Requirements

Linux Command Line and Shell Scripting Bible doesn't focus on any specific Linux distribution, so you can follow along in the book using any Linux system you have available. The bulk of the book references the bash shell, which is the default shell for most Linux systems.

Where to Go from Here

After you've finished reading *Linux Command Line and Shell Scripting Bible*, you're well on your way to incorporating Linux commands in your daily Linux work. In the ever-changing world of Linux, it's always a good idea to stay in touch with new developments. Often, Linux distributions change, adding new features and removing older ones. To keep your knowledge of Linux fresh, always stay well-informed. Find a good Linux forum site and monitor what's happening in the Linux world. Many popular Linux news sites, such as Slashdot and Distrowatch, provide up-to-the-minute information about new advances in Linux.

Part I

The Linux Command Line

IN THIS PART

Starting with Linux Shells

B efore you can dive into working with the Linux command line and shells, you should first understand what Linux is, where it came from, and how it works. This chapter walks you through what Linux is and explains where the shell and command line fit in the overall Linux picture.

What Is Linux?

If you've never worked with Linux before, you may be confused about why so many different versions are available. I'm sure you have been confused by various terms such as distribution, LiveCD, and GNU when looking at Linux packages. Wading through the world of Linux for the first time can be a tricky experience. This chapter takes some of the mystery out of the Linux system before you start working on commands and scripts.

First, four main parts make up a Linux system:

- The Linux kernel
- The GNU utilities
- A graphical desktop environment
- Application software

Each of these parts has a specific job in the Linux system. No part is very useful by itself. Figure 1-1 shows a basic diagram of how the parts fit together to create the overall Linux system.

FIGURE 1-1

The Linux system

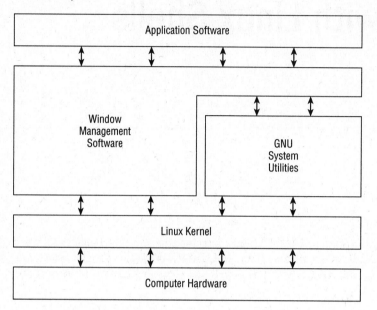

This section describes these four main parts in detail and gives you an overview of how they work together to create a complete Linux system.

Looking into the Linux Kernel

The core of the Linux system is the *kernel*. The kernel controls all the hardware and software on the computer system, allocating hardware when necessary and executing software when required.

If you've been following the Linux world at all, no doubt you've heard the name Linus Torvalds. Linus is the person responsible for creating the first Linux kernel software when he was a student at the University of Helsinki. He intended it to be a copy of the Unix system, at the time a popular operating system used at many universities.

After developing the Linux kernel, Linus released it to the Internet community and solicited suggestions for improving it. This simple process started a revolution in the world of computer operating systems. Soon Linus was receiving suggestions from students as well as professional programmers from around the world.

Allowing anyone to change programming code in the kernel would result in complete chaos. To simplify things, Linus acted as a central point for all improvement suggestions. It was ultimately Linus's decision whether or not to incorporate suggested code in the kernel.

This same concept is still in place with the Linux kernel code, except that instead of just Linus controlling the kernel code, a team of developers has taken on the task.

The kernel is primarily responsible for four main functions:

- System memory management
- Software program management
- Hardware management
- Filesystem management

The following sections explore each of these functions in more detail.

System Memory Management

One of the primary functions of the operating system kernel is memory management. Not only does the kernel manage the physical memory available on the server, but it can also create and manage virtual memory, or memory that does not actually exist.

It does this by using space on the hard disk, called the *swap space*. The kernel swaps the contents of virtual memory locations back and forth from the swap space to the actual physical memory. This allows the system to think there is more memory available than what physically exists, as shown in Figure 1-2.

FIGURE 1-2

The Linux system memory map

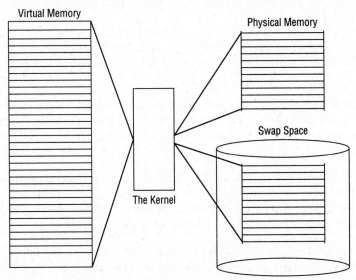

The memory locations are grouped into blocks called *pages*. The kernel locates each page of memory either in the physical memory or the swap space. The kernel then maintains a table of the memory pages that indicates which pages are in physical memory and which pages are swapped out to disk.

The kernel keeps track of which memory pages are in use and automatically copies memory pages that have not been accessed for a period of time to the swap space area (called *swapping out*), even if there's other memory available. When a program wants to access a memory page that has been swapped out, the kernel must make room for it in physical memory by swapping out a different memory page and swapping in the required page from the swap space. Obviously, this process takes time and can slow down a running process. The process of swapping out memory pages for running applications continues for as long as the Linux system is running.

Software Program Management

The Linux operating system calls a running program a *process*. A process can run in the foreground, displaying output on a display, or it can run in the background, behind the scenes. The kernel controls how the Linux system manages all the processes running on the system.

The kernel creates the first process, called the *init process*, to start all other processes on the system. When the kernel starts, it loads the init process into virtual memory. As the kernel starts each additional process, it gives it a unique area in virtual memory to store the data and code that the process uses.

Some Linux implementations contain a table of processes to start automatically on bootup. On Linux systems, this table is usually located in the special file /etc/inittabs.

Other systems (such as the popular Ubuntu Linux distribution) utilize the /etc/init.d folder, which contains scripts for starting and stopping individual applications at boot time. The scripts are started via entries under the /etc/rcX.d folders, where X is a *run level*.

The Linux operating system uses an init system that utilizes run levels. A run level can be used to direct the init process to run only certain types of processes, as defined in the /etc/inittabs file or the /etc/rcX.d folders. There are five init run levels in the Linux operating system.

At run level 1, only the basic system processes are started, along with one console terminal process. This is called *single-user* mode. Single-user mode is most often used for emergency filesystem maintenance when something is broken. Obviously, in this mode, only one person (usually the administrator) can log in to the system to manipulate data.

The standard init run level is 3. At this run level, most application software, such as network support software, is started. Another popular run level in Linux is run level 5. This is the run level where the system starts the graphical X Window software and allows you to log in using a graphical desktop window.

The Linux system can control the overall system functionality by controlling the init run level. By changing the run level from 3 to 5, the system can change from a console-based system to an advanced, graphical X Window system.

In Chapter 4, you'll see how to use the ps command to view the processes currently running on the Linux system.

Hardware Management

Still another responsibility for the kernel is hardware management. Any device that the Linux system must communicate with needs driver code inserted inside the kernel code. The driver code allows the kernel to pass data back and forth to the device, acting as a middle man between applications and the hardware. Two methods are used for inserting device driver code in the Linux kernel:

- Drivers compiled in the kernel
- Driver modules added to the kernel

Previously, the only way to insert device driver code was to recompile the kernel. Each time you added a new device to the system, you had to recompile the kernel code. This process became even more inefficient as Linux kernels supported more hardware. Fortunately, Linux developers devised a better method to insert driver code into the running kernel.

Programmers developed the concept of kernel modules to allow you to insert driver code into a running kernel without having to recompile the kernel. Also, a kernel module could be removed from the kernel when the device was finished being used. This greatly simplified and expanded using hardware with Linux.

The Linux system identifies hardware devices as special files, called *device files*. There are three classifications of device files:

- Character
- Block
- Network

Character device files are for devices that can only handle data one character at a time. Most types of modems and terminals are created as character files. Block files are for devices that can handle data in large blocks at a time, such as disk drives.

The network file types are used for devices that use packets to send and receive data. This includes network cards and a special loopback device that allows the Linux system to communicate with itself using common network programming protocols.

Linux creates special files, called *nodes*, for each device on the system. All communication with the device is performed through the device node. Each node has a unique number pair that identifies it to the Linux kernel. The number pair includes a major and a minor device number. Similar devices are grouped into the same major device number. The minor device number is used to identify a specific device within the major device group.

Filesystem Management

Unlike some other operating systems, the Linux kernel can support different types of filesystems to read and write data to and from hard drives. Besides having over a dozen filesystems of its own, Linux can read and write to and from filesystems used by other operating systems, such as Microsoft Windows. The kernel must be compiled with support for all types of filesystems that the system will use. Table 1-1 lists the standard filesystems that a Linux system can use to read and write data.

TABLE 1-1 Linux Filesystems

Filesystem	Description
ext	Linux Extended filesystem — the original Linux filesystem
ext2	Second extended filesystem, provided advanced features over ext
ext3	Third extended filesystem, supports journaling
ext4	Fourth extended filesystem, supports advanced journaling
hpfs	OS/2 high-performance filesystem
jfs	IBM's journaling filesystem
iso9660	ISO 9660 filesystem (CD-ROMs)
minix	MINIX filesystem
msdos	Microsoft FAT16
ncp	Netware filesystem
nfs	Network File System
ntfs	Support for Microsoft NT filesystem
proc	Access to system information
ReiserFS	Advanced Linux filesystem for better performance and disk recovery
smb	Samba SMB filesystem for network access
sysv	Older Unix filesystem
ufs	BSD filesystem
umsdos	Unix-like filesystem that resides on top of msdos
vfat	Windows 95 filesystem (FAT32)
XFS	High-performance 64-bit journaling filesystem

Any hard drive that a Linux server accesses must be formatted using one of the filesystem types listed in Table 1-1.

The Linux kernel interfaces with each filesystem using the Virtual File System (VFS). This provides a standard interface for the kernel to communicate with any type of filesystem. VFS caches information in memory as each filesystem is mounted and used.

The GNU Utilities

Besides having a kernel to control hardware devices, a computer operating system needs utilities to perform standard functions, such as controlling files and programs. While Linus created the Linux system kernel, he had no system utilities to run on it. Fortunately for him, at the same time he was working, a group of people were working together on the Internet trying to develop a standard set of computer system utilities that mimicked the popular Unix operating system.

The GNU organization (GNU stands for GNU's Not Unix) developed a complete set of Unix utilities, but had no kernel system to run them on. These utilities were developed under a software philosophy called open source software (OSS).

The concept of OSS allows programmers to develop software and then release it to the world with no licensing fees attached. Anyone can use the software, modify it, or incorporate it into his or her own system without having to pay a license fee. Uniting Linus's Linux kernel with the GNU operating system utilities created a complete, functional, free operating system.

While the bundling of the Linux kernel and GNU utilities is often just called Linux, you will see some Linux purists on the Internet refer to it as the GNU/Linux system to give credit to the GNU organization for its contributions to the cause.

The Core GNU Utilities

The GNU project was mainly designed for Unix system administrators to have a Unix-like environment available. This focus resulted in the project porting many common Unix system command line utilities. The core bundle of utilities supplied for Linux systems is called the *coreutils* package.

The GNU coreutils package consists of three parts:

- Utilities for handling files
- Utilities for manipulating text
- Utilities for managing processes

Each of these three main groups of utilities contains several utility programs that are invaluable to the Linux system administrator and programmer. This book covers each of the utilities contained in the GNU coreutils package in detail.

The Shell

The GNU/Linux shell is a special interactive utility. It provides a way for users to start programs, manage files on the filesystem, and manage processes running on the Linux system. The core of the shell is the command prompt. The command prompt is the interactive part of the shell. It allows you to enter text commands, and then it interprets the commands and executes them in the kernel.

The shell contains a set of internal commands that you use to control things such as copying files, moving files, renaming files, displaying the programs currently running on the system, and stopping programs running on the system. Besides the internal commands, the shell also allows you to enter the name of a program at the command prompt. The shell passes the program name off to the kernel to start it.

You can also group shell commands into files to execute as a program. Those files are called *shell scripts*. Any command that you can execute from the command line can be placed in a shell script and run as a group of commands. This provides great flexibility in creating utilities for commonly run commands, or processes that require several commands grouped together.

There are quite a few Linux shells available to use on a Linux system. Different shells have different characteristics, some being more useful for creating scripts and some being more useful for managing processes. The default shell used in all Linux distributions is the bash shell. The bash shell was developed by the GNU project as a replacement for the standard Unix shell, called the Bourne shell (after its creator). The bash shell name is a play on this wording, referred to as the "Bourne again shell."

In addition to the bash shell, we will cover several other popular shells in this book. Table 1-2 lists the different shells we will examine.

TABLE 1-2 Linux Shells

Shell	Description
ash	A simple, lightweight shell that runs in low-memory environments but has full compatibility with the bash shell
korn	A programming shell compatible with the Bourne shell but supporting advanced programming features like associative arrays and floating-point arithmetic
tcsh	A shell that incorporates elements from the C programming language into shell scripts
zsh	An advanced shell that incorporates features from bash, tcsh, and korn, providing advanced programming features, shared history files, and themed prompts

Most Linux distributions include more than one shell, although usually they pick one of them to be the default. If your Linux distribution includes multiple shells, feel free to experiment with different shells and see which one fits your needs.

The Linux Desktop Environment

In the early days of Linux (the early 1990s) all that was available was a simple text interface to the Linux operating system. This text interface allowed administrators to start programs, control program operations, and move files around on the system.

With the popularity of Microsoft Windows, computer users expected more than the old text interface to work with. This spurred more development in the OSS community, and the Linux graphical desktops emerged.

Linux is famous for being able to do things in more than one way, and no place is this more relevant than in graphical desktops. There are a plethora of graphical desktops you can choose from in Linux. The following sections describe a few of the more popular ones.

The X Window System

Two basic elements control your video environment: the video card in your PC and your monitor. To display fancy graphics on your computer, the Linux software needs to know how to talk to both of them. The X Window software is the core element in presenting graphics.

The X Window software is a low-level program that works directly with the video card and monitor in the PC, and it controls how Linux applications can present fancy windows and graphics on your computer.

Linux isn't the only operating system that uses X Window; versions are written for many different operating systems. In the Linux world, several different software packages can implement it.

The most popular package is X.org. It provides an open source software implementation of the X Window system and supports many of the newer video cards used today.

Two other X Window packages are gaining in popularity. The Fedora Linux distribution is experimenting with the Wayland software, and the Ubuntu Linux distribution has developed the Mir display server for use with its desktop environment.

When you first install a Linux distribution, it attempts to detect your video card and monitor, and then it creates an X Window configuration file that contains the required information. During installation, you may notice a time when the installation program scans your monitor for supported video modes. Sometimes, this causes your monitor to go blank for a few seconds. Because there are lots of different types of video cards and monitors, this process can take a while to complete.

The core X Window software produces a graphical display environment, but nothing else. Although this is fine for running individual applications, it is not useful for day-to-day computer use. No desktop environment allows users to manipulate files or launch programs. To do that, you need a desktop environment on top of the X Window system software.

The KDE Desktop

The K Desktop Environment (KDE) was first released in 1996 as an open source project to produce a graphical desktop similar to the Microsoft Windows environment. The KDE desktop incorporates all the features you are probably familiar with if you are a Windows user. Figure 1-3 shows a sample KDE 4 desktop running in the openSUSE Linux distribution.

FIGURE 1-3

The KDE 4 desktop on an openSUSE Linux system

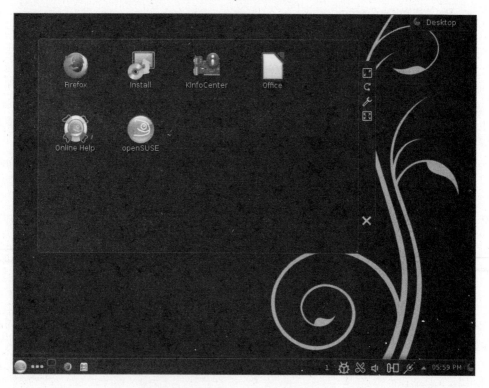

The KDE desktop allows you to place both application and file icons in a special area on the desktop. If you click an application icon, the Linux system starts the application. If you click a file icon, the KDE desktop attempts to determine what application to start to handle the file.

The bar at the bottom of the desktop is called the Panel. The Panel consists of four parts:

- **The K menu:** Much like the Windows Start menu, the K menu contains links to start installed applications.
- **Program shortcuts:** These are quick links to start applications directly from the Panel.
- **The taskbar:** The taskbar shows icons for applications currently running on the desktop.
- **Applets:** These are small applications that have an icon in the Panel that often can change depending on information from the application.

The Panel features are similar to what you would find in Windows. In addition to the desktop features, the KDE project has produced a wide assortment of applications that run in the KDE environment.

The GNOME Desktop

The GNU Network Object Model Environment (GNOME) is another popular Linux desktop environment. First released in 1999, GNOME has become the default desktop environment for many Linux distributions. (However, the most popular is Red Hat Linux.)

Although GNOME chose to depart from the standard Microsoft Windows look-and-feel, it incorporates many features that most Windows users are comfortable with:

- A desktop area for icons
- A panel area for showing running applications
- Drag-and-drop capabilities

Figure 1-4 shows the standard GNOME desktop used in the CentOS Linux distribution.

Not to be outdone by KDE, the GNOME developers have also produced a host of graphical applications that integrate with the GNOME desktop.

The Unity Desktop

If you're using the Ubuntu Linux distribution, you'll notice that it's somewhat different from both the KDE and GNOME desktop environments. Canonical, the company responsible for developing Ubuntu, has decided to embark on its own Linux desktop environment, called Unity.

FIGURE 1-4

A GNOME desktop on a CentOS Linux system

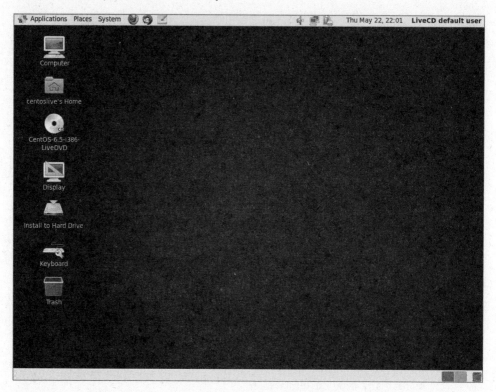

The Unity desktop gets its name from the goal of the project — to provide a single desktop experience for workstations, tablet devices, and mobile devices. The Unity desktop works the same whether you're running Ubuntu on a workstation or a mobile phone! Figure 1-5 shows an example of the Unity desktop in Ubuntu 14.04 LTS.

Other Desktops

The downside to a graphical desktop environment is that it requires a fair amount of system resources to operate properly. In the early days of Linux, a hallmark and selling feature of Linux was its ability to operate on older, less powerful PCs that the newer Microsoft desktop products couldn't run on. However, with the popularity of KDE and GNOME desktops, this has changed, because it takes just as much memory to run a KDE or GNOME desktop as the latest Microsoft desktop environment.

FIGURE 1-5

The Unity desktop on the Ubuntu Linux distribution

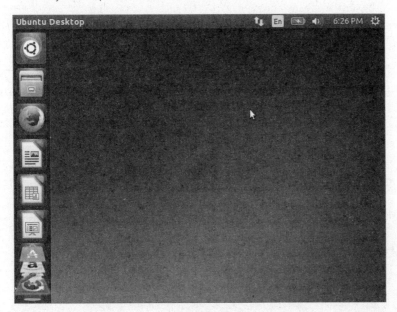

If you have an older PC, don't be discouraged. The Linux developers have banded together to take Linux back to its roots. They've created several low-memory–oriented graphical desktop applications that provide basic features that run perfectly fine on older PCs.

Although these graphical desktops don't have a plethora of applications designed around them, they still run many basic graphical applications that support features such as word processing, spreadsheets, databases, drawing, and, of course, multimedia support.

Table 1-3 shows some of the smaller Linux graphical desktop environments that can be used on lower-powered PCs and laptops.

TABLE 1-3 **Other Linux Graphical Desktops**

Desktop	Description
Fluxbox	A bare-bones desktop that doesn't include a Panel, only a pop-up menu to launch applications
Xfce	A desktop that's similar to the KDE desktop, but with fewer graphics for low-memory environments
JWM	Joe's Window Manager, a very lightweight desktop ideal for low-memory and low-disk space environments
Fvwm	Supports some advanced desktop features such as virtual desktops and Panels, but runs in low-memory environments
fvwm95	Derived from fvwm, but made to look like a Windows 95 desktop

These graphical desktop environments are not as fancy as the KDE and GNOME desktops, but they provide basic graphical functionality just fine. Figure 1-6 shows what the JWM desktop used in the Puppy Linux antiX distribution looks like.

FIGURE 1-6

The JWM desktop as seen in the Puppy Linux distribution

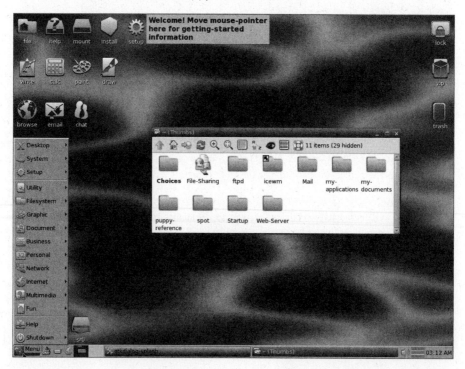

If you are using an older PC, try a Linux distribution that uses one of these desktops and see what happens. You may be pleasantly surprised.

Linux Distributions

Now that you have seen the four main components required for a complete Linux system, you may be wondering how you are going to get them all put together to make a Linux system. Fortunately, other people have already done that for you.

A complete Linux system package is called a *distribution*. Many different Linux distributions are available to meet just about any computing requirement you could have. Most distributions are customized for a specific user group, such as business users, multimedia enthusiasts, software developers, or average home users. Each customized distribution includes the software packages required to support specialized functions, such as audio- and video-editing software for multimedia enthusiasts, or compilers and integrated development environments (IDEs) for software developers.

The different Linux distributions are often divided into three categories:

- Full core Linux distributions
- Specialized distributions
- LiveCD test distributions

The following sections describe these different types of Linux distributions and show some examples of Linux distributions in each category.

Core Linux Distributions

A core Linux distribution contains a kernel, one or more graphical desktop environments, and just about every Linux application that is available, precompiled for the kernel. It provides one-stop shopping for a complete Linux installation. Table 1-4 shows some of the more popular core Linux distributions.

TABLE 1-4 **Core Linux Distributions**

Distribution	Description
Slackware	One of the original Linux distribution sets, popular with Linux geeks
Red Hat	A commercial business distribution used mainly for Internet servers
Fedora	A spin-off from Red Hat but designed for home use

Continues

TABLE 1-4   *(continued)*

Distribution	Description
Gentoo	A distribution designed for advanced Linux users, containing only Linux source code
openSUSE	Different distributions for business and home use
Debian	Popular with Linux experts and commercial Linux products

In the early days of Linux, a distribution was released as a set of floppy disks. You had to download groups of files and then copy them onto disks. It would usually take 20 or more disks to make an entire distribution! Needless to say, this was a painful experience.

Nowadays, with home computers commonly having CD and DVD players built in, Linux distributions are released as either a CD set or a single DVD. This makes installing Linux much easier.

However, beginners still often run into problems when they install one of the core Linux distributions. To cover just about any situation in which someone might want to use Linux, a single distribution must include lots of application software. They include everything from high-end Internet database servers to common games. Because of the quantity of applications available for Linux, a complete distribution often takes four or more CDs.

Although having lots of options available in a distribution is great for Linux geeks, it can become a nightmare for beginning Linux users. Most distributions ask a series of questions during the installation process to determine which applications to load by default, what hardware is connected to the PC, and how to configure the hardware. Beginners often find these questions confusing. As a result, they often either load way too many programs on their computer or don't load enough and later discover that their computer won't do what they want it to.

Fortunately for beginners, there's a much simpler way to install Linux.

Specialized Linux Distributions

A new subgroup of Linux distributions has started to appear. These are typically based on one of the main distributions but contain only a subset of applications that would make sense for a specific area of use.

In addition to providing specialized software (such as only office products for business users), customized Linux distributions also attempt to help beginning Linux users by autodetecting and autoconfiguring common hardware devices. This makes installing Linux a much more enjoyable process.

Table 1-5 shows some of the specialized Linux distributions available and what they specialize in.

TABLE 1-5   Specialized Linux Distributions

Distribution	Description
CentOS	A free distribution built from the Red Hat Enterprise Linux source code
Ubuntu	A free distribution for school and home use
PCLinuxOS	A free distribution for home and office use
Mint	A free distribution for home entertainment use
dyne:bolic	A free distribution designed for audio and MIDI applications
Puppy Linux	A free small distribution that runs well on older PCs

That's just a small sampling of specialized Linux distributions. There are literally hundreds of specialized Linux distributions, and more are popping up all the time on the Internet. No matter what your specialty, you'll probably find a Linux distribution made for you.

Many of the specialized Linux distributions are based on the Debian Linux distribution. They use the same installation files as Debian but package only a small fraction of a full-blown Debian system.

The Linux LiveCD

A relatively new phenomenon in the Linux world is the bootable Linux CD distribution. This lets you see what a Linux system is like without actually installing it. Most modern PCs can boot from a CD instead of the standard hard drive. To take advantage of this, some Linux distributions create a bootable CD that contains a sample Linux system (called a *Linux LiveCD*). Because of the limitations of the single CD size, the sample can't contain a complete Linux system, but you'd be surprised at all the software they can cram in there. The result is that you can boot your PC from the CD and run a Linux distribution without having to install anything on your hard drive!

This is an excellent way to test various Linux distributions without having to mess with your PC. Just pop in a CD and boot! All the Linux software will run directly from the CD. You can download lots of Linux LiveCDs from the Internet and burn onto a CD to test drive.

Table 1-6 shows some popular Linux LiveCDs that are available.

TABLE 1-6   Linux LiveCD Distributions

Distribution	Description
Knoppix	A German Linux, the first Linux LiveCD developed
PCLinuxOS	Full-blown Linux distribution on a LiveCD
Ubuntu	A worldwide Linux project, designed for many languages
Slax	A live Linux CD based on Slackware Linux
Puppy Linux	A full-featured Linux designed for older PCs

You may notice a familiarity in this table. Many specialized Linux distributions also have a Linux LiveCD version. Some Linux LiveCD distributions, such as Ubuntu, allow you to install the Linux distribution directly from the LiveCD. This enables you to boot with the CD, test drive the Linux distribution, and then if you like it, install it on your hard drive. This feature is extremely handy and user-friendly.

As with all good things, Linux LiveCDs have a few drawbacks. Because you access everything from the CD, applications run more slowly, especially if you're using older, slower computers and CD drives. Also, because you can't write to the CD, any changes you make to the Linux system will be gone the next time you reboot.

But advances are being made in the Linux LiveCD world that will help to solve some of these problems. These advances include the ability to:

- Copy Linux system files from the CD to memory
- Copy system files to a file on the hard drive
- Store system settings on a USB memory stick
- Store user settings on a USB memory stick

Some Linux LiveCDs, such as Puppy Linux, are designed with a minimum number of Linux system files. The LiveCD boot scripts copy them directly into memory when the CD boots. This allows you to remove the CD from the computer as soon as Linux boots. Not only does this make your applications run much faster (because applications run faster from memory), but it also gives you a free CD tray to use for ripping audio CDs or playing video DVDs from the software included in Puppy Linux.

Other Linux LiveCDs use an alternative method that allows you to remove the CD from the tray after booting. It involves copying the core Linux files onto the Windows hard drive as a single file. After the CD boots, it looks for that file and reads the system files from it. The dyne:bolic Linux LiveCD uses this technique, which is called docking. Of course, you must copy the system file to your hard drive before you can boot from the CD.

A very popular technique for storing data from a live Linux CD session is to use a common USB memory stick (also called a flash drive or a thumb drive). Just about every Linux LiveCD can recognize a plugged-in USB memory stick (even if the stick is formatted for Windows) and read and write files to and from it. This allows you to boot a Linux LiveCD, use the Linux applications to create files, store those files on your memory stick, and then access them from your Windows applications later (or from a different computer). How cool is that?

Summary

This chapter discussed the Linux system and the basics of how it works. The Linux kernel is the core of the system, controlling how memory, programs, and hardware all interact with one another. The GNU utilities are also an important piece in the Linux system. The Linux shell, which is the main focus of this book, is part of the GNU core utilities. The chapter also discussed the final piece of a Linux system, the Linux desktop environment. Things have changed over the years, and Linux now supports several graphical desktop environments.

The chapter also discussed the various Linux distributions. A Linux distribution bundles the various parts of a Linux system into a simple package that you can easily install on your PC. The Linux distribution world consists of full-blown Linux distributions that include just about every application imaginable, as well as specialized Linux distributions that include applications focused only on a special function. The Linux LiveCD craze has created another group of Linux distributions that allow you to easily test-drive Linux without even having to install it on your hard drive.

In the next chapter, you look at what you need to start your command line and shell scripting experience. You'll see what you need to do to get to the Linux shell utility from your fancy graphical desktop environment. These days, that's not always an easy thing.

Getting to the Shell

I n the old days of Linux, all you had to work with was the shell. System administrators, programmers, and system users all sat at something called a Linux console terminal entering shell commands and viewing text output. These days, with graphical desktop environments, it's getting harder to find a shell prompt on the system in order to enter shell commands. This chapter discusses what is required to reach a command line environment. It walks you through the terminal emulation packages that you may run into in the various Linux distributions.

Reaching the Command Line

Before the days of graphical desktops, the only way to interact with a Unix system was through a text *command line interface* (CLI) provided by the shell. The CLI allowed text input only and could display only text and rudimentary graphics output.

Because of these restrictions, output devices were not very fancy. Often, you needed only a simple dumb terminal to interact with the Unix system. A dumb terminal was usually nothing more than a monitor and keyboard connected to the Unix system via a communication cable (usually a multi-wire serial cable). This simple combination provided an easy way to enter text data into the Unix system and view text results.

As you well know, things are significantly different in today's Linux environment. Just about every Linux distribution uses some type of graphical desktop environment. However, to enter shell commands, you still need a text display to access the shell's CLI. The problem now is getting to one. Sometimes finding a way to get a CLI in a Linux distribution is not an easy task.

Console Terminals

One way to get to a CLI is to take the Linux system out of graphical desktop mode and place it in text mode. This provides nothing more than a simple shell CLI on the monitor, just like the days before graphical desktops. This mode is called the *Linux console* because it emulates the old days of a hard-wired console terminal and is a direct interface to the Linux system.

When the Linux system starts, it automatically creates several *virtual consoles*. A virtual console is a terminal session that runs in Linux system memory. Instead of having several dumb terminals connected to the computer, most Linux distributions start five or six (or sometimes even more) virtual consoles that you can access from a single computer keyboard and monitor.

Graphical Terminals

The alternative to using a virtual console terminal is to use a *terminal emulation package* from within the Linux graphical desktop environment. A terminal emulation package simulates working on a console terminal, but within a desktop graphical window. Figure 2-1 shows an example of a terminal emulator running in a Linux graphical desktop environment.

FIGURE 2-1

A simple terminal emulator running on a Linux desktop

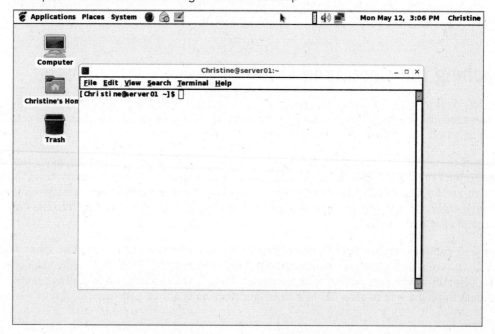

Graphical terminal emulation is responsible only for a portion of the Linux graphical experience. As a whole, the experience is accomplished via several components, including graphical terminal emulation software (called a *client*). Table 2-1 shows the different components in the Linux graphical desktop environment.

TABLE 2-1 **Graphical Interface Elements**

Name	Examples	Description
Client	Graphical terminal emulator, desktop environment, network browser	An application that requests graphical services
Display Server	Mir, Wayland Compositor, Xserver	Element that manages the display (screen) and the input devices (keyboard, mouse, touch screen)
Window Manager	Compiz, Metacity, Kwin	Element that adds borders to windows and provides features to move and manage windows
Widgets Library	Athena(Xaw), X Intrinsics	Element that adds menus and appearance items for desktop environment clients

For dealing with the command line from the desktop, the focus is on the graphical terminal emulator. You can think of graphical terminal emulators as CLI terminals "in the GUI" and virtual console terminals as CLI terminals "outside the GUI." Understanding the various terminals and their features can enhance your command line experience.

Accessing CLI via a Linux Console Terminal

In the early days of Linux, when you booted up your system you would see a login prompt on your monitor, and that's all. As mentioned earlier, this is called the Linux console. It was the only place you could enter commands for the system.

Even though several virtual consoles are created at boot time, many Linux distributions switch to a graphical environment after the boot sequence completes. This provides the user with a graphical login and desktop experience. Therefore, in this case, accessing a virtual console is done manually.

In most Linux distributions, you can access one of the Linux virtual consoles using a simple keystroke combination. Usually, you must hold down the Ctrl+Alt key combination and then press a function key (F1 through F7) for the virtual console you want to use. Function key F2 produces virtual console 2, key F3 produces virtual console 3, key F4 produces virtual console 4, and so on.

NOTE

Linux distributions typically use the Ctrl+Alt key combination with either F1 or F7 to reach the graphical interface. Ubuntu uses F7, while RHEL uses F1. It is best to test and see where your distribution puts the graphical interface.

Text mode virtual consoles use the whole screen and start with the text login screen displayed. An example of a text login screen from a virtual console is shown in Figure 2-2.

FIGURE 2-2

Linux virtual console login screen

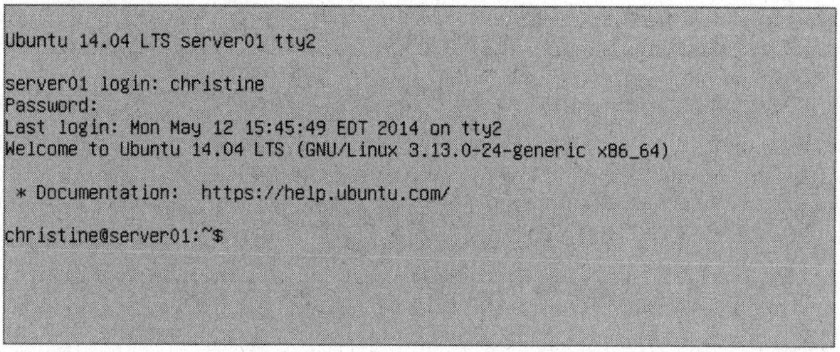
Ubuntu 14.04 LTS server01 tty2
server01 login: christine
Password:
Last login: Mon May 12 15:45:49 EDT 2014 on tty2
Welcome to Ubuntu 14.04 LTS (GNU/Linux 3.13.0-24-generic x86_64)
* Documentation: https://help.ubuntu.com/
christine@server01:~$

Notice in Figure 2-2 the words `tty2` at the end of the first text line. The `2` in `tty2` indicates that it is virtual console 2 and was reached by pressing the Ctrl+Alt+F2 key sequence. `tty` stands for teletypewriter. *Teletypewriter* is an old term, indicating a machine used for sending messages.

NOTE

Not all Linux distributions show the virtual console's tty number at the login screen.

You log into a console terminal by entering your user ID after the `login:` prompt and typing your password after the `Password:` prompt. If you have never logged in this way before, be aware that typing your password is a different experience than in a graphical environment. In a graphical environment, you may see dots or asterisks indicating the password characters as you type. However, at the virtual console, *nothing* is displayed when you type your password.

After logging into a virtual console, you are taken to the Linux CLI. Keep in mind that, within the Linux virtual console, you do not have the ability to run *any* graphical programs.

After you have logged in to a virtual console, you can keep it active and switch to another virtual console without losing your active session. You can switch between all the virtual consoles, with multiple active sessions running. This feature provides a great deal of flexibility while you work at the CLI.

Additional flexibility deals with the virtual console's appearance. Even though it is a text mode console terminal, you can modify the text and background colors.

For example, it may be easier on your eyes to set the background of the terminal to white and the text to black. After you have logged in, you can accomplish this modification in a couple of ways. One way is to type in the command **setterm -inversescreen on** and press the Enter key, as shown in Figure 2-3. Notice in the figure that the inversescreen feature is being turned on using the option on. You can also turn it off using the off option.

FIGURE 2-3

Linux virtual console with inversescreen being turned on

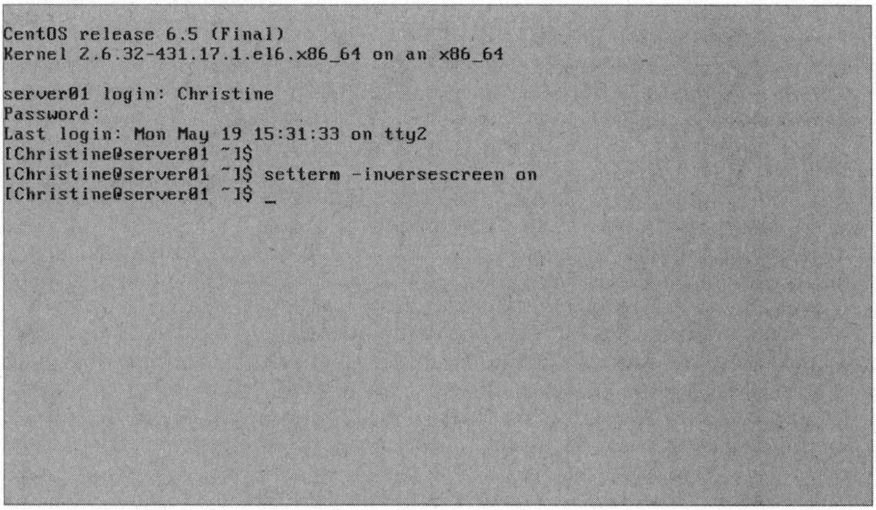

```
CentOS release 6.5 (Final)
Kernel 2.6.32-431.17.1.el6.x86_64 on an x86_64

server01 login: Christine
Password:
Last login: Mon May 19 15:31:33 on tty2
[Christine@server01 ~]$
[Christine@server01 ~]$ setterm -inversescreen on
[Christine@server01 ~]$ _
```

Another way is to type two commands, one after the other. Type **setterm -background white** and press Enter, and then type **setterm -foreground black** and press Enter. Be careful because, when you change your terminal background first, it may be hard to see the commands you are typing.

With the commands in the preceding paragraph, you are not turning features on and off, as with inversescreen. Instead, you have a choice of eight colors. The choices are black, red, green, yellow, blue, magenta, cyan, and white (which looks gray on some distributions). You can get rather creative with your plain text mode console terminals. Table 2-2 shows some options you can use with the `setterm` command to help improve your console terminal's readability or appearance.

TABLE 2-2 setterm Options for Foreground and Background Appearance

Option	Parameter Choices	Description
`-background`	`black, red, green, yellow, blue, magenta, cyan,` or `white`	Changes the terminal's background color to the one specified
`-foreground`	`black, red, green, yellow, blue, magenta, cyan,` or `white`	Changes the terminal's foreground color, specifically text, to the one specified
`-inversescreen`	on or off	Switches the background color to the foreground color and the foreground color to the background color
`-reset`	None	Changes the terminal appearance back to its default setting and clears the screen
`-store`	None	Sets the current terminal's foreground and background colors as the values to be used for `-reset`

Virtual console terminals are great for accessing the CLI outside the GUI. However, sometimes, you need to access the CLI and run graphical programs. Using a terminal emulation package solves this problem and is a popular way to access the shell CLI from within the GUI. The following sections describe common software packages that provide graphical terminal emulation.

Accessing CLI via Graphical Terminal Emulation

The graphical desktop environment offers a great deal more variety for CLI access than the virtual console terminal does. Many graphical terminal emulator packages are available for the graphical environment. Each package provides its own unique set of features and options. Some popular graphical terminal emulator packages are shown in Table 2-3 along with their websites.

TABLE 2-3 **Popular Graphical Terminal Emulator Packages**

Name	Website
Eterm	http://www.eterm.org
Final Term	http://finalterm.org
GNOME Terminal	https://help.gnome.org/users/gnome-terminal/stable
Guake	https://github.com/Guake/guake
Konsole Terminal	http://konsole.kde.org
LillyTerm	http://lilyterm.luna.com.tw/index.html
LXTerminal	http://wiki.lxde.org/en/LXTerminal
mrxvt	https://code.google.com/p/mrxvt
ROXTerm	http://roxterm.sourceforge.net
rxvt	http://sourceforge.net/projects/rxvt
rxvt-unicode	http://software.schmorp.de/pkg/rxvt-unicode
Sakura	https://launchpad.net/sakura
st	http://st.suckless.org
Terminator	https://launchpad.net/terminator
Terminology	http://www.enlightenment.org/p.php?p=about/terminology
tilda	http://tilda.sourceforge.net/tildaabout.php
UXterm	http://manpages.ubuntu.com/manpages/gutsy/man1/uxterm.1.html
Wterm	http://sourceforge.net/projects/wterm
xterm	http://invisible-island.net/xterm
Xfce4 Terminal	http://docs.xfce.org/apps/terminal/start
Yakuake	http://extragear.kde.org/apps/yakuake

Although many graphical terminal emulator packages are available, the focus in this chapter is on three commonly used ones. Often installed in Linux distributions by default, they are GNOME Terminal, Konsole Terminal, and xterm.

Using the GNOME Terminal Emulator

GNOME Terminal is the GNOME desktop environment's default terminal emulator. Many distributions, such as RHEL, Fedora, and CentOS, use the GNOME desktop environment by default, and therefore use GNOME Terminal by default. However, other desktop environments, such as Ubuntu Unity, also use the GNOME terminal as their default terminal emulator package. It is fairly easy to use and a good terminal emulator for individuals who are new to Linux. This chapter section walks you through the various parts of accessing, configuring and using the GNOME terminal emulator.

Accessing the GNOME Terminal

Each graphical desktop environment has different methods for accessing the GNOME terminal emulator. This section looks at accessing the GNOME Terminal in the GNOME, Unity, and KDE desktop environments.

> **NOTE**
>
> If you are using a different desktop environment than the ones listed in Table 2.3, you must look through the various menus offered in your environment to find the GNOME terminal emulator. In the menus, it is typically named **Terminal**.

In the GNOME desktop environment, accessing the GNOME Terminal is fairly straightforward. From the menu system in the upper-left corner of the window, click Applications, then select System Tools from the drop-down menu, and finally click Terminal. Written in shorthand, the directions look like the following: Applications ➪ System Tools ➪ Terminal.

Refer to Figure 2-1 to see a picture of the GNOME Terminal. It was accessed in a GNOME desktop environment on a CentOS distribution.

In the Unity desktop environment, accessing the GNOME terminal takes a little more effort. The simplest access method is Dash ➪ Search and type **Terminal**. The GNOME terminal shows up in the Dash home area as an application named Terminal. Click that icon to open the GNOME terminal emulator.

> **TIP**
>
> In some Linux distribution desktop environments, such as Ubuntu's Unity, you can quickly access the GNOME terminal using the shortcut key combination Ctrl+Alt+T.

In the KDE desktop environment, the Konsole terminal emulator is the default emulator. Therefore, you must dig down through the menus to access GNOME Terminal. Start with the icon labeled Kickoff Application Launcher in the lower-left corner of the screen and then click Applications ➪ Utilities ➪ Terminal.

In most desktop environments, you can create a *launcher* for accessing GNOME Terminal. A launcher is an icon you create on your desktop that allows you to start a chosen application. This is a great feature that allows you to quickly access a terminal emulator in the graphical desktop. It is especially helpful if you do not want to use shortcut keys or the shortcut key feature is not available in your desktop environment of choice.

For example, in the GNOME desktop environment, to create a launcher, right-click your mouse in the middle of the desktop area; a drop-down menu appears. Select Create Launcher... from the menu; the Create Launcher application window opens. In the Type field, select Application. Type a name for your icon in the Name field. In the Command field, type **gnome-terminal**. Click Ok to save your new launcher. An icon with the name you gave the launcher now appears on your desktop. Double-click it to open the GNOME terminal emulator.

NOTE

When you type **gnome-terminal** in the Command field, you are typing the shell command for starting the GNOME terminal emulator. You learn in Chapter 3 how to add special options to commands, such as gnome-terminal, to provide special configuration options, and how to view all the options available to you.

Several configuration options are provided by menus and short-cut keys in the application, which you can apply after you get the GNOME terminal emulation started. Understanding these options can enhance your GNOME Terminal CLI experience.

The Menu Bar

The GNOME Terminal menu bar contains the configuration and customization options you need to make your GNOME Terminal just the way you want it. The following tables briefly describe the different configuration options in the menu bar and shortcut keys associated with the options.

NOTE

As you read through these GNOME Terminal menu options, keep in mind that your Linux distribution's GNOME Terminal may have slightly different menu options available. This is because several Linux distributions use older versions of GNOME Terminal.

Table 2-4 shows the configuration options available within the GNOME Terminal File menu system. The File menu item contains items to create and manage your overall CLI terminal sessions.

TABLE 2-4 The File Menu

Name	Shortcut Key	Description
Open Terminal	Shift+Ctrl+N	Starts a new shell session in a new GNOME Terminal window
Open Tab	Shift+Ctrl+T	Starts a new shell session in a new tab in the existing GNOME Terminal window
New Profile	None	Customizes a session and saves as a profile, which can be recalled for later use
Save Contents	None	Saves the scrollback buffer contents to a text file
Close Tab	Shift+Ctrl+W	Closes the current tab session
Close Window	Shift+Ctrl+Q	Closes the current GNOME Terminal session

Notice that, as in a network browser, you can open new tabs within the GNOME Terminal session to start a whole new CLI session. Each tab session is considered to be an independent CLI session.

> **TIP**
> You do not have to click through the menu to reach options in the File menu. Most of the items are also available by right-clicking in the session area.

The Edit menu contains items, shown in Table 2-5, for handling text within the tabs. You can use your mouse to copy and paste text anywhere within the session window.

TABLE 2-5 The Edit Menu

Name	Shortcut Key	Description
Copy	Shift+Ctrl+C	Copies selected text to the GNOME clipboard
Paste	Shift+Ctrl+V	Pastes text from the GNOME clipboard into a session
Paste Filenames		Properly pastes copied filenames and their paths
Select All	None	Selects output in the entire scrollback buffer
Profiles	None	Adds, deletes, or modifies GNOME Terminal profiles
Keyboard Shortcuts	None	Creates key combinations to quickly access GNOME Terminal features
Profile Preferences	None	Edits the current session profile

The Paste Filenames menu option is available only in later versions of GNOME Terminal. Therefore, you may not see that menu option on your system.

The View menu, shown in Table 2-6, contains items for controlling how the CLI session windows appear. These options can be helpful for individuals with visual impairment.

TABLE 2-6   The View Menu

Name	Shortcut Key	Description
Show Menubar	None	Toggles on/off the menu bar display
Full Screen	F11	Toggles on/off the terminal window filling the entire desktop
Zoom In	Ctrl++	Enlarges the font size in the window incrementally
Zoom Out	Ctrl+-	Reduces the font size in the window incrementally
Normal Size	Ctrl+0	Returns the font size to default

Be aware that if you toggle off the menu bar display, the session's menu bar disappears. However, you can easily get the menu bar to display again by right-clicking in any terminal session window and toggling on the Show Menubar option.

The Search menu, shown in Table 2-7, contains items for conducting simple searches within the terminal session. These searches are similar to ones you may have conducted in a network browser or word processor.

TABLE 2-7   The Search Menu

Name	Shortcut Key	Description
Find	Shift+Ctrl+F	Opens Find window to provide designated text search options
Find Next	Shift+Ctrl+H	Searches forward from current terminal session location for designated text
Find Previous	Shift+Ctrl+G	Searches backward from current terminal session location for designated text

The Terminal menu, shown in Table 2-8, contains options for controlling the terminal emulation session features. There are no shortcut keys to access these items.

TABLE 2-8   The Terminal Menu

Name	Description
Change Profile	Switches to a new profile configuration
Set Title	Modifies session tab title bar setting
Set Character Encoding	Selects character set used to send and display characters
Reset	Sends reset terminal session control code
Reset and Clear	Sends reset terminal session control code and clears terminal session screen
Window Size List	Lists window sizes for adjusting the current terminal window size

The Reset option is extremely useful. One day, you may accidently cause your terminal session to display random characters and symbols. When this occurs, the text is unreadable. It is typically caused by displaying a non-text file to the screen. You can quickly get the terminal session back to normal by selecting Reset or Reset and Clear.

The Tabs menu, shown in Table 2-9, provides items for controlling the location of the tabs and selecting which tab is active. This menu displays only when you have more than one tab session open.

TABLE 2-9   The Tabs Menu

Name	Shortcut Key	Description
Next Tab	Ctrl+Page Down	Makes the next tab in the list active
Previous Tab	Ctrl+Page Up	Makes the previous tab in the list active
Move Tab Left	Shift+Ctrl+Page Up	Shuffles the current tab in front of the previous tab
Move Tab Right	Shift+Ctrl+Page Down	Shuffles the current tab in front of the next tab
Detach Tab	None	Removes the tab and starts a new GNOME Terminal window using this tab session
Tab List	None	Lists the currently running tabs (Select a tab to jump to that session.)
Terminal List	None	Lists the currently running terminals (Select a terminal to jump to that session. This is displayed only if multiple window sessions are open.)

Finally, the Help menu contains two menu options. Contents provides a full GNOME Terminal manual so you can research individual GNOME Terminal items and features. The About option shows you the current GNOME Terminal version that's running.

Besides the GNOME terminal emulator package, another commonly used package is Konsole Terminal. In many ways, Konsole Terminal is similar to GNOME Terminal. However, enough differences exist to warrant its own section.

Using the Konsole Terminal Emulator

The KDE Desktop Project created its own terminal emulation package called *Konsole Terminal*. The Konsole package incorporates basic terminal emulation features, along with more advanced ones expected from a graphical application. This section describes Konsole Terminal features and shows you how to use them.

Accessing the Konsole Terminal

The Konsole Terminal is the default terminal emulator for the KDE desktop environment. You can easily access it via the KDE environment's menu system. In other desktop environments, accessing the Konsole Terminal can be a little more difficult.

In the KDE desktop environment, you can access the Konsole Terminal by clicking the icon labeled Kickoff Application Launcher in the lower-left corner of the screen. Then click Applications ⇨ System ⇨ Terminal (Konsole).

> **NOTE**
> You may see two terminal menu options within the KDE menu environment. If you do, the **Terminal** menu option with the words Konsole beneath it is the Konsole terminal.

In the GNOME desktop environment, the Konsole terminal is typically not installed by default. If Konsole Terminal has been installed, you can access it via the GNOME menu system. In the upper-left corner of the window, click Applications ⇨ System Tools ⇨ Konsole.

> **NOTE**
> You may not have the Konsole terminal emulation package installed on your system. If you would like to install it, read through Chapter 9 to learn how to install software via the command line.

In the Unity desktop environment, if Konsole has been installed, you can access it via Dash ➪ Search and type **Konsole.** The Konsole Terminal shows up in the Dash home area as an application named Konsole. Click that icon to open the Konsole terminal emulator.

Figure 2-4 shows the Konsole Terminal. It was accessed on a KDE desktop environment in a CentOS Linux distribution.

FIGURE 2-4

The Konsole Terminal

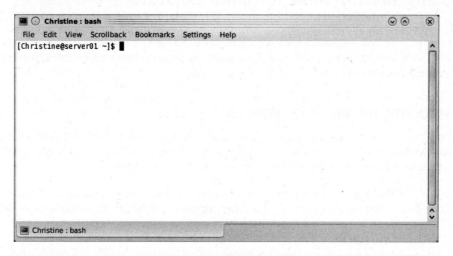

Remember that, in most desktop environments, you can create a launcher to access applications such as the Konsole Terminal. The command you need to type for the launcher to start up the Konsole terminal emulator is **konsole**. Also, if the Konsole Terminal is installed, you can start it from another terminal emulator by typing **konsole** and pressing Enter.

The Konsole Terminal, similar to GNOME Terminal, has several configuration options provided by menus and shortcut keys. The following section describes these various options.

The Menu Bar

The Konsole Terminal menu bar contains the configuration and customization options you need to easily view and change features in your terminal emulation session. The following tables briefly describe the menu options and associated shortcut keys.

The `File` menu, shown in Table 2-10, provides options for starting a new tab in the current window or in a new window.

TABLE 2-10 The File Menu

Name	Shortcut Key	Description
New Tab	Ctrl+Shift+N	Starts a new shell session in a new tab in the existing Konsole Terminal window
New Window	Ctrl+Shift+M	Starts a new shell session in a new Konsole Terminal window
Shell	None	Opens the default profile, Shell
Open Browser Here	None	Opens the default file browser application
Close Tab	Ctrl+Shift+W	Closes the current tab session
Quit	Ctrl+Shift+Q	Quits the Konsole Terminal emulation application

When you first start the Konsole Terminal, the only profile listed in the menu is `Shell`. As more profiles are created and saved, their names appear in the menu list.

The Edit menu, shown in Table 2-11, provides options for handling text in the session. Also, managing tab names is in this options list.

TABLE 2-11 **The Edit Menu**

Name	Shortcut Key	Description
Copy	Ctrl+Shift+C	Copies selected text to the Konsole clipboard
Paste	Ctrl+Shift+V	Pastes text from the Konsole clipboard into a session
Rename Tab	Ctrl+Alt+S	Modifies session tab title bar setting
Copy Input To	None	Starts/stops session input copies to chosen additional sessions
Clear Display	None	Clears the terminal session screen
Clear & Reset	None	Clears the terminal session screen and sends the reset terminal session control code

Konsole provides an excellent method for tracking what function is taking place in each tab session. Using the Rename Tab menu option, you can name a tab to match its current task. This helps in tracking which open tab session is performing what function.

The View menu, shown in Table 2-12, contains items for controlling individual session views in the Konsole Terminal window. In addition, options are available that aid in monitoring terminal session activity.

TABLE 2-12 **The View Menu**

Name	Shortcut Key	Description
Split View	None	Controls the multiple tab session display within the current Konsole Terminal window
Detach View	Ctrl+Shift+H	Removes a tab session and starts a new Konsole Terminal window using this tab session
Show Menu Bar	None	Toggles on/off Menu bar display
Full Screen Mode	Ctrl+Shift+F11	Toggles on/off the terminal window filling the entire monitor display area
Monitor for Silence	Ctrl+Shift+I	Toggles on/off a special message for tab silence
Monitor for Activity	Ctrl+Shift+A	Toggles on/off a special message for tab activity
Character Encoding	None	Selects the character set used to send and display characters

Increase Text Size	Ctrl++	Enlarges the font size in the window incrementally
Decrease Text Size	Ctrl+-	Reduces the font size in the window incrementally

The `Monitor for Silence` menu option is used for indicating *tab silence*. Tab silence occurs when no new text appears in the current tab session for 10 seconds. This allows you to switch to another tab while waiting for application output to stop.

Tab activity, toggled by the `Monitor for Activity` option, issues a special message when new text appears in the tab session. This option allows you to be notified when output from an application occurs.

Konsole retains a history, formally called a *scrollback buffer*, for each tab. The history contains output text that has scrolled out of the terminal viewing area. By default, the last 1,000 lines in the scrollback buffer are retained. The `Scrollback` menu, shown in Table 2-13, contains options for viewing this buffer.

TABLE 2-13   The Scrollback Menu

Name	Shortcut Key	Description
Search Output	Ctrl+Shift+F	Opens the Find window at the bottom of the Konsole Terminal window to provide scrollback text search options
Find Next	F3	Finds the next text match in more recent scrollback buffer history
Find Previous	Shift+F3	Finds the next text match in older scrollback buffer history
Save Output	None	Saves scrollback buffer contents to a text or HTML file
Scrollback Options	None	Opens the Scrollback Options window to configure scrollback buffer options
Clear Scrollback	None	Removes scrollback buffer contents
Clear Scrollback & Reset	Ctrl+Shift+X	Removes scrollback buffer contents and resets the terminal window

You can scroll back through the scrollback buffer by simply using the scrollbar in the viewing area. Also, you can scroll back line by line by pressing the Shift+Up Arrow or scroll back a page (24 lines) at a time by pressing Shift+Page Up.

The `Bookmarks` menu options, shown in Table 2-14, provide a way to manage *bookmarks* set in the Konsole Terminal window. A bookmark enables you to save your active session's directory location and then easily return there in either the same session or a new session.

TABLE 2-14   The Bookmarks Menu

Name	Shortcut Key	Description
Add Bookmark	Ctrl+Shift+B	Creates a new bookmark at the current directory location
Bookmark Tabs as Folder	None	Creates a new bookmark for all current terminal tab sessions
New Bookmark Folder	None	Creates a new bookmark storage folder
Edit Bookmarks	None	Edits existing bookmarks

The `Settings` menu, shown in Table 2-15, allows you to customize and manage your profiles. Also, you can add a little more functionality to your current tab session. There are no shortcut keys to access these items.

TABLE 2-15   The Settings Menu

Name	Description
Change Profile	Applies to the current tab a selected profile
Edit Current Profile	Opens the Edit Profile window to provide profile configuration options
Manage Profiles	Opens the Manage Profile window to provide profile management options
Configure Shortcuts	Creates Konsole Terminal command keyboard shortcuts
Configure Notifications	Creates custom Konsole Terminal schemas and sessions

`Configure Notifications` allows you to associate specific events that can occur within a session with different actions. When one of the events occurs, the defined action (or actions) is taken.

The `Help` menu, shown in Table 2-16, provides the full Konsole handbook (if KDE handbooks were installed in your Linux distribution) and the standard About Konsole dialog box.

TABLE 2-16 **The Help Menu**

Name	Shortcut Key	Description
Konsole Handbook	None	Contains the full Konsole Handbook
What's This?	Shift+F1	Contains help messages for terminal widgets
Report Bug	None	Opens the Submit Bug Report form
Switch Application Language	None	Opens the Switch Application's Language form
About Konsole	None	Displays the current Konsole Terminal version
About KDE		Displays the current KDE desktop environment version

Rather extensive documentation is provided to help you use the Konsole terminal emulator package. In addition to help items, you are provided with a Bug Report form to submit to the Konsole Terminal developers when you encounter a program bug.

The Konsole terminal emulator package is young compared to another popular package, xterm. In the next section, we explore the "old-timer" xterm.

Using the xterm Terminal Emulator

The oldest and most basic of terminal emulation packages is *xterm*. The xterm package has been around since before the original days of X Window, a popular display server, and it's often included by default in distributions.

Although xterm is a full terminal emulation package, it doesn't require many resources (such as memory) to operate. Because of this, the xterm package is still popular in Linux distributions designed to run on older hardware. Some graphical desktop environments use it as the default terminal emulation package.

Although it doesn't offer many fancy features, the xterm package does one thing extremely well: It emulates older terminals, such as the Digital Equipment Corporation (DEC) VT102, VT220, and Tektronix 4014 terminals. For the VT102 and VT220 terminals, xterm can even emulate the VT series of color control codes, allowing you to use color in your scripts.

NOTE
The DEC VT102 and VT220 were dumb text terminals popular for connecting to Unix systems in the 1980s and early 1990s. A VT102/VT220 could display text and display rudimentary graphics using block mode graphics. This style of terminal access is still used in many business environments today, thus keeping VT102/VT220 emulation popular.

Figure 2-5 shows what the basic xterm display looks like running on a graphical Linux desktop. You can see it is very basic.

FIGURE 2-5

The xterm Terminal

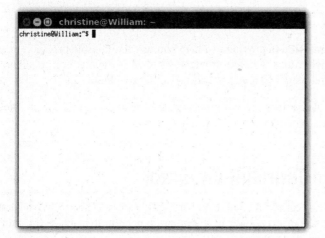

The xterm terminal emulator can be tricky to find these days. Often, it is not included in a desktop environment graphical menu arrangement.

Accessing xterm

In Ubuntu's Unity desktop, xterm is installed by default. You can access it via Dash ⇨ Search and type **xterm.** xterm shows up in the Dash home area as an application named XTerm. Click that icon to open the xterm terminal emulator.

NOTE
You may see another terminal called UXTerm when you search for xterm on Ubuntu. This is simply the xterm emulator package with Unicode support.

In the GNOME and KDE desktop environment, xterm is not installed by default. You must install it first (see Chapter 9 for help on installing software packages). After it's installed, you must start xterm from another terminal emulator. Open a terminal emulator for CLI access, type **xterm**, and press Enter. Also, remember that you can create your own desktop launcher to startup xterm.

The xterm package allows you to set individual features using command line parameters. The following sections discuss these features and how to change them.

Command Line Parameters

The list of xterm command line parameters is extensive. You can control lots of features to customize the terminal emulation features, such as enabling or disabling individual VT emulations.

> **NOTE**
>
> xterm has a huge number of configuration options — so many that they cannot all be covered here. Extensive documentation is available via the bash manual. Accessing the bash manual is covered in Chapter 3. In addition, the xterm development team provides some excellent help on its website: http://invisible-island.net/xterm/.

You can invoke certain configuration options by adding a parameter to the xterm command. For example, to have the xterm emulate a DEC VT100 terminal, type the command **xterm -ti vt100** and press Enter. Table 2-17 shows some parameters you can include when invoking the xterm terminal emulator software.

TABLE 2-17   xterm Command Line Parameters

Parameter	Description
-bg color	Specifies the color to use for the terminal background
-fb font	Specifies the font to use for bold text
-fg color	Specifies the color to use for the foreground text
-fn font	Specifies the font to use for text
-fw font	Specifies the font to use for wide text
-lf filename	Specifies the filename to use for screen logging
-ms color	Specifies the color used for the text cursor
-name name	Specifies the name of the application that appears in the title bar
-ti terminal	Specifies the terminal type to emulate

Some xterm command line parameters use a plus sign (+) or minus sign (-) to signify how a feature is set. A plus sign may turn a feature on, while a minus sign turns it off. However, the opposite can be true as well. A plus sign may disable a feature, while a minus sign enables it, such as when using the bc parameter. Table 2-18 lists some of the more common features you can set using the +/- command line parameters.

TABLE 2-18   xterm +/- Command Line Parameters

Parameter	Description
ah	Enables/disables highlighted text cursor
aw	Enables/disables auto-line-wrap
bc	Enables/disables text cursor blinking
cm	Enables/disables recognition of ANSI color change control codes
fullscreen	Enables/disables full screen mode
j	Enables/disables jump scrolling
l	Enables/disables logging screen data to a log file
mb	Enables/disables margin bell
rv	Enables/disables reverse video colors
t	Enables/disables Tektronix mode

It is important to note that not all implementations of xterm support all these command line parameters. You can determine which parameters your xterm implements by using the -help parameter when you start xterm on your system.

Now that you have been introduced to three terminal emulator packages, the big question is which is the best terminal emulator to use? There is no definite answer to that question. Which terminal emulator package you use depends upon your individual needs and desires. But it is great to have so many choices.

Summary

To start learning Linux command line commands, you need access to a CLI. In the world of graphical interfaces, this can sometimes be challenging. This chapter discussed different interfaces you should consider to get to the Linux command line.

First, this chapter discussed the difference between accessing the CLI via a virtual console terminal (a terminal outside the GUI) and a graphical terminal emulation package (a terminal inside the GUI). We took a brief look at the basic differences between these two access methods.

Next, we explored in detail accessing the CLI via a virtual console terminal, including specifics on how to change console terminal configuration options such as background color.

After looking at virtual console terminals, the chapter traveled through accessing the CLI via a graphical terminal emulator. Primarily, we covered three different types of terminal emulators: GNOME Terminal, Konsole Terminal, and xterm.

This chapter also covered the GNOME desktop project's GNOME terminal emulation package. GNOME Terminal is typically installed by default on the GNOME desktop environment. It provides convenient ways to set many terminal features via menu options and shortcut keys.

We also covered the KDE desktop project's Konsole terminal emulation package. The Konsole Terminal is typically installed by default on the KDE desktop environment. It provides several nice features, such as the ability to monitor a terminal for silence.

Finally, we covered the xterm terminal emulator package. xterm was the first terminal emulator available for Linux. It can emulate older terminal hardware such as the VT and Tektronix terminals.

In the next chapter, you start looking at the Linux command line commands. It walks you through the commands necessary to navigate around the Linux filesystem, and to create, delete, and manipulate files.

2

Basic bash Shell Commands

IN THIS CHAPTER

Interacting with the shell

Using the bash manual

Traversing the filesystem

Listing files and directories

Managing files and directories

Viewing file contents

The default shell used in many Linux distributions is the GNU bash shell. This chapter describes the basic features available in the bash shell, such as the bash manual, tab auto-completion and how to display a file's contents. You will walk through how to work with Linux files and directories using the basic commands provided by the bash shell. If you're already comfortable with the basics in the Linux environment, feel free to skip this chapter and continue with Chapter 4 to see more advanced commands.

Starting the Shell

The GNU bash shell is a program that provides interactive access to the Linux system. It runs as a regular program and is normally started whenever a user logs in to a terminal. The shell that the system starts depends on your user ID configuration.

The /etc/passwd file contains a list of all the system user accounts, along with some basic configuration information about each user. Here's a sample entry from a /etc/passwd file:

```
christine:x:501:501:Christine Bresnahan:/home/christine:/bin/bash
```

Each entry has seven data fields, with fields separated by colons. The system uses the data in these fields to assign specific features for the user. Most of these entries are discussed in more detail in Chapter 7. For now, just pay attention to the last field, which specifies the user's shell program.

NOTE

Though the focus is on the GNU bash shell, additional shells are reviewed in this book. Chapter 23 covers working with alternative shells, such as dash and tcsh.

In the earlier /etc/passwd sample entry, the user christine has /bin/bash set as her default shell program. This means when christine logs into the Linux system, the bash shell program is automatically started.

Although the bash shell program is automatically started at login, whether a shell command line interface (CLI) is presented depends on which login method is used. If a virtual console terminal is used to log in, the CLI prompt is automatically presented, and you can begin to type shell commands. However, if you log into the Linux system via a graphical desktop environment, you need to start a graphical terminal emulator to access the shell CLI prompt.

Using the Shell Prompt

After you start a terminal emulation package or log in to a Linux virtual console, you get access to the shell CLI *prompt*. The prompt is your gateway to the shell. This is the place where you enter shell commands.

The default prompt symbol for the bash shell is the dollar sign ($). This symbol indicates that the shell is waiting for you to enter text. Different Linux distributions use different formats for the prompt. On this Ubuntu Linux system, the shell prompt looks like this:

```
christine@server01:~$
```

On the CentOS Linux system, it looks like this:

```
[christine@server01 ~]$
```

Besides acting as your access point to the shell, the prompt can provide additional helpful information. In the two preceding examples, the current user ID name, christine, is shown in the prompt. Also, the name of the system is shown, server01. You learn later in this chapter about additional items shown in the prompt.

TIP

If you are new to the CLI, keep in mind that, after you type in a shell command at the prompt, you need to press the Enter key for the shell to act upon your command.

The shell prompt is not static. It can be changed to suit your needs. Chapter 6, "Using Linux Environment Variables," covers modifying your shell CLI prompt configuration.

Think of the shell CLI prompt as a helpmate, assisting you with your Linux system, giving you helpful insights, and letting you know when the shell is ready for new commands. Another helpful item in the shell is the bash Manual.

Interacting with the bash Manual

Most Linux distributions include an online manual for looking up information on shell commands, as well as lots of other GNU utilities included in the distribution. You should become familiar with the manual, because it's invaluable for working with commands, especially when you're trying to figure out various command line parameters.

The man command provides access to the manual pages stored on the Linux system. Entering the man command followed by a specific command name provides that utility's manual entry. Figure 3-1 shows an example of looking up the xterm command's manual pages. This page was reached by typing the command **man xterm**.

FIGURE 3-1

Manual pages for the xterm command

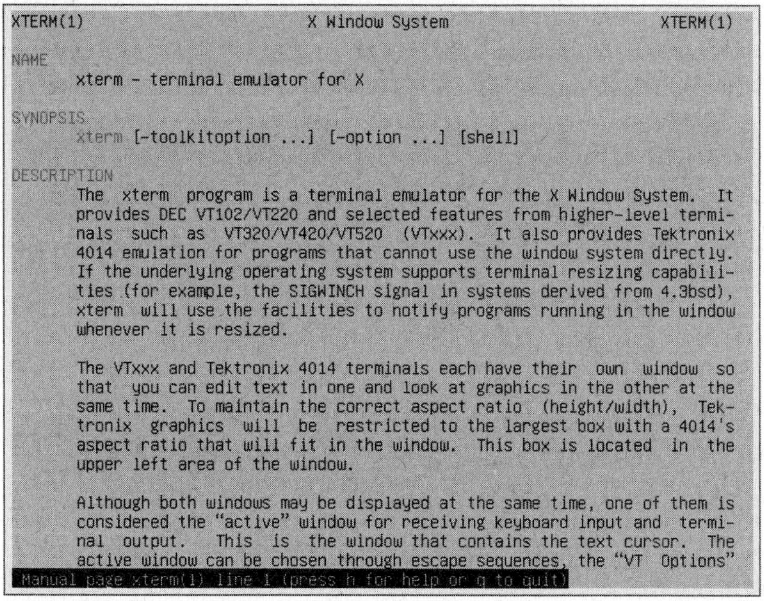

```
XTERM(1)                        X Window System                        XTERM(1)

NAME
       xterm - terminal emulator for X

SYNOPSIS
       xterm [-toolkitoption ...] [-option ...] [shell]

DESCRIPTION
       The  xterm  program is a terminal emulator for the X Window System.  It
       provides DEC VT102/VT220 and selected features from higher-level termi-
       nals  such  as  VT320/VT420/VT520  (VTxxx).  It also provides Tektronix
       4014 emulation for programs that cannot use the window system directly.
       If the underlying operating system supports terminal resizing capabili-
       ties (for example, the SIGWINCH signal in systems derived from 4.3bsd),
       xterm  will use the facilities to notify programs running in the window
       whenever it is resized.

       The VTxxx and Tektronix 4014 terminals each have their  own  window  so
       that  you can edit text in one and look at graphics in the other at the
       same time.  To maintain the correct aspect ratio (height/width),  Tek-
       tronix  graphics  will  be  restricted to the largest box with a 4014's
       aspect ratio that will fit in the window.  This box is located  in  the
       upper left area of the window.

       Although both windows may be displayed at the same time, one of them is
       considered  the "active" window for receiving keyboard input and termi-
       nal  output.   This  is  the window that contains the text cursor.  The
       active window can be chosen through escape sequences, the "VT  Options"
Manual page xterm(1) line 1 (press h for help or q to quit)
```

Notice the xterm command DESCRIPTION paragraphs in Figure 3-1. They are rather sparse and full of technical jargon. The bash manual is not a step-by-step guide, but instead a quick reference.

When you use the man command to view a command's manual pages, they are displayed with something called a *pager*. A pager is a utility that allows you to page through displayed text. Thus, you can page through the man pages by pressing the spacebar, or you can go line by line using the Enter key. In addition, you can use the arrow keys to scroll forward and backward through the man page text (assuming that your terminal emulation package supports the arrow key functions).

When you are finished with the man pages, press the q key to quit. When you quit the man pages, you receive a shell CLI prompt, indicating the shell is waiting for your next command.

The manual page divides information about a command into separate sections. Each section has a conventional naming standard as shown in Table 3-1.

TABLE 3-1 The Linux man Page Conventional Section Names

Section	Description
Name	Displays command name and a short description
Synopsis	Shows command syntax
Configuration	Provides configuration information
Description	Describes command generally
Options	Describes command option(s)
Exit Status	Defines command exit status indicator(s)
Return Value	Describes command return value(s)
Errors	Provides command error messages
Environment	Describes environment variable(s) used
Files	Defines files used by command
Versions	Describes command version information

Conforming To	Provides standards followed
Notes	Describes additional helpful command material
Bugs	Provides the location to report found bugs
Example	Shows command use examples
Authors	Provides information on command developers
Copyright	Defines command code copyright status
See Also	Refers similar available commands

Not every command's man page has all the section names described in Table 3-1. Also, some commands have section names that are not listed in the conventional standard.

TIP

What if you can't remember the command name? You can search the man pages using keywords. The syntax is `man -k keyword`. For example, to find commands dealing with the terminals, you type **man -k terminal**.

In addition to the conventionally named sections for a man page, there are man page section areas. Each section area has an assigned number, starting at 1 and going to 9; they are listed in Table 3-2.

TABLE 3-2   The Linux man Page Section Areas

Section Number	Area Contents
1	Executable programs or shell commands
2	System calls
3	Library calls
4	Special files
5	File formats and conventions
6	Games
7	Overviews, conventions, and miscellaneous
8	Super user and system administration commands
9	Kernel routines

Typically, the man utility provides the lowest numbered content area for the command. For example, looking back to Figure 3-1 where the command **man xterm** was entered, notice that in the upper-left and upper-right display corners, the word XTERM is followed by a number in parentheses, (1). This means the man pages displayed are coming from content area 1 (executable programs or shell commands).

Occasionally, a command has man pages in multiple section content areas. For example, there is a command called hostname. The man pages contain information on the command as well as an overview section on system hostnames. To see the pages desired, you type **man** *section# topic*. For the command's man pages in section 1, type **man 1 hostname**. For the overview man pages in section 7, type **man 7 hostname**.

You can also step through an introduction to the various section content areas by typing **man 1 intro** to read about section 1, **man 2 intro** to read about section 2, **man 3 intro** to read about section 3, and so on.

The man pages are not the only reference. There are also the information pages called info pages. You can learn about the info pages by typing **info info**.

In addition, most commands accept the -help or --help option. For example, you can type **hostname -help** to see a help screen. For more information on using help, type **help help**. (See a pattern here?)

Obviously, several helpful resources are available for reference. However, many basic shell concepts still need detailed explanation. In the next section, we cover navigating through the Linux filesystem.

Navigating the Filesystem

When you log into the system and reach the shell command prompt, you are usually placed in your home directory. Often, you want to explore other areas in the Linux system besides just your home directory. This section describes how to do that using shell commands. To start, you need to take a tour of just what the Linux filesystem looks like so you know where you are going.

Looking at the Linux filesystem

If you're new to the Linux system, you may be confused by how it references files and directories, especially if you're used to the way the Microsoft Windows operating system does that. Before exploring the Linux system, it helps to have an understanding of how it's laid out.

The first difference you'll notice is that Linux does not use drive letters in pathnames. In the Windows world, the physical drives installed on the computer determine the pathname of the file. Windows assigns a letter to each physical disk drive, and each drive contains its own directory structure for accessing files stored on it.

For example, in Windows you may be used to seeing the file paths such as:

```
c:\Users\Rich\Documents\test.doc
```

The Windows file path tells you exactly which physical disk partition contains the file named test.doc. For example, if you saved test.doc on a flash drive, designated by the J drive, the file path would be J:\test.doc. This path indicates that the file is located at the root of the drive assigned the letter J.

This is not the method used by Linux. Linux stores files within a single directory structure, called a *virtual directory*. The virtual directory contains file paths from all the storage devices installed on the computer, merged into a single directory structure.

The Linux virtual directory structure contains a single base directory, called the root. Directories and files beneath the root directory are listed based on the directory path used to get to them, similar to the way Windows does it.

> **TIP**
>
> You'll notice that Linux uses a forward slash (/) instead of a backward slash (\) to denote directories in file paths. The backslash character in Linux denotes an escape character and causes all sorts of problems when you use it in a file path. This may take some getting used to if you're coming from a Windows environment.

In Linux, you will see file paths similar to the following:

```
/home/Rich/Documents/test.doc
```

This indicates the file test.doc is in the directory Documents, under the directory rich, which is contained in the directory home. Notice that the path doesn't provide any information as to which physical disk the file is stored on.

The tricky part about the Linux virtual directory is how it incorporates each storage device. The first hard drive installed in a Linux system is called the *root drive*. The root drive contains the virtual directory core. Everything else builds from there.

On the root drive, Linux can use special directories as *mount points*. Mount points are directories in the virtual directory where you can assign additional storage devices. Linux causes files and directories to appear within these mount point directories, even though they are physically stored on a different drive.

Often system files are physically stored on the root drive. User files are typically stored on a separate drive or drives, as shown in Figure 3-2.

FIGURE 3-2

The Linux file structure

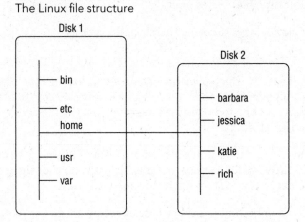

Figure 3-2 shows two hard drives on the computer. One hard drive is associated with the root of the virtual directory (indicated by a single forward slash). Other hard drives can be mounted anywhere in the virtual directory structure. In this example, the second hard drive is mounted at the location /home, which is where the user directories are located.

The Linux filesystem structure originally evolved from the Unix file structure. In a Linux filesystem, common directory names are used for common functions. Table 3-3 lists some of the more common Linux virtual top-level directory names and their contents.

TABLE 3-3 Common Linux Directory Names

Directory	Usage
/	root of the virtual directory, where normally, no files are placed
/bin	binary directory, where many GNU user-level utilities are stored
/boot	boot directory, where boot files are stored
/dev	device directory, where Linux creates device nodes
/etc	system configuration files directory
/home	home directory, where Linux creates user directories
/lib	library directory, where system and application library files are stored
/media	media directory, a common place for mount points used for removable media
/mnt	mount directory, another common place for mount points used for removable media
/opt	optional directory, often used to store third-party software packages and data files

/proc	process directory, where current hardware and process information is stored
/root	root home directory
/sbin	system binary directory, where many GNU admin-level utilities are stored
/run	run directory, where runtime data is held during system operation
/srv	service directory, where local services store their files
/sys	system directory, where system hardware information files are stored
/tmp	temporary directory, where temporary work files can be created and destroyed
/usr	user binary directory, where the bulk of GNU user-level utilities and data files are stored
/var	variable directory, for files that change frequently, such as log files

The common Linux directory names are based upon the Filesystem Hierarchy Standard (FHS). Many Linux distributions maintain compliance with FHS. Therefore, you should be able to easily find files on any FHS-compliant Linux systems.

> **NOTE**
>
> The FHS is occasionally updated. You may find that some Linux distributions are still using an older FHS standard, while other distributions only partially implement the current standard. To keep up to date on the FHS standard, visit its official home at http://www.pathname.com/fhs/.

3

When you log in to your system and reach a shell CLI prompt, your session starts in your home directory. Your home directory is a unique directory assigned to your user account. When a user account is created, the system normally assigns a unique directory for the account (see Chapter 7).

You can move around the virtual directory using a graphical interface. However, to move around the virtual directory from a CLI prompt, you need to learn to use the cd command.

Traversing directories

You use the change directory command (cd) to move your shell session to another directory in the Linux filesystem. The cd command syntax is pretty simplistic: cd *destination*.

The cd command may take a single parameter, *destination*, which specifies the directory name you want to go to. If you don't specify a destination on the cd command, it takes you to your home directory.

The `destination` parameter can be expressed using two different methods. One method is using an absolute directory reference. The other method uses a relative directory reference.

The following sections describe each of these methods. The differences between these two methods are important to understand as you traverse the filesystem.

Using absolute directory references

You can reference a directory name within the virtual directory system using an *absolute directory reference*. The absolute directory reference defines exactly where the directory is in the virtual directory structure, starting at the root. Think of the absolute directory reference as the full name for a directory.

An absolute directory reference always begins with a forward slash (/), indicating the virtual directory system's root. Thus, to reference user binaries, contained within the `bin` directory stored within the `usr` directory, you would use an absolute directory reference as follows:

```
/usr/bin
```

With the absolute directory reference, there's no doubt as to exactly where you want to go. To move to a specific location in the filesystem using the absolute directory reference, you just specify the full pathname in the `cd` command:

```
christine@server01:~$ cd /usr/bin
christine@server01:/usr/bin$
```

Notice in the preceding example that the prompt originally had a tilde (~) in it. After the change to a new directory occurred, the tilde was replaced by /usr/bin. This is where a CLI prompt can help you keep track of where you are in the virtual directory structure. The tilde indicates that your shell session is located in your home directory. After you move out of your home directory, the absolute directory reference is shown in the prompt, if the prompt has been configured to do so.

> **NOTE**
> If your shell CLI prompt does not show your shell session's current location, then it has not been configured to do so. Chapter 6 shows you how to make configuration changes, if you desire modifications to your CLI prompt.

If your prompt has not been configured to show the shell session's current absolute directory location, then you can display the location via a shell command. The `pwd` command displays the shell session's current directory location, which is called the *present working directory*. An example of using the `pwd` command is shown here.

```
christine@server01:/usr/bin$ pwd
/usr/bin
christine@server01:/usr/bin$
```

TIP

It is a good habit to use the pwd command whenever you change to a new present working directory. Because many shell commands operate on the present working directory, you always want to make sure you are in the correct directory before issuing a command.

You can move to any level within the entire Linux virtual directory structure from any level using the absolute directory reference:

```
christine@server01:/usr/bin$ cd /var/log
christine@server01:/var/log$
christine@server01:/var/log$ pwd
/var/log
christine@server01:/var/log$
```

You can also quickly jump to your home directory from any level within the Linux virtual directory structure:

```
christine@server01:/var/log$ cd
christine@server01:~$
christine@server01:~$ pwd
/home/christine
christine@server01:~$
```

However, if you're just working within your own home directory structure, often using absolute directory references can get tedious. For example, if you're already in the directory /home/christine, it seems somewhat cumbersome to have to type the command:

```
cd /home/christine/Documents
```

just to get to your Documents directory. Fortunately, there's a simpler solution.

Using relative directory references

Relative directory references allow you to specify a destination directory reference relative to your current location. A relative directory reference doesn't start with a forward slash (/).

Instead, a relative directory reference starts with either a directory name (if you're traversing to a directory under your current directory) or a special character. For example, if you are in your home directory and want to move to your Documents subdirectory, you can use the cd command along with a relative directory reference:

```
christine@server01:~$ pwd
/home/christine
christine@server01:~$
christine@server01:~$ cd Documents
christine@server01:~/Documents$ pwd
/home/christine/Documents
christine@server01:~/Documents$
```

In the preceding example, note that no forward slash (/) was used. Instead a relative directory reference was used and the present work directory was changed from /home/christine to /home/christine/Documents, with much less typing.

Also notice in the example that if the prompt is configured to display the present working directory, it keeps the tilde in the display. This shows that the present working directory is in a directory under the user's home directory.

TIP

If you are new to the command line and the Linux directory structure, it is recommended that you stick with absolute directory references for a while. After you become more familiar with the directory layout, switch to using relative directory references.

You can use a relative directory reference with the cd command in any directory containing subdirectories. You can also use a special character to indicate a relative directory location.

The two special characters used for relative directory references are:

- The single dot (.) to represent the current directory
- The double dot (..) to represent the parent directory

You *can* use the single dot, but it doesn't make sense to use it with the cd command. Later in the chapter, you will see how another command uses the single dot for relative directory references effectively.

The double dot character is extremely handy when trying to traverse a directory hierarchy. For example, if you are in the Documents directory under your home directory and need to go to your Downloads directory, also under your home directory, you can do this:

```
christine@server01:~/Documents$ pwd
/home/christine/Documents
christine@server01:~/Documents$ cd ../Downloads
christine@server01:~/Downloads$ pwd
/home/christine/Downloads
christine@server01:~/Downloads$
```

The double dot character takes you back up one level to your home directory; then the /Downloads portion of the command takes you back down into the Downloads directory. You can use as many double dot characters as necessary to move around. For example, if you are in your home directory (/home/christine) and want to go to the /etc directory, you could type the following:

```
christine@server01:~$ cd ../../etc
christine@server01:/etc$ pwd
/etc
christine@server01:/etc$
```

Of course, in a case like this, you actually have to do more typing rather than just typing the absolute directory reference, /etc. Thus, use a relative directory reference only if it makes sense to do so.

> **NOTE**
>
> It's helpful to have a long informative shell CLI prompt, as used in this chapter section. However, for clarity purposes, a simple $ prompt is used in the rest of the book's examples.

Now that you know how to traverse the directory system and confirm your present working directory, you can start to explore what's contained within the various directories. The next section takes you through the process of looking at files within the directory structure.

Listing Files and Directories

To see what files are available on the system, use the list command (ls). This section describes the ls command and options available to format the information it can display.

Displaying a basic listing

The ls command at its most basic form displays the files and directories located in your current directory:

```
$ ls
Desktop      Downloads         Music     Pictures  Templates  Videos
Documents    examples.desktop  my_script Public    test_file
$
```

Notice that the ls command produces the listing in alphabetical order (in columns rather than rows). If you're using a terminal emulator that supports color, the ls command may also show different types of entries in different colors. The LS_COLORS environment variable controls this feature. (Environment variables are covered in Chapter 6). Different Linux distributions set this environment variable depending on the capabilities of the terminal emulator.

If you don't have a color terminal emulator, you can use the -F parameter with the ls command to easily distinguish files from directories. Using the -F parameter produces the following output:

```
$ ls -F
Desktop/      Downloads/         Music/     Pictures/  Templates/ Videos/
Documents/    examples.desktop   my_script* Public/    test_file
$
```

The -F parameter flags the directories with a forward slash (/), to help identify them in the listing. Similarly, it flags executable files (like the my_script file in the preceding code) with an asterisk (*), to help you more easily find files that can be run on the system.

The basic ls command can be somewhat misleading. It shows the files and directories contained in the current directory, but not necessarily all of them. Linux often uses *hidden files* to store configuration information. In Linux, hidden files are files with filenames starting with a period (.). These files don't appear in the default ls listing. Thus, they are called hidden files.

To display hidden files along with normal files and directories, use the -a parameter. Here is an example of using the -a parameter with the ls command.

```
$ ls -a
.                 .compiz    examples.desktop  Music       test_file
..                .config    .gconf            my_script   Videos
.bash_history     Desktop    .gstreamer-0.10   Pictures    .Xauthority
.bash_logout      .dmrc      .ICEauthority     .profile    .xsession-errors
.bashrc           Documents  .local            Public      .xsession-errors.old
.cache            Downloads  .mozilla          Templates
$
```

All the files beginning with a period, hidden files, are now shown. Notice that three files begin with .bash. These are hidden files that are used by the bash shell environment. These features are covered in detail in Chapter 6.

The -R parameter is another option the ls command can use. Called the recursive option, it shows files that are contained within subdirectories in the current directory. If you have lots of subdirectories, this can be quite a long listing. Here's a simple example of what the -R parameter produces. The -F option was tacked on to help you see the file types:

```
$ ls -F -R
.:
Desktop/     Downloads/         Music/       Pictures/  Templates/  Videos/
Documents/   examples.desktop   my_script*   Public/    test_file

./Desktop:

./Documents:

./Downloads:

./Music:
ILoveLinux.mp3*

./Pictures:

./Public:
```

```
./Templates:

./Videos:
$
```

Notice that the -R parameter shows the contents of the current directory, which are the files from a user's home directory shown in earlier examples. It also shows each subdirectory in the user's home directory and their contents. The only subdirectory containing a file is the Music subdirectory, and it contains the executable file, ILoveLinux.mp3.

> **TIP**
> Option parameters don't have to be entered separately as shown in the nearby example: ls -F -R. They can often be combined as follows: ls -FR.

In the previous example, there were no subdirectories within subdirectories. If there had been further subdirectories, the -R parameter would have continued to traverse those as well. As you can see, for large directory structures, this can become quite a large output listing.

Displaying a long listing

In the basic listings, the ls command doesn't produce much information about each file. For listing additional information, another popular parameter is -l. The -l parameter produces a long listing format, providing more information about each file in the directory:

```
$ ls -l
total 48
drwxr-xr-x 2 christine christine 4096 Apr 22 20:37 Desktop
drwxr-xr-x 2 christine christine 4096 Apr 22 20:37 Documents
drwxr-xr-x 2 christine christine 4096 Apr 22 20:37 Downloads
-rw-r--r-- 1 christine christine 8980 Apr 22 13:36 examples.desktop
-rw-rw-r-- 1 christine christine    0 May 21 13:44 fall
-rw-rw-r-- 1 christine christine    0 May 21 13:44 fell
-rw-rw-r-- 1 christine christine    0 May 21 13:44 fill
-rw-rw-r-- 1 christine christine    0 May 21 13:44 full
drwxr-xr-x 2 christine christine 4096 May 21 11:39 Music
-rw-rw-r-- 1 christine christine    0 May 21 13:25 my_file
-rw-rw-r-- 1 christine christine    0 May 21 13:25 my_scrapt
-rwxrw-r-- 1 christine christine   54 May 21 11:26 my_script
-rw-rw-r-- 1 christine christine    0 May 21 13:42 new_file
drwxr-xr-x 2 christine christine 4096 Apr 22 20:37 Pictures
drwxr-xr-x 2 christine christine 4096 Apr 22 20:37 Public
drwxr-xr-x 2 christine christine 4096 Apr 22 20:37 Templates
-rw-rw-r-- 1 christine christine    0 May 21 11:28 test_file
drwxr-xr-x 2 christine christine 4096 Apr 22 20:37 Videos
$
```

The long listing format lists each file and subdirectory on a single line. In addition to the filename, the listing shows additional useful information. The first line in the output shows the total number of blocks contained within the directory. After that, each line contains the following information about each file (or directory):

- The file type — such as directory (d), file (-), linked file (l), character device (c), or block device (b)
- The file permissions (see Chapter 6)
- The number of file hard links (See the section "Linking Files" in Chapter 7.)
- The file owner username
- The file primary group name
- The file byte size
- The last time the file was modified
- The filename or directory name

The -l parameter is a powerful tool to have. Armed with this parameter, you can see most of the information you need for any file or directory.

The ls command has lots of parameters that can come in handy as you do file management. If you type at the shell prompt **man   ls**, you see several pages of available parameters for you to use to modify the ls command output.

Don't forget that you can also combine many of the parameters. You can often find a parameter combination that not only displays the desired output, but also is easy to remember, such as ls   -alF.

Filtering listing output

As you've seen in the examples, by default the ls command lists all the non-hidden directory files. Sometimes, this can be overkill, especially when you're just looking for information on a few files.

Fortunately, the ls command also provides a way for you to define a filter on the command line. It uses the filter to determine which files or directories it should display in the output.

The filter works as a simple text-matching string. Include the filter after any command line parameters you want to use:

```
$ ls -l my_script
-rwxrw-r-- 1 christine christine 54 May 21 11:26 my_script
$
```

When you specify the name of a specific file as the filter, the ls command only shows that file's information. Sometimes, you might not know the exact filename you're looking for.

The `ls` command also recognizes standard wildcard characters and uses them to match patterns within the filter:

- A question mark (?) to represent one character
- An asterisk (*) to represent any number of characters

The question mark can be used to replace exactly one character anywhere in the filter string. For example:

```
$ ls -l my_scr?pt
-rw-rw-r-- 1 christine christine  0 May 21 13:25 my_scrapt
-rwxrw-r-- 1 christine christine 54 May 21 11:26 my_script
$
```

The filter `my_scr?pt` matched two files in the directory. Similarly, the asterisk can be used to match zero or more characters:

```
$ ls -l my*
-rw-rw-r-- 1 christine christine  0 May 21 13:25 my_file
-rw-rw-r-- 1 christine christine  0 May 21 13:25 my_scrapt
-rwxrw-r-- 1 christine christine 54 May 21 11:26 my_script
$
```

Using the asterisk finds three different files, starting with the name `my`. As with the question mark, you can place the asterisks anywhere in the filter:

```
$ ls -l my_s*t
-rw-rw-r-- 1 christine christine  0 May 21 13:25 my_scrapt
-rwxrw-r-- 1 christine christine 54 May 21 11:26 my_script
$
```

Using the asterisk and question mark in the filter is called *file globbing*. File globbing is the processing of pattern matching using wildcards. The wildcards are officially called *metacharacter wildcards*. You can use more metacharacter wildcards for file globbing than just the asterisk and question mark. You can also use brackets:

```
$ ls -l my_scr[ai]pt
-rw-rw-r-- 1 christine christine  0 May 21 13:25 my_scrapt
-rwxrw-r-- 1 christine christine 54 May 21 11:26 my_script
$
```

In this example, we used the brackets along with two potential choices for a single character in that position, a or i. The brackets represent a single character position and give you multiple options for file globbing. You can list choices of characters, as shown in the preceding example, and you can specify a range of characters, such as an alphabetic range [a - i]:

```
$ ls -l f[a-i]ll
-rw-rw-r-- 1 christine christine 0 May 21 13:44 fall
-rw-rw-r-- 1 christine christine 0 May 21 13:44 fell
-rw-rw-r-- 1 christine christine 0 May 21 13:44 fill
$
```

3

Also, you can specify what should not be included in the pattern match by using the exclamation point (!):

```
$ ls -l f[!a]ll
-rw-rw-r-- 1 christine christine 0 May 21 13:44 fell
-rw-rw-r-- 1 christine christine 0 May 21 13:44 fill
-rw-rw-r-- 1 christine christine 0 May 21 13:44 full
$
```

File globbing is a powerful feature when searching for files. It can also be used with other shell commands besides ls. You find out more about this later in the chapter.

Handling Files

The shell provides many file manipulation commands on the Linux filesystem. This section walks you through the basic shell commands you need to handle files.

Creating files

Every once in a while you run into a situation where you need to create an empty file. For example, sometimes applications expect a log file to be present before they can write to it. In these situations, you can use the touch command to easily create an empty file:

```
$ touch test_one
$ ls -l test_one
-rw-rw-r-- 1 christine christine 0 May 21 14:17 test_one
$
```

The touch command creates the new file you specify and assigns your username as the file owner. Notice in the preceding example that the file size is zero because the touch command just created an empty file.

The touch command can also be used to change the modification time. This is done without changing the file contents:

```
$ ls -l test_one
-rw-rw-r-- 1 christine christine 0 May 21 14:17 test_one
$ touch test_one
$ ls -l test_one
-rw-rw-r-- 1 christine christine 0 May 21 14:35 test_one
$
```

The modification time of test_one is now updated to 14:35 from the original time, 14:17. To change only the access time, use the -a parameter with the touch command:

```
$ ls -l test_one
-rw-rw-r-- 1 christine christine 0 May 21 14:35 test_one
$ touch -a test_one
```

```
$ ls -l test_one
-rw-rw-r-- 1 christine christine 0 May 21 14:35 test_one
$ ls -l --time=atime test_one
-rw-rw-r-- 1 christine christine 0 May 21 14:55 test_one
$
```

In the preceding example, notice that by using only the ls -l command, the access time does not display. This is because the modification time is shown by default. To see a file's access time, you need to add an additional parameter, --time=atime. After we add that parameter in the preceding example, the file's altered access time is displayed.

Creating empty files and altering file timestamps is not something you will do on a Linux system daily. However, copying files is an action you will do often while using the shell.

Copying files

Copying files and directories from one location in the filesystem to another is a common practice for system administrators. The cp command provides this feature.

In its most basic form, the cp command uses two parameters — the source object and the destination object: cp *source destination*.

When both the source and destination parameters are filenames, the cp command copies the source file to a new destination file. The new file acts like a brand new file, with an updated modification time:

```
$ cp test_one  test_two
$ ls -l test_*
-rw-rw-r-- 1 christine christine 0 May 21 14:35 test_one
-rw-rw-r-- 1 christine christine 0 May 21 15:15 test_two
$
```

The new file test_two shows a different modification time than the test_one file. If the destination file already exists, the cp command may not prompt you to this fact. It is best to add the -i option to force the shell to ask whether you want to overwrite a file:

```
$ ls -l test_*
-rw-rw-r-- 1 christine christine 0 May 21 14:35 test_one
-rw-rw-r-- 1 christine christine 0 May 21 15:15 test_two
$
$ cp -i test_one  test_two
cp: overwrite 'test_two'? n
$
```

If you don't answer y, the file copy does not proceed. You can also copy a file into a pre-existing directory:

```
$ cp -i test_one  /home/christine/Documents/
$
```

```
$ ls -l /home/christine/Documents
total 0
-rw-rw-r-- 1 christine christine 0 May 21 15:25 test_one
$
```

The new file is now under the `Documents` subdirectory, using the same filename as the original.

This last example used an absolute directory reference, but you can just as easily use a relative directory reference:

```
$ cp -i test_one  Documents/
cp: overwrite 'Documents/test_one'? y
$
$ ls -l Documents
total 0
-rw-rw-r-- 1 christine christine 0 May 21 15:28 test_one
$
```

Earlier in this chapter, you read about the special symbols that can be used in relative directory references. One of them, the single dot (.), is great to use with the `cp` command. Remember that the single dot represents your present working directory. If you need to copy a file with a long source object name to your present working directory, the single dot can simplify the task:

```
$ cp -i /etc/NetworkManager/NetworkManager.conf  .
$
$ ls -l NetworkManager.conf
-rw-r--r-- 1 christine christine 76 May 21 15:55 NetworkManager.conf
$
```

It's hard to see that single dot! If you look closely, you'll see it at the end of the first example code line. Using the single dot symbol is much easier than typing a full destination object name, when you have long source object names.

The `-R` parameter is a powerful `cp` command option. It allows you to recursively copy the contents of an entire directory in one command:

```
$ ls -Fd *Scripts
Scripts/
$ ls -l Scripts/
total 25
-rwxrw-r-- 1 christine christine 929 Apr  2 08:23 file_mod.sh
-rwxrw-r-- 1 christine christine 254 Jan  2 14:18 SGID_search.sh
-rwxrw-r-- 1 christine christine 243 Jan  2 13:42 SUID_search.sh
$
$ cp -R Scripts/  Mod_Scripts
$ ls -Fd *Scripts
Mod_Scripts/  Scripts/
$ ls -l Mod_Scripts
total 25
-rwxrw-r-- 1 christine christine 929 May 21 16:16 file_mod.sh
-rwxrw-r-- 1 christine christine 254 May 21 16:16 SGID_search.sh
-rwxrw-r-- 1 christine christine 243 May 21 16:16 SUID_search.sh
$
```

The directory `Mod_Scripts` did not exist prior to the `cp -R` command. It was created with the `cp -R` command, and the entire `Scripts` directory's contents were copied into it. Notice that all the files in the new `Mod_Scripts` directory have new dates associated with them. Now `Mod_Scripts` is a complete copy of the `Scripts` directory.

> **NOTE**
>
> In the preceding example, the options `-Fd` were added to the `ls` command. You read about the `-F` option earlier in this chapter. However, the `-d` option may be new to you. The `-d` option lists a directory's information but not its contents.

You can also use wildcard metacharacters in your `cp` commands:

```
$ cp *script  Mod_Scripts/
$ ls -l Mod_Scripts
total 26
-rwxrw-r-- 1 christine christine 929 May 21 16:16 file_mod.sh
-rwxrw-r-- 1 christine christine 54  May 21 16:27 my_script
-rwxrw-r-- 1 christine christine 254 May 21 16:16 SGID_search.sh
-rwxrw-r-- 1 christine christine 243 May 21 16:16 SUID_search.sh
$
```

This command copied any files that ended with `script` to `Mod_Scripts`. In this case, only one file needed to be copied: `my_script`.

When copying files, another shell feature can help you besides the single dot and wildcard metacharacters. It is called tab auto-complete.

Using tab auto-complete

When working at the command line, you can easily mistype a command, directory name, or filename. In fact, the longer a directory reference or filename, the greater the chance that you will mistype it.

This is where *tab auto-complete* can be a lifesaver. Tab auto-complete allows you to start typing a filename or directory name and then press the tab key to have the shell complete it for you:

```
$ ls really*
really_ridiculously_long_file_name
$
$ cp really_ridiculously_long_file_name  Mod_Scripts/
ls -l Mod_Scripts
total 26
-rwxrw-r-- 1 christine christine 929 May 21 16:16 file_mod.sh
-rwxrw-r-- 1 christine christine 54  May 21 16:27 my_script
-rw-rw-r-- 1 christine christine  0  May 21 17:08
really_ridiculously_long_file_name
-rwxrw-r-- 1 christine christine 254 May 21 16:16 SGID_search.sh
-rwxrw-r-- 1 christine christine 243 May 21 16:16 SUID_search.sh
$
```

In the preceding example, we typed the command **cp really** and pressed the tab key, and the shell auto-completed the rest of the filename! Of course, the destination directory had to be typed, but still tab auto-complete saved the command from several potential typographical errors.

The trick to using tab auto-complete is to give the shell enough filename characters so it can distinguish the desired file from other files. For example, if another filename started with really, pressing the tab key would not auto-complete the filename. Instead, you would hear a beep. If this happens, you can press the tab key again, and the shell shows you all the filenames starting with really. This feature allows you to see what needs to be typed for tab auto-complete to work properly.

Linking files

Linking files is a great option available in the Linux filesystem. If you need to maintain two (or more) copies of the same file on the system, instead of having separate physical copies, you can use one physical copy and multiple virtual copies, called *links*. A link is a placeholder in a directory that points to the real location of the file. Two types of file links are available in Linux:

- A symbolic link
- A hard link

A *symbolic link* is simply a physical file that points to another file somewhere in the virtual directory structure. The two symbolically linked together files do not share the same contents.

To create a symbolic link to a file, the original file must pre-exist. We can then use the ln command with the -s option to create the symbolic link:

```
$ ls -l data_file
-rw-rw-r-- 1 christine christine 1092 May 21 17:27 data_file
$
$ ln -s data_file  sl_data_file
$
$ ls -l *data_file
-rw-rw-r-- 1 christine christine 1092 May 21 17:27 data_file
lrwxrwxrwx 1 christine christine    9 May 21 17:29 sl_data_file -> data_file
$
```

In the preceding example, notice that the name of the symbolic link, sl_data_file, is listed second in the ln command. The —> symbol displayed after the symbolic link file's long listing shows that it is symbolically linked to the file data_file.

Also note the symbolic link's file size versus the data file's file size. The symbolic link, sl_data_file, is only 9 bytes, whereas the data_file is 1092 bytes. This is because sl_data_file is only pointing to data_file. They do not share contents and are two physically separate files.

Another way to tell that these linked files are separate physical files is by viewing their *inode* number. The inode number of a file or directory is a unique identification number that the kernel assigns to each object in the filesystem. To view a file or directory's inode number, add the -i parameter to the ls command:

```
$ ls -i *data_file
296890 data_file  296891 sl_data_file
$
```

The example shows that the data file's inode number is 296890, while the sl_data_file inode number is different. It is 296891. Thus, they are different files.

A *hard link* creates a separate virtual file that contains information about the original file and where to locate it. However, they are physically the same file. When you reference the hard link file, it's just as if you're referencing the original file. To create a hard link, again the original file must pre-exist, except that this time no parameter is needed on the ln command:

```
$ ls -l code_file
-rw-rw-r-- 1 christine christine 189 May 21 17:56 code_file
$
$ ln code_file  hl_code_file
```

```
$
$ ls -li *code_file
296892 -rw-rw-r-- 2 christine christine 189 May 21 17:56
code_file
296892 -rw-rw-r-- 2 christine christine 189 May 21 17:56
hl_code_file
$
```

In the preceding example, we used the ls -li command to show both the inode numbers and a long listing for the *code_files. Notice that both files, which are hard linked together, share the name inode number. This is because they are physically the same file. Also notice that the link count (the third item in the listing) now shows that both files have two links. In addition, their file size is exactly the same size as well.

> **NOTE**
> You can only create a hard link between files on the same physical medium. To create a link between files under separate physical mediums, you must use a symbolic link.

Be careful when copying linked files. If you use the cp command to copy a file that's linked to another source file, all you're doing is making another copy of the source file. This can quickly get confusing. Instead of copying the linked file, you can create another link to the original file. You can have many links to the same file with no problems. However, you also don't want to create soft links to other soft-linked files. This creates a chain of links that can be confusing — and easily broken — causing all sorts of problems.

You may find symbolic and hard links difficult concepts. Fortunately, renaming files in the next section is a great deal easier to understand.

Renaming files

In the Linux world, renaming files is called *moving files*. The mv command is available to move both files and directories to another location or a new name:

```
$ ls -li f?ll
296730 -rw-rw-r-- 1 christine christine 0 May 21 13:44 fall
296717 -rw-rw-r-- 1 christine christine 0 May 21 13:44 fell
294561 -rw-rw-r-- 1 christine christine 0 May 21 13:44 fill
296742 -rw-rw-r-- 1 christine christine 0 May 21 13:44 full
$
$ mv fall  fzll
$
$ ls -li f?ll
296717 -rw-rw-r-- 1 christine christine 0 May 21 13:44 fell
294561 -rw-rw-r-- 1 christine christine 0 May 21 13:44 fill
296742 -rw-rw-r-- 1 christine christine 0 May 21 13:44 full
296730 -rw-rw-r-- 1 christine christine 0 May 21 13:44 fzll
$
```

Notice that moving the file changed the name from `fall` to `fzll`, but it kept the same inode number and timestamp value. This is because `mv` affects only a file's name.

You can also use `mv` to change a file's location:

```
$ ls -li /home/christine/fzll
296730 -rw-rw-r-- 1 christine christine 0 May 21 13:44
/home/christine/fzll
$
$ ls -li /home/christine/Pictures/
total 0
$ mv fzll  Pictures/
$
$ ls -li /home/christine/Pictures/
total 0
296730 -rw-rw-r-- 1 christine christine 0 May 21 13:44 fzll
$
$ ls -li /home/christine/fzll
ls: cannot access /home/christine/fzll: No such file or directory
$
```

In the preceding example, we moved the file `fzll` from /home/christine to /home/christine/Pictures using the `mv` command. Again, there were no changes to the file's inode number or timestamp value.

> **TIP**
>
> Like the `cp` command, you can use the `-i` option on the `mv` command. Thus, you are asked before the command attempts to overwrite any pre-existing files.

The only change was to the file's location. The `fzll` file no longer exists in /home/christine, because a copy of it was not left in its original location, as the `cp` command would have done.

You can use the `mv` command to move a file's location and rename it, all in one easy step:

```
$ ls -li Pictures/fzll
296730 -rw-rw-r-- 1 christine christine 0 May 21 13:44
Pictures/fzll
$
$ mv /home/christine/Pictures/fzll  /home/christine/fall
$
$ ls -li /home/christine/fall
296730 -rw-rw-r-- 1 christine christine 0 May 21 13:44
/home/christine/fall
$
$ ls -li /home/christine/Pictures/fzll
ls: cannot access /home/christine/Pictures/fzll:
No such file or directory
```

For this example, we moved the file `fzll` from a subdirectory, `Pictures`, to the home directory, `/home/christine`, and renamed it to `fall`. Neither the timestamp value nor the inode number changed. Only the location and name were altered.

You can also use the `mv` command to move entire directories and their contents:

```
$ ls -li Mod_Scripts
total 26
296886 -rwxrw-r-- 1 christine christine 929 May 21 16:16
file_mod.sh
296887 -rwxrw-r-- 1 christine christine  54 May 21 16:27
my_script
296885 -rwxrw-r-- 1 christine christine 254 May 21 16:16
SGID_search.sh
296884 -rwxrw-r-- 1 christine christine 243 May 21 16:16
SUID_search.sh
$
$ mv Mod_Scripts  Old_Scripts
$
$ ls -li Mod_Scripts
ls: cannot access Mod_Scripts: No such file or directory
$
$ ls -li Old_Scripts
total 26
296886 -rwxrw-r-- 1 christine christine 929 May 21 16:16
file_mod.sh
296887 -rwxrw-r-- 1 christine christine  54 May 21 16:27
my_script
296885 -rwxrw-r-- 1 christine christine 254 May 21 16:16
SGID_search.sh
296884 -rwxrw-r-- 1 christine christine 243 May 21 16:16
SUID_search.sh
$
```

The directory's entire contents are unchanged. The only thing that changes is the name of the directory.

After you know how to rename...err...*move* files with the `mv` command, you realize how simple it is to accomplish. Another easy, but potentially dangerous, task is deleting files.

Deleting files

Most likely at some point you'll want to be able to delete existing files. Whether it's to clean up a filesystem or to remove a software package, you always have opportunities to delete files.

In the Linux world, deleting is called *removing*. The command to remove files in the bash shell is `rm`. The basic form of the `rm` command is simple:

```
$ rm -i fall
rm: remove regular empty file 'fall'? y
$
$ ls -l fall
ls: cannot access fall: No such file or directory
$
```

Notice that the -i command parameter prompts you to make sure that you're serious about removing the file. The shell has no recycle bin or trashcan. After you remove a file, it's gone forever. Therefore, a good habit is to always tack on the -i parameter to the rm command.

You can also use wildcard metacharacters to remove groups of files. However, again, use that -i option to protect yourself:

```
$ rm -i f?ll
rm: remove regular empty file 'fell'? y
rm: remove regular empty file 'fill'? y
rm: remove regular empty file 'full'? y
$
$ ls -l f?ll
ls: cannot access f?ll: No such file or directory
$
```

One other feature of the rm command, if you're removing lots of files and don't want to be bothered with the prompt, is to use the -f parameter to force the removal. Just be careful!

Managing Directories

Linux has a few commands that work for both files and directories (such as the cp command), and some that work only for directories. To create a new directory, you need to use a specific command, which is covered in this section. Removing directories can get interesting, so that is covered in this section as well.

Creating directories

Creating a new directory in Linux is easy — just use the mkdir command:

```
$ mkdir New_Dir
$ ls -ld New_Dir
drwxrwxr-x 2 christine christine 4096 May 22 09:48 New_Dir
$
```

The system creates a new directory named New_Dir. Notice in the new directory's long listing that the directory's record begins with a d. This indicates that New_Dir is not a file, but a directory.

You can create directories and subdirectories in "bulk" if needed. However, if you attempt this with just the mkdir command, you get the following error message:

```
$ mkdir New_Dir/Sub_Dir/Under_Dir
mkdir: cannot create directory 'New_Dir/Sub_Dir/Under_Dir':
No such file or directory
$
```

To create several directories and subdirectories at the same time, you need to add the -p parameter:

```
$ mkdir -p New_Dir/Sub_Dir/Under_Dir
$
$ ls -R New_Dir
New_Dir:
Sub_Dir

New_Dir/Sub_Dir:
Under_Dir

New_Dir/Sub_Dir/Under_Dir:
$
```

The -p option on the mkdir command makes any missing *parent directories* as needed. A parent directory is a directory that contains other directories at the next level down the directory tree.

Of course, after you make something, you need to know how to delete it. This is especially useful if you created a directory in the wrong location.

Deleting directories

Removing directories can be tricky, and for good reason. There are lots of opportunities for bad things to happen when you start deleting directories. The shell tries to protect us from accidental catastrophes as much as possible. The basic command for removing a directory is rmdir:

```
$ touch New_Dir/my_file
$ ls -li New_Dir/
total 0
294561 -rw-rw-r-- 1 christine christine 0 May 22 09:52 my_file
$
$ rmdir New_Dir
rmdir: failed to remove 'New_Dir': Directory not empty
$
```

By default, the rmdir command works only for removing **empty** directories. Because we created a file, my_file, in the New_Dir directory, the rmdir command refuses to remove it.

To fix this, we must remove the file first. Then we can use the `rmdir` command on the now empty directory:

```
$ rm -i New_Dir/my_file
rm: remove regular empty file 'New_Dir/my_file'? y
$
$ rmdir New_Dir
$
$ ls -ld New_Dir
ls: cannot access New_Dir: No such file or directory
```

The `rmdir` has no `-i` option to ask if you want to remove the directory. This is one reason it is helpful that `rmdir` removes only empty directories.

You can also use the `rm` command on entire non-empty directories. Using the `-r` option allows the command to descend into the directory, remove the files, and then remove the directory itself:

```
$ ls -l My_Dir
total 0
-rw-rw-r-- 1 christine christine 0 May 22 10:02 another_file
$
$ rm -ri My_Dir
rm: descend into directory 'My_Dir'? y
rm: remove regular empty file 'My_Dir/another_file'? y
rm: remove directory 'My_Dir'? y
$
$ ls -l My_Dir
ls: cannot access My_Dir: No such file or directory
$
```

This also works for descending into multiple subdirectories and is especially useful when you have lots of directories and files to delete:

```
$ ls -FR Small_Dir
Small_Dir:
a_file  b_file  c_file  Teeny_Dir/  Tiny_Dir/

Small_Dir/Teeny_Dir:
e_file

Small_Dir/Tiny_Dir:
d_file
$
$ rm -ir Small_Dir
rm: descend into directory 'Small_Dir'? y
rm: remove regular empty file 'Small_Dir/a_file'? y
rm: descend into directory 'Small_Dir/Tiny_Dir'? y
rm: remove regular empty file 'Small_Dir/Tiny_Dir/d_file'? y
```

```
rm: remove directory 'Small_Dir/Tiny_Dir'? y
rm: descend into directory 'Small_Dir/Teeny_Dir'? y
rm: remove regular empty file 'Small_Dir/Teeny_Dir/e_file'? y
rm: remove directory 'Small_Dir/Teeny_Dir'? y
rm: remove regular empty file 'Small_Dir/c_file'? y
rm: remove regular empty file 'Small_Dir/b_file'? y
rm: remove directory 'Small_Dir'? y
$
$ ls -FR Small_Dir
ls: cannot access Small_Dir: No such file or directory
$
```

Although this works, it's somewhat awkward. Notice that you still must verify each and every file that gets removed. For a directory with lots of files and subdirectories, this can become tedious.

> **NOTE**
>
> For the rm command, the -r parameter and the -R parameter work exactly the same. When used with the rm command, the -R parameter also recursively traverses through the directory removing files. It is unusual for a shell command to have different cased parameters with the same function.

The ultimate solution for throwing caution to the wind and removing an entire directory, contents and all, is the rm command with both the -r and -f parameters:

```
$ tree Small_Dir
Small_Dir
├── a_file
├── b_file
├── c_file
├── Teeny_Dir
│   └── e_file
└── Tiny_Dir
    └── d_file

2 directories, 5 files
$
$ rm -rf Small_Dir
$
$ tree Small_Dir
Small_Dir [error opening dir]

0 directories, 0 files
$
```

The rm -rf command gives no warnings and no fanfare. This, of course, is an extremely dangerous tool to have, especially if have superuser privileges. Use it sparingly, and only after triple checking to make sure that you're doing exactly what you want to do!

In the last few sections, you looked at managing both files and directories. So far we covered everything you need to know about files, except for how to peek inside of them.

Viewing File Contents

You can use several commands for looking inside files without having to pull out a text editor utility (see Chapter 10). This section demonstrates a few of the commands you have available to help you examine files.

Viewing the file type

Before you go charging off trying to display a file, try to get a handle on what type of file it is. If you try to display a binary file, you get lots of gibberish on your monitor and may even lock up your terminal emulator.

The `file` command is a handy little utility to have around. It can peek inside of a file and determine just what kind of file it is:

```
$ file my_file
my_file: ASCII text
$
```

The file in the preceding example is a `text` file. The `file` command determined not only that the file contains text but also the character code format of the text file, `ASCII`.

This following example shows a file that is simply a directory. Thus, the `file` command gives you another method to distinguish a directory:

```
$ file New_Dir
New_Dir: directory
$
```

This third `file` command example shows a file, which is a symbolic link. Note that the `file` command even tells you to which file it is symbolically linked:

```
$ file sl_data_file
sl_data_file: symbolic link to 'data_file'
$
```

The following example shows what the `file` command returns for a script file. Although the file is `ASCII text`, because it's a script file, you can execute (run) it on the system:

```
$ file my_script
my_script: Bourne-Again shell script, ASCII text executable
$
```

The final example is a binary executable program. The `file` command determines the platform that the program was compiled for and what types of libraries it requires. This is an especially handy feature if you have a binary executable program from an unknown source:

```
$ file /bin/ls
/bin/ls: ELF 64-bit LSB  executable, x86-64, version 1 (SYSV),
dynamically linked (uses shared libs), for GNU/Linux 2.6.24,
[...]
$
```

Now that you know a quick method for viewing a file's type, you can start displaying and viewing files.

Viewing the whole file

If you have a large text file on your hands, you may want to be able to see what's inside of it. Linux has three different commands that can help you here.

Using the cat command

The `cat` command is a handy tool for displaying all the data inside a text file:

```
$ cat test1
hello

This is a test file.


That we'll use to        test the cat command.
$
```

Nothing too exciting, just the contents of the text file. However, the `cat` command has a few parameters that can help you out.

The `-n` parameter numbers all the lines for you:

```
$ cat -n test1
    1  hello
    2
    3  This is a test file.
    4
    5
    6  That we'll use to      test the cat command.
$
```

That feature will come in handy when you're examining scripts. If you just want to number the lines that have text in them, the -b parameter is for you:

```
$ cat -b test1
    1  hello

    2  This is a test file.


    3  That we'll use to      test the cat command.
$
```

Finally, if you don't want tab characters to appear, use the -T parameter:

```
$ cat -T test1
hello

This is a test file.


That we'll use to^Itest the cat command.
$
```

The -T parameter replaces any tabs in the text with the ^I character combination.

For large files, the cat command can be somewhat annoying. The text in the file just quickly scrolls off the display without stopping. Fortunately, we have a simple way to solve this problem.

Using the more command

The main drawback of the cat command is that you can't control what's happening after you start it. To solve that problem, developers created the more command. The more command displays a text file, but stops after it displays each page of data. We typed the command **more /etc/bash.bashrc** to produce the sample more screen shown in Figure 3-3.

FIGURE 3-3

Using the more command to display a text file

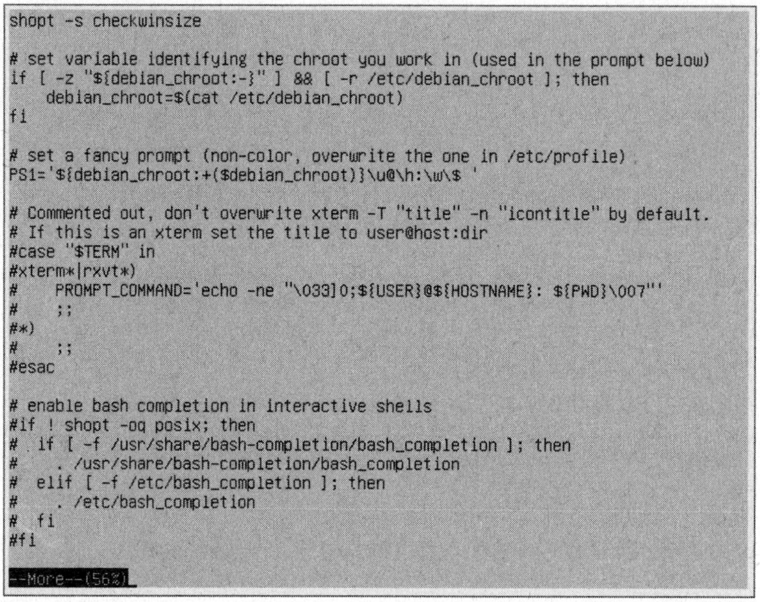

```
shopt -s checkwinsize

# set variable identifying the chroot you work in (used in the prompt below)
if [ -z "${debian_chroot:-}" ] && [ -r /etc/debian_chroot ]; then
    debian_chroot=$(cat /etc/debian_chroot)
fi

# set a fancy prompt (non-color, overwrite the one in /etc/profile)
PS1='${debian_chroot:+($debian_chroot)}\u@\h:\w\$ '

# Commented out, don't overwrite xterm -T "title" -n "icontitle" by default.
# If this is an xterm set the title to user@host:dir
#case "$TERM" in
#xterm*|rxvt*)
#    PROMPT_COMMAND='echo -ne "\033]0;${USER}@${HOSTNAME}: ${PWD}\007"'
#    ;;
#*)
#    ;;
#esac

# enable bash completion in interactive shells
#if ! shopt -oq posix; then
#  if [ -f /usr/share/bash-completion/bash_completion ]; then
#    . /usr/share/bash-completion/bash_completion
#  elif [ -f /etc/bash_completion ]; then
#    . /etc/bash_completion
#  fi
#fi
--More--(56%)
```

Notice at the bottom of the screen in Figure 3-3 that the more command displays a tag showing that you're still in the more application and how far along (56%) in the text file you are. This is the prompt for the more command.

The more command is a pager utility. Remember from earlier in this chapter a pager utility displays selected bash manual pages when you use the man command. Similarly to navigating through the man pages, you can use more to navigate through a text file by pressing the spacebar or you can go forward line by line using the Enter key. When you are finished navigating through the file using more, press the q key to quit.

The more command allows some rudimentary movement through the text file. For more advanced features, try the less command.

Using the less command

From its name, it sounds like it shouldn't be as advanced as the more command. However, the less command name is actually a play on words and is an advanced version of the more command (the less command name comes from the phrase "less is more"). It provides several very handy features for scrolling both forward and backward through a text file, as well as some pretty advanced searching capabilities.

The less command can also display a file's contents before it finishes reading the entire file. The cat and more commands cannot do this.

The `less` command operates much the same as the `more` command, displaying one screen of text from a file at a time. It supports the same command set as the `more` command, plus many more options.

One set of features is that the `less` command recognizes the up and down arrow keys as well as the Page Up and Page Down keys (assuming that you're using a properly defined terminal). This gives you full control when viewing a file.

Viewing parts of a file

Often the data you want to view is located either right at the top or buried at the bottom of a text file. If the information is at the top of a large file, you still need to wait for the `cat` or `more` commands to load the entire file before you can view it. If the information is located at the bottom of a file (such as a log file), you need to wade through thousands of lines of text just to get to the last few entries. Fortunately, Linux has specialized commands to solve both of these problems.

Using the tail command

The `tail` command displays the last lines in a file (the file's "tail"). By default, it shows the last 10 lines in the file.

For these examples, we created a text file containing 20 text lines. It is displayed here in its entirety using the `cat` command:

```
$ cat log_file
line1
line2
line3
line4
line5
Hello World - line 6
line7
line8
line9
line10
line11
Hello again - line 12
line13
line14
line15
Sweet - line16
```

```
line17
line18
line19
Last line - line20
$
```

Now that you have seen the entire text file, you can see the effect of using `tail` to view the file's last 10 lines:

```
$ tail log_file
line11
Hello again - line 12
line13
line14
line15
Sweet - line16
line17
line18
line19
Last line - line20
$
```

You can change the number of lines shown using `tail` by including the `-n` parameter. In this example, only the last two lines of the file are displayed, by adding `-n  2` to the `tail` command:

```
$ tail -n 2 log_file
line19
Last line - line20
$
```

The `-f` parameter is a pretty cool feature of the `tail` command. It allows you to peek inside a file as the file is being used by other processes. The `tail` command stays active and continues to display new lines as they appear in the text file. This is a great way to monitor the system log files in real-time mode.

Using the head command

The `head` command does what you'd expect; it displays a file's first group of lines (the file's "head"). By default, it displays the first 10 lines of text:

```
$ head log_file
line1
line2
line3
line4
line5
Hello World - line 6
```

```
line7
line8
line9
line10
$
```

Similar to the `tail` command, the `head` command supports the -n parameter so you can alter what's displayed. Both commands also allow you to simply type a dash along with the number of lines to display, as shown here:

```
$ head -5 log_file
line1
line2
line3
line4
line5
$
```

Usually the beginning of a file doesn't change, so the `head` command doesn't support the -f parameter feature as the `tail` command does. The `head` command is a handy way to just peek at the beginning of a file.

Summary

This chapter covered the basics of working with the Linux filesystem from a shell prompt. We began with a discussion of the bash shell and showed you how to interact with the shell. The command line interface (CLI) uses a prompt string to indicate when it's ready for you to enter commands.

The shell provides a wealth of utilities you can use to create and manipulate files. Before you start playing with files, you should understand how Linux stores them. This chapter discussed the basics of the Linux virtual directory and showed you how Linux references storage media devices. After describing the Linux filesystem, the chapter walked you through using the `cd` command to move around the virtual directory.

After showing you how to get to a directory, the chapter demonstrated how to use the `ls` command to list the files and subdirectories. Lots of parameters can customize the output of the `ls` command. You can obtain information on files and directories by using the `ls` command.

The `touch` command is useful for creating empty files and for changing the access or modification times on an existing file. The chapter also discussed using the `cp` command to copy existing files from one location to another. It walked you through the process of linking files instead of copying them, providing an easy way to have the same file in two locations without making a separate copy. The `ln` command provides this linking ability.

Next, you learned how to rename files (called *moving*) in Linux using the mv command and saw how to delete files (called *removing*) using the rm command. This chapter also showed you how to perform the same tasks with directories, using the mkdir and rmdir commands.

Finally, the chapter closed with a discussion on viewing the contents of files. The cat, more, and less commands provide easy methods for viewing the entire contents of a file, while the tail and head commands are great for peeking inside a file to just see a small portion of it.

The next chapter continues the discussion on bash shell commands. We'll look at more advanced administrator commands that come in handy as you administer your Linux system.

More bash Shell Commands

C hapter 3 covered the basics of walking through the Linux filesystem and working with files and directories. File and directory management is a major feature of the Linux shell; however, we should look at some other things before we start our script programming. This chapter digs into the Linux system management commands, showing you how to peek inside your Linux system using command line commands. After that, we show you a few handy commands that you can use to work with data files on the system.

Monitoring Programs

One of the toughest jobs of being a Linux system administrator is keeping track of what's running on the system — especially now, when graphical desktops take a handful of programs just to produce a single desktop. You always have lots of programs running on the system.

Fortunately, a few command line tools are available to help make life easier for you. This section covers a few of the basic tools you need to know how to use to manage programs on your Linux system.

Peeking at the processes

When a program runs on the system, it's referred to as a *process*. To examine these processes, you need to become familiar with the ps command, the Swiss Army knife of utilities. It can produce lots of information about all the programs running on your system.

Unfortunately, with this robustness comes complexity — in the form of numerous parameters — making the ps command probably one of the most difficult commands to master. Most system administrators find a subset of these parameters that provide the information they want, and they stick with using only those.

That said, however, the basic ps command doesn't really provide all that much information:

```
$ ps
  PID TTY          TIME CMD
 3081 pts/0    00:00:00 bash
 3209 pts/0    00:00:00 ps
$
```

Not too exciting. By default, the ps command shows only the processes that belong to the current user and that are running on the current terminal. In this case, we had only our bash shell running (remember, the shell is just another program running on the system) and, of course, the ps command itself.

The basic output shows the process ID (PID) of the programs, the terminal (TTY) that they are running from, and the CPU time the process has used.

NOTE

The tricky feature of the ps command (and the part that makes it so complicated) is that at one time there were two versions of it. Each version had its own set of command line parameters controlling what information it displayed and how. Recently, Linux developers have combined the two ps command formats into a single ps program (and of course added their own touches).

The GNU ps command that's used in Linux systems supports three different types of command line parameters:

- Unix-style parameters, which are preceded by a dash
- BSD-style parameters, which are not preceded by a dash
- GNU long parameters, which are preceded by a double dash

The following sections examine the three different parameter types and show examples of how they work.

Unix-style parameters

The Unix-style parameters originated with the original ps command that ran on the AT&T Unix systems invented by Bell Labs. Table 4-1 shows these parameters.

TABLE 4-1 **The ps Command Unix Parameters**

Parameter	Description
-A	Shows all processes
-N	Shows the opposite of the specified parameters
-a	Shows all processes except session headers and processes without a terminal
-d	Shows all processes except session headers
-e	Shows all processes
-C cmslist	Shows processes contained in the list cmdlist
-G grplist	Shows processes with a group ID listed in grplist
-U userlist	Shows processes owned by a userid listed in userlist
-g grplist	Shows processes by session or by groupid contained in grplist
-p pidlist	Shows processes with PIDs in the list pidlist
-s sesslist	Shows processes with session ID in the list sesslist
-t ttylist	Shows processes with terminal ID in the list ttylist
-u userlist	Shows processes by effective userid in the list userlist
-F	Uses extra full output
-O format	Displays specific columns in the list format, along with the default columns
-M	Displays security information about the process
-c	Shows additional scheduler information about the process
-f	Displays a full format listing
-j	Shows job information
-l	Displays a long listing
-o format	Displays only specific columns listed in format
-y	Prevents display of process flags
-Z	Displays the security context information
-H	Displays processes in a hierarchical format (showing parent processes)
-n namelist	Defines the values to display in the WCHAN column
-w	Uses wide output format, for unlimited width displays
-L	Shows process threads
-V	Displays the version of ps

4

That's a lot of parameters, and there are still more! The key to using the ps command is not to memorize all the available parameters — only those you find most useful. Most Linux system administrators have their own sets of parameters that they use for extracting pertinent information. For example, if you need to see everything running on the system, use the -ef parameter combination (the ps command lets you combine parameters like this):

```
$ ps -ef
UID         PID   PPID  C STIME TTY          TIME CMD
root          1      0  0 11:29 ?        00:00:01 init [5]
root          2      0  0 11:29 ?        00:00:00 [kthreadd]
root          3      2  0 11:29 ?        00:00:00 [migration/0]
root          4      2  0 11:29 ?        00:00:00 [ksoftirqd/0]
root          5      2  0 11:29 ?        00:00:00 [watchdog/0]
root          6      2  0 11:29 ?        00:00:00 [events/0]
root          7      2  0 11:29 ?        00:00:00 [khelper]
root         47      2  0 11:29 ?        00:00:00 [kblockd/0]
root         48      2  0 11:29 ?        00:00:00 [kacpid]
68         2349      1  0 11:30 ?        00:00:00 hald
root       3078   1981  0 12:00 ?        00:00:00 sshd: rich [priv]
rich       3080   3078  0 12:00 ?        00:00:00 sshd: rich@pts/0
rich       3081   3080  0 12:00 pts/0    00:00:00 -bash
rich       4445   3081  3 13:48 pts/0    00:00:00 ps -ef
$
```

Quite a few lines have been cut from the output to save space, but you can see that lots of processes are running on a Linux system. This example uses two parameters: the -e parameter, which shows all the processes running on the system, and the -f parameter, which expands the output to show a few useful columns of information:

- **UID:** The user responsible for launching the process
- **PID:** The process ID of the process
- **PPID:** The PID of the parent process (if a process is started by another process)
- **C:** Processor utilization over the lifetime of the process
- **STIME:** The system time when the process started
- **TTY:** The terminal device from which the process was launched
- **TIME:** The cumulative CPU time required to run the process
- **CMD:** The name of the program that was started

This produces a reasonable amount of information, which is what many system administrators want to see. For even more information, you can use the -l parameter, which produces the long format output:

```
$ ps -l
F S  UID PID  PPID  C PRI  NI ADDR SZ WCHAN  TTY       TIME    CMD
```

```
0 S  500 3081  3080  0 80   0 -  1173 wait pts/0   00:00:00 bash
0 R  500 4463  3081  1 80   0 -  1116 -    pts/0   00:00:00 ps
$
```

Notice the extra columns that appear when you use the -l parameter:

- F: System flags assigned to the process by the kernel
- S: The state of the process (O = running on processor; S = sleeping; R = runnable, waiting to run; Z = zombie, process terminated but parent not available; T = process stopped)
- PRI: The priority of the process (higher numbers mean lower priority)
- NI: The nice value, which is used for determining priorities
- ADDR: The memory address of the process
- SZ: Approximate amount of swap space required if the process was swapped out
- WCHAN: Address of the kernel function where the process is sleeping

BSD-style parameters

Now that you've seen the Unix parameters, let's look at the BSD-style parameters. The Berkeley Software Distribution (BSD) was a version of Unix developed at (of course) the University of California, Berkeley. It had many subtle differences from the AT&T Unix system, thus sparking many Unix wars over the years. Table 4-2 shows the BSD version of the ps command parameters.

TABLE 4-2   The ps Command BSD Parameters

Parameter	Description
T	Shows all processes associated with this terminal
a	Shows all processes associated with any terminal
g	Shows all processes including session headers
r	Shows only running processes
x	Shows all processes, even those without a terminal device assigned
U userlist	Shows processes owned by a userid listed in userlist
p pidlist	Shows processes with a PID listed in pidlist
t ttylist	Shows processes associated with a terminal listed in ttylist
O format	Lists specific columns in format to display along with the standard columns
X	Displays data in the register format
Z	Includes security information in the output
j	Shows job information
l	Uses the long format

Continues

TABLE 4-2 *(continued)*

Parameter	Description
o *format*	Displays only columns specified in *format*
s	Uses the signal format
u	Uses the user-oriented format
v	Uses the virtual memory format
N *namelist*	Defines the values to use in the WCHAN column
O *order*	Defines the order in which to display the information columns
S	Sums numerical information, such as CPU and memory usage, for child processes into the parent process
c	Displays the true command name (the name of the program used to start the process)
e	Displays any environment variables used by the command
f	Displays processes in a hierarchical format, showing which processes started which processes
h	Prevents display of the header information
k *sort*	Defines the column(s) to use for sorting the output
n	Uses numeric values for user and group IDs, along with WCHAN information
w	Produces wide output for wider terminals
H	Displays threads as if they were processes
m	Displays threads after their processes
L	Lists all format specifiers
V	Displays the version of ps

As you can see, the Unix and BSD types of parameters have lots of overlap. Most of the information you can get from one you can also get from the other. Most of the time, you choose a parameter type based on which format you're more comfortable with (for example, if you were used to a BSD environment before using Linux).

When you use the BSD-style parameters, the ps command automatically changes the output to simulate the BSD format. Here's an example using the l parameter:

```
$ ps l
F   UID   PID PPID PRI  NI  VSZ  RSS WCHAN   STAT TTY       TIME COMMAND
0   500 3081 3080  20   0 4692 1432 wait    Ss   pts/0     0:00 -bash
0   500 5104 3081  20   0 4468  844 -       R+   pts/0     0:00 ps l
$
```

Notice that while many of the output columns are the same as when we used the Unix-style parameters, some different ones appear as well:

- **VSZ:** The size in kilobytes of the process in memory
- **RSS:** The physical memory that a process has used that isn't swapped out
- **STAT:** A two-character state code representing the current process state

Many system administrators like the BSD-style l parameter because it produces a more detailed state code for processes (the STAT column). The two-character code more precisely defines exactly what's happening with the process than the single-character Unix-style output.

The first character uses the same values as the Unix-style S output column, showing when a process is sleeping, running, or waiting. The second character further defines the process's status:

- <: The process is running at high priority.
- N: The process is running at low priority.
- L: The process has pages locked in memory.
- s: The process is a session leader.
- l: The process is multi-threaded.
- +: The process is running in the foreground.

From the simple example shown previously, you can see that the bash command is sleeping, but it is a session leader (it's the main process in my session), whereas the ps command was running in the foreground on the system.

The GNU long parameters

Finally, the GNU developers put their own touches on the new, improved ps command by adding a few more options to the parameter mix. Some of the GNU long parameters copy existing Unix- or BSD-style parameters, while others provide new features. Table 4-3 lists the available GNU long parameters.

TABLE 4-3   The ps Command GNU Parameters

Parameter	Description
--deselect	Shows all processes except those listed in the command line
--Group grplist	Shows processes whose group ID is listed in grplist
--User userlist	Shows processes whose user ID is listed in userlist
--group grplist	Shows processes whose effective group ID is listed in grplist

Continues

TABLE 4-3   *(continued)*

Parameter	Description
--pid *pidlist*	Shows processes whose process ID is listed in *pidlist*
--ppid *pidlist*	Shows processes whose parent process ID is listed in *pidlist*
--sid *sidlist*	Shows processes whose session ID is listed in *sidlist*
--tty *ttylist*	Shows processes whose terminal device ID is listed in *ttylist*
--user *userlist*	Shows processes whose effective user ID is listed in *userlist*
--format *format*	Displays only columns specified in the *format*
--context	Displays additional security information
--cols *n*	Sets screen width to *n* columns
--columns *n*	Sets screen width to *n* columns
--cumulative	Includes stopped child process information
--forest	Displays processes in a hierarchical listing showing parent processes
--headers	Repeats column headers on each page of output
--no-headers	Prevents display of column headers
--lines *n*	Sets the screen height to *n* lines
--rows *n*	Sets the screen height to *n* rows
--sort *order*	Defines the column(s) to use for sorting the output
--width *n*	Sets the screen width to *n* columns
--help	Displays the help information
--info	Displays debugging information
--version	Displays the version of the ps program

You can combine GNU long parameters with either Unix- or BSD-style parameters to really customize your display. One cool feature of GNU long parameters that we really like is the --forest parameter. It displays the hierarchical process information, but using ASCII characters to draw cute charts:

```
 1981 ?          00:00:00 sshd
 3078 ?          00:00:00  \_ sshd
 3080 ?          00:00:00      \_ sshd
 3081 pts/0      00:00:00          \_ bash
16676 pts/0      00:00:00              \_ ps
```

This format makes tracing child and parent processes a snap!

Real-time process monitoring

The ps command is great for gleaning information about processes running on the system, but it has one drawback. The ps command can display information only for a specific point in time. If you're trying to find trends about processes that are frequently swapped in and out of memory, it's hard to do that with the ps command.

Instead, the top command can solve this problem. The top command displays process information similarly to the ps command, but it does it in real-time mode. Figure 4-1 is a snapshot of the top command in action.

FIGURE 4-1

The output of the top command while it is running

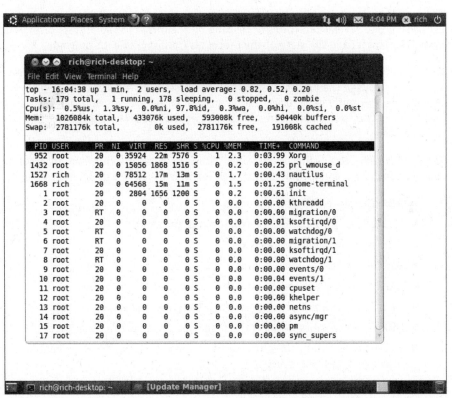

The first section of the output shows general system information. The first line shows the current time, how long the system has been up, the number of users logged in, and the load average on the system.

The load average appears as three numbers: the 1-minute, 5-minute, and 15-minute load averages. The higher the values, the more load the system is experiencing. It's not uncommon for the 1-minute load value to be high for short bursts of activity. If the 15-minute load value is high, your system may be in trouble.

NOTE

The trick in Linux system administration is defining what exactly a high load average value is. This value depends on what's normally running on your system and the hardware configuration. What's high for one system might be normal for another. Usually, if your load averages start getting over 2, things are getting busy on your system.

The second line shows general process information (called *tasks* in top): how many processes are running, sleeping, stopped, and zombie (have finished but their parent process hasn't responded).

The next line shows general CPU information. The top display breaks down the CPU utilization into several categories depending on the owner of the process (user versus system processes) and the state of the processes (running, idle, or waiting).

Following that are two lines that detail the status of the system memory. The first line shows the status of the physical memory in the system, how much total memory there is, how much is currently being used, and how much is free. The second memory line shows the status of the swap memory area in the system (if any is installed), with the same information.

Finally, the next section shows a detailed list of the currently running processes, with some information columns that should look familiar from the ps command output:

- **PID:** The process ID of the process
- **USER:** The user name of the owner of the process
- **PR:** The priority of the process
- **NI:** The nice value of the process
- **VIRT:** The total amount of virtual memory used by the process
- **RES:** The amount of physical memory the process is using
- **SHR:** The amount of memory the process is sharing with other processes
- **S:** The process status (D = interruptible sleep, R = running, S = sleeping, T = traced or stopped, or Z = zombie)
- **%CPU:** The share of CPU time that the process is using
- **%MEM:** The share of available physical memory the process is using
- **TIME+:** The total CPU time the process has used since starting
- **COMMAND:** The command line name of the process (program started)

By default, when you start top, it sorts the processes based on the %CPU value. You can change the sort order by using one of several interactive commands while top is running. Each interactive command is a single character that you can press while top is running and changes the behavior of the program. Pressing f allows you to select the field to use to sort the output, and pressing d allows you to change the polling interval. Press q to exit the top display.

You have lots of control over the output of the top command. Using this tool, you can often find offending processes that have taken over your system. Of course, after you find one, the next job is to stop it, which brings us to the next topic.

Stopping processes

A crucial part of being a system administrator is knowing when and how to stop a process. Sometimes, a process gets hung up and needs a gentle nudge to either get going again or stop. Other times, a process runs away with the CPU and refuses to give it up. In both cases, you need a command that allows you to control a process. Linux follows the Unix method of interprocess communication.

In Linux, processes communicate with each other using *signals*. A process signal is a predefined message that processes recognize and may choose to ignore or act on. The developers program how a process handles signals. Most well-written applications have the ability to receive and act on the standard Unix process signals. Table 4-4 shows these signals.

TABLE 4-4 Linux Process Signals

Signal	Name	Description
1	HUP	Hangs up
2	INT	Interrupts
3	QUIT	Stops running
9	KILL	Unconditionally terminates
11	SEGV	Produces segment violation
15	TERM	Terminates if possible
17	STOP	Stops unconditionally, but doesn't terminate
18	TSTP	Stops or pauses, but continues to run in background
19	CONT	Resumes execution after STOP or TSTP

Two commands available in Linux allow you to send process signals to running processes.

The kill command

The kill command allows you to send signals to processes based on their process ID (PID). By default, the kill command sends a TERM signal to all the PIDs listed on the command line. Unfortunately, you can only use the process PID instead of its command name, making the kill command difficult to use sometimes.

To send a process signal, you must either be the owner of the process or be logged in as the root user.

```
$ kill 3940
-bash: kill: (3940) - Operation not permitted
$
```

The TERM signal tells the process to kindly stop running. Unfortunately, if you have a runaway process, most likely it ignores the request. When you need to get forceful, the -s parameter allows you to specify other signals (either using their name or signal number).

As you can see from the following example, no output is associated with the kill command.

```
# kill -s HUP 3940
#
```

To see if the command was effective, you must perform another ps or top command to see if the offending process stopped.

The killall command

The killall command is a powerful way to stop processes by using their names rather than the PID numbers. The killall command allows you to use wildcard characters as well, making it a very useful tool when you have a system that's gone awry:

```
# killall http*
#
```

This example kills all the processes that start with http, such as the httpd services for the Apache web server.

CAUTION

Be extremely careful using the killall command when logged in as the root user. It's easy to get carried away with wildcard characters and accidentally stop important system processes. This could lead to a damaged filesystem.

Monitoring Disk Space

Another important task of the system administrator is to keep track of the disk usage on the system. Whether you're running a simple Linux desktop or a large Linux server, you need to know how much space you have for your applications.

Some command line commands can help you manage the media environment on your Linux system. This section describes the core commands you'll likely run into during your system administration duties.

Mounting media

As discussed in Chapter 3, the Linux filesystem combines all media disks into a single virtual directory. Before you can use a new media disk on your system, you must place it in the virtual directory. This task is called *mounting*.

In today's graphical desktop world, most Linux distributions have the ability to automatically mount specific types of *removable media*. A removable media device is a medium that (obviously) can be easily removed from the PC, such as CD-ROMs and USB memory sticks.

If you're not using a distribution that automatically mounts and unmounts removable media, you have to do it yourself. This section describes the Linux command line commands to help you manage your removable media devices.

The mount command

Oddly enough, the command used to mount media is called mount. By default, the mount command displays a list of media devices currently mounted on the system:

```
$ mount
/dev/mapper/VolGroup00-LogVol00 on / type ext3 (rw)
proc on /proc type proc (rw)
sysfs on /sys type sysfs (rw)
devpts on /dev/pts type devpts (rw,gid=5,mode=620)
/dev/sda1 on /boot type ext3 (rw)
tmpfs on /dev/shm type tmpfs (rw)
none on /proc/sys/fs/binfmt_misc type binfmt_misc (rw)
sunrpc on /var/lib/nfs/rpc_pipefs type rpc_pipefs (rw)
/dev/sdb1 on /media/disk type vfat
(rw,nosuid,nodev,uhelper=hal,shortname=lower,uid=503)
$
```

The mount command provides four pieces of information:

- The device filename of the media
- The mount point in the virtual directory where the media is mounted
- The filesystem type
- The access status of the mounted media

The last entry in the preceding example is a USB memory stick that the GNOME desktop automatically mounted at the /media/disk mount point. The vfat filesystem type shows that it was formatted on a Microsoft Windows PC.

To manually mount a media device in the virtual directory, you must be logged in as the root user or use the sudo command to run the command as the root user. The following is the basic command for manually mounting a media device:

```
mount -t type device directory
```

The `type` parameter defines the filesystem type under which the disk was formatted. Linux recognizes lots of different filesystem types. If you share removable media devices with your Windows PCs, you are most likely to run into these types:

- **vfat:** Windows long filesystem
- **ntfs:** Windows advanced filesystem used in Windows NT, XP, and Vista
- **iso9660:** The standard CD-ROM filesystem

Most USB memory sticks and floppies are formatted using the vfat filesystem. If you need to mount a data CD, you must use the iso9660 filesystem type.

The next two parameters define the location of the device file for the media device and the location in the virtual directory for the mount point. For example, to manually mount the USB memory stick at device `/dev/sdb1` at location `/media/disk`, you use the following command:

```
mount -t vfat /dev/sdb1 /media/disk
```

After a media device is mounted in the virtual directory, the root user has full access to the device, but access by other users is restricted. You can control who has access to the device using directory permissions (discussed in Chapter 7).

In case you need to use some of the more exotic features of the `mount` command, Table 4-5 shows the available parameters .

TABLE 4-5   The mount Command Parameters

Parameter	Description
`-a`	Mounts all filesystems specified in the `/etc/fstab` file
`-f`	Causes the mount command to simulate mounting a device, but not actually mount it
`-F`	Mounts all filesystems at the same time when used with the `-a` parameter
`-v`	Explains all the steps required to mount the device; stands for verbose mode
`-I`	Tells you not to use any filesystem helper files under `/sbin/mount .filesystem`
`-l`	Adds the filesystem labels automatically for ext2, ext3, or XFS filesystems
`-n`	Mounts the device without registering it in the `/etc/mstab` mounted device file
`-p num`	For encrypted mounting, reads the passphrase from the file descriptor *num*
`-s`	Ignores mount options not supported by the filesystem
`-r`	Mounts the device as read-only

-w	Mounts the device as read-write (the default)
-L label	Mounts the device with the specified *label*
-U uuid	Mounts the device with the specified *uuid*
-O	When used with the -a parameter, limits the set of filesystems applied
-o	Adds specific options to the filesystem

The -o option allows you to mount the filesystem with a comma-separated list of additional options. These are popular options to use:

- ro: Mounts as read-only
- rw: Mounts as read-write
- user: Allows an ordinary user to mount the filesystem
- check=none: Mounts the filesystem without performing an integrity check
- loop: Mounts a file

The unmount command

To remove a removable media device, you should never just remove it from the system. Instead, you should always *unmount* it first.

> **TIP**
>
> Linux doesn't allow you to eject a mounted CD. If you ever have trouble removing a CD from the drive, most likely it means the CD is still mounted in the virtual directory. Unmount it first, and then try to eject it.

The command used to unmount devices is umount (yes, there's no "n" in the command, which gets confusing sometimes). The format for the umount command is pretty simple:

```
umount [directory | device ]
```

The umount command gives you the choice of defining the media device by either its device location or its mounted directory name. If any program has a file open on a device, the system won't let you unmount it.

```
[root@testbox mnt]# umount /home/rich/mnt
umount: /home/rich/mnt: device is busy
umount: /home/rich/mnt: device is busy
[root@testbox mnt]# cd /home/rich
[root@testbox rich]# umount /home/rich/mnt
[root@testbox rich]# ls -l mnt
total 0
[root@testbox rich]#
```

4

In this example, the command prompt was still in a directory within the filesystem structure, so the umount command couldn't unmount the image file. After the command prompt was moved out of the image file filesystem, the umount command successfully unmounted the image file.

Using the df command

Sometimes, you need to see how much disk space is available on an individual device. The df command allows you to easily see what's happening on all the mounted disks:

```
$ df
Filesystem          1K-blocks     Used Available Use% Mounted on
/dev/sda2            18251068  7703964   9605024  45% /
/dev/sda1              101086    18680     77187  20% /boot
tmpfs                 119536        0    119536   0% /dev/shm
/dev/sdb1             127462   113892     13570  90% /media/disk
$
```

The df command shows each mounted filesystem that contains data. As you can see from the mount command earlier, some mounted devices are used for internal system purposes. The command displays the following:

- The device location of the device
- How many 1024-byte blocks of data it can hold
- How many 1024-byte blocks are used
- How many 1024-byte blocks are available
- The amount of used space as a percentage
- The mount point where the device is mounted

A few different command line parameters are available with the df command, most of which you'll never use. One popular parameter is -h, which shows the disk space in human-readable form, usually as an M for megabytes or a G for gigabytes:

```
$ df -h
Filesystem      Size  Used Avail Use% Mounted on
/dev/sdb2        18G  7.4G  9.2G  45% /
/dev/sda1        99M   19M   76M  20% /boot
tmpfs           117M     0  117M   0% /dev/shm
/dev/sdb1       125M  112M   14M  90% /media/disk
$
```

Now instead of having to decode those ugly block numbers, all the disk sizes are shown using "normal" sizes. The df command is invaluable in troubleshooting disk space problems on the system.

> **NOTE**
>
> Remember that the Linux system always has processes running in the background that handle files. The values from the df command reflect what the Linux system thinks are the current values at that point in time. It's possible that you have a process running that has created or deleted a file but has not released the file yet. This value is not included in the free space calculation.

Using the du command

With the df command, you can easily see when a disk is running out of space. The next problem for the system administrator is to know what to do when that happens.

Another useful command to help you is the du command. The du command shows the disk usage for a specific directory (by default, the current directory). This is a quick way to determine if you have any obvious disk hogs on the system.

By default, the du command displays all the files, directories, and subdirectories under the current directory, and it shows how many disk blocks each file or directory takes. For a standard-sized directory, this can be quite a listing. Here's a partial listing of using the du command:

```
$ du
484      ./.gstreamer-0.10
8        ./Templates
8        ./Download
8        ./.ccache/7/0
24       ./.ccache/7
368      ./.ccache/a/d
384      ./.ccache/a
424      ./.ccache
8        ./Public
8        ./.gphpedit/plugins
32       ./.gphpedit
72       ./.gconfd
128      ./.nautilus/metafiles
384      ./.nautilus
72       ./.bittorrent/data/metainfo
20       ./.bittorrent/data/resume
144      ./.bittorrent/data
152      ./.bittorrent
8        ./Videos
8        ./Music
16       ./.config/gtk-2.0
40       ./.config
8        ./Documents
```

The number at the left of each line is the number of disk blocks that each file or directory takes. Notice that the listing starts at the bottom of a directory and works its way up through the files and subdirectories contained within the directory.

The du command by itself can be somewhat useless. It's nice to be able to see how much disk space each individual file and directory takes up, but it can be meaningless when you have to wade through pages and pages of information before you find what you're looking for.

You can use a few command line parameters with the du command to make things a little more legible:

- -c: Produces a grand total of all the files listed
- -h: Prints sizes in human-readable form, using K for kilobyte, M for megabyte, and G for gigabyte
- -s: Summarizes each argument

The next step for the system administrator is to use some file-handling commands for manipulating large amounts of data. That's exactly what the next section covers.

Working with Data Files

When you have a large amount of data, handling the information and making it useful can be difficult. As you saw with the du command in the previous section, it's easy to get data overload when working with system commands.

The Linux system provides several command line tools to help you manage large amounts of data. This section covers the basic commands that every system administrator — as well as any everyday Linux user — should know how to use to make their lives easier.

Sorting data

The sort command is a popular function that comes in handy when working with large amounts of data. The sort command does what it says: It sorts data.

By default, the sort command sorts the data lines in a text file using standard sorting rules for the language you specify as the default for the session.

```
$ cat file1
one
two
three
four
```

```
five
$ sort file1
five
four
one
three
two
$
```

It's pretty simple, but things aren't always as easy as they appear. Look at this example:

```
$ cat file2
1
2
100
45
3
10
145
75
$ sort file2
1
10
100
145
2
3
45
75
$
```

If you were expecting the numbers to sort in numerical order, you were disappointed. By default, the sort command interprets numbers as characters and performs a standard character sort, producing output that might not be what you want. To solve this problem, use the -n parameter, which tells the sort command to recognize numbers as numbers instead of characters and to sort them based on their numerical values:

```
$ sort -n file2
1
2
3
10
45
75
100
145
$
```

4

Now, that's much better! Another common parameter that's used is -M, the month sort. Linux log files usually contain a timestamp at the beginning of the line to indicate when the event occurred:

```
Sep 13 07:10:09 testbox smartd[2718]: Device: /dev/sda, opened
```

If you sort a file that uses timestamp dates using the default sort, you get something like this:

```
$ sort file3
Apr
Aug
Dec
Feb
Jan
Jul
Jun
Mar
May
Nov
Oct
Sep
$
```

It's not exactly what you wanted. If you use the -M parameter, the sort command recognizes the three-character month nomenclature and sorts appropriately:

```
$ sort -M file3
Jan
Feb
Mar
Apr
May
Jun
Jul
Aug
Sep
Oct
Nov
Dec
$
```

Table 4-6 shows other handy sort parameters you can use.

TABLE 4-6 **The sort Command Parameters**

Single Dash	Double Dash	Description
-b	--ignore-leading-blanks	Ignores leading blanks when sorting
-C	--check = quiet	Doesn't sort, but doesn't report if data is out of sort order
-c	--check	Doesn't sort, but checks if the input data is already sorted, and reports if not sorted
-d	--dictionary-order	Considers only blanks and alphanumeric characters; doesn't consider special characters
-f	--ignore-case	By default, sort orders capitalized letters first; ignores case
-g	--general-numeric-sort	Uses general numerical value to sort
-i	--ignore-nonprinting	Ignores nonprintable characters in the sort
-k	--key = *POS1*[,*POS2*]	Sorts based on position POS1, and ends at POS2 if specified
-M	--month-sort	Sorts by month order using three-character month names
-m	--merge	Merges two already sorted data files
-n	--numeric-sort	Sorts by string numerical value
-o	--output = *file*	Writes results to file specified
-R	--random-sort	Sorts by a random hash of keys
	--random-source = *FILE*	Specifies the file for random bytes used by the -R parameter
-r	--reverse	Reverses the sort order (descending instead of ascending
-S	--buffer-size = *SIZE*	Specifies the amount of memory to use
-s	--stable	Disables last-resort comparison
-T	--temporary-direction = *DIR*	Specifies a location to store temporary working files
-t	--field-separator = *SEP*	Specifies the character used to distinguish key positions
-u	--unique	With the -c parameter, checks for strict ordering; without the -c parameter, outputs only the first occurrence of two similar lines
-z	--zero-terminated	Ends all lines with a NULL character instead of a new line

4

The -k and -t parameters are handy when sorting data that uses fields, such as the /etc/passwd file. Use the -t parameter to specify the field separator character, and use the -k parameter to specify which field to sort on. For example, to sort the password file based on numerical userid, just do this:

```
$ sort -t ':' -k 3 -n /etc/passwd
root:x:0:0:root:/root:/bin/bash
bin:x:1:1:bin:/bin:/sbin/nologin
daemon:x:2:2:daemon:/sbin:/sbin/nologin
adm:x:3:4:adm:/var/adm:/sbin/nologin
lp:x:4:7:lp:/var/spool/lpd:/sbin/nologin
sync:x:5:0:sync:/sbin:/bin/sync
shutdown:x:6:0:shutdown:/sbin:/sbin/shutdown
halt:x:7:0:halt:/sbin:/sbin/halt
mail:x:8:12:mail:/var/spool/mail:/sbin/nologin
news:x:9:13:news:/etc/news:
uucp:x:10:14:uucp:/var/spool/uucp:/sbin/nologin
operator:x:11:0:operator:/root:/sbin/nologin
games:x:12:100:games:/usr/games:/sbin/nologin
gopher:x:13:30:gopher:/var/gopher:/sbin/nologin
ftp:x:14:50:FTP User:/var/ftp:/sbin/nologin
```

Now the data is perfectly sorted based on the third field, which is the numerical userid value.

The -n parameter is great for sorting numerical outputs, such as the output of the du command:

```
$ du -sh * | sort -nr
1008k    mrtg-2.9.29.tar.gz
972k     bldg1
888k     fbs2.pdf
760k     Printtest
680k     rsync-2.6.6.tar.gz
660k     code
516k     fig1001.tiff
496k     test
496k     php-common-4.0.4pl1-6mdk.i586.rpm
448k     MesaGLUT-6.5.1.tar.gz
400k     plp
```

Notice that the -r option also sorts the values in descending order, so you can easily see what files are taking up the most space in your directory.

NOTE

The pipe command (|) used in this example redirects the output of the du command to the sort command. That's discussed in more detail in Chapter 11.

Searching for data

Often in a large file, you must look for a specific line of data buried somewhere in the middle of the file. Instead of manually scrolling through the entire file, you can let the grep command search for you. The command line format for the grep command is:

```
grep [options] pattern [file]
```

The grep command searches either the input or the file you specify for lines that contain characters that match the specified pattern. The output from grep is the lines that contain the matching pattern.

Here are two simple examples of using the grep command with the file1 file used in the "Sorting data" section:

```
$ grep three file1
three
$ grep t file1
two
three
$
```

The first example searches the file file1 for text matching the pattern *three*. The grep command produces the line that contains the matching pattern. The next example searches the file file1 for the text matching the pattern *t*. In this case, two lines matched the specified pattern, and both are displayed.

Because of the popularity of the grep command, it has undergone lots of development changes over its lifetime. Lots of features have been added to the grep command. If you look over the man pages for the grep command, you'll see how versatile it really is.

If you want to reverse the search (output lines that don't match the pattern), use the -v parameter:

```
$ grep -v t file1
one
four
five
$
```

If you need to find the line numbers where the matching patterns are found, use the -n parameter:

```
$ grep -n t file1
2:two
3:three
$
```

If you just need to see a count of how many lines contain the matching pattern, use the `-c` parameter:

```
$ grep -c t file1
2
$
```

If you need to specify more than one matching pattern, use the `-e` parameter to specify each individual pattern:

```
$ grep -e t -e f file1
two
three
four
five
$
```

This example outputs lines that contain either the string t or the string f.

By default, the grep command uses basic Unix-style regular expressions to match patterns. A Unix-style regular expression uses special characters to define how to look for matching patterns.

For a more detailed explanation of regular expressions, see Chapter 20.

Here's a simple example of using a regular expression in a grep search:

```
$ grep [tf] file1
two
three
four
five
$
```

The square brackets in the regular expression indicate that grep should look for matches that contain either a *t* or an *f* character. Without the regular expression, grep would search for text that would match the string tf.

The egrep command is an offshoot of grep, which allows you to specify POSIX extended regular expressions, which contain more characters for specifying the matching pattern (again, see Chapter 20 for more details). The fgrep command is another version that allows you to specify matching patterns as a list of fixed-string values, separated by newline characters. This allows you to place a list of strings in a file and then use that list in the fgrep command to search for the strings in a larger file.

Compressing data

If you've done any work in the Microsoft Windows world, no doubt you've used zip files. It became such a popular feature that Microsoft eventually incorporated it into the Windows operating system starting with XP. The zip utility allows you to easily compress large files (both text and executable) into smaller files that take up less space.

Linux contains several file compression utilities. Although this may sound great, it often leads to confusion and chaos when trying to download files. Table 4-7 lists the file compression utilities available for Linux.

TABLE 4-7   **Linux File Compression Utilities**

Utility	File Extension	Description
bzip2	.bz2	Uses the Burrows-Wheeler block sorting text compression algorithm and Huffman coding
compress	.Z	Original Unix file compression utility; starting to fade away into obscurity
gzip	.gz	The GNU Project's compression utility; uses Lempel-Ziv coding
zip	.zip	The Unix version of the PKZIP program for Windows

The compress file compression utility is not often found on Linux systems. If you download a file with a .Z extension, you can usually install the compress package (called ncompress in many Linux distributions) using the software installation methods discussed in Chapter 9 and then uncompress the file with the uncompress command. The gzip utility is the most popular compression tool used in Linux.

The gzip package is a creation of the GNU Project, in their attempt to create a free version of the original Unix compress utility. This package includes these files:

- gzip for compressing files
- gzcat for displaying the contents of compressed text files
- gunzip for uncompressing files

These utilities work the same way as the bzip2 utilities:

```
$ gzip myprog
$ ls -l my*
-rwxrwxr-x 1 rich rich 2197 2007-09-13 11:29 myprog.gz
$
```

The gzip command compresses the file you specify on the command line. You can also specify more than one filename or even use wildcard characters to compress multiple files at once:

```
$ gzip my*
$ ls -l my*
```

```
-rwxr--r--    1 rich     rich          103 Sep  6 13:43 myprog.c.gz
-rwxr-xr-x    1 rich     rich         5178 Sep  6 13:43 myprog.gz
-rwxr--r--    1 rich     rich           59 Sep  6 13:46 myscript.gz
-rwxr--r--    1 rich     rich           60 Sep  6 13:44 myscript2.gz
$
```

The gzip command compresses every file in the directory that matches the wildcard pattern.

Archiving data

Although the zip command works great for compressing and archiving data into a single file, it's not the standard utility used in the Unix and Linux worlds. By far the most popular archiving tool used in Unix and Linux is the tar command.

The tar command was originally used to write files to a tape device for archiving. However, it can also write the output to a file, which has become a popular way to archive data in Linux.

The following is the format of the tar command:

```
tar function [options] object1 object2 ...
```

The function parameter defines what the tar command should do, as shown in Table 4-8.

TABLE 4-8   The tar Command Functions

Function	Long Name	Description
-A	--concatenate	Appends an existing tar archive file to another existing tar archive file
-c	--create	Creates a new tar archive file
-d	--diff	Checks the differences between a tar archive file and the filesystem
	--delete	Deletes from an existing tar archive file
-r	--append	Appends files to the end of an existing tar archive file
-t	--list	Lists the contents of an existing tar archive file
-u	--update	Appends files to an existing tar archive file that are newer than a file with the same name in the existing archive
-x	--extract	Extracts files from an existing archive file

Each function uses *options* to define a specific behavior for the tar archive file. Table 4-9 lists the common options that you can use with the tar command.

TABLE 4-9 **The tar Command Options**

Option	Description
-C *dir*	Changes to the specified directory
-f *file*	Outputs results to file (or device) *file*
-j	Redirects output to the bzip2 command for compression
-p	Preserves all file permissions
-v	Lists files as they are processed
-z	Redirects the output to the gzip command for compression

These options are usually combined to create the following scenarios. First, you want to create an archive file using this command:

```
tar -cvf test.tar test/ test2/
```

The above command creates an archive file called test.tar containing the contents of both the test directory and the test2 directory. Next, this command:

```
tar -tf test.tar
```

lists (but doesn't extract) the contents of the tar file test.tar. Finally, this command:

```
tar -xvf test.tar
```

extracts the contents of the tar file test.tar. If the tar file was created from a directory structure, the entire directory structure is re-created starting at the current directory.

As you can see, using the tar command is a simple way to create archive files of entire directory structures. This is a common method for distributing source code files for open source applications in the Linux world.

> **TIP**
> If you download open source software, often you see filenames that end in .tgz. These are gzipped tar files, which can be extracted using the command tar -zxvf filename.tgz.

Summary

This chapter discussed some of the more advanced bash commands used by Linux system administrators and programmers. The ps and top commands are vital in determining the status of the system, allowing you to see what applications are running and how many resources they are consuming.

In this day of removable media, another popular topic for system administrators is mounting storage devices. The `mount` command allows you to mount a physical storage device into the Linux virtual directory structure. To remove the device, use the `umount` command.

Finally, the chapter discussed various utilities used for handling data. The `sort` utility easily sorts large data files to help you organize data, and the `grep` utility allows you to quickly scan through large data files looking for specific information. Several file compression utilities are available in Linux, including `gzip` and `zip`. Each one allows you to compress large files to help save space on your filesystem. The Linux `tar` utility is a popular way to archive directory structures into a single file that can easily be ported to another system.

The next chapter discusses Linux shells and how to interact with them. Linux allows you to communicate between shells, which can come in handy when creating subshells in your scripts.

Understanding the Shell

N ow that you know a few shell basics, such as reaching the shell and rudimentary shell commands, it is time to explore the actual shell process. To understand the shell, you need to understand a few CLI basics.

A shell is not just a CLI. It is a complicated interactive running program. Entering commands and using the shell to run scripts can raise some interesting and confusing issues. Understanding the shell process and its relationships helps you resolve these issues or avoid them altogether.

This chapter takes you through learning about the shell process. You see how subshells are created and their relationship to the parent shell. The varied commands that create child processes are explored as well as built-in commands. You even read about some shell tips and tricks to try.

Exploring Shell Types

The shell program that the system starts depends on your user ID configuration. In the /etc/ passwd file, the user ID has its default shell program listed in field #7 of its record. The default shell program is started whenever the user logs into a virtual console terminal or starts a terminal emulator in the GUI.

In the following example, user christine has the GNU bash shell as her default shell program:

```
$ cat /etc/passwd
[...]
Christine:x:501:501:Christine B:/home/Christine:/bin/bash
$
```

The bash shell program resides in the /bin directory. A long listing reveals /bin/bash (the bash shell) is an executable program:

```
$ ls -lF /bin/bash
-rwxr-xr-x. 1 root root 938832 Jul 18  2013 /bin/bash*
$
```

Several other shell programs are on this particular CentOS distribution. They include tcsh, which is based off the original C shell:

```
$ ls -lF /bin/tcsh
-rwxr-xr-x. 1 root root 387328 Feb 21  2013 /bin/tcsh*
$
```

Also, the Debian based version of the ash shell, dash, is included:

```
$ ls -lF /bin/dash
-rwxr-xr-x. 1 root root 109672 Oct 17  2012 /bin/dash*
$
```

Finally, a soft link (see Chapter 3) of the C shell points to the tcsh shell:

```
$ ls -lF /bin/csh
lrwxrwxrwx. 1 root root 4 Mar 18 15:16 /bin/csh -> tcsh*
$
```

Each of these different shell programs could be set as a user's default shell. However, due to the bash shell's popularity, it's rare to use any other shell as a default shell.

> **NOTE**
>
> A brief description of various shells was included in Chapter 1. You may be interested in learning even more about shells other than the GNU bash shell. Additional alternative shell information is in Chapter 23.

The *default interactive shell* starts whenever a user logs into a virtual console terminal or starts a terminal emulator in the GUI. However, another default shell, /bin/sh, is the *default system shell*. The default system shell is used for system shell scripts, such as those needed at startup.

Often, you see a distribution with its default system shell set to the bash shell using a soft link as shown here on this CentOS distribution:

```
$ ls -l /bin/sh
lrwxrwxrwx. 1 root root 4 Mar 18 15:05 /bin/sh -> bash
$
```

However, be aware that on some distributions, the default system shell is different than the default interactive shell, such as on this Ubuntu distribution:

```
$ cat /etc/passwd
[...]
christine:x:1000:1000:Christine,,,:/home/christine:/bin/bash
$
$ ls -l /bin/sh
lrwxrwxrwx 1 root root 4 Apr 22 12:33 /bin/sh -> dash
$
```

Note that the user, christine, has her default interactive shell set to /bin/bash, the bash shell. But the default system shell, /bin/sh, is set to the dash shell.

> **TIP**
>
> For bash shell scripts, these two different shells, default interactive shell and default system shell, can cause problems. Be sure to read about the important syntax needed for a bash shell script's first line in Chapter 11 to avoid these issues.

You are not forced to stick with your default interactive shell. You can start any shell available on your distribution, simply by typing its filename. For example, to start the dash shell, you can run it directly by typing the command **/bin/dash**:

```
$ /bin/dash
$
```

It doesn't look like anything happened, but the dash shell program started. The $ prompt is a CLI prompt for the dash shell. You can leave the dash shell program by typing the command **exit**:

```
$ exit
exit
$
```

Again, it looks like nothing happened. However, the dash shell program was exited. To understand this process, the next section explores the relationship between a login shell program and a newly started shell program.

Exploring Parent and Child Shell Relationships

The default interactive shell started when a user logs into a virtual console terminal or starts a terminal emulator in the GUI is a *parent shell*. As you have read so far in this book, a parent shell process provides a CLI prompt and waits for commands to be entered.

When the /bin/bash command or the equivalent bash command is entered at the CLI prompt, a new shell program is created. This is a *child shell*. A child shell also has a CLI prompt and waits for commands to be entered.

5

Because you do not see any relevant messages when you type **bash** and spawn a child shell, another command can help bring clarity. The ps command was covered in Chapter 4. Using this with the -f option before and after entering a child shell is useful:

```
$ ps -f
UID          PID   PPID  C STIME TTY          TIME CMD
501         1841   1840  0 11:50 pts/0     00:00:00 -bash
501         2429   1841  4 13:44 pts/0     00:00:00 ps -f
$
$ bash
$
$ ps -f
UID          PID   PPID  C STIME TTY          TIME CMD
501         1841   1840  0 11:50 pts/0     00:00:00 -bash
501         2430   1841  0 13:44 pts/0     00:00:00 bash
501         2444   2430  1 13:44 pts/0     00:00:00 ps -f
$
```

The first use of ps -f shows two processes. One process has a process ID of 1841 (second column) and is running the bash shell program (last column). The second process (process ID 2429) is the actual ps -f command running.

> **NOTE**
> A *process* is a running program. The bash shell is a program, and when it runs, it is a process. A running shell is simply one type of process. Therefore, when reading about running a bash shell, you often see the word "shell" and the word "process" used interchangeably.

After the command bash is entered, a child shell is created. The second ps -f is executed from within the child shell. From this display, you can see that *two* bash shell programs are running. The first bash shell program, the parent shell process, has the original process ID (PID) of 1841. The second bash shell program, the child shell process, has a PID of 2430. Note that the child shell has a parent process ID (PPID) of 1841, denoting that the parent shell process is its parent. Figure 5-1 diagrams this relationship.

FIGURE 5-1

Parent and child bash shell processes

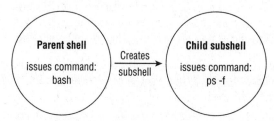

116

When a child shell process is spawned, only some of the parent's environment is copied to the child shell environment. This can cause problems with items such as variables, and it is covered in Chapter 6.

A child shell is also called a *subshell*. A subshell can be created from a parent shell, and a subshell can be created from another subshell:

```
$ ps -f
UID         PID  PPID  C STIME TTY          TIME CMD
501        1841  1840  0 11:50 pts/0     00:00:00 -bash
501        2532  1841  1 14:22 pts/0     00:00:00 ps -f
$
$ bash
$
$ bash
$
$ bash
$
$ ps --forest
  PID TTY          TIME CMD
 1841 pts/0     00:00:00 bash
 2533 pts/0     00:00:00  \_ bash
 2546 pts/0     00:00:00      \_ bash
 2562 pts/0     00:00:00          \_ bash
 2576 pts/0     00:00:00              \_ ps
$
```

In the preceding example, the bash shell command was entered three times. Effectively, this created three subshells. The ps --forest command shows the nesting of these subshells. Figure 5-2 also shows this subshell nesting.

The ps -f command can be useful in subshell nesting, because it displays who is whose parent via the PPID column:

```
$ ps -f
UID         PID  PPID  C STIME TTY          TIME CMD
501        1841  1840  0 11:50 pts/0     00:00:00 -bash
501        2533  1841  0 14:22 pts/0     00:00:00 bash
501        2546  2533  0 14:22 pts/0     00:00:00 bash
501        2562  2546  0 14:24 pts/0     00:00:00 bash
501        2585  2562  1 14:29 pts/0     00:00:00 ps -f
$
```

The bash shell program can use command line parameters to modify the shell start. Table 5-1 lists the command line parameters available in bash.

5

FIGURE 5-2

Subshell nesting

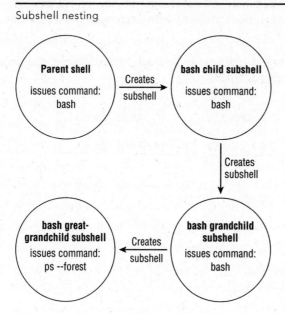

TABLE 5-1 The bash Command Line Parameters

Parameter	Description
-c string	Reads commands from string and processes them
-i	Starts an interactive shell, allowing input from the user
-l	Acts as if invoked as a login shell
-r	Starts a restricted shell, limiting the user to the default directory
-s	Reads commands from the standard input

You can find more help on the bash command and even more command line parameters by typing **man bash**. The bash --help command provides additional assistance as well.

You can gracefully exit out of each subshell by entering the exit command:

```
$ exit
exit
$
$ ps --forest
  PID TTY          TIME CMD
 1841 pts/0    00:00:00 bash
```

```
  2533 pts/0    00:00:00  \_ bash
  2546 pts/0    00:00:00     \_ bash
  2602 pts/0    00:00:00        \_ ps
$
$ exit
exit
$
$ exit
exit
$
$ ps --forest
  PID TTY          TIME CMD
  1841 pts/0    00:00:00 bash
  2604 pts/0    00:00:00  \_ ps
$
```

Not only does the exit command allow you to leave child subshells, but you can also log out of your current virtual console terminal or terminal emulation software as well. Just type **exit** in the parent shell, and you gracefully exit the CLI.

Another time a subshell can be created is when you run a shell script. You learn more about that topic in Chapter 11.

Also, you can spawn subshells without using the bash shell command or running a shell script. One way is by using a process list.

Looking at process lists

On a single line, you can designate a list of commands to be run one after another. This is done by entering a command list using a semicolon (;) between commands:

```
$ pwd ; ls ; cd /etc ; pwd ; cd ; pwd ; ls
/home/Christine
Desktop     Downloads  Music     Public     Videos
Documents   junk.dat   Pictures  Templates
/etc
/home/Christine
Desktop     Downloads  Music     Public     Videos
Documents   junk.dat   Pictures  Templates
$
```

In the preceding example, the commands all executed one after another with no problems. However, this is not a process list. For a command list to be considered a process list, the commands must be encased in parentheses:

```
$ (pwd ; ls ; cd /etc ; pwd ; cd ; pwd ; ls)
/home/Christine
Desktop     Downloads   Music       Public      Videos
Documents   junk.dat    Pictures    Templates
/etc
/home/Christine
Desktop     Downloads   Music       Public      Videos
Documents   junk.dat    Pictures    Templates
$
```

Though the parentheses addition may not appear to be a big difference, they do cause a very different effect. Adding parentheses and turning the command list into a process list created a subshell to execute the commands.

> **NOTE**
>
> A process list is a *command grouping* type. Another command grouping type puts the commands between curly brackets and ends the command list with a semicolon (;). The syntax is as follows: { `command;` }. Using curly brackets for command grouping does not create a subshell as a process list does.

To indicate if a subshell was spawned, a command using an environment variable is needed here. (Environment variables are covered in detail in Chapter 6). The command needed is echo $BASH_SUBSHELL. If it returns a 0, then there is no subshell. If it returns 1 or more, then there is a subshell.

First, the example using just a command list is executed with the echo $BASH_SUBSHELL tacked onto the end:

```
$ pwd ; ls ; cd /etc ; pwd ; cd ; pwd ; ls ; echo $BASH_SUBSHELL
/home/Christine
Desktop     Downloads   Music       Public      Videos
Documents   junk.dat    Pictures    Templates
/etc
/home/Christine
Desktop     Downloads   Music       Public      Videos
Documents   junk.dat    Pictures    Templates
0
```

At the very end of the commands' output, you can see the number zero (0) is displayed. This indicates a subshell was not created to execute these commands.

The results are different using a process list. The list is executed with echo $BASH_SUBSHELL tacked onto the end:

```
$ (pwd ; ls ; cd /etc ; pwd ; cd ; pwd ; ls ; echo $BASH_SUBSHELL)
/home/Christine
Desktop     Downloads   Music       Public      Videos
Documents   junk.dat    Pictures    Templates
/etc
```

```
/home/Christine
Desktop     Downloads   Music     Public      Videos
Documents   junk.dat    Pictures  Templates
1
```

In this case, the number one (1) displayed at the output's end. This indicates a subshell was indeed created and used for executing these commands.

Thus, a *process list* is a command grouping enclosed with parentheses, which creates a subshell to execute the command(s). You can even create a grandchild subshell by embedding parentheses within a process list:

```
$ ( pwd ; echo $BASH_SUBSHELL)
/home/Christine
1
$ ( pwd ; (echo $BASH_SUBSHELL))
/home/Christine
2
```

Notice in the first process list, the number one (1) is displayed indicating a child subshell as you would expect. However in the example's second process list, additional parentheses were added around the echo $BASH_SUBSHELL command. These additional parentheses caused a grandchild subshell to be created for the command's execution. Thus, a number two (2) was displayed indicating a subshell within a subshell.

Subshells are often used for multi-processing in shell scripts. However, entering into a subshell is an expensive method and can significantly slow down processing. Subshell issues exist also for an interactive CLI shell session. It is not truly multi-processing, because the terminal gets tied up with the subshell's I/O.

Creatively using subshells

At the interactive shell CLI, you have more productive ways to use subshells. Process lists, co-processes, and pipes (covered in Chapter 11) use subshells. They all can be used effectively within the interactive shell.

One productive subshell method in the interactive shell uses background mode. Before discussing how to use background mode and subshells together, you need to understand background mode itself.

Investigating background mode

Running a command in background mode allows the command to be processed and frees up your CLI for other use. A classic command to demonstrate background mode is the sleep command.

5

The sleep command accepts as a parameter the number of seconds you want the process to wait (sleep). This command is often used to introduce pauses in shell scripts. The command sleep 10 causes the session to pause for 10 seconds and then return a shell CLI prompt:

```
$ sleep 10
$
```

To put a command into background mode, the & character is tacked onto its end. Putting the sleep command into background mode allows a little investigation with the ps command:

```
$ sleep 3000&
[1] 2396
$ ps -f
UID        PID  PPID  C STIME TTY          TIME CMD
christi+   2338  2337  0 10:13 pts/9    00:00:00 -bash
christi+   2396  2338  0 10:17 pts/9    00:00:00 sleep 3000
christi+   2397  2338  0 10:17 pts/9    00:00:00 ps -f
$
```

The sleep command was told to sleep for 3000 seconds (50 minutes) in the background (&). When it was put into the background, two informational items were displayed before the shell CLI prompt was returned. The first informational item is the background job's number (1) displayed in brackets. The second item is the background job's process ID (2396).

The ps command was used to display the various processes. Notice that the sleep 3000 command is listed. Also note that its process ID (PID) in the second column is the same PID displayed when the command went into the background, 2396.

In addition to the ps command, you can use the jobs command to display background job information. The jobs command displays any user's processes (jobs) currently running in background mode:

```
$ jobs
[1]+  Running                 sleep 3000 &
$
```

The jobs command shows the job number (1) in brackets. It also displays the job's current status (running) as well as the command itself, (sleep 3000 &).

You can see even more information by using the -l (lowercase L) parameter on the jobs command. The -l parameter displays the command's PID in addition to the other information:

```
$ jobs -l
[1]+  2396 Running                 sleep 3000 &
$
```

When the background job is finished, its completion status is displayed:

```
[1]+   Done                         sleep 3000 &
$
```

Background mode is very handy. And it provides a method for creating useful subshells at the CLI.

Putting process lists into the background

As stated earlier, a process list is a command or series of commands executed within a sub-shell. Using a process list including sleep commands and displaying the BASH_SUBSHELL variable operates as you would expect:

```
$ (sleep 2 ; echo $BASH_SUBSHELL ; sleep 2)
1
$
```

In the preceding example, a two-second pause occurs, the number one (1) is displayed indicating a single subshell level (child subshell), and then another two-second pause occurs before the prompt returns. Nothing too dramatic here.

Putting the same process list into background mode can cause a slightly different effect with command output:

```
$ (sleep 2 ; echo $BASH_SUBSHELL ; sleep 2)&
[2] 2401
$ 1

[2]+   Done                    ( sleep 2; echo $BASH_SUBSHELL; sleep 2 )
$
```

Putting the process list into the background causes a job number and process ID to appear, and the prompt returns. However, the odd event is that the displayed number one (1), indicating a single-level subshell, is displayed by the prompt! Don't let this confuse you. Simply press the Enter key, and you get another prompt back.

Using a process list in background mode is one creative method for using subshells at the CLI. You can do large amounts of processing within a subshell and not have your terminal tied up with the subshell's I/O.

5

Of course, the process list of `sleep` and `echo` commands are just for example purposes. Creating backup files with `tar` (see Chapter 4) is a more practical example of using background process lists effectively:

```
$ (tar -cf Rich.tar /home/rich ; tar -cf My.tar /home/christine)&
[3] 2423
$
```

Putting a process list in background mode is not the only way to use subshells creatively at the CLI. Co-processing is another method.

Looking at co-processing

Co-processing does two things at the same time. It spawns a subshell in background mode and executes a command within that subshell.

To perform co-processing, the `coproc` command is used along with the command to be executed in the subshell:

```
$ coproc sleep 10
[1] 2544
$
```

Co-processing performs almost identically to putting a command in background mode, except for the fact that it creates a subshell. You'll notice that when the `coproc` command and its parameters were entered, a background job was started. The background job number (1) and process ID (2544) were displayed on the screen.

The `jobs` command allows you to display the co-processing status:

```
$ jobs
[1]+  Running                 coproc COPROC sleep 10 &
$
```

From the preceding example, you can see the background command executing in the subshell is `coproc COPROC sleep 10`. The COPROC is a name given to the process by the `coproc` command. You can set the name yourself by using extended syntax for the command:

```
$ coproc My_Job { sleep 10; }
[1] 2570
$
$ jobs
[1]+  Running                 coproc My_Job { sleep 10; } &
$
```

By using the extended syntax, the co-processing name was set to My_Job. Be careful here, because the extended syntax is a little tricky. You have to make sure that a space appears after the first curly bracket ({) and before the start of your command. Also, you have to make sure the command ends with a semicolon (;). And you have to ensure that a space appears after the semicolon and before the closing curly bracket (}).

You can be really clever and combine co-processing with process lists creating nested subshells. Just type your process list and put the command coproc in front of it:

```
$ coproc ( sleep 10; sleep 2 )
[1] 2574
$
$ jobs
[1]+  Running       coproc COPROC ( sleep 10; sleep 2 ) &
$
$ ps --forest
  PID TTY          TIME CMD
 2483 pts/12    00:00:00 bash
 2574 pts/12    00:00:00  \_ bash
 2575 pts/12    00:00:00  |   \_ sleep
 2576 pts/12    00:00:00  \_ ps
$
```

Just remember that spawning a subshell can be expensive and slow. Creating nested subshells is even more so!

Using subshells can provide flexibility at the command line as well as convenience. Understanding their behavior is important to obtaining this flexibility and convenience. Command behavior is also important to understand. In the next section, the behavior differences between built-in and external commands are explored.

Understanding Shell Built-In Commands

While learning about the GNU bash shell, you likely have heard the term built-in command. It is important to understand both shell built-in and non-built-in (external) commands. Built-in commands and non-built-in commands operate very differently.

Looking at external commands

An *external command*, sometimes called a filesystem command, is a program that exists outside of the bash shell. They are not built into the shell program. An external command program is typically located in /bin, /usr/bin, /sbin, or /usr/sbin.

The ps command is an external command. You can find its filename by using both the which and the type commands:

```
$ which ps
/bin/ps
$
$ type -a ps
ps is /bin/ps
$
$ ls -l /bin/ps
-rwxr-xr-x 1 root root 93232 Jan  6 18:32 /bin/ps
$
```

Whenever an external command is executed, a child process is created. This action is termed *forking*. Conveniently, the external command ps displays its current parent as well as its own forked child processes:

```
$ ps -f
UID         PID  PPID  C STIME TTY          TIME CMD
christi+    2743  2742  0 17:09 pts/9    00:00:00 -bash
christi+    2801  2743  0 17:16 pts/9    00:00:00 ps -f
$
```

Because it is an external command, when the ps command executes, a child process is created. In this case, the ps command's PID is 2801 and the parent PID is 2743. The bash shell process, which is the parent, has a PID of 2743. Figure 5-3 illustrates the forking that occurs when an external command is executed.

FIGURE 5-3

External command forking

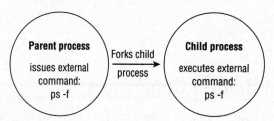

Whenever a process must fork, it takes time and effort to set up the new child process's environment. Thus, external commands can be a little expensive.

When using a built-in command, no forking is required. Therefore, built-in commands are less expensive.

Looking at built-in commands

Built-in commands are different in that they do not need a child process to execute. They were compiled into the shell and thus are part of the shell's toolkit. No external program file exists to run them.

Both the cd and exit commands are built into the bash shell. You can tell a command is built-in by using the type command:

```
$ type cd
cd is a shell builtin
$
$ type exit
exit is a shell builtin
$
```

Because they do not need to fork a child process to execute or open a program file, built-in commands are faster and more efficient. A list of GNU bash shell built-in commands is provided in Appendix A.

Be aware that some commands have multiple flavors. For example, both echo and pwd have a built-in command flavor as well as an external command flavor. These flavors are slightly different. To see multiple flavors for commands, use the -a option on the type command:

```
$ type -a echo
echo is a shell builtin
echo is /bin/echo
$
$ which echo
/bin/echo
$
$ type -a pwd
pwd is a shell builtin
pwd is /bin/pwd
```

5

```
$
$ which pwd
/bin/pwd
$
```

Using the `type -a` command shows both types for each of the two commands. Note that the `which` command shows only the external command file.

> **TIP**
>
> To use the external command for a command that has multiple flavors, directly reference the file. For example, to use the `pwd` external command, type `/bin/pwd`.

Using the history command

A useful built-in command is the `history` command. The bash shell keeps track of the commands you have used. You can recall these commands and even reuse them.

To see a recently used commands list, just type the `history` command with no options:

```
$ history
    1  ps -f
    2  pwd
    3  ls
    4  coproc ( sleep 10; sleep 2 )
    5  jobs
    6  ps --forest
    7  ls
    8  ps -f
    9  pwd
   10  ls -l /bin/ps
   11  history
   12  cd /etc
   13  pwd
   14  ls
   15  cd
   16  type pwd
   17  which pwd
   18  type echo
   19  which echo
   20  type -a pwd
   21  type -a echo
   22  pwd
   23  history
```

In this example, only the last 23 commands are shown. Typically, the last 1,000 commands are kept in history. That is lots of commands!

TIP

You can set the number of commands to keep in the bash history. To do so, you need to modify an environment variable called HISTSIZE (see Chapter 6).

You can recall and reuse the last command in your history list. This can save time and typing. To recall and reuse your last command, type !! and press the Enter key:

```
$ ps --forest
  PID TTY          TIME CMD
 2089 pts/0    00:00:00 bash
 2744 pts/0    00:00:00  \_ ps
$
$ !!
ps --forest
  PID TTY          TIME CMD
 2089 pts/0    00:00:00 bash
 2745 pts/0    00:00:00  \_ ps
$
```

When !! was entered, the bash shell first displayed the command it was recalling from the shell's history. After the command was displayed, it was executed.

Command history is kept in the hidden .bash_history file, which is located in the user's home directory. Be careful here. The bash command history is stored in memory and then written out into the history file when the shell is exited:

```
$ history
[...]
   25  ps --forest
   26  history
   27  ps --forest
   28  history
$
$ cat .bash_history
pwd
ls
history
exit
$
```

Notice when the history command is run, 28 commands are listed. In the example, the listing is snipped for brevity. However, when the .bash_history file is displayed, only four commands are listed, and they don't match the history command's list.

You can force the command history to be written to the `.bash_history` file before leaving a shell session. In order to force this write, use the -a option on the history command:

```
$ history -a
$
$ history
[...]
    25  ps --forest
    26  history
    27  ps --forest
    28  history
    29  ls -a
    30  cat .bash_history
    31  history -a
    32  history
$
$ cat .bash_history
[...]
ps --forest
history
ps --forest
history
ls -a
cat .bash_history
history -a
```

This time both listings need to be snipped because they are so long. Notice that contents from both the history command and the `.bash_history` file match, except for the very last command listed for the history command, because it came after the history -a command was issued.

> **NOTE**
>
> If you have multiple terminal sessions open, you can still append the `.bash_history` in each open session using the history -a command. However, the histories are not automatically updated for your other open terminal sessions. This is because the `.bash_history` file is read only when a terminal session is first started. To force the `.bash_history` file to be reread and a terminal session's history to be updated, use the history -n command.

You can recall any command from the history list. Just enter an exclamation point and the command's number from the history list:

```
$ history
[...]
    13  pwd
    14  ls
    15  cd
```

```
   16   type pwd
   17   which pwd
   18   type echo
   19   which echo
   20   type -a pwd
   21   type -a echo
[...]
   32   history -a
   33   history
   34   cat .bash_history
   35   history
$
$ !20
type -a pwd
pwd is a shell builtin
pwd is /bin/pwd
$
```

Command number 20 was pulled from command history. Notice that similar to executing the last command in history, the bash shell first displays the command it is recalling from the shell's history. After the command is displayed, it is executed.

Using bash shell command history can be a great timesaver. You can do even more with the built-in `history` command. Be sure to view the bash manual pages for `history`, by typing **man history**.

Using command aliases

The `alias` command is another shell built-in command. A *command alias* allows you to create an alias name for common commands (along with their parameters) to help keep your typing to a minimum.

Most likely, your Linux distribution has already set some common command aliases for you. To see a list of the active aliases, use the `alias` command with the `-p` parameter:

```
$ alias -p
[...]
alias egrep='egrep --color=auto'
alias fgrep='fgrep --color=auto'
alias grep='grep --color=auto'
alias l='ls -CF'
alias la='ls -A'
alias ll='ls -alF'
alias ls='ls --color=auto'
$
```

Notice that, on this Ubuntu Linux distribution, an alias is used to override the standard `ls` command. It automatically provides the `--color` parameter, indicating that the terminal supports color mode listings.

5

You can create your own aliases using the `alias` command:

```
$ alias li='ls -li'
$
$ li
total 36
529581 drwxr-xr-x. 2 Christine Christine 4096 May 19 18:17 Desktop
529585 drwxr-xr-x. 2 Christine Christine 4096 Apr 25 16:59 Documents
529582 drwxr-xr-x. 2 Christine Christine 4096 Apr 25 16:59 Downloads
529586 drwxr-xr-x. 2 Christine Christine 4096 Apr 25 16:59 Music
529587 drwxr-xr-x. 2 Christine Christine 4096 Apr 25 16:59 Pictures
529584 drwxr-xr-x. 2 Christine Christine 4096 Apr 25 16:59 Public
529583 drwxr-xr-x. 2 Christine Christine 4096 Apr 25 16:59 Templates
532891 -rwxrw-r--. 1 Christine Christine   36 May 30 07:21 test.sh
529588 drwxr-xr-x. 2 Christine Christine 4096 Apr 25 16:59 Videos
$
```

After you define an alias value, you can use it at any time in your shell, including in shell scripts. Be aware that because command aliases are built-in commands, an alias is valid only for the shell process in which it is defined:

```
$ alias li='ls -li'
$
$ bash
$
$ li
bash: li: command not found
$
$ exit
exit
$
```

Fortunately, you can make an alias value permanent across subshells. The next chapter covers how to do that, along with environment variables.

Summary

This chapter discussed the complicated interactive program, the GNU bash shell. It covered understanding the shell process and its relationships, including how subshells are spawned and their relationship to the parent shell. We also explored commands that create child processes and commands that don't.

The default interactive shell is normally started whenever a user logs in to a terminal. The shell that the system starts depends upon a user ID configuration. Typically, it is /bin/bash. The default system shell, /bin/sh, is used for system shell scripts, such as those needed at startup.

A subshell or child shell can be spawned using the bash command. They are also created when a process list or the coproc command is used. Using subshells at the command line can allow for creative and productive use of the CLI. Subshells can be nested, spawning grandchild shells and great-grandchild shells. Creating a subshell is an expensive process as a new environment for the shell must be created as well.

Finally, the chapter looked at two different types of shell commands: built-in and external commands. External commands create a child process with a new environment, but a built-in command does not. This causes external commands to be more expensive to use. Because a new environment is not needed, built-in commands are more efficient and not affected by any environment changes.

Shells, subshells, processes, and forked processes are all affected by environment variables. How the variables affect and can be used within these different contexts are explored in the next chapter.

5

Using Linux Environment Variables

L inux environment variables help define your Linux shell experience. Many programs and scripts use environment variables to obtain system information and store temporary data and configuration information. Environment variables are set in lots of places on the Linux system, and you should know where these places are.

This chapter walks you through the world of Linux environment variables, showing where they are, how to use them, and even how to create your own. The chapter finishes off with how to use variable arrays.

Exploring Environment Variables

The bash shell uses a feature called *environment variables* to store information about the shell session and the working environment (thus the name environment variables). This feature also allows you to store data in memory that can be easily accessed by any program or script running from the shell. It is a handy way to store needed persistent data.

There are two environment variable types in the bash shell:

- Global variables
- Local variables

135

This section describes each type of environment variable and shows how to see and use them.

Looking at global environment variables

Global environment variables are visible from the shell session and from any spawned child subshells. Local variables are available only in the shell that creates them. This makes global environment variables useful in applications that create child subshells, which require parent shell information.

The Linux system sets several global environment variables when you start your bash session. (For more details about what variables are started at that time, see the "Locating System Environment Variables" section later in this chapter.) The system environment variables almost always use all capital letters to differentiate them from normal user environment variables.

To view global environment variables, use the env or the printenv command:

```
$ printenv
HOSTNAME=server01.class.edu
SELINUX_ROLE_REQUESTED=
TERM=xterm
SHELL=/bin/bash
HISTSIZE=1000
[...]
HOME=/home/Christine
LOGNAME=Christine
[...]
G_BROKEN_FILENAMES=1
_=/usr/bin/printenv
```

So many global environment variables get set for the bash shell that the display had to be snipped. Not only are many set during the login process, but how you log in can affect which ones are set as well.

To display an individual environment variable's value, you can use the printenv command, but not the env command:

```
$ printenv HOME
/home/Christine
```

```
$
$ env HOME
env: HOME: No such file or directory
$
```

You can also use the echo command to display a variable's value. When referencing an environment variable in this case, you must place a dollar sign ($) before the environment variable name:

```
$ echo $HOME
/home/Christine
$
```

Using the dollar sign along with the variable name does more than just display its current definition when used with the echo command. The dollar sign before a variable name allows the variable to be passed as a command parameter:

```
$ ls $HOME
Desktop      Downloads   Music     Public      test.sh
Documents    junk.dat    Pictures  Templates   Videos
$
$ ls /home/Christine
Desktop      Downloads   Music     Public      test.sh
Documents    junk.dat    Pictures  Templates   Videos
$
```

As mentioned earlier, global environment variables are also available to any process's subshells:

```
$ bash
$
$ ps -f
UID         PID   PPID  C STIME TTY          TIME CMD
501         2017  2016  0 16:00 pts/0    00:00:00 -bash
501         2082  2017  0 16:08 pts/0    00:00:00 bash
501         2095  2082  0 16:08 pts/0    00:00:00 ps -f
$
$ echo $HOME
/home/Christine
$
$ exit
exit
$
```

In this example, after spawning a subshell using the bash command, the HOME environment variable's current value is shown. It is set to the exact same value, /home/Christine, as it was in the parent shell.

Looking at local environment variables

Local environment variables, as their name implies, can be seen only in the local process in which they are defined. Even though they are local, they are just as important as global environment variables. In fact, the Linux system also defines standard local environment variables for you by default. However, you can also define your own local variables. These, as you would assume, are called user-defined local variables.

Trying to see the local variables list is a little tricky at the CLI. Unfortunately, there isn't a command that displays only these variables. The set command displays all variables defined for a specific process, including both local and global environment variables and user-defined variables:

```
$ set
BASH=/bin/bash
[...]
BASH_ALIASES=()
BASH_ARGC=()
BASH_ARGV=()
BASH_CMDS=()
BASH_LINENO=()
BASH_SOURCE=()
[...]
colors=/etc/DIR_COLORS
my_variable='Hello World'
[...]
$
```

All global environment variables displayed using the env or printenv commands appear in the set command's output. The additional environment variables are the local environment and user-defined variables.

> **NOTE**
>
> The differences between the commands env, printenv, and set are subtle. The set command displays both global and local environment variables and user-defined variables. It also sorts the display alphabetically. The env and printenv are different from set in that they do not sort the variables, nor do they include local environment or local user-defined variables. Used in this context, env and printenv produce duplicate listings. However, the env command has additional functionality that printenv does not have, making it the slightly more powerful command.

Setting User-Defined Variables

You can set your own variables directly from the bash shell. This section shows you how to create your own variables and reference them from an interactive shell or shell script program.

Setting local user-defined variables

After you start a bash shell (or spawn a shell script), you're allowed to create local user-defined variables that are visible within your shell process. You can assign either a numeric or a string value to an environment variable by assigning the variable to a value using the equal sign:

```
$ echo $my_variable

$ my_variable=Hello
$
$ echo $my_variable
Hello
```

That was simple! Now, any time you need to reference the my_variable user-defined variable's value, just reference it by the name $my_variable.

If you need to assign a string value that contains spaces, you need to use a single or double quotation mark to delineate the beginning and the end of the string:

```
$ my_variable=Hello World
-bash: World: command not found
$
$ my_variable="Hello World"
$
$ echo $my_variable
Hello World
$
```

Without the quotation marks, the bash shell assumes that the next word is another command to process. Notice that for the local variable you defined, you used lowercase letters, while the system environment variables you've seen so far have all used uppercase letters.

> **TIP**
>
> The standard bash shell convention is for all environment variables to use uppercase letters. If you are creating a local variable for yourself and your own shell scripts, use lowercase letters. Variables are case sensitive. By keeping your user-defined local variables lowercase, you avoid the potential disaster of redefining a system environment variable.

It's extremely important that you not use spaces between the variable name, the equal sign, and the value. If you put any spaces in the assignment, the bash shell interprets the value as a separate command:

```
$ my_variable = "Hello World"
-bash: my_variable: command not found
$
```

After you set a local variable, it's available for use anywhere within your shell process. However, if you spawn another shell, it's not available in the child shell:

```
$ my_variable="Hello World"
$
$ bash
$
$ echo $my_variable

$ exit
exit
$
$ echo $my_variable
Hello World
$
```

In this example, a child shell was spawned. The user-defined my_variable was not available in the child shell. This is demonstrated by the blank line returned after the echo $my_variable command. After the child shell was exited and returned to the original shell, the local variable was still available.

Similarly, if you set a local variable in a child process, after you leave the child process, the local variable is no longer available:

```
$ echo $my_child_variable

$ bash
$
$ my_child_variable="Hello Little World"
$
$ echo $my_child_variable
Hello Little World
$
$ exit
exit
$
$ echo $my_child_variable

$
```

The local variable set within the child shell doesn't exist after a return to the parent shell. You can change this behavior by turning your local user-defined variable into a global environment variable.

Setting global environment variables

Global environment variables are visible from any child processes created by the parent process that sets the variable. The method used to create a global environment variable is to first create a local variable and then export it to the global environment.

This is done by using the `export` command and the variable name minus the dollar sign:

```
$ my_variable="I am Global now"
$
$ export my_variable
$
$ echo $my_variable
I am Global now
$
$ bash
$
$ echo $my_variable
I am Global now
$
$ exit
exit
$
$ echo $my_variable
I am Global now
$
```

After defining and exporting the local variable my_variable, a child shell was started by the bash command. The child shell was able to properly display the my_variable variable's value. The variable kept its value, because the export command made it a global environment variable.

Changing a global environment variable within a child shell does not affect the variable's value in the parent shell:

```
$ my_variable="I am Global now"
$ export my_variable
$
$ echo $my_variable
I am Global now
$
$ bash
$
$ echo $my_variable
I am Global now
$
$ my_variable="Null"
$
$ echo $my_variable
Null
$
$ exit
exit
$
```

```
$ echo $my_variable
I am Global now
$
```

After defining and exporting the variable my_variable, a subshell was started by the bash command. The subshell properly displayed the value of the my_variable global environment variable. The variable's value was then changed by the child shell. However, the variable's value was modified only within the child shell and not in the parent's shell.

A child shell cannot even use the export command to change the parent shell's global environment variable's value:

```
$ my_variable="I am Global now"
$ export my_variable
$
$ echo $my_variable
I am Global now
$
$ bash
$
$ echo $my_variable
I am Global now
$
$ my_variable="Null"
$
$ export my_variable
$
$ echo $my_variable
Null
$
$ exit
exit
$
$ echo $my_variable
I am Global now
$
```

Even though the child shell redefined and exported the variable my_variable, the parent shell's my_variable variable kept its original value.

Removing Environment Variables

Of course, if you can create a new environment variable, it makes sense that you can also remove an existing environment variable. You can do this with the unset command. When referencing the environment variable in the unset command, remember not to use the dollar sign:

```
$ echo $my_variable
I am Global now
```

```
$
$ unset my_variable
$
$ echo $my_variable

$
```

> **TIP**
>
> It can be confusing to remember when to use and when not to use the dollar sign with environment variables. Just remember this: If you are doing anything *with* the variable, use the dollar sign. If you are doing anything *to* the variable, don't use the dollar sign. The exception to this rule is using `printenv` to display a variable's value.

When dealing with global environment variables, things get a little tricky. If you're in a child process and unset a global environment variable, it applies only to the child process. The global environment variable is still available in the parent process:

```
$ my_variable="I am Global now"
$
$ export my_variable
$
$ echo $my_variable
I am Global now
$
$ bash
$
$ echo $my_variable
I am Global now
$
$ unset my_variable
$
$ echo $my_variable

$ exit
exit
$
$ echo $my_variable
I am Global now
$
```

Just as with modifying a variable, you cannot unset it in a child shell and have the variable be unset in the parent's shell.

Uncovering Default Shell Environment Variables

The bash shell uses specific environment variables by default to define the system environment. You can always count on these variables being set or available to be set on your

Linux system. Because the bash shell is a derivative of the original Unix Bourne shell, it also includes environment variables originally defined in that shell.

Table 6-1 shows the environment variables that the bash shell provides that are compatible with the original Unix Bourne shell.

TABLE 6-1 The bash Shell Bourne Variables

Variable	Description
CDPATH	A colon-separated list of directories used as a search path for the cd command
HOME	The current user's home directory
IFS	A list of characters that separate fields used by the shell to split text strings
MAIL	The filename for the current user's mailbox (The bash shell checks this file for new mail.)
MAILPATH	A colon-separated list of multiple filenames for the current user's mailbox (The bash shell checks each file in this list for new mail.)
OPTARG	The value of the last option argument processed by the getopt command
OPTIND	The index value of the last option argument processed by the getopt command
PATH	A colon-separated list of directories where the shell looks for commands
PS1	The primary shell command line interface prompt string
PS2	The secondary shell command line interface prompt string

Besides the default Bourne environment variables, the bash shell also provides a few variables of its own, as shown in Table 6-2.

TABLE 6-2 The bash Shell Environment Variables

Variable	Description
BASH	The full pathname to execute the current instance of the bash shell
BASH_ALIASES	An associative array of currently set aliases
BASH_ARGC	A variable array that contains the number of parameters being passed to a subroutine or shell script
BASH_ARCV	A variable array that contains the parameters being passed to a subroutine or shell script
BASH_CMDS	An associative array of locations of commands the shell has executed

BASH_COMMAND	The shell command currently being or about to be executed
BASH_ENV	When set, each bash script attempts to execute a startup file defined by this variable before running.
BASH_EXECUTION_STRING	The command(s) passed using the bash -c option
BASH_LINENO	A variable array containing the source code line number of the currently executing shell function
BASH_REMATCH	A read-only variable array containing patterns and their sub-patterns for positive matches using the regular expression comparison operator, =~
BASH_SOURCE	A variable array containing the source code filename of the currently executing shell function
BASH_SUBSHELL	The current nesting level of a subshell environment (The initial value is 0.)
BASH_VERSINFO	A variable array that contains the individual major and minor version numbers of the current instance of the bash shell
BASH_VERSION	The version number of the current instance of the bash shell
BASH_XTRACEFD	If set to a valid file descriptor (0,1,2), trace output generated from the 'set -x' debugging option can be redirected. This is often used to separate trace output into a file.
BASHOPTS	A list of bash shell options that are currently enabled
BASHPID	Process ID of the current bash process
COLUMNS	Contains the terminal width of the terminal used for the current instance of the bash shell
COMP_CWORD	An index into the variable COMP_WORDS, which contains the current cursor position
COMP_LINE	The current command line
COMP_POINT	The index of the current cursor position relative to the beginning of the current command
COMP_KEY	The final key used to invoke the current completion of a shell function
COMP_TYPE	An integer value representing the type of completion attempted that caused a completion shell function to be invoked
COMP_WORDBREAKS	The Readline library word separator characters for performing word completion
COMP_WORDS	An array variable that contains the individual words on the current command line
COMPREPLY	An array variable that contains the possible completion codes generated by a shell function

Continues

TABLE 6-2   *(continued)*

Variable	Description
COPROC	An array variable that holds an unnamed coprocess' I/O file descriptors
DIRSTACK	An array variable that contains the current contents of the directory stack
EMACS	Indicates the emacs shell buffer is executing and line editing is disabled, when set to 't'
ENV	When set, executes the startup file defined before a bash shell script runs (It is used only when the bash shell has been invoked in POSIX mode.)
EUID	The numeric effective user ID of the current user
FCEDIT	The default editor used by the fc command
FIGNORE	A colon-separated list of suffixes to ignore when performing file name completion
FUNCNAME	The name of the currently executing shell function
FUNCNEST	Sets the maximum allowed function nesting level, when set to a number greater than zero (If it is exceeded, the current command aborts.)
GLOBIGNORE	A colon-separated list of patterns defining the set of filenames to be ignored by file name expansion
GROUPS	A variable array containing the list of groups of which the current user is a member
histchars	Up to three characters, which control history expansion
HISTCMD	The history number of the current command
HISTCONTROL	Controls what commands are entered in the shell history list
HISTFILE	The name of the file in which to save the shell history list (.bash_history by default)
HISTFILESIZE	The maximum number of lines to save in the history file
HISTTIMEFORMAT	Used as a formatting string to print each command's timestamp in bash history, if set and not null
HISTIGNORE	A colon-separated list of patterns used to decide which commands are ignored for the history file
HISTSIZE	The maximum number of commands stored in the history file
HOSTFILE	Contains the name of the file that should be read when the shell needs to complete a hostname
HOSTNAME	The name of the current host
HOSTTYPE	A string describing the machine the bash shell is running on

IGNOREEOF	The number of consecutive EOF characters the shell must receive before exiting (If this value doesn't exist, the default is 1.)
INPUTRC	The name of the Readline initialization file (The default is .inputrc.)
LANG	The locale category for the shell
LC_ALL	Overrides the LANG variable, defining a locale category
LC_COLLATE	Sets the collation order used when sorting string values
LC_CTYPE	Determines the interpretation of characters used in filename expansion and pattern matching
LC_MESSAGES	Determines the locale setting used when interpreting double-quoted strings preceded by a dollar sign
LC_NUMERIC	Determines the locale setting used when formatting numbers
LINENO	The line number in a script currently executing
LINES	Defines the number of lines available on the terminal
MACHTYPE	A string defining the system type in cpu-company-system format
MAPFILE	An array variable that holds read-in text from the mapfile command when no array variable name is given
MAILCHECK	How often (in seconds) the shell should check for new mail (The default is 60.)
OLDPWD	The previous working directory used in the shell
OPTERR	If set to 1, the bash shell displays errors generated by the getopts command.
OSTYPE	A string defining the operating system the shell is running on
PIPESTATUS	A variable array containing a list of exit status values from the processes in the foreground process
POSIXLY_CORRECT	If set, bash starts in POSIX mode.
PPID	The process ID (PID) of the bash shell's parent process
PROMPT_COMMAND	If set, the command to execute before displaying the primary prompt
PROMPT_DIRTRIM	An integer used to indicate the number of trailing directory names to display when using the \w and \W prompt string escapes (The directory names removed are replaced with one set of ellipses.)
PS3	The prompt to use for the select command
PS4	The prompt displayed before the command line is echoed if the bash -x parameter is used
PWD	The current working directory

Continues

TABLE 6-2   *(continued)*

Variable	Description
RANDOM	Returns a random number between 0 and 32767 (Assigning a value to this variable seeds the pseudo-random number generator.)
READLINE_LINE	Readline buffer contents when using bind -x command
READLINE_POINT	Readline buffer content insertion point's current position when using bind -x command
REPLY	The default variable for the read command
SECONDS	The number of seconds since the shell was started (Assigning a value resets the timer to the value.)
SHELL	The full pathname to the bash shell
SHELLOPTS	A colon-separated list of enabled bash shell options
SHLVL	Indicates the shell level, incremented by one each time a new bash shell is started
TIMEFORMAT	A format specifying how the shell displays time values
TMOUT	The value of how long (in seconds) the select and read commands should wait for input (The default of zero indicates to wait indefinitely.)
TMPDIR	Directory name where the bash shell creates temporary files for its use
UID	The numeric real user ID of the current user

You may notice that not all default environment variables are shown when the set command is used. When not in use, the default environment variables are not all required to contain a value.

Setting the PATH Environment Variable

When you enter an external command (see Chapter 5) in the shell command line interface (CLI), the shell must search the system to find the program. The PATH environment variable defines the directories it searches looking for commands and programs. On this Ubuntu Linux system, the PATH environment variable looks like this:

```
$ echo $PATH
/usr/local/sbin:/usr/local/bin:/usr/sbin:/usr/bin:
/sbin:/bin:/usr/games:/usr/local/games
$
```

This shows that there are eight directories where the shell looks for commands and programs. The directories in the PATH are separated by colons.

If a command's or program's location is not included in the PATH variable, the shell cannot find it without an absolute directory reference. If the shell cannot find the command or program, it produces an error message:

```
$ myprog
-bash: myprog: command not found
$
```

The problem is that often applications place their executable programs in directories that aren't in the PATH environment variable. The trick is ensuring that your PATH environment variable includes all the directories where your applications reside.

You can add new search directories to the existing PATH environment variable without having to rebuild it from scratch. The individual directories listed in the PATH are separated by colons. All you need to do is reference the original PATH value and add any new directories to the string. This looks something like this:

```
$ echo $PATH
/usr/local/sbin:/usr/local/bin:/usr/sbin:/usr/bin:
/sbin:/bin:/usr/games:/usr/local/games
$
$ PATH=$PATH:/home/christine/Scripts
$
$ echo $PATH
/usr/local/sbin:/usr/local/bin:/usr/sbin:/usr/bin:/sbin:/bin:/usr/
    games:/usr/local/games:/home/christine/Scripts
$
$ myprog
The factorial of 5 is 120.
$
```

By adding the directory to the PATH environment variable, you can now execute your program from anywhere in the virtual directory structure:

```
$ cd /etc
$
$ myprog
The factorial of 5 is 120
$
```

> **TIP**
>
> If you want your program's location to be available to subshells, be sure to export your modified PATH environment variable.

A common trick for programmers is to include the single dot symbol in their PATH environment variable. The single dot symbol represents the current directory (see Chapter 3):

```
$ PATH=$PATH:.
$
```

```
$ cd /home/christine/Old_Scripts
$
$ myprog2
The factorial of 6 is 720
$
```

Changes to the PATH variable last only until you exit the system or the system reboots. The changes are not persistent. In the next section, you see how you can make changes to environment variables permanent.

Locating System Environment Variables

The Linux system uses environment variables for many purposes. You know now how to modify system environment variables and create your own variables. The trick is in how these environment variables are made persistent.

When you start a bash shell by logging in to the Linux system, by default bash checks several files for commands. These files are called *startup files* or *environment files*. The startup files that bash processes depend on the method you use to start the bash shell. You can start a bash shell in three ways:

- As a default login shell at login time
- As an interactive shell that is started by spawning a subshell
- As a non-interactive shell to run a script

The following sections describe the startup files the bash shell executes in each of these startup methods.

Understanding the login shell process

When you log in to the Linux system, the bash shell starts as a login shell. The login shell typically looks for five different startup files to process commands from:

- /etc/profile
- $HOME/.bash_profile
- $HOME/.bashrc
- $HOME/.bash_login
- $HOME/.profile

The /etc/profile file is the main default startup file for the bash shell on the system. All users on the system execute this startup file when they log in.

> **NOTE**
>
> Be aware that some Linux distributions use Pluggable Authentication Modules (PAM). In this case, before the bash shell is started, PAM files are processed, including ones that may contain environment variables. PAM file examples include the /etc/environment file and the $HOME/.pam_environment file. Find more information about PAM at http://linux-pam.org.

The other four startup files are specific for each user and can be customized for an individual user's requirements. Let's look closer at these files.

Viewing the /etc/profile file

The /etc/profile file is the main default startup file for the bash shell. Whenever you log in to the Linux system, bash executes the commands in the /etc/profile startup file first. Different Linux distributions place different commands in this file. On this Ubuntu Linux system, the file looks like this:

```
$ cat /etc/profile
# /etc/profile: system-wide .profile file for the Bourne shell (sh(1))
# and Bourne compatible shells (bash(1), ksh(1), ash(1), ...).

if [ "$PS1" ]; then
  if [ "$BASH" ] && [ "$BASH" != "/bin/sh" ]; then
    # The file bash.bashrc already sets the default PS1.
    # PS1='\h:\w\$ '
    if [ -f /etc/bash.bashrc ]; then
      . /etc/bash.bashrc
    fi
  else
    if [ "`id -u`" -eq 0 ]; then
      PS1='# '
    else
      PS1='$ '
    fi
  fi
fi

# The default umask is now handled by pam_umask.
# See pam_umask(8) and /etc/login.defs.

if [ -d /etc/profile.d ]; then
  for i in /etc/profile.d/*.sh; do
    if [ -r $i ]; then
      . $i
    fi
  done
  unset i
fi
$
```

Most of the commands and syntax you see in this file are covered in more detail in Chapter 12 and beyond. Each distribution's /etc/profile file has different settings and commands. For example, notice that a file is mentioned in this Ubuntu distribution's /etc/profile file above, called /etc/bash.bashrc. It contains system environment variables.

However, in this CentOS distribution's /etc/profile file listed below, no /etc/bash.bashrc file is called. Also note that it sets and exports some system environment variables within itself:

```
$ cat /etc/profile
# /etc/profile

# System wide environment and startup programs, for login setup
# Functions and aliases go in /etc/bashrc

# It's NOT a good idea to change this file unless you know what you
# are doing. It's much better to create a custom.sh shell script in
# /etc/profile.d/ to make custom changes to your environment, to
# prevent the need for merging in future updates.

pathmunge () {
    case ":${PATH}:" in
        *:"$1":*)
            ;;
        *)
            if [ "$2" = "after" ] ; then
                PATH=$PATH:$1
            else
                PATH=$1:$PATH
            fi
    esac
}


if [ -x /usr/bin/id ]; then
    if [ -z "$EUID" ]; then
        # ksh workaround
        EUID=`id -u`
        UID=`id -ru`
    fi
    USER="`id -un`"
    LOGNAME=$USER
    MAIL="/var/spool/mail/$USER"
fi

# Path manipulation
if [ "$EUID" = "0" ]; then
    pathmunge /sbin
```

```
      pathmunge /usr/sbin
      pathmunge /usr/local/sbin
else
      pathmunge /usr/local/sbin after
      pathmunge /usr/sbin after
      pathmunge /sbin after
fi

HOSTNAME=`/bin/hostname 2>/dev/null`
HISTSIZE=1000
if [ "$HISTCONTROL" = "ignorespace" ] ; then
    export HISTCONTROL=ignoreboth
else
    export HISTCONTROL=ignoredups
fi

export PATH USER LOGNAME MAIL HOSTNAME HISTSIZE HISTCONTROL

# By default, we want umask to get set. This sets it for login shell
# Current threshold for system reserved uid/gids is 200
# You could check uidgid reservation validity in
# /usr/share/doc/setup-*/uidgid file
if [ $UID -gt 199 ] && [ "`id -gn`" = "`id -un`" ]; then
    umask 002
else
    umask 022
fi

for i in /etc/profile.d/*.sh ; do
    if [ -r "$i" ]; then
        if [ "${-#*i}" != "$-" ]; then
            . "$i"
        else
            . "$i" >/dev/null 2>&1
        fi
    fi
done

unset i
unset -f pathmunge
$
```

Both distributions' /etc/profile files use a certain feature. It is a for statement that iterates through any files located in the /etc/profile.d directory. (for statements are discussed in detail in Chapter 13.) This provides a place for the Linux system to place application-specific startup files that is executed by the shell when you log in. On this Ubuntu Linux system, the following files are in the profile.d directory:

```
$ ls -l /etc/profile.d
total 12
-rw-r--r-- 1 root root   40 Apr 15 06:26 appmenu-qt5.sh
-rw-r--r-- 1 root root  663 Apr  7 10:10 bash_completion.sh
-rw-r--r-- 1 root root 1947 Nov 22  2013 vte.sh
$
```

You can see that this CentOs system has quite a few more files in /etc/profile.d:

```
$ ls -l /etc/profile.d
total 80
-rw-r--r--. 1 root root 1127 Mar  5 07:17 colorls.csh
-rw-r--r--. 1 root root 1143 Mar  5 07:17 colorls.sh
-rw-r--r--. 1 root root   92 Nov 22  2013 cvs.csh
-rw-r--r--. 1 root root   78 Nov 22  2013 cvs.sh
-rw-r--r--. 1 root root  192 Feb 24 09:24 glib2.csh
-rw-r--r--. 1 root root  192 Feb 24 09:24 glib2.sh
-rw-r--r--. 1 root root   58 Nov 22  2013 gnome-ssh-askpass.csh
-rw-r--r--. 1 root root   70 Nov 22  2013 gnome-ssh-askpass.sh
-rwxr-xr-x. 1 root root  373 Sep 23  2009 kde.csh
-rwxr-xr-x. 1 root root  288 Sep 23  2009 kde.sh
-rw-r--r--. 1 root root 1741 Feb 20 05:44 lang.csh
-rw-r--r--. 1 root root 2706 Feb 20 05:44 lang.sh
-rw-r--r--. 1 root root  122 Feb  7  2007 less.csh
-rw-r--r--. 1 root root  108 Feb  7  2007 less.sh
-rw-r--r--. 1 root root  976 Sep 23  2011 qt.csh
-rw-r--r--. 1 root root  912 Sep 23  2011 qt.sh
-rw-r--r--. 1 root root 2142 Mar 13 15:37 udisks-bash-completion.sh
-rw-r--r--. 1 root root   97 Apr  5  2012 vim.csh
-rw-r--r--. 1 root root  269 Apr  5  2012 vim.sh
-rw-r--r--. 1 root root  169 May 20  2009 which2.sh
$
```

Notice that several files are related to specific applications on the system. Most applications create two startup files — one for the bash shell (using the .sh extension) and one for the c shell (using the .csh extension).

The lang.csh and lang.sh files attempt to determine the default language character set used on the system and set the LANG environment variable appropriately.

Viewing the $HOME startup files

The remaining startup files are all used for the same function — to provide a user-specific startup file for defining user-specific environment variables. Most Linux distributions use only one or two of these four startup files:

- $HOME/.bash_profile
- $HOME/.bashrc

- $HOME/.bash_login
- $HOME/.profile

Notice that all four files start with a dot, making them hidden files (they don't appear in a normal ls command listing). Because they are in the user's HOME directory, each user can edit the files and add his or her own environment variables that are active for every bash shell session they start.

NOTE

Environment files are one area where Linux distributions vary greatly. Not every $HOME file listed in this section exists for every user. For example, some users may have only the $HOME/.bash_profile file. This is normal.

The first file found in the following ordered list is run, and the rest are ignored:

```
$HOME/.bash_profile
$HOME/.bash_login
$HOME/.profile
```

Notice that $HOME/.bashrc is not in this list. This is because it is typically run from one of the other files.

TIP

Remember that $HOME represents a user's home directory. Also, the tilde (~) is used to represent a user's home directory.

This CentOS Linux system contains the following .bash_profile file:

```
$ cat $HOME/.bash_profile
# .bash_profile

# Get the aliases and functions
if [ -f ~/.bashrc ]; then
        . ~/.bashrc
fi

# User specific environment and startup programs

PATH=$PATH:$HOME/bin

export PATH
$
```

The .bash_profile startup file first checks to see if the startup file, .bashrc, is present in the HOME directory. If it's there, the startup file executes the commands in it.

Understanding the interactive shell process

If you start a bash shell without logging into a system (if you just type `bash` at a CLI prompt, for example), you start what's called an *interactive shell*. The interactive shell doesn't act like the login shell, but it still provides a CLI prompt for you to enter commands.

If bash is started as an interactive shell, it doesn't process the `/etc/profile` file. Instead, it only checks for the `.bashrc` file in the user's HOME directory.

On this Linux CentOS distribution, this file looks like this:

```
$ cat .bashrc

# .bashrc
# Source global definitions
if [ -f /etc/bashrc ]; then
        . /etc/bashrc
fi

# User specific aliases and functions
$
```

The `.bashrc` file does two things. First, it checks for a common `bashrc` file in the `/etc` directory. Second, it provides a place for the user to enter personal command aliases (discussed in Chapter 5) and private script functions (described in Chapter 17).

Understanding the non-interactive shell process

The last type of shell is a non-interactive subshell. This is the shell where the system can start to execute a shell script. This is different in that there isn't a CLI prompt to worry about. However, you may want to run specific startup commands each time you start a script on your system.

> **TIP**
> Scripts can be executed in different ways. Only some execution methods start a subshell. You learn about the different shell execution methods in Chapter 11.

To accommodate that situation, the bash shell provides the BASH_ENV environment variable. When the shell starts a non-interactive subshell process, it checks this environment variable for the startup file name to execute. If one is present, the shell executes the file's commands, which typically include variables set for the shell scripts.

On this CentOS Linux distribution, this environment value is not set by default. When a variable is not set, the `printenv` command simply returns the CLI prompt:

```
$ printenv BASH_ENV
$
```

On this Ubuntu distribution, the BASH_ENV variable isn't set either. Remember that, when a variable is not set, the echo command displays a blank line and returns the CLI prompt:

```
$ echo $BASH_ENV

$
```

So if the BASH_ENV variable isn't set, how do the shell scripts get their environment variables? Remember that some shell script execution methods start a subshell, also called a child shell (see Chapter 5). A child shell inherits its parent shell's exported variables.

For example, if the parent shell was a login shell and had variables set and exported in the /etc/profile file, /etc/profile.d/*.sh files, and the $HOME/.bashrc file, the child shell for the script inherits these variables.

However, remember that any variables set but not exported by the parent shell are local variables. Local variables are not inherited by a subshell.

For scripts that do not start a subshell, the variables are already available in the current shell. Thus, even if BASH_ENV is not set, both the current shell's local and global variables are present to be used.

Making environment variables persistent

Now that you know you way around the various shell process types and their various environment files, locating the permanent environment variables is much easier. You can also set your own permanent global or local variables using these files.

For global environment variables (those variables needed by all the users on a Linux system), it may be tempting to put new or modified variable settings in the /etc/ profile, but this is a bad idea. The file could be changed when your distribution is upgraded, and you would lose all the customized variable settings.

It is a better idea to create a file ending with .sh in the /etc/profile.d directory. In that file, place all your new or modified global environment variable settings.

On most distributions, the best place to store an individual user's persistent bash shell variables is in the $HOME/.bashrc file. This is true for all shell process types. However, if the BASH_ENV variable is set, keep in mind that unless it points to $HOME/.bashrc, you may need to store a user's variables for non-interactive shell types elsewhere.

> **NOTE**
> Keep in mind that user environment variables for graphical interface elements, such as the GUI client, may need to be set in different configuration files than where bash shell environment variables are set.

Recall back in Chapter 5 that command alias settings are also not persistent. You can also store your personal alias settings in the $HOME/.bashrc startup file to make them permanent.

Learning about Variable Arrays

A really cool feature of environment variables is that they can be used as *arrays*. An array is a variable that can hold multiple values. Values can be referenced either individually or as a whole for the entire array.

To set multiple values for an environment variable, just list them in parentheses, with values separated by spaces:

```
$ mytest=(one two three four five)
$
```

Not much excitement there. If you try to display the array as a normal environment variable, you'll be disappointed:

```
$ echo $mytest
one
$
```

Only the first value in the array appears. To reference an individual array element, you must use a numerical index value, which represents its place in the array. The numeric value is enclosed in square brackets:

```
$ echo ${mytest[2]}
three
$
```

To display an entire array variable, you use the asterisk wildcard character as the index value:

```
$ echo ${mytest[*]}
one two three four five
$
```

You can also change the value of an individual index position:

```
$ mytest[2]=seven
$
$ echo ${mytest[*]}
one two seven four five
$
```

You can even use the unset command to remove an individual value within the array, but be careful, because this gets tricky. Watch this example:

```
$ unset mytest[2]
$
$ echo ${mytest[*]}
one two four five
$
$ echo ${mytest[2]}

$ echo ${mytest[3]}
four
$
```

This example uses the unset command to remove the value at index value 2. When you display the array, it appears that the other index values just dropped down one. However, if you specifically display the data at index value 2, you see that that location is empty.

Finally, you can remove the entire array just by using the array name in the unset command:

```
$ unset mytest
$
$ echo ${mytest[*]}

$
```

Sometimes variable arrays just complicate matters, so they're often not used in shell script programming. They're not very portable to other shell environments, which is a downside if you do lots of shell programming for different shells. Some bash system environment variables use arrays (such as BASH_VERSINFO), but overall you probably won't run into them very often.

Summary

This chapter examined the world of Linux environment variables. Global environment variables can be accessed from any child shell spawned by the parent shell in which they're defined. Local environment variables can be accessed only from the process in which they're defined.

The Linux system uses both global and local environment variables to store information about the system environment. You can access this information from the shell command line interface, as well as within shell scripts. The bash shell uses the system environment variables defined in the original Unix Bourne shell, as well as lots of new environment variables. The PATH environment variable defines the search pattern the bash shell takes to find an executable command. You can modify the PATH environment variable to add your own directories, or even the current directory symbol, to make running your programs easier.

You can also create your own global and local environment variables for your own use. After you create an environment variable, it's accessible for the entire duration of your shell session.

The bash shell executes several startup files when it starts up. These startup files can contain environment variable definitions to set standard environment variables for each bash session. When you log in to the Linux system, the bash shell accesses the /etc/profile startup file and three local startup files for each user, $HOME/.bash_profile, $HOME/.bash_login, and $HOME/.profile. Users can customize these files to include environment variables and startup scripts for their own use.

Finally, this chapter discussed the use of environment variable arrays. These environment variables can contain multiple values in a single variable. You can access the values either individually by referencing an index value or as a whole by referencing the entire environment variable array name.

The next chapter dives into the world of Linux file permissions. This is possibly the most difficult topic for novice Linux users. However, to write good shell scripts, you need to understand how file permissions work and be able to use them on your Linux system.

Understanding Linux File Permissions

N o system is complete without some form of security. There must be a mechanism available to protect files from unauthorized viewing or modification. The Linux system follows the Unix method of file permissions, allowing individual users and groups access to files based on a set of security settings for each file and directory. This chapter discusses how to use the Linux file security system to protect data when necessary and share data when desired.

Linux Security

The core of the Linux security system is the *user account*. Each individual who accesses a Linux system should have a unique user account assigned. The users' permissions to objects on the system depend on the user account they log in with.

User permissions are tracked using a *user ID* (often called a UID), which is assigned to an account when it's created. The UID is a numerical value, unique for each user. However, you don't log in to a Linux system using your UID. Instead, you use a *login name*. The login name is an alphanumeric text string of eight characters or fewer that the user uses to log in to the system (along with an associated password).

The Linux system uses special files and utilities to track and manage user accounts on the system. Before we can discuss file permissions, we need to discuss how Linux handles user accounts. This section describes the files and utilities required for user accounts so that you can understand how to use them when working with file permissions.

The /etc/passwd file

The Linux system uses a special file to match the login name to a corresponding UID value. This file is the /etc/passwd file. The /etc/passwd file contains several pieces of information about the user. Here's what a typical /etc/passwd file looks like on a Linux system:

```
$ cat /etc/passwd
root:x:0:0:root:/root:/bin/bash
bin:x:1:1:bin:/bin:/sbin/nologin
daemon:x:2:2:daemon:/sbin:/sbin/nologin
adm:x:3:4:adm:/var/adm:/sbin/nologin
lp:x:4:7:lp:/var/spool/lpd:/sbin/nologin
sync:x:5:0:sync:/sbin:/bin/sync
shutdown:x:6:0:shutdown:/sbin:/sbin/shutdown
halt:x:7:0:halt:/sbin:/sbin/halt
mail:x:8:12:mail:/var/spool/mail:/sbin/nologin
news:x:9:13:news:/etc/news:
uucp:x:10:14:uucp:/var/spool/uucp:/sbin/nologin
operator:x:11:0:operator:/root:/sbin/nologin
games:x:12:100:games:/usr/games:/sbin/nologin
gopher:x:13:30:gopher:/var/gopher:/sbin/nologin
ftp:x:14:50:FTP User:/var/ftp:/sbin/nologin
nobody:x:99:99:Nobody:/:/sbin/nologin
rpm:x:37:37::/var/lib/rpm:/sbin/nologin
vcsa:x:69:69:virtual console memory owner:/dev:/sbin/nologin
mailnull:x:47:47::/var/spool/mqueue:/sbin/nologin
smmsp:x:51:51::/var/spool/mqueue:/sbin/nologin
apache:x:48:48:Apache:/var/www:/sbin/nologin
rpc:x:32:32:Rpcbind Daemon:/var/lib/rpcbind:/sbin/nologin
ntp:x:38:38::/etc/ntp:/sbin/nologin
nscd:x:28:28:NSCD Daemon:/:/sbin/nologin
tcpdump:x:72:72::/:/sbin/nologin
dbus:x:81:81:System message bus:/:/sbin/nologin
avahi:x:70:70:Avahi daemon:/:/sbin/nologin
hsqldb:x:96:96::/var/lib/hsqldb:/sbin/nologin
sshd:x:74:74:Privilege-separated SSH:/var/empty/sshd:/sbin/nologin
rpcuser:x:29:29:RPC Service User:/var/lib/nfs:/sbin/nologin
nfsnobody:x:65534:65534:Anonymous NFS User:/var/lib/nfs:/sbin/nologin
haldaemon:x:68:68:HAL daemon:/:/sbin/nologin
xfs:x:43:43:X Font Server:/etc/X11/fs:/sbin/nologin
gdm:x:42:42::/var/gdm:/sbin/nologin
rich:x:500:500:Rich Blum:/home/rich:/bin/bash
mama:x:501:501:Mama:/home/mama:/bin/bash
katie:x:502:502:katie:/home/katie:/bin/bash
jessica:x:503:503:Jessica:/home/jessica:/bin/bash
mysql:x:27:27:MySQL Server:/var/lib/mysql:/bin/bash
$
```

The `root` user account is the administrator for the Linux system and is always assigned UID 0. As you can see, the Linux system creates lots of user accounts for various functions that aren't actual users. These are called *system accounts*. A system account is a special account that services running on the system use to gain access to resources on the system. All services that run in background mode need to be logged in to the Linux system under a system user account.

Before security became a big issue, these services often just logged in using the `root` user account. Unfortunately, if an unauthorized person broke into one of these services, he instantly gained access to the system as the `root` user. To prevent this, now just about every service that runs in background on a Linux server has its own user account to log in with. This way, if a troublemaker compromises a service, he still can't necessarily get access to the whole system.

Linux reserves UIDs below 500 for system accounts. Some services even require specific UIDs to work properly. When you create accounts for normal users, most Linux systems assign the first available UID starting at 500 (although this is not necessarily true for all Linux distributions).

You probably noticed that the `/etc/passwd` file contains much more than just the login name and UID for the user. The fields of the `/etc/passwd` file contain the following information:

- The login username
- The password for the user
- The numerical UID of the user account
- The numerical group ID (GID) of the user account
- A text description of the user account (called the comment field)
- The location of the HOME directory for the user
- The default shell for the user

The password field in the `/etc/passwd` file is set to an *x*. This doesn't mean that all the user accounts have the same password. In the old days of Linux, the `/etc/passwd` file contained an encrypted version of the user's password. However, because lots of programs need to access the `/etc/passwd` file for user information, this became a security problem. With the advent of software that could easily decrypt encrypted passwords, the bad guys had a field day trying to break user passwords stored in the `/etc/passwd` file. Linux developers needed to rethink that policy.

Now, most Linux systems hold user passwords in a separate file (called the *shadow* file, located at `/etc/shadow`). Only special programs (such as the login program) are allowed access to this file.

The /etc/passwd file is a standard text file. You can use any text editor to manually perform user management functions (such as adding, modifying, or removing user accounts) directly in the /etc/passwd file. However, this is an extremely dangerous practice. If the /etc/passwd file becomes corrupt, the system can't read it, and it prevents anyone (even the root user) from logging in. Instead, it's safer to use the standard Linux user management utilities to perform all user management functions.

The /etc/shadow file

The /etc/shadow file provides more control over how the Linux system manages passwords. Only the root user has access to the /etc/shadow file, making it more secure than the /etc/passwd file.

The /etc/shadow file contains one record for each user account on the system. A record looks like this:

```
rich:$1$.FfcK0ns$f1UgiyHQ25wrB/hykCn020:11627:0:99999:7:::
```

There are nine fields in each /etc/shadow file record:

- The login name corresponding to the login name in the /etc/passwd file
- The encrypted password
- The number of days since January 1, 1970, that the password was last changed
- The minimum number of days before the password can be changed
- The number of days before the password must be changed
- The number of days before password expiration that the user is warned to change the password
- The number of days after a password expires before the account will be disabled
- The date (stored as the number of days since January 1, 1970) since the user account was disabled
- A field reserved for future use

Using the shadow password system, the Linux system has much finer control over user passwords. It can control how often a user must change his or her password and when to disable the account if the password hasn't been changed.

Adding a new user

The primary tool used to add new users to your Linux system is useradd. This command provides an easy way to create a new user account and set up the user's HOME directory structure all at once. The useradd command uses a combination of system default values and command line parameters to define a user account. The system defaults are set in the

/etc/default/useradd file. To see the system default values used on your Linux distribution, enter the useradd command with the -D parameter:

```
# /usr/sbin/useradd -D
GROUP=100
HOME=/home
INACTIVE=-1
EXPIRE=
SHELL=/bin/bash
SKEL=/etc/skel
CREATE_MAIL_SPOOL=yes
#
```

> **NOTE**
>
> Some Linux distributions place the Linux user and group utilities in the /usr/sbin directory, which may not be in your PATH environment variable. If that's the case in your Linux distribution, either add the directory to your PATH or use the absolute file path to run it.

7

The -D parameter shows what defaults the useradd command uses if you don't specify them in the command line when creating a new user account. This example shows the following default values:

- The new user is added to a common group with group ID 100.
- The new user has a HOME account created in the directory /home/loginname.
- The account can't be disabled when the password expires.
- The new account can't be set to expire at a set date.
- The new account uses the bash shell as the default shell.
- The system copies the contents of the /etc/skel directory to the user's HOME directory.
- The system creates a file in the mail directory for the user account to receive mail.

The penultimate value is interesting. The useradd command allows an administrator to create a default HOME directory configuration and then uses that as a template to create the new user's HOME directory. This allows you to place default files for the system in every new user's HOME directory automatically. In the Ubuntu Linux system, the /etc/skel directory has the following files:

```
$ ls -al /etc/skel
total 32
drwxr-xr-x   2 root root  4096 2010-04-29 08:26 .
drwxr-xr-x 135 root root 12288 2010-09-23 18:49 ..
-rw-r--r--   1 root root   220 2010-04-18 21:51 .bash_logout
```

```
-rw-r--r--    1 root  root   3103 2010-04-18 21:51 .bashrc
-rw-r--r--    1 root  root    179 2010-03-26 08:31 examples.desktop
-rw-r--r--    1 root  root    675 2010-04-18 21:51 .profile
$
```

You should recognize these files from Chapter 6. These are the standard startup files for the bash shell environment. The system automatically copies these default files into every user's HOME directory you create.

You can test this by creating a new user account using the default system parameters and then looking at the HOME directory for the new user:

```
# useradd -m test
# ls -al /home/test
total 24
drwxr-xr-x 2 test test 4096 2010-09-23 19:01 .
drwxr-xr-x 4 root root 4096 2010-09-23 19:01 ..
-rw-r--r-- 1 test test  220 2010-04-18 21:51 .bash_logout
-rw-r--r-- 1 test test 3103 2010-04-18 21:51 .bashrc
-rw-r--r-- 1 test test  179 2010-03-26 08:31 examples.desktop
-rw-r--r-- 1 test test  675 2010-04-18 21:51 .profile
#
```

By default, the useradd command doesn't create a HOME directory, but the −m command line option tells it to create the HOME directory. As you can see in the example, the useradd command created the new HOME directory, using the files contained in the /etc/skel directory.

> **NOTE**
> To run the user account administration commands in this chapter, you either need to be logged in as the special root user account or use the sudo command to run the commands as the root user account.

If you want to override a default value or behavior when creating a new user, you can do that with command line parameters. These are shown in Table 7-1.

TABLE 7-1 The useradd Command Line Parameters

Parameter	Description
-c comment	Adds text to the new user's comment field
-d home_dir	Specifies a different name for the HOME directory other than the login name

-e *expire_date*	Specifies a date, in YYYY-MM-DD format, when the account will expire
-f *inactive_days*	Specifies the number of days after a password expires when the account will be disabled. A value of 0 disables the account as soon as the password expires; a value of -1 disables this feature.
-g *initial_group*	Specifies the group name or GID of the user's login group
-G *group . . .*	Specifies one or more supplementary groups the user belongs to
-k	Copies the /etc/skel directory contents into the user's HOME directory (must use -m as well)
-m	Creates the user's HOME directory
-M	Doesn't create a user's HOME directory (used if the default setting is to create one)
-n	Creates a new group using the same name as the user's login name
-r	Creates a system account
-p *passwd*	Specifies a default password for the user account
-s *shell*	Specifies the default login shell
-u *uid*	Specifies a unique UID for the account

As you can see, you can override all the system default values when creating a new user account just by using command line parameters. However, if you find yourself having to override a value all the time, it's easier to just change the system default value.

You can change the system default new user values by using the -D parameter, along with a parameter representing the value you need to change. These parameters are shown in Table 7-2.

TABLE 7-2   The useradd Change Default Values Parameters

Parameter	Description
-b *default_home*	Changes the location where users' HOME directories are created
-e *expiration_date*	Changes the expiration date on new accounts
-f *inactive*	Changes the number of days after a password has expired before the account is disabled
-g *group*	Changes the default group name or GID used
-s *shell*	Changes the default login shell

Changing the default values is a snap:

```
# useradd -D -s /bin/tsch
# useradd -D
GROUP=100
HOME=/home
INACTIVE=-1
EXPIRE=
SHELL=/bin/tsch
SKEL=/etc/skel
CREATE_MAIL_SPOOL=yes
#
```

Now, the useradd command uses the tsch shell as the default login shell for all new user accounts you create.

Removing a user

If you want to remove a user from the system, the userdel command is what you need. By default, the userdel command removes only the user information from the /etc/passwd file. It doesn't remove any files the account owns on the system.

If you use the -r parameter, userdel removes the user's HOME directory, along with the user's mail directory. However, other files owned by the deleted user account may still be on the system. This can be a problem in some environments.

Here's an example of using the userdel command to remove an existing user account:

```
# /usr/sbin/userdel -r test
# ls -al /home/test
ls: cannot access /home/test: No such file or directory
#
```

After using the -r parameter, the user's old /home/test directory no longer exists.

> **CAUTION**
>
> Be careful when using the -r parameter in an environment with lots of users. You never know if a user had important files stored in his or her HOME directory that are used by someone else or another program. Always check before removing a user's HOME directory!

Modifying a user

Linux provides a few different utilities for modifying the information for existing user accounts. Table 7-3 shows these utilities.

TABLE 7-3   User Account Modification Utilities

Command	Description
usermod	Edits user account fields, as well as specifying primary and secondary group membership
passwd	Changes the password for an existing user
chpasswd	Reads a file of login name and password pairs, and updates the passwords
chage	Changes the password's expiration date
chfn	Changes the user account's comment information
chsh	Changes the user account's default shell

Each of these utilities provides a specific function for changing information about user accounts. The following sections describe each of these utilities.

usermod

The usermod command is the most robust of the user account modification utilities. It provides options for changing most of the fields in the /etc/passwd file. To do that, you just need to use the command line parameter that corresponds to the value you want to change. The parameters are mostly the same as the useradd parameters (such as -c to change the comment field, -e to change the expiration date, and -g to change the default login group). However, a couple of additional parameters might come in handy:

- -l changes the login name of the user account.
- -L locks the account so the user can't log in.
- -p changes the password for the account.
- -U unlocks the account so the user can log in.

The -L parameter is especially handy. Use this to lock an account so a user can't log in without having to remove the account and the user's data. To return the account to normal, just use the -U parameter.

passwd and chpasswd

A quick way to change just the password for a user is the passwd command:

```
# passwd test
Changing password for user test.
New UNIX password:
```

```
Retype new UNIX password:
passwd: all authentication tokens updated successfully.
#
```

If you just use the passwd command by itself, it changes your own password. Any user in the system can change his or her own password, but only the root user can change someone else's password.

The -e option is a handy way to force a user to change the password on the next log in. This allows you to set the user's password to a simple value and forces them to change it to something harder that they can remember.

If you ever need to do a mass password change for lots of users on the system, the chpasswd command can be a lifesaver. The chpasswd command reads a list of login name and password pairs (separated by a colon) from the standard input, automatically encrypts the password, and sets it for the user account. You can also use the redirection command to redirect a file of *userid:password* pairs into the command:

```
# chpasswd < users.txt
#
```

chsh, chfn, and chage

The chsh, chfn, and chage utilities are specialized for specific account modification functions. The chsh command allows you to quickly change the default login shell for a user. You must use the full pathname for the shell, and not just the shell name:

```
#  chsh -s /bin/csh test
Changing shell for test.
Shell changed.
#
```

The chfn command provides a standard method for storing information in the comments field in the /etc/passwd file. Instead of just inserting random text, such as names or nicknames, or even just leaving the comment field blank, the chfn command uses specific information used in the Unix finger command to store information in the comment field. The finger command allows you to easily find information about people on your Linux system:

```
# finger rich
Login: rich                             Name: Rich Blum
Directory: /home/rich                   Shell: /bin/bash
On since Thu Sep 20 18:03 (EDT) on pts/0 from 192.168.1.2
No mail.
No Plan.
#
```

> **NOTE**
>
> Because of security concerns, many Linux system administrators disable the `finger` command on their systems, and many Linux distributions don't even install it by default.

If you use the `chfn` command with no parameters, it queries you for the appropriate values to enter in to the comment field:

```
# chfn test
Changing finger information for test.
Name []: Ima Test
Office []: Director of Technology
Office Phone []: (123)555-1234
Home Phone []: (123)555-9876

Finger information changed.
# finger test
Login: test                          Name: Ima Test
Directory: /home/test                Shell: /bin/csh
Office: Director of Technology       Office Phone: (123)555-1234
Home Phone: (123)555-9876
Never logged in.
No mail.
No Plan.
#
```

If you now look at the entry in the /etc/passwd file, it looks like this:

```
# grep test /etc/passwd
test:x:504:504:Ima Test,Director of Technology,(123)555-
1234,(123)555-9876:/home/test:/bin/csh
#
```

All the finger information is neatly stored away in the /etc/passwd file entry.

Finally, the `chage` command helps you manage the password aging process for user accounts. You need to set several parameters to individual values, shown in Table 7-4.

TABLE 7-4 The chage Command Parameters

Parameter	Description
-d	Sets the number of days since the password was last changed
-E	Sets the date the password expires

Continues

TABLE 7-4   *(continued)*

Parameter	Description
-I	Sets the number of days of inactivity after the password expires to lock the account
-m	Sets the minimum number of days between password changes
-W	Sets the number of days before the password expires that a warning message appears

The chage date values can be expressed using one of two methods:

- A date in YYYY-MM-DD format
- A numerical value representing the number of days since January 1, 1970

One neat feature of the chage command is that it allows you to set an expiration date for an account. Using this feature, you can create temporary user accounts that automatically expire on a set date, without your having to remember to delete them! Expired accounts are similar to locked accounts. The account still exists, but the user can't log in with it.

Using Linux Groups

User accounts are great for controlling security for individual users, but they aren't so good at allowing groups of users to share resources. To accomplish this, the Linux system uses another security concept, called *groups*.

Group permissions allow multiple users to share a common set of permissions for an object on the system, such as a file, directory, or device (more on that later in the "Decoding File Permissions" section).

Linux distributions differ somewhat on how they handle default group memberships. Some Linux distributions create just one group that contains all the user accounts as members. You need to be careful if your Linux distribution does this, because your files may be readable by all other users on the system. Other distributions create a separate group account for each user to provide a little more security.

Each group has a unique GID, which, like UIDs, is a unique numerical value on the system. Along with the GID, each group has a unique group name. You can use some group utilities to create and manage your own groups on the Linux system. This section discusses how group information is stored and how to use the group utilities to create new groups and modify existing groups.

The /etc/group file

Just like user accounts, group information is stored in a file on the system. The /etc/ group file contains information about each group used on the system. These are examples from a typical /etc/group file on a Linux system:

```
root:x:0:root
bin:x:1:root,bin,daemon
daemon:x:2:root,bin,daemon
sys:x:3:root,bin,adm
adm:x:4:root,adm,daemon
rich:x:500:
mama:x:501:
katie:x:502:
jessica:x:503:
mysql:x:27:
test:x:504:
```

Like UIDs, GIDs are assigned using a special format. Groups used for system accounts are assigned GIDs below 500, and user groups are assigned GIDs starting at 500. The /etc/ group file uses four fields:

- The group name
- The group password
- The GID
- The list of user accounts that belong to the group

The group password allows a non-group member to temporarily become a member of the group by using the password. This feature is not used all that commonly, but it does exist.

You should never add users to groups by editing the /etc/group file. Instead, use the usermod command (discussed earlier in the "Linux Security" section) to add a user account to a group. Before you can add users to different groups, you must create the groups.

> **NOTE**
>
> The list of user accounts is somewhat misleading. You'll notice that there are several groups in the list that don't have any users listed. This isn't because they don't have any members. When a user account uses a group as the default group in the /etc/passwd file, the user account doesn't appear in the /etc/group file as a member. This has caused confusion for more than one system administrator over the years!

Creating new groups

The groupadd command allows you to create new groups on your system:

```
# /usr/sbin/groupadd shared
# tail /etc/group
haldaemon:x:68:
xfs:x:43:
gdm:x:42:
rich:x:500:
mama:x:501:
katie:x:502:
jessica:x:503:
mysql:x:27:
test:x:504:
shared:x:505:
#
```

When you create a new group, no users are assigned to it by default. The groupadd command doesn't provide an option for adding user accounts to the group. Instead, to add new users, use the usermod command:

```
# /usr/sbin/usermod -G shared rich
# /usr/sbin/usermod -G shared test
# tail /etc/group
haldaemon:x:68:
xfs:x:43:
gdm:x:42:
rich:x:500:
mama:x:501:
katie:x:502:
jessica:x:503:
mysql:x:27:
test:x:504:
shared:x:505:rich, test
#
```

The shared group now has two members, test and rich. The -G parameter in usermod appends the new group to the list of groups for the user account.

NOTE

If you change the user groups for an account that is currently logged into the system, the user must log out and then log back in for the group changes to take effect.

> **CAUTION**
>
> Be careful when assigning groups for user accounts. If you use the -g parameter, the group name you specify replaces the default group for the user account. The -G parameter adds the group to the list of groups the user belongs to, keeping the default group intact.

Modifying groups

As you can see from the /etc/group file, you don't need to modify much information about a group. The groupmod command allows you to change the GID (using the -g parameter) or the group name (using the -n parameter) of an existing group:

```
# /usr/sbin/groupmod -n sharing shared
# tail /etc/group
haldaemon:x:68:
xfs:x:43:
gdm:x:42:
rich:x:500:
mama:x:501:
katie:x:502:
jessica:x:503:
mysql:x:27:
test:x:504:
sharing:x:505:test,rich
#
```

When changing the name of a group, the GID and group members remain the same, only the group name changes. Because all security permissions are based on the GID, you can change the name of a group as often as you wish without adversely affecting file security.

Decoding File Permissions

Now that you know about users and groups, it's time to decode the cryptic file permissions you've seen when using the ls command. This section describes how to decipher the permissions and where they come from.

Using file permission symbols

If you remember from Chapter 3, the `ls` command allows you to see the file permissions for files, directories, and devices on the Linux system:

```
$ ls -l
total 68
-rw-rw-r-- 1 rich rich   50 2010-09-13 07:49 file1.gz
-rw-rw-r-- 1 rich rich   23 2010-09-13 07:50 file2
-rw-rw-r-- 1 rich rich   48 2010-09-13 07:56 file3
-rw-rw-r-- 1 rich rich   34 2010-09-13 08:59 file4
-rwxrwxr-x 1 rich rich 4882 2010-09-18 13:58 myprog
-rw-rw-r-- 1 rich rich  237 2010-09-18 13:58 myprog.c
drwxrwxr-x 2 rich rich 4096 2010-09-03 15:12 test1
drwxrwxr-x 2 rich rich 4096 2010-09-03 15:12 test2
$
```

The first field in the output listing is a code that describes the permissions for the files and directories. The first character in the field defines the type of the object:

- – for files
- d for directories
- l for links
- c for character devices
- b for block devices
- n for network devices

After that, you see three sets of three characters. Each set of three characters defines an access permission triplet:

- r for read permission for the object
- w for write permission for the object
- x for execute permission for the object

If a permission is denied, a dash appears in the location. The three sets relate the three levels of security for the object:

- The owner of the object
- The group that owns the object
- Everyone else on the system

This is broken down in Figure 7-1.

FIGURE 7-1

The Linux file permissions

-rwxrwxr-x 1 rich rich   4882   2010-09-18 13:58 myprog

permissions for everyone else

permissions for group members

permissions for the file owner

The easiest way to discuss this is to take an example and decode the file permissions one by one:

```
-rwxrwxr-x 1 rich rich 4882 2010-09-18 13:58 myprog
```

The file `myprog` has the following sets of permissions:

- `rwx` for the file owner (set to the login name rich)
- `rwx` for the file group owner (set to the group name rich)
- `r-x` for everyone else on the system

These permissions indicate that the user login name rich can read, write, and execute the file (considered full permissions). Likewise, members in the group rich can also read, write, and execute the file. However, anyone else not in the rich group can only read and execute the file; the *w* is replaced with a dash, indicating that write permissions are not assigned to this security level.

Default file permissions

You may be wondering about where these file permissions come from. The answer is *umask*. The `umask` command sets the default permissions for any file or directory you create:

```
$ touch newfile
$ ls -al newfile
-rw-r--r--    1 rich     rich            0 Sep 20 19:16 newfile
$
```

The `touch` command created the file using the default permissions assigned to my user account. The `umask` command shows and sets the default permissions:

```
$ umask
0022
$
```

Unfortunately, the umask command setting isn't overtly clear, and trying to understand exactly how it works makes things even muddier. The first digit represents a special security feature called the *sticky bit*. We'll talk more about that later on in this chapter in the "Sharing Files" section.

The next three digits represent the octal values of the umask for a file or directory. To understand how umask works, you first need to understand octal mode security settings.

Octal mode security settings take the three rwx permission values and convert them into a 3-bit binary value, represented by a single octal value. In the binary representation, each position is a binary bit. Thus, if the read permission is the only permission set, the value becomes r--, relating to a binary value of 100, indicating the octal value of 4. Table 7-5 shows the possible combinations you'll run into.

TABLE 7-5   Linux File Permission Codes

Permissions	Binary	Octal	Description
---	000	0	No permissions
--x	001	1	Execute-only permission
-w-	010	2	Write-only permission
-wx	011	3	Write and execute permissions
r--	100	4	Read-only permission
r-x	101	5	Read and execute permissions
rw-	110	6	Read and write permissions
rwx	111	7	Read, write, and execute permissions

Octal mode takes the octal permissions and lists three of them in order for the three security levels (user, group, and everyone). Thus, the octal mode value 664 represents read and write permissions for the user and group, but read-only permission for everyone else.

Now that you know about octal mode permissions, the umask value becomes even more confusing. The octal mode shown for the default umask on my Linux system is 0022, but the file I created had an octal mode permission of 644. How did that happen?

The umask value is just that, a mask. It masks out the permissions you don't want to give to the security level. Now we have to dive into some octal arithmetic to figure out the rest of the story.

The umask value is subtracted from the full permission set for an object. The full permission for a file is mode 666 (read/write permission for all), but for a directory it's 777 (read/write/execute permission for all).

Thus, in the example, the file starts out with permissions 666, and the umask of 022 is applied, leaving a file permission of 644.

The umask value is normally set in the /etc/profile startup file in most Linux distributions (see Chapter 6), but some prefer to set it in the /etc/login.defs file (such as in Ubuntu). You can specify a different default umask setting using the umask command:

```
$ umask 026
$ touch newfile2
$ ls -l newfile2
-rw-r-----   1 rich     rich              0 Sep 20 19:46 newfile2
$
```

By setting the umask value to 026, the default file permissions become 640, so the new file now is restricted to read-only for the group members, and everyone else on the system has no permissions to the file.

The umask value also applies to making new directories:

```
$ mkdir newdir
$ ls -l
drwxr-x--x   2 rich     rich           4096 Sep 20 20:11 newdir/
$
```

Because the default permissions for a directory are 777, the resulting permissions from the umask are different from those of a new file. The 026 umask value is subtracted from 777, leaving the 751 directory permission setting.

Changing Security Settings

If you've already created a file or directory and need to change the security settings on it, Linux has a few different utilities available for this. This section shows you how to change the existing permissions, the default owner, and the default group settings for a file or directory.

Changing permissions

The chmod command allows you to change the security settings for files and directories. The format of the chmod command is:

```
chmod options mode file
```

The mode parameter allows you to set the security settings using either octal or symbolic mode. The octal mode settings are pretty straightforward; just use the standard three-digit octal code you want the file to have:

```
$ chmod 760 newfile
$ ls -l newfile
-rwxrw----   1 rich     rich              0 Sep 20 19:16 newfile
$
```

The octal file permissions are automatically applied to the file indicated. The symbolic mode permissions are not so easy to implement.

Instead of using the normal string of three sets of three characters, the chmod command takes a different approach. The following is the format for specifying a permission in symbolic mode:

```
[ugoa…] [ [+-=] [rwxXstugo…]
```

Makes perfectly good sense, doesn't it? The first group of characters defines to whom the new permissions apply:

- u for the user
- g for the group
- o for others (everyone else)
- a for all of the above

Next, a symbol is used to indicate whether you want to add the permission to the existing permissions (+), subtract the permission from the existing permission (–), or set the permissions to the value (=).

Finally, the third symbol is the permission used for the setting. You may notice that there are more than the normal rwx values here. These are the additional settings:

- X assigns execute permissions only if the object is a directory or if it already had execute permissions.
- s sets the UID or GID on execution.
- t saves program text.
- u sets the permissions to the owner's permissions.
- g sets the permissions to the group's permissions.
- o sets the permissions to the other's permissions.

Using these permissions looks like this:

```
$ chmod o+r newfile
$ ls -lF newfile
-rwxrw-r--   1 rich     rich              0 Sep 20 19:16 newfile*
$
```

The o+r entry adds the read permission to whatever permissions the everyone security level already had.

```
$ chmod u-x newfile
$ ls -lF newfile
-rw-rw-r--    1 rich       rich              0 Sep 20 19:16 newfile
$
```

The u-x entry removes the execute permission that the user already had. Note that the -F option for the ls command indicates whether a file has execution permissions by adding an asterisk to the filename.

The *options* parameters provide a few additional features to augment the behavior of the chmod command. The -R parameter performs the file and directory changes recursively. You can use wildcard characters for the filename specified, changing the permissions on multiple files with just one command.

Changing ownership

Sometimes, you need to change the owner of a file, such as when someone leaves an orga-nization or a developer creates an application that needs to be owned by a system account when it's in production. Linux provides two commands for doing that. The chown command makes it easy to change the owner of a file, and the chgrp command allows you to change the default group of a file.

The format of the chown command is:

```
chown options owner[.group] file
```

You can specify either the login name or the numeric UID for the new owner of the file:

```
# chown dan newfile
# ls -l newfile
-rw-rw-r--    1 dan        rich              0 Sep 20 19:16 newfile
#
```

Simple. The chown command also allows you to change both the user and group of a file:

```
# chown dan.shared newfile
# ls -l newfile
-rw-rw-r--    1 dan        shared            0 Sep 20 19:16 newfile
#
```

If you really want to get tricky, you can just change the default group for a file:

```
# chown .rich newfile
# ls -l newfile
-rw-rw-r--    1 dan        rich              0 Sep 20 19:16 newfile
#
```

Finally, if your Linux system uses individual group names that match user login names, you can change both with just one entry:

```
# chown test. newfile
# ls -l newfile
-rw-rw-r--    1 test    test          0 Sep 20 19:16 newfile
#
```

The chown command uses a few different option parameters. The -R parameter allows you to make changes recursively through subdirectories and files, using a wildcard character. The -h parameter also changes the ownership of any files that are symbolically linked to the file.

> **NOTE**
> Only the root user can change the owner of a file. Any user can change the default group of a file, but the user must be a member of the groups the file is changed from and to.

The chgrp command provides an easy way to change just the default group for a file or directory:

```
$ chgrp shared newfile
$ ls -l newfile
-rw-rw-r--    1 rich    shared        0 Sep 20 19:16 newfile
$
```

The user account must own the file, and be a member of the new group as well to be able to change the group. Now any member in the shared group can write to the file. This is one way to share files on a Linux system. However, sharing files among a group of people on the system can get tricky. The next section discusses how to do this.

Sharing Files

As you've probably already figured out, creating groups is the way to share access to files on the Linux system. However, for a complete file-sharing environment, things are more complicated.

As you've already seen in the "Decoding File Permissions" section, when you create a new file, Linux assigns the file permissions of the new file using your default UID and GID. To allow others access to the file, you need to either change the security permissions for the everyone security group or assign the file a different default group that contains other users.

This can be a pain in a large environment if you want to create and share documents among several people. Fortunately, there's a simple solution for how to solve this problem.

There are three additional bits of information that Linux stores for each file and directory:

- **The set user id (SUID):** When a file is executed by a user, the program runs under the permissions of the file owner.
- **The set group id (SGID):** For a file, the program runs under the permissions of the file group. For a directory, new files created in the directory use the directory group as the default group.
- **The sticky bit:** The file remains (sticks) in memory after the process ends.

The SGID bit is important for sharing files. By enabling the SGID bit, you can force all new files created in a shared directory to be owned by the directory's group and now the individual user's group.

The SGID is set using the chmod command. It's added to the beginning of the standard three-digit octal value (making a four-digit octal value), or you can use the symbol s in symbolic mode.

If you're using octal mode, you'll need to know the arrangement of the bits, shown in Table 7-6.

TABLE 7-6: The chmod SUID, SGID, and Sticky Bit Octal Values

Binary	Octal	Description
000	0	All bits are cleared.
001	1	The sticky bit is set.
010	2	The SGID bit is set.
011	3	The SGID and sticky bits are set.
100	4	The SUID bit is set.
101	5	The SUID and sticky bits are set.
110	6	The SUID and SGID bits are set.
111	7	All bits are set.

So, to create a shared directory that always sets the directory group for all new files, all you need to do is set the SGID bit for the directory:

```
$ mkdir testdir
$ ls -l
drwxrwxr-x    2 rich     rich          4096 Sep 20 23:12 testdir/
```

```
$ chgrp shared testdir
$ chmod g+s testdir
$ ls -l
drwxrwsr-x    2 rich      shared      4096 Sep 20 23:12 testdir/
$ umask 002
$ cd testdir
$ touch testfile
$ ls -l
total 0
-rw-rw-r--    1 rich      shared         0 Sep 20 23:13 testfile
$
```

The first step is to create a directory that you want to share using the mkdir command. Next, use the chgrp command to change the default group for the directory to a group that contains the members who need to share files (you must be a member of that group for this to work). Finally, set the SGID bit for the directory to ensure that any files created in the directory use the shared group name as the default group.

For this environment to work properly, all the group members must have their umask values set to make files writable by group members. In the preceding example, the umask is changed to 002 so the files are writable by the group.

After all that's done, any member of the group can go to the shared directory and create a new file. As expected, the new file uses the default group of the directory, not the user account's default group. Now any user in the shared group can access this file.

Summary

This chapter discussed the command line commands you need to know to manage the Linux security on your system. Linux uses a system of user IDs and group IDs to protect access to files, directories, and devices. Linux stores information about user accounts in the /etc/passwd file and information about groups in the /etc/group file. Each user is assigned a unique numeric user ID, along with a text login name to identify the user in the system. Groups are also assigned unique numerical group IDs and text group names. A group can contain one or more users to allowed shared access to system resources.

Several commands are available for managing user accounts and groups. The useradd command allows you to create new user accounts, and the groupadd command allows you to create new group accounts. To modify an existing user account, use the usermod command. Similarly, use the groupmod command to modify group account information.

Linux uses a complicated system of bits to determine access permissions for files and directories. Each file contains three security levels of protection: the file's owner, a default group that has access to the file, and a level for everyone else on the system. Each security level is defined by three access bits: read, write, and execute. The combination of three bits is often referred to by the symbols `rwx`, for read, write, and execute. If a permission is denied, its symbol is replaced with a dash (such as `r--` for read-only permission).

The symbolic permissions are often referred to as octal values, with the three bits combined into one octal value and three octal values representing the three security levels. Use the `umask` command to set the default security settings for files and directories created on the system. The system administrator normally sets a default umask value in the `/etc /profile` file, but you can use the `umask` command to change your umask value at any time.

Use the `chmod` command to change security settings for files and directories. Only the file's owner can change permissions for a file or directory. However, the root user can change the security settings for any file or directory on the system. You can use the `chown` and `chgrp` commands to change the default owner and group of the file.

The chapter closed with a discussion on how to use the set GID bit to create a shared directory. The SGID bit forces any new files or directories created in a directory to use the default group name of the parent directory, not that of the user who created them. This provides an easy way to share files between users on the system.

Now that you're up to speed with file permissions, it's time to take a closer look at how to work with the actual filesystem in Linux. The next chapter shows you how to create new partitions in Linux from the command line and then how to format the new partitions so that they can be used in the Linux virtual directory.

7

Managing Filesystems

IN THIS CHAPTER

Understanding filesystem basics

Exploring journaling and copy-on-write filesystems

Managing filesystems

Investigating the logical volume layout

Using the Linux Logical Volume Manager

W hen you're working with your Linux system, one of the decisions you'll need to make is what filesystem to use for the storage devices. Most Linux distributions kindly provide a default filesystem for you at installation time, and most beginning Linux users just use it without giving the topic another thought.

Although using the default filesystem choice isn't necessarily a bad thing, sometimes it helps to know the other options available to you. This chapter discusses the different filesystem options you have available in the Linux world and shows you how to create and manage them from the Linux command line.

Exploring Linux Filesystems

Chapter 3 discussed how Linux uses a *filesystem* to store files and folders on a storage device. The filesystem provides a way for Linux to bridge the gap between the ones and zeroes stored in the hard drive and the files and folders you work with in your applications.

Linux supports several types of filesystems to manage files and folders. Each filesystem implements the virtual directory structure on storage devices using slightly different features. This section walks you through the strengths and weaknesses of the more common filesystems used in the Linux environment.

Understanding the basic Linux filesystems

The original Linux system used a simple filesystem that mimicked the functionality of the Unix filesystem. This section discusses the evolution of that filesystem.

Looking at the ext Filesystem

The original filesystem introduced with the Linux operating system is called the *extended filesystem* (or just ext for short). It provides a basic Unix-like filesystem for Linux, using virtual directories to handle physical devices, and storing data in fixed-length blocks on the physical devices.

The ext filesystem uses a system called *inodes* to track information about the files stored in the virtual directory. The inode system creates a separate table on each physical device, called the *inode table*, to store file information. Each stored file in the virtual directory has an entry in the inode table. The *extended* part of the name comes from the additional data that it tracks on each file, which consists of these items:

- The filename
- The file size
- The owner of the file
- The group the file belongs to
- Access permissions for the file
- Pointers to each disk block that contains data from the file

Linux references each inode in the inode table using a unique number (called the *inode number*), assigned by the filesystem as data files are created. The filesystem uses the inode number to identify the file rather than having to use the full filename and path.

Looking at the ext2 Filesystem

The original ext filesystem had quite a few limitations, such as restraining files to only 2GB in size. Not too long after Linux was first introduced, the ext filesystem was upgraded to create the second extended filesystem, called *ext2*.

As you can guess, the ext2 filesystem is an expansion of the basic abilities of the ext filesystem, but maintains the same structure. The ext2 filesystem expands the inode table format to track additional information about each file on the system.

The ext2 inode table adds the created, modified, and last accessed time values for files to help system administrators track file access on the system. The ext2 filesystem also increases the maximum file size allowed to 2TB (then in later versions of ext2, that was increased to 32TB) to help accommodate large files commonly found in database servers.

In addition to expanding the inode table, the ext2 filesystem also changed the way in which files are stored in the data blocks. A common problem with the ext filesystem was that as a file is written to the physical device, the blocks used to store the data tend to be scattered throughout the device (called *fragmentation*). Fragmentation of data blocks can reduce the filesystem performance, because it takes longer to search the storage device to access all the blocks for a specific file.

The ext2 filesystem helps reduce fragmentation by allocating disk blocks in groups when you save a file. By grouping the data blocks for a file, the filesystem doesn't have to search all over the physical device for the data blocks to read the file.

The ext2 filesystem was the default filesystem used in Linux distributions for many years, but it, too, had its limitations. The inode table, although a nice feature that allows the filesystem to track additional information about files, can cause problems that can be fatal to the system. Each time the filesystem stores or updates a file, it must modify the inode table with the new information. The problem is that this isn't always a fluid action.

If something should happen to the computer system between the file being stored and the inode table being updated, the two would become out of sync. The ext2 filesystem is notorious for easily becoming corrupted due to system crashes and power outages. Even if the file data is stored just fine on the physical device, if the inode table entry isn't completed, the ext2 filesystem doesn't even know that the file existed!

It wasn't long before developers were exploring a different avenue of Linux filesystems.

Understanding journaling filesystems

Journaling filesystems provide a new level of safety to the Linux system. Instead of writing data directly to the storage device and then updating the inode table, journaling filesystems write file changes into a temporary file (called the *journal*) first. After data is successfully written to the storage device and the inode table, the journal entry is deleted.

If the system should crash or suffer a power outage before the data can be written to the storage device, the journaling filesystem just reads through the journal file and processes any uncommitted data left over.

Linux commonly uses three different methods of journaling, each with different levels of protection. These are shown in Table 8-1.

TABLE 8-1 Journaling Filesystem Methods

Method	Description
Data mode	Both inode and file data are journaled. Low risk of losing data, but poor performance.
Ordered mode	Only inode data is written to the journal, but not removed until file data is successfully written. Good compromise between performance and safety.
Writeback mode	Only inode data is written to the journal, no control over when the file data is written. Higher risk of losing data, but still better than not using journaling.

8

The data mode journaling method is by far the safest for protecting data, but it is also the slowest. All the data written to a storage device must be written twice, once to the journal and again to the actual storage device. This can cause poor performance, especially for systems that do lots of data writing.

Over the years, a few different journaling filesystems have appeared in Linux. The following sections describe the popular Linux journaling filesystems available.

Looking at the ext3 Filesystem

The *ext3* filesystem was added to the Linux kernel in 2001, and up until recently was the default filesystem used by just about all Linux distributions. It uses the same inode table structure as the ext2 filesystem, but adds a journal file to each storage device to journal the data written to the storage device.

By default, the ext3 filesystem uses the ordered mode method of journaling, only writing the inode information to the journal file, but not removing it until the data blocks have been successfully written to the storage device. You can change the journaling method used in the ext3 filesystem to either data or writeback modes with a simple command line option when creating the filesystem.

Although the ext3 filesystem added basic journaling to the Linux filesystem, it still lacked a few things. For example, the ext3 filesystem doesn't provide any recovery from accidental deletion of files, no built-in data compression is available (although a patch can be installed separately that provides this feature), and the ext3 filesystem doesn't support encrypting files. For those reasons, developers in the Linux project chose to continue work on improving the ext3 filesystem.

Looking at the ext4 Filesystem

The result of expanding the ext3 filesystem was (as you probably guessed) the *ext4* filesystem. The ext4 filesystem was officially supported in the Linux kernel in 2008 and is now the default filesystem used in popular Linux distributions, such as Ubuntu.

In addition to supporting compression and encryption, the ext4 filesystem also supports a feature called *extents*. Extents allocate space on a storage device in blocks and only store the starting block location in the inode table. This helps save space in the inode table by not having to list all the data blocks used to store data from the file.

The ext4 filesystem also incorporates *block preallocation*. If you want to reserve space on a storage device for a file that you know will grow in size, with the ext4 filesystem it's possible to allocate all the expected blocks for the file, not just the blocks that physically exist. The ext4 filesystem fills in the reserved data blocks with zeroes and knows not to allocate them for any other file.

Looking at the Reiser Filesystem

In 2001, Hans Reiser created the first journaling filesystem for Linux, called *ReiserFS*. The ReiserFS filesystem supports only writeback journaling mode, writing only the inode table data to the journal file. Because it writes only the inode table data to the journal, the ReiserFS filesystem is one of the faster Linux journaling filesystems.

Two interesting features incorporated into the ReiserFS filesystem are that you can resize an existing filesystem while it's still active and that it uses a technique called *tailpacking*, which stuffs data from one file into empty space in a data block from another file. The active filesystem resizing feature is great if you have to expand an already created filesystem to accommodate more data.

The ReiserFS development team began working on a new version called *Reiser4* in 2004. The Reiser4 filesystem has several improvements over ResierFS, including extremely efficient handling of small files. However, most current mainstream Linux distributions don't use the Reiser4 filesystem. Yet, you may still run into a Linux system that employs it.

Looking at the Journaled Filesystem

Possibly one of the oldest journaling filesystems around, the *Journaled File System* (JFS) was developed by IBM in 1990 for its AIX flavor of Unix. However, it wasn't until its second version that it was ported to the Linux environment.

> **NOTE**
> The official IBM name of the second version of the JFS filesystem is JFS2, but most Linux systems refer to it as just JFS.

The JFS filesystem uses the ordered journaling method, storing only the inode table data in the journal, but not removing it until the actual file data is written to the storage device. This method is a compromise between the speed of the Reiser4 and the integrity of the data mode journaling method.

The JFS filesystem uses extent-based file allocation, allocating a group of blocks for each file written to the storage device. This method provides for less fragmentation on the storage device.

Outside of the IBM Linux offerings, the JFS filesystem isn't popularly used, but you may run into it in your Linux journey.

Looking at the XFS Filesystem

The *XFS* journaling filesystem is yet another filesystem originally created for a commercial Unix system that made its way into the Linux world. Silicon Graphics Incorporated (SGI) originally created XFS in 1994 for its commercial IRIX Unix system. It was released to the Linux environment for common use in 2002. The XFS filesystem has recently become more popular and is used as the default filesystem in mainstream Linux distributions, such as RHEL.

The XFS filesystem uses the writeback mode of journaling, which provides high performance but does introduce an amount of risk because the actual data isn't stored in the

8

journal file. The XFS filesystem also allows online resizing of the filesystem, similar to the Reiser4 filesystem, except XFS filesystems can only be expanded and not shrunk.

Understanding the copy-on-write filesystems

With journaling, you must choose between safety and performance. Although data mode journaling provides the highest safety, performance suffers because both inode and data is journaled. With writeback mode journaling, performance is acceptable, but safety is compromised.

For filesystems, an alternative to journaling is a technique called *copy-on-write* (COW). COW offers both safety and performance via *snapshots*. For modifying data, a *clone* or *writable-snapshot* is used. Instead of writing modified data over current data, the modified data is put in a new filesystem location. Even when data modification is completed, the old data is never overwritten.

COW filesystems are gaining in popularity. Two of the most popular, Btrfs and ZFS, are briefly reviewed in the following sections.

Looking at the ZFS Filesystem

The COW filesystem *ZFS* was developed in 2005 by Sun Microsystems for the OpenSolaris operating system. It began being ported to Linux in 2008 and was finally available for Linux production use in 2012.

ZFS is a stable filesystem and competes well against Resier4, Btrfs, and ext4. Its biggest detractor is that ZFS does not have a GPL license. The OpenZFS project was launched in 2013, which may help to change this situation. However, it's possible that until a GPL license is obtained, ZFS will never be a default Linux filesystem.

Looking at the Btrfs Filesystem

The COW newcomer is the *Btrfs* filesystem, also called the B-tree filesystem. Oracle started development on Btrfs in 2007. It was based on many of Reiser4's features, but offered improvements in reliability. Additional developers eventually joined in and helped Btrfs quickly rise toward the top of the popular filesystems list. This popularity is due to stability, ease of use, as well as the ability to dynamically resize a mounted filesystem. The openSUSE Linux distribution recently established Btrfs as its default filesystem. It is also offered in other Linux distributions, such as RHEL, although not as the default filesystem.

Working with Filesystems

Linux provides a few different utilities that make it easier to work with filesystems from the command line. You can add new filesystems or change existing filesystems from the comfort of your own keyboard. This section walks you through the commands for interacting with filesystems from a command line environment.

Creating partitions

To start out, you need to create a *partition* on the storage device to contain the filesystem. The partition can be an entire disk or a subset of a disk that contains a portion of the virtual directory.

The fdisk utility is used to help you organize partitions on any storage device installed on the system. The fdisk command is an interactive program that allows you to enter commands to walk through the steps of partitioning a hard drive.

To start the fdisk command, you need to specify the device name of the storage device you want to partition and you need to have superuser privileges. When you don't have superuser privileges and attempt to use fdisk, you'll receive some sort of error message, like this one:

```
$ fdisk /dev/sdb

Unable to open /dev/sdb
$
```

> **NOTE**
>
> Sometimes, the hardest part of creating a new disk partition is trying to find the physical disk on your Linux system. Linux uses a standard format for assigning device names to hard drives, but you need to be familiar with the format. For older IDE drives, Linux uses /dev/hdx, where x is a letter based on the order the drive is detected (a for the first drive, b for the second, and so on). For both the newer SATA drives and SCSI drives, Linux uses /dev/sdx, where x is a letter based on the order the drive is detected (again, a for the first drive, b for the second, and so on). It's always a good idea to double-check to make sure you are referencing the correct drive before formatting the partition!

If you do have superuser privileges and the correct device name, the fdisk command allows you entrance into the utility as demonstrated here on a CentOS distribution:

```
$ sudo fdisk /dev/sdb
[sudo] password for Christine:
Device contains neither a valid DOS partition table,
nor Sun, SGI or OSF disklabel
Building a new DOS disklabel with disk identifier 0xd3f759b5.
Changes will remain in memory only
until you decide to write them.
After that, of course, the previous content won't be recoverable.

Warning: invalid flag 0x0000 of partition table 4 will
be corrected by w(rite)

[...]
Command (m for help):
```

8

TIP

If this is the first time you're partitioning the storage device, `fdisk` gives you a warning that a partition table is not on the device.

The `fdisk` interactive command prompt uses single letter commands to instruct `fdisk` what to do. Table 8-2 shows the commands available at the `fdisk` command prompt.

TABLE 8-2 The fdisk Commands

Command	Description
a	Toggles a flag indicating if the partition is bootable
b	Edits the disklabel used by BSD Unix systems
c	Toggles the DOS compatibility flag
d	Deletes the partition
l	Lists the available partition types
m	Displays the command options
n	Adds a new partition
o	Creates a DOS partition table
p	Displays the current partition table
q	Quits without saving changes
s	Creates a new disklabel for Sun Unix systems
t	Changes the partition system ID
u	Changes the storage units used
v	Verifies the partition table
w	Writes the partition table to the disk
x	Advanced functions

Although this list may look intimidating, usually you need just a few basic commands in day-to-day work.

For starters, you can display the details of a storage device using the p command:

```
Command (m for help): p

Disk /dev/sdb: 5368 MB, 5368709120 bytes
255 heads, 63 sectors/track, 652 cylinders
Units = cylinders of 16065 * 512 = 8225280 bytes
Sector size (logical/physical): 512 bytes / 512 bytes
I/O size (minimum/optimal): 512 bytes / 512 bytes
```

```
Disk identifier: 0x11747e88

  Device Boot      Start        End       Blocks   Id  System

Command (m for help):
```

The output shows that the storage device has 5368MB of space on it (5GB). The listing under the storage device details shows whether there are any existing partitions on the device. The listing in this example doesn't show any partitions, so the device is not partitioned yet.

Next, you'll want to create a new partition on the storage device. Use the n command for that:

```
Command (m for help): n
Command action
   e   extended
   p   primary partition (1-4)
p
Partition number (1-4): 1
First cylinder (1-652, default 1): 1
Last cylinder, +cylinders or +size{K,M,G} (1-652, default 652): +2G

Command (m for help):
```

Partitions can be created as either a *primary partition* or an *extended partition*. Primary partitions can be formatted with a filesystem directly, whereas extended partitions can only contain other primary partitions. The reason for extended partitions is that there can only be four partitions on a single storage device. You can extend that by creating multiple extended partitions and then creating primary partitions inside the extended partitions. This example creates a primary storage device, assigns it partition number 1, and then allocates 2GB of the storage device space to it. You can see the results using the p command again:

```
Command (m for help): p

Disk /dev/sdb: 5368 MB, 5368709120 bytes
255 heads, 63 sectors/track, 652 cylinders
Units = cylinders of 16065 * 512 = 8225280 bytes
Sector size (logical/physical): 512 bytes / 512 bytes
I/O size (minimum/optimal): 512 bytes / 512 bytes
Disk identifier: 0x029aa6af

  Device Boot      Start        End       Blocks   Id  System
/dev/sdb1             1         262     2104483+   83  Linux

Command (m for help):
```

Now in the output there's a partition shown on the storage device (called /dev/sdb1). The Id entry defines how Linux treats the partition. fdisk allows you to create lots of partition types. Using the l command lists the different types available. The default is type 83, which defines a Linux filesystem. If you want to create a partition for a different filesystem (such as a Windows NTFS partition), just select a different partition type.

8

You can repeat the process to allocate the remaining space on the storage device to another Linux partition. After you've created the partitions you want, use the w command to save the changes to the storage device:

```
Command (m for help): w
The partition table has been altered!

Calling ioctl() to re-read partition table.
Syncing disks.
$
```

The storage device partition information was written to the partition table, and Linux was informed of the new partition via the ioctl() call. Now that you have set up a partition on the storage device, you're ready to format it with a Linux filesystem.

> **TIP**
> Some distributions and older distribution versions do not automatically inform your Linux system of a new partition after it is made. In this case, you need to use either the partprobe or hdparm command (see their man pages), or reboot your system so it reads the updated partition table.

Creating a filesystem

Before you can store data on the partition, you must format it with a filesystem so Linux can use it. Each filesystem type uses its own command line program to format partitions. Table 8-3 lists the utilities used for the different filesystems discussed in this chapter.

TABLE 8-3   Command Line Programs to Create Filesystems

Utility	Purpose
mkefs	Creates an ext filesystem
mke2fs	Creates an ext2 filesystem
mkfs.ext3	Creates an ext3 filesystem
mkfs.ext4	Creates an ext4 filesystem
mkreiserfs	Creates a ReiserFS filesystem
jfs_mkfs	Creates a JFS filesystem
mkfs.xfs	Creates an XFS filesystem
mkfs.zfs	Creates a ZFS filesystem
mkfs.btrfs	Creates a Btrfs filesystem

Not all filesystem utilities are installed by default. To determine whether you have a particular filesystem utility, use the type command:

```
$ type mkfs.ext4
mkfs.ext4 is /sbin/mkfs.ext4
$
$ type mkfs.btrfs
-bash: type: mkfs.btrfs: not found
$
```

The preceding example on an Ubuntu system shows that the mkfs.ext4 utility is available. However, the Btrfs utility is not. See Chapter 9 on how to install additional software and utilities on your Linux distribution.

Each filesystem utility command has lots of command line options that allow you to customize just how the filesystem is created in the partition. To see all the command line options available, use the man command to display the manual pages for the filesystem command (see Chapter 3). All the filesystem commands allow you to create a default filesystem with just the simple command with no options:

```
$ sudo mkfs.ext4 /dev/sdb1
[sudo] password for Christine:
mke2fs 1.41.12 (17-May-2010)
Filesystem label=
OS type: Linux
Block size=4096 (log=2)
Fragment size=4096 (log=2)
Stride=0 blocks, Stripe width=0 blocks
131648 inodes, 526120 blocks
26306 blocks (5.00%) reserved for the super user
First data block=0
Maximum filesystem blocks=541065216
17 block groups
32768 blocks per group, 32768 fragments per group
7744 inodes per group
Superblock backups stored on blocks:
        32768, 98304, 163840, 229376, 294912

Writing inode tables: done
Creating journal (16384 blocks): done
Writing superblocks and filesystem accounting information: done

This filesystem will be automatically checked every 23 mounts or
180 days, whichever comes first. Use tune2fs -c or -i to override.
$
```

The new filesystem uses the ext4 filesystem type, which is a journaling filesystem in Linux. Notice that part of the creation process was to create the new journal.

After you create the filesystem for a partition, the next step is to mount it on a virtual directory mount point so you can store data in the new filesystem. You can mount the new filesystem anywhere in your virtual directory where you need the extra space.

8

```
$ ls /mnt
$
$ sudo mkdir /mnt/my_partition
$
$ ls -al /mnt/my_partition/
$
$ ls -dF /mnt/my_partition
/mnt/my_partition/
$
$ sudo  mount -t ext4  /dev/sdb1  /mnt/my_partition
$
$ ls -al /mnt/my_partition/
total 24
drwxr-xr-x. 3 root root  4096 Jun 11 09:53 .
drwxr-xr-x. 3 root root  4096 Jun 11 09:58 ..
drwx------. 2 root root 16384 Jun 11 09:53 lost+found
$
```

The mkdir command (Chapter 3) creates the mount point in the virtual directory, and the mount command adds the new hard drive partition to the mount point. The -t option on the mount command indicates what filesystem type, ext4, you are mounting. Now you can save new files and folders on the new partition!

> **NOTE**
> This method of mounting a filesystem only temporarily mounts the filesystem. When you reboot your Linux system, the filesystem doesn't automatically mount. To force Linux to automatically mount the new filesystem at boot time, add the new filesystem to the /etc/fstab file.

Now that the filesystem is mounted within the virtual directory system, it can start to be used on a regular basis. Unfortunately, with regular use comes the potential for serious problems, such as filesystem corruption. The next section looks at how to deal with these issues.

Checking and repairing a filesystem

Even with modern filesystems, things can go wrong if power is unexpectedly lost, or if a wayward application locks up the system while file access is in progress. Fortunately, some command line tools are available to help you make an attempt to restore the filesystem back to order.

Each filesystem has its own recovery command for interacting with the filesystem. That has the potential of getting ugly, because more and more filesystems are available in the Linux environment, making for lots of individual commands you have to know. Fortunately, a common front-end program available can determine the filesystem on the storage device and use the appropriate filesystem recovery command based on the filesystem being recovered.

The `fsck` command is used to check and repair most Linux filesystem types, including ones discussed earlier in this chapter — ext, ext2, ext3, ext4, Reiser4, JFS, and XFS. The format of the command is:

```
fsck options filesystem
```

You can list multiple *filesystem* entries on the command line to check. Filesystems can be referenced using either the device name, the mount point in the virtual directory, or a special Linux UUID value assigned to the filesystem.

> **TIP**
>
> Although journaling filesystems users do need the `fsck` command, it is arguable as to whether COW filesystems users do. In fact, the ZFS filesystem does not even have an interface to the `fsck` utility.

The `fsck` command uses the /etc/fstab file to automatically determine the filesystem on a storage device that's normally mounted on the system. If the storage device isn't normally mounted (such as if you just created a filesystem on a new storage device), you need to use the `-t` command line option to specify the filesystem type. Table 8-4 lists the other command line options available.

TABLE 8-4 The fsck Command Line Options

Option	Description
-a	Automatically repairs the filesystem if errors are detected
-A	Checks all the filesystems listed in the /etc/fstab file
-C	Displays a progress bar for filesystems that support that feature (only ext2 and ext3)
-N	Doesn't run the check, only displays what checks would be performed
-r	Prompts to fix if errors found
-R	Skips the root filesystem if using the -A option
-s	If checking multiple filesystems, performs the checks one at a time
-t	Specifies the filesystem type to check
-T	Doesn't show the header information when starting
-V	Produces verbose output during the checks
-y	Automatically repairs the filesystem if errors detected

You may notice that some of the command line options are redundant. That's part of the problem of trying to implement a common front-end for multiple commands. Some of the individual filesystem repair commands have additional options that can be used. If you

8

need to do more advanced error checking, you'll need to check the man pages for the individual filesystem repair tool to see if there are extended options specific to that filesystem.

> **TIP**
>
> You can run the fsck command on unmounted filesystems only. For most filesystems, you can just unmount the filesystem to check it and then remount it when you're finished. However, because the root filesystem contains all the core Linux commands and log files, you can't unmount it on a running system.
>
> This is a time where having a Linux LiveCD comes in handy! Just boot your system with the LiveCD, and then run the fsck command on the root filesystem!

This chapter has showed how to handle filesystems contained in physical storage devices. Linux also provides a couple of different ways to create logical storage devices for filesystems. The next section examines how you can use a logical storage device for your filesystems.

Managing Logical Volumes

If you create your filesystems using standard partitions on hard drives, trying to add additional space to an existing filesystem can be somewhat of a painful experience. You can only expand a partition to the extent of the available space on the same physical hard drive. If no more space is available on that hard drive, you're stuck having to get a larger hard drive and manually moving the existing filesystem to the new drive.

What would come in handy is a way to dynamically add more space to an existing filesystem by just adding a partition from another hard drive to the existing filesystem. The Linux *Logical Volume Manager* (LVM) software package allows you to do just that. It provides an easy way for you to manipulate disk space on a Linux system without having to rebuild entire filesystems.

Exploring logical volume management layout

The core of logical volume management is how it handles the physical hard drive partitions installed on the system. In the logical volume management world, hard drives are called *physical volumes* (PV). Each PV maps to a specific physical partition created on a hard drive.

Multiple PV elements are pooled together to create a *volume group* (VG). The logical volume management system treats the VG like a physical hard drive, but in reality the VG may consist of multiple physical partitions spread across multiple hard drives. The VG provides a platform to create the logical partitions, which actually contain the filesystem.

The final layer in the structure is the *logical volume* (LV). The LV creates the partition environment for Linux to create a filesystem, acting similar to a physical hard disk partition as far as Linux is concerned. The Linux system treats the LV just like a physical partition.

You can format the LV using any one of the standard Linux filesystems and then add it to the Linux virtual directory at a mount point.

Figure 8-1 shows the basic layout of a typical Linux logical volume management environment.

FIGURE 8-1

The logical volume management environment

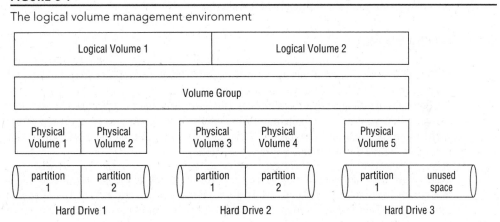

The volume group, shown in Figure 8-1, spans across three separate physical hard drives, which contain five separate physical partitions. Inside the volume group are two separate logical volumes. The Linux system treats each logical volume just like a physical partition. Each logical volume can be formatted as an ext4 filesystem and then mounted to a specific location in the virtual directory.

Notice in Figure 8-1 that the third physical hard drive has an unused partition. Using logical volume management, you can easily assign this unused partition to the existing volume group at a later time, and then either use it to create a new logical volume or add it to expand one of the existing logical volumes when you need more space.

Likewise, if you add a new hard drive to the system, the local volume management system allows you to add it to the existing volume group, and then create more space for one of the existing logical volumes, or start a new logical volume to be mounted. That's a much better way of handling expanding filesystems!

Using the LVM in Linux

The Linux LVM was developed by Heinz Mauelshagen and released to the Linux community in 1998. It allows you to manage a complete logical volume management environment in Linux using simple command line commands.

Two versions of Linux LVM are available:

8

- **LVM1:** The original LVM package released in 1998 and available in only the 2.4 Linux kernels. It provides only basic logical volume management features.
- **LVM2:** An updated version of the LVM, available in the 2.6 Linux kernels. It provides additional features over the standard LVM1 features.

Most modern Linux distributions using the 2.6 kernel version or above provide support for LVM2. Besides the standard logical volume management features, LVM2 provides a few other nice things for you to use in your Linux system.

Taking a Snapshot

The original Linux LVM allows you to copy an existing logical volume to another device while the logical volume is active. This feature is called a *snapshot*. Snapshots are great for backing up important data that can't be locked due to high availability requirements. Traditional backup methods usually lock files as they're being copied to the backup media. The snapshot allows you to continue running mission critical web or database servers while performing the copy. Unfortunately, LVM1 allows you to create only a read-only snapshot. After you create the snapshot, you can't write to it.

LVM2 allows you to create a read-write snapshot of an active logical volume. With the read-write copy, you can remove the original logical volume and mount the snapshot as a replacement. This feature is great for fast fail-overs or for experimenting with applications that modify data that may need to be restored if something fails.

Striping

Another interesting feature that LVM2 provides is *striping*. With striping, a logical volume is created across multiple physical hard drives. When the Linux LVM writes a file to the logical volume, the data blocks in the file are spread across the multiple hard drives. Each successive block of data is written to the next hard drive.

Striping helps improve disk performance, because Linux can write the multiple data blocks for a file to the multiple hard drives simultaneously, rather than having to wait for a single hard drive to move the read/write head to different locations. This improvement also applies to reading sequentially accessed files, because the LVM can read data from the multiple hard drives simultaneously.

> **NOTE**
>
> LVM striping is not the same as RAID striping. LVM striping doesn't provide a parity entry, which creates the fault-tolerant environment. In fact, LVM striping may increase the chance of a file being lost due to a hard drive failure. A single disk failure can result in multiple logical volumes being inaccessible.

Mirroring

Just because you install a filesystem using LVM doesn't mean that things can't still go wrong in the filesystem. Just as in a physical partition, LVM logical volumes are susceptible to power outages and disk crashes. After a filesystem becomes corrupt, there's always a possibility that you won't be able to recover it.

The LVM snapshot process provides some comfort knowing that you can create a backup copy of a logical volume at any time, but for some environments that may not be enough. Systems that have lots of data changes, such as database servers, may store hundreds or thousands of records since the last snapshot.

A solution to this problem is the LVM *mirror*. A mirror is a complete copy of a logical volume that's updated in real time. When you create the mirror logical volume, LVM synchronizes the original logical volume to the mirror copy. Depending on the size of the original logical volume, this may take some time to complete.

After the original synchronization is complete, LVM performs two writes for each write process in the filesystem — one to the main logical volume and one to the mirrored copy. As you can guess, this process does slow down write performance on the system. However, if the original logical volume should become corrupt for some reason, you have a complete up-to-date copy at your fingertips!

Using the Linux LVM

Now that you've seen what the Linux LVM can do, this section discusses how to implement it to help organize the disk space on your system. The Linux LVM package only provides command line programs for creating and managing all the components in the logical volume management system. Some Linux distributions include graphical front-ends to the command line commands, but for complete control of your LVM environment, it's best to get comfortable working directly with the commands.

Defining Physical Volumes

The first step in the process is to convert the physical partitions on the hard drive into physical volume extents used by the Linux LVM. Our friend the fdisk command helps us here. After creating the basic Linux partition, you need to change the partition type using the t command:

```
[...]
Command (m for help): t
Selected partition 1
Hex code (type L to list codes): 8e
Changed system type of partition 1 to 8e (Linux LVM)

Command (m for help): p

Disk /dev/sdb: 5368 MB, 5368709120 bytes
255 heads, 63 sectors/track, 652 cylinders
Units = cylinders of 16065 * 512 = 8225280 bytes
Sector size (logical/physical): 512 bytes / 512 bytes
```

8

```
I/O size (minimum/optimal): 512 bytes / 512 bytes
Disk identifier: 0xa8661341

   Device Boot      Start          End       Blocks   Id  System
/dev/sdb1               1          262    2104483+   8e  Linux LVM

Command (m for help): w
The partition table has been altered!

Calling ioctl() to re-read partition table.
Syncing disks.
$
```

The 8e partition type denotes that the partition will be used as part of a Linux LVM system and not as a direct filesystem, as you saw with the 83 partition type earlier.

> **NOTE**
> If the pvcreate command in the next step does not work for you, it's most likely due to the LVM2 package not being installed by default. To install the package, use the package name lvm2 and see Chapter 9 for how to install software packages.

The next step is to use the partition to create the actual physical volume. That's done using the pvcreate command. The pvcreate command defines the physical partition to use for the PV. It simply tags the partition as a physical volume in the Linux LVM system:

```
$ sudo pvcreate /dev/sdb1
  dev_is_mpath: failed to get device for 8:17
  Physical volume "/dev/sdb1" successfully created
$
```

> **NOTE**
> Don't let the daunting message dev_is_mpath: failed to get device for 8:17 or similar messages frighten you. As long as you receive the successfully created message, all is well. The pvcreate command checks to see whether the partition is a multi-path (mpath) device. If it is not, it issues the daunting message.

You can use the pvdisplay command to display a list of physical volumes you've created if you'd like to see your progress along the way:

```
$ sudo pvdisplay /dev/sdb1
  "/dev/sdb1" is a new physical volume of "2.01 GiB"
  --- NEW Physical volume ---
  PV Name               /dev/sdb1
  VG Name
  PV Size               2.01 GiB
```

```
Allocatable           NO
PE Size               0
Total PE              0
Free PE               0
Allocated PE          0
PV UUID               0FIuq2-LBod-IOWt-8VeN-tglm-Q2ik-rGU2w7

$
```

The `pvdisplay` command shows that /dev/sdb1 is now tagged as a PV. Notice, however, that in the output, the VG Name is blank. The PV does not yet belong to a volume group.

Creating Volume Groups

The next step in the process is to create one or more volume groups from the physical volumes. There are no set rules for how many volume groups you need to create for your system — you can add all the available physical volumes to a single volume group, or you can create multiple volume groups by combining different physical volumes.

To create the volume group from the command line, you need to use the `vgcreate` command. The `vgcreate` command requires a few command line parameters to define the volume group name, as well as the name of the physical volumes you're using to create the volume group:

```
$ sudo vgcreate Vol1 /dev/sdb1
    Volume group "Vol1" successfully created
$
```

That's not all too exciting for output! If you'd like to see some details about the newly created volume group, use the `vgdisplay` command:

```
$ sudo vgdisplay Vol1
    --- Volume group ---
    VG Name               Vol1
    System ID
    Format                lvm2
    Metadata Areas        1
    Metadata Sequence No  1
    VG Access             read/write
    VG Status             resizable
    MAX LV                0
    Cur LV                0
    Open LV               0
    Max PV                0
    Cur PV                1
    Act PV                1
    VG Size               2.00 GiB
    PE Size               4.00 MiB
```

8

```
Total PE          513
Alloc PE / Size   0 / 0
Free  PE / Size   513 / 2.00 GiB
VG UUID           oe4I7e-5RA9-G9ti-ANoI-QKLz-qkX4-58Wj6e

$
```

This example creates a volume group named Vol1, using the physical volume created on the /dev/sdb1 partition.

Now that you have one or more volume groups created, you're ready to create the logical volume.

Creating Logical Volumes

The logical volume is what the Linux system uses to emulate a physical partition, and it holds the filesystem. The Linux system handles the logical volumes just like a physical partition, allowing you to define filesystems in the logical volume and then mount the filesystem into the virtual directory.

To create the logical volume, use the lvcreate command. Although you can usually get away without using command line options in the other Linux LVM commands, the lvcreate command requires at least some options to be entered. Table 8-5 shows the available command line options.

TABLE 8-5   The lvcreate Options

Option	Long Option Name	Description
-c	--chunksize	Specifies the chunksize of the snapshot logical volume
-C	--contiguous	Sets or resets the contiguous allocation policy
-i	--stripes	Specifies the number of stripes
-I	--stripsize	Specifies the size of each stripe
-l	--extents	Specifies the number of logical extents to allocate to a new logical volume or the percent of the logical extents to use
-L	--size	Specifies the disk size to allocate to a new logical volume
	--minor	Specifies the minor number of the device
-m	--mirrors	Creates a mirrored logical volume
-M	--persistent	Makes the minor number persistent
-n	--name	Specifies the name of the new logical volume
-p	--permission	Sets read/write permission for the logical volume
-r	--readahead	Sets the read ahead sector count

-R	--regionsize	Specifies the size to divide the mirror regions into
-s	--snapshot	Creates a snapshot logical volume
-Z	--zero	Sets the first 1KB of data on the new logical volume to zeros

Although the command line options may look intimidating, for most situations, you can get by with a minimal amount of options:

```
$ sudo lvcreate -l 100%FREE -n lvtest Vol1
  Logical volume "lvtest" created
$
```

If you want to see the details of what you created, use the lvdisplay command:

```
$ sudo lvdisplay Vol1
  --- Logical volume ---
  LV Path                /dev/Vol1/lvtest
  LV Name                lvtest
  VG Name                Vol1
  LV UUID                4W2369-pLXy-jWmb-1IFN-SMNX-xZnN-3KN208
  LV Write Access        read/write
  LV Creation host, time ... -0400
  LV Status              available
  # open                 0
  LV Size                2.00 GiB
  Current LE             513
  Segments               1
  Allocation             inherit
  Read ahead sectors     auto
  - currently set to     256
  Block device           253:2

$
```

Now you can see just what you created! Notice that the volume group name (Vol1) is used to identify the volume group to use when creating the new logical volume.

The -l parameter defines how much of the available space on the volume group specified to use for the logical volume. Notice that you can specify the value as a percent of the free space in the volume group. This example used all (100%) of the free space for the new logical volume.

You can use the -l parameter to specify the size as a percentage of the available space or the -L parameter to specify the actual size in bytes, kilobytes (KB), megabytes (MB), or gigabytes (GB). The -n parameter allows you to provide a name for the logical volume (called lvtest in this example).

8

Creating the Filesystem

After you run the `lvcreate` command, the logical volume exists but doesn't have a filesystem. To do that, you need to use the appropriate command line program for the filesystem you want to create:

```
$ sudo mkfs.ext4 /dev/Vol1/lvtest
mke2fs 1.41.12 (17-May-2010)
Filesystem label=
OS type: Linux
Block size=4096 (log=2)
Fragment size=4096 (log=2)
Stride=0 blocks, Stripe width=0 blocks
131376 inodes, 525312 blocks
26265 blocks (5.00%) reserved for the super user
First data block=0
Maximum filesystem blocks=541065216
17 block groups
32768 blocks per group, 32768 fragments per group
7728 inodes per group
Superblock backups stored on blocks:
        32768, 98304, 163840, 229376, 294912

Writing inode tables: done
Creating journal (16384 blocks): done
Writing superblocks and filesystem accounting information: done

This filesystem will be automatically checked every 28 mounts or
180 days, whichever comes first.Use tune2fs -c or -i to override.
$
```

After you've created the new filesystem, you can mount the volume in the virtual directory using the standard Linux mount command, just as if it were a physical partition. The only difference is that you use a special path that identifies the logical volume:

```
$ sudo mount /dev/Vol1/lvtest /mnt/my_partition
$
$ mount
/dev/mapper/vg_server01-lv_root on / type ext4 (rw)
[...]
/dev/mapper/Vol1-lvtest on /mnt/my_partition type ext4 (rw)
$
$ cd /mnt/my_partition
$
$ ls -al
total 24
drwxr-xr-x. 3 root root  4096 Jun 12 10:22 .
drwxr-xr-x. 3 root root  4096 Jun 11 09:58 ..
drwx------. 2 root root 16384 Jun 12 10:22 lost+found
$
```

Notice that the path used in both the `mkfs.ext4` and `mount` commands is a little odd. Instead of a physical partition path, the path uses the volume group name, along with the logical volume name. After the filesystem is mounted, you can access the new area in the virtual directory.

Modifying the LVM

Because the benefit of using the Linux LVM is to dynamically modify filesystems, you'd expect that some tools would allow you to do that. Some tools are available in Linux that allow you to modify the existing logical volume management configuration.

If you don't have access to a fancy graphical interface for managing your Linux LVM environment, all is not lost. You've already seen some of the Linux LVM command line programs in action in this chapter. You can use a host of other command line programs to manage the LVM setup after you've installed it. Table 8-6 lists the common commands that are available in the Linux LVM package.

TABLE 8-6   The Linux LVM Commands

Command	Function
vgchange	Activates and deactivates a volume group
vgremove	Removes a volume group
vgextend	Adds physical volumes to a volume group
vgreduce	Removes physical volumes from a volume group
lvextend	Increases the size of a logical volume
lvreduce	Decreases the size of a logical volume

Using these command line programs, you have full control over your Linux LVM environment.

> **TIP**
>
> Be careful when manually increasing or decreasing the size of a logical volume. The filesystem stored in the logical volume must be manually fixed to handle the change in size. Most filesystems include command line programs for reformatting the filesystem, such as the `resize2fs` program for the ext2, ext3, and ext4 filesystems.

8

Summary

Working with storage devices in Linux requires that you know a little bit about filesystems. Knowing how to create and work with filesystems from the command line can come in handy as you work on Linux systems. This chapter discussed how to handle filesystems from the Linux command line.

The Linux system is different from Windows in that it supports lots of different methods for storing files and folders. Each filesystem method has different features that make it ideal for different situations. Also, each filesystem method uses different commands for interacting with the storage device.

Before you can install a filesystem on a storage device, you must first prepare the device. The fdisk command is used to partition storage devices to get them ready for the filesystem. When you partition the storage device, you must define what type of filesystem will be used on it.

After you partition a storage device, you can use one of several different filesystems for the partition. Popular Linux filesystems include ext4 and XFS. Both of these filesystems provide journaling filesystem features, making them less prone to errors and problems if the Linux system should crash.

One limiting factor to creating filesystems directly on a storage device partition is that you can't easily change the size of the filesystem if you run out of disk space. However, Linux supports logical volume management, a method of creating virtual partitions across multiple storage devices. This method allows you to easily expand an existing filesystem without having to completely rebuild it. The Linux LVM package provides command line commands to create logical volumes across multiple storage devices on which to build filesystems.

Now that you've seen the core Linux command line commands, it's close to the time to start creating some shell script programs. However, before you start coding, we need to discuss another element: installing software. If you plan to write shell scripts, you need an environment in which to create your masterpieces. The next chapter discusses how to install and manage software packages from the command line in different Linux environments.

Installing Software

IN THIS CHAPTER

Installing software

Using Debian packages

Working with Red Hat packages

In the old days of Linux, installing software could be a painful experience. Fortunately, the Linux developers have made life a little easier for us by bundling software into pre-built packages that are much easier to install. However, you still have a little work to do to get the software packages installed, especially if you want to do that from the command line. This chapter looks at the various Package Management Systems available in Linux and the command line tools used for software installation, management, and removal.

Package Management Primer

Before diving into the world of Linux software package management, this chapter goes through a few of the basics first. Each of the major Linux distributions utilizes some form of a Package Management System (PMS) to control installing software applications and libraries. A PMS utilizes a database that keeps track of these items:

- What software packages are installed on the Linux system
- What files have been installed for each package
- Versions of each of the software packages installed

Software packages are stored on servers, called *repositories*, and are accessed across the Internet via PMS utilities running on your local Linux system. You can use the PMS utilities to search for new software packages or even updates to software packages already installed on the system.

A software package often has *dependencies* or other packages that must be installed first for the software to run properly. The PMS utilities detect these dependencies and offer to install any additionally needed software packages before installing the desired package.

The downside to PMS is that there isn't a single standard utility. Whereas all the bash shell commands discussed so far in this book work no matter which Linux distribution you use, this is not true with software package management.

The PMS utilities and their associated commands are vastly different between the various Linux distributions. The two primary PMS base utilities commonly used in the Linux world are dpkg and rpm.

Debian-based distributions such as Ubuntu and Linux Mint use, at the base of their PMS utilities, the dpkg command. This command interacts directly with the PMS on the Linux system and is used for installing, managing, and removing software packages.

The Red Hat–based distributions, such as Fedora, openSUSE, and Mandriva, use the rpm command at the base of their PMS. Similar to the dpkg command, the rpm command can list installed packages, install new packages, and remove existing software.

Note that these two commands are the core of their respective PMS, not the entire PMS itself. Many Linux distributions that use the dpkg or rpm methods have built additional specialty PMS utilities upon these base commands to help make your life much easier. The following sections walk through various PMS utility commands you'll run into in the popular Linux distributions.

The Debian-Based Systems

The dpkg command is at the core of the Debian-based family of PMS tools. These other tools are included in this PMS:

- apt-get
- apt-cache
- aptitude

By far the most common command line tool is aptitude, and for good reason. The aptitude tool is essentially a front-end for both the apt tools and dpkg. Whereas dpkg is a PMS tool, aptitude is a complete Package Management System.

Using the aptitude command at the command line helps you avoid common software installation problems, such as missing software dependencies, unstable system environments, and just a whole lot of unnecessary hassle. This section looks at how to use the aptitude command tool from the Linux command line.

Managing packages with aptitude

A common task faced by Linux system administrators is to determine what packages are already installed on the system. Fortunately, aptitude has a handy interactive interface that makes this task an easy one.

If you have aptitude installed in your Linux distribution, at the shell prompt just type aptitude and press Enter. You are thrown into aptitude's full-screen mode, as you can see in Figure 9-1.

FIGURE 9.1

The aptitude main window

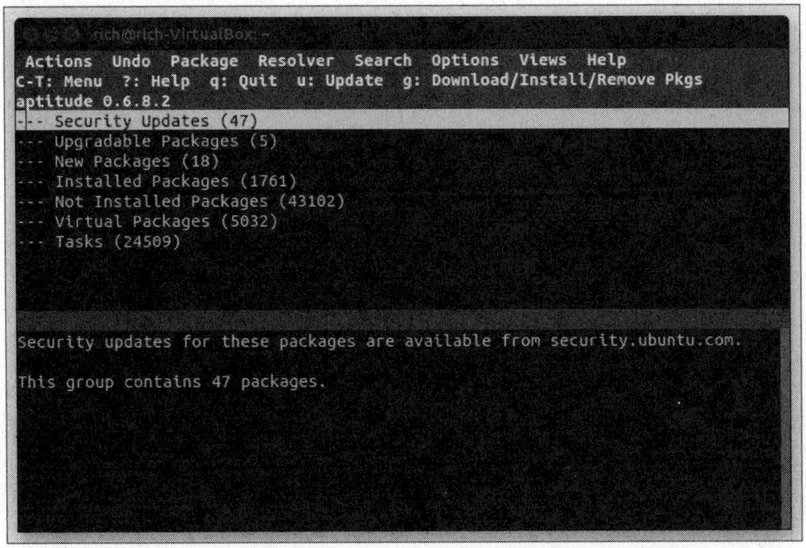

Use the arrow keys to maneuver around the menu. Select the menu option Installed Packages to see what packages are installed. You will see several groups of software packages, such as editors, and so on. A number in parentheses follows each group, which indicates the number of packages the group contains.

Use the arrow keys to highlight a group, and press Enter to see each subgroup of packages. You then see the individual package names and their version numbers. Press Enter on individual packages to get very detailed information, such as the package's description, home page, size, maintainer, and so on.

When you're finished viewing the installed packages, press q to quit the display. You can then go back to the arrow keys. and use Enter to toggle open or closed the packages and their subgroups. When you are all finished, just press q multiple times until you receive the pop-up screen "Really quit Aptitude?"

If you already know the packages on your system and want to quickly display detailed information about a particular package, you don't need to go into aptitude's interactive interface. You can use aptitude as a single command at the command line:

```
aptitude show package_name
```

Here's an example of displaying the details of the package `mysql-client`:

```
$ aptitude show mysql-client
Package: mysql-client
State: not installed
Version: 5.5.38-0ubuntu0.14.04.1
Priority: optional
Section: database
Maintainer: Ubuntu Developers <ubuntu-devel-discuss@lists.ubuntu.com>
Architecture: all
Uncompressed Size: 129 k
Depends: mysql-client-5.5
Provided by: mysql-client-5.5
Description: MySQL database client (metapackage depending on the latest version)
 This is an empty package that depends on the current "best" version of
 mysql-client (currently mysql-client-5.5), as determined by the MySQL
 maintainers.  Install this package if in doubt about which MySQL version you
 want, as this is the one considered to be in the best shape by the Maintainers.
Homepage: http://dev.mysql.com/

$
```

> **NOTE**
>
> The `aptitude show` command indicates that the package is not installed on the system. It also shows detailed package information from the software repository.

One detail you cannot get with `aptitude` is a listing of all the files associated with a particular software package. To get this list, you must go to the `dpkg` tool itself:

```
dpkg -L package_name
```

Here's an example of using `dpkg` to list all the files installed as part of the `vim-common` package:

```
$
$ dpkg -L vim-common
/.
/usr
/usr/bin
/usr/bin/xxd
/usr/bin/helpztags
/usr/lib
/usr/lib/mime
/usr/lib/mime/packages
/usr/lib/mime/packages/vim-common
/usr/share
/usr/share/man
/usr/share/man/ru
```

```
/usr/share/man/ru/man1
/usr/share/man/ru/man1/vim.1.gz
/usr/share/man/ru/man1/vimdiff.1.gz
/usr/share/man/ru/man1/xxd.1.gz
/usr/share/man/it
/usr/share/man/it/man1
[...]
$
```

You can also do the reverse — find what package a particular file belongs to:

```
dpkg --search absolute_file_name
```

Note that you need to use an absolute file reference for this to work:

```
$
$ dpkg --search /usr/bin/xxd
vim-common: /usr/bin/xxd
$
```

The output shows the /usr/bin/xxd file was installed as part of the vim-common package.

Installing software packages with aptitude

Now that you know more about listing software package information on your system, this section walks through a software package install. First, you'll want to determine the package name to install. How do you find a particular software package? Use the aptitude command with the search option:

```
aptitude search package_name
```

The beauty of the search option is that you do not need to insert wildcards around package_name. Wildcards are implied. Here's an example of using aptitude to look for the wine software package:

```
$
$ aptitude search wine
p   gnome-wine-icon-theme        - red variation of the GNOME- ...
v   libkwineffects1-api          -
p   libkwineffects1a             - library used by effects...
p   q4wine                       - Qt4 GUI for wine (W.I.N.E)
p   shiki-wine-theme             - red variation of the Shiki- ...
p   wine                         - Microsoft Windows Compatibility ...
p   wine-dev                     - Microsoft Windows Compatibility ...
p   wine-gecko                   - Microsoft Windows Compatibility ...
p   wine1.0                      - Microsoft Windows Compatibility ...
p   wine1.0-dev                  - Microsoft Windows Compatibility ...
```

9

```
p    winel.0-gecko              - Microsoft Windows Compatibility ...
p    winel.2                    - Microsoft Windows Compatibility ...
p    winel.2-dbg                - Microsoft Windows Compatibility ...
p    winel.2-dev                - Microsoft Windows Compatibility ...
p    winel.2-gecko              - Microsoft Windows Compatibility ...
p    winefish                   - LaTeX Editor based on Bluefish
$
```

Notice that before each package name is either a p or i. If you see an i u, the package is currently installed on your system. If you see a p or v, it is available but not installed. As you can see from the preceding listing, this system does not have wine currently installed, but the package is available from the software repository.

Installing a software package on a system from a repository using aptitude is as easy as this:

```
aptitude install package_name
```

After you find the software package name from the search option, just plug it into the aptitude command using the install option:

```
$
$ sudo aptitude install wine
The following NEW packages will be installed:
  cabextract{a} esound-clients{a} esound-common{a} gnome-exe-thumbnailer
{a}
  icoutils{a} imagemagick{a} libaudio2{a} libaudiofile0{a} libcdt4{a}
  libesd0{a} libgraph4{a} libgvc5{a} libilmbase6{a} libmagickcore3-extra
{a}
  libmpg123-0{a} libnetpbm10{a} libopenal1{a} libopenexr6{a}
  libpathplan4{a} libxdot4{a} netpbm{a} ttf-mscorefonts-installer{a}
  ttf-symbol-replacement{a} winbind{a} wine winel.2{a} winel.2-gecko{a}
0 packages upgraded, 27 newly installed, 0 to remove and 0 not upgraded.
Need to get 0B/27.6MB of archives. After unpacking 121MB will be used.
Do you want to continue? [Y/n/?] Y
Preconfiguring packages ...
[...]
All done, no errors.
All fonts downloaded and installed.
Updating fontconfig cache for /usr/share/fonts/truetype/msttcorefonts
Setting up winbind (2:3.5.4~dfsg-1ubuntu7) ...
 * Starting the Winbind daemon winbind
 [ OK ]
Setting up wine (1.2-0ubuntu5) ...
Setting up gnome-exe-thumbnailer (0.6-0ubuntu1) ...
Processing triggers for libc-bin ...
ldconfig deferred processing now taking place

$
```

> **NOTE**
>
> Before the `aptitude` command in the preceding listing, the `sudo` command is used. The `sudo` command allows you to run a command as the root user. You can use the `sudo` command to run administrative tasks, such as installing software.

To check if the installation processed properly, just use the `search` option again. This time you should see an `i u` listed in front of the wine software package, indicating it is installed.

You may also notice that there are additional packages with the `i u` in front of them. This is because `aptitude` automatically resolved any necessary package dependencies for us and installs the needed additional library and software packages. This is a wonderful feature included in many Package Management Systems.

Updating software with aptitude

While `aptitude` helps protect you from problems installing software, trying to coordinate a multiple-package update with dependencies can get tricky. To safely update all the software packages on a system with any new versions in the repository, use the `safe-upgrade` option:

```
aptitude safe-upgrade
```

Notice that this command doesn't take a software package name as an argument. That's because the `safe-upgrade` option upgrades all the installed packages to the most recent version available in the repository, which is safer for system stabilization.

Here's a sample output from running the `aptitude safe-update` command:

```
$
$ sudo aptitude safe-upgrade
The following packages will be upgraded:
  evolution evolution-common evolution-plugins gsfonts libevolution
  xserver-xorg-video-geode
6 packages upgraded, 0 newly installed, 0 to remove and 0 not upgraded.
Need to get 9,312kB of archives. After unpacking 0B will be used.
Do you want to continue? [Y/n/?] Y
Get:1 http://us.archive.ubuntu.com/ubuntu/ maverick/main
 libevolution i386 2.30.3-1ubuntu4 [2,096kB]
[...]
Preparing to replace xserver-xorg-video-geode 2.11.9-2
(using .../xserver-xorg-video-geode_2.11.9-3_i386.deb) ...
Unpacking replacement xserver-xorg-video-geode ...
Processing triggers for man-db ...
Processing triggers for desktop-file-utils ...
Processing triggers for python-gmenu ...
[...]
Current status: 0 updates [-6].
$
```

9

You can also use less-conservative options for software upgrades:

- `aptitude full-upgrade`
- `aptitude dist-upgrade`

These options perform the same task, upgrading all the software packages to the latest versions. Where they differ from `safe-upgrade` is that they do not check dependencies between packages. The whole package dependency issue can get real ugly. If you're not exactly sure of the dependencies for the various packages, stick with the `safe-upgrade` option.

> **NOTE**
>
> Obviously, running aptitude's `safe-upgrade` option is something you should do on a regular basis to keep your system up to date. However, it is especially important to run it after a fresh distribution installation. Usually, lots of security patches and updates have been released since the last full release of a distribution.

Uninstalling software with aptitude

Getting rid of software packages with aptitude is as easy as installing and upgrading them. The only real choice you have to make is whether to keep the software's data and configuration files around afterward.

To remove a software package, but not the data and configuration files, use the `remove` option of aptitude. To remove a software package and the related data and configuration files, use the `purge` option:

```
$ sudo aptitude purge wine
[sudo] password for user:
The following packages will be REMOVED:
  cabextract{u} esound-clients{u} esound-common{u} gnome-exe-thumbnailer
{u}
  icoutils{u} imagemagick{u} libaudio2{u} libaudiofile0{u} libcdt4{u}
  libesd0{u} libgraph4{u} libgvc5{u} libilmbase6{u} libmagickcore3-extra
{u}
  libmpg123-0{u} libnetpbm10{u} libopenal1{u} libopenexr6{u}
  libpathplan4{u} libxdot4{u} netpbm{u} ttf-mscorefonts-installer{u}
  ttf-symbol-replacement{u} winbind{u} wine{p} wine1.2{u} wine1.2-gecko
{u}
0 packages upgraded, 0 newly installed, 27 to remove and 6 not upgraded.
Need to get 0B of archives. After unpacking 121MB will be freed.
Do you want to continue? [Y/n/?] Y
(Reading database ... 120968 files and directories currently installed.)
Removing ttf-mscorefonts-installer ...
[...]
Processing triggers for fontconfig ...
Processing triggers for ureadahead ...
Processing triggers for python-support ...

$
```

To see if the package has been removed, you can use the `aptitude search` option again. If you see a c in front of the package name, it means the software has been removed, but the configuration files have not been purged from the system. A p in front indicates the configuration files have also been removed.

The aptitude repositories

The default software repository locations for `aptitude` are set up for you when you install your Linux distribution. The repository locations are stored in the file /etc/apt/ sources.list.

In many cases, you never need to add/remove a software repository so you don't need to touch this file. However, `aptitude` pulls software from only these repositories. Also, when searching for software to install or update, aptitude checks only these repositories. If you need to include some additional software repositories for your PMS, this is the place to do it.

> **TIP**
>
> The Linux distribution developers work hard to make sure package versions added to the repositories don't conflict with one another. Usually it's safest to upgrade or install a software package from the repository. Even if a newer version is available elsewhere, you may want to hold off installing it until that version is available in your Linux distribution's repository.

The following is an example of a sources.list file from an Ubuntu system:

```
$ cat /etc/apt/sources.list
#deb cdrom:[Ubuntu 14.04 LTS _Trusty Tahr_ - Release i386 (20140417)]/
 trusty main restricted

# See http://help.ubuntu.com/community/UpgradeNotes for how to upgrade to
# newer versions of the distribution.
deb http://us.archive.ubuntu.com/ubuntu/ trusty main restricted
deb-src http://us.archive.ubuntu.com/ubuntu/ trusty main restricted

## Major bug fix updates produced after the final release of the
## distribution.
deb http://us.archive.ubuntu.com/ubuntu/ trusty-updates main restricted
deb-src http://us.archive.ubuntu.com/ubuntu/ trusty-updates main restricted

## N.B. software from this repository is ENTIRELY UNSUPPORTED by the Ubuntu
## team. Also, please note that software in universe WILL NOT receive any
## review or updates from the Ubuntu security team.
deb http://us.archive.ubuntu.com/ubuntu/ trusty universe
deb-src http://us.archive.ubuntu.com/ubuntu/ trusty universe
deb http://us.archive.ubuntu.com/ubuntu/ trusty-updates universe
```

9

```
deb-src http://us.archive.ubuntu.com/ubuntu/ trusty-updates universe
[...]
## Uncomment the following two lines to add software from Canonical's
## 'partner' repository.
## This software is not part of Ubuntu, but is offered by Canonical and the
## respective vendors as a service to Ubuntu users.
# deb http://archive.canonical.com/ubuntu trusty partner
# deb-src http://archive.canonical.com/ubuntu trusty partner

## This software is not part of Ubuntu, but is offered by third-party
## developers who want to ship their latest software.
deb http://extras.ubuntu.com/ubuntu trusty main
deb-src http://extras.ubuntu.com/ubuntu trusty main
$
```

First, notice that the file is full of helpful comments and warnings. The repository sources specified use the following structure:

```
deb (or deb-src) address  distribution_name  package_type_list
```

The deb or deb-src value indicates the software package type. The deb value indicates it is a source of compiled programs, whereas the deb-src value indicates it is a source of source code.

The address entry is the software repository's web address. The distribution_name entry is the name of this particular software repository's distribution's version. In the example, the distribution name is trusty. This does not necessarily mean that the distribution you are running is Ubuntu's Trusty Tahr; it just means the Linux distribution is using the Ubuntu Trusty Tahr software repositories! For example, in Linux Mint's sources.list file, you see a mix of Linux Mint and Ubuntu software repositories.

Finally, the package_type_list entry may be more than one word and indicates what type of packages the repository has in it. For example, you may see values such as main, restricted, universe, or partner.

When you need to add a software repository to your sources file, you can try to wing it yourself, but that more than likely will cause problems. Often, software repository sites or various package developer sites have an exact line of text that you can copy from their website and paste into your sources.list file. It's best to choose the safer route and just copy/paste.

The front-end interface, aptitude, provides intelligent command line options for working with the Debian-based dpkg utility. Now it's time to look at the Red Hat–based distributions' rpm utility and its various front-end interfaces.

The Red Hat–Based Systems

Like the Debian-based distributions, the Red Hat–based systems have several different front-end tools that are available. These are the common ones:

- yum: Used in Red Hat and Fedora
- urpm: Used in Mandriva
- zypper: Used in openSUSE

These front-ends are all based on the rpm command line tool. The following section discusses how to manage software packages using these various rpm-based tools. The focus is on yum, but information is also included for zypper and urpm.

Listing installed packages

To find out what is currently installed on your system, at the shell prompt, type the following command:

```
yum list installed
```

The information will probably whiz by you on the display screen, so it's best to redirect the installed software listing into a file. You can then use the more or less command (or a GUI editor) to look at the list in a controlled manner.

```
yum list installed > installed_software
```

To list out the installed packages on your openSUSE or Mandriva distribution, see the commands in Table 9-1. Unfortunately, the urpm tool used in Mandriva cannot produce a currently installed software listing. Thus, you need to revert to the underlying rpm tool.

TABLE 9-1 How to List Installed Software with zypper and urpm

Distribution	Front-End Tool	Command
Mandriva	urpm	rpm -qa > installed_software
openSUSE	zypper	zipper search -I > installed_software

To find out detailed information for a particular software package, yum really shines. It gives you a very verbose description of the package, and with another simple command, you can see whether the package is installed:

```
# yum list xterm
Loaded plugins: langpacks, presto, refresh-packagekit
Adding en_US to language list
Available Packages
```

```
xterm.i686 253-1.el6
#
# yum list installed xterm
Loaded plugins: refresh-packagekit
Error: No matching Packages to list
#
```

The commands to list detailed software package information using `urpm` and `zypper` are in Table 9-2. You can acquire an even more detailed set of package information from the repository, using the `info` option on the `zypper` command.

TABLE 9-2   How to See Various Package Details with zypper and urpm

Detail Type	Front-End Tool	Command
Package Information	urpm	`urpmq -i` *package_name*
Installed?	urpm	`rpm -q` *package_name*
Package Information	zypper	`zypper search -s` *package_name*
Installed?	zypper	Same command, but look for an `i` in the Status column

Finally, if you need to find out what software package provides a particular file on your filesystem, the versatile `yum` can do that, too! Just enter the command:

```
yum provides file_name
```

Here's an example of trying to find what software provided the configuration file `/etc/yum.conf`:

```
#
# yum provides /etc/yum.conf
Loaded plugins: fastestmirror, refresh-packagekit, security
Determining fastest mirrors
 * base: mirror.web-ster.com
 * extras: centos.chi.host-engine.com
 * updates: mirror.umd.edu
yum-3.2.29-40.el6.centos.noarch : RPM package installer/updater/manager
Repo       : base
Matched from:
Filename   : /etc/yum.conf


yum-3.2.29-43.el6.centos.noarch : RPM package installer/updater/manager
Repo       : updates
Matched from:
```

```
Filename    : /etc/yum.conf


yum-3.2.29-40.el6.centos.noarch : RPM package installer/updater/manager
Repo        : installed
Matched from:
Other       : Provides-match: /etc/yum.conf



#

#
```

yum checked three separate repositories: base, updates, and installed. From both, the
answer is: the yum software package provides this file!

Installing software with yum

Installation of a software package using yum is incredibly easy. The following is the basic
command for installing a software package, all its needed libraries, and package dependencies from a repository:

```
yum install package_name
```

Here's an example of installing the xterm package that we talked about in Chapter 2:

```
$ su -
Password:
# yum install xterm
Loaded plugins: fastestmirror, refresh-packagekit, security
Determining fastest mirrors
 * base: mirrors.bluehost.com
 * extras: mirror.5ninesolutions.com
 * updates: mirror.san.fastserv.com
Setting up Install Process
Resolving Dependencies
--> Running transaction check
---> Package xterm.i686 0:253-1.el6 will be installed
--> Finished Dependency Resolution

Dependencies Resolved
[...]
Installed:
  xterm.i686 0:253-1.el6

Complete!
#
```

9

You can also manually download an `rpm` installation file and install it using `yum`. This is called a *local installation*. This is the basic command:

```
yum localinstall package_name.rpm
```

You can begin to see that one of `yum`'s strengths is that it uses very logical and user-friendly commands.

Table 9-3 shows how to perform a package install with `urpm` and `zypper`. You should note that if you are not logged in as root, you get a "command not found" error message using `urpm`.

TABLE 9-3   How to Install Software with zypper and urpm

Front-End Tool	Command
urpm	urpmi package_name
zypper	zypper install package_name

Updating software with yum

In most Linux distributions, when you're working away in the GUI, you get those nice little notification icons telling you that an update is needed. Here at the command line, it takes a little more work.

To see the list of all the available updates for your installed packages, type the following command:

```
yum list updates
```

It's always nice to get no response to this command because it means you have nothing to update! However, if you do discover a particular software package needs updating, type the following command:

```
yum update package_name
```

If you'd like to update all the packages listed in the update list, just enter the following command:

```
yum update
```

Commands for updating software packages on Mandriva and openSUSE are listed in Table 9-4. When urpm is used, the repository database is automatically refreshed as well as software packages updated.

TABLE 9-4   How to Update Software with zypper and urpm

Front-End Tool	Command
urpm	urpmi --auto-update --update
zypper	zypper update

Uninstalling software with yum

The yum tool also provides an easy way to uninstall software you no longer want on your system. As with aptitude, you need to choose whether to keep the software package's data and configuration files.

To just remove the software package and keep any configuration and data files, use the following command:

    yum remove *package_name*

To uninstall the software and all its files, use the erase option:

    yum erase *package_name*

It is equally easy to remove software using urpm and zypper in Table 9-5. Both of these tools perform a function similar to yum's erase option.

TABLE 9-5   How to Uninstall Software with zypper and urpm

Front-End Tool	Command
urpm	urpme package_name
zypper	zypper remove package_name

Although life is considerably easier with PMS packages, it's not always problem-free. Occasionally, things do go wrong. Fortunately, there's help.

Dealing with broken dependencies

Sometimes, as multiple software packages get loaded, a software dependency for one package can get overwritten by the installation of another package. This is called a *broken dependency*.

If this should happen on your system, first try the following command:

```
yum clean all
```

Then try to use the update option in the yum command. Sometimes, just cleaning up any misplaced files can help.

If that doesn't solve the problem, try the following command:

```
yum deplist package_name
```

This command displays all the package's library dependencies and what software package provides them. After you know the libraries required for a package, you can then install them. Here's an example of determining the dependencies for the xterm package:

```
# yum deplist xterm

Loaded plugins: fastestmirror, refresh-packagekit, security
Loading mirror speeds from cached hostfile
 * base: mirrors.bluehost.com
 * extras: mirror.5ninesolutions.com
 * updates: mirror.san.fastserv.com
Finding dependencies:
package: xterm.i686 253-1.el6
  dependency: libncurses.so.5
   provider: ncurses-libs.i686 5.7-3.20090208.el6
  dependency: libfontconfig.so.1
   provider: fontconfig.i686 2.8.0-3.el6
  dependency: libXft.so.2
   provider: libXft.i686 2.3.1-2.el6
  dependency: libXt.so.6
   provider: libXt.i686 1.1.3-1.el6
  dependency: libX11.so.6
   provider: libX11.i686 1.5.0-4.el6
  dependency: rtld(GNU_HASH)
   provider: glibc.i686 2.12-1.132.el6
   provider: glibc.i686 2.12-1.132.el6_5.1
   provider: glibc.i686 2.12-1.132.el6_5.2
  dependency: libICE.so.6
   provider: libICE.i686 1.0.6-1.el6
  dependency: libXaw.so.7
   provider: libXaw.i686 1.0.11-2.el6
  dependency: libtinfo.so.5
   provider: ncurses-libs.i686 5.7-3.20090208.el6
  dependency: libutempter.so.0
   provider: libutempter.i686 1.1.5-4.1.el6
  dependency: /bin/sh
   provider: bash.i686 4.1.2-15.el6_4
  dependency: libc.so.6(GLIBC_2.4)
```

```
     provider: glibc.i686 2.12-1.132.el6
     provider: glibc.i686 2.12-1.132.el6_5.1
     provider: glibc.i686 2.12-1.132.el6_5.2
   dependency: libXmu.so.6
     provider: libXmu.i686 1.1.1-2.el6
 #
```

If that doesn't solve your problem, you have one last tool:

```
yum update --skip-broken
```

The `--skip-broken` option allows you to just ignore the package with the broken dependency and update the other software packages. This may not help the broken package, but at least you can update the remaining packages on the system!

In Table 9-6, the commands to try for broken dependencies with `urpm` and `zypper` are listed. With `zypper`, there is only the one command to verify and fix a broken dependency. With `urpm`, if the clean option does not work, you can skip updates on the offensive package. To do this, you must add the name of the offending package to the file `/etc/urpmi/skip.list`.

TABLE 9-6 **Broken Dependencies with zypper and urpm**

Front End Tool	Command
urpm	urpmi --clean
zypper	zypper verify

yum repositories

Just like the `aptitude` systems, `yum` has its software repositories set up at installation. For most purposes, these pre-installed repositories work just fine for your needs. But if and when the time comes that you need to install software from a different repository, here are some things you need to know.

TIP

A wise system administrator sticks with approved repositories. An approved repository is one that is sanctioned by the distribution's official site. If you start adding unapproved repositories, you lose the guarantee of stability. And you will be heading into broken dependencies territory.

To see what repositories you are currently pulling software from, type the following command:

```
yum repolist
```

If you don't find a repository you need software from, you need to do a little configuration file editing. The yum repository definition files are located in /etc/yum.repos.d. You need to add the proper URL and gain access to any necessary encryption keys.

Good repository sites such as rpmfusion.org lay out all the steps necessary to use them. Sometimes, these repository sites offer an rpm file that you can download and install using the yum localinstall command. The installation of the rpm file does all the repository setup work for you. Now that's convenient!

urpm calls its repositories *media*. The commands for looking at urpm media and zypper's repositories are in Table 9-7. Notice with both of these front-end tools that you do not edit a configuration file. Instead, to add media or a repository, you just type the command.

TABLE 9-7 zypper and urpm Repositories

Action	Front-End Tool	Command
Display repository	urpm	urpmq --list-media
Add repository	urpm	urpmi.addmedia path_name
Display repository	zypper	zypper repos
Add repository	zypper	zypper addrepo path_name

Both Debian-based and Red Hat–based systems use Package Management Systems to ease the process of managing software. Now we are going to step out of the world of Package Management Systems and look at something a little more difficult: installing directly from source code.

Installing from Source Code

Chapter 4 discussed *tarball* packages — how to create them using the tar command line command and how to unpack them. Before the fancy rpm and dpkg tools, administrators had to know how to unpack and install software from tarballs.

If you work in the open source software environment much, there's a good chance you will still find software packed up as a tarball. This section walks you through the process of unpacking and installing a tarball software package.

For this example, the software package sysstat is used. The sysstat utility is a very nice software package that provides a variety of system monitoring tools.

First, you need to download the sysstat tarball to your Linux system. You can often find the sysstat package available on different Linux sites, but it's usually best to go straight to the source of the program. In this case, it's the website `http://sebastien.godard` `.pagesperso-orange.fr/`.

If you click the Download link, you go to the page that contains the files for downloading. The current version at the time of this writing is 11.1.1, and the distribution file name is `sysstat-11.1.1.tar.gz`.

Click the link to download the file to your Linux system. After you have downloaded the file, you can unpack it.

To unpack a software tarball, use the standard `tar` command:

```
#
# tar -zxvf sysstat-11.1.1.tar.gz
sysstat-11.1.1/
sysstat-11.1.1/cifsiostat.c
sysstat-11.1.1/FAQ
sysstat-11.1.1/ioconf.h
sysstat-11.1.1/rd_stats.h
sysstat-11.1.1/COPYING
sysstat-11.1.1/common.h
sysstat-11.1.1/sysconfig.in
sysstat-11.1.1/mpstat.h
sysstat-11.1.1/rndr_stats.h
[...]
sysstat-11.1.1/activity.c
sysstat-11.1.1/sar.c
sysstat-11.1.1/iostat.c
sysstat-11.1.1/rd_sensors.c
sysstat-11.1.1/prealloc.in
sysstat-11.1.1/sa2.in
#

#
```

Now that the tarball is unpacked and the files have neatly put themselves into a directory called `sysstat-11.1.1`, you can dive down into that directory and continue.

First, use the `cd` command to get into the new directory and list the contents of the directory:

```
$ cd sysstat-11.1.1
$ ls
activity.c      iconfig        prealloc.in    sa.h
build           INSTALL        pr_stats.c     sar.c
CHANGES         ioconf.c       pr_stats.h     sa_wrap.c
cifsiostat.c    ioconf.h       rd_sensors.c   sysconfig.in
cifsiostat.h    iostat.c       rd_sensors.h   sysstat-11.1.1.lsm
common.c        iostat.h       rd_stats.c     sysstat-11.1.1.spec
```

9

```
common.h        json_stats.c        rd_stats.h    sysstat.in
configure       json_stats.h        README        sysstat.ioconf
configure.in    Makefile.in         rndr_stats.c  sysstat.service.in
contrib         man                 rndr_stats.h  sysstat.sysconfig.in
COPYING         mpstat.c            sa1.in        version.in
count.c         mpstat.h            sa2.in        xml
count.h         nfsiostat-sysstat.c sa_common.c   xml_stats.c
CREDITS         nfsiostat-sysstat.h sadc.c        xml_stats.h
cron            nls                 sadf.c
FAQ             pidstat.c           sadf.h
format.c        pidstat.h           sadf_misc.c
$
```

In the listing of the directory, you should typically see a README or AAAREADME file. It is very important to read this file. The actual instructions you need to finish the software's installation are in this file.

Following the advice contained in the README file, the next step is to configure sysstat for your system. This checks your Linux system to ensure it has the proper library dependencies, in addition to the proper compiler to compile the source code:

```
# ./configure

Check programs:
.
checking for gcc... gcc
checking whether the C compiler works... yes
checking for C compiler default output file name... a.out
[...]
checking for ANSI C header files... (cached) yes
checking for dirent.h that defines DIR... yes
checking for library containing opendir... none required
checking ctype.h usability... yes
checking ctype.h presence... yes
checking for ctype.h... yes
checking errno.h usability... yes
checking errno.h presence... yes
checking for errno.h... yes
[...]
Check library functions:
.
checking for strchr... yes
checking for strcspn... yes
checking for strspn... yes
checking for strstr... yes
checking for sensors support... yes
checking for sensors_get_detected_chips in -lsensors... no
checking for sensors lib... no
.
```

```
Check system services:
.
checking for special C compiler options needed for large files... no
checking for _FILE_OFFSET_BITS value needed for large files... 64
.
Check configuration:
[...]
Now create files:
[...]
config.status: creating Makefile

    Sysstat version:            11.1.1
    Installation prefix:        /usr/local
    rc directory:               /etc/rc.d
    Init directory:             /etc/rc.d/init.d
    Systemd unit dir:
    Configuration directory:        /etc/sysconfig
    Man pages directory:            ${datarootdir}/man
    Compiler:                   gcc
    Compiler flags:             -g -O2

#
```

If anything does go wrong, the configure step displays an error message explaining what's missing. If you don't have the GNU C compiler installed in your Linux distribution, you get a single error message, but for all other issues you should see multiple messages indicating what's installed and what isn't.

The next stage is to build the various binary files using the make command. The make command compiles the source code and then the linker to create the final executable files for the package. As with the configure command, the make command produces lots of output as it goes through the steps of compiling and linking all the source code files:

```
# make
-gcc -o sadc.o -c -g -O2 -Wall -Wstrict-prototypes -pipe -O2
 -DSA_DIR=\"/var/log/sa\" -DSADC_PATH=\"/usr/local/lib/sa/sadc\"
 -DUSE_NLS -DPACKAGE=\"sysstat\"
 -DLOCALEDIR=\"/usr/local/share/locale\" sadc.c
gcc -o act_sadc.o -c -g -O2 -Wall -Wstrict-prototypes -pipe -O2
 -DSOURCE_SADC  -DSA_DIR=\"/var/log/sa\"
 -DSADC_PATH=\"/usr/local/lib/sa/sadc\"
 -DUSE_NLS -DPACKAGE=\"sysstat\"
 -DLOCALEDIR=\"/usr/local/share/locale\" activity.c
[...]
#
```

When make is finished, you have the actual sysstat software program available in the directory! However, it's somewhat inconvenient to have to run it from that directory.

Instead, you'll want to install it in a common location on your Linux system. To do that, you need to log in as the root user account (or use the `sudo` command if your Linux distribution prefers) and then use the `install` option of the `make` command:

```
# make install
mkdir -p /usr/local/share/man/man1
mkdir -p /usr/local/share/man/man5
mkdir -p /usr/local/share/man/man8
rm -f /usr/local/share/man/man8/sa1.8*
install -m 644 -g man man/sa1.8 /usr/local/share/man/man8
rm -f /usr/local/share/man/man8/sa2.8*
install -m 644 -g man man/sa2.8 /usr/local/share/man/man8
rm -f /usr/local/share/man/man8/sadc.8*
[...]
install -m 644 -g man man/sadc.8 /usr/local/share/man/man8
install -m 644 FAQ /usr/local/share/doc/sysstat-11.1.1
install -m 644 *.lsm /usr/local/share/doc/sysstat-11.1.1
#
```

Now the `sysstat` package is installed on the system! Although it's not quite as easy as installing a software package via a PMS, installing software using tarballs is not that difficult.

Summary

This chapter discussed how to work with a Package Management Systems (PMS) to install, update, or remove software from the command line. Although most of the Linux distributions use fancy GUI tools for software package management, you can also perform package management from the command line.

The Debian-based Linux distributions use the `dpkg` utility to interface with the PMS from the command line. A front-end to the `dpkg` utility is `aptitude`. It provides simple command line options for working with software packages in the dpkg format.

The Red Hat–based Linux distributions are based on the `rpm` utility but use different front-end tools at the command line. Red Hat and Fedora use `yum` for installing and managing software packages. The openSUSE distribution uses `zypper` for managing software, while the Mandriva distribution uses `urpm`.

The chapter closed with a discussion on how to install software packages that are only distributed in source code tarballs. The `tar` command allows you to unpack the source code files from the tarball, and `configure` and `make` allow you to build the final executable program from the source code.

The next chapter looks at the different editors available in Linux distributions. As you get ready to start working on shell scripts, it will come in handy to know what editors are available to use!

Working with Editors

B
efore you can start your shell scripting career, you need to know how to use at least one text editor in Linux. The more you know about how to use features such as searching, cutting, and pasting, the quicker you can develop your shell scripts.

You can choose from several editors. Many individuals find a particular editor whose features they love and exclusively use that text editor. This chapter discusses just a few of the text editors you'll see in the Linux world.

Visiting the vim Editor

The vi editor was the original editor used on Unix systems. It used the console graphics mode to emulate a text-editing window, allowing you to see the lines of your file, move around within the file, and insert, edit, and replace text.

Although it was quite possibly the most complicated editor in the world (at least in the opinion of those who hate it), it provides many features that have made it a staple for Unix administrators for decades.

When the GNU Project ported the vi editor to the open source world, they chose to make some improvements to it. Because it no longer resembled the original vi editor found in the Unix world, the developers also renamed it, to vi improved, or *vim*.

This section walks you through the basics of using the vim editor to edit your text shell script files.

Checking your vim package

Before you begin your exploration of the vim editor, it's a good idea to understand what vim package your Linux system has installed. On some distributions, you will have the full vim package installed and an alias for the vi command, as shown on this CentOS distribution:

```
$ alias vi
alias vi='vim'
$
$ which vim
/usr/bin/vim
$
$ ls -l /usr/bin/vim
-rwxr-xr-x. 1 root root 1967072 Apr  5  2012 /usr/bin/vim
$
```

Notice that the program file's long listing does not show any linked files (see Chapter 3 for more information on linked files). If the vim program is linked, it may be linked to a less than full-featured editor. Thus, it's a good idea to check for linked files.

On other distributions, you will find various flavors of the vim editor. Notice on this Ubuntu distribution that not only is there no alias for the vi command, but the /usr/bin/vi program file belongs to a series of file links:

```
$ alias vi
-bash: alias: vi: not found
$
$ which vi
/usr/bin/vi
$
$ ls -l /usr/bin/vi
lrwxrwxrwx 1 root root 20 Apr 22 12:39
/usr/bin/vi -> /etc/alternatives/vi
$
$ ls -l /etc/alternatives/vi
lrwxrwxrwx 1 root root 17 Apr 22 12:33
/etc/alternatives/vi -> /usr/bin/vim.tiny
$
$ ls -l /usr/bin/vim.tiny
-rwxr-xr-x 1 root root 884360 Jan  2 14:40
/usr/bin/vim.tiny
$
$ readlink -f /usr/bin/vi
/usr/bin/vim.tiny
```

Thus, when the vi command is entered, the /usr/bin/vim.tiny program is executed. The vim.tiny program provides only a few vim editor features. If you are serious about using the vim editor and have Ubuntu, you should install at least the basic vim package.

NOTE

Notice in the preceding example that, instead of having to use the ls -l command multiple times to find a series of linked files' final object, you can use the readlink -f command. It immediately produces the linked file series' final object.

Software installations were covered in detail in Chapter 9. Installing the basic vim package on this Ubuntu distribution is fairly straightforward:

```
$ sudo apt-get install vim
[...]
The following extra packages will be installed:
  vim-runtime
Suggested packages:
  ctags vim-doc vim-scripts
The following NEW packages will be installed:
  vim vim-runtime
[...]
$
$ readlink -f /usr/bin/vi
/usr/bin/vim.basic
$
```

The basic vim editor is now installed on this Ubuntu distribution, and the /usr/bin/vi program file's link was automatically changed to point to /usr/bin/vim.basic. Thus, when the vi command is entered on this Ubuntu system, the basic vim editor is used instead of tiny vim.

Exploring vim basics

The vim editor works with data in a memory buffer. To start the vim editor, just type the vim command (or vi if there's an alias or linked file) and the name of the file you want to edit:

```
$ vim myprog.c
```

If you start vim without a filename, or if the file doesn't exist, vim opens a new buffer area for editing. If you specify an existing file on the command line, vim reads the entire file's contents into a buffer area, where it is ready for editing, as shown in Figure 10-1.

10

FIGURE 10-1

The vim main window.

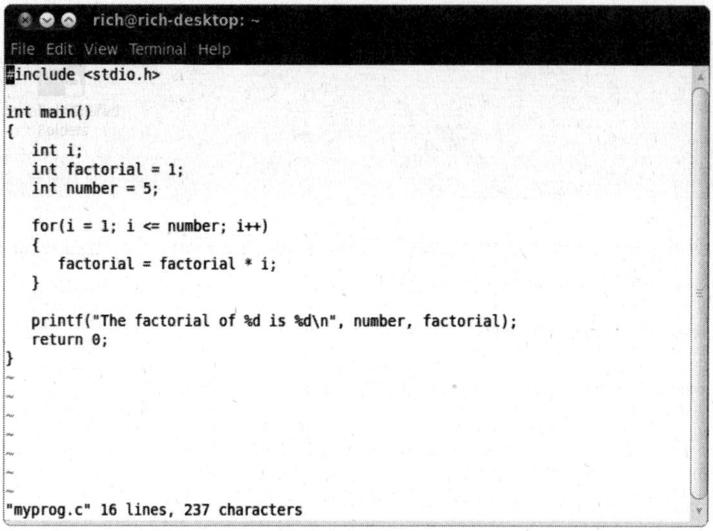

```
#include <stdio.h>

int main()
{
    int i;
    int factorial = 1;
    int number = 5;

    for(i = 1; i <= number; i++)
    {
        factorial = factorial * i;
    }

    printf("The factorial of %d is %d\n", number, factorial);
    return 0;
}
~
~
~
~
~
~
~
"myprog.c" 16 lines, 237 characters
```

The vim editor detects the terminal type for the session (see Chapter 2) and uses a full-screen mode to use the entire console window for the editor area.

The initial vim edit window shows the contents of the file (if there are any) along with a message line at the bottom of the window. If the file contents don't take up the entire screen, vim places a tilde on lines that are not part of the file (as shown in Figure 10-1).

The message line at the bottom indicates information about the edited file, depending on the file's status, and the default settings in your vim installation. If the file is new, the message [New File] appears.

The vim editor has two modes of operation:

- Normal mode
- Insert mode

When you first open a file (or start a new file) for editing, the vim editor enters *normal* mode. In normal mode, the vim editor interprets keystrokes as commands (more on those later).

In *insert* mode, vim inserts every key you type at the current cursor location in the buffer. To enter insert mode, press the i key. To get out of insert mode and go back into normal mode, press the Escape key on the keyboard.

In normal mode, you can move the cursor around the text area by using the arrow keys (as long as your terminal type is detected properly by vim). If you happen to be on a flaky terminal connection that doesn't have the arrow keys defined, all hope is not lost. The vim commands include commands for moving the cursor:

- h to move left one character
- j to move down one line (the next line in the text)
- k to move up one line (the previous line in the text)
- l to move right one character

Moving around within large text files line by line can get tedious. Fortunately, vim provides a few commands to help speed things along:

- PageDown (or Ctrl+F) to move forward one screen of data
- PageUp (or Ctrl+B) to move backward one screen of data
- G to move to the last line in the buffer
- *num* G to move to the line number *num* in the buffer
- gg to move to the first line in the buffer

The vim editor has a special feature within normal mode called *command line mode*. The command line mode provides an interactive command line where you can enter additional commands to control the actions in vim. To get to command line mode, press the colon key in normal mode. The cursor moves to the message line, and a colon (:) appears, waiting for you to enter a command.

Within the command line mode are several commands for saving the buffer to the file and exiting vim:

- q to quit if no changes have been made to the buffer data
- q! to quit and discard any changes made to the buffer data
- w *filename* to save the file under a different filename
- wq to save the buffer data to the file and quit

After seeing just a few basic vim commands, you might understand why some people absolutely hate the vim editor. To be able to use vim to its fullest, you must know plenty of obscure commands. However, after you get a few of the basic vim commands down, you can quickly edit files directly from the command line, no matter what type of environment you're in. Plus, after you get comfortable typing commands, it almost seems second nature to type both data and editing commands, and it becomes odd having to jump back to using a mouse!

10

Editing data

While in insert mode, you can insert data into the buffer; however, sometimes you need to add or remove data after you've already entered it into the buffer. While in normal mode, the vim editor provides several commands for editing the data in the buffer. Table 10-1 lists some common editing commands for vim.

TABLE 10-1 vim Editing Commands

Command	Description
x	Deletes the character at the current cursor position
dd	Deletes the line at the current cursor position
dw	Deletes the word at the current cursor position
d$	Deletes to the end of the line from the current cursor position
J	Deletes the line break at the end of the line at the current cursor position (joins lines)
u	Undoes the previous edit command
a	Appends data after the current cursor position
A	Appends data to the end of the line at the current cursor position
r char	Replaces a single character at the current cursor position with char
R text	Overwrites the data at the current cursor position with text, until you press Escape

Some of the editing commands also allow you to use a numeric modifier to indicate how many times to perform the command. For example, the command 2x deletes two characters, starting from the current cursor position, and the command 5dd deletes five lines, starting at the line from the current cursor position.

> **NOTE**
> Be careful when trying to use the keyboard Backspace or Delete keys while in the vim editor's normal mode. The vim editor usually recognizes the Delete key as the functionality of the x command, deleting the character at the current cursor location. Usually, the vim editor doesn't recognize the Backspace key in normal mode.

Copying and pasting

A standard editor feature is the ability to cut or copy data and paste it elsewhere in the document. The vim editor provides a way to do this.

Cutting and pasting is relatively easy. You've already seen the commands in Table 10-1 that can remove data from the buffer. However, when vim removes data, it actually keeps it stored in a separate register. You can retrieve that data by using the p command.

For example, you can use the dd command to delete a line of text, move the cursor to the buffer location where you want to place it, and then use the p command. The p command inserts the text after the line at the current cursor position. You can do this with any command that removes text.

Copying text is a little bit trickier. The copy command in vim is y (for yank). You can use the same second character with y as with the d command (yw to yank a word, y$ to yank to the end of a line). After you yank the text, move the cursor to the location where you want to place the text and use the p command. The yanked text now appears at that location.

Yanking is tricky in that you can't see what happened because you're not affecting the text that you yank. You never know for sure what you yanked until you paste it somewhere. But there's another feature in vim that helps you out with yanking.

The *visual mode* highlights text as you move the cursor. You use visual mode to select text to yank for pasting. To enter visual mode, move the cursor to the location where you want to start yanking, and press v. Notice that the text at the cursor position is now highlighted. Next, move the cursor to cover the text you want to yank (you can even move down lines to yank more than one line of text). As you move the cursor, vim highlights the text in the yank area. After you've covered the text you want to copy, press the y key to activate the yank command. Now that you have the text in the register, just move the cursor to where you want to paste and use the p command.

Searching and substituting

You can easily search for data in the buffer using the vim search command. To enter a search string, press the forward slash (/) key. The cursor goes to the message line, and vim displays a forward slash. Enter the text you want to find, and press the Enter key. The vim editor responds with one of three actions:

■ If the word appears after the current cursor location, it jumps to the first location where the text appears.

■ If the word doesn't appear after the current cursor location, it wraps around the end of the file to the first location in the file where the text appears (and indicates this with a message).

■ It produces an error message stating that the text was not found in the file.

To continue searching for the same word, press the forward slash character and then press the Enter key, or you can use the n key, for *next*.

10

The substitute command allows you to quickly replace (substitute) one word for another in the text. To get to the substitute command, you must be in command line mode. The format for the substitute command is:

```
:s/old/new/
```

The vim editor jumps to the first occurrence of the text old and replaces it with the text new. You can make a few modifications to the substitute command to substitute more than one occurrence of the text:

- :s/old/new/g to replace all occurrences of old in a line
- :n,ms/old/new/g to replace all occurrences of old between line numbers n and m
- :%s/old/new/g to replace all occurrences of old in the entire file
- :%s/old/new/gc to replace all occurrences of old in the entire file, but prompt for each occurrence

As you can see, for a console mode text editor, vim contains quite a few advanced features. Because every Linux distribution includes it, it's a good idea to at least know the basics of the vim editor so you can always edit scripts, no matter where you are or what you have available.

Navigating the nano Editor

Although vim is a very complicated editor with many powerful features, nano is a very simple editor. For individuals who need a simple console mode text editor that is easy to navigate, nano is the tool to use. It's also a great text editor for kids who are starting on their Linux command line adventure.

The nano text editor is a clone of the Unix systems' Pico editor. Although Pico also is a light and simple text editor, it is not licensed under the GPL. Not only is the nano text editor licensed under the GPL, it is also part of the GNU project.

The nano text editor is installed on most Linux distributions by default. Everything about the nano text editor is simple. To open a file at the command line with nano:

```
$ nano myprog.c
```

If you start nano without a filename, or if the file doesn't exist, nano simply opens a new buffer area for editing. If you specify an existing file on the command line, nano reads the entire contents of the file into a buffer area, where it is ready for editing, as shown in Figure 10-2.

FIGURE 10-2

The nano editor window

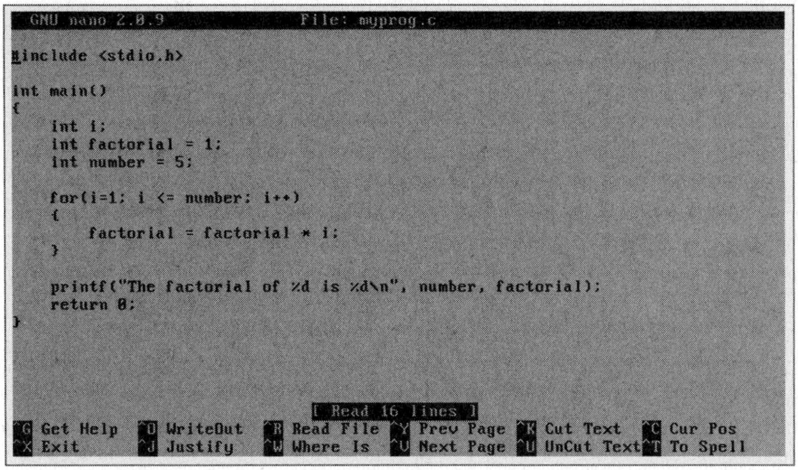

```
  GNU nano 2.0.9              File: myprog.c

#include <stdio.h>

int main()
{
    int i;
    int factorial = 1;
    int number = 5;

    for(i=1; i <= number; i++)
    {
        factorial = factorial * i;
    }

    printf("The factorial of %d is %d\n", number, factorial);
    return 0;
}


                         [ Read 16 lines ]
^G Get Help  ^O WriteOut  ^R Read File ^Y Prev Page ^K Cut Text  ^C Cur Pos
^X Exit      ^J Justify   ^W Where Is  ^V Next Page ^U UnCut Text^T To Spell
```

Notice at the bottom of the nano editor window various commands with a brief description are shown. These commands are the nano control commands. The caret (^) symbol shown represents the Ctrl key. Therefore, ^X stands for the keyboard sequence Ctrl+X.

> **TIP**
>
> Though the nano control commands list capital letters in the keyboard sequences, you can use either lowercase or uppercase characters for control commands.

Having all the basic commands listed right in front of you is great. No need to memorize what control command does what. Table 10-2 presents the various nano control commands.

TABLE 10-2 nano Control Commands

Command	Description
CTRL+C	Displays the cursor's position within the text editing buffer
CTRL+G	Displays nano's main help window
CTRL+J	Justifies the current text paragraph
CTRL+K	Cuts the text line and stores it in cut buffer
CTRL+O	Writes out the current text editing buffer to a file

Continues

10

TABLE 10-2 *(continued)*

Command	Description
CTRL+R	Reads a file into the current text editing buffer
CTRL+T	Starts the available spell checker
CTRL+U	Pastes text stored in cut buffer and places in current line
CTRL+V	Scrolls text editing buffer to next page
CTRL+W	Searches for word or phrases within text editing buffer
CTRL+X	Closes the current text editing buffer, exits nano, and returns to the shell
CTRL+Y	Scrolls text editing buffer to previous page

The control commands listed in Table 10-2 are really all you need. However, if you desire more powerful control features than those listed, nano has them. To see more control commands, type Ctrl+G in the nano text editor to display its main help window containing additional control commands.

> **NOTE**
>
> If you try to use the nano spell checker via the Ctrl+T command and get the error message `Spell checking failed: Error invoking 'Spell'`, there are some potential solutions. Install the spell checker software package, `aspell`, on your Linux distribution using Chapter 9 as a guide.
>
> If installing the `aspell` software package does not solve the problem, as superuser edit the `/etc/nanorc` file, using your favorite text editor. Find the line, `# set speller "aspell -x -c"` and delete the hash mark (#) from the line. Save and exit the file.

Additional powerful features are available at the command line. You can use command line options to control nano editor features, such as creating a backup file before editing. Type **man nano** to see these additional command line options for starting nano.

The vim and nano text editors offer a choice between powerful and simple console mode text editors. However, neither offers the ability to use graphical features for editing. Some text editors can operate in both worlds, as explored in the next section.

Exploring the emacs Editor

The emacs editor is an extremely popular editor that appeared before even Unix was around. Developers liked it so much that they ported it to the Unix environment, and now it's been ported to the Linux environment. The emacs editor started out life as a console editor, much like vi, but has migrated to the graphical world.

The emacs editor still provides the original console mode editor, and now it also has the ability to use a graphical window to allow editing text in a graphical environment. Typically, when you start the emacs editor from a command line, the editor determines whether you have an available graphical session and starts in graphical mode. If you don't, it starts in console mode.

This section describes both the console mode and graphical mode emacs editors so that you'll know how to use either one if you want (or need) to.

Checking your emacs package

Many distributions do not come with the emacs editor installed by default. You can check your Red Hat-based distribution, by using the which and/or yum list command as shown on this CentOS distribution:

```
$ which emacs
/usr/bin/which: no emacs in (/usr/lib64/qt-3.3
/bin:/usr/local/bin:/bin:/usr/bin:/usr/local/sbin:
/usr/sbin:/sbin:/home/Christine/bin)
$
$ yum list emacs
[...]
Available Packages
emacs.x86_64                    1:23.1-25.el6                    base
```

The emacs editor package is not currently installed on this CentOS distribution. However, it is available to be installed. (For a more thorough discussion on displaying installed software, see Chapter 9).

For a Debian-based distribution, check for the emacs editor package by using the which and/or apt-cache show command as shown on this Ubuntu distribution:

```
$ which emacs
$
$ sudo apt-cache show emacs
Package: emacs
Priority: optional
Section: editors
Installed-Size: 25
[...]
Description-en: GNU Emacs editor (metapackage)
 GNU Emacs is the extensible self-documenting text editor.
 This is a metapackage that will always depend on the latest
 recommended Emacs release.
Description-md5: 21fb7da111336097a2378959f6d6e6a8
Bugs: https://bugs.launchpad.net/ubuntu/+filebug
```

10

```
Origin: Ubuntu
Supported: 5y
$
```

The which command operates a little differently here. When it does not find the installed command, it simply returns the bash shell prompt. The emacs editor package is optional for this Ubuntu distribution, but is available to be installed. The following shows the emacs editor being installed on Ubuntu:

```
$ sudo apt-get install emacs
Reading package lists... Done
Building dependency tree
Reading state information... Done
The following extra packages will be installed:
[...]
Install emacsen-common for emacs24
emacsen-common: Handling install of emacsen flavor emacs24
Wrote /etc/emacs24/site-start.d/00debian-vars.elc
Wrote /usr/share/emacs24/site-lisp/debian-startup.elc
Setting up emacs (45.0ubuntu1) ...
Processing triggers for libc-bin (2.19-0ubuntu6) ...
$
$ which emacs
/usr/bin/emacs
$
```

Now when the which command is used, it points to the emacs program file. The emacs editor is ready to be used on this Ubuntu distribution.

For the CentOS distribution, install the emacs editor using the yum install command:

```
$ sudo yum install emacs
[sudo] password for Christine:
[...]
Setting up Install Process
Resolving Dependencies
[...]
Installed:
  emacs.x86_64 1:23.1-25.el6

Dependency Installed:
  emacs-common.x86_64 1:23.1-25.el6
  libotf.x86_64 0:0.9.9-3.1.el6
  m17n-db-datafiles.noarch 0:1.5.5-1.1.el6

Complete!
$
$ which emacs
/usr/bin/emacs
$
$ yum list emacs
```

```
[...]
Installed Packages
emacs.x86_64            1:23.1-25.el6            @base
$
```

With the emacs editor successfully installed on your Linux distribution, you can begin to explore its different features, staring with using it on the console.

Using emacs on the console

The console mode version of emacs is another editor that uses lots of key commands to perform editing functions. The emacs editor uses key combinations involving the Control key (the Ctrl key on the keyboard) and the Meta key. In most terminal emulator packages, the Meta key is mapped to the Alt key. The official emacs documents abbreviate the Ctrl key as C- and the Meta key as M-. Thus, if you enter a Ctrl+x key combination, the document shows C-x. This chapter does the same so as not to confuse you.

Exploring the basics of emacs

To edit a file using emacs, from the command line, enter:

```
$ emacs myprog.c
```

The emacs console mode window appears with a short introduction and help screen. Don't be alarmed; as soon as you press a key, emacs loads the file into the active buffer and displays the text, as shown in Figure 10-3.

FIGURE 10-3

Editing a file using the emacs editor in console mode

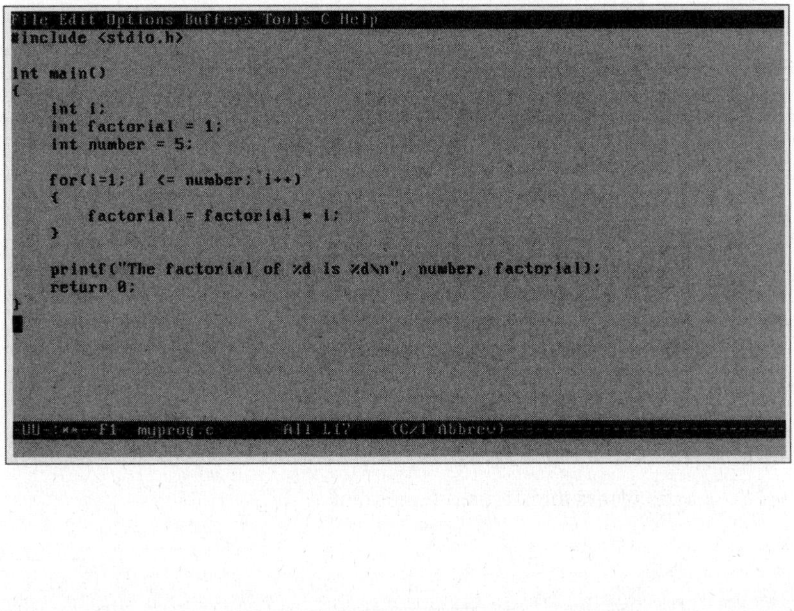

10

You'll notice that the top of the console mode window shows a typical menu bar. Unfortunately, you can't use the menu bar in console mode, only in graphical mode.

Unlike the vim editor, where you have to move into and out of insert mode to switch between entering commands and inserting text, the emacs editor has only one mode. If you type a printable character, emacs inserts it at the current cursor position. If you type a command, emacs executes the command.

To move the cursor around the buffer area, you can use the arrow keys and the PageUp and PageDown keys, assuming that emacs detected your terminal emulator correctly. If not, these commands move the cursor around:

- `C-p` moves up one line (the previous line in the text).
- `C-b` moves left (back) one character.
- `C-f` moves right (forward) one character.
- `C-n` moves down one line (the next line in the text).

These commands make longer jumps with the cursor within the text:

- `M-f` moves right (forward) to the next word.
- `M-b` moves left (backward) to the previous word.
- `C-a` moves to the beginning of the current line.
- `C-e` moves to the end of the current line.
- `M-a` moves to the beginning of the current sentence.
- `M-e` moves to the end of the current sentence.
- `M-v` moves back one screen of data.
- `C-v` moves forward one screen of data.
- `M-<` moves the first line of the text.
- `M->` moves to the last line of the text.

You should know these commands for saving the editor buffer back into the file and exiting emacs:

- `C-x C-s` saves the current buffer contents to the file.
- `C-z` exits emacs but keeps it running in your session so you can come back to it.
- `C-x C-c` exits emacs and stops the program.

You'll notice that two of these features require two key commands. The C-x command is called the *extend command*. This provides yet another whole set of commands to work with.

Editing data

The emacs editor is pretty robust about inserting and deleting text in the buffer. To insert text, just move the cursor to the location where you want to insert the text and start typing. To delete text, emacs uses the Backspace key to delete the character before the current cursor position and the Delete key to delete the character at the current cursor location.

The emacs editor also has commands for killing text. The difference between deleting text and killing text is that when you kill text, emacs places it in a temporary area where you can retrieve it (see the next section, "Copying and pasting"). Deleted text is gone forever.

These commands are for killing text in the buffer:

- M-Backspace kills the word before the current cursor position.
- M-d kills the word after the current cursor position.
- C-k kills from the current cursor position to the end of the line.
- M-k kills from the current cursor position to the end of the sentence.

The emacs editor also includes a fancy way of mass-killing text. Just move the cursor to the start of the area you want to kill, and press either the C-@ or C-Spacebar keys. Then move the cursor to the end of the area you want to kill, and press the C-w command keys. All the text between the two locations is killed.

If you happen to make a mistake when killing text, the C-/ command undoes the kill command and returns the data to the state it was in before you killed it.

Copying and pasting

You've seen how to cut data from the emacs buffer area; now it's time to see how to paste it somewhere else. Unfortunately, if you use the vim editor, this process may confuse you when you use the emacs editor.

In an unfortunate coincidence, pasting data in emacs is called *yanking*. In the vim editor, copying is called yanking, which is what makes this a difficult thing to remember if you happen to use both editors.

After you kill data using one of the kill commands, move the cursor to the location where you want to paste the data, and use the C-y command. This yanks the text out of the temporary area and pastes it at the current cursor position. The C-y command yanks the text from the last kill command. If you've performed multiple kill commands, you can cycle through them using the M-y command.

To copy text, just yank it back into the same location you killed it from and then move to the new location and use the C-y command again. You can yank text back as many times as you desire.

10

Searching and Replacing

Searching for text in the emacs editor is done by using the C-s and C-r commands. The C-s command performs a forward search in the buffer area from the current cursor position to the end of the buffer, whereas the C-r command performs a backward search in the buffer area from the current cursor position to the start of the buffer.

When you enter either the C-s or C-r command, a prompt appears in the bottom line, querying you for the text to search. You can perform two types of searches in emacs.

In an *incremental* search, the emacs editor performs the text search in real-time mode as you type the word. When you type the first letter, it highlights all the occurrences of that letter in the buffer. When you type the second letter, it highlights all the occurrences of the two-letter combination in the text and so on until you complete the text you're searching for.

In a *non-incremental* search, press the Enter key after the C-s or C-r commands. This locks the search query into the bottom line area and allows you to type the search text in full before searching.

To replace an existing text string with a new text string, you must use the M-x command. This command requires a text command, along with parameters.

The text command is replace-string. After typing the command, press the Enter key, and emacs queries you for the existing text string. After entering that, press the Enter key again and emacs queries you for the new replacement text string.

Using buffers in emacs

The emacs editor allows you to edit multiple files at the same time by having multiple buffer areas. You can load files into a buffer and switch between buffers while editing.

To load a new file into a buffer while you're in emacs, use the C-x C-f key combination. This is the emacs Find a File mode. It takes you to the bottom line in the window and allows you to enter the name of the file you want to start to edit. If you don't know the name or location of the file, just press the Enter key. This brings up a file browser in the edit window, as shown in Figure 10-4.

From here, you can browse to the file you want to edit. To traverse up a directory level, go to the double dot entry and press the Enter key. To traverse down a directory, go to the directory entry and press the Enter key. When you've found the file you want to edit, press the Enter key and emacs loads it into a new buffer area.

You can list the active buffer areas by pressing the C-x C-b extended command combination. The emacs editor splits the editor window and displays a list of buffers in the bottom window. emacs provides two buffers in addition to your main editing buffer:

- A scratch area called *scratch*
- A message area called *Messages*

FIGURE 10-4

The emacs Find a File mode browser

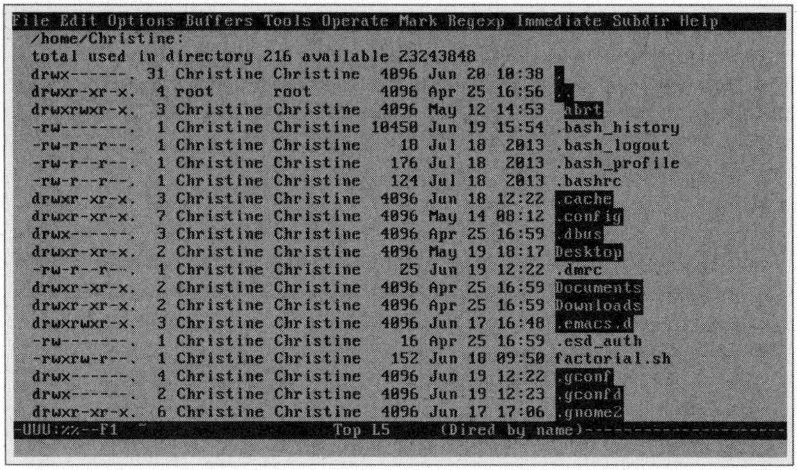

```
File Edit Options Buffers Tools Operate Mark Regexp Immediate Subdir Help
  /home/Christine:
  total used in directory 216 available 23243848
  drwx------. 31 Christine Christine  4096 Jun 20 10:38 .
  drwxr-xr-x.  4 root      root       4096 Apr 25 16:56 ..
  drwxrwxr-x.  3 Christine Christine  4096 May 12 14:53 abrt
  -rw-------.  1 Christine Christine 10450 Jun 19 15:54 .bash_history
  -rw-r--r--.  1 Christine Christine    18 Jul 18 2013 .bash_logout
  -rw-r--r--.  1 Christine Christine   176 Jul 18 2013 .bash_profile
  -rw-r--r--.  1 Christine Christine   124 Jul 18 2013 .bashrc
  drwxr-xr-x.  3 Christine Christine  4096 Jun 18 12:22 .cache
  drwxr-xr-x.  7 Christine Christine  4096 May 14 08:12 .config
  drwx------.  3 Christine Christine  4096 Apr 25 16:59 .dbus
  drwxr-xr-x.  2 Christine Christine  4096 May 19 10:17 Desktop
  -rw-r--r--.  1 Christine Christine    25 Jun 19 12:22 .dmrc
  drwxr-xr-x.  2 Christine Christine  4096 Apr 25 16:59 Documents
  drwxr-xr-x.  2 Christine Christine  4096 Apr 25 16:59 Downloads
  drwxrwxr-x.  3 Christine Christine  4096 Jun 17 16:48 .emacs.d
  -rw-------.  1 Christine Christine    16 Apr 25 16:59 .esd_auth
  -rwxrw-r--.  1 Christine Christine   152 Jun 18 09:50 factorial.sh
  drwx------.  4 Christine Christine  4096 Jun 19 12:22 .gconf
  drwx------.  2 Christine Christine  4096 Jun 19 12:23 .gconfd
  drwxr-xr-x.  6 Christine Christine  4096 Jun 17 17:06 .gnome2
-UUU:%%--F1              Top L5      (Dired by name)-------------------
```

The scratch area allows you to enter LISP programming commands as well as enter notes to yourself. The message area shows messages generated by emacs while operating. If any errors occur while using emacs, they appear in the message area.

You can switch to a different buffer area in the window in two ways:

- Use C-x o to switch to the buffer listing window. Use the arrow keys to move to the buffer area you want and press the Enter key.
- Use C-x b to type in the name of the buffer area you want to switch to.

When you select the option to switch to the buffer listing window, emacs opens the buffer area in the new window area. The emacs editor allows you to have multiple windows open in a single session. The following section discusses how to manage multiple windows in emacs.

Using windows in console mode emacs

The console mode emacs editor was developed many years before the idea of graphical windows appeared. However, it was advanced for its time, in that it could support multiple editing windows within the main emacs window.

You can split the emacs editing window into multiple windows by using one of two commands:

- C-x 2 splits the window horizontally into two windows.
- C-x 3 splits the window vertically into two windows.

10

To move from one window to another, use the C-x o command. Notice that when you create a new window, emacs uses the buffer area from the original window in the new window. After you move into the new window, you can use the C-x C-f command to load a new file or use one of the commands to switch to a different buffer area in the new window.

To close a window, move to it and use the C-x 0 (that's a zero) command. If you want to close all the windows except the one you're in, use the C-x 1 (that's a numerical one) command.

Using emacs in a GUI

If you use emacs from a GUI environment (such as the Unity or GNOME desktops), it starts in graphical mode, as shown in Figure 10-5.

FIGURE 10-5

The emacs graphical window

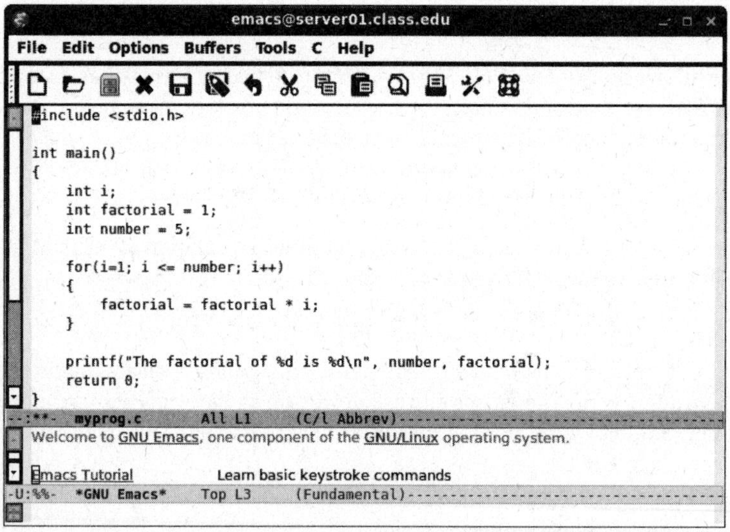

If you've already used emacs in console mode, you should be fairly familiar with the graphical mode. All the key commands are available as menu bar items. The emacs menu bar contains the following items:

- **File** allows you to open files in the window, create new windows, close windows, save buffers, and print buffers.
- **Edit** allows you to cut and copy selected text to the clipboard, paste clipboard data to the current cursor position, search for text, and replace text.

- **Options** provides settings for many more emacs features, such as highlighting, word wrap, cursor type, and setting fonts.
- **Buffers** lists the current buffers available and allows you to easily switch between buffer areas.
- **Tools** provides access to the advanced features in emacs, such as the command line interface access, spell checking, comparing text between files (called diff), sending an e-mail message, calendar, and the calculator.
- **Help** provides the emacs manual online for access to help on specific emacs functions.

In addition to the normal graphical emacs menu bar items, there is often a separate item specific to the file type in the editor buffer. Figure 10-5 shows opening a C program, so emacs provided a C menu item, allowing advanced settings for highlighting C syntax, and compiling, running, and debugging the code from a command prompt.

The graphical emacs window is an example of an older console application making the migration to the graphical world. Now that many Linux distributions provide graphical desktops (even on servers that don't need them), graphical editors are becoming more commonplace. Popular Linux desktop environments (such as KDE and GNOME) have also provided graphical text editors specifically for their environments, which are covered in the rest of this chapter.

Exploring the KDE Family of Editors

If you're using a Linux distribution that uses the KDE desktop (see Chapter 1), you have a couple of options when it comes to text editors. The KDE project officially supports two popular text editors:

- **KWrite:** A single-screen text-editing package
- **Kate:** A full-featured, multi-window text-editing package

Both of these editors are graphical text editors that contain many advanced features. The Kate editor provides more advanced features, plus extra niceties not often found in standard text editors. This section describes each of the editors and shows some of the features you can use to help with your shell script editing.

Looking at the KWrite editor

The basic editor for the KDE environment is KWrite. It provides simple word-processing–style text editing, along with support for code syntax highlighting and editing. The default KWrite editing window is shown in Figure 10-6.

10

FIGURE 10-6

The default KWrite window editing a shell script program

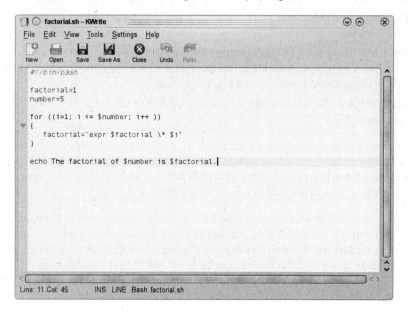

You can't tell from Figure 10-6, but the KWrite editor recognizes several types of programming languages and uses color coding to distinguish constants, functions, and comments. Also, notice that the for loop has an icon that links the opening and closing braces. This is called a *folding marker*. By clicking the icon, you can collapse the function into a single line. This is a great feature when working through large applications.

The KWrite editing window provides full cut and paste capabilities, using the mouse and the arrow keys. As in a word processor, you can highlight and cut (or copy) text anywhere in the buffer area and paste it at any other place.

To edit a file using KWrite, you can either select KWrite from the KDE menu system on your desktop (some Linux distributions even create a Panel icon for it) or start it from the command line prompt:

```
$ kwrite factorial.sh
```

The kwrite command has several command line parameters you can use to customize how it starts:

- --stdin causes KWrite to read data from the standard input device instead of a file.
- --encoding specifies a character encoding type to use for the file.

- --line specifies a line number in the file to start at in the editor window.
- --column specifies a column number in the file to start at in the editor window.

The KWrite editor provides both a menu bar and a toolbar at the top of the edit window, allowing you to select features and change configuration settings of the KWrite editor.

The menu bar contains these items:

- **File** loads, saves, prints, and exports text from files.
- **Edit** manipulates text in the buffer area.
- **View** manages how the text appears in the editor window.
- **Bookmarks** handle pointers to return to specific locations in the text; this option may need to be enabled in the configurations.
- **Tools** contains specialized features to manipulate the text.
- **Settings** configures the way the editor handles text.
- **Help** gives you information about the editor and commands.

The Edit menu bar item provides commands for all your text-editing needs. Instead of having to remember cryptic key commands (which by the way, KWrite also supports), you can just select items in the Edit menu bar, as shown in Table 10-3.

TABLE 10-3   The KWrite Edit Menu Items

Item	Description
Undo	Reverses the last action or operation
Redo	Reverses the last undo action
Cut	Deletes the selected text and places it in the clipboard
Copy	Copies the selected text to the clipboard
Paste	Inserts the current contents of the clipboard at the current cursor position
Select All	Selects all text in the editor
Deselect	Deselects any text that is currently selected
Overwrite Mode	Toggles insert mode to overwrite mode, replacing text with new typed text instead of just inserting the new text
Find	Produces the Find Text dialog box, which allows you to customize a text search
Find Next	Repeats the last find operation forward in the buffer area
Find Previous	Repeats the last find operation backwards in the buffer area

Continues

10

TABLE 10-3 *(continued)*

Item	Description
Replace	Produces the Replace With dialog box, which allows you to customize a text search and replace
Find Selected	Finds the next occurrence of the selected text
Find Selected Backwards	Finds the previous occurrence of the selected text
Go to Line	Produces the Goto dialog box, which allows you to enter a line number. The cursor moves to the specified line

The Find feature has two modes. Normal mode performs simple text searches and power searches. Replace mode lets you do advanced searching and replacing if necessary. You toggle between the two modes using the green arrow in the Find section, as shown in Figure 10-7.

FIGURE 10-7

The KWrite Find section

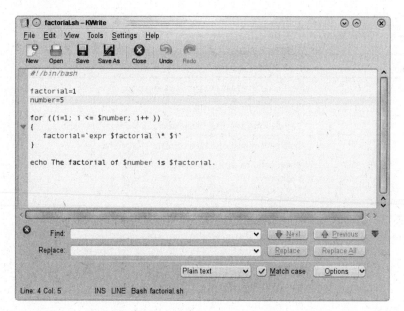

The Find power mode allows you to search not only with words, but with a regular expression (discussed in Chapter 20) for the search. You can use some other options to customize the search as well, indicating, for example, whether or not to perform a case-sensitive search or to look only for whole words instead of finding the text within words.

The Tools menu bar item provides several handy features for working with the text in the buffer area. Table 10-4 describes the tools available in KWrite.

TABLE 10-4 The KWrite Tools

Tool	Description
Read Only Mode	Locks the text so no changes can be made while in the editor
Encoding	Sets the character set encoding used by the text
Spelling	Starts the spell-check program at the start of the text
Spelling (from cursor)	Starts the spell-check program from the current cursor position
Spellcheck Selection	Starts the spell-check program only on the selected section of text
Indent	Increases the paragraph indentation by one
Unindent	Decreases the paragraph indentation by one
Clean Indentation	Returns all paragraph indentation to the original settings
Align	Forces the current line or the selected lines to return to the default indentation settings
Uppercase	Sets the selected text, or the character at the current cursor position, to uppercase
Lowercase	Sets the selected text, or the character at the current cursor position, to lowercase
Capitalize	Capitalizes the first letter of the selected text or the word at the current cursor position
Join Lines	Combines the selected lines, or the line at the current cursor position and the next line, into one line
Word Wrap Document	Enables word wrapping in the text. If a line extends past the editor window edge, the line continues on the next line.

There are lots of tools for a simple text editor!

The Settings menu includes the Configure Editor dialog box, shown in Figure 10-8.

10

FIGURE 10-8

The KWrite Configure Editor dialog box

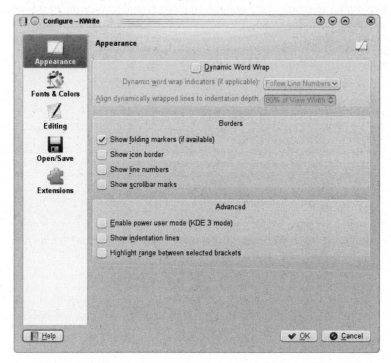

The Configuration dialog box uses icons on the left side for you to select the feature in KWrite to configure. When you select an icon, the right side of the dialog box shows the configuration settings for the feature.

The Appearance feature allows you to set several features that control how the text appears in the text editor window. You can enable word wrap, line numbers (great for programmers), and the folder markers from here. With the Fonts & Colors feature, you can customize the complete color scheme for the editor, determining what colors to make each category of text in the program code.

Looking at the Kate editor

The Kate editor is the flagship editor for the KDE Project. It uses the same text editor as the KWrite application (so most of those features are the same), but it incorporates lots of other features into a single package.

When you start the Kate editor from the KDE menu system, the first thing you notice is that the editor doesn't start! Instead, you get a dialog box, as shown in Figure 10-9.

FIGURE 10-9

The Kate session dialog box

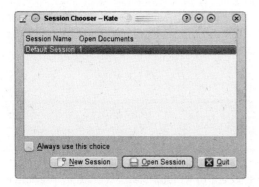

The Kate editor handles files in sessions. You can have multiple files open in a session, and you can have multiple sessions saved. When you start Kate, it provides you with the choice of which session to return to. When you close your Kate session, it remembers the documents you had open and displays them the next time you start Kate. This allows you to easily manage files from multiple projects by using separate workspaces for each project.

After selecting a session, you see the main Kate editor window, shown in Figure 10-10.

The left side frame shows the documents currently open in the session. You can switch between documents just by clicking the document name. To edit a new file, click the Filesystem Browser tab on the left side. The left frame is now a full graphical filesystem browser, allowing you to graphically browse to locate your files.

A great feature of the Kate editor is the built-in terminal window, shown in Figure 10-11.

10

FIGURE 10-10

The main Kate editing window

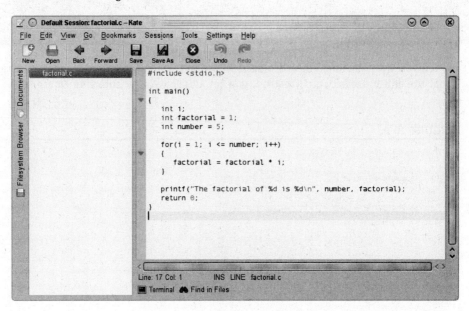

The terminal tab at the bottom of the text editor window starts the built-in terminal emulator in Kate (using the KDE Konsole terminal emulator). This feature horizontally splits the current editing window, creating a new window with Konsole running in it. You can now enter command line commands, start programs, or check on system settings without having to leave the editor! To close the terminal window, just type **exit** at the command prompt.

As you can tell from the terminal feature, Kate also supports multiple windows. The Window menu bar item (View) provides options to perform these tasks:

- Create a new Kate window using the current session
- Split the current window vertically to create a new window
- Split the current window horizontally to create a new window
- Close the current window

FIGURE 10-11

The Kate built-in terminal window

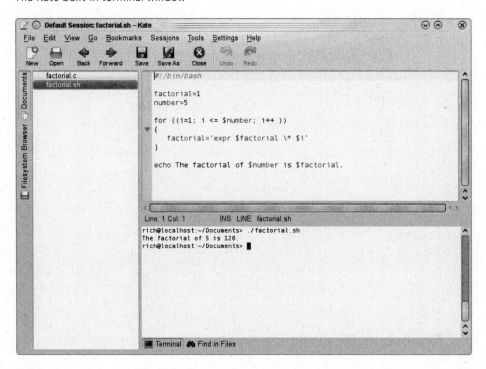

To set the configuration settings in Kate, select the Configure Kate item under the Settings menu bar item. The Configuration dialog box, shown in Figure 10-12, appears.

Notice that the Editor settings area is exactly the same as for KWrite. This is because the two editors share the same text editor engine. The Application settings area allows you to configure settings for the Kate items, such as controlling sessions (shown in Figure 10-12), the documents list, and the filesystem browser. Kate also supports external plug-in applications, which can be activated here.

10

FIGURE 10-12

The Kate configuration settings dialog box

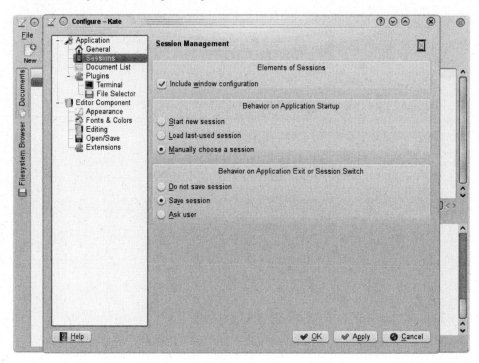

Exploring the GNOME Editor

If you're working on a Linux system using the GNOME or Unity desktop environment, there's a graphical text editor that you can use as well. The gedit text editor is a basic text editor, with a few advanced features thrown in just for fun. This section walks you through the features of gedit and demonstrates how to use it for your shell script programming.

Starting gedit

Most GNOME desktop environments include gedit in the Accessories Panel menu item. For the Unity desktop environment, go to Dash ⇨ Search and type **gedit**. If you can't find gedit via the menu system, you can start it from the command line prompt in a GUI terminal emulator:

```
$ gedit factorial.sh myprog.c
```

When you start gedit with multiple files, it loads all the files into separate buffers and displays each one as a tabbed window within the main editor window, as shown in Figure 10-13.

FIGURE 10-13

The gedit main editor window

The left frame in the gedit main editor window shows the documents you're currently editing. If your gedit doesn't show the left frame when started, you can press the F9 function key or enable Side Pane from the View menu.

> **NOTE**
> Different desktops may have gedit options that are available in slightly different menu locations than shown in these figures. Additional options may also be available. Consult your distribution's gedit Help menu for more assistance.

The right side shows the tabbed windows that contain the buffer text. If you hover your mouse pointer over each tab, a dialog box appears, showing the full pathname of the file, the MIME type, and the character set encoding it uses.

10

Understanding basic gedit features

In addition to the editor windows, gedit uses both a menu bar and toolbar that allow you to set features and configure settings. The toolbar provides quick access to menu bar items. These menu bar items are available:

- **File** handles new files, saves existing files, and prints files.
- **Edit** manipulates text in the active buffer area and sets the editor preferences.
- **View** sets the editor features to display in the window and sets the text highlighting mode.
- **Search** finds and replaces text in the active editor buffer area.
- **Tools** accesses plug-in tools installed in gedit.
- **Documents** manages files open in the buffer areas.
- **Help** provides access to the full gedit manual.

There shouldn't be anything too surprising here. The Edit menu contains the standard cut, copy, and paste functions, along with a neat feature that allows you to easily enter the date and time in the text in several different formats. The Search menu provides a standard find function, which produces a dialog box where you can enter the text to find, along with the capability to select how the find feature should work (matching case, matching the whole word, and the search direction). It also provides an incremental search feature, which works in real-time mode, finding text as you type the characters of the word.

Setting preferences

The Edit menu contains a Preferences item, which produces the gedit Preferences dialog box, shown in Figure 10-14.

This is where you can customize the operation of the gedit editor. The Preferences dialog box contains five tabbed areas for setting the features and behavior of the editor.

Setting View preferences

The View tab provides options for how gedit displays the text in the editor window:

- **Text Wrapping:** Determines how to handle long lines of text in the editor. The Enabling text wrapping option wraps long lines to the next line of the editor. The Do Not Split Words Over Two Lines option prevents the auto-inserting of hyphens into long words, to prevent them being split between two lines.
- **Line Numbers:** Displays line numbers in the left margin in the editor window.

- **Current Line:** Highlights the line where the cursor is currently positioned, enabling you to easily find the cursor position.

- **Right Margin:** Enables the right margin and allows you to set how many columns should be in the editor window. The default value is 80 columns.

- **Bracket Matching:** When enabled, highlights bracket pairs in programming code, allowing you to easily match brackets in `if-then` statements, `for` and `while` loops, and other coding elements that use brackets.

The line-numbering and bracket-matching features provide an environment for programmers to troubleshoot code that's not often found in text editors.

FIGURE 10-14

The GNOME desktop gedit Preferences dialog box

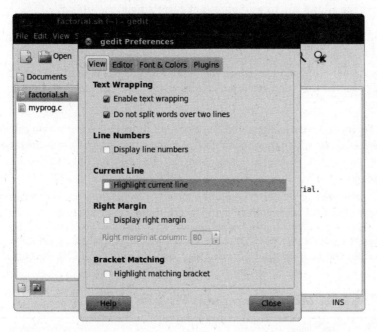

Setting Editor preferences

The Editor tab provides options for how the gedit editor handles tabs and indentation, along with how files are saved:

10

- **Tab Stops:** Sets the number of spaces skipped when you press the Tab key. The default value is eight. This feature also includes a check box that, when selected, inserts spaces instead of a tab skip.

- **Automatic Indentation:** When enabled, causes gedit to automatically indent lines in the text for paragraphs and code elements (such as if-then statements and loops).

- **File Saving:** Provides two features for saving files: whether or not to create a backup copy of the file when opened in the edit window, and whether or not to automatically save the file at a preselected interval.

The auto-save feature is a great way to ensure that your changes are saved on a regular basis to prevent catastrophes from crashes or power outages.

Setting Font & Color preferences

The Font & Colors tab allows you to configure (not surprisingly) two items:

- **Font:** Allows you to select the default font, or to select a customized font and font size from a dialog box.

- **Color Scheme:** Allows you to select the default color scheme used for text, background, selected text, and selection colors, or choose a custom color for each category.

The default colors for gedit normally match the standard GNOME desktop theme selected for the desktop. These colors will change to match the scheme you select for the desktop.

Managing plug-ins

The Plugins tab provides control over the plug-ins used in gedit. Plug-ins are separate programs that can interface with gedit to provide additional functionality.

Several plug-ins are available for gedit, but not all of them are installed by default. Table 10-5 describes the plug-ins that are currently available in the GNOME desktop's gedit.

TABLE 10-5 The GNOME desktop gedit Plug-ins

Plug-In	Description
Change Case	Changes the case of selected text
Document Statistics	Reports the number of words, lines, characters, and non-space characters
External Tools	Provides a shell environment in the editor to execute commands and scripts
File Browser Pane	Provides a simple file browser to make selecting files for editing easier

Indent Lines	Provides selected lines to be indented or un-indented
Insert Date/Time	Inserts the current date and time in several formats at the current cursor position
Modelines	Provides emacs-style message lines at the bottom of the editor window
Python Console	Provides an interactive console at the bottom of the editor window for entering commands using the Python programming language
Quick Open	Opens files directly in the gedit edit window
Snippets	Allows you to store often-used pieces of text for easy retrieval anywhere in the text
Sort	Quickly sorts the entire file or selected text
Spell Checker	Provides dictionary spellchecking for the text file
Tag List	Provides a list of commonly used strings you can easily enter into your text

Plug-ins that are enabled show a check mark in the check box next to their name. Some plug-ins, such as the External Tools plug-in, also provide additional configuration features after you select them. It allows you to set a shortcut key to start the terminal, where gedit displays output, and the command to use to start the shell session.

Unfortunately, not all plug-ins are installed in the same place in the gedit menu bar. Some plug-ins appear in the Tools menu bar item (such as the Spell Checker and External Tools plug-ins), while others appear in the Edit menu bar item (such as the Change Case and Insert Date/Time plug-ins).

This chapter has covered just a few of the text editors available on Linux. If you find that the text editors described here don't meet your needs, you have options. Many more Linux editors are available, such as geany, Eclipse, jed, Bluefish, and leafpad to name a few. All these editors can help you as you begin your bash shell script writing journey.

Summary

When it comes to creating shell scripts, you need some type of text editor. Several popular text editors are available for the Linux environment. The most popular editor in the Unix world, vi, has been ported to the Linux world as the vim editor. The vim editor provides simple text editing from the console, using a rudimentary full-screen graphical mode. The vim editor provides many advanced editor features, such as text searching and replacement.

Another editor that has been ported from the Unix world to Linux is the nano text editor. The vim editor can be rather complex, but the nano editor offers simplicity. The nano editor allows quick text editing in console mode.

10

Another popular Unix editor — emacs — has also made its way to the Linux world. The Linux version of emacs has both console and a graphical mode, making it the bridge between the old world and the new. The emacs editor provides multiple buffer areas, allowing you to edit multiple files simultaneously.

The KDE Project created two editors for use in the KDE desktop. The KWrite editor is a simple editor that provides the basic text-editing features, along with a few advanced features, such as syntax highlighting for programming code, line numbering, and code folding. The Kate editor provides more advanced features for programmers. One great feature in Kate is a built-in terminal window. You can open a command line interface session directly in the Kate editor without having to open a separate terminal emulator window. The Kate editor also allows you to open multiple files, providing different windows for each opened file.

The GNOME Project also provides a simple text editor for programmers. The gedit editor is a basic text editor that provides some advanced features such as code syntax highlighting and line numbering, but it was designed to be a bare-bones editor. To spruce up the gedit editor, developers created plug-ins, which expand the features available in gedit. Current plug-ins include a spell-checker, a terminal emulator, and a file browser.

This wraps up the background chapters on working with the command line in Linux. The next part of the book dives into the shell-scripting world. The next chapter starts off by showing you how to create a shell script file and how to run it on your Linux system. It also shows you the basics of shell scripts, allowing you to create simple programs by stringing multiple commands together into a script you can run.

Part II

Shell Scripting Basics

IN THIS PART

Basic Script Building

IN THIS CHAPTER

Using multiple commands

Creating a script file

Displaying messages

Using variables

Redirecting input and output

Pipes

Performing math

Exiting the script

N ow that we've covered the basics of the Linux system and the command line, it's time to start coding. This chapter discusses the basics of writing shell scripts. You need to know these basic concepts before you can start writing your own shell script masterpieces.

Using Multiple Commands

So far you've seen how to use the command line interface (CLI) prompt of the shell to enter commands and view the command results. The key to shell scripts is the ability to enter multiple commands and process the results from each command, even possibly passing the results of one command to another. The shell allows you to chain commands together into a single step.

If you want to run two commands together, you can enter them on the same prompt line, separated with a semicolon:

```
$ date ; who
Mon Feb 21 15:36:09 EST 2014
Christine tty2         2014-02-21 15:26
Samantha tty3         2014-02-21 15:26
Timothy  tty1         2014-02-21 15:26
user     tty7         2014-02-19 14:03 (:0)
```

```
user       pts/0        2014-02-21 15:21 (:0.0)
$
```

Congratulations, you just wrote a shell script! This simple script uses just two bash shell commands. The date command runs first, displaying the current date and time, followed by the output of the who command, showing who is currently logged on to the system. Using this technique, you can string together as many commands as you wish, up to the maximum command line character count of 255 characters.

Using this technique is fine for small scripts, but it has a major drawback: You must enter the entire command at the command prompt every time you want to run it. Instead of having to manually enter the commands onto a command line, you can combine the commands into a simple text file. When you need to run the commands, just simply run the text file.

Creating a Script File

To place shell commands in a text file, first you need to use a text editor (see Chapter 10) to create a file and then enter the commands into the file.

When creating a shell script file, you must specify the shell you are using in the first line of the file. Here's the format for this:

```
#!/bin/bash
```

In a normal shell script line, the pound sign (#) is used as a comment line. A comment line in a shell script isn't processed by the shell. However, the first line of a shell script file is a special case, and the pound sign followed by the exclamation point tells the shell what shell to run the script under (yes, you can be using a bash shell and run your script using another shell).

After indicating the shell, commands are entered onto each line of the file, followed by a carriage return. As mentioned, comments can be added by using the pound sign. An example looks like this:

```
#!/bin/bash
# This script displays the date and who's logged on
date
who
```

And that's all there is to it. You can use the semicolon and put both commands on the same line if you want to, but in a shell script, you can list commands on separate lines. The shell processes commands in the order in which they appear in the file.

Also notice that another line was included that starts with the pound symbol and adds a comment. Lines that start with the pound symbol (other than the first #! line) aren't interpreted by the shell. This is a great way to leave comments for yourself about what's happening in the script, so when you come back to it two years later, you can easily remember what you did.

Save this script in a file called `test1`, and you are almost ready. You need to do a couple of things before you can run your new shell script file.

If you try running the file now, you'll be somewhat disappointed to see this:

```
$ test1
bash: test1: command not found
$
```

The first hurdle to jump is getting the bash shell to find your script file. If you remember from Chapter 6, the shell uses an environment variable called PATH to find commands. A quick look at the PATH environment variable demonstrates our problem:

```
$ echo $PATH
/usr/kerberos/sbin:/usr/kerberos/bin:/usr/local/bin:/usr/bin
:/bin:/usr/local/sbin:/usr/sbin:/sbin:/home/user/bin $
```

The PATH environment variable is set to look for commands only in a handful of directories. To get the shell to find the `test1` script, we need to do one of two things:

- Add the directory where our shell script file is located to the PATH environment variable.
- Use an absolute or relative file path to reference our shell script file in the prompt.

TIP

Some Linux distributions add the $HOME/bin directory to the PATH environment variable. This creates a place in every user's HOME directory to place files where the shell can find them to execute.

For this example, we use the second method to tell the shell exactly where the script file is located. Remember that to reference a file in the current directory, you can use the single dot operator in the shell:

```
$ ./test1
bash: ./test1: Permission denied
$
```

The shell found the shell script file just fine, but there's another problem. The shell indicated that you don't have permission to execute the file. A quick look at the file permissions should show what's going on here:

```
$ ls -l test1
-rw-rw-r--    1 user     user           73 Sep 24 19:56 test1
$
```

When the new test1 file was created, the umask value determined the default permission settings for the new file. Because the umask variable is set to 002 (see Chapter 7) in Ubuntu, the system created the file with only read/write permissions for the file's owner and group.

The next step is to give the file owner permission to execute the file, using the chmod command (see Chapter 7):

```
$ chmod u+x test1
$ ./test1
Mon Feb 21 15:38:19 EST 2014
Christine tty2        2014-02-21 15:26
Samantha tty3        2014-02-21 15:26
Timothy  tty1        2014-02-21 15:26
user     tty7        2014-02-19 14:03 (:0)
user     pts/0       2014-02-21 15:21 (:0.0) $
```

Success! Now all the pieces are in the right places to execute the new shell script file.

Displaying Messages

Most shell commands produce their own output, which is displayed on the console monitor where the script is running. Many times, however, you will want to add your own text messages to help the script user know what is happening within the script. You can do this with the echo command. The echo command can display a simple text string if you add the string following the command:

```
$ echo This is a test
This is a test
$
```

Notice that by default you don't need to use quotes to delineate the string you're displaying. However, sometimes this can get tricky if you are using quotes within your string:

```
$ echo Let's see if this'll work
Lets see if thisll work
$
```

The echo command uses either double or single quotes to delineate text strings. If you use them within your string, you need to use one type of quote within the text and the other type to delineate the string:

```
$ echo "This is a test to see if you're paying attention"
This is a test to see if you're paying attention
$ echo 'Rich says "scripting is easy".'
Rich says "scripting is easy".
$
```

Now all the quotation marks appear properly in the output.

You can add echo statements anywhere in your shell scripts where you need to display additional information:

```
$ cat test1
#!/bin/bash
# This script displays the date and who's logged on
echo  The time and date are:
date
echo "Let's see who's logged into the system:"
who
$
```

When you run this script, it produces the following output:

```
$ ./test1
The time and date are:
Mon Feb 21 15:41:13 EST 2014
Let's see who's logged into the system:
Christine tty2         2014-02-21 15:26
Samantha tty3          2014-02-21 15:26
Timothy  tty1          2014-02-21 15:26
user     tty7          2014-02-19 14:03 (:0)
user     pts/0         2014-02-21 15:21 (:0.0)
$
```

That's nice, but what if you want to echo a text string on the same line as a command output? You can use the -n parameter for the echo statement to do that. Just change the first echo statement line to this:

```
echo -n "The time and date are: "
```

You need to use quotes around the string to ensure that there's a space at the end of the echoed string. The command output begins exactly where the string output stops. The output now looks like this:

```
$ ./test1
The time and date are: Mon Feb 21 15:42:23 EST 2014
Let's see who's logged into the system:
Christine tty2         2014-02-21 15:26
Samantha tty3          2014-02-21 15:26
Timothy  tty1          2014-02-21 15:26
user     tty7          2014-02-19 14:03 (:0)
user     pts/0         2014-02-21 15:21 (:0.0)
$
```

Perfect! The echo command is a crucial piece of shell scripts that interact with users. You'll find yourself using it in many situations, especially when you want to display the values of script variables. Let's look at that next.

Using Variables

Just running individual commands from the shell script is useful, but this has its limitations. Often, you'll want to incorporate other data in your shell commands to process information. You can do this by using *variables*. Variables allow you to temporarily store information within the shell script for use with other commands in the script. This section shows how to use variables in your shell scripts.

Environment variables

You've already seen one type of Linux variable in action. Chapter 6 described the environment variables available in the Linux system. You can access these values from your shell scripts as well.

The shell maintains environment variables that track specific system information, such as the name of the system, the name of the user logged in to the system, the user's system ID (called UID), the default home directory of the user, and the search path used by the shell to find programs. You can display a complete list of active environment variables available by using the set command:

```
$ set
BASH=/bin/bash
[...]
HOME=/home/Samantha
HOSTNAME=localhost.localdomain
HOSTTYPE=i386
IFS=$' \t\n'
IMSETTINGS_INTEGRATE_DESKTOP=yes
IMSETTINGS_MODULE=none
LANG=en_US.utf8
LESSOPEN='|/usr/bin/lesspipe.sh %s'
LINES=24
LOGNAME=Samantha
[...]
```

You can tap into these environment variables from within your scripts by using the environment variable's name preceded by a dollar sign. This is demonstrated in the following script:

```
$ cat test2
#!/bin/bash
# display user information from the system.
echo "User info for userid: $USER"
echo UID: $UID
echo HOME: $HOME
$
```

The *$USER*, *$UID*, and *$HOME* environment variables are used to display the pertinent information about the logged-in user. The output should look something like this:

```
$chmod u+x test2
$ ./test2
User info for userid: Samantha
UID: 1001
HOME: /home/Samantha
$
```

Notice that the environment variables in the echo commands are replaced by their current values when the script runs. Also notice that we were able to place the *$USER* system variable within the double quotation marks in the first string, and the shell script still figured out what we meant. There is a drawback to using this method, however. Look at what happens in this example:

```
$ echo "The cost of the item is $15"
The cost of the item is 5
```

That is obviously not what was intended. Whenever the script sees a dollar sign within quotes, it assumes you're referencing a variable. In this example, the script attempted to display the variable *$1* (which was not defined) and then the number 5. To display an actual dollar sign, you must precede it with a backslash character:

```
$ echo "The cost of the item is \$15"
The cost of the item is $15
```

That's better. The backslash allowed the shell script to interpret the dollar sign as an actual dollar sign and not a variable. The next section shows how to create your own variables in your scripts.

> **NOTE**
> You may also see variables referenced using the format ${variable}. The extra braces around the variable name are often used to help identify the variable name from the dollar sign.

User variables

In addition to the environment variables, a shell script allows you to set and use your own variables within the script. Setting variables allows you to temporarily store data and use it throughout the script, making the shell script more like a real computer program.

User variables can be any text string of up to 20 letters, digits, or an underscore character. User variables are case sensitive, so the variable *Var1* is different from the variable *var1*. This little rule often gets novice script programmers in trouble.

Values are assigned to user variables using an equal sign. No spaces can appear between the variable, the equal sign, and the value (another trouble spot for novices). Here are a few examples of assigning values to user variables:

```
var1=10
var2=-57
var3=testing
var4="still more testing"
```

The shell script automatically determines the data type used for the variable value. Variables defined within the shell script maintain their values throughout the life of the shell script but are deleted when the shell script completes.

Just like system variables, user variables can be referenced using the dollar sign:

```
$ cat test3
#!/bin/bash
# testing variables
days=10
guest="Katie"
echo "$guest checked in $days days ago"
days=5
guest="Jessica"
echo "$guest checked in $days days ago"
$
```

Running the script produces the following output:

```
$ chmod u+x test3
$ ./test3
Katie checked in 10 days ago
Jessica checked in 5 days ago
$
```

Each time the variable is referenced, it produces the value currently assigned to it. It's important to remember that when referencing a variable value you use the dollar sign, but when referencing the variable to assign a value to it, you do not use the dollar sign. Here's an example of what I mean:

```
$ cat test4
#!/bin/bash
# assigning a variable value to another variable

value1=10
value2=$value1
echo The resulting value is $value2
$
```

When you use the value of the *value1* variable in the assignment statement, you must still use the dollar sign. This code produces the following output:

```
$ chmod u+x test4
$ ./test4
The resulting value is 10
$
```

If you forget the dollar sign and make the *value2* assignment line look like this:

```
value2=value1
```

you get the following output:

```
$ ./test4
The resulting value is value1
$
```

Without the dollar sign, the shell interprets the variable name as a normal text string, which is most likely not what you wanted.

Command substitution

One of the most useful features of shell scripts is the ability to extract information from the output of a command and assign it to a variable. After you assign the output to a variable, you can use that value anywhere in your script. This comes in handy when processing data in your scripts.

There are two ways to assign the output of a command to a variable:

- The backtick character (`)
- The $() format

Be careful with the backtick character; it is not the normal single quotation mark character you are used to using for strings. Because it is not used very often outside of shell scripts, you may not even know where to find it on your keyboard. You should become familiar with it because it's a crucial component of many shell scripts. Hint: On a U.S. keyboard, it is usually on the same key as the tilde symbol (~).

Command substitution allows you to assign the output of a shell command to a variable. Although this doesn't seem like much, it is a major building block in script programming.

You must either surround the entire command line command with two backtick characters:

```
testing=`date`
```

or use the $() format:

```
testing=$(date)
```

The shell runs the command within the command substitution characters and assigns the output to the variable testing. Notice that there are no spaces between the assignment equal sign and the command substitution character. Here's an example of creating a variable using the output from a normal shell command:

```
$ cat test5
#!/bin/bash
testing=$(date)
echo "The date and time are: " $testing
$
```

The variable testing receives the output from the date command, and it is used in the echo statement to display it. Running the shell script produces the following output:

```
$ chmod u+x test5
$ ./test5
The date and time are:  Mon Jan 31 20:23:25 EDT 2014
$
```

That's not all that exciting in this example (you could just as easily just put the command in the echo statement), but after you capture the command output in a variable, you can do anything with it.

Here's a popular example of how command substitution is used to capture the current date and use it to create a unique filename in a script:

```
#!/bin/bash
# copy the /usr/bin directory listing to a log file
today=$(date +%y%m%d)
ls /usr/bin -al > log.$today
```

The today variable is assigned the output of a formatted date command. This is a common technique used to extract date information for log filenames. The +%y%m%d format instructs the date command to display the date as a two-digit year, month, and day:

```
$ date +%y%m%d
140131
$
```

The script assigns the value to a variable, which is then used as part of a filename. The file itself contains the redirected output (discussed in the "Redirecting Input and Output" section) of a directory listing. After running the script, you should see a new file in your directory:

```
 -rw-r--r--    1 user     user           769 Jan 31 10:15 log.140131
```

The log file appears in the directory using the value of the $today variable as part of the filename. The contents of the log file are the directory listing from the /usr/bin directory. If the script runs the next day, the log filename is log.140201, thus creating a new file for the new day.

11

CAUTION

Command substitution creates what's called a `subshell` to run the enclosed command. A subshell is a separate child shell generated from the shell that's running the script. Because of that, any variables you create in the script aren't available to the subshell command.

Subshells are also created if you run a command from the command prompt using the ./ path, but they aren't created if you just run the command without a path. However, if you use a built-in shell command, that doesn't generate a subshell. Be careful when running scripts from the command prompt!

Redirecting Input and Output

Sometimes, you want to save the output from a command instead of just having it displayed on the monitor. The bash shell provides a few different operators that allow you to *redirect* the output of a command to an alternative location (such as a file). Redirection can be used for input as well as output, redirecting a file to a command for input. This section describes what you need to do to use redirection in your shell scripts.

Output redirection

The most basic type of redirection is sending output from a command to a file. The bash shell uses the greater-than symbol (>) for this:

```
command > outputfile
```

Anything that would appear on the monitor from the command instead is stored in the output file specified:

```
$ date > test6
$ ls -l test6
-rw-r--r--    1 user      user            29 Feb 10 17:56 test6
$ cat test6
Thu Feb 10 17:56:58 EDT 2014
$
```

The redirect operator created the file test6 (using the default umask settings) and redirected the output from the date command to the test6 file. If the output file already exists, the redirect operator overwrites the existing file with the new file data:

```
$ who > test6
$ cat test6
user     pts/0     Feb 10 17:55
$
```

Now the contents of the test6 file contain the output from the who command.

Sometimes, instead of overwriting the file's contents, you may need to append output from a command to an existing file — for example, if you're creating a log file to document an action on the system. In this situation, you can use the double greater-than symbol (>>) to append data:

```
$ date >> test6
$ cat test6
user       pts/0     Feb 10 17:55
Thu Feb 10 18:02:14 EDT 2014
$
```

The test6 file still contains the original data from the who command processed earlier — and now it contains the new output from the date command.

Input redirection

Input redirection is the opposite of output redirection. Instead of taking the output of a command and redirecting it to a file, input redirection takes the content of a file and redirects it to a command.

The input redirection symbol is the less-than symbol (<):

```
command < inputfile
```

The easy way to remember this is that the command is always listed first in the command line, and the redirection symbol "points" to the way the data is flowing. The less-than symbol indicates that the data is flowing from the input file to the command.

Here's an example of using input redirection with the wc command:

```
$ wc < test6
     2      11      60
$
```

The wc command provides a count of text in the data. By default, it produces three values:

- The number of lines in the text
- The number of words in the text
- The number of bytes in the text

By redirecting a text file to the wc command, you can get a quick count of the lines, words, and bytes in the file. The example shows that there are 2 lines, 11 words, and 60 bytes in the test6 file.

Another method of input redirection is called *inline input redirection*. This method allows you to specify the data for input redirection on the command line instead of in a file. This may seem somewhat odd at first, but a few applications are available for this process (such as those shown in the "Performing Math" section).

The inline input redirection symbol is the double less-than symbol (<<). Besides this symbol, you must specify a text marker that delineates the beginning and end of the data used for input. You can use any string value for the text marker, but it must be the same at the beginning of the data and the end of the data:

```
command << marker
data
marker
```

When using inline input redirection on the command line, the shell prompts for data using the secondary prompt, defined in the *PS2* environment variable (see Chapter 6). Here's how this looks when you use it:

```
$ wc << EOF
> test string 1
> test string 2
> test string 3
> EOF
      3       9      42
$
```

The secondary prompt continues to prompt for more data until you enter the string value for the text marker. The wc command performs the line, word, and byte counts of the data supplied by the inline input redirection.

Pipes

Sometimes, you need to send the output of one command to the input of another command. This is possible using redirection, but somewhat clunky:

```
$ rpm -qa > rpm.list
$ sort < rpm.list
abrt-1.1.14-1.fc14.i686
abrt-addon-ccpp-1.1.14-1.fc14.i686
abrt-addon-kerneloops-1.1.14-1.fc14.i686
abrt-addon-python-1.1.14-1.fc14.i686
abrt-desktop-1.1.14-1.fc14.i686
abrt-gui-1.1.14-1.fc14.i686
abrt-libs-1.1.14-1.fc14.i686
abrt-plugin-bugzilla-1.1.14-1.fc14.i686
abrt-plugin-logger-1.1.14-1.fc14.i686
abrt-plugin-runapp-1.1.14-1.fc14.i686
acl-2.2.49-8.fc14.i686

[...]
```

The rpm command manages the software packages installed on systems using the Red Hat Package Management system (RPM), such as the Fedora system as shown. When used with the -qa parameters, it produces a list of the existing packages installed, but not necessarily in any specific order. If you're looking for a specific package or group of packages, it can be difficult to find it using the output of the rpm command.

Using the standard output redirection, the output was redirected from the rpm command to a file, called rpm.list. After the command finished, the rpm.list file contained a list of all the installed software packages on my system. Next, input redirection was used to send the contents of the rpm.list file to the sort command to sort the package names alphabetically.

That was useful, but again, a somewhat clunky way of producing the information. Instead of redirecting the output of a command to a file, you can redirect the output to another command. This process is called *piping*.

Like the command substitution backtick, the symbol for piping is not used often outside of shell scripting. The symbol is two vertical lines, one above the other. However, the pipe symbol often looks like a single vertical line in print (|). On a U.S. keyboard, it is usually on the same key as the backslash (\). The pipe is put between the commands to redirect the output from one to the other:

```
command1 | command2
```

Don't think of piping as running two commands back to back. The Linux system actually runs both commands at the same time, linking them together internally in the system. As the first command produces output, it's sent immediately to the second command. No intermediate files or buffer areas are used to transfer the data.

Now, using piping you can easily pipe the output of the rpm command directly to the sort command to produce your results:

```
$ rpm -qa | sort
abrt-1.1.14-1.fc14.i686
abrt-addon-ccpp-1.1.14-1.fc14.i686
abrt-addon-kerneloops-1.1.14-1.fc14.i686
abrt-addon-python-1.1.14-1.fc14.i686
abrt-desktop-1.1.14-1.fc14.i686
abrt-gui-1.1.14-1.fc14.i686
abrt-libs-1.1.14-1.fc14.i686
abrt-plugin-bugzilla-1.1.14-1.fc14.i686
abrt-plugin-logger-1.1.14-1.fc14.i686
abrt-plugin-runapp-1.1.14-1.fc14.i686
acl-2.2.49-8.fc14.i686

[...]
```

Unless you're a (very) quick reader, you probably couldn't keep up with the output generated by this command. Because the piping feature operates in real time, as soon as the `rpm` command produces data, the `sort` command gets busy sorting it. By the time the `rpm` command finishes outputting data, the `sort` command already has the data sorted and starts displaying it on the monitor.

There's no limit to the number of `pipes` you can use in a command. You can continue piping the output of commands to other commands to refine your operation.

In this case, because the output of the `sort` command zooms by so quickly, you can use one of the text paging commands (such as `less` or `more`) to force the output to stop at every screen of data:

```
$ rpm -qa | sort | more
```

This command sequence runs the `rpm` command, `pipes` the output to the `sort` command, and then `pipes` that output to the `more` command to display the data, stopping after every screen of information. This now lets you pause and read what's on the display before continuing, as shown in Figure 11-1.

FIGURE 11-1

Using piping to send data to the more command

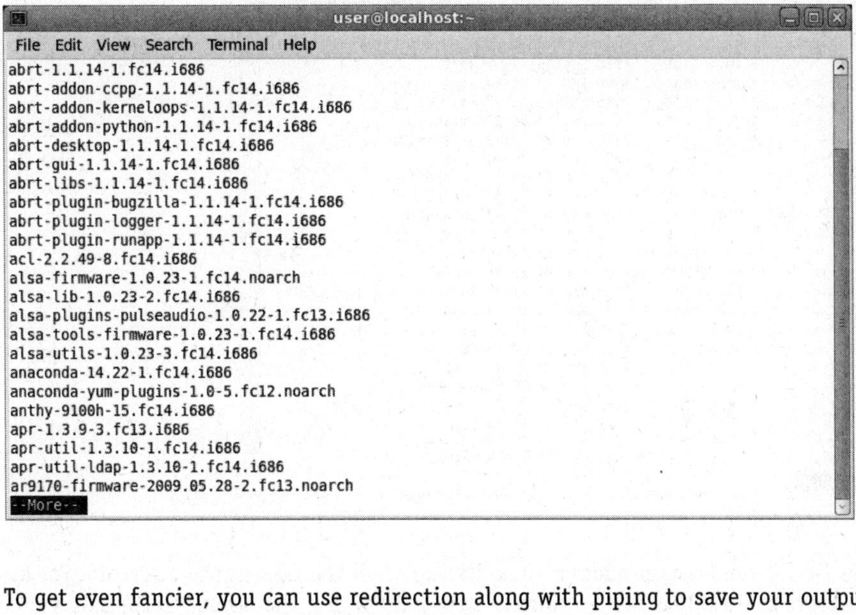
user@localhost:~
File Edit View Search Terminal Help
abrt-1.1.14-1.fc14.i686
abrt-addon-ccpp-1.1.14-1.fc14.i686
abrt-addon-kerneloops-1.1.14-1.fc14.i686
abrt-addon-python-1.1.14-1.fc14.i686
abrt-desktop-1.1.14-1.fc14.i686
abrt-gui-1.1.14-1.fc14.i686
abrt-libs-1.1.14-1.fc14.i686
abrt-plugin-bugzilla-1.1.14-1.fc14.i686
abrt-plugin-logger-1.1.14-1.fc14.i686
abrt-plugin-runapp-1.1.14-1.fc14.i686
acl-2.2.49-8.fc14.i686
alsa-firmware-1.0.23-1.fc14.noarch
alsa-lib-1.0.23-2.fc14.i686
alsa-plugins-pulseaudio-1.0.22-1.fc13.i686
alsa-tools-firmware-1.0.23-1.fc14.i686
alsa-utils-1.0.23-3.fc14.i686
anaconda-14.22-1.fc14.i686
anaconda-yum-plugins-1.0-5.fc12.noarch
anthy-9100h-15.fc14.i686
apr-1.3.9-3.fc13.i686
apr-util-1.3.10-1.fc14.i686
apr-util-ldap-1.3.10-1.fc14.i686
ar9170-firmware-2009.05.28-2.fc13.noarch
--More--

To get even fancier, you can use redirection along with piping to save your output to a file:

```
$ rpm -qa | sort > rpm.list
$ more rpm.list
```

```
abrt-1.1.14-1.fc14.i686
abrt-addon-ccpp-1.1.14-1.fc14.i686
abrt-addon-kerneloops-1.1.14-1.fc14.i686
abrt-addon-python-1.1.14-1.fc14.i686
abrt-desktop-1.1.14-1.fc14.i686
abrt-gui-1.1.14-1.fc14.i686
abrt-libs-1.1.14-1.fc14.i686
abrt-plugin-bugzilla-1.1.14-1.fc14.i686
abrt-plugin-logger-1.1.14-1.fc14.i686
abrt-plugin-runapp-1.1.14-1.fc14.i686
acl-2.2.49-8.fc14.i686
[...]
```

As expected, the data in the rpm.list file is now sorted!

By far one of the most popular uses of piping is piping the results of commands that produce long output to the more command. This is especially common with the ls command, as shown in Figure 11-2.

FIGURE 11-2

Using the more command with the ls command

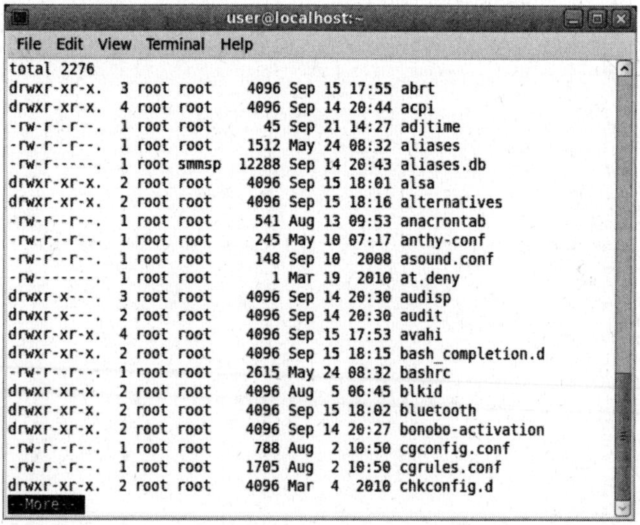

The ls -l command produces a long listing of all the files in the directory. For directories with lots of files, this can be quite a listing. By piping the output to the more command, you force the output to stop at the end of every screen of data.

Performing Math

Another feature crucial to any programming language is the ability to manipulate numbers. Unfortunately, for shell scripts this process is a bit awkward. There are two different ways to perform mathematical operations in your shell scripts.

The expr command

Originally, the Bourne shell provided a special command that was used for processing mathematical equations. The `expr` command allowed the processing of equations from the command line, but it is extremely clunky:

```
$ expr 1 + 5
6
```

The `expr` command recognizes a few different mathematical and string operators, shown in Table 11-1.

TABLE 11-1 The expr Command Operators

Operator	Description
ARG1 | ARG2	Returns ARG1 if neither argument is null or zero; otherwise, returns ARG2
ARG1 & ARG2	Returns ARG1 if neither argument is null or zero; otherwise, returns 0
ARG1 < ARG2	Returns 1 if ARG1 is less than ARG2; otherwise, returns 0
ARG1 <= ARG2	Returns 1 if ARG1 is less than or equal to ARG2; otherwise, returns 0
ARG1 = ARG2	Returns 1 if ARG1 is equal to ARG2; otherwise, returns 0
ARG1 != ARG2	Returns 1 if ARG1 is not equal to ARG2; otherwise, returns 0
ARG1 >= ARG2	Returns 1 if ARG1 is greater than or equal to ARG2; otherwise, returns 0
ARG1 > ARG2	Returns 1 if ARG1 is greater than ARG2; otherwise, returns 0
ARG1 + ARG2	Returns the arithmetic sum of ARG1 and ARG2
ARG1 - ARG2	Returns the arithmetic difference of ARG1 and ARG2
ARG1 * ARG2	Returns the arithmetic product of ARG1 and ARG2
ARG1 / ARG2	Returns the arithmetic quotient of ARG1 divided by ARG2
ARG1 % ARG2	Returns the arithmetic remainder of ARG1 divided by ARG2
STRING : REGEXP	Returns the pattern match if REGEXP matches a pattern in STRING

Continues

TABLE 11-1 *(continued)*

Operator	Description
match STRING REGEXP	Returns the pattern match if REGEXP matches a pattern in STRING
substr STRING POS LENGTH	Returns the substring LENGTH characters in length, starting at position POS (starting at 1)
index STRING CHARS	Returns position in STRING where CHARS is found; otherwise, returns 0
length STRING	Returns the numeric length of the string STRING
+ TOKEN	Interprets TOKEN as a string, even if it's a keyword
(EXPRESSION)	Returns the value of EXPRESSION

Although the standard operators work fine in the expr command, the problem occurs when using them from a script or the command line. Many of the expr command operators have other meanings in the shell (such as the asterisk). Using them in the expr command produces odd results:

```
$ expr 5 * 2
expr: syntax error
$
```

To solve this problem, you need to use the shell escape character (the backslash) to identify any characters that may be misinterpreted by the shell before being passed to the expr command:

```
$ expr 5 \* 2
10
$
```

Now that's really starting to get ugly! Using the expr command in a shell script is equally cumbersome:

```
$ cat test6
#!/bin/bash
# An example of using the expr command
var1=10
var2=20
var3=$(expr $var2 / $var1)
echo The result is $var3
```

To assign the result of a mathematical equation to a variable, you have to use command substitution to extract the output from the expr command:

```
$ chmod u+x test6
$ ./test6
The result is 2
$
```

Fortunately, the bash shell has an improvement for processing mathematical operators as you shall see in the next section.

Using brackets

The bash shell includes the `expr` command to stay compatible with the Bourne shell; however, it also provides a much easier way of performing mathematical equations. In bash, when assigning a mathematical value to a variable, you can enclose the mathematical equation using a dollar sign and square brackets (`$[ operation ]`):

```
$ var1=$[1 + 5]
$ echo $var1
6
$ var2=$[$var1 * 2]
$ echo $var2
12
$
```

Using brackets makes shell math much easier than with the `expr` command. This same technique also works in shell scripts:

```
$ cat test7
#!/bin/bash
var1=100
var2=50
var3=45
var4=$[$var1 * ($var2 - $var3)]
echo The final result is $var4
$
```

Running this script produces the output:

```
$ chmod u+x test7
$ ./test7
The final result is 500
$
```

Also, notice that when using the square brackets method for calculating equations, you don't need to worry about the multiplication symbol, or any other characters, being misinterpreted by the shell. The shell knows that it's not a wildcard character because it is within the square brackets.

There's one major limitation to performing math in the bash shell script. Look at this example:

```
$ cat test8
#!/bin/bash
var1=100
```

```
var2=45
var3=$[$var1 / $var2]
echo The final result is $var3
$
```

Now run it and see what happens:

```
$ chmod u+x test8
$ ./test8
The final result is 2
$
```

The bash shell mathematical operators support only integer arithmetic. This is a huge limitation if you're trying to do any sort of real-world mathematical calculations.

> **NOTE**
>
> The z shell (zsh) provides full floating-point arithmetic operations. If you require floating-point calculations in your shell scripts, you might consider checking out the z shell (discussed in Chapter 23).

A floating-point solution

You can use several solutions for overcoming the bash integer limitation. The most popular solution uses the built-in bash calculator, called bc.

The basics of bc

The bash calculator is actually a programming language that allows you to enter floating-point expressions at a command line and then interprets the expressions, calculates them, and returns the result. The bash calculator recognizes these:

- Numbers (both integer and floating point)
- Variables (both simple variables and arrays)
- Comments (lines starting with a pound sign or the C language /* */ pair)
- Expressions
- Programming statements (such as if-then statements)
- Functions

You can access the bash calculator from the shell prompt using the bc command:

```
$ bc
bc 1.06.95
Copyright 1991-1994, 1997, 1998, 2000, 2004, 2006 Free Software Foundation, Inc.
This is free software with ABSOLUTELY NO WARRANTY.
For details type 'warranty'.
```

```
12 * 5.4
64.8
3.156 * (3 + 5)
25.248
quit
$
```

The example starts out by entering the expression 12 * 5.4. The bash calculator returns the answer. Each subsequent expression entered into the calculator is evaluated, and the result is displayed. To exit the bash calculator, you must enter quit.

The floating-point arithmetic is controlled by a built-in variable called *scale*. You must set this value to the desired number of decimal places you want in your answers, or you won't get what you were looking for:

```
$ bc -q
3.44 / 5
0
scale=4
3.44 / 5
.6880
quit
$
```

The default value for the *scale* variable is zero. Before the *scale* value is set, the bash calculator provides the answer to zero decimal places. After you set the *scale* variable value to four, the bash calculator displays the answer to four decimal places. The -q command line parameter suppresses the lengthy welcome banner from the bash calculator.

In addition to normal numbers, the bash calculator also understands variables:

```
$ bc -q
var1=10
var1 * 4
40
var2 = var1 / 5
print var2
2
quit
$
```

After a variable value is defined, you can use the variable throughout the bash calculator session. The print statement allows you to print variables and numbers.

Using bc in scripts

Now you may be wondering how the bash calculator is going to help you with floating-point arithmetic in your shell scripts. Do you remember command substitution? Yes, you can use the command substitution character to run a bc command and assign the output to a variable! The basic format to use is this:

```
variable=$(echo "options; expression" | bc)
```

The first portion, options, allows you to set variables. If you need to set more than one variable, separate them using the semicolon. The expression parameter defines the mathematical expression to evaluate using bc. Here's a quick example of doing this in a script:

```
$ cat test9
#!/bin/bash
var1=$(echo "scale=4; 3.44 / 5" | bc)
echo The answer is $var1
$
```

This example sets the scale variable to four decimal places and then specifies a specific calculation for the expression. Running this script produces the following output:

```
$ chmod u+x test9
$ ./test9
The answer is .6880
$
```

Now that's fancy! You aren't limited to just using numbers for the expression value. You can also use variables defined in the shell script:

```
$ cat test10
#!/bin/bash
var1=100
var2=45
var3=$(echo "scale=4; $var1 / $var2" | bc)
echo The answer for this is $var3
$
```

The script defines two variables, which are used within the expression sent to the bc command. Remember to use the dollar sign to signify the value for the variables and not the variables themselves. The output of this script is as follows:

```
$ ./test10
The answer for this is 2.2222
$
```

And of course, after a value is assigned to a variable, that variable can be used in yet another calculation:

```
$ cat test11
#!/bin/bash
var1=20
var2=3.14159
```

```
var3=$(echo "scale=4; $var1 * $var1" | bc)
var4=$(echo "scale=4; $var3 * $var2" | bc)
echo The final result is $var4
$
```

This method works fine for short calculations, but sometimes you need to get more involved with your numbers. If you have more than just a couple of calculations, it gets confusing trying to list multiple expressions on the same command line.

There's a solution to this problem. The bc command recognizes input redirection, allowing you to redirect a file to the bc command for processing. However, this also can get confusing, because you'd need to store your expressions in a file.

The best method is to use inline input redirection, which allows you to redirect data directly from the command line. In the shell script, you assign the output to a variable:

```
variable=$(bc << EOF
options
statements
expressions
EOF
)
```

The EOF text string indicates the beginning and end of the inline redirection data. Remember that the command substitution characters are still needed to assign the output of the bc command to the variable.

Now you can place all the individual bash calculator elements on separate lines in the script file. Here's an example of using this technique in a script:

```
$ cat test12
#!/bin/bash

var1=10.46
var2=43.67
var3=33.2
var4=71

var5=$(bc << EOF
scale = 4
a1 = ( $var1 * $var2)
b1 = ($var3 * $var4)
a1 + b1
EOF
)

echo The final answer for this mess is $var5
$
```

Placing each option and expression on a separate line in your script makes things cleaner and easier to read and follow. The EOF string indicates the start and end of the data to redirect to the bc command. Of course, you must use the command substitution characters to indicate the command to assign to the variable.

You'll also notice in this example that you can assign variables within the bash calculator. It's important to remember that any variables created within the bash calculator are valid only within the bash calculator and can't be used in the shell script.

Exiting the Script

So far in our sample scripts, we terminated things pretty abruptly. When we were finished with our last command, we just ended the script. There's a more elegant way of completing things available to us.

Every command that runs in the shell uses an *exit status* to indicate to the shell that it's finished processing. The exit status is an integer value between 0 and 255 that's passed by the command to the shell when the command finishes running. You can capture this value and use it in your scripts.

Checking the exit status

Linux provides the $? special variable that holds the exit status value from the last command that executed. You must view or use the $? variable immediately after the command you want to check. It changes values to the exit status of the last command executed by the shell:

```
$ date
Sat Jan 15 10:01:30 EDT 2014
$ echo $?
0
$
```

By convention, the exit status of a command that successfully completes is zero. If a command completes with an error, then a positive integer value is placed in the exit status:

```
$ asdfg
-bash: asdfg: command not found
$ echo $?
127
$
```

The invalid command returns an exit status of 127. There's not much of a standard convention to Linux error exit status codes. However, you can use the guidelines shown in Table 11-2.

TABLE 11-2 **Linux Exit Status Codes**

Code	Description
0	Successful completion of the command
1	General unknown error
2	Misuse of shell command
126	The command can't execute
127	Command not found
128	Invalid exit argument
128+x	Fatal error with Linux signal x
130	Command terminated with Ctrl+C
255	Exit status out of range

An exit status value of 126 indicates that the user didn't have the proper permissions set to execute the command:

```
$ ./myprog.c
-bash: ./myprog.c: Permission denied
$ echo $?
126
$
```

Another common error you'll encounter occurs if you supply an invalid parameter to a command:

```
$ date %t
date: invalid date '%t'
$ echo $?
1
$
```

This generates the general exit status code of 1, indicating that an unknown error occurred in the command.

The exit command

By default, your shell script exits with the exit status of the last command in your script:

```
$ ./test6
The result is 2
$ echo $?
0
$
```

You can change that to return your own exit status code. The exit command allows you to specify an exit status when your script ends:

```
$ cat test13
#!/bin/bash
# testing the exit status
var1=10
var2=30
var3=$[$var1 + $var2]
echo The answer is $var3
exit 5
$
```

When you check the exit status of the script, you get the value used as the parameter of the exit command:

```
$ chmod u+x test13
$ ./test13
The answer is 40
$ echo $?
5
$
```

You can also use variables in the exit command parameter:

```
$ cat test14
#!/bin/bash
# testing the exit status
var1=10
var2=30
var3=$[$var1 + $var2]
exit $var3
$
```

When you run this command, it produces the following exit status:

```
$ chmod u+x test14
$ ./test14
$ echo $?
40
$
```

You should be careful with this feature, however, because the exit status codes can only go up to 255. Watch what happens in this example:

```
$ cat test14b
#!/bin/bash
# testing the exit status
var1=10
```

```
var2=30
var3=$[$var1 * $var2]
echo The value is $var3
exit $var3
$
```

Now when you run it, you get the following:

```
$ ./test14b
The value is 300
$ echo $?
44
$
```

The exit status code is reduced to fit in the 0 to 255 range. The shell does this by using modulo arithmetic. The *modulo* of a value is the remainder after a division. The resulting number is the remainder of the specified number divided by 256. In the case of 300 (the result value), the remainder is 44, which is what appears as the exit status code.

In Chapter 12, you'll see how you can use the if-then statement to check the error status returned by a command to see whether the command was successful.

Summary

The bash shell script allows you to string commands together into a script. The most basic way to create a script is to separate multiple commands on the command line using a semicolon. The shell executes each command in order, displaying the output of each command on the monitor.

You can also create a shell script file, placing multiple commands in the file for the shell to execute in order. The shell script file must define the shell used to run the script. This is done in the first line of the script file, using the #! symbol, followed by the full path of the shell.

Within the shell script you can reference environment variable values by using a dollar sign in front of the variable. You can also define your own variables for use within the script, and assign values and even the output of a command by using the backtick character or the $() format. The variable value can be used within the script by placing a dollar sign in front of the variable name.

The bash shell allows you to redirect both the input and output of a command from the standard behavior. You can redirect the output of any command from the monitor display to a file by using the greater-than symbol, followed by the name of the file to capture the output. You can append output data to an existing file by using two greater-than symbols.

The less-than symbol is used to redirect input to a command. You can redirect input from a file to a command.

The Linux pipe command (the broken bar symbol) allows you to redirect the output of a command directly to the input of another command. The Linux system runs both commands at the same time, sending the output of the first command to the input of the second command without using any redirect files.

The bash shell provides a couple of ways for you to perform mathematical operations in your shell scripts. The expr command is a simple way to perform integer math. In the bash shell, you can also perform basic math calculations by enclosing equations in square brackets, preceded by a dollar sign. To perform floating-point arithmetic, you need to utilize the bc calculator command, redirecting input from inline data and storing the output in a user variable.

Finally, the chapter discussed how to use the exit status in your shell script. Every command that runs in the shell produces an exit status. The exit status is an integer value between 0 and 255 that indicates if the command completed successfully, and if not, what the reason may have been. An exit status of 0 indicates that the command completed successfully. You can use the exit command in your shell script to declare a specific exit status upon the completion of your script.

So far in your shell scripts, things have proceeded in an orderly fashion from one command to the next. In the next chapter, you'll see how you can use some logic flow control to alter which commands are executed within the script.

Using Structured Commands

IN THIS CHAPTER

Working with the if-then statement

Nesting ifs

Understanding the test command

Testing compound conditions

Using double brackets and parentheses

Looking at case

In the shell scripts presented in Chapter 11, the shell processed each individual command in the shell script in the order it appeared. This works out fine for sequential operations, where you want all the commands to process in the proper order. However, this isn't how all programs operate.

Many programs require some sort of logic flow control between the commands in the script. There is a whole command class that allows the script to skip over executed commands based on tested conditions. These commands are generally referred to as *structured commands*.

The structured commands allow you to alter the operation flow of a program. Quite a few structured commands are available in the bash shell, so we'll look at them individually. In this chapter, we look at if-then and case statements.

Working with the if-then Statement

The most basic type of structured command is the if-then statement. The if-then statement has the following format:

```
if command
then
     commands
fi
```

If you're using if-then statements in other programming languages, this format may be somewhat confusing. In other programming languages, the object after the if statement is an equation that is evaluated for a TRUE or FALSE value. That's not how the bash shell if statement works.

The bash shell `if` statement runs the command defined on the `if` line. If the exit status of the command (see Chapter 11) is zero (the command completed successfully), the commands listed under the `then` section are executed. If the exit status of the command is anything else, the `then` commands aren't executed, and the bash shell moves on to the next command in the script. The `fi` statement delineates the `if-then` statement's end.

Here's a simple example to demonstrate this concept:

```
$ cat test1.sh
#!/bin/bash
# testing the if statement
if pwd
then
    echo "It worked"
fi
$
```

This script uses the `pwd` command on the `if` line. If the command completes successfully, the `echo` statement should display the text string. When you run this script from the command line, you get the following results:

```
$ ./test1.sh
/home/Christine
It worked
$
```

The shell executed the `pwd` command listed on the `if` line. Because the exit status was zero, it also executed the `echo` statement listed in the `then` section.

Here's another example:

```
$ cat test2.sh
#!/bin/bash
# testing a bad command
if IamNotaCommand
then
    echo "It worked"
fi
echo "We are outside the if statement"
$
$ ./test2.sh
./test2.sh: line 3: IamNotaCommand: command not found
We are outside the if statement
$
```

In this example, we deliberately used a command, `IamNotaCommand`, that does not work in the `if` statement line. Because this is a bad command, it produces an exit status that's non-zero, and the bash shell skips the `echo` statement in the `then` section. Also notice that the error message generated from running the command in the `if` statement still appears in the script's output. There may be times when you don't want an error statement to appear. Chapter 15 discusses how this can be avoided.

You are not limited to just one command in the `then` section. You can list commands just as in the rest of the shell script. The bash shell treats the commands as a block, executing all of them when the command in the `if` statement line returns a zero exit status or skipping all of them when the command returns a non-zero exit status:

```
$ cat test3.sh
#!/bin/bash
# testing multiple commands in the then section
#
testuser=Christine
#
if grep $testuser /etc/passwd
then
    echo "This is my first command"
    echo "This is my second command"
    echo "I can even put in other commands besides echo:"
    ls -a /home/$testuser/.b*
fi
$
```

The `if` statement line uses the `grep` comment to search the /etc/passwd file to see if a specific username is currently used on the system. If there's a user with that logon name, the script displays some text and then lists the bash files in the user's *HOME* directory:

```
$ ./test3.sh
Christine:x:501:501:Christine B:/home/Christine:/bin/bash
This is my first command
This is my second command
I can even put in other commands besides echo:
/home/Christine/.bash_history   /home/Christine/.bash_profile
/home/Christine/.bash_logout    /home/Christine/.bashrc
$
```

However, if you set the *testuser* variable to a user that doesn't exist on the system, nothing happens:

```
$ cat test3.sh
#!/bin/bash
# testing multiple commands in the then section
#
testuser=NoSuchUser
#
if grep $testuser /etc/passwd
then
    echo "This is my first command"
    echo "This is my second command"
    echo "I can even put in other commands besides echo:"
    ls -a /home/$testuser/.b*
fi
$
$ ./test3.sh
$
```

It's not all that exciting. It would be nice if we could display a little message saying that the username wasn't found on the system. Well, we can, using another feature of the if-then statement.

Exploring the if-then-else Statement

In the if-then statement, you have only one option for whether a command is successful. If the command returns a non-zero exit status code, the bash shell just moves on to the next command in the script. In this situation, it would be nice to be able to execute an alternate set of commands. That's exactly what the if-then-else statement is for.

The if-then-else statement provides another group of commands in the statement:

```
if command
then
    commands
else
    commands
fi
```

When the command in the if statement line returns with a zero exit status code, the commands listed in the then section are executed, just as in a normal if-then statement. When the command in the if statement line returns a non-zero exit status code, the bash shell executes the commands in the else section.

Now you can copy and modify the test script to include an else section:

```
$ cp test3.sh test4.sh
$
$ nano test4.sh
$
```

```
$ cat test4.sh
#!/bin/bash
# testing the else section
#
testuser=NoSuchUser
#
if grep $testuser /etc/passwd
then
    echo "The bash files for user $testuser are:"
    ls -a /home/$testuser/.b*
    echo
else
    echo "The user $testuser does not exist on this system."
    echo
fi
$
$ ./test4.sh
The user NoSuchUser does not exist on this system.

$
```

That's more user-friendly. Just like the then section, the else section can contain multiple commands. The fi statement delineates the end of the else section.

Nesting ifs

Sometimes, you must check for several situations in your script code. For these situations, you can nest the if-then statements:

To check if a logon name is not in the /etc/passwd file and yet a directory for that user still exists, use a nested if-then statement. In this case, the nested if-then statement is within the primary if-then-else statement's else code block:

```
$ ls -d /home/NoSuchUser/
/home/NoSuchUser/
$
$ cat test5.sh
#!/bin/bash
# Testing nested ifs
#
testuser=NoSuchUser
#
if grep $testuser /etc/passwd
then
    echo "The user $testuser exists on this system."
else
    echo "The user $testuser does not exist on this system."
```

```
      if ls -d /home/$testuser/
      then
          echo "However, $testuser has a directory."
      fi
fi
$
$ ./test5.sh
The user NoSuchUser does not exist on this system.
/home/NoSuchUser/
However, NoSuchUser has a directory.
$
```

The script correctly finds that although the login name has been removed from the /etc/ passwd file, the user's directory is still on the system. The problem with using this manner of nested if-then statements in a script is that the code can get hard to read, and the logic flow becomes difficult to follow.

Instead of having to write separate if-then statements, you can use an alternative version of the else section, called elif. The elif continues an else section with another if-then statement:

```
if command1
then
    commands
elif command2
then
    more commands
fi
```

The elif statement line provides another command to evaluate, similar to the original if statement line. If the exit status code from the elif command is zero, bash executes the commands in the second then statement section. Using this method of nesting provides cleaner code with an easier-to-follow logic flow:

```
$ cat test5.sh
#!/bin/bash
# Testing nested ifs - use elif
#
testuser=NoSuchUser
#
if grep $testuser /etc/passwd
then
    echo "The user $testuser exists on this system."
#
elif ls -d /home/$testuser
then
    echo "The user $testuser does not exist on this system."
    echo "However, $testuser has a directory."
#
```

```
fi
$
$ ./test5.sh
/home/NoSuchUser
The user NoSuchUser does not exist on this system.
However, NoSuchUser has a directory.
$
```

You can even take this script a step further and have it check for both a non-existent user with a directory and a non-existent user without a directory. This is accomplished by adding an else statement within the nested elif:

```
$ cat test5.sh
#!/bin/bash
# Testing nested ifs - use elif & else
#
testuser=NoSuchUser
#
if grep $testuser /etc/passwd
then
    echo "The user $testuser exists on this system."
#
elif ls -d /home/$testuser
then
    echo "The user $testuser does not exist on this system."
    echo "However, $testuser has a directory."
#
else
    echo "The user $testuser does not exist on this system."
    echo "And, $testuser does not have a directory."
fi
$
$ ./test5.sh
/home/NoSuchUser
The user NoSuchUser does not exist on this system.
However, NoSuchUser has a directory.
$
$ sudo rmdir /home/NoSuchUser
[sudo] password for Christine:
$
$ ./test5.sh
ls: cannot access /home/NoSuchUser: No such file or directory
The user NoSuchUser does not exist on this system.
And, NoSuchUser does not have a directory.
$
```

Before the /home/NoSuchUser directory was removed and the test script executed the elif statement, a zero exit status was returned. Thus, the statements within the elif's then code block were executed. After the /home/NoSuchUser directory was removed, a non-zero exit status was returned for the elif statement. This caused the statements in the else block within the elif block to be executed.

> **TIP**
>
> Keep in mind that, with an elif statement, any else statements immediately following it are for that elif code block. They are not part of a preceding if-then statement code block.

You can continue to string elif statements together, creating one huge if-then-elif conglomeration:

```
if command1
then
     command set 1
elif command2
then
    command set 2
elif command3
then
    command set 3
elif command4
then
    command set 4
fi
```

Each block of commands is executed depending on which command returns the zero exit status code. Remember that the bash shell executes the if statements in order, and only the first one that returns a zero exit status results in the then section being executed.

Even though the code looks cleaner with elif statements, it still can be confusing to follow the script's logic. Later in the "Considering the case Command" section, you'll see how to use the case command instead of having to nest lots of if-then statements.

Trying the test Command

So far, all you've seen in the if statement line are normal shell commands. You might be wondering if the bash if-then statement has the ability to evaluate any condition other than a command's exit status code.

The answer is no, it can't. However, there's a neat utility available in the bash shell that helps you evaluate other things, using the if-then statement.

The test command provides a way to test different conditions in an if-then statement. If the condition listed in the test command evaluates to TRUE, the test command exits with a zero exit status code. This makes the if-then statement behave in much the same way that if-then statements work in other programming languages. If the condition is FALSE, the test command exits with a non-zero exit status code, which causes the if-then statement to exit.

The format of the test command is pretty simple:

```
test condition
```

The *condition* is a series of parameters and values that the test command evaluates. When used in an if-then statement, the test command looks like this:

```
if test condition
then
    commands
fi
```

If you leave out the *condition* portion of the test command statement, it exits with a non-zero exit status code and triggers any else block statements:

```
$ cat test6.sh
#!/bin/bash
# Testing the test command
#
if test
then
    echo "No expression returns a True"
else
    echo "No expression returns a False"
fi
$
$ ./test6.sh
No expression returns a False
$
```

When you add in a condition, it is tested by the test command. For example, using the test command, you can determine whether a variable has content. A simple condition expression is needed to determine whether a variable has content:

```
$ cat test6.sh
#!/bin/bash
# Testing the test command
#
my_variable="Full"
#
if test $my_variable
then
    echo "The $my_variable expression returns a True"
#
else
```

```
        echo "The $my_variable expression returns a False"
fi
$
$ ./test6.sh
The Full expression returns a True
$
```

The variable my_variable contains content (Full), so when the test command checks the condition, the exit status returns a zero. This triggers the statement in the then code block.

As you would suspect, the opposite occurs when the variable does not contain content:

```
$ cat test6.sh
#!/bin/bash
# Testing the test command
#
my_variable=""
#
if test $my_variable
then
    echo "The $my_variable expression returns a True"
#
else
    echo "The $my_variable expression returns a False"
fi
$
$ ./test6.sh
The  expression returns a False
$
```

The bash shell provides an alternative way of testing a condition without declaring the test command in an if-then statement:

```
if [ condition ]
then
    commands
fi
```

The square brackets define the test condition. Be careful; you *must* have a space after the first bracket and a space before the last bracket, or you'll get an error message.

The test command and test conditions can evaluate three classes of conditions:

- Numeric comparisons
- String comparisons
- File comparisons

The next sections describe how to use each of these test classes in your if-then statements.

Using numeric comparisons

The most common test evaluation method is to perform a comparison of two numeric values. Table 12-1 shows the list of condition parameters used for testing two values.

TABLE 12-1 The test Numeric Comparisons

Comparison	Description
n1 -eq n2	Checks if n1 is equal to n2
n1 -ge n2	Checks if n1 is greater than or equal to n2
n1 -gt n2	Checks if n1 is greater than n2
n1 -le n2	Checks if n1 is less than or equal to n2
n1 -lt n2	Checks if n1 is less than n2
n1 -ne n2	Checks if n1 is not equal to n2

The numeric test conditions can be used to evaluate both numbers and variables. Here's an example of doing that:

```
$ cat numeric_test.sh
#!/bin/bash
# Using numeric test evaluations
#
value1=10
value2=11
#
if [ $value1 -gt 5 ]
then
    echo "The test value $value1 is greater than 5"
fi
#
if [ $value1 -eq $value2 ]
then
    echo "The values are equal"
else
    echo "The values are different"
fi
#
$
```

The first test condition:

```
if [ $value1 -gt 5 ]
```

tests if the value of the variable *value1* is greater than 5. The second test condition:

```
if [ $value1 -eq $value2 ]
```

tests if the value of the variable *value1* is equal to the value of the variable *value2*. Both numeric test conditions evaluate as expected:

```
$ ./numeric_test.sh
The test value 10 is greater than 5
The values are different
$
```

There is a limitation to the test numeric conditions concerning floating-point values:

```
$ cat floating_point_test.sh
#!/bin/bash
# Using floating point numbers in test evaluations
#
value1=5.555
#
echo "The test value is $value1"
#
if [ $value1 -gt 5 ]
then
    echo "The test value $value1 is greater than 5"
fi
#
$ ./floating_point_test.sh
The test value is 5.555
./floating_point_test.sh: line 8:
[: 5.555: integer expression expected
$
```

This example uses a floating-point value, stored in the *value1* variable. Next, it evaluates the value. Something obviously went wrong.

Remember that the only numbers the bash shell can handle are integers. This works perfectly fine if all you need to do is display the result, using an echo statement. However, this doesn't work in numeric-oriented functions, such as our numeric test condition. The bottom line is that you cannot use floating-point values for test conditions.

Using string comparisons

Test conditions also allow you to perform comparisons on string values. Performing comparisons on strings can get tricky, as you'll see. Table 12-2 shows the comparison functions you can use to evaluate two string values.

TABLE 12-2 **The test String Comparisons**

Comparison	Description
str1 = str2	Checks if str1 is the same as string str2
str1 != str2	Checks if str1 is not the same as str2
str1 < str2	Checks if str1 is less than str2
str1 > str2	Checks if str1 is greater than str2
-n str1	Checks if str1 has a length greater than zero
-z str1	Checks if str1 has a length of zero

The following sections describe the different string comparisons available.

Looking at string equality

The equal and not equal conditions are fairly self-explanatory with strings. It's pretty easy to know when two string values are the same or not:

```
$ cat test7.sh
#!/bin/bash
# testing string equality
testuser=rich
#
if [ $USER = $testuser ]
then
    echo "Welcome $testuser"
fi
$
$ ./test7.sh
Welcome rich
$
```

Also, using the not equals string comparison allows you to determine if two strings have the same value or not:

```
$ cat test8.sh
#!/bin/bash
# testing string equality
testuser=baduser
#
if [ $USER != $testuser ]
then
    echo "This is not $testuser"
else
    echo "Welcome $testuser"
fi
```

```
$
$ ./test8.sh
This is not baduser
$
```

Keep in mind that the test comparison takes all punctuation and capitalization into account when comparing strings for equality.

Looking at string order

Trying to determine if one string is less than or greater than another is where things start getting tricky. Two problems often plague shell programmers when trying to use the greater-than or less-than features of test conditions:

- The greater-than and less-than symbols must be escaped, or the shell uses them as redirection symbols, with the string values as filenames.

- The greater-than and less-than order is not the same as that used with the sort command.

The first item can result in a huge problem that often goes undetected when programming your scripts. Here's an example of what sometimes happens to novice shell script programmers:

```
$ cat badtest.sh
#!/bin/bash
# mis-using string comparisons
#
val1=baseball
val2=hockey
#
if [ $val1 > $val2 ]
then
    echo "$val1 is greater than $val2"
else
    echo "$val1 is less than $val2"
fi
$
$ ./badtest.sh
baseball is greater than hockey
$ ls -l hockey
-rw-r--r--    1 rich     rich            0 Sep 30 19:08 hockey
$
```

By just using the greater-than symbol itself in the script, no errors are generated, but the results are wrong. The script interpreted the greater-than symbol as an output redirection (see Chapter 15). Thus, it created a file called hockey. Because the redirection completed successfully, the test condition returns a zero exit status code, which the if statement evaluates as though things completed successfully!

To fix this problem, you need to properly escape the greater-than symbol:

```
$ cat test9.sh
#!/bin/bash
# mis-using string comparisons
#
val1=baseball
val2=hockey
#
if [ $val1 \> $val2 ]
then
   echo "$val1 is greater than $val2"
else
    echo "$val1 is less than $val2"
fi
$
$ ./test9.sh
baseball is less than hockey
$
```

Now that answer is more along the lines of what you would expect from the string comparison.

The second issue is a little more subtle, and you may not even run across it unless you are working with uppercase and lowercase letters. The sort command handles uppercase letters opposite to the way the test conditions consider them:

```
$ cat test9b.sh
#!/bin/bash
# testing string sort order
val1=Testing
val2=testing
#
if [ $val1 \> $val2 ]
then
    echo "$val1 is greater than $val2"
else
    echo "$val1 is less than $val2"
fi
$
$ ./test9b.sh
Testing is less than testing
$
$ sort testfile
testing
Testing
$
```

Capitalized letters are treated as less than lowercase letters in test comparisons. However, the sort command does the opposite. When you put the same strings in a file and use the sort command, the lowercase letters appear first. This is due to different ordering techniques.

Test comparisons use standard ASCII ordering, using each character's ASCII numeric value to determine the sort order. The sort command uses the sorting order defined for the system locale language settings. For the English language, the locale settings specify that lowercase letters appear before uppercase letters in sorted order.

> **NOTE**
>
> The test command and test expressions use the standard mathematical comparison symbols for string comparisons and text codes for numerical comparisons. This is a subtle feature that many programmers manage to get reversed. If you use the mathematical comparison symbols for numeric values, the shell interprets them as string values and may not produce the correct results.

Looking at string size

The -n and -z comparisons are handy when trying to evaluate whether a variable contains data:

```
$ cat test10.sh
#!/bin/bash
# testing string length
val1=testing
val2=''
#
if [ -n $val1 ]
then
    echo "The string '$val1' is not empty"
else
    echo "The string '$val1' is empty"
fi
#
if [ -z $val2 ]
then
    echo "The string '$val2' is empty"
else
    echo "The string '$val2' is not empty"
fi
#
if [ -z $val3 ]
then
    echo "The string '$val3' is empty"
else
    echo "The string '$val3' is not empty"
fi
```

```
$
$ ./test10.sh
The string 'testing' is not empty
The string '' is empty
The string '' is empty
$
```

This example creates two string variables. The val1 variable contains a string, and the val2 variable is created as an empty string. The following comparisons are made as shown below:

```
if [ -n $val1 ]
```

The preceding code determines whether the val1 variable is non-zero in length, which it is, so its then section is processed.

```
if [ -z $var2 ]
```

This preceding code determines whether the val2 variable is zero in length, which it is, so its then section is processed.

```
if [ -z $val3 ]
```

The preceding determines whether the val3 variable is zero in length. This variable was never defined in the shell script, so it indicates that the string length is still zero, even though it wasn't defined.

> **TIP**
>
> Empty and uninitialized variables can have catastrophic effects on your shell script tests. If you're not sure of the contents of a variable, it's always best to test if the variable contains a value using -n or -z before using it in a numeric or string comparison.

Using file comparisons

The last category of test comparisons is quite possibly the most powerful and most used comparisons in shell scripting. This category allows you to test the status of files and directories on the Linux filesystem. Table 12-3 lists these comparisons.

TABLE 12-3   The test File Comparisons

Comparison	Description
-d file	Checks if file exists and is a directory
-e file	Checks if file exists
-f file	Checks if file exists and is a file

Continues

TABLE 12.3   *(continued)*

Comparison	Description
-r file	Checks if file exists and is readable
-s file	Checks if file exists and is not empty
-w file	Checks if file exists and is writable
-x file	Checks if file exists and is executable
-O file	Checks if file exists and is owned by the current user
-G file	Checks if file exists and the default group is the same as the current user
file1 -nt file2	Checks if file1 is newer than file2
file1 -ot file2	Checks if file1 is older than file2

These conditions give you the ability to check filesystem files within shell scripts. They are often used in scripts that access files. Because they're used so often, let's look at each of these individually.

Checking directories

The -d test checks to see if a specified directory exists on the system. This is usually a good thing to do if you're trying to write a file to a directory or before you try to change to a directory location:

```
$ cat test11.sh
#!/bin/bash
# Look before you leap
#
jump_directory=/home/arthur
#
if [ -d $jump_directory ]
then
    echo "The $jump_directory directory exists"
    cd $jump_directory
    ls
else
    echo "The $jump_directory directory does not exist"
fi
#
$
$ ./test11.sh
The /home/arthur directory does not exist
$
```

The -d test condition checks to see if the jump_directory variable's directory exists. If it does, it proceeds to use the cd command to change to the current directory and performs a directory listing. If it does not, the script emits a warning message and exits the script.

Checking whether an object exists

The -e comparison allows you to check if either a file or directory object exists before you attempt to use it in your script:

```
$ cat test12.sh
#!/bin/bash
# Check if either a directory or file exists
#
location=$HOME
file_name="sentinel"
#
if [ -e $location ]
then   #Directory does exist
    echo "OK on the $location directory."
    echo "Now checking on the file, $file_name."
    #
    if [ -e $location/$file_name ]
    then #File does exist
        echo "OK on the filename"
        echo "Updating Current Date..."
        date >> $location/$file_name
    #
    else #File does not exist
        echo "File does not exist"
        echo "Nothing to update"
    fi
#
else   #Directory does not exist
    echo "The $location directory does not exist."
    echo "Nothing to update"
fi
#
$
$ ./test12.sh
OK on the /home/Christine directory.
Now checking on the file, sentinel.
File does not exist
Nothing to update
$
$ touch sentinel
$
$ ./test12.sh
OK on the /home/Christine directory.
Now checking on the file, sentinel.
OK on the filename
Updating Current Date...
$
```

The first check uses the -e comparison to determine whether the user has a *$HOME* directory. If so, the next -e comparison checks to determine whether the sentinel file exists in the *$HOME* directory. If the file doesn't exist, the shell script notes that the file is missing and that there is nothing to update.

To ensure that the update will work, the sentinel file was created and the shell script was run a second time. This time when the conditions are tested, both the $HOME and the sentinel file are found, and the current date and time is appended to the file.

Checking for a file

The -e comparison works for both files and directories. To be sure that the object specified is a file and not a directory, you must use the -f comparison:

```
$ cat test13.sh
#!/bin/bash
# Check if either a directory or file exists
#
item_name=$HOME
echo
echo "The item being checked: $item_name"
echo
#
if [ -e $item_name ]
then #Item does exist
    echo "The item, $item_name, does exist."
    echo "But is it a file?"
    echo
    #
    if [ -f $item_name ]
    then #Item is a file
        echo "Yes, $item_name is a file."
    #
    else #Item is not a file
        echo "No, $item_name is not a file."
    fi
#
else   #Item does not exist
    echo "The item, $item_name, does not exist."
    echo "Nothing to update"
fi
#
$ ./test13.sh

The item being checked: /home/Christine

The item, /home/Christine, does exist.
But is it a file?

No, /home/Christine is not a file.
$
```

This little script does lots of checking! First, it uses the -e comparison to test whether *$HOME* exists. If it does, it uses -f to test whether it's a file. If it isn't a file (which of course it isn't), a message is displayed stating that it is not a file.

A slight modification to the variable, item_name, replacing the directory $HOME with a file, $HOME/sentinel, causes a different outcome:

```
$ nano test13.sh
$
$ cat test13.sh
#!/bin/bash
# Check if either a directory or file exists
#
item_name=$HOME/sentinel
[...]
$
$ ./test13.sh

The item being checked: /home/Christine/sentinel

The item, /home/Christine/sentinel, does exist.
But is it a file?

Yes, /home/Christine/sentinel is a file.
$
```

The test13.sh script listing is snipped, because the only item changed in the shell script was the item_name variable's value. Now when the script is run, the -f test on $HOME/ sentinel exits with a zero status, triggering the then statement, which in turn outputs the message Yes, /home/Christine/sentinel is a file.

Checking for read access

Before trying to read data from a file, it's usually a good idea to test whether you can read from the file first. You do this with the -r comparison:

```
$ cat test14.sh
#!/bin/bash
# testing if you can read a file
pwfile=/etc/shadow
#
# first, test if the file exists, and is a file
if [ -f $pwfile ]
then
    # now test if you can read it
    if [ -r $pwfile ]
```

```
    then
        tail $pwfile
    else
        echo "Sorry, I am unable to read the $pwfile file"
    fi
else
    echo "Sorry, the file $file does not exist"
fi
$
$ ./test14.sh
Sorry, I am unable to read the /etc/shadow file
$
```

The /etc/shadow file contains the encrypted passwords for system users, so it's not readable by normal users on the system. The -r comparison determined that read access to the file wasn't allowed, so the test command failed and the bash shell executed the else section of the if-then statement.

Checking for empty files

You should use -s comparison to check whether a file is empty, especially if you don't want to remove a non-empty file. Be careful because when the -s comparison succeeds, it indicates that a file has data in it:

```
$ cat test15.sh
#!/bin/bash
# Testing if a file is empty
#
file_name=$HOME/sentinel
#
if [ -f $file_name ]
then
    if [ -s $file_name ]
    then
        echo "The $file_name file exists and has data in it."
        echo "Will not remove this file."
#
    else
        echo "The $file_name file exists, but is empty."
        echo "Deleting empty file..."
        rm $file_name
    fi
else
    echo "File, $file_name, does not exist."
fi
#
$ ls -l $HOME/sentinel
-rw-rw-r--. 1 Christine Christine 29 Jun 25 05:32 /home/Christine/sentinel
```

```
$
$ ./test15.sh
The /home/Christine/sentinel file exists and has data in it.
Will not remove this file.
$
```

First, the -f comparison tests whether the file exists. If it does exist, the -s comparison is triggered to determine whether the file is empty. An empty file will be deleted. You can see from the ls -l that the sentinel file is not empty, and therefore the script does not delete it.

Checking whether you can write to a file

The -w comparison determines whether you have permission to write to a file. The test16.sh script is simply an update of the test13.sh script. Now instead of just checking whether the item_name exists and is a file, the script also checks to see whether it has permission to write to the file:

```
$ cat test16.sh
#!/bin/bash
# Check if a file is writable.
#
item_name=$HOME/sentinel
echo
echo "The item being checked: $item_name"
echo
[...]
        echo "Yes, $item_name is a file."
        echo "But is it writable?"
        echo
        #
        if [ -w $item_name ]
        then #Item is writable
            echo "Writing current time to $item_name"
            date +%H%M >> $item_name
        #
        else #Item is not writable
            echo "Unable to write to $item_name"
        fi
    #
    else #Item is not a file
        echo "No, $item_name is not a file."
    fi
[...]
$
$ ls -l sentinel
-rw-rw-r--. 1 Christine Christine 0 Jun 27 05:38 sentinel
$
```

12

```
$ ./test16.sh

The item being checked: /home/Christine/sentinel

The item, /home/Christine/sentinel, does exist.
But is it a file?

Yes, /home/Christine/sentinel is a file.
But is it writable?

Writing current time to /home/Christine/sentinel
$
$ cat sentinel
0543
$
```

The item_name variable is set to $HOME/sentinel, and this file allows user write access (see Chapter 7 for more information on file permissions). Thus, when the script is run, the -w test expressions returns a non-zero exit status and the then code block is executed, which writes a time stamp into the sentinel file.

When the sentinel file user's write access is removed via chmod, the -w test expression returns a non-zero status, and a time stamp is not written to the file:

```
$ chmod u-w sentinel
$
$ ls -l sentinel
-r--rw-r--. 1 Christine Christine 5 Jun 27 05:43 sentinel
$
$ ./test16.sh

The item being checked: /home/Christine/sentinel

The item, /home/Christine/sentinel, does exist.
But is it a file?

Yes, /home/Christine/sentinel is a file.
But is it writable?

Unable to write to /home/Christine/sentinel
$
```

The chmod command could be used again to grant the write permission back for the user. This would make the write test expression return a zero exit status and allow a write attempt to the file.

Checking whether you can run a file

The -x comparison is a handy way to determine whether you have execute permission for a specific file. Although this may not be needed for most commands, if you run lots of scripts from your shell scripts, it could be useful:

```
$ cat test17.sh
#!/bin/bash
# testing file execution
#
if [ -x test16.sh ]
then
    echo "You can run the script: "
    ./test16.sh
else
    echo "Sorry, you are unable to execute the script"
fi
$
$ ./test17.sh
You can run the script:
[...]
$
$ chmod u-x test16.sh
$
$ ./test17.sh
Sorry, you are unable to execute the script
$
```

This example shell script uses the -x comparison to test whether you have permission to execute the test16.sh script. If so, it runs the script. After successfully running the test16.sh script the first time, the permissions were changed. This time, the -x comparison failed, because execute permission had been removed for the test16.sh script.

Checking ownership

The -O comparison allows you to easily test whether you're the owner of a file:

```
$ cat test18.sh
#!/bin/bash
# check file ownership
#
if [ -O /etc/passwd ]
then
    echo "You are the owner of the /etc/passwd file"
else
    echo "Sorry, you are not the owner of the /etc/passwd file"
fi
```

12

```
$
$ ./test18.sh
Sorry, you are not the owner of the /etc/passwd file
$
```

The script uses the -O comparison to test whether the user running the script is the owner of the /etc/passwd file. The script is run under a normal user account, so the test fails.

Checking default group membership

The -G comparison checks the default group of a file, and it succeeds if it matches the group of the default group for the user. This can be somewhat confusing because the -G comparison checks the default groups only and not all the groups to which the user belongs. Here's an example of this:

```
$ cat test19.sh
#!/bin/bash
# check file group test
#
if [ -G $HOME/testing ]
then
    echo "You are in the same group as the file"
else
    echo "The file is not owned by your group"
fi
$
$ ls -l $HOME/testing
-rw-rw-r-- 1 rich rich 58 2014-07-30 15:51 /home/rich/testing
$
$ ./test19.sh
You are in the same group as the file
$
$ chgrp sharing $HOME/testing
$
$ ./test19
The file is not owned by your group
$
```

The first time the script is run, the *$HOME/testing* file is in the rich group, and the -G comparison succeeds. Next, the group is changed to the sharing group, of which the user is also a member. However, the -G comparison failed, because it compares only the default groups, not any additional group memberships.

Checking file date

The last set of comparisons deal with comparing the creation times of two files. This comes in handy when writing scripts to install software. Sometimes, you don't want to install a file that is older than a file already installed on the system.

The -nt comparison determines whether a file is newer than another file. If a file is newer, it has a more recent file creation time. The -ot comparison determines whether a file is older than another file. If the file is older, it has an older file creation time:

```
$ cat test20.sh
#!/bin/bash
# testing file dates
#
if [ test19.sh -nt test18.sh ]
then
    echo "The test19 file is newer than test18"
else
    echo "The test18 file is newer than test19"
fi
if [ test17.sh -ot test19.sh ]
then
   echo "The test17 file is older than the test19 file"
fi
$
$ ./test20.sh
The test19 file is newer than test18
The test17 file is older than the test19 file
$
$ ls -l test17.sh test18.sh test19.sh
-rwxrw-r-- 1 rich rich 167 2014-07-30 16:31 test17.sh
-rwxrw-r-- 1 rich rich 185 2014-07-30 17:46 test18.sh
-rwxrw-r-- 1 rich rich 167 2014-07-30 17:50 test19.sh
$
```

The file paths used in the comparisons are relative to the directory from which you run the script. This can cause problems if the files being checked are moved around. Another problem is that neither of these comparisons checks whether the file exists first. Try this test:

```
$ cat test21.sh
#!/bin/bash
# testing file dates
#
if [ badfile1 -nt badfile2 ]
then
    echo "The badfile1 file is newer than badfile2"
else
    echo "The badfile2 file is newer than badfile1"
fi
$
$ ./test21.sh
The badfile2 file is newer than badfile1
$
```

This little example demonstrates that if the files don't exist, the -nt comparison just returns a failed condition. It's imperative to ensure that the files exist before trying to use them in the -nt or -ot comparison.

Considering Compound Testing

The if-then statement allows you to use Boolean logic to combine tests. You can use these two Boolean operators:

- [condition1] && [condition2]
- [condition1] || [condition2]

The first Boolean operation uses the AND Boolean operator to combine two conditions. Both conditions must be met for the then section to execute.

> **TIP**
> Boolean logic is a method that reduces the potential returned values to be either TRUE or FALSE.

The second Boolean operation uses the OR Boolean operator to combine two conditions. If either condition evaluates to a TRUE condition, the then section is executed.

The following shows the AND Boolean operator in use:

```
$ cat test22.sh
#!/bin/bash
# testing compound comparisons
#
if [ -d $HOME ] && [ -w $HOME/testing ]
then
    echo "The file exists and you can write to it"
else
    echo "I cannot write to the file"
fi
$
$ ./test22.sh
I cannot write to the file
$
$ touch $HOME/testing
$
$ ./test22.sh
The file exists and you can write to it
$
```

Using the AND Boolean operator, both of the comparisons must be met. The first comparison checks to see if the *$HOME* directory exists for the user. The second comparison checks to see if there's a file called `testing` in the user's *$HOME* directory, and if the user has write permissions for the file. If either of these comparisons fails, the `if` statement fails and the shell executes the `else` section. If both of the comparisons succeed, the `if` statement succeeds, and the shell executes the `then` section.

Working with Advanced if-then Features

Two additions to the bash shell provide advanced features that you can use in `if-then` statements:

- Double parentheses for mathematical expressions
- Double square brackets for advanced string handling functions

The following sections describe each of these features in more detail.

Using double parentheses

The *double parentheses* command allows you to incorporate advanced mathematical formulas in your comparisons. The `test` command allows for only simple arithmetic operations in the comparison. The double parentheses command provides more mathematical symbols, which programmers who have used other programming languages may be familiar with using. Here's the format of the double parentheses command:

```
(( expression ))
```

The *expression* term can be any mathematical assignment or comparison expression. Besides the standard mathematical operators that the `test` command uses, Table 12-4 shows the list of additional operators available for use in the double parentheses command.

TABLE 12-4 **The Double Parentheses Command Symbols**

Symbol	Description
`val++`	Post-increment
`val--`	Post-decrement
`++val`	Pre-increment
`--val`	Pre-decrement
`!`	Logical negation
`~`	Bitwise negation
`**`	Exponentiation

Continues

TABLE 12.4   *(continued)*

Symbol	Description
<<	Left bitwise shift
>>	Right bitwise shift
&	Bitwise Boolean AND
|	Bitwise Boolean OR
&&	Logical AND
||	Logical OR

You can use the double parentheses command in an `if` statement, as well as in a normal command in the script for assigning values:

```
$ cat test23.sh
#!/bin/bash
# using double parenthesis
#
val1=10
#
if (( $val1 ** 2 > 90 ))
then
   (( val2 = $val1 ** 2 ))
   echo "The square of $val1 is $val2"
fi
$
$ ./test23.sh
The square of 10 is 100
$
```

Notice that you don't need to escape the greater-than symbol in the expression within the double parentheses. This is yet another advanced feature besides the double parentheses command.

Using double brackets

The *double bracket* command provides advanced features for string comparisons. Here's the double bracket command format:

```
[[ expression ]]
```

The double bracketed *expression* uses the standard string comparison used in the test evaluations. However, it provides an additional feature that the test evaluations don't — *pattern matching*.

> **NOTE**
> Double brackets work fine in the bash shell. Be aware, however, that not all shells support double brackets.

In pattern matching, you can define a regular expression (discussed in detail in Chapter 20) that's matched against the string value:

```
$ cat test24.sh
#!/bin/bash
# using pattern matching
#
if [[ $USER == r* ]]
then
    echo "Hello $USER"
else
    echo "Sorry, I do not know you"
fi
$
$ ./test24.sh
Hello rich
$
```

Notice in the preceding script that double equal signs (==) are used. These double equal signs designate the string to the right (r*) as a pattern, and pattern matching rules are applied. The double bracket command matches the *$USER* environment variable to see whether it starts with the letter r. If so, the comparison succeeds, and the shell executes the then section commands.

Considering the case Command

Often, you'll find yourself trying to evaluate a variable's value, looking for a specific value within a set of possible values. In this scenario, you end up having to write a lengthy if-then-else statement, like this:

```
$ cat test25.sh
#!/bin/bash
# looking for a possible value
#
if [ $USER = "rich" ]
then
    echo "Welcome $USER"
    echo "Please enjoy your visit"
elif [ $USER = "barbara" ]
then
    echo "Welcome $USER"
    echo "Please enjoy your visit"
elif [ $USER = "testing" ]
then
    echo "Special testing account"
elif [ $USER = "jessica" ]
```

```
then
   echo "Do not forget to logout when you're done"
else
   echo "Sorry, you are not allowed here"
fi
$
$ ./test25.sh
Welcome rich
Please enjoy your visit
$
```

The elif statements continue the if-then checking, looking for a specific value for the single comparison variable.

Instead of having to write all the elif statements to continue checking the same variable value, you can use the case command. The case command checks multiple values of a single variable in a list-oriented format:

```
case variable in
pattern1 | pattern2) commands1;;
pattern3) commands2;;
*) default commands;;
esac
```

The case command compares the variable specified against the different patterns. If the variable matches the pattern, the shell executes the commands specified for the pattern. You can list more than one pattern on a line, using the bar operator to separate each pattern. The asterisk symbol is the catch-all for values that don't match any of the listed patterns. Here's an example of converting the if-then-else program to using the case command:

```
$ cat test26.sh
#!/bin/bash
# using the case command
#
case $USER in
rich | barbara)
   echo "Welcome, $USER"
   echo "Please enjoy your visit";;
testing)
   echo "Special testing account";;
jessica)
   echo "Do not forget to log off when you're done";;
*)
   echo "Sorry, you are not allowed here";;
esac
$
$ ./test26.sh
```

```
Welcome, rich
Please enjoy your visit
$
```

The case command provides a much cleaner way of specifying the various options for each possible variable value.

Summary

Structured commands allow you to alter the normal flow of shell script execution. The most basic structured command is the if-then statement. This statement provides a command evaluation and performs other commands based on the evaluated command's output.

You can expand the if-then statement to include a set of commands the bash shell executes if the specified command fails as well. The if-then-else statement executes commands only if the command being evaluated returns a non-zero exit status code.

You can also link if-then-else statements together, using the elif statement. The elif is equivalent to using an else if statement, providing for additional checking of whether the original command that was evaluated failed.

In most scripts, instead of evaluating a command, you'll want to evaluate a condition, such as a numeric value, the contents of a string, or the status of a file or directory. The test command provides an easy way for you to evaluate all these conditions. If the condition evaluates to a TRUE condition, the test command produces a zero exit status code for the if-then statement. If the condition evaluates to a FALSE condition, the test command produces a non-zero exit status code for the if-then statement.

The square bracket is a special bash command that is a synonym for the test command. You can enclose a test condition in square brackets in the if-then statement to test for numeric, string, and file conditions.

The double parentheses command provides advanced mathematical evaluations using additional operators. The double square bracket command allows you to perform advanced string pattern-matching evaluations.

Finally, the chapter discussed the case command, which is a shorthand way of performing multiple if-then-else commands, checking the value of a single variable against a list of values.

The next chapter continues the discussion of structured commands by examining the shell looping commands. The for and while commands let you create loops that iterate through commands for a given period of time.

More Structured Commands

In the previous chapter, you saw how to manipulate the flow of a shell script program by checking the output of commands and the values of variables. In this chapter, we continue to look at structured commands that control the flow of your shell scripts. You'll see how you can perform repeating processes, commands that can loop through a set of commands until an indicated condition has been met. This chapter discusses and demonstrates the for, while, and until bash shell looping commands.

The for Command

Iterating through a series of commands is a common programming practice. Often, you need to repeat a set of commands until a specific condition has been met, such as processing all the files in a directory, all the users on a system, or all the lines in a text file.

The bash shell provides the for command to allow you to create a loop that iterates through a series of values. Each iteration performs a defined set of commands using one of the values in the series. Here's the basic format of the bash shell for command:

```
for var in list
do
    commands
done
```

You supply the series of values used in the iterations in the *list* parameter. You can specify the values in the list in several ways.

In each iteration, the variable *var* contains the current value in the list. The first iteration uses the first item in the list, the second iteration the second item, and so on until all the items in the list have been used.

The *commands* entered between the do and done statements can be one or more standard bash shell commands. Within the commands, the $var variable contains the current list item value for the iteration.

> **NOTE**
>
> If you prefer, you can include the do statement on the same line as the for statement, but you must separate it from the list items using a semicolon: for var in list; do.

We mentioned that there are several different ways to specify the values in the list. The following sections show the various ways to do that.

Reading values in a list

The most basic use of the for command is to iterate through a list of values defined within the for command itself:

```
$ cat test1
#!/bin/bash
# basic for command

for test in Alabama Alaska Arizona Arkansas California Colorado
do
    echo The next state is $test
done
$ ./test1
The next state is Alabama
The next state is Alaska
The next state is Arizona
The next state is Arkansas
The next state is California
The next state is Colorado
$
```

Each time the for command iterates through the list of values provided, it assigns the $test variable the next value in the list. The $test variable can be used just like any other script variable within the for command statements. After the last iteration, the $test variable remains valid throughout the remainder of the shell script. It retains the last iteration value (unless you change its value):

```
$ cat test1b
#!/bin/bash
```

```
# testing the for variable after the looping
for test in Alabama Alaska Arizona Arkansas California Colorado
do
    echo "The next state is $test"
done
echo "The last state we visited was $test"
test=Connecticut
echo "Wait, now we're visiting $test"
$ ./test1b
The next state is Alabama
The next state is Alaska
The next state is Arizona
The next state is Arkansas
The next state is California
The next state is Colorado
The last state we visited was Colorado
Wait, now we're visiting Connecticut
$
```

The $test variable retained its value and allowed us to change the value and use it outside of the for command loop, as any other variable would.

Reading complex values in a list

Things aren't always as easy as they seem with the for loop. There are times when you run into data that causes problems. Here's a classic example of what can cause problems for shell script programmers:

```
$ cat badtest1
#!/bin/bash
# another example of how not to use the for command

for test in I don't know if this'll work
do
    echo "word:$test"
done
$ ./badtest1
word:I
word:dont know if thisll
word:work
$
```

Ouch, that hurts. The shell saw the single quotation marks within the list values and attempted to use them to define a single data value, and it really messed things up in the process.

You have two ways to solve this problem:

- Use the escape character (the backslash) to escape the single quotation mark.
- Use double quotation marks to define the values that use single quotation marks.

Neither solution is all that fantastic, but each one helps solve the problem:

```
$ cat test2
#!/bin/bash
# another example of how not to use the for command

for test in I don\'t know if "this'll" work
do
    echo "word:$test"
done
$ ./test2
word:I
word:don't
word:know
word:if
word:this'll
word:work
$
```

In the first problem value, you added the backslash character to escape the single quotation mark in the don't value. In the second problem value, you enclosed the this'll value in double quotation marks. Both methods worked fine to distinguish the value.

Another problem you may run into is multi-word values. Remember that the for loop assumes that each value is separated with a space. If you have data values that contain spaces, you run into yet another problem:

```
$ cat badtest2
#!/bin/bash
# another example of how not to use the for command

for test in Nevada New Hampshire New Mexico New York North Carolina
do
    echo "Now going to $test"
done
$ ./badtest1
Now going to Nevada
Now going to New
Now going to Hampshire
Now going to New
Now going to Mexico
Now going to New
Now going to York
```

```
Now going to North
Now going to Carolina
$
```

Oops, that's not exactly what we wanted. The `for` command separates each value in the list with a space. If there are spaces in the individual data values, you must accommodate them using double quotation marks:

```
$ cat test3
#!/bin/bash
# an example of how to properly define values

for test in Nevada "New Hampshire" "New Mexico" "New York"
do
    echo "Now going to $test"
done
$ ./test3
Now going to Nevada
Now going to New Hampshire
Now going to New Mexico
Now going to New York
$
```

Now the `for` command can properly distinguish between the different values. Also, notice that when you use double quotation marks around a value, the shell doesn't include the quotation marks as part of the value.

Reading a list from a variable

Often what happens in a shell script is that you accumulate a list of values stored in a variable and then need to iterate through the list. You can do this using the `for` command as well:

```
$ cat test4
#!/bin/bash
# using a variable to hold the list

list="Alabama Alaska Arizona Arkansas Colorado"
list=$list" Connecticut"

for state in $list
do
    echo "Have you ever visited $state?"
done
$ ./test4
Have you ever visited Alabama?
Have you ever visited Alaska?
Have you ever visited Arizona?
```

13

```
Have you ever visited Arkansas?
Have you ever visited Colorado?
Have you ever visited Connecticut?
$
```

The $list variable contains the standard text list of values to use for the iterations. Notice that the code also uses another assignment statement to add (or concatenate) an item to the existing list contained in the $list variable. This is a common method for adding text to the end of an existing text string stored in a variable.

Reading values from a command

Another way to generate values for use in the list is to use the output of a command. You use command substitution to execute any command that produces output and then use the output of the command in the for command:

```
$ cat test5
#!/bin/bash
# reading values from a file

file="states"

for state in $(cat $file)
do
    echo "Visit beautiful $state"
done
$ cat states
Alabama
Alaska
Arizona
Arkansas
Colorado
Connecticut
Delaware
Florida
Georgia
$ ./test5
Visit beautiful Alabama
Visit beautiful Alaska
Visit beautiful Arizona
Visit beautiful Arkansas
Visit beautiful Colorado
Visit beautiful Connecticut
Visit beautiful Delaware
Visit beautiful Florida
Visit beautiful Georgia
$
```

This example uses the `cat` command in the command substitution to display the contents of the file states. Notice that the states file includes each state on a separate line, not separated by spaces. The `for` command still iterates through the output of the `cat` command one line at a time, assuming that each state is on a separate line. However, this doesn't solve the problem of having spaces in data. If you list a state with a space in it, the `for` command still takes each word as a separate value. There's a reason for this, which we look at in the next section.

> **NOTE**
>
> The `test5` code example assigned the filename to the variable using just the filename without a path. This requires that the file be in the same directory as the script. If this isn't the case, you need to use a full pathname (either absolute or relative) to reference the file location.

Changing the field separator

The cause of this problem is the special environment variable IFS, called the *internal field separator*. The IFS environment variable defines a list of characters the bash shell uses as field separators. By default, the bash shell considers the following characters as field separators:

- A space
- A tab
- A newline

If the bash shell sees any of these characters in the data, it assumes that you're starting a new data field in the list. When working with data that can contain spaces (such as filenames), this can be annoying, as you saw in the previous script example.

To solve this problem, you can temporarily change the IFS environment variable values in your shell script to restrict the characters the bash shell recognizes as field separators. For example, if you want to change the IFS value to recognize only the newline character, you need to do this:

```
IFS=$'\n'
```

Adding this statement to your script tells the bash shell to ignore spaces and tabs in data values. Applying this technique to the previous script yields the following:

```
$ cat test5b
#!/bin/bash
# reading values from a file

file="states"

IFS=$'\n'
```

```
for state in $(cat $file)
do
    echo "Visit beautiful $state"
done
$ ./test5b
Visit beautiful Alabama
Visit beautiful Alaska
Visit beautiful Arizona
Visit beautiful Arkansas
Visit beautiful Colorado
Visit beautiful Connecticut
Visit beautiful Delaware
Visit beautiful Florida
Visit beautiful Georgia
Visit beautiful New York
Visit beautiful New Hampshire
Visit beautiful North Carolina
$
```

Now the shell script can use values in the list that contain spaces.

CAUTION

When working on long scripts, it's possible to change the IFS value in one place, and then forget about it and assume the default value elsewhere in the script. A safe practice to get into is to save the original IFS value before changing it and then restore it when you're finished.

This technique can be coded like this:

```
IFS.OLD=$IFS
IFS=$'\n'
<use the new IFS value in code>
IFS=$IFS.OLD
```

This ensures that the IFS value is returned to the default value for future operations within the script.

Other excellent applications of the IFS environment variable are possible. Suppose you want to iterate through values in a file that are separated by a colon (such as in the /etc/passwd file). You just need to set the IFS value to a colon:

```
IFS=:
```

If you want to specify more than one IFS character, just string them together on the assignment line:

```
IFS=$'\n':;"
```

This assignment uses the newline, colon, semicolon, and double quotation mark characters as field separators. There's no limit to how you can parse your data using the IFS characters.

Reading a directory using wildcards

Finally, you can use the `for` command to automatically iterate through a directory of files. To do this, you must use a wildcard character in the file or pathname. This forces the shell to use *file globbing*. File globbing is the process of producing filenames or pathnames that match a specified wildcard character.

This feature is great for processing files in a directory when you don't know all the filenames:

```
$ cat test6
#!/bin/bash
# iterate through all the files in a directory

for file in /home/rich/test/*
do

   if [ -d "$file" ]
   then
      echo "$file is a directory"
   elif [ -f "$file" ]
   then
      echo "$file is a file"
   fi
done
$ ./test6
/home/rich/test/dir1 is a directory
/home/rich/test/myprog.c is a file
/home/rich/test/myprog is a file
/home/rich/test/myscript is a file
/home/rich/test/newdir is a directory
/home/rich/test/newfile is a file
/home/rich/test/newfile2 is a file
/home/rich/test/testdir is a directory
/home/rich/test/testing is a file
/home/rich/test/testprog is a file
/home/rich/test/testprog.c is a file
$
```

The `for` command iterates through the results of the `/home/rich/test/*` listing. The code tests each entry using the `test` command (using the square bracket method) to see if it's a directory, using the `-d` parameter, or a file, using the `-f` parameter (See Chapter 12).

Notice in this example that we did something different in the `if` statement tests:

```
if [ -d "$file" ]
```

In Linux, it's perfectly legal to have directory and filenames that contain spaces. To accommodate that, you should enclose the $file variable in double quotation marks. If you don't, you'll get an error if you run into a directory or filename that contains spaces:

```
./test6: line 6: [: too many arguments
./test6: line 9: [: too many arguments
```

The bash shell interprets the additional words as arguments within the test command, causing an error.

You can also combine both the directory search method and the list method in the same for statement by listing a series of directory wildcards in the for command:

```
$ cat test7
#!/bin/bash
# iterating through multiple directories

for file in /home/rich/.b* /home/rich/badtest
do
    if [ -d "$file" ]
    then
        echo "$file is a directory"
    elif [ -f "$file" ]
    then
        echo "$file is a file"
    else
        echo "$file doesn't exist"
    fi
done
$ ./test7
/home/rich/.backup.timestamp is a file
/home/rich/.bash_history is a file
/home/rich/.bash_logout is a file
/home/rich/.bash_profile is a file
/home/rich/.bashrc is a file
/home/rich/badtest doesn't exist
$
```

The for statement first uses file globbing to iterate through the list of files that result from the wildcard character; then it iterates through the next file in the list. You can combine any number of wildcard entries in the list to iterate through.

CAUTION

Notice that you can enter anything in the list data. Even if the file or directory doesn't exist, the for statement attempts to process whatever you place in the list. This can be a problem when working with files and directories. You have no way of knowing if you're trying to iterate through a nonexistent directory: It's always a good idea to test each file or directory before trying to process it.

The C-Style for Command

If you've done any programming using the C programming language, you're probably surprised by the way the bash shell uses the for command. In the C language, a for loop normally defines a variable, which it then alters automatically during each iteration. Typically, programmers use this variable as a counter and either increment or decrement the counter by one in each iteration. The bash for command can also provide this functionality. This section shows you how to use a C-style for command in a bash shell script.

The C language for command

The C language for command has a specific method for specifying a variable, a condition that must remain true for the iterations to continue, and a method for altering the variable for each iteration. When the specified condition becomes false, the for loop stops. The condition equation is defined using standard mathematical symbols. For example, consider the following C language code:

```
for (i = 0; i < 10; i++)
{
    printf("The next number is %d\n", i);
}
```

This code produces a simple iteration loop, where the variable i is used as a counter. The first section assigns a default value to the variable. The middle section defines the condition under which the loop will iterate. When the defined condition becomes false, the for loop stops iterations. The last section defines the iteration process. After each iteration, the expression defined in the last section is executed. In this example, the i variable is incremented by one after each iteration.

The bash shell also supports a version of the for loop that looks similar to the C-style for loop, although it does have some subtle differences, including a couple of things that will confuse shell script programmers. Here's the basic format of the C-style bash for loop:

```
for (( variable assignment ; condition ; iteration process ))
```

The format of the C-style for loop can be confusing for bash shell script programmers, because it uses C-style variable references instead of the shell-style variable references. Here's what a C-style for command looks like:

```
for (( a = 1; a < 10; a++ ))
```

Notice that there are a couple of things that don't follow the standard bash shell for method:

- The assignment of the variable value can contain spaces.
- The variable in the condition isn't preceded with a dollar sign.
- The equation for the iteration process doesn't use the expr command format.

The shell developers created this format to more closely resemble the C-style `for` command. Although this is great for C programmers, it can throw even expert shell programmers into a tizzy. Be careful when using the C-style `for` loop in your scripts.

Here's an example of using the C-style `for` command in a bash shell program:

```
$ cat test8
#!/bin/bash
# testing the C-style for loop

for (( i=1; i <= 10; i++ ))
do
    echo "The next number is $i"
done
$ ./test8
The next number is 1
The next number is 2
The next number is 3
The next number is 4
The next number is 5
The next number is 6
The next number is 7
The next number is 8
The next number is 9
The next number is 10
$
```

The `for` loop iterates through the commands using the variable defined in the `for` loop (the letter *i* in this example). In each iteration, the $i variable contains the value assigned in the `for` loop. After each iteration, the loop iteration process is applied to the variable, which in this example, increments the variable by one.

Using multiple variables

The C-style `for` command also allows you to use multiple variables for the iteration. The loop handles each variable separately, allowing you to define a different iteration process for each variable. Although you can have multiple variables, you can define only one condition in the `for` loop:

```
$ cat test9
#!/bin/bash
# multiple variables

for (( a=1, b=10; a <= 10; a++, b-- ))
do
    echo "$a - $b"
done
$ ./test9
```

```
 1 - 10
 2 - 9
 3 - 8
 4 - 7
 5 - 6
 6 - 5
 7 - 4
 8 - 3
 9 - 2
10 - 1
$
```

The a and b variables are each initialized with different values, and different iteration processes are defined. While the loop increases the a variable, it decreases the b variable for each iteration.

The while Command

The while command is somewhat of a cross between the if-then statement and the for loop. The while command allows you to define a command to test and then loop through a set of commands for as long as the defined test command returns a zero exit status. It tests the test command at the start of each iteration. When the test command returns a non-zero exit status, the while command stops executing the set of commands.

Basic while format

Here's fhe format of the while command:

```
while test command
do
 other commands
done
```

The test command defined in the while command is the exact same format as in if-then statements (see Chapter 12). As in the if-then statement, you can use any normal bash shell command, or you can use the test command to test for conditions, such as variable values.

The key to the while command is that the exit status of the test command specified must change, based on the commands run during the loop. If the exit status never changes, the while loop will get stuck in an infinite loop.

The most common use of the test command is to use brackets to check a value of a shell variable that's used in the loop commands:

```
$ cat test10
#!/bin/bash
```

```
# while command test

var1=10
while [ $var1 -gt 0 ]
do
    echo $var1
    var1=$[ $var1 - 1 ]
done
$ ./test10
10
9
8
7
6
5
4
3
2
1
$
```

The while command defines the test condition to check for each iteration:

```
while [ $var1 -gt 0 ]
```

As long as the test condition is true, the while command continues to loop through the commands defined. Within the commands, the variable used in the test condition must be modified, or you'll have an infinite loop. In this example, we use shell arithmetic to decrease the variable value by one:

```
var1=$[ $var1 - 1 ]
```

The while loop stops when the test condition is no longer true.

Using multiple test commands

The while command allows you to define multiple test commands on the while statement line. Only the exit status of the last test command is used to determine when the loop stops. This can cause some interesting results if you're not careful. Here's an example of what we mean:

```
$ cat test11
#!/bin/bash
# testing a multicommand while loop

var1=10

while echo $var1
```

```
        [ $var1 -ge 0 ]
do
    echo "This is inside the loop"
    var1=$[ $var1 - 1 ]
done
$ ./test11
10
This is inside the loop
9
This is inside the loop
8
This is inside the loop
7
This is inside the loop
6
This is inside the loop
5
This is inside the loop
4
This is inside the loop
3
This is inside the loop
2
This is inside the loop
1
This is inside the loop
0
This is inside the loop
-1
$
```

Pay close attention to what happened in this example. Two test commands were defined in the while statement:

```
while echo $var1
      [ $var1 -ge 0 ]
```

The first test simply displays the current value of the var1 variable. The second test uses brackets to determine the value of the var1 variable. Inside the loop, an echo statement displays a simple message, indicating that the loop was processed. Notice when you run the example how the output ends:

```
This is inside the loop
-1
$
```

The while loop executed the echo statement when the var1 variable was equal to zero and then decreased the var1 variable value. Next, the test commands were executed for the next iteration. The echo test command was executed, displaying the value of the var1 variable, which is now less than zero. It's not until the shell executes the test test command that the while loop terminates.

This demonstrates that in a multi-command while statement, all the test commands are executed in each iteration, including the last iteration when the last test command fails. Be careful of this. Another thing to be careful of is how you specify the multiple test commands. Note that each test command is on a separate line!

The until Command

The until command works in exactly the opposite way from the while command. The until command requires that you specify a test command that normally produces a non-zero exit status. As long as the exit status of the test command is non-zero, the bash shell executes the commands listed in the loop. When the test command returns a zero exit status, the loop stops.

As you would expect, the format of the until command is:

```
until test commands
do
    other commands
done
```

Similar to the while command, you can have more than one *test command* in the until command statement. Only the exit status of the last command determines if the bash shell executes the *other commands* defined.

The following is an example of using the until command:

```
$ cat test12
#!/bin/bash
# using the until command

var1=100

until [ $var1 -eq 0 ]
do
    echo $var1
    var1=$[ $var1 - 25 ]
done
$ ./test12
100
75
50
25
$
```

This example tests the var1 variable to determine when the until loop should stop. As soon as the value of the variable is equal to zero, the until command stops the loop. The same caution as for the while command applies when you use multiple test commands with the until command:

```
$ cat test13
#!/bin/bash
# using the until command

var1=100

until echo $var1
      [ $var1 -eq 0 ]
do
    echo Inside the loop: $var1
    var1=$[ $var1 - 25 ]
done
$ ./test13
100
Inside the loop: 100
75
Inside the loop: 75
50
Inside the loop: 50
25
Inside the loop: 25
0
$
```

The shell executes the test commands specified and stops only when the last command is true.

Nesting Loops

A loop statement can use any other type of command within the loop, including other loop commands. This is called a *nested loop*. Care should be taken when using nested loops, because you're performing an iteration within an iteration, which multiplies the number of times commands are being run. If you don't pay close attention to this, it can cause problems in your scripts.

Here's a simple example of nesting a for loop inside another for loop:

```
$ cat test14
#!/bin/bash
```

```
# nesting for loops

for (( a = 1; a <= 3; a++ ))
do
    echo "Starting loop $a:"
    for (( b = 1; b <= 3; b++ ))
    do
        echo "   Inside loop: $b"
    done
done
$ ./test14
Starting loop 1:
    Inside loop: 1
    Inside loop: 2
    Inside loop: 3
Starting loop 2:
    Inside loop: 1
    Inside loop: 2
    Inside loop: 3
Starting loop 3:
    Inside loop: 1
    Inside loop: 2
    Inside loop: 3
$
```

The nested loop (also called the *inner loop*) iterates through its values for each iteration of the outer loop. Notice that there's no difference between the do and done commands for the two loops. The bash shell knows when the first done command is executed that it refers to the inner loop and not the outer loop.

The same applies when you mix loop commands, such as placing a for loop inside a while loop:

```
$ cat test15
#!/bin/bash
# placing a for loop inside a while loop

var1=5

while [ $var1 -ge 0 ]
do
    echo "Outer loop: $var1"
    for (( var2 = 1; $var2 < 3; var2++ ))
    do
        var3=$[ $var1 * $var2 ]
        echo "  Inner loop: $var1 * $var2 = $var3"
    done
    var1=$[ $var1 - 1 ]
done
$ ./test15
```

```
Outer loop: 5
   Inner loop: 5 * 1 = 5
   Inner loop: 5 * 2 = 10
Outer loop: 4
   Inner loop: 4 * 1 = 4
   Inner loop: 4 * 2 = 8
Outer loop: 3
   Inner loop: 3 * 1 = 3
   Inner loop: 3 * 2 = 6
Outer loop: 2
   Inner loop: 2 * 1 = 2
   Inner loop: 2 * 2 = 4
Outer loop: 1
   Inner loop: 1 * 1 = 1
   Inner loop: 1 * 2 = 2
Outer loop: 0
   Inner loop: 0 * 1 = 0
   Inner loop: 0 * 2 = 0
$
```

Again, the shell distinguished between the do and done commands of the inner for loop from the same commands in the outer while loop.

If you really want to test your brain, you can even combine until and while loops:

```
$ cat test16
#!/bin/bash
# using until and while loops

var1=3

until [ $var1 -eq 0 ]
do
    echo "Outer loop: $var1"
    var2=1
    while [ $var2 -lt 5 ]
    do
        var3=$(echo "scale=4; $var1 / $var2" | bc)
        echo "   Inner loop: $var1 / $var2 = $var3"
        var2=$[ $var2 + 1 ]
    done
    var1=$[ $var1 - 1 ]
done
$ ./test16
Outer loop: 3
   Inner loop: 3 / 1 = 3.0000
   Inner loop: 3 / 2 = 1.5000
   Inner loop: 3 / 3 = 1.0000
   Inner loop: 3 / 4 = .7500
```

```
Outer loop: 2
   Inner loop: 2 / 1 = 2.0000
   Inner loop: 2 / 2 = 1.0000
   Inner loop: 2 / 3 = .6666
   Inner loop: 2 / 4 = .5000
Outer loop: 1
   Inner loop: 1 / 1 = 1.0000
   Inner loop: 1 / 2 = .5000
   Inner loop: 1 / 3 = .3333
   Inner loop: 1 / 4 = .2500
$
```

The outer until loop starts with a value of 3 and continues until the value equals 0. The inner while loop starts with a value of 1 and continues as long as the value is less than 5. Each loop must change the value used in the test condition, or the loop will get stuck infinitely.

Looping on File Data

Often, you must iterate through items stored inside a file. This requires combining two of the techniques covered:

- Using nested loops
- Changing the IFS environment variable

By changing the IFS environment variable, you can force the for command to handle each line in the file as a separate item for processing, even if the data contains spaces. After you've extracted an individual line in the file, you may have to loop again to extract data contained within it.

The classic example of this is processing data in the /etc/passwd file. This requires that you iterate through the /etc/passwd file line by line and then change the IFS variable value to a colon so you can separate the individual components in each line.

The following is an example of doing just that:

```
#!/bin/bash
# changing the IFS value

IFS.OLD=$IFS
IFS=$'\n'
for entry in $(cat /etc/passwd)
do
    echo "Values in $entry -"
    IFS=:
    for value in $entry
```

```
    do
        echo "    $value"
    done
done
$
```

This script uses two different IFS values to parse the data. The first IFS value parses the individual lines in the /etc/passwd file. The inner for loop next changes the IFS value to the colon, which allows you to parse the individual values within the /etc/passwd lines.

When you run this script, you get output something like this:

```
Values in rich:x:501:501:Rich Blum:/home/rich:/bin/bash -
    rich
    x
    501
    501
    Rich Blum
    /home/rich
    /bin/bash
Values in katie:x:502:502:Katie Blum:/home/katie:/bin/bash -
    katie
    x
    506
    509
    Katie Blum
    /home/katie
    /bin/bash
```

The inner loop parses each individual value in the /etc/passwd entry. This is also a great way to process comma-separated data, a common way to import spreadsheet data.

Controlling the Loop

You might be tempted to think that after you start a loop, you're stuck until the loop finishes all its iterations. This is not true. A couple of commands help us control what happens inside of a loop:

- The break command
- The continue command

Each command has a different use in how to control the operation of a loop. The following sections describe how you can use these commands to control the operation of your loops.

The break command

The break command is a simple way to escape a loop in progress. You can use the break command to exit any type of loop, including while and until loops.

You can use the break command in several situations. This section shows each of these methods.

Breaking out of a single loop

When the shell executes a break command, it attempts to break out of the loop that's currently processing:

```
$ cat test17
#!/bin/bash
# breaking out of a for loop

for var1 in 1 2 3 4 5 6 7 8 9 10
do
    if [ $var1 -eq 5 ]
    then
        break
    fi
    echo "Iteration number: $var1"
done
echo "The for loop is completed"
$ ./test17
Iteration number: 1
Iteration number: 2
Iteration number: 3
Iteration number: 4
The for loop is completed
$
```

The for loop should normally have iterated through all the values specified in the list. However, when the if-then condition was satisfied, the shell executed the break command, which stopped the for loop.

This technique also works for while and until loops:

```
$ cat test18
#!/bin/bash
# breaking out of a while loop

var1=1

while [ $var1 -lt 10 ]
do
    if [ $var1 -eq 5 ]
```

```
        then
            break
        fi
        echo "Iteration: $var1"
        var1=$[ $var1 + 1 ]
    done
    echo "The while loop is completed"
$ ./test18
Iteration: 1
Iteration: 2
Iteration: 3
Iteration: 4
The while loop is completed
$
```

The while loop terminated when the if-then condition was met, executing the break command.

Breaking out of an inner loop

When you're working with multiple loops, the break command automatically terminates the innermost loop you're in:

```
$ cat test19
#!/bin/bash
# breaking out of an inner loop

for (( a = 1; a < 4; a++ ))
do
    echo "Outer loop: $a"
    for (( b = 1; b < 100; b++ ))
    do
        if [ $b -eq 5 ]
        then
            break
        fi
        echo "   Inner loop: $b"
    done
done
$ ./test19
Outer loop: 1
    Inner loop: 1
    Inner loop: 2
    Inner loop: 3
    Inner loop: 4
Outer loop: 2
    Inner loop: 1
    Inner loop: 2
    Inner loop: 3
```

```
        Inner loop: 4
Outer loop: 3
        Inner loop: 1
        Inner loop: 2
        Inner loop: 3
        Inner loop: 4
$
```

The `for` statement in the inner loop specifies to iterate until the b variable is equal to 100. However, the `if-then` statement in the inner loop specifies that when the b variable value is equal to 5, the `break` command is executed. Notice that even though the inner loop is terminated with the `break` command, the outer loop continues working as specified.

Breaking out of an outer loop

There may be times when you're in an inner loop but need to stop the outer loop. The `break` command includes a single command line parameter value:

```
break n
```

where *n* indicates the level of the loop to break out of. By default, *n* is 1, indicating to break out of the current loop. If you set *n* to a value of 2, the `break` command stops the next level of the outer loop:

```
$ cat test20
#!/bin/bash
# breaking out of an outer loop

for (( a = 1; a < 4; a++ ))
do
    echo "Outer loop: $a"
    for (( b = 1; b < 100; b++ ))
    do
        if [ $b -gt 4 ]
        then
            break 2
        fi
        echo "    Inner loop: $b"
    done
done
$ ./test20
Outer loop: 1
        Inner loop: 1
        Inner loop: 2
        Inner loop: 3
        Inner loop: 4
$
```

Now when the shell executes the `break` command, the outer loop stops.

The continue command

The continue command is a way to prematurely stop processing commands inside of a loop but not terminate the loop completely. This allows you to set conditions within a loop where the shell won't execute commands. Here's a simple example of using the continue command in a for loop:

```
$ cat test21
#!/bin/bash
# using the continue command

for (( var1 = 1; var1 < 15; var1++ ))
do
    if [ $var1 -gt 5 ] && [ $var1 -lt 10 ]
    then
        continue
    fi
    echo "Iteration number: $var1"
done
$ ./test21
Iteration number: 1
Iteration number: 2
Iteration number: 3
Iteration number: 4
Iteration number: 5
Iteration number: 10
Iteration number: 11
Iteration number: 12
Iteration number: 13
Iteration number: 14
$
```

When the conditions of the if-then statement are met (the value is greater than 5 and less than 10), the shell executes the continue command, which skips the rest of the commands in the loop, but keeps the loop going. When the if-then condition is no longer met, things return to normal.

You can use the continue command in while and until loops, but be extremely careful with what you're doing. Remember that when the shell executes the continue command, it skips the remaining commands. If you're incrementing your test condition variable in one of those conditions, bad things happen:

```
$ cat badtest3
#!/bin/bash
# improperly using the continue command in a while loop

var1=0

while echo "while iteration: $var1"
```

```
        [ $var1 -lt 15 ]
do
    if [ $var1 -gt 5 ] && [ $var1 -lt 10 ]
    then
        continue
    fi
    echo "   Inside iteration number: $var1"
    var1=$[ $var1 + 1 ]
done
$ ./badtest3 | more
while iteration: 0
    Inside iteration number: 0
while iteration: 1
    Inside iteration number: 1
while iteration: 2
    Inside iteration number: 2
while iteration: 3
    Inside iteration number: 3
while iteration: 4
    Inside iteration number: 4
while iteration: 5
    Inside iteration number: 5
while iteration: 6
while iteration: 6
while iteration: 6
while iteration: 6
while iteration: 6
while iteration: 6
while iteration: 6
while iteration: 6
while iteration: 6
while iteration: 6
while iteration: 6
$
```

You'll want to make sure you redirect the output of this script to the more command so you can stop things. Everything seems to be going just fine until the if-then condition is met, and the shell executes the continue command. When the shell executes the continue command, it skips the remaining commands in the while loop. Unfortunately, that's where the $var1 counter variable that is tested in the while test command is incremented. That means that the variable isn't incremented, as you can see from the continually displaying output.

As with the break command, the continue command allows you to specify what level of loop to continue with a command line parameter:

```
continue n
```

where *n* defines the loop level to continue. Here's an example of continuing an outer `for` loop:

```
$ cat test22
#!/bin/bash
# continuing an outer loop

for (( a = 1; a <= 5; a++ ))
do
    echo "Iteration $a:"
    for (( b = 1; b < 3; b++ ))
    do
        if [ $a -gt 2 ] && [ $a -lt 4 ]
        then
            continue 2
        fi
        var3=$[ $a * $b ]
        echo "   The result of $a * $b is $var3"
    done
done
$ ./test22
Iteration 1:
   The result of 1 * 1 is 1
   The result of 1 * 2 is 2
Iteration 2:
   The result of 2 * 1 is 2
   The result of 2 * 2 is 4
Iteration 3:
Iteration 4:
   The result of 4 * 1 is 4
   The result of 4 * 2 is 8
Iteration 5:
   The result of 5 * 1 is 5
   The result of 5 * 2 is 10
$
```

The `if-then` statement:

```
if [ $a -gt 2 ] && [ $a -lt 4 ]
    then
        continue 2
    fi
```

uses the `continue` command to stop processing the commands inside the loop but continue the outer loop. Notice in the script output that the iteration for the value 3 doesn't process any inner loop statements, because the `continue` command stopped the processing, but it continues with the outer loop processing.

Processing the Output of a Loop

Finally, you can either pipe or redirect the output of a loop within your shell script. You do this by adding the processing command to the end of the `done` command:

```
for file in /home/rich/*
 do
    if [ -d "$file" ]
    then
       echo "$file is a directory"
    elif
       echo "$file is a file"
    fi
done > output.txt
```

Instead of displaying the results on the monitor, the shell redirects the results of the `for` command to the file `output.txt`.

Consider the following example of redirecting the output of a `for` command to a file:

```
$ cat test23
#!/bin/bash
# redirecting the for output to a file

for (( a = 1; a < 10; a++ ))
do
    echo "The number is $a"
done > test23.txt
echo "The command is finished."
$ ./test23
The command is finished.
$ cat test23.txt
The number is 1
The number is 2
The number is 3
The number is 4
The number is 5
The number is 6
The number is 7
The number is 8
The number is 9
$
```

The shell creates the file `test23.txt` and redirects the output of the `for` command only to the file. The shell displays the `echo` statement after the `for` command just as normal.

This same technique also works for piping the output of a loop to another command:

```
$ cat test24
#!/bin/bash
```

```
# piping a loop to another command

for state in "North Dakota" Connecticut Illinois Alabama Tennessee
do
    echo "$state is the next place to go"
done | sort
echo "This completes our travels"
$ ./test24
Alabama is the next place to go
Connecticut is the next place to go
Illinois is the next place to go
North Dakota is the next place to go
Tennessee is the next place to go
This completes our travels
$
```

The state values aren't listed in any particular order in the for command list. The output
of the for command is piped to the sort command, which changes the order of the for
command output. Running the script indeed shows that the output was properly sorted
within the script.

Practical Examples

Now that you've seen how to use the different ways to create loops in shell scripts, let's
look at some practical examples of how to use them. Looping is a common way to iterate
through data on the system, whether it's files in folders or data contained in a file. Here are
a couple of examples that demonstrate using simple loops to work with data.

Finding executable files

When you run a program from the command line, the Linux system searches a series of
folders looking for that file. Those folders are defined in the PATH environment variable. If
you want to find out just what executable files are available on your system for you to use,
just scan all the folders in the PATH environment variable. That may take some time to do
manually, but it's a breeze working out a small shell script to do that.

The first step is to create a for loop to iterate through the folders stored in the PATH environment variable. When you do that, don't forget to set the IFS separator character:

```
IFS=:
for folder in $PATH
do
```

Now that you have the individual folders in the $folder variable, you can use another
for loop to iterate through all the files inside that particular folder:

```
for file in $folder/*
do
```

The last step is to check whether the individual files have the executable permission set, which you can do using the if-then test feature:

```
if [ -x $file ]
then
    echo "    $file"
fi
```

And there you have it! Putting all the pieces together into a script looks like this:

```
$ cat test25
#!/bin/bash
# finding files in the PATH

IFS=:
for folder in $PATH
do
    echo "$folder:"
    for file in $folder/*
    do
        if [ -x $file ]
        then
            echo "    $file"
        fi
    done
done
$
```

When you run the code, you get a listing of the executable files that you can use from the command line:

```
$ ./test25 | more
/usr/local/bin:
/usr/bin:
    /usr/bin/Mail
    /usr/bin/Thunar
    /usr/bin/X
    /usr/bin/Xorg
    /usr/bin/[
    /usr/bin/a2p
    /usr/bin/abiword
    /usr/bin/ac
    /usr/bin/activation-client
    /usr/bin/addr2line
...
```

The output shows all the executable files found in all the folders defined in the PATH environment variable, which is quite a few!

Creating multiple user accounts

The goal of shell scripts is to make life easier for the system administrator. If you happen to work in an environment with lots of users, one of the most boring tasks can be creating new user accounts. Fortunately, you can use the while loop to make your job a little easier!

Instead of having to manually enter useradd commands for every new user account you need to create, you can place the new user accounts in a text file and create a simple shell script to do that work for you. The format of the text file that we'll use looks like this:

```
userid,user name
```

The first entry is the userid you want to use for the new user account. The second entry is the full name of the user. The two values are separated by a comma, making this a comma-separated file format, or .csv. This is a very common file format used in spreadsheets, so you can easily create the user account list in a spreadsheet program and save it in .csv format for your shell script to read and process.

To read the file data, we're going to use a little shell scripting trick. We'll actually set the IFS separator character to a comma as the test part of the while statement. Then to read the individual lines, we'll use the read command. That looks like this:

```
while IFS=',' read -r userid name
```

The read command does the work of moving onto the next line of text in the .csv text file, so we don't need another loop to do that. The while command exits when the read command returns a FALSE value, which happens when it runs out of lines to read in the file. Tricky!

To feed the data from the file into the while command, you just use a redirection symbol at the end of the while command.

Putting everything together results in this script:

```
$ cat test26
#!/bin/bash
# process new user accounts

input="users.csv"
while IFS=',' read -r userid name
do
   echo "adding $userid"
   useradd -c "$name" -m $userid
done < "$input"
$
```

The $input variable points to the data file and is used as the redirect data for the while command. The users.csv file looks like this:

```
$ cat users.csv
rich,Richard Blum
```

```
christine,Christine Bresnahan
barbara,Barbara Blum
tim,Timothy Bresnahan
$
```

To run the problem, you must be the root user account, because the `useradd` command requires root privileges:

```
# ./test26
adding rich
adding christine
adding barbara
adding tim
#
```

Then by taking a quick look at the `/etc/passwd` file, you can see that the accounts have been created:

```
# tail /etc/passwd
rich:x:1001:1001:Richard Blum:/home/rich:/bin/bash
christine:x:1002:1002:Christine Bresnahan:/home/christine:/bin/bash
barbara:x:1003:1003:Barbara Blum:/home/barbara:/bin/bash
tim:x:1004:1004:Timothy Bresnahan:/home/tim:/bin/bash
#
```

Congratulations, you've saved yourself lots of time in adding user accounts!

Summary

Looping is an integral part of programming. The bash shell provides three looping commands that you can use in your scripts.

The `for` command allows you to iterate through a list of values, either supplied within the command line, contained in a variable, or obtained by using file globbing, to extract file and directory names from a wildcard character.

The `while` command provides a method to loop based on the condition of a command, using either ordinary commands or the test command, which allows you to test conditions of variables. As long as the command (or condition) produces a zero exit status, the `while` loop continues to iterate through the specified set of commands.

The `until` command also provides a method to iterate through commands, but it bases its iterations on a command (or condition) producing a non-zero exit status. This feature allows you to set a condition that must be met before the iteration stops.

You can combine loops in shell scripts, producing multiple layers of loops. The bash shell provides the continue and break commands, which allow you to alter the flow of the normal loop process based on different values within the loop.

The bash shell also allows you to use standard command redirection and piping to alter the output of a loop. You can use redirection to redirect the output of a loop to a file or piping to redirect the output of a loop to another command. This provides a wealth of features with which you can control your shell script execution.

The next chapter discusses how to interact with your shell script user. Often, shell scripts aren't completely self-contained. They require some sort of external data that must be supplied at the time you run them. The next chapter discusses different methods with which you can provide real-time data to your shell scripts for processing.

13

Handling User Input

S o far you've seen how to write scripts that interact with data, variables, and files on the Linux system. Sometimes, you need to write a script that has to interact with the person running the script. The bash shell provides a few different methods for retrieving data from people, including command line parameters (data values added after the command), command line options (single-letter values that modify the behavior of the command), and the capability to read input directly from the keyboard. This chapter discusses how to incorporate these different methods into your bash shell scripts to obtain data from the person running your script.

Passing Parameters

The most basic method of passing data to your shell script is to use *command line parameters*. Command line parameters allow you to add data values to the command line when you execute the script:

```
$ ./addem 10 30
```

This example passes two command line parameters (10 and 30) to the script addem. The script handles the command line parameters using special variables. The following sections describe how to use command line parameters in your bash shell scripts.

Reading parameters

The bash shell assigns special variables, called *positional parameters,* to all of the command line parameters entered. This includes the name of the script the shell is executing. The positional parameter variables are standard numbers, with *$0* being the script's name, *$1* being the first parameter, *$2* being the second parameter, and so on, up to *$9* for the ninth parameter.

Here's a simple example of using one command line parameter in a shell script:

```
$ cat test1.sh
#!/bin/bash
# using one command line parameter
#
factorial=1
for (( number = 1; number <= $1 ; number++ ))
do
    factorial=$[ $factorial * $number ]
done
echo The factorial of $1 is $factorial
$
$ ./test1.sh 5
The factorial of 5 is 120
$
```

You can use the *$1* variable just like any other variable in the shell script. The shell script automatically assigns the value from the command line parameter to the variable; you don't need to do anything with it.

If you need to enter more command line parameters, each parameter must be separated by a space on the command line:

```
$ cat test2.sh
#!/bin/bash
# testing two command line parameters
#
total=$[ $1 * $2 ]
echo The first parameter is $1.
echo The second parameter is $2.
echo The total value is $total.
$
$ ./test2.sh 2 5
The first parameter is 2.
The second parameter is 5.
The total value is 10.
$
```

The shell assigns each parameter to the appropriate variable.

In the preceding example, the command line parameters used were both numerical values. You can also use text strings in the command line:

```
$ cat test3.sh
#!/bin/bash
# testing string parameters
#
echo Hello $1, glad to meet you.
$
$ ./test3.sh Rich
Hello Rich, glad to meet you.
$
```

The shell passes the string value entered into the command line to the script. However, you'll have a problem if you try to do this with a text string that contains spaces:

```
$ ./test3.sh Rich Blum
Hello Rich, glad to meet you.
$
```

Remember that each of the parameters is separated by a space, so the shell interpreted the space as just separating the two values. To include a space as a parameter value, you must use quotation marks (either single or double quotation marks):

```
$ ./test3.sh 'Rich Blum'
Hello Rich Blum, glad to meet you.
$
$ ./test3.sh "Rich Blum"
Hello Rich Blum, glad to meet you.
$
```

NOTE

The quotation marks used when you pass text strings as parameters are not part of the data. They just delineate the beginning and the end of the data.

14

If your script needs more than nine command line parameters, you can continue, but the variable names change slightly. After the ninth variable, you must use braces around the variable number, such as ${10}. Here's an example of doing that:

```
$ cat test4.sh
#!/bin/bash
# handling lots of parameters
#
total=$[ ${10} * ${11} ]
echo The tenth parameter is ${10}
echo The eleventh parameter is ${11}
echo The total is $total
```

```
$
$ ./test4.sh 1 2 3 4 5 6 7 8 9 10 11 12
The tenth parameter is 10
The eleventh parameter is 11
The total is 110
$
```

This technique allows you to add as many command line parameters to your scripts as you could possibly need.

Reading the script name

You can use the $0 parameter to determine the script name the shell started from the command line. This can come in handy if you're writing a utility that can have multiple functions.

```
$ cat test5.sh
#!/bin/bash
# Testing the $0 parameter
#
echo The zero parameter is set to: $0
#
$
$ bash test5.sh
The zero parameter is set to: test5.sh
$
```

However, there is a potential problem. When using a different command to run the shell script, the command becomes entangled with the script name in the $0 parameter:

```
$ ./test5.sh
The zero parameter is set to: ./test5.sh
$
```

There is another potential problem. When the actual string passed is the full script path, and not just the script's name, the $0 variable gets set to the full script path and name:

```
$ bash /home/Christine/test5.sh
The zero parameter is set to: /home/Christine/test5.sh
$
```

If you want to write a script that performs different functions based on just the script's name, you'll have to do a little work. You need to be able to strip off whatever path is used to run the script. Also, you need to be able to remove any entangled commands from the script.

Fortunately, there's a handy little command available that does just that. The basename command returns just the script's name without the path:

```
$ cat test5b.sh
#!/bin/bash
```

```
# Using basename with the $0 parameter
#
name=$(basename $0)
echo
echo The script name is: $name
#
$ bash /home/Christine/test5b.sh

The script name is: test5b.sh
$
$ ./test5b.sh

The script name is: test5b.sh
$
```

Now that's much better. You can use this technique to write scripts that perform different functions based on the script name used. Here's a simple example:

```
$ cat test6.sh
#!/bin/bash
# Testing a Multi-function script
#
name=$(basename $0)
#
if [ $name = "addem" ]
then
    total=$[ $1 + $2 ]
#
elif [ $name = "multem" ]
then
    total=$[ $1 * $2 ]
fi
#
echo
echo The calculated value is $total
#
$
$ cp test6.sh addem
$ chmod u+x addem
$
$ ln -s test6.sh multem
$
$ ls -l *em
-rwxrw-r--. 1 Christine Christine 224 Jun 30 23:50 addem
lrwxrwxrwx. 1 Christine Christine   8 Jun 30 23:50 multem -> test6.sh
$
$ ./addem 2 5

The calculated value is 7
```

```
$
$ ./multem 2 5

The calculated value is 10
$
```

The example creates two separate filenames from the test6.sh script, one by just copying the file to a new script (addem) and the other by using a symbolic link (see Chapter 3) to create the new script (multem). In both cases, the script determines the script's base name and performs the appropriate function based on that value.

Testing parameters

Be careful when using command line parameters in your shell scripts. If the script is run without the parameters, bad things can happen:

```
$ ./addem 2
./addem: line 8: 2 +  : syntax error: operand expected (error
 token is " ")
The calculated value is
$
```

When the script assumes there is data in a parameter variable, and no data is present, most likely you'll get an error message from your script. This is a poor way to write scripts. Always check your parameters to make sure the data is there before using it:

```
$ cat test7.sh
#!/bin/bash
# testing parameters before use
#
if [ -n "$1" ]
then
    echo Hello $1, glad to meet you.
else
    echo "Sorry, you did not identify yourself. "
fi
$
$ ./test7.sh Rich
Hello Rich, glad to meet you.
$
$ ./test7.sh
Sorry, you did not identify yourself.
$
```

In this example, the -n test evaluation was used to check for data in the $1 command line parameter. In the next section, you'll learn another way to check command line parameters.

Using Special Parameter Variables

A few special bash shell variables track command line parameters. This section describes what they are and how to use them.

Counting parameters

As you saw in the last section, you should verify command line parameters before using them in your script. For scripts that use multiple command line parameters, this checking can get tedious.

Instead of testing each parameter, you can count how many parameters were entered on the command line. The bash shell provides a special variable for this purpose.

The special $# variable contains the number of command line parameters included when the script was run. You can use this special variable anywhere in the script, just like a normal variable:

```
$ cat test8.sh
#!/bin/bash
# getting the number of parameters
#
echo There were $# parameters supplied.
$
$ ./test8.sh
There were 0 parameters supplied.
$
$ ./test8.sh 1 2 3 4 5
There were 5 parameters supplied.
$
$ ./test8.sh 1 2 3 4 5 6 7 8 9 10
There were 10 parameters supplied.
$
$ ./test8.sh "Rich Blum"
There were 1 parameters supplied.
$
```

Now you have the ability to test the number of parameters present before trying to use them:

```
$ cat test9.sh
#!/bin/bash
# Testing parameters
#
if [ $# -ne 2 ]
then
    echo
```

```
        echo Usage: test9.sh a b
        echo
    else
        total=$[ $1 + $2 ]
        echo
        echo The total is $total
        echo
    fi
    #
    $
    $ bash test9.sh

    Usage: test9.sh a b

    $ bash test9.sh 10

    Usage: test9.sh a b

    $ bash test9.sh 10 15

    The total is 25

    $
```

The if-then statement uses the -ne evaluation to perform a numeric test of the command line parameters supplied. If the correct number of parameters isn't present, an error message displays showing the correct usage of the script.

This variable also provides a cool way of grabbing the last parameter on the command line without having to know how many parameters were used. However, you need to use a little trick to get there.

If you think this through, you might think that because the *$#* variable contains the value of the number of parameters, using the variable *${$#}* would represent the last command line parameter variable. Try that and see what happens:

```
    $ cat badtest1.sh
    #!/bin/bash
    # testing grabbing last parameter
    #
    echo The last parameter was ${$#}
    $
    $ ./badtest1.sh 10
    The last parameter was 15354
    $
```

Wow, what happened? Obviously, something went wrong. It turns out that you can't use the dollar sign within the braces. Instead, you must replace the dollar sign with an exclamation mark. Odd, but it works:

```
$ cat test10.sh
#!/bin/bash
# Grabbing the last parameter
#
params=$#
echo
echo The last parameter is $params
echo The last parameter is ${!#}
echo
#
$
$ bash test10.sh 1 2 3 4 5

The last parameter is 5
The last parameter is 5

$
$ bash test10.sh

The last parameter is 0
The last parameter is test10.sh

$
```

Perfect. This script also assigned the *$#* variable value to the variable *params* and then used that variable within the special command line parameter variable format as well. Both versions worked. It's also important to notice that, when there weren't any parameters on the command line, the *$#* value was zero, which is what appears in the *params* variable, but the *${!#}* variable returns the script name used on the command line.

Grabbing all the data

In some situations you want to grab all the parameters provided on the command line. Instead of having to mess with using the *$#* variable to determine how many parameters are on the command line and having to loop through all of them, you can use a couple of other special variables.

The *$** and *$@* variables provide easy access to all your parameters. Both of these variables include all the command line parameters within a single variable.

The *$** variable takes all the parameters supplied on the command line as a single word. The word contains each of the values as they appear on the command line. Basically, instead of treating the parameters as multiple objects, the *$** variable treats them all as one parameter.

The *$@* variable, on the other hand, takes all the parameters supplied on the command line as separate words in the same string. It allows you to iterate through the values, separating out each parameter supplied. This is most often accomplished using the `for` command.

14

It can easily get confusing to figure out how these two variables operate. Let's look at the difference between the two:

```
$ cat test11.sh
#!/bin/bash
# testing $* and $@
#
echo
echo "Using the \$* method: $*"
echo
echo "Using the \$@ method: $@"
$
$ ./test11.sh rich barbara katie jessica

Using the $* method: rich barbara katie jessica

Using the $@ method: rich barbara katie jessica
$
```

Notice that on the surface, both variables produce the same output, showing all the command line parameters provided at once.

The following example demonstrates where the differences are:

```
$ cat test12.sh
#!/bin/bash
# testing $* and $@
#
echo
count=1
#
for param in "$*"
do
    echo "\$* Parameter #$count = $param"
    count=$[ $count + 1 ]
done
#
echo
count=1
#
for param in "$@"
do
    echo "\$@ Parameter #$count = $param"
    count=$[ $count + 1 ]
done
$
$ ./test12.sh rich barbara katie jessica

$* Parameter #1 = rich barbara katie jessica

$@ Parameter #1 = rich
```

```
$@ Parameter #2 = barbara
$@ Parameter #3 = katie
$@ Parameter #4 = jessica
$
```

Now we're getting somewhere. By using the `for` command to iterate through the special variables, you can see how they each treat the command line parameters differently. The `$*` variable treated all the parameters as a single parameter, while the `$@` variable treated each parameter separately. This is a great way to iterate through command line parameters.

Being Shifty

Another tool you have in your bash shell tool belt is the `shift` command. The bash shell provides the `shift` command to help you manipulate command line parameters. The `shift` command literally shifts the command line parameters in their relative positions.

When you use the `shift` command, it moves each parameter variable one position to the left by default. Thus, the value for variable `$3` is moved to `$2`, the value for variable `$2` is moved to `$1`, and the value for variable `$1` is discarded (note that the value for variable `$0`, the program name, remains unchanged).

This is another great way to iterate through command line parameters, especially if you don't know how many parameters are available. You can just operate on the first parameter, shift the parameters over, and then operate on the first parameter again.

Here's a short demonstration of how this works:

```
$ cat test13.sh
#!/bin/bash
# demonstrating the shift command
echo
count=1
while [ -n "$1" ]
do
    echo "Parameter #$count = $1"
    count=$[ $count + 1 ]
    shift
done
$
$ ./test13.sh rich barbara katie jessica

Parameter #1 = rich
Parameter #2 = barbara
Parameter #3 = katie
Parameter #4 = jessica
$
```

14

The script performs a `while` loop, testing the length of the first parameter's value. When the first parameter's length is zero, the loop ends. After testing the first parameter, the `shift` command is used to shift all the parameters one position.

Alternatively, you can perform a multiple location shift by providing a parameter to the `shift` command. Just provide the number of places you want to shift:

```
$ cat test14.sh
#!/bin/bash
# demonstrating a multi-position shift
#
echo
echo "The original parameters: $*"
shift 2
echo "Here's the new first parameter: $1"
$
$ ./test14.sh 1 2 3 4 5

The original parameters: 1 2 3 4 5
Here's the new first parameter: 3
$
```

By using values in the `shift` command, you can easily skip over parameters you don't need.

Working with Options

If you've been following along in the book, you've seen several bash commands that provide both parameters and options. *Options* are single letters preceded by a dash that alter the behavior of a command. This section shows three methods for working with options in your shell scripts.

Finding your options

On the surface, there's nothing all that special about command line options. They appear on the command line immediately after the script name, just the same as command line parameters. In fact, if you want, you can process command line options the same way you process command line parameters.

Processing simple options

In the test13.sh script earlier, you saw how to use the shift command to work your way down the command line parameters provided with the script program. You can use this same technique to process command line options.

As you extract each individual parameter, use the case statement (see Chapter 12) to determine when a parameter is formatted as an option:

```
$ cat test15.sh
#!/bin/bash
# extracting command line options as parameters
#
echo
while [ -n "$1" ]
do
    case "$1" in
      -a) echo "Found the -a option" ;;
      -b) echo "Found the -b option" ;;
      -c) echo "Found the -c option" ;;
       *) echo "$1 is not an option" ;;
    esac
    shift
done
$
$ ./test15.sh -a -b -c -d

Found the -a option
Found the -b option
Found the -c option
-d is not an option
$
```

The case statement checks each parameter for valid options. When one is found, the appropriate commands are run in the case statement.

This method works, no matter in what order the options are presented on the command line:

```
$ ./test15.sh -d -c -a

-d is not an option
Found the -c option
Found the -a option
$
```

The case statement processes each option as it finds it in the command line parameters. If any other parameters are included on the command line, you can include commands in the catch-all part of the case statement to process them.

Separating options from parameters

Often you'll run into situations where you'll want to use both options and parameters for a shell script. The standard way to do this in Linux is to separate the two with a special character code that tells the script when the options are finished and when the normal parameters start.

For Linux, this special character is the double dash (--). The shell uses the double dash to indicate the end of the option list. After seeing the double dash, your script can safely process the remaining command line parameters as parameters and not options.

To check for the double dash, simply add another entry in the case statement:

```
$ cat test16.sh
#!/bin/bash
# extracting options and parameters
echo
while [ -n "$1" ]
do
    case "$1" in
        -a) echo "Found the -a option" ;;
        -b) echo "Found the -b option";;
        -c) echo "Found the -c option" ;;
        --) shift
            break ;;
        *) echo "$1 is not an option";;
    esac
    shift
done
#
count=1
for param in $@
do
    echo "Parameter #$count: $param"
    count=$[ $count + 1 ]
done
$
```

This script uses the break command to break out of the while loop when it encounters the double dash. Because we're breaking out prematurely, we need to ensure that we stick in another shift command to get the double dash out of the parameter variables.

For the first test, try running the script using a normal set of options and parameters:

```
$ ./test16.sh -c -a -b test1 test2 test3

Found the -c option
Found the -a option
Found the -b option
test1 is not an option
```

```
test2 is not an option
test3 is not an option
$
```

The results show that the script assumed that all the command line parameters were options when it processed them. Next, try the same thing, only this time using the double dash to separate the options from the parameters on the command line:

```
$ ./test16.sh -c -a -b -- test1 test2 test3

Found the -c option
Found the -a option
Found the -b option
Parameter #1: test1
Parameter #2: test2
Parameter #3: test3
$
```

When the script reaches the double dash, it stops processing options and assumes that any remaining parameters are command line parameters.

Processing options with values

Some options require an additional parameter value. In these situations, the command line looks something like this:

```
$ ./testing.sh -a test1 -b -c -d test2
```

Your script must be able to detect when your command line option requires an additional parameter and be able to process it appropriately. Here's an example of how to do that:

```
$ cat test17.sh
#!/bin/bash
# extracting command line options and values
echo
while [ -n "$1" ]
do
   case "$1" in
      -a) echo "Found the -a option";;
      -b) param="$2"
          echo "Found the -b option, with parameter value $param"
          shift ;;
      -c) echo "Found the -c option";;
      --) shift
          break ;;
       *) echo "$1 is not an option";;
   esac
   shift
done
```

```
#
count=1
for param in "$@"
do
    echo "Parameter #$count: $param"
    count=$[ $count + 1 ]
done
$
$ ./test17.sh -a -b test1 -d

Found the -a option
Found the -b option, with parameter value test1
-d is not an option
$
```

In this example, the case statement defines three options that it processes. The -b option also requires an additional parameter value. Because the parameter being processed is *$1*, you know that the additional parameter value is located in *$2* (because all the parameters are shifted after they are processed). Just extract the parameter value from the *$2* variable. Of course, because we used two parameter spots for this option, you also need to set the shift command to shift one additional position.

Just as with the basic feature, this process works no matter what order you place the options in (just remember to include the appropriate option parameter with the each option):

```
$ ./test17.sh -b test1 -a -d
Found the -b option, with parameter value test1
Found the -a option
-d is not an option
$
```

Now you have the basic ability to process command line options in your shell scripts, but there are limitations. For example, this doesn't work if you try to combine multiple options in one parameter:

```
$ ./test17.sh -ac
-ac is not an option
$
```

It is a common practice in Linux to combine options, and if your script is going to be user-friendly, you'll want to offer this feature for your users as well. Fortunately, there's another method for processing options that can help you.

Using the getopt command

The getopt command is a great tool to have handy when processing command line options and parameters. It reorganizes the command line parameters to make parsing them in your script easier.

Looking at the command format

The `getopt` command can take a list of command line options and parameters, in any form, and automatically turn them into the proper format. It uses the following command format:

getopt optstring *parameters*

The *optstring* is the key to the process. It defines the valid option letters that can be used in the command line. It also defines which option letters require a parameter value.

First, list each command line option letter you're going to use in your script in the *optstring*. Then place a colon after each option letter that requires a parameter value. The `getopt` command parses the supplied parameters based on the *optstring* you define.

> **TIP**
>
> A more advanced version of the `getopt` command, called `getopts` (notice it is plural), is available. The `getopts` command is covered later in this chapter. Because of their nearly identical spelling, it's easy to get these two commands confused. Be careful!

Here's a simple example of how `getopt` works:

```
$ getopt ab:cd -a -b test1 -cd test2 test3
 -a -b test1 -c -d -- test2 test3
$
```

The *optstring* defines four valid option letters, a, b, c, and d. A colon (:) is placed behind the letter b in order to require option b to have a parameter value. When the `getopt` command runs, it examines the provided parameter list (-a -b test1 -cd test2 test3) and parses it based on the supplied *optstring*. Notice that it automatically separated the -cd options into two separate options and inserted the double dash to separate the additional parameters on the line.

If you specify a parameter option not in the *optstring*, by default the `getopt` command produces an error message:

```
$ getopt ab:cd -a -b test1 -cde test2 test3
getopt: invalid option -- e
 -a -b test1 -c -d -- test2 test3
$
```

If you prefer to just ignore the error messages, use `getopt` with the -q option:

```
$ getopt -q ab:cd -a -b test1 -cde test2 test3
 -a -b 'test1' -c -d -- 'test2' 'test3'
$
```

Note that the `getopt` command options must be listed before the *optstring*. Now you should be ready to use this command in your scripts to process command line options.

14

Using getopt in your scripts

You can use the getopt command in your scripts to format any command line options or parameters entered for your script. It's a little tricky, however, to use.

The trick is to replace the existing command line options and parameters with the formatted version produced by the getopt command. The way to do that is to use the set command.

You saw the set command back in Chapter 6. The set command works with the different variables in the shell.

One of the set command options is the double dash (--). The double dash instructs set to replace the command line parameter variables with the values on the set command's command line.

The trick then is to feed the original script command line parameters to the getopt command and then feed the output of the getopt command to the set command to replace the original command line parameters with the nicely formatted ones from getopt. This looks something like this:

```
set -- $(getopt -q ab:cd "$@")
```

Now the values of the original command line parameter variables are replaced with the output from the getopt command, which formats the command line parameters for us.

Using this technique, we can now write scripts that handle our command line parameters for us:

```
$ cat test18.sh
#!/bin/bash
# Extract command line options & values with getopt
#
set -- $(getopt -q ab:cd "$@")
#
echo
while [ -n "$1" ]
do
   case "$1" in
   -a) echo "Found the -a option" ;;
   -b) param="$2"
       echo "Found the -b option, with parameter value $param"
       shift ;;
   -c) echo "Found the -c option" ;;
   --) shift
       break ;;
    *) echo "$1 is not an option";;
   esac
   shift
```

```
done
#
count=1
for param in "$@"
do
    echo "Parameter #$count: $param"
    count=$[ $count + 1 ]
done
#
$
```

You'll notice this is basically the same script as in test17.sh. The only thing that changed is the addition of the getopt command to help format our command line parameters.

Now when you run the script with complex options, things work much better:

```
$ ./test18.sh -ac

Found the -a option
Found the -c option
$
```

And of course, all the original features work just fine as well:

```
$ ./test18.sh -a -b test1 -cd test2 test3 test4

Found the -a option
Found the -b option, with parameter value 'test1'
Found the -c option
Parameter #1: 'test2'
Parameter #2: 'test3'
Parameter #3: 'test4'
$
```

Now things are looking pretty fancy. However, there's still one small bug that lurks in the getopt command. Check out this example:

```
$ ./test18.sh -a -b test1 -cd "test2 test3" test4

Found the -a option
Found the -b option, with parameter value 'test1'
Found the -c option
Parameter #1: 'test2
Parameter #2: test3'
Parameter #3: 'test4'
$
```

The getopt command isn't good at dealing with parameter values with spaces and quotation marks. It interpreted the space as the parameter separator, instead of following the double quotation marks and combining the two values into one parameter. Fortunately, this problem has another solution.

Advancing to getopts

The `getopts` command (notice that it is plural) is built into the bash shell. It looks much like its `getopt` cousin, but has some expanded features.

Unlike `getopt`, which produces one output for all the processed options and parameters found in the command line, the `getopts` command works on the existing shell parameter variables sequentially.

It processes the parameters it detects in the command line one at a time each time it's called. When it runs out of parameters, it exits with an exit status greater than zero. This makes it great for using in loops to parse all the parameters on the command line.

Here's the format of the `getopts` command:

```
getopts optstring variable
```

The *optstring* value is similar to the one used in the `getopt` command. Valid option letters are listed in the *optstring*, along with a colon if the option letter requires a parameter value. To suppress error messages, start the *optstring* with a colon. The getopts command places the current parameter in the *variable* defined in the command line.

The `getopts` command uses two environment variables. The *OPTARG* environment variable contains the value to be used if an option requires a parameter value. The *OPTIND* environment variable contains the value of the current location within the parameter list where getopts left off. This allows you to continue processing other command line parameters after finishing the options.

Let's look at a simple example that uses the `getopts` command:

```
$ cat test19.sh
#!/bin/bash
# simple demonstration of the getopts command
#
echo
while getopts :ab:c opt
do
   case "$opt" in
      a) echo "Found the -a option" ;;
      b) echo "Found the -b option, with value $OPTARG";;
      c) echo "Found the -c option" ;;
      *) echo "Unknown option: $opt";;
   esac
done
$
```

```
$ ./test19.sh -ab test1 -c

Found the -a option
Found the -b option, with value test1
Found the -c option
$
```

The while statement defines the getopts command, specifying what command line options to look for, along with the variable name (*opt*) to store them in for each iteration.

You'll notice something different about the case statement in this example. When the getopts command parses the command line options, it strips off the leading dash, so you don't need leading dashes in the case definitions.

The getopts command offers several nice features. For starters, you can include spaces in your parameter values:

```
$ ./test19.sh -b "test1 test2" -a

Found the -b option, with value test1 test2
Found the -a option
$
```

Another nice feature is that you can run the option letter and the parameter value together without a space:

```
$ ./test19.sh -abtest1

Found the -a option
Found the -b option, with value test1
$
```

The getopts command correctly parsed the test1 value from the -b option. In addition, the getopts command bundles any undefined option it finds in the command line into a single output, the question mark:

```
$ ./test19.sh -d

Unknown option: ?
$
$ ./test19.sh -acde

Found the -a option
Found the -c option
Unknown option: ?
Unknown option: ?
$
```

Any option letter not defined in the *optstring* value is sent to your code as a question mark.

The getopts command knows when to stop processing options and leave the parameters for you to process. As getopts processes each option, it increments the *OPTIND* environment variable by one. When you've reached the end of the getopts processing, you can use the *OPTIND* value with the shift command to move to the parameters:

```
$ cat test20.sh
#!/bin/bash
# Processing options & parameters with getopts
#
echo
while getopts :ab:cd opt
do
    case "$opt" in
    a) echo "Found the -a option"  ;;
    b) echo "Found the -b option, with value $OPTARG" ;;
    c) echo "Found the -c option"  ;;
    d) echo "Found the -d option"  ;;
    *) echo "Unknown option: $opt" ;;
    esac
done
#
shift $[ $OPTIND - 1 ]
#
echo
count=1
for param in "$@"
do
    echo "Parameter $count: $param"
    count=$[ $count + 1 ]
done
#
$
$ ./test20.sh -a -b test1 -d test2 test3 test4

Found the -a option
Found the -b option, with value test1
Found the -d option

Parameter 1: test2
Parameter 2: test3
Parameter 3: test4
$
```

Now you have a full-featured command line option and parameter processing utility you can use in all your shell scripts!

Standardizing Options

When you create your shell script, obviously you're in control of what happens. It's completely up to you as to which letter options you select to use and how you select to use them.

However, a few letter options have achieved a somewhat standard meaning in the Linux world. If you leverage these options in your shell script, your scripts will be more user-friendly.

Table 14-1 shows some of the common meanings for command line options used in Linux.

TABLE 14-1 Common Linux Command Line Options

Option	Description
-a	Shows all objects
-c	Produces a count
-d	Specifies a directory
-e	Expands an object
-f	Specifies a file to read data from
-h	Displays a help message for the command
-i	Ignores text case
-l	Produces a long format version of the output
-n	Uses a non-interactive (batch) mode
-o	Specifies an output file to redirect all output to
-q	Runs in quiet mode
-r	Processes directories and files recursively
-s	Runs in silent mode
-v	Produces verbose output
-x	Excludes an object
-y	Answers yes to all questions

You'll probably recognize most of these option meanings just from working with the various bash commands throughout the book. Using the same meaning for your options helps users interact with your script without having to worry about manuals.

Getting User Input

Although providing command line options and parameters is a great way to get data from your script users, sometimes your script needs to be more interactive. Sometimes you need to ask a question while the script is running and wait for a response from the person running your script. The bash shell provides the `read` command just for this purpose.

Reading basics

The `read` command accepts input either from standard input (such as from the keyboard) or from another file descriptor. After receiving the input, the `read` command places the data into a variable. Here's the `read` command at its simplest:

```
$ cat test21.sh
#!/bin/bash
# testing the read command
#
echo -n "Enter your name: "
read name
echo "Hello $name, welcome to my program. "
#
$
$ ./test21.sh
Enter your name: Rich Blum
Hello Rich Blum, welcome to my program.
$
```

That's pretty simple. Notice that the `echo` command that produced the prompt uses the `-n` option. This suppresses the newline character at the end of the string, allowing the script user to enter data immediately after the string, instead of on the next line. This gives your scripts a more form-like appearance.

In fact, the `read` command includes the `-p` option, which allows you to specify a prompt directly in the read command line:

```
$ cat test22.sh
#!/bin/bash
# testing the read -p option
#
read -p "Please enter your age: " age
days=$[ $age * 365 ]
echo "That makes you over $days days old! "
#
$
$ ./test22.sh
Please enter your age: 10
That makes you over 3650 days old!
$
```

You'll notice in the first example that when a name was entered, the read command assigned both the first name and last name to the same variable. The read command assigns all data entered at the prompt to a single variable, or you can specify multiple variables. Each data value entered is assigned to the next variable in the list. If the list of variables runs out before the data does, the remaining data is assigned to the last variable:

```
$ cat test23.sh
#!/bin/bash
# entering multiple variables
#
read -p "Enter your name: " first last
echo "Checking data for $last, $first…"
$
$ ./test23.sh
Enter your name: Rich Blum
Checking data for Blum, Rich...
$
```

You can also specify no variables on the read command line. If you do that, the read command places any data it receives in the special environment variable REPLY:

```
$ cat test24.sh
#!/bin/bash
# Testing the REPLY Environment variable
#
read -p "Enter your name: "
echo
echo Hello $REPLY, welcome to my program.
#
$
$ ./test24.sh
Enter your name: Christine

Hello Christine, welcome to my program.
$
```

The REPLY environment variable contains all the data entered in the input, and it can be used in the shell script as any other variable.

Timing out

Be careful when using the read command. Your script may get stuck waiting for the script user to enter data. If the script must go on regardless of whether any data was entered, you can use the -t option to specify a timer. The -t option specifies the number of seconds for the read command to wait for input. When the timer expires, the read command returns a non-zero exit status:

```
$ cat test25.sh
#!/bin/bash
```

```
# timing the data entry
#
if read -t 5 -p "Please enter your name: " name
then
    echo "Hello $name, welcome to my script"
else
    echo
    echo "Sorry, too slow! "
fi
$
$ ./test25.sh
Please enter your name: Rich
Hello Rich, welcome to my script
$
$ ./test25.sh
Please enter your name:
Sorry, too slow!
$
```

Because the read command exits with a non-zero exit status if the timer expires, it's easy to use the standard structured statements, such as an if-then statement or a while loop to track what happened. In this example, when the timer expires, the if statement fails, and the shell executes the commands in the else section.

Instead of timing the input, you can also set the read command to count the input characters. When a preset number of characters has been entered, it automatically exits, assigning the entered data to the variable:

```
$ cat test26.sh
#!/bin/bash
# getting just one character of input
#
read -n1 -p "Do you want to continue [Y/N]? " answer
case $answer in
Y | y) echo
        echo "fine, continue on...";;
N | n) echo
        echo OK, goodbye
        exit;;
esac
echo "This is the end of the script"
$
$ ./test26.sh
Do you want to continue [Y/N]? Y
fine, continue on...
This is the end of the script
$
$ ./test26.sh
```

```
Do you want to continue [Y/N]? n
OK, goodbye
$
```

This example uses the -n option with the value of 1, instructing the read command to accept only a single character before exiting. As soon as you press the single character to answer, the read command accepts the input and passes it to the variable. You don't need to press the Enter key.

Reading with no display

Sometimes you need input from the script user, but you don't want that input to display on the monitor. The classic example is when entering passwords, but there are plenty of other types of data that you need to hide.

The -s option prevents the data entered in the read command from being displayed on the monitor; actually, the data is displayed, but the read command sets the text color to the same as the background color. Here's an example of using the -s option in a script:

```
$ cat test27.sh
#!/bin/bash
# hiding input data from the monitor
#
read -s -p "Enter your password: " pass
echo
echo "Is your password really $pass? "
$
$ ./test27.sh
Enter your password:
Is your password really T3st1ng?
$
```

The data typed at the input prompt doesn't appear on the monitor but is assigned to the variable for use in the script.

Reading from a file

Finally, you can also use the read command to read data stored in a file on the Linux system. Each call to the read command reads a single line of text from the file. When no more lines are left in the file, the read command exits with a non-zero exit status.

The tricky part is getting the data from the file to the read command. The most common method is to pipe the result of the cat command of the file directly to a while command that contains the read command. Here's an example:

```
$ cat test28.sh
#!/bin/bash
```

14

```
# reading data from a file
#
count=1
cat test | while read line
do
    echo "Line $count: $line"
    count=$[ $count + 1]
done
echo "Finished processing the file"
$
$ cat test
The quick brown dog jumps over the lazy fox.
This is a test, this is only a test.
O Romeo, Romeo! Wherefore art thou Romeo?
$
$ ./test28.sh
Line 1: The quick brown dog jumps over the lazy fox.
Line 2: This is a test, this is only a test.
Line 3: O Romeo, Romeo! Wherefore art thou Romeo?
Finished processing the file
$
```

The while command loop continues processing lines of the file with the read command, until the read command exits with a non-zero exit status.

Summary

This chapter showed three methods for retrieving data from the script user. Command line parameters allow users to enter data directly on the command line when they run the script. The script uses positional parameters to retrieve the command line parameters and assign them to variables.

The shift command allows you to manipulate the command line parameters by rotating them within the positional parameters. This command allows you to easily iterate through the parameters without knowing how many parameters are available.

You can use three special variables when working with command line parameters. The shell sets the $# variable to the number of parameters entered on the command line. The $* variable contains all the parameters as a single string, and the $@ variable contains all the parameters as separate words. These variables come in handy when you're trying to process long parameter lists.

Besides parameters, your script users can use command line options to pass information to your script. Command line options are single letters preceded by a dash. Different options can be assigned to alter the behavior of your script.

The bash shell provides three ways to handle command line options.

The first way is to handle them just like command line parameters. You can iterate through the options using the positional parameter variables, processing each option as it appears on the command line.

Another way to handle command line options is with the getopt command. This command converts command line options and parameters into a standard format that you can process in your script. The getopt command allows you to specify which letters it recognizes as options and which options require an additional parameter value. The getopt command processes the standard command line parameters and outputs the options and parameters in the proper order.

The final method for handling command line options is via the getopts command (note that it's plural). The getopts command provides more advanced processing of the command line parameters. It allows for multi-value parameters, along with identifying options not defined by the script.

An interactive method to obtain data from your script users is the read command. The read command allows your scripts to query users for information and wait. The read command places any data entered by the script user into one or more variables, which you can use within the script.

Several options are available for the read command that allow you to customize the data input into your script, such as using hidden data entry, applying timed data entry, and requesting a specific number of input characters.

In the next chapter, we look further into how bash shell scripts output data. So far, you've seen how to display data on the monitor and redirect it to a file. Next, we explore a few other options that you have available not only to direct data to specific locations but also to direct specific types of data to specific locations. This will help make your shell scripts look professional!

14

Presenting Data

So far the scripts shown in this book display information either by echoing data to the monitor or by redirecting data to a file. Chapter 11 demonstrated how to redirect the output of a command to a file. This chapter expands on that topic by showing you how you can redirect the output of your script to different locations on your Linux system.

Understanding Input and Output

So far, you've seen two methods for displaying the output from your scripts:

- Displaying output on the monitor screen
- Redirecting output to a file

Both methods produced an all-or-nothing approach to data output. There are times, however, when it would be nice to display some data on the monitor and other data in a file. For these instances, it comes in handy to know how Linux handles input and output so you can get your script output to the right place.

The following sections describe how to use the standard Linux input and output system to your advantage, to help direct script output to specific locations.

Standard file descriptors

The Linux system handles every object as a file. This includes the input and output process. Linux identifies each file object using a *file descriptor*. The file descriptor is a non-negative integer that uniquely identifies open files in a session. Each process is allowed to have up to nine open file descriptors at a time. The bash shell reserves the first three file descriptors (0, 1, and 2) for special purposes. These are shown in Table 15-1.

TABLE 15-1 **Linux Standard File Descriptors**

File Descriptor	Abbreviation	Description
0	STDIN	Standard input
1	STDOUT	Standard output
2	STDERR	Standard error

These three special file descriptors handle the input and output from your script. The shell uses them to direct the default input and output in the shell to the appropriate location, which by default is usually your monitor. The following sections describe each of these standard file descriptors in greater detail.

STDIN

The STDIN file descriptor references the standard input to the shell. For a terminal interface, the standard input is the keyboard. The shell receives input from the keyboard on the STDIN file descriptor and processes each character as you type it.

When you use the input redirect symbol (<), Linux replaces the standard input file descriptor with the file referenced by the redirection. It reads the file and retrieves data just as if it were typed on the keyboard.

Many bash commands accept input from STDIN, especially if no files are specified on the command line. Here's an example of using the cat command with data entered from STDIN:

```
$ cat
this is a test
this is a test
this is a second test.
this is a second test.
```

When you enter the cat command on the command line by itself, it accepts input from STDIN. As you enter each line, the cat command echoes the line to the display.

However, you can also use the STDIN redirect symbol to force the cat command to accept input from another file other than STDIN:

```
$ cat < testfile
This is the first line.
This is the second line.
```

```
This is the third line.
$
```

Now the `cat` command uses the lines that are contained in the `testfile` file as the input. You can use this technique to input data to any shell command that accepts data from STDIN.

STDOUT

The STDOUT file descriptor references the standard output for the shell. On a terminal interface, the standard output is the terminal monitor. All output from the shell (including programs and scripts you run in the shell) is directed to the standard output, which is the monitor.

Most bash commands direct their output to the STDOUT file descriptor by default. As shown in Chapter 11, you can change that using output redirection:

```
$ ls -l > test2
$ cat test2
total 20
-rw-rw-r-- 1 rich rich 53 2014-10-16 11:30 test
-rw-rw-r-- 1 rich rich  0 2014-10-16 11:32 test2
-rw-rw-r-- 1 rich rich 73 2014-10-16 11:23 testfile
$
```

With the output redirection symbol, all the output that normally would go to the monitor is instead redirected to the designated redirection file by the shell.

You can also append data to a file. You do this using the `>>` symbol:

```
$ who >> test2
$ cat test2
total 20
-rw-rw-r-- 1 rich rich 53 2014-10-16 11:30 test
-rw-rw-r-- 1 rich rich  0 2014-10-16 11:32 test2
-rw-rw-r-- 1 rich rich 73 2014-10-16 11:23 testfile
rich     pts/0        2014-10-17 15:34 (192.168.1.2)
$
```

The output generated by the `who` command is appended to the data already in the `test2` file.

However, if you use the standard output redirection for your scripts, you can run into a problem. Here's an example of what can happen in your script:

```
$ ls -al badfile > test3
ls: cannot access badfile: No such file or directory
$ cat test3
$
```

15

When a command produces an error message, the shell doesn't redirect the error message to the output redirection file. The shell created the output redirection file, but the error message appeared on the monitor screen. Notice that there isn't an error when trying to display the contents of the test3 file. The test3 file was created just fine, but it's empty.

The shell handles error messages separately from the normal output. If you're creating a shell script that runs in background mode, often you must rely on the output messages being sent to a log file. Using this technique, if any error messages occur, they don't appear in the log file. You need to do something different.

STDERR

The shell handles error messages using the special STDERR file descriptor. The STDERR file descriptor references the standard error output for the shell. This is the location where the shell sends error messages generated by the shell or programs and scripts running in the shell.

By default, the STDERR file descriptor points to the same place as the STDOUT file descriptor (even though they are assigned different file descriptor values). This means that, by default, all error messages go to the monitor display.

However, as you saw in the example, when you redirect STDOUT, this doesn't automatically redirect STDERR. When working with scripts, you'll often want to change that behavior, especially if you're interested in logging error messages to a log file.

Redirecting errors

You've already seen how to redirect the STDOUT data by using the redirection symbol. Redirecting the STDERR data isn't much different; you just need to define the STDERR file descriptor when you use the redirection symbol. You can do this in a couple of ways.

Redirecting errors only

As you saw in Table 15-1, the STDERR file descriptor is set to the value 2. You can select to redirect only error messages by placing this file descriptor value immediately before the redirection symbol. The value must appear immediately before the redirection symbol or it doesn't work:

```
$ ls -al badfile 2> test4
$ cat test4
ls: cannot access badfile: No such file or directory
$
```

Now when you run the command, the error message doesn't appear on the monitor. Instead, the output file contains any error messages that are generated by the command. Using this method, the shell redirects the error messages only, not the normal data. Here's another example of mixing STDOUT and STDERR messages in the same output:

```
$ ls -al test badtest test2 2> test5
-rw-rw-r-- 1 rich rich 158 2014-10-16 11:32 test2
```

```
$ cat test5
ls: cannot access test: No such file or directory
ls: cannot access badtest: No such file or directory
$
```

The normal STDOUT output from the ls command still goes to the default STDOUT file descriptor, which is the monitor. Because the command redirects file descriptor 2 output (STDERR) to an output file, the shell sends any error messages generated directly to the specified redirection file.

Redirecting errors and data

If you want to redirect both errors and the normal output, you need to use two redirection symbols. You need to precede each with the appropriate file descriptor for the data you want to redirect and then have them point to the appropriate output file for holding the data:

```
$ ls -al test test2 test3 badtest 2> test6 1> test7
$ cat test6
ls: cannot access test: No such file or directory
ls: cannot access badtest: No such file or directory
$ cat test7
-rw-rw-r-- 1 rich rich 158 2014-10-16 11:32 test2
-rw-rw-r-- 1 rich rich   0 2014-10-16 11:33 test3
$
```

The shell redirects the normal output of the ls command that would have gone to STDOUT to the test7 file using the 1> symbol. Any error messages that would have gone to STDERR were redirected to the test6 file using the 2> symbol.

You can use this technique to separate normal script output from any error messages that occur in the script. This allows you to easily identify errors without having to wade through thousands of lines of normal output data.

Alternatively, if you want, you can redirect both STDERR and STDOUT output to the same output file. The bash shell provides a special redirection symbol just for this purpose, the &> symbol:

```
$ ls -al test test2 test3 badtest &> test7
$ cat test7
ls: cannot access test: No such file or directory
ls: cannot access badtest: No such file or directory
-rw-rw-r-- 1 rich rich 158 2014-10-16 11:32 test2
-rw-rw-r-- 1 rich rich   0 2014-10-16 11:33 test3
$
```

When you use the &> symbol, all the output generated by the command is sent to the same location, both data and errors. Notice that one of the error messages is out of order from what you'd expect. The error message for the badtest file (the last file to be listed) appears second in the output file. The bash shell automatically gives error messages a higher priority than the standard output. This allows you to view the error messages together, rather than scattered throughout the output file.

Redirecting Output in Scripts

You can use the STDOUT and STDERR file descriptors in your scripts to produce output in multiple locations simply by redirecting the appropriate file descriptors. There are two methods for redirecting output in the script:

- Temporarily redirecting each line
- Permanently redirecting all commands in the script

The following sections describe how each of these methods works.

Temporary redirections

If you want to purposely generate error messages in your script, you can redirect an individual output line to STDERR. You just need to use the output redirection symbol to redirect the output to the STDERR file descriptor. When you redirect to a file descriptor, you must precede the file descriptor number with an ampersand (&):

```
echo "This is an error message" >&2
```

This line displays the text wherever the STDERR file descriptor for the script is pointing, instead of the normal STDOUT. The following is an example of a script that uses this feature:

```
$ cat test8
#!/bin/bash
# testing STDERR messages

echo "This is an error" >&2
echo "This is normal output"
$
```

If you run the script as normal, you don't notice any difference:

```
$ ./test8
This is an error
This is normal output
$
```

Remember that, by default, Linux directs the STDERR output to STDOUT. However, if you redirect STDERR when running the script, any text directed to STDERR in the script is redirected:

```
$ ./test8 2> test9
This is normal output
```

```
$ cat test9
This is an error
$
```

Perfect! The text displayed using STDOUT appears on the monitor, while the echo statement text sent to STDERR is redirected to the output file.

This method is great for generating error messages in your scripts. If someone uses your scripts, they can easily redirect the error messages using the STDERR file descriptor, as shown.

Permanent redirections

If you have lots of data that you're redirecting in your script, it can get tedious having to redirect every echo statement. Instead, you can tell the shell to redirect a specific file descriptor for the duration of the script by using the exec command:

```
$ cat test10
#!/bin/bash
# redirecting all output to a file
exec 1>testout

echo "This is a test of redirecting all output"
echo "from a script to another file."
echo "without having to redirect every individual line"
$ ./test10
$ cat testout
This is a test of redirecting all output
from a script to another file.
without having to redirect every individual line
$
```

The exec command starts a new shell and redirects the STDOUT file descriptor to a file. All output in the script that goes to STDOUT is instead redirected to the file.

You can also redirect the STDOUT in the middle of a script:

```
$ cat test11
#!/bin/bash
# redirecting output to different locations

exec 2>testerror

echo "This is the start of the script"
echo "now redirecting all output to another location"

exec 1>testout

echo "This output should go to the testout file"
```

```
        echo "but this should go to the testerror file" >&2
        $
        $ ./test11
        This is the start of the script
        now redirecting all output to another location
        $ cat testout
        This output should go to the testout file
        $ cat testerror
        but this should go to the testerror file
        $
```

The script uses the exec command to redirect any output going to STDERR to the file testerror. Next, the script uses the echo statement to display a few lines to STDOUT. After that, the exec command is used again to redirect STDOUT to the testout file. Notice that even when STDOUT is redirected, you can still specify the output from an echo statement to go to STDERR, which in this case is still redirected to the testerror file.

This feature can come in handy when you want to redirect the output of just parts of a script to an alternative location, such as an error log. There's just one problem you run into when using this.

After you redirect STDOUT or STDERR, you can't easily redirect them back to their original location. If you need to switch back and forth with your redirection, you need to learn a trick. The "Creating Your Own Redirection" section later in this chapter discusses this trick and how to use it in your shell scripts.

Redirecting Input in Scripts

You can use the same technique used to redirect STDOUT and STDERR in your scripts to redirect STDIN from the keyboard. The exec command allows you to redirect STDIN from a file on the Linux system:

```
        exec 0< testfile
```

This command informs the shell that it should retrieve input from the file testfile instead of STDIN. This redirection applies anytime the script requests input. Here's an example of this in action:

```
        $ cat test12
        #!/bin/bash
        # redirecting file input

        exec 0< testfile
        count=1

        while read line
```

```
do
    echo "Line #$count: $line"
    count=$[ $count + 1 ]
done
$ ./test12
Line #1: This is the first line.
Line #2: This is the second line.
Line #3: This is the third line.
$
```

Chapter 14 showed you how to use the read command to read data entered from the keyboard by a user. By redirecting STDIN from a file, when the read command attempts to read from STDIN, it retrieves data from the file instead of the keyboard.

This is an excellent technique to read data in files for processing in your scripts. A common task for Linux system administrators is to read data from log files for processing. This is the easiest way to accomplish that task.

Creating Your Own Redirection

When you redirect input and output in your script, you're not limited to the three default file descriptors. I mentioned that you could have up to nine open file descriptors in the shell. The other six file descriptors are numbered from 3 through 8 and are available for you to use as either input or output redirection. You can assign any of these file descriptors to a file and then use them in your scripts as well. This section shows you how to use the other file descriptors in your scripts.

Creating output file descriptors

You assign a file descriptor for output by using the exec command. As with the standard file descriptors, after you assign an alternative file descriptor to a file location, that redirection stays permanent until you reassign it. Here's a simple example of using an alternative file descriptor in a script:

```
$ cat test13
#!/bin/bash
# using an alternative file descriptor

exec 3>test13out

echo "This should display on the monitor"
echo "and this should be stored in the file" >&3
echo "Then this should be back on the monitor"
$ ./test13
This should display on the monitor
```

15

```
Then this should be back on the monitor
$ cat test13out
and this should be stored in the file
$
```

The script uses the exec command to redirect file descriptor 3 to an alternative file location. When the script executes the echo statements, they display on STDOUT as you would expect. However, the echo statements that you redirect to file descriptor 3 go to the alternative file. This allows you to keep normal output for the monitor and redirect special information to files, such as log files.

You can also use the exec command to append data to an existing file instead of creating a new file:

```
exec 3>>test13out
```

Now the output is appended to the test13out file instead of creating a new file.

Redirecting file descriptors

Here's the trick to help you bring back a redirected file descriptor. You can assign an alternative file descriptor to a standard file descriptor, and vice versa. This means that you can redirect the original location of STDOUT to an alternative file descriptor and then redirect that file descriptor back to STDOUT. This might sound somewhat complicated, but in practice it's fairly straightforward. This example will clear things up for you:

```
$ cat test14
#!/bin/bash
# storing STDOUT, then coming back to it

exec 3>&1
exec 1>test14out

echo "This should store in the output file"
echo "along with this line."

exec 1>&3

echo "Now things should be back to normal"
$
$ ./test14
Now things should be back to normal
$ cat test14out
This should store in the output file
along with this line.
$
```

This example is a little crazy so let's walk through it piece by piece. First, the script redirects file descriptor 3 to the current location of file descriptor 1, which is STDOUT. This means that any output sent to file descriptor 3 goes to the monitor.

The second exec command redirects STDOUT to a file. The shell now redirects any output sent to STDOUT directly to the output file. However, file descriptor 3 still points to the original location of STDOUT, which is the monitor. If you send output data to file descriptor 3 at this point, it still goes to the monitor, even though STDOUT is redirected.

After sending some output to STDOUT, which points to a file, the script then redirects STDOUT to the current location of file descriptor 3, which is still set to the monitor. This means that now STDOUT points to its original location, the monitor.

This method can get confusing, but it's a common way to temporarily redirect output in script files and then set the output back to the normal settings.

Creating input file descriptors

You can redirect input file descriptors exactly the same way as output file descriptors. Save the STDIN file descriptor location to another file descriptor before redirecting it to a file; when you're finished reading the file, you can restore STDIN to its original location:

```
$ cat test15
#!/bin/bash
# redirecting input file descriptors

exec 6<&0

exec 0< testfile

count=1
while read line
do
    echo "Line #$count: $line"
    count=$[ $count + 1 ]
done
exec 0<&6
read -p "Are you done now? " answer
case $answer in
Y|y) echo "Goodbye";;
N|n) echo "Sorry, this is the end.";;
esac
$ ./test15
Line #1: This is the first line.
Line #2: This is the second line.
Line #3: This is the third line.
Are you done now? y
Goodbye
$
```

15

In this example, file descriptor 6 is used to hold the location for STDIN. The script then redirects STDIN to a file. All the input for the read command comes from the redirected STDIN, which is now the input file.

When all the lines have been read, the script returns STDIN to its original location by redirecting it to file descriptor 6. The script tests to make sure that STDIN is back to normal by using another read command, which this time waits for input from the keyboard.

Creating a read/write file descriptor

As odd as it may seem, you can also open a single file descriptor for both input and output. You can then use the same file descriptor to both read data from a file and write data to the same file.

You need to be especially careful with this method, however. As you read and write data to and from a file, the shell maintains an internal pointer, indicating where it is in the file. Any reading or writing occurs where the file pointer last left off. This can produce some interesting results if you're not careful. Look at this example:

```
$ cat test16
#!/bin/bash
# testing input/output file descriptor

exec 3<> testfile
read line <&3
echo "Read: $line"
echo "This is a test line" >&3
$ cat testfile
This is the first line.
This is the second line.
This is the third line.
$ ./test16
Read: This is the first line.
$ cat testfile
This is the first line.
This is a test line
ine.
This is the third line.
$
```

This example uses the exec command to assign file descriptor 3 for both input and output sent to and from the file testfile. Next, it uses the read command to read the first line in the file, using the assigned file descriptor, and then it displays the read line of data in STDOUT. After that, it uses the echo statement to write a line of data to the file opened with the same file descriptor.

When you run the script, at first things look just fine. The output shows that the script read the first line in the testfile file. However, if you display the contents of the testfile file after running the script, you see that the data written to the file overwrote the existing data.

When the script writes data to the file, it starts where the file pointer is located. The read command reads the first line of data, so it left the file pointer pointing to the first character in the second line of data. When the echo statement outputs data to the file, it places the data at the current location of the file pointer, overwriting whatever data was there.

Closing file descriptors

If you create new input or output file descriptors, the shell automatically closes them when the script exits. There are situations, however, when you need to manually close a file descriptor before the end of the script.

To close a file descriptor, redirect it to the special symbol &-. This is how this looks in the script:

```
exec 3>&-
```

This statement closes file descriptor 3, preventing it from being used any more in the script. Here's an example of what happens when you try to use a closed file descriptor:

```
$ cat badtest
#!/bin/bash
# testing closing file descriptors

exec 3> test17file

echo "This is a test line of data" >&3

exec 3>&-

echo "This won't work" >&3
$ ./badtest
./badtest: 3: Bad file descriptor
$
```

After you close the file descriptor, you can't write any data to it in your script or the shell produces an error message.

There's yet another thing to be careful of when closing file descriptors. If you open the same output file later on in your script, the shell replaces the existing file with a new file. This means that if you output any data, it overwrites the existing file. Consider the following example of this problem:

```
$ cat test17
#!/bin/bash
# testing closing file descriptors

exec 3> test17file
echo "This is a test line of data" >&3
exec 3>&-

cat test17file

exec 3> test17file
echo "This'll be bad" >&3
$ ./test17
This is a test line of data
$ cat test17file
This'll be bad
$
```

After sending a data string to the test17file file and closing the file descriptor, the script uses the cat command to display the contents of the file. So far, so good. Next, the script reopens the output file and sends another data string to it. When you display the contents of the output file, all you see is the second data string. The shell overwrote the original output file.

Listing Open File Descriptors

With only nine file descriptors available to you, you'd think that it wouldn't be hard to keep things straight. Sometimes, however, it's easy to get lost when trying to keep track of which file descriptor is redirected where. To help you keep your sanity, the bash shell provides the lsof command.

The lsof command lists all the open file descriptors on the entire Linux system. This is somewhat of a controversial feature, because it can provide information about the Linux system to non-system-administrators. That's why many Linux systems hide this command so users don't accidentally stumble across it.

On many Linux systems (such as Fedora) the lsof command is located in the /usr/sbin directory. To run it with a normal user account, I have to reference it by its full pathname:

```
$ /usr/sbin/lsof
```

This produces an amazing amount of output. It displays information about every file currently open on the Linux system. This includes all the processes running on background, as well as any user accounts logged in to the system.

Plenty of command line parameters and options are available to help filter out the lsof output. The most commonly used are -p, which allows you to specify a process ID (PID), and -d, which allows you to specify the file descriptor numbers to display.

To easily determine the current PID of the process, you can use the special environment variable $$, which the shell sets to the current PID. The -a option is used to perform a Boolean AND of the results of the other two options, to produce the following:

```
$ /usr/sbin/lsof -a -p $$ -d 0,1,2
COMMAND  PID USER    FD    TYPE DEVICE SIZE NODE NAME
bash    3344 rich    0u    CHR  136,0       2 /dev/pts/0
bash    3344 rich    1u    CHR  136,0       2 /dev/pts/0
bash    3344 rich    2u    CHR  136,0       2 /dev/pts/0
$
```

This shows the default file descriptors (0, 1, and 2) for the current process (the bash shell). The default output of lsof contains several columns of information, described in Table 15-2.

TABLE 15-2 Default lsof Output

Column	Description
COMMAND	The first nine characters of the name of the command in the process
PID	The process ID of the process
USER	The login name of the user who owns the process
FD	The file descriptor number and access type [r—(read), w—(write), u—(read/write)]
TYPE	The type of file [CHR—(character), BLK— (block), DIR— (directory), REG—(regular file)]
DEVICE	The device numbers (major and minor) of the device
SIZE	If available, the size of the file
NODE	The node number of the local file
NAME	The name of the file

The file type associated with STDIN, STDOUT, and STDERR is character mode. Because the STDIN, STDOUT, and STDERR file descriptors all point to the terminal, the name of the output file is the device name of the terminal. All three standard files are available for both reading and writing (although it does seem odd to be able to write to STDIN and read from STDOUT).

Now, let's look at the results of the lsof command from inside a script that's opened a couple of alternative file descriptors:

15

```
$ cat test18
#!/bin/bash
# testing lsof with file descriptors

exec 3> test18file1
exec 6> test18file2
exec 7< testfile

/usr/sbin/lsof -a -p $$ -d0,1,2,3,6,7
$ ./test18
COMMAND  PID USER    FD    TYPE DEVICE SIZE    NODE NAME
test18  3594 rich     0u    CHR  136,0            2 /dev/pts/0
test18  3594 rich     1u    CHR  136,0            2 /dev/pts/0
test18  3594 rich     2u    CHR  136,0            2 /dev/pts/0
18      3594 rich     3w    REG  253,0      0 360712 /home/rich/test18file1
18      3594 rich     6w    REG  253,0      0 360715 /home/rich/test18file2
18      3594 rich     7r    REG  253,0     73 360717 /home/rich/testfile
$
```

The script creates three alternative file descriptors, two for output (3 and 6) and one for input (7). When the script runs the lsof command, you can see the new file descriptors in the output. We truncated the first part of the output so you could see the results of the filename. The filename shows the complete pathname for the files used in the file descriptors. It shows each of the files as type REG, which indicates that they are regular files on the filesystem.

Suppressing Command Output

Sometimes, you may not want to display any output from your script. This often occurs if you're running a script as a background process (see Chapter 16). If any error messages occur from the script while it's running in the background, the shell e-mails them to the owner of the process. This can get tedious, especially if you run scripts that generate minor nuisance errors.

To solve that problem, you can redirect STDERR to a special file called the *null file*. The null file is pretty much what it says it is — a file that contains nothing. Any data that the shell outputs to the null file is not saved, thus the data are lost.

The standard location for the null file on Linux systems is /dev/null. Any data you redirect to that location is thrown away and doesn't appear:

```
$ ls -al > /dev/null
$ cat /dev/null
$
```

This is a common way to suppress any error messages without actually saving them:

```
$ ls -al badfile test16 2> /dev/null
-rwxr--r--    1 rich      rich          135 Oct 29 19:57 test16*
$
```

You can also use the /dev/null file for input redirection as an input file. Because the /dev/null file contains nothing, it is often used by programmers to quickly remove data from an existing file without having to remove the file and re-create it:

```
$ cat testfile
This is the first line.
This is the second line.
This is the third line.
$ cat /dev/null > testfile
$ cat testfile
$
```

The file testfile still exists on the system, but now it is empty. This is a common method used to clear out log files that must remain in place for applications to operate.

Using Temporary Files

The Linux system contains a special directory location reserved for temporary files. Linux uses the /tmp directory for files that don't need to be kept indefinitely. Most Linux distributions configure the system to automatically remove any files in the /tmp directory at bootup.

Any user account on the system has privileges to read and write files in the /tmp directory. This feature provides an easy way for you to create temporary files that you don't necessarily have to worry about cleaning up.

There's even a specific command to use for creating a temporary file. The mktemp command allows you to easily create a unique temporary file in the /tmp folder. The shell creates the file but doesn't use your default umask value (see Chapter 7). Instead, it only assigns read and write permissions to the file's owner and makes you the owner of the file. After you create the file, you have full access to read and write to and from it from your script, but no one else can access it (other than the root user, of course).

Creating a local temporary file

By default, mktemp creates a file in the local directory. To create a temporary file in a local directory with the mktemp command, you just need to specify a filename template. The template consists of any text filename, plus six X's appended to the end of the filename:

```
$ mktemp testing.XXXXXX
$ ls -al testing*
-rw-------    1 rich      rich            0 Oct 17 21:30 testing.UfIi13
$
```

15

The `mktemp` command replaces the six X's with a six-character code to ensure the filename is unique in the directory. You can create multiple temporary files and be assured that each one is unique:

```
$ mktemp testing.XXXXXX
testing.1DRLuV
$ mktemp testing.XXXXXX
testing.1VBtkW
$ mktemp testing.XXXXXX
testing.PgqNKG
$ ls -l testing*
-rw-------    1 rich      rich         0 Oct 17 21:57 testing.1DRLuV
-rw-------    1 rich      rich         0 Oct 17 21:57 testing.PgqNKG
-rw-------    1 rich      rich         0 Oct 17 21:30 testing.UfIi13
-rw-------    1 rich      rich         0 Oct 17 21:57 testing.1VBtkW
$
```

As you can see, the output of the `mktemp` command is the name of the file that it creates. When you use the `mktemp` command in a script, you'll want to save that filename in a variable, so you can refer to it later on in the script:

```
$ cat test19
#!/bin/bash
# creating and using a temp file

tempfile=$(mktemp test19.XXXXXX)

exec 3>$tempfile

echo "This script writes to temp file $tempfile"

echo "This is the first line" >&3
echo "This is the second line." >&3
echo "This is the last line." >&3
exec 3>&-

echo "Done creating temp file. The contents are:"
cat $tempfile
rm -f $tempfile 2> /dev/null
$ ./test19
This script writes to temp file test19.vCHoya
Done creating temp file. The contents are:
This is the first line
This is the second line.
This is the last line.
$ ls -al test19*
-rwxr--r--    1 rich      rich       356 Oct 29 22:03 test19*
$
```

The script uses the mktemp command to create a temporary file and assigns the filename to the $tempfile variable. It then uses the temporary file as the output redirection file for file descriptor 3. After displaying the temporary filename on STDOUT, it writes a few lines to the temporary file, and then it closes the file descriptor. Finally, it displays the contents of the temporary file and then uses the rm command to remove it.

Creating a temporary file in /tmp

The -t option forces mktemp to create the file in the temporary directory of the system. When you use this feature, the mktemp command returns the full pathname used to create the temporary file, not just the filename:

```
$ mktemp -t test.XXXXXX
/tmp/test.xG3374
$ ls -al /tmp/test*
-rw------- 1 rich rich 0 2014-10-29 18:41 /tmp/test.xG3374
$
```

Because the mktemp command returns the full pathname, you can then reference the temporary file from any directory on the Linux system, no matter where it places the temporary directory:

```
$ cat test20
#!/bin/bash
# creating a temp file in /tmp

tempfile=$(mktemp -t tmp.XXXXXX)

echo "This is a test file." > $tempfile
echo "This is the second line of the test." >> $tempfile

echo "The temp file is located at: $tempfile"
cat $tempfile
rm -f $tempfile
$ ./test20
The temp file is located at: /tmp/tmp.Ma3390
This is a test file.
This is the second line of the test.
$
```

When mktemp creates the temporary file, it returns the full pathname to the environment variable. You can then use that value in any command to reference the temporary file.

Creating a temporary directory

The -d option tells the mktemp command to create a temporary directory instead of a file. You can then use that directory for whatever purposes you need, such as creating additional temporary files:

15

```
$ cat test21
#!/bin/bash
# using a temporary directory

tempdir=$(mktemp -d dir.XXXXXX)
cd $tempdir
tempfile1=$(mktemp temp.XXXXXX)
tempfile2=$(mktemp temp.XXXXXX)
exec 7> $tempfile1
exec 8> $tempfile2

echo "Sending data to directory $tempdir"
echo "This is a test line of data for $tempfile1" >&7
echo "This is a test line of data for $tempfile2" >&8
$ ./test21
Sending data to directory dir.ouT8S8
$ ls -al
total 72
drwxr-xr-x    3 rich      rich          4096 Oct 17 22:20 ./
drwxr-xr-x    9 rich      rich          4096 Oct 17 09:44 ../
drwx------    2 rich      rich          4096 Oct 17 22:20 dir.ouT8S8/
-rwxr--r--    1 rich      rich           338 Oct 17 22:20 test21*
$ cd dir.ouT8S8
[dir.ouT8S8]$ ls -al
total 16
drwx------    2 rich      rich          4096 Oct 17 22:20 ./
drwxr-xr-x    3 rich      rich          4096 Oct 17 22:20 ../
-rw-------    1 rich      rich            44 Oct 17 22:20 temp.N5F3O6
-rw-------    1 rich      rich            44 Oct 17 22:20 temp.SQslb7
[dir.ouT8S8]$ cat temp.N5F3O6
This is a test line of data for temp.N5F3O6
[dir.ouT8S8]$ cat temp.SQslb7
This is a test line of data for temp.SQslb7
[dir.ouT8S8]$
```

The script creates a directory in the current directory and uses the cd command to change to that directory before creating two temporary files. The two temporary files are then assigned to file descriptors and used to store output from the script.

Logging Messages

Sometimes, it's beneficial to send output both to the monitor and to a file for logging. Instead of having to redirect output twice, you can use the special tee command.

The tee command is like a T-connector for pipes. It sends data from STDIN to two destinations at the same time. One destination is STDOUT. The other destination is a filename specified on the tee command line:

```
tee filename
```

Because `tee` redirects data from STDIN, you can use it with the pipe command to redirect output from any command:

```
$ date | tee testfile
Sun Oct 19 18:56:21 EDT 2014
$ cat testfile
Sun Oct 19 18:56:21 EDT 2014
$
```

The output appears in STDOUT and is written to the file specified. Be careful: By default, the `tee` command overwrites the output file on each use:

```
$ who | tee testfile
rich      pts/0        2014-10-17 18:41 (192.168.1.2)
$ cat testfile
rich      pts/0        2014-10-17 18:41 (192.168.1.2)
$
```

If you want to append data to the file, you must use the -a option:

```
$ date | tee -a testfile
Sun Oct 19 18:58:05 EDT 2014
$ cat testfile
rich      pts/0        2014-10-17 18:41 (192.168.1.2)
Sun Oct 19 18:58:05 EDT 2014
$
```

Using this technique, you can both save data in files and display the data on the monitor for your users:

```
$ cat test22
#!/bin/bash
# using the tee command for logging

tempfile=test22file

echo "This is the start of the test" | tee $tempfile
echo "This is the second line of the test" | tee -a $tempfile
echo "This is the end of the test" | tee -a $tempfile
$ ./test22
This is the start of the test
This is the second line of the test
This is the end of the test
$ cat test22file
This is the start of the test
This is the second line of the test
This is the end of the test
$
```

Now you can save a permanent copy of your output at the same time as you're displaying it to your users.

Practical Example

File redirection is very common both when reading files into scripts and when outputting data from a script into a file. This example script does both of those things. It reads a .csv-formatted data file and outputs SQL INSERT statements to insert the data into a database (see Chapter 25).

The shell script uses a command line parameter to define the name of the .csv file from which to read the data. The .csv format is used to export data from spreadsheets, so you can place the database data into a spreadsheet, save the spreadsheet in .csv format, read the file, and create INSERT statements to insert the data into a MySQL database.

Here's what the script looks like:

```
$cat test23
#!/bin/bash
# read file and create INSERT statements for MySQL

outfile='members.sql'
IFS=','
while read lname fname address city state zip
do
   cat >> $outfile << EOF
   INSERT INTO members (lname,fname,address,city,state,zip) VALUES
('$lname', '$fname', '$address', '$city', '$state', '$zip');
EOF
done < ${1}
$
```

That's a pretty short script, thanks to the file redirection that goes on! There are three redirection operations happening in the script. The while loop uses the read statement (discussed in Chapter 14) to read text from the data file. Notice in the done statement the redirection symbol:

```
done < ${1}
```

The $1 represents the first command line parameter when you run the test23 program. That specifies the data file from which to read the data. The read statement parses the text using the IFS character, which we specify as a comma.

The other two redirection operations in the script both appear in the same statement:

```
cat >> $outfile << EOF
```

This one statement has one output append redirection (the double greater-than symbol) and one input append redirection (the double less-than symbol). The output redirection appends the cat command output to the file specified by the $outfile variable. The input to the cat command is redirected from the standard input to use the data stored inside the script. The EOF symbol marks the start and end delimiter of the data that's appended to the file:

```
INSERT INTO members (lname,fname,address,city,state,zip) VALUES
('$lname', '$fname', '$address', '$city', '$state', '$zip');
```

The text creates a standard SQL INSERT statement. Notice that the data values are replaced with the variables for the data read from the read statement.

So basically the while loop reads on the data one line at a time, plugs those data values into the INSERT statement template, then outputs the result to the output file.

For this experiment, I used this as the input data file:

```
$ cat members.csv
Blum,Richard,123 Main St.,Chicago,IL,60601
Blum,Barbara,123 Main St.,Chicago,IL,60601
Bresnahan,Christine,456 Oak Ave.,Columbus,OH,43201
Bresnahan,Timothy,456 Oak Ave.,Columbus,OH,43201
$
```

When you run the script, nothing appears in the output on the monitor:

```
$ ./test23 < members.csv
$
```

But when you look at the members.sql output file, you should see the output data:

```
$ cat members.sql
   INSERT INTO members (lname,fname,address,city,state,zip) VALUES ('Blum',
'Richard', '123 Main St.', 'Chicago', 'IL', '60601');
   INSERT INTO members (lname,fname,address,city,state,zip) VALUES ('Blum',
'Barbara', '123 Main St.', 'Chicago', 'IL', '60601');
   INSERT INTO members (lname,fname,address,city,state,zip) VALUES ('Bresnahan',
'Christine', '456 Oak Ave.', 'Columbus', 'OH', '43201');
   INSERT INTO members (lname,fname,address,city,state,zip) VALUES ('Bresnahan',
'Timothy', '456 Oak Ave.', 'Columbus', 'OH', '43201');
$
```

The script worked exactly as expected! Now you can easily import the members.sql file into a MySQL database table (see Chapter 25).

15

Summary

Understanding how the bash shell handles input and output can come in handy when creating your scripts. You can manipulate both how the script receives data and how it displays data, to customize your script for any environment. You can redirect the input of a script from the standard input (STDIN) to any file on the system. You can also redirect the output of the script from the standard output (STDOUT) to any file on the system.

Besides the STDOUT, you can redirect any error messages your script generates by redirecting the STDERR output. This is accomplished by redirecting the file descriptor associated with the STDERR output, which is file descriptor 2. You can redirect STDERR output to the same file as the STDOUT output or to a completely separate file. This enables you to separate normal script messages from any error messages generated by the script.

The bash shell allows you to create your own file descriptors for use in your scripts. You can create file descriptors 3 through 8 and assign them to any output file you desire. After you create a file descriptor, you can redirect the output of any command to it, using the standard redirection symbols.

The bash shell also allows you to redirect input to a file descriptor, providing an easy way to read data contained in a file into your script. You can use the lsof command to display the active file descriptors in your shell.

Linux systems provide a special file, called /dev/null, to allow you to redirect output that you don't want. The Linux system discards anything redirected to the /dev/null file. You can also use this file to produce an empty file by redirecting the contents of the /dev/null file to the file.

The mktemp command is a handy feature of the bash shell that allows you to easily create temporary files and directories. Simply specify a template for the mktemp command, and it creates a unique file each time you call it, based on the file template format. You can also create temporary files and directories in the /tmp directory on the Linux system, which is a special location that isn't preserved between system boots.

The tee command is a handy way to send output both to the standard output and to a log file. This enables you to display messages from your script on the monitor and store them in a log file at the same time.

In Chapter 16, you'll see how to control and run your scripts. Linux provides several different methods for running scripts other than directly from the command line interface prompt. You'll see how to schedule your scripts to run at a specific time, as well as learn how to pause them while they're running.

Script Control

IN THIS CHAPTER

A s you start building advanced scripts, you'll probably wonder how to run and control them on your Linux system. So far in this book, the only way we've run scripts is directly from the command line interface in real-time mode. This isn't the only way to run scripts in Linux. Quite a few options are available for running your shell scripts. There are also options for controlling your scripts. Various control methods include sending signals to your script, modifying a script's priority, and switching the run mode while a script is running. This chapter examines the different ways you can control your shell scripts.

Handling Signals

Linux uses signals to communicate with processes running on the system. Chapter 4 described the different Linux signals and how the Linux system uses these signals to stop, start, and kill processes. You can control the operation of your shell script by programming the script to perform certain commands when it receives specific signals.

Signaling the bash shell

There are more than 30 Linux signals that can be generated by the system and applications. Table 16-1 lists the most common Linux system signals that you'll run across in your shell script writing.

TABLE 16-1 **Linux Signals**

Signal	Value	Description
1	SIGHUP	Hangs up the process
2	SIGINT	Interrupts the process
3	SIGQUIT	Stops the process
9	SIGKILL	Unconditionally terminates the process
15	SIGTERM	Terminates the process if possible
17	SIGSTOP	Unconditionally stops, but doesn't terminate, the process
18	SIGTSTP	Stops or pauses the process, but doesn't terminate
19	SIGCONT	Continues a stopped process

By default, the bash shell ignores any SIGQUIT (3) and SIGTERM (15) signals it receives (so an interactive shell cannot be accidentally terminated). However, the bash shell does not ignore any SIGHUP (1) and SIGINT (2) signals it receives.

If the bash shell receives a SIGHUP signal, such as when you leave an interactive shell, it exits. Before it exits, however, it passes the SIGHUP signal to any processes started by the shell, including any running shell scripts.

With a SIGINT signal, the shell is just interrupted. The Linux kernel stops giving the shell processing time on the CPU. When this happens, the shell passes the SIGINT signal to any processes started by the shell to notify them of the situation.

As you probably have noticed, the shell passes these signals on to your shell script program for processing. However, a shell script's default behavior does not govern these signals, which may have an adverse effect on the script's operation. To avoid this situation, you can program your script to recognize signals and perform commands to prepare the script for the consequences of the signal.

Generating signals

The bash shell allows you to generate two basic Linux signals using key combinations on the keyboard. This feature comes in handy if you need to stop or pause a runaway script.

Interrupting a process

The Ctrl+C key combination generates a SIGINT signal and sends it to any processes currently running in the shell. You can test this by running a command that normally takes a long time to finish and pressing the Ctrl+C key combination:

```
$ sleep 100
^C
$
```

The Ctrl+C key combination sends a SIGINT signal, which simply stops the current process running in the shell. The sleep command pauses the shell's operation for the specified number of seconds and returns the shell prompt. By pressing the Ctrl+C key combination before the time passed, the sleep command terminated prematurely.

Pausing a process

Instead of terminating a process, you can pause it in the middle of whatever it's doing. Sometimes, this can be a dangerous thing (for example, if a script has a file lock open on a crucial system file), but often it allows you to peek inside what a script is doing without actually terminating the process.

The Ctrl+Z key combination generates a SIGTSTP signal, stopping any processes running in the shell. Stopping a process is different than terminating the process. Stopping the process leaves the program in memory and able to continue running from where it left off. In the "Controlling the Job" section later in this chapter, you learn how to restart a process that's been stopped.

When you use the Ctrl+Z key combination, the shell informs you that the process has been stopped:

```
$ sleep 100
^Z
[1]+  Stopped                 sleep 100
$
```

The number in the square brackets is the *job number* assigned by the shell. The shell refers to each process running in the shell as a *job* and assigns each job a unique job number within the current shell. It assigns the first started process job number 1, the second job number 2, and so on.

If you have a stopped job assigned to your shell session, bash warns you if you try to exit the shell:

```
$ sleep 100
^Z
[1]+  Stopped                 sleep 100
$ exit
exit
There are stopped jobs.
$
```

You can view the stopped jobs using the ps command:

```
$ sleep 100
^Z
[1]+  Stopped                 sleep 100
$
$ ps -l
```

```
F S UID    PID   PPID  C PRI NI ADDR SZ WCHAN  TTY          TIME CMD
0 S 501   2431   2430  0  80  0 - 27118 wait   pts/0    00:00:00 bash
0 T 501   2456   2431  0  80  0 - 25227 signal pts/0    00:00:00 sleep
0 R 501   2458   2431  0  80  0 - 27034 -      pts/0    00:00:00 ps
$
```

In the S column (process state), the ps command shows the stopped job's state as T. This indicates the command is either being traced or is stopped.

If you really want to exit the shell with a stopped job still active, just type the exit command again. The shell exits, terminating the stopped job. Alternately, now that you know the PID of the stopped job, you can use the kill command to send a SIGKILL signal to terminate it:

```
$ kill -9 2456
$
[1]+  Killed                  sleep 100
$
```

When you kill the job, initially you don't get any response. However, the next time you do something that produces a shell prompt (such as pressing the Enter key), you'll see a message indicating that the job was killed. Each time the shell produces a prompt, it also displays the status of any jobs that have changed states in the shell. After you kill a job, the next time you force the shell to produce a prompt, it displays a message showing that the job was killed while running.

Trapping signals

Instead of allowing your script to leave signals ungoverned, you can trap them when they appear and perform other commands. The trap command allows you to specify which Linux signals your shell script can watch for and intercept from the shell. If the script receives a signal listed in the trap command, it prevents it from being processed by the shell and instead handles it locally.

The format of the trap command is:

```
trap commands signals
```

On the trap command line, you just list the commands you want the shell to execute, along with a space-separated list of signals you want to trap. You can specify the signals either by their numeric value or by their Linux signal name.

Here's a simple example of using the trap command to capture the SIGINT signal and govern the script's behavior when the signal is sent:

```
$ cat test1.sh
#!/bin/bash
# Testing signal trapping
#
```

```
trap "echo ' Sorry! I have trapped Ctrl-C'" SIGINT
#
echo This is a test script
#
count=1
while [ $count -le 10 ]
do
    echo "Loop #$count"
    sleep 1
    count=$[ $count + 1 ]
done
#
echo "This is the end of the test script"
#
```

The `trap` command used in this example displays a simple text message each time it detects the SIGINT signal. Trapping this signal makes this script impervious to the user attempting to stop the program by using the bash shell keyboard Ctrl+C command:

```
$ ./test1.sh
This is a test script
Loop #1
Loop #2
Loop #3
Loop #4
Loop #5
^C Sorry! I have trapped Ctrl-C
Loop #6
Loop #7
Loop #8
^C Sorry! I have trapped Ctrl-C
Loop #9
Loop #10
This is the end of the test script
$
```

Each time the Ctrl+C key combination was used, the script executed the echo statement specified in the `trap` command instead of not managing the signal and allowing the shell to stop the script.

Trapping a script exit

Besides trapping signals in your shell script, you can trap them when the shell script exits. This is a convenient way to perform commands just as the shell finishes its job.

To trap the shell script exiting, just add the EXIT signal to the `trap` command:

```
$ cat test2.sh
#!/bin/bash
```

```
# Trapping the script exit
#
trap "echo Goodbye..." EXIT
#
count=1
while [ $count -le 5 ]
do
    echo "Loop #$count"
    sleep 1
    count=$[ $count + 1 ]
done
#
$
$ ./test2.sh
Loop #1
Loop #2
Loop #3
Loop #4
Loop #5
Goodbye...
$
```

When the script gets to the normal exit point, the trap is triggered, and the shell executes the command you specify on the trap command line. The EXIT trap also works if you prematurely exit the script:

```
$ ./test2.sh
Loop #1
Loop #2
Loop #3
^CGoodbye...

$
```

Because the SIGINT signal isn't listed in the trap command list, when the Ctrl+C key combination is used to send that signal, the script exits. However, before the script exits, because the EXIT is trapped, the shell executes the trap command.

Modifying or removing a trap

To handle traps differently in various sections of your shell script, you simply reissue the trap command with new options:

```
$ cat test3.sh
#!/bin/bash
# Modifying a set trap
#
trap "echo ' Sorry... Ctrl-C is trapped.'" SIGINT
```

```
#
count=1
while [ $count -le 5 ]
do
    echo "Loop #$count"
    sleep 1
    count=$[ $count + 1 ]
done
#
trap "echo ' I modified the trap!'" SIGINT
#
count=1
while [ $count -le 5 ]
do
    echo "Second Loop #$count"
    sleep 1
    count=$[ $count + 1 ]
done
#
$
```

After the signal trap is modified, the script manages the signal or signals differently. However, if a signal is received before the trap is modified, the script processes it per the original trap command:

```
$ ./test3.sh
Loop #1
Loop #2
Loop #3
^C Sorry... Ctrl-C is trapped.
Loop #4
Loop #5
Second Loop #1
Second Loop #2
^C I modified the trap!
Second Loop #3
Second Loop #4
Second Loop #5
$
```

You can also remove a set trap. Simply add two dashes after the trap command and a list of the signals you want to return to default behavior:

```
$ cat test3b.sh
#!/bin/bash
# Removing a set trap
#
trap "echo ' Sorry... Ctrl-C is trapped.'" SIGINT
#
```

```
      count=1
      while [ $count -le 5 ]
      do
         echo "Loop #$count"
         sleep 1
         count=$[ $count + 1 ]
      done
      #
      # Remove the trap
      trap -- SIGINT
      echo "I just removed the trap"
      #
      count=1
      while [ $count -le 5 ]
      do
         echo "Second Loop #$count"
         sleep 1
         count=$[ $count + 1 ]
      done
      #
      $ ./test3b.sh
      Loop #1
      Loop #2
      Loop #3
      Loop #4
      Loop #5
      I just removed the trap
      Second Loop #1
      Second Loop #2
      Second Loop #3
      ^C
      $
```

> **TIP**
>
> You can use a single dash instead of a double dash after the `trap` command to return signals to their default behavior. Both the single and double dash work properly.

After the signal trap is removed, the script handles the SIGINT signal in its default manner, terminating the script. However, if a signal is received before the trap is removed, the script processes it per the original `trap` command:

```
      $ ./test3b.sh
      Loop #1
      Loop #2
      Loop #3
      ^C Sorry... Ctrl-C is trapped.
      Loop #4
```

```
Loop #5
I just removed the trap
Second Loop #1
Second Loop #2
^C
$
```

In this example, the first Ctrl+C key combination was used to attempt to terminate the script prematurely. Because the signal was received before the trap was removed, the script executed the command specified in the trap. After the script executed the trap removal, then Ctrl+C could prematurely terminate the script.

Running Scripts in Background Mode

Sometimes, running a shell script directly from the command line interface is inconvenient. Some scripts can take a long time to process, and you may not want to tie up the command line interface waiting. While the script is running, you can't do anything else in your terminal session. Fortunately, there's a simple solution to that problem.

When you use the ps command, you see a whole bunch of different processes running on the Linux system. Obviously, all these processes are not running on your terminal monitor. This is called running processes in the *background*. In background mode, a process runs without being associated with a STDIN, STDOUT, and STDERR on a terminal session (see Chapter 15).

You can exploit this feature with your shell scripts as well, allowing them to run behind the scenes and not lock up your terminal session. The following sections describe how to run your scripts in background mode on your Linux system.

Running in the background

Running a shell script in background mode is a fairly easy thing to do. To run a shell script in background mode from the command line interface, just place an ampersand symbol (&) after the command:

```
$ cat test4.sh
#!/bin/bash
# Test running in the background
#
count=1
while [ $count -le 10 ]
do
    sleep 1
    count=$[ $count + 1 ]
done
```

```
#
$
$ ./test4.sh &
[1] 3231
$
```

When you place the ampersand symbol after a command, it separates the command from the bash shell and runs it as a separate background process on the system. The first thing that displays is the line:

```
[1] 3231
```

The number in the square brackets is the job number assigned by the shell to the background process. The next number is the Process ID (PID) the Linux system assigns to the process. Every process running on the Linux system must have a unique PID.

As soon as the system displays these items, a new command line interface prompt appears. You are returned to the shell, and the command you executed runs safely in background mode. At this point, you can enter new commands at the prompt.

When the background process finishes, it displays a message on the terminal:

```
[1]     Done                        ./test4.sh
```

This shows the job number and the status of the job (Done), along with the command used to start the job.

Be aware that while the background process is running, it still uses your terminal monitor for STDOUT and STDERR messages:

```
$ cat test5.sh
#!/bin/bash
# Test running in the background with output
#
echo "Start the test script"
count=1
while [ $count -le 5 ]
do
    echo "Loop #$count"
    sleep 5
    count=$[ $count + 1 ]
done
#
echo "Test script is complete"
#
$
$ ./test5.sh &
[1] 3275
```

```
$ Start the test script
Loop #1
Loop #2
Loop #3
Loop #4
Loop #5
Test script is complete

[1]    Done                        ./test5.sh
$
```

You'll notice from the example that the output from the test5.sh script displays. The output intermixes with the shell prompt, which is why Start the test script appears next to the $ prompt.

You can still issue commands while this output is occurring:

```
$ ./test5.sh &
[1] 3319
$ Start the test script
Loop #1
Loop #2
Loop #3
ls myprog*
myprog   myprog.c
$ Loop #4
Loop #5
Test script is complete

[1]+   Done                        ./test5.sh
$$
```

While the test5.sh script is running in the background, the command ls   myprog* was entered. The script's output, the typed command, and the command's output all inter-mixed with each other's output display. This can be confusing! It is a good idea to redirect STDOUT and STDERR for scripts you will be running in the background (Chapter 15) to avoid this messy output.

Running multiple background jobs

You can start any number of background jobs at the same time from the command line prompt:

```
$ ./test6.sh &
[1] 3568
$ This is Test Script #1

$ ./test7.sh &
```

```
[2] 3570
$ This is Test Script #2

$ ./test8.sh &
[3] 3573
$ And...another Test script

$ ./test9.sh &
[4] 3576
$ Then...there was one more test script

$
```

Each time you start a new job, the Linux system assigns it a new job number and PID. You can see that all the scripts are running using the ps command:

```
$ ps
  PID TTY          TIME CMD
 2431 pts/0    00:00:00 bash
 3568 pts/0    00:00:00 test6.sh
 3570 pts/0    00:00:00 test7.sh
 3573 pts/0    00:00:00 test8.sh
 3574 pts/0    00:00:00 sleep
 3575 pts/0    00:00:00 sleep
 3576 pts/0    00:00:00 test9.sh
 3577 pts/0    00:00:00 sleep
 3578 pts/0    00:00:00 sleep
 3579 pts/0    00:00:00 ps
$
```

You must be careful when using background processes from a terminal session. Notice in the output from the ps command that each of the background processes is tied to the terminal session (pts/0) terminal. If the terminal session exits, the background process also exits.

NOTE

Earlier in this chapter we mentioned that when you attempt to exit a terminal session, a warning is issued if there are stopped processes. However, with background processes, only some terminal emulators remind you that a background job is running, before you attempt to exit the terminal session.

If you want your script to continue running in background mode after you have logged off the console, there's something else you need to do. The next section discusses that process.

Running Scripts without a Hang-Up

Sometimes, you may want to start a shell script from a terminal session and let the script run in background mode until it finishes, even if you exit the terminal session. You can do this by using the nohup command.

The nohup command runs another command blocking any SIGHUP signals that are sent to the process. This prevents the process from exiting when you exit your terminal session.

The format used for the nohup command is as follows:

```
$ nohup ./test1.sh &
[1] 3856
$ nohup: ignoring input and appending output to 'nohup.out'

$
```

As with a normal background process, the shell assigns the command a job number, and the Linux system assigns a PID number. The difference is that when you use the nohup command, the script ignores any SIGHUP signals sent by the terminal session if you close the session.

Because the nohup command disassociates the process from the terminal, the process loses the STDOUT and STDERR output links. To accommodate any output generated by the command, the nohup command automatically redirects STDOUT and STDERR messages to a file, called nohup.out.

NOTE

If you run another command using nohup, the output is appended to the existing nohup.out file. Be careful when running multiple commands from the same directory, because all the output is sent to the same nohup.out file, which can get confusing.

The nohup.out file contains all the output that would normally be sent to the terminal monitor. After the process finishes running, you can view the nohup.out file for the output results:

```
$ cat nohup.out
This is a test script
Loop 1
Loop 2
Loop 3
Loop 4
Loop 5
Loop 6
Loop 7
Loop 8
Loop 9
Loop 10
This is the end of the test script
$
```

The output appears in the nohup.out file just as if the process ran on the command line.

Controlling the Job

Earlier in this chapter, you saw how to use the Ctrl+C key combination to stop a job running in the shell. After you stop a job, the Linux system lets you either kill or restart it. You can kill the process by using the `kill` command. Restarting a stopped process requires that you send it a SIGCONT signal.

The function of starting, stopping, killing, and resuming jobs is called *job control*. With job control, you have full control over how processes run in your shell environment. This section describes the commands used to view and control jobs running in your shell.

Viewing jobs

The key command for job control is the `jobs` command. The `jobs` command allows you to view the current jobs being handled by the shell:

```
$ cat test10.sh
#!/bin/bash
# Test job control
#
echo "Script Process ID: $$"
#
count=1
while [ $count -le 10 ]
do
    echo "Loop #$count"
    sleep 10
    count=$[ $count + 1 ]
done
#
echo "End of script..."
#
$
```

The script uses the *$$* variable to display the PID that the Linux system assigns to the script; then it goes into a loop, sleeping for 10 seconds at a time for each iteration.

You can start the script from the command line interface and then stop it using the Ctrl+Z key combination:

```
$ ./test10.sh
Script Process ID: 1897
Loop #1
Loop #2
^Z
[1]+  Stopped                 ./test10.sh
$
```

Using the same script, another job is started as a background process, using the ampersand symbol. To make life a little easier, the output of that script is redirected to a file so it doesn't appear on the screen:

```
$ ./test10.sh > test10.out &
[2] 1917
$
```

The jobs command enables you to view the jobs assigned to the shell. The jobs command shows both the stopped and the running jobs, along with their job numbers and the commands used in the jobs:

```
$ jobs
[1]+  Stopped                 ./test10.sh
[2]-  Running                 ./test10.sh > test10.out &
$
```

You can view the various jobs' PIDs by adding the -l parameter (lowercase L) on the jobs command:

```
$ jobs -l
[1]+  1897 Stopped            ./test10.sh
[2]-  1917 Running            ./test10.sh > test10.out &
$
```

The jobs command uses a few different command line parameters, as shown in Table 16-2.

TABLE 16-2   The jobs Command Parameters

Parameter	Description
-l	Lists the PID of the process along with the job number
-n	Lists only jobs that have changed their status since the last notification from the shell
-p	Lists only the PIDs of the jobs
-r	Lists only the running jobs
-s	Lists only stopped jobs

You probably noticed the plus and minus signs in the jobs command output. The job with the plus sign is considered the default job. It would be the job referenced by any job control commands if a job number wasn't specified in the command line.

The job with the minus sign is the job that would become the default job when the current default job finishes processing. There will be only one job with the plus sign and one job with the minus sign at any time, no matter how many jobs are running in the shell.

The following is an example showing how the next job in line takes over the default status, when the default job is removed. Three separate processes are started in the background. The jobs command listing shows the three processes, their PID, and their status. Note that the default process (the one listed with the plus sign) is the last process started, job #3.

```
$ ./test10.sh > test10a.out &
[1] 1950
$ ./test10.sh > test10b.out &
[2] 1952
$ ./test10.sh > test10c.out &
[3] 1955
$
$ jobs -l
[1]    1950 Running                ./test10.sh > test10a.out &
[2]-   1952 Running                ./test10.sh > test10b.out &
[3]+   1955 Running                ./test10.sh > test10c.out &
$
```

Using the kill command to send a SIGHUP signal to the default process causes the job to terminate. In the next jobs listing, the job that previously had the minus sign now has the plus sign and is the default job:

```
$ kill 1955
$
[3]+  Terminated               ./test10.sh > test10c.out
$
$ jobs -l
[1]-  1950 Running                ./test10.sh > test10a.out &
[2]+  1952 Running                ./test10.sh > test10b.out &
$
$ kill 1952
$
[2]+  Terminated               ./test10.sh > test10b.out
$
$ jobs -l
[1]+  1950 Running                ./test10.sh > test10a.out &
$
```

Although changing a background job to the default process is interesting, it doesn't seem very useful. In the next section, you learn how to use commands to interact with the default process using no PID or job number.

Restarting stopped jobs

Under bash job control, you can restart any stopped job as either a background process or a foreground process. A foreground process takes over control of the terminal you're working on, so be careful about using that feature.

To restart a job in background mode, use the bg command:

```
$ ./test11.sh
^Z
[1]+  Stopped                 ./test11.sh
$
$ bg
[1]+ ./test11.sh &
$
$ jobs
[1]+  Running                 ./test11.sh &
$
```

Because the job was the default job, indicated by the plus sign, only the bg command was needed to restart it in background mode. Notice that no PID is listed when the job is moved into background mode.

If you have additional jobs, you need to use the job number along with the bg command:

```
$ ./test11.sh
^Z
[1]+  Stopped                 ./test11.sh
$
$ ./test12.sh
^Z
[2]+  Stopped                 ./test12.sh
$
$ bg 2
[2]+ ./test12.sh &
$
$ jobs
[1]+  Stopped                 ./test11.sh
[2]-  Running                 ./test12.sh &
$
```

The command bg 2 was used to send the second job into background mode. Notice that when the jobs command was used, it listed both jobs with their status, even though the default job is not currently in background mode.

To restart a job in foreground mode, use the fg command, along with the job number:

```
$ fg 2
./test12.sh
This is the script's end...
$
```

Because the job is running in foreground mode, the command line interface prompt does not appear until the job finishes.

16

Being Nice

In a multitasking operating system (which Linux is), the kernel is responsible for assigning CPU time for each process running on the system. The *scheduling priority* is the amount of CPU time the kernel assigns to the process relative to the other processes. By default, all processes started from the shell have the same scheduling priority on the Linux system.

The scheduling priority is an integer value, from -20 (the highest priority) to +19 (the lowest priority). By default, the bash shell starts all processes with a scheduling priority of 0.

> **TIP**
>
> It's confusing to remember that -20, the lowest value, is the highest priority and 19, the highest value, is the lowest priority. Just remember the phrase, "Nice guys finish last." The "nicer" or higher you are in value, the lower your chance of getting the CPU.

Sometimes, you want to change the priority of a shell script, either lowering its priority so it doesn't take as much processing power away from other processes or giving it a higher priority so it gets more processing time. You can do this by using the nice command.

Using the nice command

The nice command allows you to set the scheduling priority of a command as you start it. To make a command run with less priority, just use the -n command line option for nice to specify a new priority level:

```
$ nice -n 10 ./test4.sh > test4.out &
[1] 4973
$
$ ps -p 4973 -o pid,ppid,ni,cmd
  PID  PPID  NI CMD
 4973  4721  10 /bin/bash ./test4.sh
$
```

Notice that you must use the nice command on the same line as the command you are starting. The output from the ps command confirms that the nice value (column NI) has been set to 10.

The nice command causes the script to run at a lower priority. However, if you try to increase the priority of one of your commands, you might be in for a surprise:

```
$ nice -n -10 ./test4.sh > test4.out &
[1] 4985
$ nice: cannot set niceness: Permission denied

  [1]+  Done                    nice -n -10 ./test4.sh > test4.out
$
```

The nice command prevents normal system users from increasing the priority of their commands. Notice that the job does run, even though the attempt to raise its priority with the nice command failed.

You don't have to use the -n option with the nice command. You can simply type the priority preceded by a dash:

```
$ nice -10 ./test4.sh > test4.out &
[1] 4993
$
$ ps -p 4993 -o pid,ppid,ni,cmd
  PID  PPID  NI CMD
 4993  4721  10 /bin/bash ./test4.sh
$
```

However, this can get confusing when the priority is a negative number, because you must have a double-dash. It's best just to use the -n option to avoid confusion.

Using the renice command

Sometimes, you'd like to change the priority of a command that's already running on the system. That's what the renice command is for. It allows you to specify the PID of a running process to change its priority:

```
$ ./test11.sh &
[1] 5055
$
$ ps -p 5055 -o pid,ppid,ni,cmd
  PID  PPID  NI CMD
 5055  4721   0 /bin/bash ./test11.sh
$
$ renice -n 10 -p 5055
5055: old priority 0, new priority 10
$
$ ps -p 5055 -o pid,ppid,ni,cmd
  PID  PPID  NI CMD
 5055  4721  10 /bin/bash ./test11.sh
$
```

The renice command automatically updates the scheduling priority of the running process. As with the nice command, the renice command has some limitations:

- You can only renice processes that you own.
- You can only renice your processes to a lower priority.
- The root user can renice any process to any priority.

If you want to fully control running processes, you must be logged in as the root account or use the sudo command.

Running Like Clockwork

When you start working with scripts, you may want to run a script at a preset time, usually at a time when you're not there. The Linux system provides a couple of ways to run a script at a preselected time: the at command and the cron table. Each method uses a different technique for scheduling when and how often to run scripts. The following sections describe each of these methods.

Scheduling a job using the at command

The at command allows you to specify a time when the Linux system will run a script. The at command submits a job to a queue with directions on when the shell should run the job. The at daemon, atd, runs in the background and checks the job queue for jobs to run. Most Linux distributions start this daemon automatically at boot time.

The atd daemon checks a special directory on the system (usually /var/spool/at) for jobs submitted using the at command. By default, the atd daemon checks this directory every 60 seconds. When a job is present, the atd daemon checks the time the job is set to be run. If the time matches the current time, the atd daemon runs the job.

The following sections describe how to use the at command to submit jobs to run and how to manage these jobs.

Understanding the at command format

The basic at command format is pretty simple:

```
at [-f filename] time
```

By default, the at command submits input from STDIN to the queue. You can specify a filename used to read commands (your script file) using the -f parameter.

The *time* parameter specifies when you want the Linux system to run the job. If you specify a time that has already passed, the at command runs the job at that time on the next day.

You can get pretty creative with how you specify the time. The at command recognizes lots of different time formats:

- A standard hour and minute, such as 10:15
- An AM/PM indicator, such as 10:15PM
- A specific named time, such as now, noon, midnight, or teatime (4PM)

In addition to specifying the time to run the job, you can also include a specific date, using a few different date formats:

- A standard date format, such as MMDDYY, MM/DD/YY, or DD.MM.YY

- A text date, such as Jul 4 or Dec 25, with or without the year

- A time increment:

    - Now + 25 minutes
    - 10:15PM tomorrow
    - 10:15 + 7 days

When you use the at command, the job is submitted into a *job queue*. The job queue holds the jobs submitted by the at command for processing. There are 26 different job queues available for different priority levels. Job queues are referenced using lowercase letters, *a* through *z*, and uppercase letters *A* through *Z*.

NOTE

A few years ago, the batch command was another method that allowed a script to be run at a later time. The batch command was unique because you could schedule a script to run when the system was at a lower usage level. However, nowadays, the batch command is just simply a script, /usr/bin/batch, that calls the at command and submits your job to the b queue.

The higher alphabetically the job queue, the lower the priority (higher nice value) the job will run under. By default, at jobs are submitted to the at job a queue. If you want to run a job at a lower priority, you can specify a different queue letter using the -q parameter.

Retrieving job output

When the job runs on the Linux system, there's no monitor associated with the job. Instead, the Linux system uses the e-mail address of the user who submitted the job as STDOUT and STDERR. Any output destined to STDOUT or STDERR is mailed to the user via the mail system.

Here's a simple example using the at command to schedule a job to run on a CentOS distribution:

```
$ cat test13.sh
#!/bin/bash
# Test using at command
#
echo "This script ran at $(date +%B%d,%T)"
echo
sleep 5
echo "This is the script's end..."
#
```

```
$ at -f test13.sh now
job 7 at 2015-07-14 12:38
$
```

The `at` command displays the job number assigned to the job along with the time the job is scheduled to run. The `-f` option tells what script file to use and the `now` time designation directs `at` to run the script immediately.

Using e-mail for the `at` command's output is inconvenient at best. The `at` command sends e-mail via the sendmail application. If your system does not use sendmail, you won't get any output! Therefore, it's best to redirect STDOUT and STDERR in your scripts (see Chapter 15) when using the `at` command, as the following example shows:

```
$ cat test13b.sh
#!/bin/bash
# Test using at command
#
echo "This script ran at $(date +%B%d,%T)" > test13b.out
echo >> test13b.out
sleep 5
echo "This is the script's end..." >> test13b.out
#
$
$ at -M -f test13b.sh now
job 8 at 2015-07-14 12:48
$
$ cat test13b.out
This script ran at July14,12:48:18

This is the script's end...
$
```

If you don't want to use e-mail or redirection with `at`, it is best to add the `-M` option to suppress any output generated by jobs using the `at` command.

Listing pending jobs

The `atq` command allows you to view what jobs are pending on the system:

```
$ at -M -f test13b.sh teatime
job 17 at 2015-07-14 16:00
$
$ at -M -f test13b.sh tomorrow
job 18 at 2015-07-15 13:03
$
$ at -M -f test13b.sh 13:30
job 19 at 2015-07-14 13:30
$
$ at -M -f test13b.sh now
```

```
job 20 at 2015-07-14 13:03
$
$ atq
20        2015-07-14 13:03 = Christine
18        2015-07-15 13:03 a Christine
17        2015-07-14 16:00 a Christine
19        2015-07-14 13:30 a Christine
$
```

The job listing shows the job number, the date and time the system will run the job, and the job queue the job is stored in.

Removing jobs

After you know the information about what jobs are pending in the job queues, you can use the atrm command to remove a pending job:

```
$ atq
18        2015-07-15 13:03 a Christine
17        2015-07-14 16:00 a Christine
19        2015-07-14 13:30 a Christine
$
$ atrm 18
$
$ atq
17        2015-07-14 16:00 a Christine
19        2015-07-14 13:30 a Christine
$
```

Just specify the job number you want to remove. You can only remove jobs that you submit for execution. You can't remove jobs submitted by others.

Scheduling regular scripts

Using the at command to schedule a script to run at a preset time is great, but what if you need that script to run at the same time every day or once a week or once a month? Instead of having to continually submit at jobs, you can use another feature of the Linux system.

The Linux system uses the cron program to allow you to schedule jobs that need to run on a regular basis. The cron program runs in the background and checks special tables, called *cron tables,* for jobs that are scheduled to run.

Looking at the cron table

The cron table uses a special format for allowing you to specify when a job should be run. The format for the cron table is:

```
min hour dayofmonth month dayofweek command
```

The cron table allows you to specify entries as specific values, ranges of values (such as 1–5), or as a wildcard character (the asterisk). For example, if you want to run a command at 10:15 on every day, you would use this cron table entry:

```
15 10 * * * command
```

The wildcard character used in the *dayofmonth*, *month*, and *dayofweek* fields indicates that cron will execute the command every day of every month at 10:15. To specify a command to run at 4:15 PM every Monday, you would use the following:

```
15 16 * * 1 command
```

You can specify the *dayofweek* entry as either a three-character text value (mon, tue, wed, thu, fri, sat, sun) or as a numeric value, with 0 being Sunday and 6 being Saturday.

Here's another example: to execute a command at 12 noon on the first day of every month, you would use the following format:

```
00 12 1 * * command
```

The *dayofmonth* entry specifies a date value (1–31) for the month.

The command list must specify the full command pathname or shell script to run. You can add any command line parameters or redirection symbols you like, as a regular command line:

```
15 10 * * * /home/rich/test4.sh > test4out
```

The cron program runs the script using the user account that submitted the job. Thus, you must have the proper permissions to access the command and output files specified in the command listing.

Building the cron table

Each system user can have their own cron table (including the root user) for running scheduled jobs. Linux provides the crontab command for handling the cron table. To list an existing cron table, use the -l parameter:

```
$ crontab -l
no crontab for rich
$
```

By default, each user's cron table file doesn't exist. To add entries to your cron table, use the -e parameter. When you do that, the crontab command starts a text editor (see Chapter 10) with the existing cron table (or an empty file if it doesn't yet exist).

Viewing cron directories

When you create a script that has less precise execution time needs, it is easier to use one of the pre-configured cron script directories. There are four basic directories: hourly, daily, monthly, and weekly.

```
$ ls /etc/cron.*ly
/etc/cron.daily:
cups          makewhatis.cron  prelink          tmpwatch
logrotate     mlocate.cron     readahead.cron

/etc/cron.hourly:
0anacron

/etc/cron.monthly:
readahead-monthly.cron

/etc/cron.weekly:
$
```

Thus, if you have a script that needs to be run one time per day, just copy the script to the daily directory and cron executes it each day.

Looking at the anacron program

The only problem with the cron program is that it assumes that your Linux system is operational 24 hours a day, 7 days a week. Unless you're running Linux in a server environment, this may not necessarily be true.

If the Linux system is turned off at the time a job is scheduled to run in the cron table, the job doesn't run. The cron program doesn't retroactively run missed jobs when the system is turned back on. To resolve this issue, many Linux distributions also include the anacron program.

If anacron determines that a job has missed a scheduled running, it runs the job as soon as possible. This means that if your Linux system is turned off for a few days, when it starts back up, any jobs scheduled to run during the time it was off are automatically run.

This feature is often used for scripts that perform routine log maintenance. If the system is always off when the script should run, the log files would never get trimmed and could grow to undesirable sizes. With `anacron`, you're guaranteed that the log files are trimmed at least each time the system is started.

The `anacron` program deals only with programs located in the `cron` directories, such as `/etc/cron.monthly`. It uses timestamps to determine if the jobs have been run at the proper scheduled interval. A timestamp file exists for each `cron` directory and is located in `/var/spool/anacron`:

```
$ sudo cat /var/spool/anacron/cron.monthly
20150626
$
```

The `anacron` program has its own table (usually located at `/etc/anacrontab`) to check the job directories:

```
$ sudo cat /etc/anacrontab
# /etc/anacrontab: configuration file for anacron

# See anacron(8) and anacrontab(5) for details.

SHELL=/bin/sh
PATH=/sbin:/bin:/usr/sbin:/usr/bin
MAILTO=root
# the maximal random delay added to the base delay of the jobs
RANDOM_DELAY=45
# the jobs will be started during the following hours only
START_HOURS_RANGE=3-22

#period in days   delay in minutes   job-identifier   command
1       5         cron.daily              nice run-parts /etc/cron.daily
7       25        cron.weekly             nice run-parts /etc/cron.weekly
@monthly 45       cron.monthly            nice run-parts /etc/cron.monthly
$
```

The basic format of the `anacron` table is slightly different from that of the `cron` table:

```
period delay identifier command
```

The period entry defines how often the jobs should be run, specified in days. The `anacron` program uses this entry to check against the jobs' timestamp file. The delay entry specifies how many minutes after the system starts the `anacron` program should run missed scripts. The command entry contains the `run-parts` program and a `cron` script directory name. The `run-parts` program is responsible for running any script in the directory passed to it.

Notice that anacron does not run the scripts located in `/etc/cron.hourly`. This is because the `anacron` program does not deal with scripts that have execution time needs of less than daily.

The identifier entry is a unique non-blank character string — for example, `cron-weekly`. It is used to uniquely identify the job in log messages and error e-mails.

Starting scripts with a new shell

The ability to run a script every time a user starts a new bash shell (even just when a specific user starts a bash shell) can come in handy. Sometimes, you want to set shell features for a shell session or just ensure that a specific file has been set.

Recall the startup files run when a user logs into the bash shell (covered in detail in Chapter6). Also, remember that not every distribution has all the startup files. Essentially, the first file found in the following ordered list is run and the rest are ignored:

- `$HOME/.bash_profile`
- `$HOME/.bash_login`
- `$HOME/.profile`

Therefore, you should place any scripts you want run at login time in the first file listed.

The bash shell runs the `.bashrc` file any time a new shell is started. You can test this by adding a simple echo statement to the `.bashrc` file in your home directory and starting a new shell:

```
$ cat .bashrc
# .bashrc

# Source global definitions
if [ -f /etc/bashrc ]; then
        . /etc/bashrc
fi

# User specific aliases and functions
echo "I'm in a new shell!"
$
$ bash
I'm in a new shell!
$
$ exit
exit
$
```

The `.bashrc` file is also typically run from one of the bash startup files. Because the `.bashrc` file runs both when you log into the bash shell and when you start a bash shell, if you need a script to run in both instances, place your shell script inside this file.

Summary

The Linux system allows you to control your shell scripts by using signals. The bash shell accepts signals and passes them on to any process running under the shell process. Linux signals allow you to easily kill a runaway process or temporarily pause a long-running process.

You can use the `trap` statement in your scripts to catch signals and perform commands. This feature provides a simple way to control whether a user can interrupt your script while it's running.

By default, when you run a script in a terminal session shell, the interactive shell is suspended until the script completes. You can cause a script or command to run in background mode by adding an ampersand sign (&) after the command name. When you run a script or command in background mode, the interactive shell returns, allowing you to continue entering more commands. Any background processes run using this method are still tied to the terminal session. If you exit the terminal session, the background processes also exit.

To prevent this from happening, use the `nohup` command. This command intercepts any signals intended for the command that would stop it — for example, when you exit the terminal session. This allows scripts to continue running in background mode even if you exit the terminal session.

When you move a process to background mode, you can still control what happens to it. The jobs command allows you to view processes started from the shell session. After you know the job ID of a background process, you can use the `kill` command to send Linux signals to the process or use the `fg` command to bring the process back to the foreground in the shell session. You can suspend a running foreground process by using the Ctrl+Z key combination and place it back in background mode, using the `bg` command.

The `nice` and `renice` commands allow you to change the priority level of a process. By giving a process a lower priority, you allow the CPU to allocate less time to it. This comes in handy when running long processes that can take lots of CPU time.

In addition to controlling processes while they're running, you can also determine when a process starts on the system. Instead of running a script directly from the command line interface prompt, you can schedule the process to run at an alternative time. You can accomplish this in several different ways. The `at` command enables you to run a script once at a preset time. The `cron` program provides an interface that can run scripts at a regularly scheduled interval.

Finally, the Linux system provides script files for you to use for scheduling your scripts to run whenever a user starts a new bash shell. Similarly, the startup files, such as `.bashrc`, are located in every user's home directory to provide a location to place scripts and commands that run with a new shell.

In the next chapter, we look at how to write script functions. Script functions allow you to write code blocks once and then use them in multiple locations throughout your script.

Part III

Advanced Shell Scripting

IN THIS PART

17

Creating Functions

IN THIS CHAPTER

Basic script functions

Returning a value

Using variables in functions

Array and variable functions

Function recursion

Creating a library

Using functions on the command line

O ften while writing shell scripts, you'll find yourself using the same code in multiple locations. If it's just a small code snippet, it's usually not that big of a deal. However, rewriting large chunks of code multiple times in your shell script can get tiring. The bash shell provides a way to help you out by supporting user-defined functions. You can encapsulate your shell script code into a function and use it as many times as you want anywhere in your script. This chapter walks you through the process of creating your own shell script functions and demonstrates how to use them in other shell script applications.

Basic Script Functions

As you start writing more complex shell scripts, you'll find yourself reusing parts of code that perform specific tasks. Sometimes, it's something simple, such as displaying a text message and retrieving an answer from the script users. Other times, it's a complicated calculation that's used multiple times in your script as part of a larger process.

In each of these situations, it can get tiresome writing the same blocks of code over and over in your script. It would be nice to just write the block of code once and be able to refer to that block of code anywhere in your script without having to rewrite it.

The bash shell provides a feature allowing you to do just that. *Functions* are blocks of script code that you assign a name to and reuse anywhere in your code. Anytime you need to use that block of code in your script, you simply use the function name you assigned it (referred to as *calling* the function). This section describes how to create and use functions in your shell scripts.

Creating a function

There are two formats you can use to create functions in bash shell scripts. The first format uses the keyword `function`, along with the function name you assign to the block of code:

```
function name {
    commands
}
```

The `name` attribute defines a unique name assigned to the function. Each function you define in your script must be assigned a unique name.

The `commands` are one or more bash shell commands that make up your function. When you call the function, the bash shell executes each of the commands in the order they appear in the function, just as in a normal script.

The second format for defining a function in a bash shell script more closely follows how functions are defined in other programming languages:

```
name() {
commands
}
```

The empty parentheses after the function name indicate that you're defining a function. The same naming rules apply in this format as in the original shell script function format.

Using functions

To use a function in your script, specify the function name on a line, just as you would any other shell command:

```
$ cat test1
#!/bin/bash
# using a function in a script

function func1 {
    echo "This is an example of a function"
}

count=1
while [ $count -le 5 ]
do
    func1
    count=$[ $count + 1 ]
```

```
done

echo "This is the end of the loop"
func1
echo "Now this is the end of the script"
$
$ ./test1
This is an example of a function
This is an example of a function
This is an example of a function
This is an example of a function
This is an example of a function
This is the end of the loop
This is an example of a function
Now this is the end of the script
$
```

Each time you reference the func1 function name, the bash shell returns to the func1 function definition and executes any commands you defined there.

The function definition doesn't have to be the first thing in your shell script, but be careful. If you attempt to use a function before it's defined, you'll get an error message:

```
$ cat test2
#!/bin/bash
# using a function located in the middle of a script

count=1
echo "This line comes before the function definition"

function func1 {
    echo "This is an example of a function"
}

while [ $count -le 5 ]
do
    func1
    count=$[ $count + 1 ]
done
echo "This is the end of the loop"
func2
echo "Now this is the end of the script"

function func2 {
    echo "This is an example of a function"
}
$
$ ./test2
This line comes before the function definition
This is an example of a function
```

```
This is an example of a function
This is an example of a function
This is an example of a function
This is an example of a function
This is the end of the loop
./test2: func2: command not found
Now this is the end of the script
$
```

The first function, func1, was defined after a couple of statements in the script, which is perfectly fine. When the func1 function was used in the script, the shell knew where to find it.

However, the script attempted to use the func2 function before it was defined. Because the func2 function wasn't defined, when the script reached the place where we used it, it produced an error message.

You also need to be careful about your function names. Remember, each function name must be unique, or you'll have a problem. If you redefine a function, the new definition overrides the original function definition, without producing any error messages:

```
$ cat test3
#!/bin/bash
# testing using a duplicate function name

function func1 {
echo "This is the first definition of the function name"
}

func1

function func1 {
    echo "This is a repeat of the same function name"
}

func1
echo "This is the end of the script"
$
$ ./test3
This is the first definition of the function name
This is a repeat of the same function name
This is the end of the script
$
```

The original definition of the func1 function works fine, but after the second definition of the func1 function, any subsequent uses of the function use the second definition.

Returning a Value

The bash shell treats functions like mini-scripts, complete with an exit status (see Chapter11). There are three different ways you can generate an exit status for your functions.

The default exit status

By default, the exit status of a function is the exit status returned by the last command in the function. After the function executes, you use the standard $? variable to determine the exit status of the function:

```
$ cat test4
#!/bin/bash
# testing the exit status of a function

func1() {
    echo "trying to display a non-existent file"
    ls -l badfile
}

echo "testing the function: "
func1
echo "The exit status is: $?"
$
$ ./test4
testing the function:
trying to display a non-existent file
ls: badfile: No such file or directory
The exit status is: 1
$
```

The exit status of the function is 1 because the last command in the function failed. However, you have no way of knowing if any of the other commands in the function completed successfully or not. Look at this example:

```
$ cat test4b
#!/bin/bash
# testing the exit status of a function

func1() {
    ls -l badfile
    echo "This was a test of a bad command"
```

```
    }

    echo "testing the function:"
    func1
    echo "The exit status is: $?"
    $
    $ ./test4b
    testing the function:
    ls: badfile: No such file or directory
    This was a test of a bad command
    The exit status is: 0
    $
```

This time, because the function ended with an echo statement that completed successfully, the exit status of the function is 0, even though one of the commands in the function failed. Using the default exit status of a function can be a dangerous practice. Fortunately, we have a couple of other solutions.

Using the return command

The bash shell uses the return command to exit a function with a specific exit status. The return command allows you to specify a single integer value to define the function exit status, providing an easy way for you to programmatically set the exit status of your function:

```
    $ cat test5
    #!/bin/bash
    # using the return command in a function

    function dbl {
        read -p "Enter a value: " value
        echo "doubling the value"
        return $[ $value * 2 ]
    }

    dbl
    echo "The new value is $?"
    $
```

The dbl function doubles the integer value contained in the *$value* variable provided by the user input. It then returns the result using the return command, which the script displays using the *$?* variable.

You must be careful, however, when using this technique to return a value from a function. Keep the following two tips in mind to avoid problems:

- Remember to retrieve the return value as soon as the function completes.
- Remember that an exit status must be in the range of 0 to 255.

If you execute any other commands before retrieving the value of the function, using the $?$ variable, the return value from the function is lost. Remember that the $?$ variable returns the exit status of the last executed command.

The second problem defines a limitation for using this return value technique. Because an exit status must be less than 256, the result of your function must produce an integer value less than 256. Any value over that returns an error value:

```
$ ./test5
Enter a value: 200
doubling the value
The new value is 1
$
```

You cannot use this return value technique if you need to return either larger integer values or a string value. Instead, you need to use another method, demonstrated in the next section.

Using function output

Just as you can capture the output of a command to a shell variable, you can also capture the output of a function to a shell variable. You can use this technique to retrieve any type of output from a function to assign to a variable:

```
result='dbl'
```

This command assigns the output of the dbl function to the $result shell variable. Here's an example of using this method in a script:

```
$ cat test5b
#!/bin/bash
# using the echo to return a value

function dbl {
    read -p "Enter a value: " value
    echo $[ $value * 2 ]
}

result=$(dbl)
echo "The new value is $result"
$
$ ./test5b
Enter a value: 200
The new value is 400
$
$ ./test5b
```

```
Enter a value: 1000
The new value is 2000
$
```

The new function now uses an echo statement to display the result of the calculation. The script just captures the output of the dbl function instead of looking at the exit status for the answer.

There's a subtle trick that this example demonstrates. You'll notice that the dbl function really outputs two messages. The read command outputs a short message querying the user for the value. The bash shell script is smart enough to not consider this as part of the STDOUT output and ignores it. If you had used an echo statement to produce this query message to the user, it would have been captured by the shell variable as well as the output value.

> **NOTE**
> Using this technique, you can also return floating point and string values, making this an extremely versatile method for returning values from functions.

Using Variables in Functions

You might have noticed in the test5 example in the previous section that we used a variable called $value within the function to hold the value that it processed. When you use variables in your functions, you need to be somewhat careful about how you define and handle them. This is a common cause of problems in shell scripts. This section goes over a few techniques for handling variables both inside and outside your shell script functions.

Passing parameters to a function

As mentioned earlier in the "Returning a Value" section, the bash shell treats functions just like mini-scripts. This means that you can pass parameters to a function just like a regular script (see Chapter 14).

Functions can use the standard parameter environment variables to represent any parameters passed to the function on the command line. For example, the name of the function is defined in the $0 variable, and any parameters on the function command line are defined using the variables $1, $2, and so on. You can also use the special variable $# to determine the number of parameters passed to the function.

When specifying the function in your script, you must provide the parameters on the same command line as the function, like this:

```
func1 $value1 10
```

The function can then retrieve the parameter values using the parameter environment variables. Here's an example of using this method to pass values to a function:

```
$ cat test6
#!/bin/bash
# passing parameters to a function

function addem {
   if [ $# -eq 0 ] || [ $# -gt 2 ]
   then
      echo -1
   elif [ $# -eq 1 ]
   then
      echo $[ $1 + $1 ]
   else
      echo $[ $1 + $2 ]
   fi
}

echo -n "Adding 10 and 15: "
value=$(addem 10 15)
echo $value
echo -n "Let's try adding just one number: "
value=$(addem 10)
echo $value
echo -n "Now trying adding no numbers: "
value=$(addem)
echo $value
echo -n "Finally, try adding three numbers: "
value=$(addem 10 15 20)
echo $value
$
$ ./test6
Adding 10 and 15: 25
Let's try adding just one number: 20
Now trying adding no numbers: -1
Finally, try adding three numbers: -1
$
```

The addem function in the text6 script first checks the number of parameters passed to it by the script. If there aren't any parameters, or if there are more than two parameters, addem returns a value of -1. If there's just one parameter, addem adds the parameter to itself for the result. If there are two parameters, addem adds them together for the result.

Because the function uses the special parameter environment variables for its own parameter values, it can't directly access the script parameter values from the command line of the script. The following example fails:

```
$ cat badtest1
#!/bin/bash
```

```
# trying to access script parameters inside a function

function badfunc1 {
    echo $[ $1 * $2 ]
}

if [ $# -eq 2 ]
then
    value=$(badfunc1)
    echo "The result is $value"
else
    echo "Usage: badtest1 a b"
fi
$
$ ./badtest1
Usage: badtest1 a b
$ ./badtest1 10 15
./badtest1: *  : syntax error: operand expected (error token is "*
")
The result is
$
```

Even though the function uses the *$1* and *$2* variables, they aren't the same *$1* and *$2* variables available in the main part of the script. Instead, if you want to use those values in your function, you have to manually pass them when you call the function:

```
$ cat test7
#!/bin/bash
# trying to access script parameters inside a function

function func7 {
    echo $[ $1 * $2 ]
}

if [ $# -eq 2 ]
then
    value=$(func7 $1 $2)
    echo "The result is $value"
else
    echo "Usage: badtest1 a b"
fi
$
$ ./test7
Usage: badtest1 a b
$ ./test7 10 15
The result is 150
$
```

By passing the $1 and $2 variables to the function, they become available for the function to use, just like any other parameter.

Handling variables in a function

One thing that causes problems for shell script programmers is the *scope* of a variable. The scope is where the variable is visible. Variables defined in functions can have a different scope than regular variables. That is, they can be hidden from the rest of the script.

Functions use two types of variables:

- Global
- Local

The following sections describe how to use both types of variables in your functions.

Global variables

Global variables are variables that are valid anywhere within the shell script. If you define a global variable in the main section of a script, you can retrieve its value inside a function. Likewise, if you define a global variable inside a function, you can retrieve its value in the main section of the script.

By default, any variables you define in the script are global variables. Variables defined outside of a function can be accessed within the function just fine:

```
$ cat test8
#!/bin/bash
# using a global variable to pass a value

function dbl {
   value=$[ $value * 2 ]
}

read -p "Enter a value: " value
dbl
echo "The new value is: $value"
$
$ ./test8
Enter a value: 450
The new value is: 900
$
```

The $value variable is defined outside of the function and assigned a value outside of the function. When the dbl function is called, the variable and its value are still valid inside the function. When the variable is assigned a new value inside the function, that new value is still valid when the script references the variable.

This can be a dangerous practice, however, especially if you intend to use your functions in different shell scripts. It requires that you know exactly what variables are used in the function, including any variables used to calculate values not returned to the script. Here's an example of how things can go bad:

```
$ cat badtest2
#!/bin/bash
# demonstrating a bad use of variables

function func1 {
    temp=$[ $value + 5 ]
    result=$[ $temp * 2 ]
}

temp=4
value=6

func1
echo "The result is $result"
if [ $temp -gt $value ]
then
    echo "temp is larger"
else
    echo "temp is smaller"
fi
$
$ ./badtest2
The result is 22
temp is larger
$
```

Because the $temp variable was used in the function, its value is compromised in the script, producing a result that you may not have intended. There's an easy way to solve this problem in your functions, as shown in the next section.

Local variables

Instead of using global variables in functions, any variables that the function uses internally can be declared as local variables. To do that, just use the local keyword in front of the variable declaration:

```
local temp
```

You can also use the local keyword in an assignment statement while assigning a value to the variable:

```
local temp=$[ $value + 5 ]
```

The `local` keyword ensures that the variable is limited to only within the function. If a variable with the same name appears outside the function in the script, the shell keeps the two variable values separate. Now you can easily keep your function variables separate from your script variables and share only the ones you want to share:

```
$ cat test9
#!/bin/bash
# demonstrating the local keyword

function func1 {
    local temp=$[ $value + 5 ]
    result=$[ $temp * 2 ]
}

temp=4
value=6

func1
echo "The result is $result"
if [ $temp -gt $value ]
then
    echo "temp is larger"
else
    echo "temp is smaller"
fi
$
$ ./test9
The result is 22
temp is smaller
$
```

Now when you use the $temp variable within the func1 function, it doesn't affect the value assigned to the $temp variable in the main script.

Array Variables and Functions

Chapter 6 discussed an advanced way of allowing a single variable to hold multiple values by using arrays. Using array variable values with functions is a little tricky, and there are some special considerations. This section describes a technique that allows you to do that.

Passing arrays to functions

The art of passing an array variable to a script function can be confusing. If you try to pass the array variable as a single parameter, it doesn't work:

```
$ cat badtest3
#!/bin/bash
```

```
# trying to pass an array variable

function testit {
    echo "The parameters are: $@"
    thisarray=$1
    echo "The received array is ${thisarray[*]}"
}

myarray=(1 2 3 4 5)
echo "The original array is: ${myarray[*]}"
testit $myarray
$
$ ./badtest3
The original array is: 1 2 3 4 5
The parameters are: 1
The received array is 1
$
```

If you try using the array variable as a function parameter, the function only picks up the first value of the array variable.

To solve this problem, you must disassemble the array variable into its individual values and use the values as function parameters. Inside the function, you can reassemble all the parameters into a new array variable. Here's an example of doing this:

```
$ cat test10
#!/bin/bash
# array variable to function test

function testit {
    local newarray
    newarray=(;'echo "$@"')
    echo "The new array value is: ${newarray[*]}"
}

myarray=(1 2 3 4 5)
echo "The original array is ${myarray[*]}"
testit ${myarray[*]}
$
$ ./test10
The original array is 1 2 3 4 5
The new array value is: 1 2 3 4 5
$
```

The script uses the $myarray variable to hold all the individual array values to place them all on the command line for the function. The function then rebuilds the array variable from the command line parameters. Once inside the function, the array can be used just like any other array:

```
$ cat test11
#!/bin/bash
```

```
# adding values in an array

function addarray {
    local sum=0
    local newarray
    newarray=($(echo "$@"))
    for value in ${newarray[*]}
    do
        sum=$[ $sum + $value ]
    done
    echo $sum
}

myarray=(1 2 3 4 5)
echo "The original array is: ${myarray[*]}"
arg1=$(echo ${myarray[*]})
result=$(addarray $arg1)
echo "The result is $result"
$
$ ./test11
The original array is: 1 2 3 4 5
The result is 15
$
```

The addarray function iterates through the array values, adding them together. You can put any number of values in the *myarray* array variable, and the addarray function adds them.

Returning arrays from functions

Passing an array variable from a function back to the shell script uses a similar technique. The function uses an echo statement to output the individual array values in the proper order, and the script must reassemble them into a new array variable:

```
$ cat test12
#!/bin/bash
# returning an array value

function arraydblr {
    local origarray
    local newarray
    local elements
    local i
    origarray=($(echo "$@"))
    newarray=($(echo "$@"))
    elements=$[ $# - 1 ]
    for (( i = 0; i <= $elements; i++ ))
    {
        newarray[$i]=$[ ${origarray[$i]} * 2 ]
    }
```

```
        echo ${newarray[*]}
}

myarray=(1 2 3 4 5)
echo "The original array is: ${myarray[*]}"
arg1=$(echo ${myarray[*]})
result=($(arraydblr $arg1))
echo "The new array is: ${result[*]}"
$
$ ./test12
The original array is: 1 2 3 4 5
The new array is: 2 4 6 8 10
```

The script passes the array value, using the *$arg1* variable to the arraydblr function. The arraydblr function reassembles the array into a new array variable, and it makes a copy for the output array variable. It then iterates through the individual array variable values, doubles each value, and places it into the copy of the array variable in the function.

The arraydblr function then uses the echo statement to output the individual values of the array variable values. The script uses the output of the arraydblr function to reassemble a new array variable with the values.

Function Recursion

One feature that local function variables provide is *self-containment.* A self-contained function doesn't use any resources outside of the function, other than whatever variables the script passes to it in the command line.

This feature enables the function to be called *recursively,* which means that the function calls itself to reach an answer. Usually, a recursive function has a base value that it eventually iterates down to. Many advanced mathematical algorithms use recursion to reduce a complex equation down one level repeatedly, until they get to the level defined by the base value.

The classic example of a recursive algorithm is calculating factorials. A factorial of a number is the value of the preceding numbers multiplied with the number. Thus, to find the factorial of 5, you'd perform the following equation:

```
5! = 1 * 2 * 3 * 4 * 5 = 120
```

Using recursion, the equation is reduced down to the following format:

```
x! = x * (x-1)!
```

or in English, the factorial of *x* is equal to *x* times the factorial of *x-1*. This can be expressed in a simple recursive script:

```
function factorial {
   if [ $1 -eq 1 ]
```

```
    then
        echo 1
    else
        local temp=$[ $1 - 1 ]
        local result='factorial $temp'
        echo $[ $result * $1 ]
    fi
}
```

The factorial function uses itself to calculate the value for the factorial:

```
$ cat test13
#!/bin/bash
# using recursion

function factorial {
    if [ $1 -eq 1 ]
    then
        echo 1
    else
        local temp=$[ $1 - 1 ]
        local result=$(factorial $temp)
        echo $[ $result * $1 ]
    fi
}

read -p "Enter value: " value
result=$(factorial $value)
echo "The factorial of $value is: $result"
$
$ ./test13
Enter value: 5
The factorial of 5 is: 120
$
```

Using the factorial function is easy. Having created a function like this, you may want to use it in other scripts. Next, we look at how to do that efficiently.

Creating a Library

It's easy to see how functions can help save typing in a single script, but what if you just happen to use the same single code block between scripts? It's obviously challenging if you have to define the same function in each script, only to use it one time in each script.

There's a solution for that problem! The bash shell allows you to create a *library file* for your functions and then reference that single library file in as many scripts as you need to.

The first step in the process is to create a common library file that contains the functions you need in your scripts. Here's a simple library file called myfuncs that defines three simple functions:

```
$ cat myfuncs
# my script functions

function addem {
    echo $[ $1 + $2 ]
}

function multem {
    echo $[ $1 * $2 ]
}

function divem {
    if [ $2 -ne 0 ]
    then
        echo $[ $1 / $2 ]
    else
        echo -1
    fi
}
$
```

The next step is to include the myfuncs library file in your script files that want to use any of the functions. This is where things get tricky.

The problem is with the scope of shell functions. As with environment variables, shell functions are valid only for the shell session in which you define them. If you run the myfuncs shell script from your shell command line interface prompt, the shell creates a new shell and runs the script in that new shell. This defines the three functions for that shell, but when you try to run another script that uses those functions, they aren't available.

This applies to scripts as well. If you try to just run the library file as a regular script file, the functions don't appear in your script:

```
$ cat badtest4
#!/bin/bash
# using a library file the wrong way
./myfuncs

result=$(addem 10 15)
echo "The result is $result"
$
$ ./badtest4
./badtest4: addem: command not found
The result is
$
```

The key to using function libraries is the source command. The source command executes commands within the current shell context instead of creating a new shell to execute them. You use the source command to run the library file script inside of your shell script. This makes the functions available to the script.

The source command has a shortcut alias, called the *dot operator*. To source the myfuncs library file in a shell script, you just need to add the following line:

```
. ./myfuncs
```

This example assumes that the myfuncs library file is located in the same directory as the shell script. If not, you need to use the appropriate path to access the file. Here's an example of creating a script that uses the myfuncs library file:

```
$ cat test14
#!/bin/bash
# using functions defined in a library file
. ./myfuncs

value1=10
value2=5
result1=$(addem $value1 $value2)
result2=$(multem $value1 $value2)
result3=$(divem $value1 $value2)
echo "The result of adding them is: $result1"
echo "The result of multiplying them is: $result2"
echo "The result of dividing them is: $result3"
$
$ ./test14
The result of adding them is: 15
The result of multiplying them is: 50
The result of dividing them is: 2
$
```

The script successfully uses the functions defined in the myfuncs library file.

Using Functions on the Command Line

You can use script functions to create some pretty complex operations. Sometimes, it would be nice to be able to use these functions directly on the command line interface prompt.

Just as you can use a script function as a command in a shell script, you can also use a script function as a command in the command line interface. This is a nice feature because after you define the function in the shell, you can use it from any directory on the system; you don't have to worry about a script being in your *PATH* environment variable. The trick is to get the shell to recognize the function. You can do that in a couple of ways.

Creating functions on the command line

Because the shell interprets commands as you type them, you can define a function directly on the command line. You can do that in two ways.

The first method defines the function all on one line:

```
$ function divem { echo $[ $1 / $2 ];  }
$ divem 100 5
20
$
```

When you define the function on the command line, you must remember to include a semi-colon at the end of each command, so the shell knows where to separate commands:

```
$ function doubleit { read -p "Enter value: " value; echo $[
 $value * 2 ]; }
$
$ doubleit
Enter value: 20
40
$
```

The other method is to use multiple lines to define the function. When you do that, the bash shell uses the secondary prompt to prompt you for more commands. Using this method, you don't need to place a semicolon at the end of each command; just press the Enter key:

```
$ function multem {
> echo $[ $1 * $2 ]
> }
$ multem 2 5
10
$
```

When you use the brace at the end of the function, the shell knows that you're finished defining the function.

CAUTION

Be extremely careful when creating functions on the command line. If you use a function with the same name as a built-in command or another command, the function overrides the original command.

Defining functions in the .bashrc file

The obvious downside to defining shell functions directly on the command line is that when you exit the shell, your function disappears. For complex functions, this can become a problem.

A much simpler method is to define the function in a place where it is reloaded by the shell each time you start a new shell.

The best place to do that is the .bashrc file. The bash shell looks for this file in your home directory each time it starts, whether interactively or as the result of starting a new shell from within an existing shell.

Directly defining functions

You can define the functions directly in the .bashrc file in your home directory. Most Linux distributions already define some things in the .bashrc file, so be careful not to remove those items. Just add your functions to the bottom of the existing file. Here's an example of doing that:

```
$ cat .bashrc
# .bashrc

# Source global definitions
if [ -r /etc/bashrc ]; then
        . /etc/bashrc
fi

function addem {
    echo $[ $1 + $2 ]
}
$
```

The function doesn't take effect until the next time you start a new bash shell. After you do that, you can use the function anywhere on the system.

Sourcing function files

Just as in a shell script, you can use the source command (or its alias the dot operator) to add functions from an existing library file to your .bashrc script:

```
$ cat .bashrc
# .bashrc

# Source global definitions
if [ -r /etc/bashrc ]; then
        . /etc/bashrc
fi

. /home/rich/libraries/myfuncs
$
```

Make sure that you include the proper pathname to reference the library file for the bash shell to find. The next time you start a shell, all the functions in your library are available at the command line interface:

```
$ addem 10 5
15
$ multem 10 5
50
$ divem 10 5
2
$
```

Even better, the shell also passes any defined functions to child shell processes so your functions are automatically available for any shell scripts you run from your shell session. You can test this by writing a script that uses the functions without defining or sourcing them:

```
$ cat test15
#!/bin/bash
# using a function defined in the .bashrc file

value1=10
value2=5
result1=$(addem $value1 $value2)
result2=$(multem $value1 $value2)
result3=$(divem $value1 $value2)
echo "The result of adding them is: $result1"
echo "The result of multiplying them is: $result2"
echo "The result of dividing them is: $result3"
$
$ ./test15
The result of adding them is: 15
The result of multiplying them is: 50
The result of dividing them is: 2
$
```

Even without sourcing the library file, the functions worked perfectly in the shell script.

Following a Practical Example

There's much more to using functions than just creating your own functions to work with. In the open source world, code sharing is key, and that also applies to shell script functions. Quite a few different shell script functions are available for you to download and use in your own applications.

This section walks through downloading, installing, and using the GNU shtool shell script function library. The shtool library provides some simple shell script functions for performing everyday shell functions, such as working with temporary files and folders or formatting output to display.

Downloading and installing

The first step in the process is to download and install the GNU shtool library to your system so you can use the library functions in your own shell scripts. To do that, you need to use an FTP client program or a browser in a graphical desktop. Use this URL to download the shtool package:

```
ftp://ftp.gnu.org/gnu/shtool/shtool-2.0.8.tar.gz
```

This downloads the file shtool-2.0.8.tar.gz to the download folder. From there, you can use the cp command line tool or the graphical file manager tool in your Linux distribution (such as Nautilus in Ubuntu) to copy the file to your Home folder.

After you copy the file to your Home folder, you can extract it using the tar command:

```
tar -zxvf shtool-2.0.8.tar.gz
```

This extracts the package files into a folder named shtool-2.0.8. Now you're ready to build the shell script library file.

Building the library

The shtool distribution file must be configured for your specific Linux environment. To do that, it uses standard configure and make commands, commonly used in the C programming environment. To build the library file, you just need to run two commands:

```
$ ./confifgure
$ make
```

The configure command checks the software necessary to build the shtool library file. As it finds the tools it needs, it modifies the configuration file with the proper paths to the tools.

The make command runs through the steps to build the shtool library file. The resulting file (shtool) is the full library package file. You can test the library file using the make command as well:

```
$ make test
Running test suite:
echo..........ok
mdate.........ok
table.........ok
prop..........ok
move..........ok
install.......ok
mkdir.........ok
mkln..........ok
```

```
mkshadow.......ok
fixperm........ok
rotate.........ok
tarball........ok
subst..........ok
platform.......ok
arx............ok
slo............ok
scpp...........ok
version........ok
path...........ok
OK: passed: 19/19
$
```

The test mode tests all the functions available in the shtool library. If all pass, then you're ready to install the library into a common location on your Linux system so all your scripts can use it. To do that, you can use the install option of the make command. However, you need to be logged in as the root user account to run it:

```
$ su
Password:
# make install
./shtool mkdir -f -p -m 755 /usr/local
./shtool mkdir -f -p -m 755 /usr/local/bin
./shtool mkdir -f -p -m 755 /usr/local/share/man/man1
./shtool mkdir -f -p -m 755 /usr/local/share/aclocal
./shtool mkdir -f -p -m 755 /usr/local/share/shtool
...
./shtool install -c -m 644 sh.version /usr/local/share/shtool/sh.version
./shtool install -c -m 644 sh.path /usr/local/share/shtool/sh.path
#
```

Now you're ready to start using the functions in your own shell scripts!

The shtool library functions

The shtool library provides quite a few functions that can come in handy when working with shell scripts. Table 17.1 shows the functions available in the library.

TABLE 17.1 The shtool Library Functions

Function	Description
Arx	Creates an archive with extended features
Echo	Displays the string value with construct expansion
fixperm	Changes file permissions inside a folder tree

install	Installs a script or file
mdate	Displays modification time of a file or directory
mkdir	Creates one or more directories
Mkln	Creates a link using relative paths
mkshadow	Creates a shadow tree
move	Moves files with substitution
Path	Works with program paths
platform	Displays the platform identity
Prop	Displays an animated progress propeller
rotate	Rotates logfiles
Scpp	The sharing C pre-processor
Slo	Separates linker options by library class
Subst	Uses sed substitution operations
Table	Displays field-separated data in a table format
tarball	Creates tar files from files and folders
version	Creates a version information file

Each of the shtool functions has lots of options and arguments that you can use to modify how it works. Here's the format to use a shtool function:

```
shtool [options] [function [options] [args]]
```

Using the library

You can use the shtool functions directly from the command line or from within your shell scripts. Here's an example of using the platform function inside a shell script:

```
$ cat test16
#!/bin/bash

shtool platform
$ ./test16
Ubuntu 14.04 (iX86)
$
```

The platform function returns the Linux distribution and the CPU hardware that the host system is using. One of my favorites is the prop function. It creates a spinning propeller from alternating the \, |, /, and – characters while something is processing. That's a great tool to help show your shell script users that something is happening in the background while the script is running.

To use the `prop` function, you just pipe the output of the function you want to monitor to the `shtool` script:

```
$ ls -al /usr/bin | shtool prop -p "waiting..."
waiting...
$
```

The `prop` function alternates between the propeller characters to indicate that something is happening. In this case, it's the output from the `ls` command. How much of that you see depends on how fast your CPU can list out all the files in the `/usr/bin folder`! The –p option allows you to customize the output text that appears before the propeller characters. Now that's getting fancy!

Summary

Shell script functions allow you to place script code that's repeated throughout the script in a single place. Instead of having to rewrite blocks of code, you can create a function containing the code block and then just reference the function name in your script. The bash shell jumps to the function code block whenever it sees the function name used in the script.

You can even create script functions that return values. This allows you to create functions that interact with the script, returning both numeric and character data. Script functions can return numeric data by using the exit status of the last command in the function or using the `return` command. The `return` command allows you to programmatically set the exit status of your function to a specific value based on the results of the function.

Functions can also return values using the standard `echo` statement. You can capture the output data using the backtick character as you would any other shell command. This enables you to return any type of data from a function, including strings and floating-point numbers.

You can use shell variables within your functions, assigning values to variables and retrieving values from existing variables. This allows you to pass any type of data both into and out of a script function from the main script program. Functions also allow you to define local variables, which are accessible only from within the function code block. Local variables allow you to create self-contained functions, which don't interfere with any variables or processes used in the main shell script.

Functions can also call other functions, including themselves. When a function calls itself, it is called recursion. A recursive function often has a base value that is the terminal value of the function. The function continues to call itself with a decreasing parameter value until the base value is reached.

If you use lots of functions in your shell scripts, you can create library files of script functions. The library files can be included in any shell script file by using the source command, or its alias, the dot operator. This is called sourcing the library file. The shell doesn't run the library file but makes the functions available within the shell that runs the script. You can use this same technique to create functions that you can use on the normal shell command line. You can either define functions directly on the command line or you can add them to your .bashrc file so they are available for each new shell session you start. This is a handy way to create utilities that can be used no matter what your $PATH$ environment variable is set to.

The next chapter discusses the use of text graphics in your scripts. In this day of modern graphical interfaces, sometimes a plain text interface just doesn't cut it. The bash shell provides some easy ways for you to incorporate simple graphics features in your scripts to help spice things up.

17

Writing Scripts for Graphical Desktops

IN THIS CHAPTER

Creating text menus

Building text window widgets

Adding X Window graphics

O ver the years, shell scripts have acquired a reputation for being dull and boring. This doesn't have to be the case, however, if you plan on running your scripts in a graphical environment. There are plenty of ways to interact with your script user that don't rely on the `read` and `echo` statements. This chapter dives into a few different methods you can use to help add life to your interactive scripts so they don't look so old-fashioned.

Creating Text Menus

The most common way to create an interactive shell script is to utilize a menu. Offering your customers a choice of various options helps guide them through exactly what the script can and can't do.

Menu scripts usually clear the display area and then show a list of options available. The customer can select an option by pressing an associated letter or number assigned to each option. Figure 18-1 shows the layout of a sample menu.

The core of a shell script menu is the `case` command (see Chapter 12). The `case` command performs specific commands, depending on what character your customer selects from the menu.

The following sections walk you through the steps you should follow to create a menu-based shell script.

FIGURE 18-1

Displaying a menu from a shell script

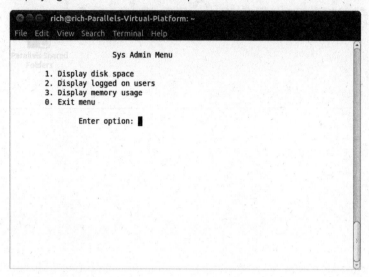

Create the menu layout

The first step in creating a menu is, obviously, to determine what elements you want to appear in the menu and lay them out the way that you want them to appear.

Before creating the menu, it's usually a good idea to clear the monitor display. This enables you to display your menu in a clean environment without distracting text.

The clear command uses the terminfo data of your terminal session (see Chapter 2) to clear any text that appears on the monitor. After the clear command, you can use the echo command to display your menu elements.

By default, the echo command can only display printable text characters. When creating menu items, it's often helpful to use nonprintable items, such as the tab and newline characters. To include these characters in your echo command, you must use the -e option. Thus, the command:

```
echo -e "1.\tDisplay disk space"
```

results in the output line:

```
1.        Display disk space
```

This greatly helps in formatting the layout of the menu items. With just a few echo commands, you can create a reasonable-looking menu:

```
clear
echo
echo -e "\t\t\tSys Admin Menu\n"
echo -e "\t1. Display disk space"
echo -e "\t2. Display logged on users"
echo -e "\t3. Display memory usage"
echo -e "\t0. Exit menu\n\n"
echo -en "\t\tEnter option: "
```

The -en option on the last line displays the line without adding the newline character at the end. This gives the menu a more professional look, because the cursor stays at the end of the line waiting for the customer's input.

The last part of creating the menu is to retrieve the input from the customer. This is done using the read command (see Chapter 14). Because we expect only single-character input, the nice thing to do is to use the -n option in the read command to retrieve only one character. This allows the customer to enter a number without having to press the Enter key:

```
read -n 1 option
```

Next, you need to create your menu functions.

Create the menu functions

Shell script menu options are easier to create as a group of separate functions. This enables you to create a simple, concise case command that is easy to follow.

To do that, you need to create separate shell functions for each of your menu options. The first step in creating a menu shell script is to determine what functions you want your script to perform and lay them out as separate functions in your code.

It is common practice to create *stub functions* for functions that aren't implemented yet. A stub function is a function that doesn't contain any commands yet or possibly just an echo statement indicating what should be there eventually:

```
function diskspace {
   clear
   echo "This is where the diskspace commands will go"
}
```

This enables your menu to operate smoothly while you work on the individual functions. You don't have to code all the functions for your menu to work. You'll notice that the function starts out with the `clear` command. This enables you to start the function on a clean monitor screen, without the menu showing.

One thing that helps out in the shell script menu is to create the menu layout itself as a function:

```
function menu {
    clear
    echo
    echo -e "\t\t\tSys Admin Menu\n"
    echo -e "\t1. Display disk space"
    echo -e "\t2. Display logged on users"
    echo -e "\t3. Display memory usage"
    echo -e "\t0. Exit program\n\n"
    echo -en "\t\tEnter option: "
    read -n 1 option
}
```

This enables you to easily redisplay the menu at any time just by calling the `menu` function.

Add the menu logic

Now that you have your menu layout and your functions, you just need to create the programming logic to put the two together. As mentioned, this requires the `case` command.

The `case` command should call the appropriate function according to the character selection expected from the menu. It's always a good idea to use the default `case` command character (the asterisk) to catch any incorrect menu entries.

The following code illustrates the use of the `case` command in a typical menu:

```
menu
case $option in
0)
    break ;;
1)
    diskspace ;;
2)
    whoseon ;;
3)
    memusage ;;
*)
    clear
    echo "Sorry, wrong selection";;
esac
```

This code first uses the `menu` function to clear the monitor screen and display the menu. The `read` command in the `menu` function pauses until the customer hits a character on the keyboard.

After that's been done, the `case` command takes over. The `case` command calls the appropriate function based on the returned character. After the function completes, the `case` command exits.

Putting it all together

Now that you've seen all the parts that make up a shell script menu, let's put them together and see how they all interoperate. Here's an example of a full menu script:

```
$ cat menu1
#!/bin/bash
# simple script menu

function diskspace {
   clear
   df -k
}

function whoseon {
   clear
   who
}

function memusage {
   clear
   cat /proc/meminfo
}

function menu {
   clear
   echo
   echo -e "\t\t\tSys Admin Menu\n"
   echo -e "\t1. Display disk space"
   echo -e "\t2. Display logged on users"
   echo -e "\t3. Display memory usage"
   echo -e "\t0. Exit program\n\n"
   echo -en "\t\tEnter option: "
   read -n 1 option
}

while [ 1 ]
do
   menu
   case $option in
   0)
      break ;;
   1)
      diskspace ;;
```

```
      2)
         whoseon ;;
      3)
         memusage ;;
      *)
         clear
         echo "Sorry, wrong selection";;
      esac
      echo -en "\n\n\t\t\tHit any key to continue"
      read -n 1 line
done
clear
$
```

This menu creates three functions to retrieve administrative information about the Linux system using common commands. It uses a `while` loop to continually loop through the menu until the customer selects option 0, which uses the `break` command to break out of the `while` loop.

You can use this same template to create any shell script menu interface. It provides a simple way to interact with your customers.

Using the select command

You may have noticed that half the challenge of creating a text menu is just creating the menu layout and retrieving the answer that you enter. The bash shell provides a handy little utility for you that does all this work automatically.

The `select` command allows you to create a menu from a single command line and then retrieve the entered answer and automatically process it. The format of the `select` command is as follows:

```
select variable in list
do
      commands
done
```

The `list` parameter is a space-separated list of text items that build the menu. The `select` command displays each item in the list as a numbered option and then displays a special prompt, defined by the PS3 environment variable, for the selection.

Here's a simple example of the `select` command in action:

```
$ cat smenu1
#!/bin/bash
# using select in the menu

function diskspace {
```

```
      clear
      df -k
}

function whoseon {
      clear
      who
}

function memusage {
      clear
      cat /proc/meminfo
}

PS3="Enter option: "
select option in "Display disk space" "Display logged on users"¬
"Display memory usage" "Exit program"
do
      case $option in
      "Exit program")
            break ;;
      "Display disk space")
            diskspace ;;
      "Display logged on users")
            whoseon ;;
      "Display memory usage")
            memusage ;;
      *)
            clear
            echo "Sorry, wrong selection";;
      esac
done
clear
$
```

The `select` statement must all be on one line in the code file. That's indicated by the continuation character in the listing. When you run the program, it automatically produces the following menu:

```
$ ./smenu1
1) Display disk space      3) Display memory usage
2) Display logged on users 4) Exit program
Enter option:
```

When you use the `select` command, remember that the result value stored in the variable is the entire text string and not the number associated with the menu item. The text string values are what you need to compare in your `case` statements.

Doing Windows

Using text menus is a step in the right direction, but there's still so much missing in our interactive scripts, especially if we try to compare them to the graphical Windows world. Fortunately for us, some very resourceful people out in the open source world have helped us out.

The *dialog* package is a nifty little tool originally created by Savio Lam and currently maintained by Thomas E. Dickey. This package recreates standard Windows dialog boxes in a text environment using ANSI escape control codes. You can easily incorporate these dialog boxes in your shell scripts to interact with your script users. This section describes the dialog package and demonstrates how to use it in shell scripts.

> **NOTE**
>
> The dialog package isn't installed in all Linux distributions by default. If it's not installed by default, because of its popularity it's almost always included in the software repository. Check your specific Linux distribution documentation for how to load the dialog package. For the Ubuntu Linux distribution, the following is the command line command to install it:
>
> ```
> sudo apt-get install dialog
> ```
>
> That package installs the dialog package plus the required libraries for your system.

The dialog package

The `dialog` command uses command line parameters to determine what type of Windows *widget* to produce. A widget is the dialog package term for a type of Windows element. The dialog package currently supports the types of widgets shown in Table 18-1.

TABLE 18-1 The dialog Widgets

Widget	Description
calendar	Provides a calendar from which to select a date
checklist	Displays multiple entries where each entry can be turned on or off
form	Allows you to build a form with labels and text fields to be filled out
fselect	Provides a file selection window to browse for a file
gauge	Displays a meter showing a percentage of completion
infobox	Displays a message without waiting for a response
inputbox	Displays a single text form box for text entry
inputmenu	Provides an editable menu
menu	Displays a list of selections from which to choose

msgbox	Displays a message and requires the user to select an OK button
pause	Displays a meter showing the status of a specified pause period
passwordbox	Displays a single textbox that hides entered text
passwordform	Displays a form with labels and hidden text fields
radiolist	Provides a group of menu items where only one item can be selected
tailbox	Displays text from a file in a scroll window using the tail command
tailboxbg	Same as tailbox, but operates in background mode
textbox	Displays the contents of a file in a scroll window
timebox	Provides a window to select an hour, minute, and second
yesno	Provides a simple message with Yes and No buttons

As you can see from Table 18-1, you can choose from lots of different widgets. This can give your scripts a more professional look with very little effort.

To specify a specific widget on the command line, you need to use the double dash format:

```
dialog --widget parameters
```

where *widget* is the widget name as seen in Table 18-1, and *parameters* defines the size of the widget window and any text required for the widget.

Each dialog widget provides output in two forms:

- Using STDERR
- Using the exit code status

The exit code status of the dialog command determines the button selected by the user. If an OK or Yes button is selected, the dialog command returns a 0 exit status. If a Cancel or No button is selected, the dialog command returns a 1 exit status. You can use the standard $? variable to determine which button was selected in the dialog widget.

If a widget returns any data, such as a menu selection, the dialog command sends the data to STDERR. You can use the standard bash shell technique of redirecting the STDERR output to another file or file descriptor:

```
dialog --inputbox "Enter your age:" 10 20 2>age.txt
```

This command redirects the text entered in the textbox to the age.txt file.

The following sections look at some examples of the more common dialog widgets you'll use in your shell scripts.

18

The msgbox widget

The msgbox widget is the most common type of dialog box. It displays a simple message in a window and waits for the user to click an OK button before disappearing. The following format is required to use a msgbox widget:

```
dialog --msgbox text height width
```

The text parameter is any string you want to place in the window. The dialog command automatically wraps the text to fit the size of the window you create, using the height and width parameters. If you want to place a title at the top of the window, you can also use the --title parameter, along with the text of the title. Here's an example of using the msgbox widget:

```
$ dialog --title Testing --msgbox "This is a test" 10 20
```

After entering this command, the message box appears on the screen of the terminal emulator session you're using. Figure 18-2 shows what this looks like.

FIGURE 18-2

Using the msgbox widget in the dialog command

If your terminal emulator supports the mouse, you can click the OK button to close the dialog box. You can also use keyboard commands to simulate a click — just press the Enter key.

The yesno widget

The `yesno` widget takes the `msgbox` widget one step further, allowing the user to answer a yes/no question displayed in the window. It produces two buttons at the bottom of the window — one for Yes and another for No. The user can switch between buttons by using the mouse, the tab key, or the keyboard arrow keys. To select the button, the user can either press the spacebar or the Enter key.

Here's an example of using the `yesno` widget:

```
$ dialog --title "Please answer" --yesno "Is this thing on?" 10 20
$ echo $?
1
$
```

This produces the widget shown in Figure 18-3.

FIGURE 18-3

Using the yesno widget in the dialog command

The exit status of the `dialog` command is set depending on which button the user selects. If the No button is selected, the exit status is 1, and if the Yes button is selected, the exit status is 0.

The inputbox widget

The `inputbox` widget provides a simple textbox area for the user to enter a text string. The dialog command sends the value of the text string to STDERR. You must redirect that to retrieve the answer. Figure 18-4 demonstrates what the `inputbox` widget looks like.

FIGURE 18-4

The inputbox widget

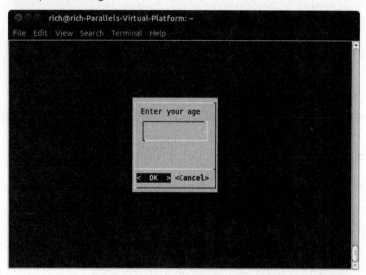

As you can see in Figure 18-4, the `inputbox` provides two buttons — OK and Cancel. If the Cancel button is selected, the exit status of the command is 1; otherwise, the exit status is 0:

```
$ dialog --inputbox "Enter your age:" 10 20 2>age.txt
$ echo $?
0
$ cat age.txt
12$
```

You'll notice when you use the `cat` command to display the contents of the text file that there's no newline character after the value. This enables you to easily redirect the file contents to a variable in a shell script to extract the string entered by the user.

The textbox widget

The `textbox` widget is a great way to display lots of information in a window. It produces a scrollable window containing the text from a file specified in the parameters:

```
$ dialog --textbox /etc/passwd 15 45
```

The contents of the /etc/passwd file are shown within the scrollable text window, as illustrated in Figure 18-5.

FIGURE 18-5

The textbox widget

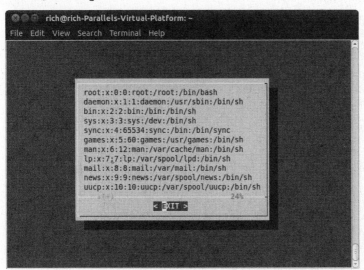

You can use the arrow keys to scroll left and right, as well as up and down in the text file. The bottom line in the window shows the percent location within the file that you're viewing. The textbox contains only a single Exit button, which should be selected to exit the widget.

The menu widget

The menu widget allows you to create a window version of the text menu we created earlier in this chapter. You simply provide a selection tag and the text for each item:

```
$ dialog --menu "Sys Admin Menu" 20 30 10 1 "Display disk space"
2 "Display users" 3 "Display memory usage" 4 "Exit" 2> test.txt
```

The first parameter defines a title for the menu. The next two parameters define the height and width of the menu window, while the third parameter defines the number of menu items that appear in the window at one time. If there are more menu items, you can scroll through them using the arrow keys.

Following those parameters, you must add menu item pairs. The first element is the tag used to select the menu item. Each tag should be unique for each menu item and can be selected by pressing the appropriate key on the keyboard. The second element is the text used in the menu. Figure 18-6 demonstrates the menu produced by the example command.

FIGURE 18-6

The menu widget with menu items

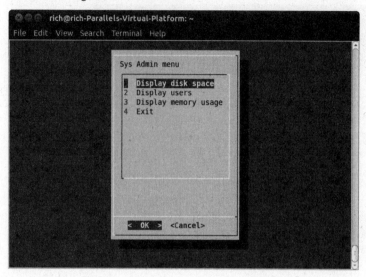

If the user selects a menu item by pressing the appropriate key for the tag, that menu item is highlighted but not selected. A selection isn't made until the OK button is selected by using either the mouse or the Enter key. The dialog command sends the selected menu item text to STDERR, which you can redirect as needed.

The fselect widget

There are several fancy built-in widgets provided by the dialog command. The fselect widget is extremely handy when working with filenames. Instead of forcing the user to type a filename, you can use the fselect widget to browse to the file location and select the file, as shown in Figure 18-7.

The fselect widget format looks like:

```
$ dialog --title "Select a file" --fselect $HOME/ 10 50 2>file.txt
```

The first parameter after the fselect option is the starting folder location used in the window. The fselect widget window consists of a directory listing on the left side, a file listing on the right side that shows all the files in the selected directory, and a simple textbox that contains the currently selected file or directory. You can manually type a filename in the textbox, or you can use the directory and file listings to select one (use the spacebar to select a file to add to the textbox).

FIGURE 18-7

The fselect widget

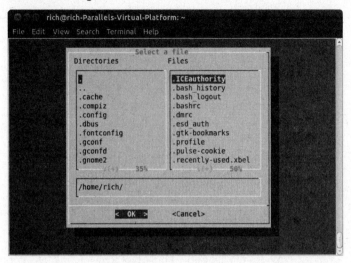

The dialog options

In addition to the standard widgets, you can customize lots of different options in the dialog command. You've already seen the --title parameter in action. This allows you to set a title for the widget that appears at the top of the window.

Lots of other options allow you to completely customize both the appearance and the behavior of your windows. Table 18-2 shows the options available for the dialog command.

TABLE 18-2 The dialog Command Options

Option	Description
--add-widget	Proceeds to the next dialog unless Esc or the Cancel button has been pressed
--aspect *ratio*	Specifies the width/height aspect ratio of the window
--backtitle *title*	Specifies a title to display on the background, at the top of the screen
--begin *x y*	Specifies the starting location of the top-left corner of the window
--cancel-label *label*	Specifies an alternative label for the Cancel button

Continues

TABLE 18-2   *(continued)*

Option	Description
`--clear`	Clears the display using the default dialog background color
`--colors`	Embeds ANSI color codes in dialog text
`--cr-wrap`	Allows newline characters in dialog text and forces a line wrap
`--create-rc` *file*	Dumps a sample configuration file to the specified file
`--defaultno`	Makes the default of a yes/no dialog No
`--default-item` *string*	Sets the default item in a checklist, form, or menu dialog
`--exit-label` *label*	Specifies an alternative label for the Exit button
`--extra-button`	Displays an extra button between the OK and Cancel buttons
`--extra-label` *label*	Specifies an alternative label for the Extra button
`--help`	Displays the dialog command help message
`--help-button`	Displays a Help button after the OK and Cancel buttons
`--help-label` *label*	Specifies an alternative label for the Help button
`--help-status`	Writes the checklist, radiolist, or form information after the help information in the Help button was selected
`--ignore`	Ignores options that dialog does not recognize
`--input-fd` *fd*	Specifies an alternative file descriptor, other than STDIN
`--insecure`	Changes the password widget to display asterisks when typing
`--item-help`	Adds a help column at the bottom of the screen for each tag in a checklist, radiolist, or menu for the tag item
`--keep-window`	Doesn't clear old widgets from the screen
`--max-input` *size*	Specifies a maximum string size for the input; default is 2048
`--nocancel`	Suppresses the Cancel button
`--no-collapse`	Doesn't convert tabs to spaces in dialog text
`--no-kill`	Places the tailboxbg dialog in background and disables SIGHUP for the process
`--no-label` *label*	Specifies an alternative label for the No button
`--no-shadow`	Doesn't display shadows for dialog windows
`--ok-label` *label*	Specifies an alternative label for the OK button
`--output-fd` *fd*	Specifies an alternative output file descriptor other than STDERR
`--print-maxsize`	Prints the maximum size of dialog windows allowed to the output

`--print-size`	Prints the size of each dialog window to the output
`--print-version`	Prints the dialog version to output
`--separate-output`	Outputs the result of a checklist widget one line at a time with no quoting
`--separator string`	Specifies a string that separates the output for each widget
`--separate-widget string`	Specifies a string that separates the output for each widget
`--shadow`	Draws a shadow to the right and bottom of each window
`--single-quoted`	Uses single quoting if needed for the checklist output
`--sleep sec`	Delays for the specified number of seconds after processing the dialog window
`--stderr`	Sends output to STDERR — the default behavior
`--stdout`	Sends output to STDOUT
`--tab-correct`	Converts tabs to spaces
`--tab-len n`	Specifies the number of spaces a tab character uses; default is 8
`--timeout sec`	Specifies the number of seconds before exiting with an error code if no user input
`--title title`	Specifies the title of the dialog window
`--trim`	Removes leading spaces and newline characters from dialog text
`--visit-items`	Modifies the tab stops in the dialog window to include the list of items
`--yes-label label`	Specifies an alternative label for the Yes button

The `--backtitle` option is a handy way to create a common title for your menu through the script. If you specify it for each dialog window, it persists throughout your application, creating a professional look to your script.

As you can tell from Table 18-2, you can overwrite any of the button labels in your dialog window. This feature allows you to create just about any window situation you need.

Using the dialog command in a script

Using the `dialog` command in your scripts is a snap. There are just two things you must remember:

- Check the exit status of the `dialog` command if there's a Cancel or No button available.
- Redirect STDERR to retrieve the output value.

If you follow these two rules, you'll have a professional-looking interactive script in no time. Here's an example using dialog widgets to reproduce the system admin menu created earlier in the chapter:

```
$ cat menu3
#!/bin/bash
# using dialog to create a menu

temp=$(mktemp -t test.XXXXXX)
temp2=$(mktemp -t test2.XXXXXX)

function diskspace {
    df -k > $temp
    dialog --textbox $temp 20 60
}

function whoseon {
    who > $temp
    dialog --textbox $temp 20 50
}

function memusage {
    cat /proc/meminfo > $temp
    dialog --textbox $temp 20 50
}

while [ 1 ]
do
dialog --menu "Sys Admin Menu" 20 30 10 1 "Display disk space" 2
"Display users" 3 "Display memory usage" 0 "Exit" 2> $temp2
if [ $? -eq 1 ]
then
    break
fi

selection=$(cat $temp2)

case $selection in
1)
    diskspace ;;
2)
    whoseon ;;
3)
    memusage ;;
0)
    break ;;
*)
    dialog --msgbox "Sorry, invalid selection" 10 30
```

```
esac
done
rm -f $temp 2> /dev/null
rm -f $temp2 2> /dev/null
$
```

The script uses the while loop with a constant true value to create an endless loop displaying the menu dialog. This means that, after every function, the script returns to displaying the menu.

The menu dialog includes a Cancel button, so the script checks the exit status of the dialog command in case the user presses the Cancel button to exit. Because it's in a while loop, exiting is as easy as using the break command to jump out of the while loop.

The script uses the mktemp command to create two temporary files for holding data for the dialog commands. The first one, $temp, is used to hold the output of the df, whoeson, and meminfo commands so they can be displayed in the textbox dialog (see Figure 18-8). The second temporary file, $temp2, is used to hold the selection value from the main menu dialog.

FIGURE 18-8

The meminfo command output displayed using the textbox dialog option

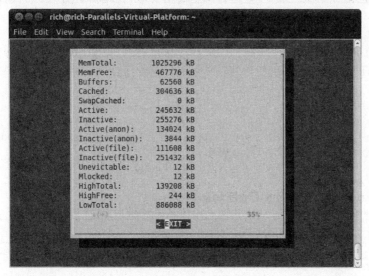

Now this is starting to look like a real application that you can show off to people!

Getting Graphic

If you're looking for even more graphics for your interactive scripts, you can go one step further. Both the KDE and GNOME desktop environments (see Chapter 1) have expanded on the `dialog` command idea and include commands that produce X Window graphical widgets for their respective environments.

This section describes the kdialog and zenity packages, which provide graphical window widgets for the KDE and GNOME desktops, respectively.

The KDE environment

The KDE graphical environment includes the kdialog package by default. The kdialog package uses the `kdialog` command to generate standard windows, similar to the dialog-style widgets, within your KDE desktop. However, instead of having the clunky feel to them, these windows blend right in with the rest of your KDE application windows! This allows you to produce Windows-quality user interfaces directly from your shell scripts!

> **NOTE**
>
> Just because your Linux distribution uses the KDE desktop doesn't necessarily mean it has the kdialog package installed by default. You may need to manually install it from the distribution repository.

kdialog widgets

Just like the `dialog` command, the `kdialog` command uses command line options to specify what type of window widget to use. The following is the format of the `kdialog` command:

```
kdialog display-options window-options arguments
```

The `window-options` options allow you to specify what type of window widget to use. The available options are shown in Table 18-3.

TABLE 18-3   kdialog Window Options

Option	Description
`--checklist` *title* *[tag item status]*	A checklist menu, with status specifying if the item is checked or not
`--error` *text*	Error message box
`--inputbox` **text** *[init]*	Input textbox where you can specify the default value using the *init* value
`--menu` **title** *[tag item]*	Menu selection box title and a list of items identified by a tag

`--msgbox` *text*	Simple message box with specified text
`--password` *text*	Password input textbox that hides user input
`--radiolist` *title [tag item status]*	A radiolist menu, with status specifying if the item is selected or not
`--separate-output`	Returns items on separate lines for checklist and radiolist menus
`--sorry` *text*	Sorry message box
`--textbox` *file [width] [height]*	Textbox displaying the contents of *file*, alternatively specified by *width* and *height*
`--title` *title*	Specifies a title for the TitleBar area of the dialog window
`--warningyesno` *text*	Warning message box with Yes and No buttons
`--warningcontinuecancel` *text*	Warning message box with Continue and Cancel buttons
`--warningyesnocancel` *text*	Warning message box with Yes, No, and Cancel buttons
`--yesno` *text*	Question box with Yes and No buttons
`--yesnocancel` *text*	Question box with Yes, No, and Cancel buttons

As you can see from Table 18-3, all the standard window dialog box types are represented. However, when you use a kdialog window widget, it appears as a separate window in the KDE desktop, not inside the terminal emulator session!

The `checklist` and `radiolist` widgets allow you to define individual items in the lists and whether they are selected by default:

```
$kdialog --checklist "Items I need" 1 "Toothbrush" on 2 "Toothpaste"
    off 3 "Hair brush" on 4 "Deodorant" off 5 "Slippers" off
```

The resulting checklist window is shown in Figure 18-9.

The items specified as "on" are highlighted in the checklist. To select or deselect an item in the checklist, just click it. If you select the OK button, the kdialog sends the tag values to STDOUT:

```
"1" "3"
$
```

When you press the Enter key, the kdialog box appears with the selections. When you click the OK or Cancel buttons, the kdialog command returns each tag as a string value to STDOUT (these are the `"1"`, and `"3"` values you see in the output). Your script must be able to parse the resulting values and match them with the original values.

18

FIGURE 18-9

A kdialog checklist dialog window

Using kdialog

You can use the `kdialog` window widgets in your shell scripts similarly to how you use the `dialog` widgets. The big difference is that the `kdialog` window widgets output values using STDOUT instead of STDERR.

Here's a script that converts the sys admin menu created earlier into a KDE application:

```
$ cat menu4
#!/bin/bash
# using kdialog to create a menu

temp=$(mktemp -t temp.XXXXXX)
temp2=$(mktemp -t temp2.XXXXXX)

function diskspace {
    df -k > $temp
    kdialog --textbox $temp 1000 10
}

function whoseon {
    who > $temp
    kdialog --textbox $temp 500 10
}

function memusage {
    cat /proc/meminfo > $temp
    kdialog --textbox $temp 300 500
}

while [ 1 ]
do
```

```
kdialog --menu "Sys Admin Menu" "1" "Display diskspace" "2" "Display
users" "3" "Display memory usage" "0" "Exit" > $temp2
if [ $? -eq 1 ]
then
   break
fi

selection=$(cat $temp2)

case $selection in
1)
   diskspace ;;
2)
   whoseon ;;
3)
   memusage ;;
0)
   break ;;
*)
   kdialog --msgbox "Sorry, invalid selection"
esac
done
$
```

There isn't much difference in the script from using the kdialog command and the dialog command. The resulting main menu generated is shown in Figure 18-10.

FIGURE 18-10

The sys admin menu script using kdialog

Now your simple shell script looks just like a real KDE application! There's no limit to what you can do with your interactive scripts now.

The GNOME environment

The GNOME graphical environment supports two popular packages that can generate standard windows:

- gdialog
- zenity

By far, zenity is the most commonly available package found in most GNOME desktop Linux distributions (it's installed by default in both Ubuntu and Fedora). This section describes the features of zenity and demonstrates how to use it in your shell scripts.

zenity Widgets

As you would expect, zenity allows you to create different windows widgets by using command line options. Table 18-4 shows the different widgets that zenity can produce.

TABLE 18-4 The zenity Windows Widgets

Option	Description
--calendar	Displays a full month calendar
--entry	Displays a text entry dialog window
--error	Displays an error message dialog window
--file-selection	Displays a full pathname and filename dialog window
--info	Displays an informational dialog window
--list	Displays a checklist or radiolist dialog window
--notification	Displays a notification icon
--progress	Displays a progress bar dialog window
--question	Displays a yes/no question dialog window
--scale	Displays a scale dialog window
--text-info	Displays a textbox containing text
--warning	Displays a warning dialog window

The zenity command line program works somewhat differently than the kdialog and dialog programs. Many of the widget types are defined using additional options on the command line, instead of including them as arguments to an option.

The zenity command does offer some pretty cool advanced dialog windows. The calendar option produces a full month calendar, as shown in Figure 18-11.

FIGURE 18-11

The zenity calendar dialog window

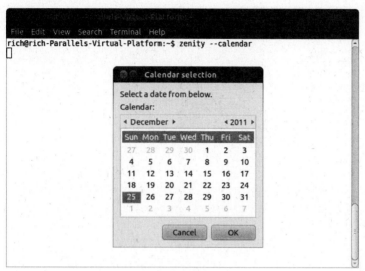

When you select a date from the calendar, the zenity command returns the value to STDOUT, just like kdialog:

```
$ zenity --calendar
12/25/2011
$
```

Another pretty cool window in zenity is the file selection option, shown in Figure 18-12.

You can use the dialog window to browse to any directory location on the system (as long as you have the privileges to view the directory) and select a file. When you select a file, the zenity command returns the full file and pathname:

```
$ zenity --file-selection
/home/ubuntu/menu5
$
```

With tools like that at your disposal, the sky's the limit with your shell script creations!

Using zenity in scripts

As you would expect, zenity performs well in shell scripts. Unfortunately, zenity chose not to follow the option convention used in dialog and kdialog, so converting any existing interactive scripts to zenity may prove challenging.

FIGURE 18-12

The zenity file selection dialog window

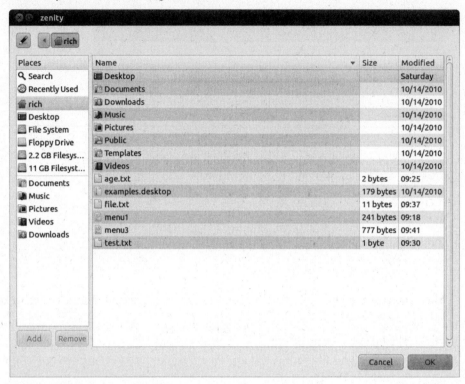

In converting the sys admin menu from kdialog to zenity, we had to do quite a bit of manipulation of the widget definitions:

```
$cat menu5
#!/bin/bash
# using zenity to create a menu

temp=$(mktemp -t temp.XXXXXX)
temp2=$(mktemp -t temp2.XXXXXX)

function diskspace {
   df -k > $temp
   zenity --text-info --title "Disk space" --filename=$temp
--width 750 --height 10
}

function whoseon {
   who > $temp
   zenity --text-info --title "Logged in users" --filename=$temp
```

```
--width 500 --height 10
}

function memusage {
   cat /proc/meminfo > $temp
   zenity --text-info --title "Memory usage" --filename=$temp
--width 300 --height 500
}

while [ 1 ]
do
zenity --list --radiolist --title "Sys Admin Menu" --column "Select"
--column "Menu Item" FALSE "Display diskspace" FALSE "Display users"
FALSE "Display memory usage" FALSE "Exit" > $temp2
if [ $? -eq 1 ]
then
   break
fi

selection=$(cat $temp2)
case $selection in
"Display disk space")
   diskspace ;;
"Display users")
   whoseon ;;
"Display memory usage")
   memusage ;;
Exit)
   break ;;
*)
   zenity --info "Sorry, invalid selection"
esac
done
$
```

Because zenity doesn't support the menu dialog window, we used a radiolist type window for the main menu, as shown in Figure 18-13.

The radiolist uses two columns, each with a column heading. The first column includes the radio buttons to select. The second column is the item text. The radiolist also doesn't use tags for the items. When you select an item, the full text of the item is returned to STDOUT. This makes life a little more interesting for the case command. You must use the full text from the items in the case options. If there are any spaces in the text, you need to use quotation marks around the text.

Using the zenity package, you can add a Windows feel to your interactive shell scripts in the GNOME desktop.

FIGURE 18-13

The sys admin menu using zenity

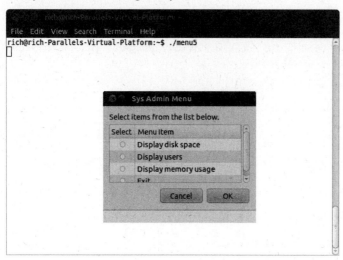

Summary

Interactive shell scripts have a reputation for being dull and boring. You can change that by using a few different techniques and tools available on most Linux systems. First, you can create menu systems for your interactive scripts by using the case command and shell script functions.

The menu command allows you to paint a menu, using the standard echo command, and read a response from the user, using the read command. The case command then selects the appropriate shell script function based on the value entered.

The dialog program provides several prebuilt text widgets for creating Windows-like objects on a text-based terminal emulator. You can create dialog boxes for displaying text, entering text, and choosing files and dates by using the dialog program. This helps bring even more life to your shell script.

If you're running your shell scripts in a graphical X Window environment, you can utilize even more tools in your interactive scripts. For the KDE desktop, there's the kdialog program. This program provides simple commands to create windows widgets for all the basic windows functions. For the GNOME desktop, there are the gdialog and zenity programs. Each of these programs provides window widgets that blend into the GNOME desktop just like a real Windows application.

The next chapter dives into the subject of editing and manipulating text data files. Often the biggest use of shell scripts revolves around parsing and displaying data in text files such as log and error files. The Linux environment includes two very useful tools, sed and gawk, for working with text data in your shell scripts. The next chapter introduces you to these tools, and shows the basics of how to use them.

Introducing sed and gawk

B y far, one of the most common functions that people use shell scripts for is to work with text files. Between examining log files, reading configuration files, and handling data elements, shell scripts can help automate the mundane tasks of manipulating any type of data contained in text files. However, trying to manipulate the contents of text files using just shell script commands can be somewhat awkward. If you perform any type of data manipulation in your shell scripts, you want to become familiar with the sed and gawk tools available in Linux. These tools can greatly simplify any data-handling tasks you need to perform.

Manipulating Text

Chapter 10 showed you how to edit text files using different editor programs available in the Linux environment. These editors enable you to easily manipulate text contained in a text file by using simple commands or mouse clicks.

There are times, however, when you'll find yourself wanting to manipulate text in a text file on the fly, without having to pull out a full-fledged interactive text editor. In these situations, it would be useful to have a simple command line editor that could easily format, insert, modify, or delete text elements automatically.

The Linux system provides two common tools for doing just that. This section describes the two most popular command line editors used in the Linux world, sed and gawk.

Getting to know the sed editor

The sed editor is called a *stream editor*, as opposed to a normal interactive text editor. In an interactive text editor, such as vim, you interactively use keyboard commands to insert, delete, or replace text in the data. A stream editor edits a stream of data based on a set of rules you supply ahead of time, before the editor processes the data.

The sed editor can manipulate data in a data stream based on commands you either enter into the command line or store in a command text file. The sed editor does these things:

1. Reads one data line at a time from the input
2. Matches that data with the supplied editor commands
3. Changes data in the stream as specified in the commands
4. Outputs the new data to STDOUT

After the stream editor matches all the commands against a line of data, it reads the next line of data and repeats the process. After the stream editor processes all the lines of data in the stream, it terminates.

Because the commands are applied sequentially line by line, the sed editor makes only one pass through the data stream to make the edits. This makes the sed editor much faster than an interactive editor and allows you to quickly make changes to data in a file on the fly.

Here's the format for using the sed command:

```
sed options script file
```

The *options* parameters allow you to customize the behavior of the sed command and include the options shown in Table 19-1.

TABLE 19-1 The sed Command Options

Option	Description
-e script	Adds commands specified in the script to the commands run while processing the input
-f file	Adds the commands specified in the file to the commands run while processing the input
-n	Doesn't produce output for each command, but waits for the print command

The script parameter specifies a single command to apply against the stream data. If more than one command is required, you must use either the -e option to specify them in the command line or the -f option to specify them in a separate file. Numerous commands are available for manipulating data. We examine some of the basic commands used by the sed editor in this chapter and then look at some of the more advanced commands in Chapter 21.

Defining an editor command in the command line

By default, the sed editor applies the specified commands to the STDIN input stream. This allows you to pipe data directly to the sed editor for processing. Here's a quick example demonstrating how to do this:

```
$ echo "This is a test" | sed 's/test/big test/'
This is a big test
$
```

This example uses the s command in the sed editor. The s command substitutes a second text string for the first text string pattern specified between the forward slashes. In this example, the words big test were substituted for the word test.

When you run this example, it should display the results almost instantaneously. That's the power of using the sed editor. You can make multiple edits to data in about the same time it takes for some of the interactive editors just to start up.

Of course, this simple test just edited one line of data. You should get the same speedy results when editing complete files of data:

```
$ cat data1.txt
The quick brown fox jumps over the lazy dog.
The quick brown fox jumps over the lazy dog.
The quick brown fox jumps over the lazy dog.
The quick brown fox jumps over the lazy dog.
$
$ sed 's/dog/cat/' data1.txt
The quick brown fox jumps over the lazy cat.
The quick brown fox jumps over the lazy cat.
The quick brown fox jumps over the lazy cat.
The quick brown fox jumps over the lazy cat.
$
```

The sed command executes and returns the data almost instantaneously. As it processes each line of data, the results are displayed. You'll start seeing results before the sed editor completes processing the entire file.

It's important to note that the sed editor doesn't modify the data in the text file itself. It only sends the modified text to STDOUT. If you look at the text file, it still contains the original data:

```
$ cat data1.txt
The quick brown fox jumps over the lazy dog.
The quick brown fox jumps over the lazy dog.
The quick brown fox jumps over the lazy dog.
The quick brown fox jumps over the lazy dog.
$
```

Using multiple editor commands in the command line

To execute more than one command from the sed command line, just use the -e option:

```
$ sed -e 's/brown/green/; s/dog/cat/' data1.txt
The quick green fox jumps over the lazy cat.
```

19

```
The quick green fox jumps over the lazy cat.
The quick green fox jumps over the lazy cat.
The quick green fox jumps over the lazy cat.
$
```

Both commands are applied to each line of data in the file. The commands must be separated with a semicolon, and there shouldn't be any spaces between the end of the command and the semicolon.

Instead of using a semicolon to separate the commands, you can use the secondary prompt in the bash shell. Just enter the first single quotation mark to open the sed program script (sed editor command list), and bash continues to prompt you for more commands until you enter the closing quotation mark:

```
$ sed -e '
> s/brown/green/
> s/fox/elephant/
> s/dog/cat/' data1.txt
The quick green elephant jumps over the lazy cat.
The quick green elephant jumps over the lazy cat.
The quick green elephant jumps over the lazy cat.
The quick green elephant jumps over the lazy cat.
$
```

You must remember to finish the command on the same line where the closing single quotation mark appears. After the bash shell detects the closing quotation mark, it processes the command. After it starts, the sed command applies each command you specified to each line of data in the text file.

Reading editor commands from a file

Finally, if you have lots of sed commands you want to process, it is often easier to just store them in a separate file. Use the -f option to specify the file in the sed command:

```
$ cat script1.sed
s/brown/green/
s/fox/elephant/
s/dog/cat/
$
$ sed -f script1.sed data1.txt
The quick green elephant jumps over the lazy cat.
The quick green elephant jumps over the lazy cat.
The quick green elephant jumps over the lazy cat.
The quick green elephant jumps over the lazy cat.
$
```

In this case, you don't put a semicolon after each command. The sed editor knows that each line contains a separate command. As with entering commands on the command line, the sed editor reads the commands from the specified file and applies them to each line in the data file.

> **TIP**
>
> It can be easy to confuse your sed editor script files with your bash shell script files. To eliminate confusion, use a .sed file extension on your sed script files.

We'll look at some other sed editor commands that come in handy for manipulating data in the "Commanding at the sed Editor Basics" section. Before that, let's quickly look at the other Linux data editor.

Getting to know the gawk program

Although the sed editor is a handy tool for modifying text files on the fly, it has its limitations. Often, you need a more advanced tool for manipulating data in a file, one that provides a more programming-like environment allowing you to modify and reorganize data in a file. This is where gawk comes in.

> **NOTE**
>
> The gawk program is not installed by default on all distributions. If your Linux distribution does not have the gawk program, install the gawk package using Chapter 9 as a guide.

The gawk program is the GNU version of the original awk program in Unix. The gawk program takes stream editing one step further than the sed editor by providing a programming language instead of just editor commands. Within the gawk programming language, you can do the following:

- Define variables to store data.
- Use arithmetic and string operators to operate on data.
- Use structured programming concepts, such as if-then statements and loops, to add logic to your data processing.
- Generate formatted reports by extracting data elements within the data file and repositioning them in another order or format.

The gawk program's report-generating capabilities are often used for extracting data elements from large bulky text files and formatting them into a readable report. The perfect example of this is formatting log files. Trying to pore through lines of errors in a log file can be difficult. The gawk program allows you to filter just the data elements you want to view from the log file, and then you can format them in a manner that makes reading the important data easier.

19

Visiting the gawk command format

Here's the basic format of the gawk program:

```
gawk options program file
```

Table 19-2 shows the options available with the gawk program.

TABLE 19-2 **The gawk Options**

Option	Description
-F fs	Specifies a file separator for delineating data fields in a line
-f file	Specifies a file name to read the program from
-v var=value	Defines a variable and default value used in the gawk program
-mf N	Specifies the maximum number of fields to process in the data file
-mr N	Specifies the maximum record size in the data file
-W keyword	Specifies the compatibility mode or warning level for gawk

The command line options provide an easy way to customize features in the gawk program. We'll look more closely at these as we explore gawk.

The power of gawk is in the program script. You can write scripts to read the data within a text line and then manipulate and display the data to create any type of output report.

Reading the program script from the command line

A gawk program script is defined by opening and closing braces. You must place script commands between the two braces ({ }). If you incorrectly use a parenthesis instead of a brace to enclose your gawk script, you get error messages, similar to the following:

```
$ gawk '(print "Hello World!"}'
gawk: (print "Hello World!"}
gawk:  ^ syntax error
```

Because the gawk command line assumes that the script is a single text string, you must also enclose your script in single quotation marks. Here's an example of a simple gawk program script specified on the command line:

```
$ gawk '{print "Hello World!"}'
```

The program script defines a single command, the print command. The print command does what it says: It prints text to STDOUT. If you try running this command, you'll be somewhat disappointed, because nothing happens right away. Because no filename was defined in the command line, the gawk program retrieves data from STDIN. When you run the program, it just waits for text to come in via STDIN.

If you type a line of text and press the Enter key, gawk runs the text through the program script. Just like the sed editor, the gawk program executes the program script on each line of text available in the data stream. Because the program script is set to display a fixed text string, no matter what text you enter in the data stream, you get the same text output:

```
$ gawk '{print "Hello World!"}'
This is a test
Hello World!
hello
Hello World!
This is another test
Hello World!
```

To terminate the gawk program, you must signal that the data stream has ended. The bash shell provides a key combination to generate an End-of-File (EOF) character. The Ctrl+D key combination generates an EOF character in bash. Using that key combination terminates the gawk program and returns you to a command line interface prompt.

Using data field variables

One of the primary features of gawk is its ability to manipulate data in the text file. It does this by automatically assigning a variable to each data element in a line. By default, gawk assigns the following variables to each data field it detects in the line of text:

- $0 represents the entire line of text.
- $1 represents the first data field in the line of text.
- $2 represents the second data field in the line of text.
- $n represents the nth data field in the line of text.

Each data field is determined in a text line by a *field separation character*. When gawk reads a line of text, it delineates each data field using the defined field separation character. The default field separation character in gawk is any whitespace character (such as the tab or space characters).

Here's an example gawk program that reads a text file and displays only the first data field value:

```
$ cat data2.txt
One line of test text.
Two lines of test text.
Three lines of test text.
$
$ gawk '{print $1}' data2.txt
One
Two
Three
$
```

This program uses the $1 field variable to display only the first data field for each line of text.

If you're reading a file that uses a different field separation character, you can specify it by using the -F option:

```
$ gawk -F: '{print $1}' /etc/passwd
root
bin
daemon
adm
lp
sync
shutdown
halt
mail
[...]
```

This short program displays the first data field in the password file on the system. Because the /etc/passwd file uses a colon to separate the data fields, if you want to separate each data element, you must specify it as the field separation character in the gawk options.

Using multiple commands in the program script

A programming language wouldn't be very useful if you could only execute one command. The gawk programming language allows you to combine commands into a normal program. To use multiple commands in the program script specified on the command line, just place a semicolon between each command:

```
$ echo "My name is Rich" | gawk '{$4="Christine"; print $0}'
My name is Christine
$
```

The first command assigns a value to the $4 field variable. The second command then prints the entire data field. Notice from the output that the gawk program replaced the fourth data field in the original text with the new value.

You can also use the secondary prompt to enter your program script commands one line at a time:

```
$ gawk '{
> $4="Christine"
> print $0}'
My name is Rich
My name is Christine
$
```

After you open the single quotation mark, the bash shell provides the secondary prompt to prompt you for more data. You can add your commands one at a time on each line until you enter the closing single quotation mark. Because no filename was defined in the command line, the gawk program retrieves data from STDIN. When you run the program, it waits for text to come in via STDIN. To exit the program, just press the Ctrl+D key combination to signal the end of the data.

Reading the program from a file

As with the sed editor, the gawk editor allows you to store your programs in a file and refer to them in the command line:

```
$ cat script2.gawk
{print $1 "'s home directory is " $6}
$
$ gawk -F: -f script2.gawk /etc/passwd
root's home directory is /root
bin's home directory is /bin
daemon's home directory is /sbin
adm's home directory is /var/adm
lp's home directory is /var/spool/lpd
[...]
Christine's home directory is /home/Christine
Samantha's home directory is /home/Samantha
Timothy's home directory is /home/Timothy
$
```

The script2.gawk program script uses the print command again to print the /etc/passwd file's home directory data field (field variable $6) and the userid data field (field variable $1).

You can specify multiple commands in the program file. To do so, just place each command on a separate line. You don't need to use semicolons:

```
$ cat script3.gawk
{
text = "'s home directory is "
print $1 text $6
}
$
$ gawk -F: -f script3.gawk /etc/passwd
root's home directory is /root
bin's home directory is /bin
daemon's home directory is /sbin
adm's home directory is /var/adm
lp's home directory is /var/spool/lpd
[...]
Christine's home directory is /home/Christine
Samantha's home directory is /home/Samantha
Timothy's home directory is /home/Timothy
$
```

19

The `script3.gawk` program script defines a variable to hold a text string used in the `print` command. Notice that gawk programs don't use a dollar sign when referencing a variable's value, as a shell script does.

Running scripts before processing data

The gawk program also allows you to specify when the program script is run. By default, gawk reads a line of text from the input and then executes the program script on the data in the line of text. Sometimes, you may need to run a script before processing data, such as to create a header section for a report. The BEGIN keyword is used to accomplish this. It forces gawk to execute the program script specified after the BEGIN keyword, before gawk reads the data:

```
$ gawk 'BEGIN {print "Hello World!"}'
Hello World!
$
```

This time the `print` command displays the text before reading any data. However, after it displays the text, it quickly exits, without waiting for any data.

The reason for this is that the BEGIN keyword only applies the specified script before it processes any data. If you want to process data with a normal program script, you must define the program using another script section:

```
$ cat data3.txt
Line 1
Line 2
Line 3
$
$ gawk 'BEGIN {print "The data3 File Contents:"}
> {print $0}' data3.txt
The data3 File Contents:
Line 1
Line 2
Line 3
$
```

Now after gawk executes the BEGIN script, it uses the second script to process any file data. Be careful when doing this; both of the scripts are still considered one text string on the gawk command line. You need to place your single quotation marks accordingly.

Running scripts after processing data

Like the BEGIN keyword, the END keyword allows you to specify a program script that gawk executes after reading the data:

```
$ gawk 'BEGIN {print "The data3 File Contents:"}
> {print $0}
```

```
> END {print "End of File"}' data3.txt
The data3 File Contents:
Line 1
Line 2
Line 3
End of File
$
```

When the gawk program is finished printing the file contents, it executes the commands in the END script. This is a great technique to use to add footer data to reports after all the normal data has been processed.

You can put all these elements together into a nice little program script file to create a full report from a simple data file:

```
$ cat script4.gawk
BEGIN {
print "The latest list of users and shells"
print " UserID \t Shell"
print "-------- \t -------"
FS=":"
}

{
print $1 "     \t "  $7
}

END {
print "This concludes the listing"
}
$
```

This script uses the BEGIN script to create a header section for the report. It also defines a special variable called FS. This is yet another way to define the field separation character. This way, you don't have to depend on the script's user to define the field separation character in the command line options.

Here's a somewhat truncated output from running this gawk program script:

```
$ gawk -f script4.gawk /etc/passwd
The latest list of users and shells
 UserID         Shell
--------        -------
root            /bin/bash
bin             /sbin/nologin
daemon          /sbin/nologin
[...]
Christine       /bin/bash
```

```
mysql            /bin/bash
Samantha         /bin/bash
Timothy          /bin/bash
This concludes the listing
$
```

As expected, the BEGIN script created the header text, the program script processed the information from the specified data file (the /etc/passwd file), and the END script produced the footer text. The \t within the print command produces some nicely formatted tabbed output.

This gives you a small taste of the power available when you use simple gawk scripts. Chapter 22 describes some more basic programming principles available for your gawk scripts, along with some even more advanced programming concepts you can use in your gawk program scripts to create professional looking reports from even the most cryptic data files.

Commanding at the sed Editor Basics

The key to successfully using the sed editor is to know its myriad of commands and formats, which help you to customize your text editing. This section describes some of the basic commands and features you can incorporate into your script to start using the sed editor.

Introducing more substitution options

You've already seen how to use the s command to substitute new text for the text in a line. However, a few additional options are available for the substitute command that can help make your life easier.

Substituting flags

There's a caveat to how the substitute command replaces matching patterns in the text string. Watch what happens in this example:

```
$ cat data4.txt
This is a test of the test script.
This is the second test of the test script.
$
$ sed 's/test/trial/' data4.txt
This is a trial of the test script.
This is the second trial of the test script.
$
```

The substitute command works fine in replacing text in multiple lines, but by default, it replaces only the first occurrence in each line. To get the substitute command to work on different occurrences of the text, you must use a *substitution flag*. The substitution flag is set after the substitution command strings:

```
s/pattern/replacement/flags
```

Four types of substitution flags are available:

- A number, indicating the pattern occurrence for which new text should be substituted
- g, indicating that new text should be substituted for all occurrences of the existing text
- p, indicating that the contents of the original line should be printed
- w *file*, which means to write the results of the substitution to a file

In the first type of substitution, you can specify which occurrence of the matching pattern the sed editor should substitute new text for:

```
$ sed 's/test/trial/2' data4.txt
This is a test of the trial script.
This is the second test of the trial script.
$
```

As a result of specifying a 2 as the substitution flag, the sed editor replaces the pattern only in the second occurrence in each line. The g substitution flag enables you to replace every occurrence of the pattern in the text:

```
$ sed 's/test/trial/g' data4.txt
This is a trial of the trial script.
This is the second trial of the trial script.
$
```

The p substitution flag prints a line that contains a matching pattern in the substitute command. This is most often used in conjunction with the -n sed option:

```
$ cat data5.txt
This is a test line.
This is a different line.
$
$ sed -n 's/test/trial/p' data5.txt
This is a trial line.
$
```

The -n option suppresses output from the sed editor. However, the p substitution flag outputs any line that has been modified. Using the two in combination produces output only for lines that have been modified by the substitute command.

The w substitution flag produces the same output but stores the output in the specified file:

```
$ sed 's/test/trial/w test.txt' data5.txt
This is a trial line.
This is a different line.
$
$ cat test.txt
This is a trial line.
$
```

The normal output of the sed editor appears in STDOUT, but only the lines that include the matching pattern are stored in the specified output file.

Replacing characters

Sometimes, you run across characters in text strings that aren't easy to use in the substitution pattern. One popular example in the Linux world is the forward slash (/).

Substituting pathnames in a file can get awkward. For example, if you wanted to substitute the C shell for the bash shell in the /etc/passwd file, you'd have to do this:

```
$ sed 's/\/bin\/bash/\/bin\/csh/' /etc/passwd
```

Because the forward slash is used as the string delimiter, you must use a backslash to escape it if it appears in the pattern text. This often leads to confusion and mistakes.

To solve this problem, the sed editor allows you to select a different character for the string delimiter in the substitute command:

```
$ sed 's!/bin/bash!/bin/csh!' /etc/passwd
```

In this example, the exclamation point is used for the string delimiter, making the pathnames much easier to read and understand.

Using addresses

By default, the commands you use in the sed editor apply to all lines of the text data. If you want to apply a command only to a specific line or a group of lines, you must use *line addressing*.

There are two forms of line addressing in the sed editor:

- A numeric range of lines
- A text pattern that filters out a line

Both forms use the same format for specifying the address:

```
[address] command
```

You can also group more than one command together for a specific address:

```
address {
    command1
    command2
    command3
}
```

The sed editor applies each of the commands you specify only to lines that match the address specified. This section demonstrates using both of these addressing techniques in your sed editor scripts.

Addressing the numeric line

When using numeric line addressing, you reference lines using their line position in the text stream. The sed editor assigns the first line in the text stream as line number one and continues sequentially for each new line.

The address you specify in the command can be a single line number or a range of lines specified by a starting line number, a comma, and an ending line number. Here's an example of specifying a line number to which the sed command will be applied:

```
$ sed '2s/dog/cat/' data1.txt
The quick brown fox jumps over the lazy dog
The quick brown fox jumps over the lazy cat
The quick brown fox jumps over the lazy dog
The quick brown fox jumps over the lazy dog
$
```

The sed editor modified the text only in line two per the address specified. Here's another example, this time using a range of line addresses:

```
$ sed '2,3s/dog/cat/' data1.txt
The quick brown fox jumps over the lazy dog
The quick brown fox jumps over the lazy cat
The quick brown fox jumps over the lazy cat
The quick brown fox jumps over the lazy dog
$
```

If you want to apply a command to a group of lines starting at some point within the text, but continuing to the end of the text, you can use the special address, the dollar sign:

```
$ sed '2,$s/dog/cat/' data1.txt
The quick brown fox jumps over the lazy dog
The quick brown fox jumps over the lazy cat
The quick brown fox jumps over the lazy cat
The quick brown fox jumps over the lazy cat
$
```

Because you may not know how many lines of data are in the text, the dollar sign often comes in handy.

Using text pattern filters

The other method of restricting which lines a command applies to is a bit more complicated. The sed editor allows you to specify a text pattern that it uses to filter lines for the command. This is the format:

/*pattern*/command

You must encapsulate the *pattern* you specify in forward slashes. The sed editor applies the command only to lines that contain the text pattern you specify.

For example, if you want to change the default shell for only the user Samantha, you'd use the sed command:

```
$ grep Samantha /etc/passwd
Samantha:x:502:502::/home/Samantha:/bin/bash
$
$ sed '/Samantha/s/bash/csh/' /etc/passwd
root:x:0:0:root:/root:/bin/bash
bin:x:1:1:bin:/bin:/sbin/nologin
[...]
Christine:x:501:501:Christine B:/home/Christine:/bin/bash
Samantha:x:502:502::/home/Samantha:/bin/csh
Timothy:x:503:503::/home/Timothy:/bin/bash
$
```

The command was applied only to the line with the matching text pattern. Although using a fixed text pattern may be useful for filtering specific values, as in the userid example, it's somewhat limited in what you can do with it. The sed editor uses a feature called *regular expressions* in text patterns to allow you to create patterns that get pretty involved.

Regular expressions allow you to create advanced text pattern-matching formulas to match all sorts of data. These formulas combine a series of wildcard characters, special characters, and fixed text characters to produce a concise pattern that can match just about any text situation. Regular expressions are one of the scarier parts of shell script programming, and Chapter 20 covers them in great detail.

Grouping commands

If you need to perform more than one command on an individual line, group the commands together using braces. The sed editor processes each command listed on the address line(s):

```
$ sed '2{
> s/fox/elephant/
> s/dog/cat/
```

```
> }' data1.txt
The quick brown fox jumps over the lazy dog.
The quick brown elephant jumps over the lazy cat.
The quick brown fox jumps over the lazy dog.
The quick brown fox jumps over the lazy dog.
$
```

Both commands are processed against the address. And of course, you can specify an address range before the grouped commands:

```
$ sed '3,${
> s/brown/green/
> s/lazy/active/
> }' data1.txt
The quick brown fox jumps over the lazy dog.
The quick brown fox jumps over the lazy dog.
The quick green fox jumps over the active dog.
The quick green fox jumps over the active dog.
$
```

The sed editor applies all the commands to all the lines in the address range.

Deleting lines

The text substitution command isn't the only command available in the sed editor. If you need to delete specific lines of text in a text stream, you can use the delete command.

The delete command, d, pretty much does what it says. It deletes any text lines that match the addressing scheme supplied. Be careful with the delete command, because if you forget to include an addressing scheme, all the lines are deleted from the stream:

```
$ cat data1.txt
The quick brown fox jumps over the lazy dog
The quick brown fox jumps over the lazy dog
The quick brown fox jumps over the lazy dog
The quick brown fox jumps over the lazy dog
$
$ sed 'd' data1.txt
$
```

The delete command is obviously most useful when used in conjunction with a specified address. This allows you to delete specific lines of text from the data stream, either by line number:

```
$ cat data6.txt
This is line number 1.
This is line number 2.
This is line number 3.
```

```
This is line number 4.
$
$ sed '3d' data6.txt
This is line number 1.
This is line number 2.
This is line number 4.
$
```

or by a specific range of lines:

```
$ sed '2,3d' data6.txt
This is line number 1.
This is line number 4.
$
```

or by using the special end-of-file character:

```
$ sed '3,$d' data6.txt
This is line number 1.
This is line number 2.
$
```

The pattern-matching feature of the sed editor also applies to the delete command:

```
$ sed '/number 1/d' data6.txt
This is line number 2.
This is line number 3.
This is line number 4.
$
```

The sed editor removes the line containing text that matches the pattern you specify.

> **NOTE**
>
> Remember that the sed editor doesn't touch the original file. Any lines you delete are only gone from the output of the sed editor. The original file still contains the "deleted" lines.

You can also delete a range of lines using two text patterns, but be careful if you do this. The first pattern you specify "turns on" the line deletion, and the second pattern "turns off" the line deletion. The sed editor deletes any lines between the two specified lines (including the specified lines):

```
$ sed '/1/,/3/d' data6.txt
This is line number 4.
$
```

In addition, you must be careful because the delete feature "turns on" whenever the sed editor detects the start pattern in the data stream. This may produce an unexpected result:

```
$ cat data7.txt
This is line number 1.
This is line number 2.
This is line number 3.
This is line number 4.
This is line number 1 again.
This is text you want to keep.
This is the last line in the file.
$
$ sed '/1/,/3/d' data7.txt
This is line number 4.
$
```

The second occurrence of a line with the number 1 in it triggered the delete command again, deleting the rest of the lines in the data stream, because the stop pattern wasn't recognized. Of course, the other obvious problem occurs if you specify a stop pattern that never appears in the text:

```
$ sed '/1/,/5/d' data7.txt
$
```

Because the delete features "turned on" at the first pattern match, but never found the end pattern match, the entire data stream was deleted.

Inserting and appending text

As you would expect, like any other editor, the sed editor allows you to insert and append text lines to the data stream. The difference between the two actions can be confusing:

- The insert command (i) adds a new line before the specified line.
- The append command (a) adds a new line after the specified line.

What is confusing about these two commands is their formats. You can't use these commands on a single command line. You must specify the line to insert or append the line to insert on a separate line by itself. Here's the format for doing this:

```
sed '[address]command\
new line'
```

The text in *new line* appears in the sed editor output in the place you specify. Remember that when you use the insert command, the text appears before the data stream text:

```
$ echo "Test Line 2" | sed 'i\Test Line 1'
Test Line 1
Test Line 2
$
```

And when you use the append command, the text appears after the data stream text:

```
$ echo "Test Line 2" | sed 'a\Test Line 1'
Test Line 2
Test Line 1
$
```

When you use the sed editor from the command line interface prompt, you get the secondary prompt to enter the new line of data. You must complete the sed editor command on this line. After you enter the ending single quotation mark, the bash shell processes the command:

```
$ echo "Test Line 2" | sed 'i\
> Test Line 1'
Test Line 1
Test Line 2
$
```

This works well for adding text before or after the text in the data stream, but what about adding text inside the data stream?

To insert or append data inside the data stream lines, you must use addressing to tell the sed editor where you want the data to appear. You can specify only a single line address when using these commands. You can match either a numeric line number or a text pattern, but you cannot use a range of addresses. This is logical, because you can only insert or append before or after a single line, and not a range of lines.

Here's an example of inserting a new line before line 3 in the data stream:

```
$ sed '3i\
> This is an inserted line.' data6.txt
This is line number 1.
This is line number 2.
This is an inserted line.
This is line number 3.
This is line number 4.
$
```

Here's an example of appending a new line after line 3 in the data stream:

```
$ sed '3a\
> This is an appended line.' data6.txt
This is line number 1.
This is line number 2.
This is line number 3.
This is an appended line.
This is line number 4.
$
```

This uses the same process as the insert command; it just places the new text line after the specified line number. If you have a multiline data stream, and you want to append a new line of text to the end of a data stream, just use the dollar sign, which represents the last line of data:

```
$ sed '$a\
> This is a new line of text.' data6.txt
This is line number 1.
This is line number 2.
This is line number 3.
This is line number 4.
This is a new line of text.
$
```

The same idea applies if you want to add a new line at the beginning of the data stream. Just insert a new line before line number one.

To insert or append more than one line of text, you must use a backslash on each line of new text until you reach the last text line where you want to insert or append text:

```
$ sed '1i\
> This is one line of new text.\
> This is another line of new text.' data6.txt
This is one line of new text.
This is another line of new text.
This is line number 1.
This is line number 2.
This is line number 3.
This is line number 4.
$
```

Both of the specified lines are added to the data stream.

Changing lines

The change command allows you to change the contents of an entire line of text in the data stream. It works the same way as the insert and append commands, in that you must specify the new line separately from the rest of the sed command:

```
$ sed '3c\
> This is a changed line of text.' data6.txt
This is line number 1.
This is line number 2.
This is a changed line of text.
This is line number 4.
$
```

In this example, the sed editor changes the text in line number 3. You can also use a text pattern for the address:

```
$ sed '/number 3/c\
> This is a changed line of text.' data6.txt
This is line number 1.
This is line number 2.
This is a changed line of text.
This is line number 4.
$
```

The text pattern change command changes any line of text in the data stream that it matches.

```
$ cat data8.txt
This is line number 1.
This is line number 2.
This is line number 3.
This is line number 4.
This is line number 1 again.
This is yet another line.
This is the last line in the file.
$
$ sed '/number 1/c\
> This is a changed line of text.' data8.txt
This is a changed line of text.
This is line number 2.
This is line number 3.
This is line number 4.
This is a changed line of text.
This is yet another line.
This is the last line in the file.
$
```

You can use an address range in the change command, but the results may not be what you expect:

```
$ sed '2,3c\
> This is a new line of text.' data6.txt
This is line number 1.
This is a new line of text.
This is line number 4.
$
```

Instead of changing both lines with the text, the sed editor uses the single line of text to replace both lines.

Transforming characters

The transform command (y) is the only sed editor command that operates on a single character. The transform command uses the format:

[address]y/inchars/outchars/

The transform command performs a one-to-one mapping of the inchars and the outchars values. The first character in inchars is converted to the first character in outchars. The second character in inchars is converted to the second character in outchars. This mapping continues throughout the length of the specified characters. If the inchars and outchars are not the same length, the sed editor produces an error message.

Here's a simple example of using the transform command:

```
$ sed 'y/123/789/' data8.txt
This is line number 7.
This is line number 8.
This is line number 9.
This is line number 4.
This is line number 7 again.
This is yet another line.
This is the last line in the file.
$
```

As you can see from the output, each instance of the characters specified in the inchars pattern has been replaced by the character in the same position in the outchars pattern.

The transform command is a global command; that is, it performs the transformation on any character found in the text line automatically, without regard to the occurrence:

```
$ echo "This 1 is a test of 1 try." | sed 'y/123/456/'
This 4 is a test of 4 try.
$
```

The sed editor transformed both instances of the matching character 1 in the text line. You can't limit the transformation to a specific occurrence of the character.

Printing revisited

The "Introducing more substitution options" section showed you how to use the p flag with the substitution command to display lines that the sed editor changed. In addition, three commands that can be used to print information from the data stream:

- The p command to print a text line
- The equal sign (=) command to print line numbers
- The l (lowercase L) command to list a line

19

The following sections look at these three printing commands in the sed editor.

Printing lines

Like the p flag in the substitution command, the p command prints a line in the sed editor output. On its own, this command doesn't offer much excitement:

```
$ echo "this is a test" | sed 'p'
this is a test
this is a test
$
```

All it does is print the data text that you already know is there. The most common use for the print command is printing lines that contain matching text from a text pattern:

```
$ cat data6.txt
This is line number 1.
This is line number 2.
This is line number 3.
This is line number 4.
$
$ sed -n '/number 3/p' data6.txt
This is line number 3.
$
```

By using the -n option on the command line, you can suppress all the other lines and print only the line that contains the matching text pattern.

You can also use this as a quick way to print a subset of lines in a data stream:

```
$ sed -n '2,3p' data6.txt
This is line number 2.
This is line number 3.
$
```

You can also use the print command when you need to see a line before it gets altered, such as with the substitution or change command. You can create a script that displays the line before it's changed:

```
$ sed -n '/3/{
> p
> s/line/test/p
> }' data6.txt
This is line number 3.
This is test number 3.
$
```

This sed editor command searches for lines that contain the number 3 and executes two commands. First, the script uses the p command to print the original version of the line;

then it uses the s command to substitute text, along with the p flag to print the resulting text. The output shows both the original line text and the new line text.

Printing line numbers

The equal sign command prints the current line number for the line within the data stream. Line numbers are determined by using the newline character in the data stream. Each time a newline character appears in the data stream, the sed editor assumes that it terminates a line of text:

```
$ cat data1.txt
The quick brown fox jumps over the lazy dog.
The quick brown fox jumps over the lazy dog.
The quick brown fox jumps over the lazy dog.
The quick brown fox jumps over the lazy dog.
$
$ sed '=' data1.txt
1
The quick brown fox jumps over the lazy dog.
2
The quick brown fox jumps over the lazy dog.
3
The quick brown fox jumps over the lazy dog.
4
The quick brown fox jumps over the lazy dog.
$
```

The sed editor prints the line number before the actual line of text. The equal sign command comes in handy if you're searching for a specific text pattern in the data stream:

```
$ sed -n '/number 4/{
> =
> p
> }' data6.txt
4
This is line number 4.
$
```

By using the -n option, you can have the sed editor display both the line number and text for the line that contains the matching text pattern.

Listing lines

The list command (l) allows you to print both the text and nonprintable characters in a data stream. Any nonprintable characters are shown using either their octal values, preceded by a backslash or the standard C-style nomenclature for common nonprintable characters, such as \t for tab characters:

```
$ cat data9.txt
This    line    contains        tabs.
```

```
$
$ sed -n 'l' data9.txt
This\tline\tcontains\ttabs.$
$
```

The tab character locations are shown with the \t nomenclature. The dollar sign at the end of the line indicates the newline character. If you have a data stream that contains an escape character, the list command displays it using the octal code if necessary:

```
$ cat data10.txt
This line contains an escape character.
$
$ sed -n 'l' data10.txt
This line contains an escape character. \a$
$
```

The data10.txt file contains an escape control code, which generates a bell sound. When you use the cat command to display the text file, you don't see the escape control code; you just hear the sound (if your speakers are turned on). However, using the list command, you can display the escape control code used.

Using files with sed

The substitution command contains flags that allow you to work with files. There are also regular sed editor commands that let you do that without having to substitute text.

Writing to a file

The w command is used to write lines to a file. Here's the format for the w command:

```
[address]w filename
```

The filename can be specified as either a relative or absolute pathname, but in either case, the person running the sed editor must have write permissions for the file. The address can be any type of addressing method used in sed, such as a single line number, a text pattern, or a range of line numbers or text patterns.

Here's an example that prints only the first two lines of a data stream to a text file:

```
$ sed '1,2w test.txt' data6.txt
This is line number 1.
This is line number 2.
This is line number 3.
This is line number 4.
$
$ cat test.txt
This is line number 1.
This is line number 2.
$
```

Of course, if you don't want the lines to display on STDOUT, you can use the -n option for the sed command.

This is a great tool to use if you need to create a data file from a master file on the basis of common text values, such as those in a mailing list:

```
$ cat data11.txt
Blum, R        Browncoat
McGuiness, A   Alliance
Bresnahan, C   Browncoat
Harken, C      Alliance
$
$ sed -n '/Browncoat/w Browncoats.txt' data11.txt
$
$ cat Browncoats.txt
Blum, R        Browncoat
Bresnahan, C   Browncoat
$
```

The sed editor writes to a destination file only the data lines that contain the text pattern.

Reading data from a file

You've already seen how to insert data into and append text to a data stream from the sed command line. The read command (r) allows you to insert data contained in a separate file.

Here's the format of the read command:

```
[address]r filename
```

The *filename* parameter specifies either an absolute or relative pathname for the file that contains the data. You can't use a range of addresses for the read command. You can only specify a single line number or text pattern address. The sed editor inserts the text from the file after the address.

```
$ cat data12.txt
This is an added line.
This is the second added line.
$
$ sed '3r data12.txt' data6.txt
This is line number 1.
This is line number 2.
This is line number 3.
This is an added line.
This is the second added line.
This is line number 4.
$
```

19

The sed editor inserts into the data stream all the text lines in the data file. The same technique works when using a text pattern address:

```
$ sed '/number 2/r data12.txt' data6.txt
This is line number 1.
This is line number 2.
This is an added line.
This is the second added line.
This is line number 3.
This is line number 4.
$
```

If you want to add text to the end of a data stream, just use the dollar sign address symbol:

```
$ sed '$r data12.txt' data6.txt
This is line number 1.
This is line number 2.
This is line number 3.
This is line number 4.
This is an added line.
This is the second added line.
$
```

A cool application of the read command is to use it in conjunction with a delete command to replace a placeholder in a file with data from another file. For example, suppose that you had a form stored in a text file that looked like this:

```
$ cat notice.std
Would the following people:
LIST
please report to the ship's captain.
$
```

The form letter uses the generic placeholder LIST in place of a list of people. To insert the list of people after the placeholder, you just use the read command. However, this still leaves the placeholder text in the output. To remove that, just use the delete command. The result looks like this:

```
$ sed '/LIST/{
> r data11.txt
> d
> }' notice.std
Would the following people:
Blum, R        Browncoat
McGuiness, A  Alliance
Bresnahan, C  Browncoat
```

```
Harken, C     Alliance
please report to the ship's captain.
$
```

Now the placeholder text is replaced with the list of names from the data file.

Summary

Shell scripts can do lots of work on their own, but it's often difficult to manipulate data with just a shell script. Linux provides two handy utilities to help with handling text data. The sed editor is a stream editor that quickly processes data on the fly as it reads it. You must provide the sed editor with a list of editing commands, which it applies to the data.

The gawk program is a utility from the GNU organization that mimics and expands on the functionality of the Unix awk program. The gawk program contains a built-in programming language that you can use to write scripts to handle and process data. You can use the gawk program to extract data elements from large data files and output them in just about any format you desire. This makes processing large log files a snap, as well as creating custom reports from data files.

A crucial element of using both the sed and gawk programs is knowing how to use regular expressions. Regular expressions are key to creating customized filters for extracting and manipulating data in text files. The next chapter dives into the often misunderstood world of regular expressions, showing you how to build regular expressions for manipulating all types of data.

19

Regular Expressions

The key to successfully working with the sed editor and the gawk program in your shell script is your comfort using regular expressions. This is not always an easy thing to do, because trying to filter specific data from a large batch of data can (and often does) get complicated. This chapter describes how to create regular expressions in both the sed editor and the gawk program that can filter out just the data you need.

What Are Regular Expressions?

The first step to understanding regular expressions is to define just exactly what they are. This section explains what a regular expression is and describes how Linux uses regular expressions.

A definition

A *regular expression* is a pattern template you define that a Linux utility uses to filter text. A Linux utility (such as the sed editor or the gawk program) matches the regular expression pattern against data as that data flows into the utility. If the data matches the pattern, it's accepted for processing. If the data doesn't match the pattern, it's rejected. This is illustrated in Figure 20-1.

The regular expression pattern makes use of wildcard characters to represent one or more characters in the data stream. There are plenty of instances in Linux where you can specify a wildcard character to represent data you don't know about. You've already seen an example of using wildcard characters with the Linux ls command for listing files and directories (see Chapter 3).

FIGURE 20-1

Matching data against a regular expression pattern

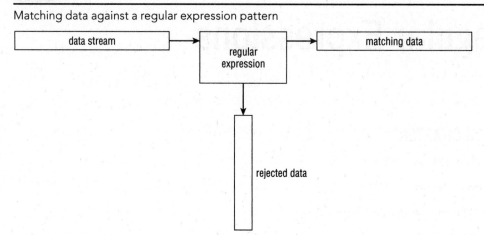

The asterisk wildcard character allows you to list only files that match a certain criteria. For example:

```
$ ls -al da*
-rw-r--r--    1 rich     rich          45 Nov 26 12:42 data
-rw-r--r--    1 rich     rich          25 Dec  4 12:40 data.tst
-rw-r--r--    1 rich     rich         180 Nov 26 12:42 data1
-rw-r--r--    1 rich     rich          45 Nov 26 12:44 data2
-rw-r--r--    1 rich     rich          73 Nov 27 12:31 data3
-rw-r--r--    1 rich     rich          79 Nov 28 14:01 data4
-rw-r--r--    1 rich     rich         187 Dec  4 09:45 datatest
$
```

The da* parameter instructs the ls command to list only the files whose name starts with *da*. There can be any number of characters after the da in the filename (including none). The ls command reads the information regarding all the files in the directory but displays only the ones that match the wildcard character.

Regular expression wildcard patterns work in a similar way. The regular expression pattern contains text and/or special characters that define a template for the sed editor and the gawk program to follow when matching data. You can use different special characters in a regular expression to define a specific pattern for filtering data.

Types of regular expressions

The biggest problem with using regular expressions is that there isn't just one set of them. Several different applications use different types of regular expressions in the Linux environment. These include such diverse applications as programming languages (Java, Perl, and

Python), Linux utilities (such as the sed editor, the gawk program, and the grep utility), and mainstream applications (such as the MySQL and PostgreSQL database servers).

A regular expression is implemented using a *regular expression engine*. A regular expression engine is the underlying software that interprets regular expression patterns and uses those patterns to match text.

The Linux world has two popular regular expression engines:

- The POSIX Basic Regular Expression (BRE) engine
- The POSIX Extended Regular Expression (ERE) engine

Most Linux utilities at a minimum conform to the POSIX BRE engine specifications, recognizing all the pattern symbols it defines. Unfortunately, some utilities (such as the sed editor) conform only to a subset of the BRE engine specifications. This is due to speed constraints, because the sed editor attempts to process text in the data stream as quickly as possible.

The POSIX ERE engine is often found in programming languages that rely on regular expressions for text filtering. It provides advanced pattern symbols as well as special symbols for common patterns, such as matching digits, words, and alphanumeric characters. The gawk program uses the ERE engine to process its regular expression patterns.

Because there are so many different ways to implement regular expressions, it's hard to present a single, concise description of all the possible regular expressions. The following sections discuss the most commonly found regular expressions and demonstrate how to use them in the sed editor and gawk program.

Defining BRE Patterns

The most basic BRE pattern is matching text characters in a data stream. This section demonstrates how you can define text in the regular expression pattern and what to expect from the results.

Plain text

Chapter 18 demonstrated how to use standard text strings in the sed editor and the gawk program to filter data. Here's an example to refresh your memory:

```
$ echo "This is a test" | sed -n '/test/p'
This is a test
$ echo "This is a test" | sed -n '/trial/p'
$
$ echo "This is a test" | gawk '/test/{print $0}'
```

20

```
This is a test
$ echo "This is a test" | gawk '/trial/{print $0}'
$
```

The first pattern defines a single word, *test*. The sed editor and gawk program scripts each use their own version of the print command to print any lines that match the regular expression pattern. Because the echo statement contains the word "test" in the text string, the data stream text matches the defined regular expression pattern, and the sed editor displays the line.

The second pattern again defines just a single word, this time the word "trial." Because the echo statement text string doesn't contain that word, the regular expression pattern doesn't match, so neither the sed editor nor the gawk program prints the line.

You probably already noticed that the regular expression doesn't care where in the data stream the pattern occurs. It also doesn't matter how many times the pattern occurs. After the regular expression can match the pattern anywhere in the text string, it passes the string along to the Linux utility that's using it.

The key is matching the regular expression pattern to the data stream text. It's important to remember that regular expressions are extremely picky about matching patterns. The first rule to remember is that regular expression patterns are case sensitive. This means they'll match only those patterns with the proper case of characters:

```
$ echo "This is a test" | sed -n '/this/p'
$
$ echo "This is a test" | sed -n '/This/p'
This is a test
$
```

The first attempt failed to match because the word "this" doesn't appear in all lowercase in the text string, while the second attempt, which uses the uppercase letter in the pattern, worked just fine.

You don't have to limit yourself to whole words in the regular expression. If the defined text appears anywhere in the data stream, the regular expression matches the following:

```
$ echo "The books are expensive" | sed -n '/book/p'
The books are expensive
$
```

Even though the text in the data stream is books, the data in the stream contains the regular expression book, so the regular expression pattern matches the data. Of course, if you try the opposite, the regular expression fails:

```
$ echo "The book is expensive" | sed -n '/books/p'
$
```

The complete regular expression text didn't appear in the data stream, so the match failed and the sed editor didn't display the text.

You also don't have to limit yourself to single text words in the regular expression. You can include spaces and numbers in your text string as well:

```
$ echo "This is line number 1" | sed -n '/ber 1/p'
This is line number 1
$
```

Spaces are treated just like any other character in the regular expression:

```
$ echo "This is line number1" | sed -n '/ber 1/p'
$
```

If you define a space in the regular expression, it must appear in the data stream. You can even create a regular expression pattern that matches multiple contiguous spaces:

```
$ cat data1
This is a normal line of text.
This is  a line with too many spaces.
$ sed -n '/  /p' data1
This is  a line with too many spaces.
$
```

The line with two spaces between words matches the regular expression pattern. This is a great way to catch spacing problems in text files!

Special characters

As you use text strings in your regular expression patterns, there's something you need to be aware of. There are a few exceptions when defining text characters in a regular expression. Regular expression patterns assign a special meaning to a few characters. If you try to use these characters in your text pattern, you won't get the results you were expecting.

These special characters are recognized by regular expressions:

.*[]^${}\+?|()

As the chapter progresses, you'll find out just what these special characters do in a regular expression. For now, however, just remember that you can't use these characters by themselves in your text pattern.

If you want to use one of the special characters as a text character, you need to *escape* it. When you escape the special characters, you add a special character in front of it to indicate to the regular expression engine that it should interpret the next character as a normal text character. The special character that does this is the backslash character (\).

20

For example, if you want to search for a dollar sign in your text, just precede it with a backslash character:

```
$ cat data2
The cost is $4.00
$ sed -n '/\$/p' data2
The cost is $4.00
$
```

Because the backslash is a special character, if you need to use it in a regular expression pattern, you need to escape it as well, producing a double backslash:

```
$ echo "\ is a special character" | sed -n '/\\/p'
\ is a special character
$
```

Finally, although the forward slash isn't a regular expression special character, if you use it in your regular expression pattern in the sed editor or the gawk program, you get an error:

```
$ echo "3 / 2" | sed -n '///p'
sed: -e expression #1, char 2: No previous regular expression
$
```

To use a forward slash, you need to escape that as well:

```
$ echo "3 / 2" | sed -n '/\//p'
3 / 2
$
```

Now the sed editor can properly interpret the regular expression pattern, and all is well.

Anchor characters

As shown in the "Plain Text" section, by default, when you specify a regular expression pattern, if the pattern appears anywhere in the data stream, it matches. You can use two special characters to anchor a pattern to either the beginning or the end of lines in the data stream.

Starting at the beginning

The caret character (^) defines a pattern that starts at the beginning of a line of text in the data stream. If the pattern is located any place other than the start of the line of text, the regular expression pattern fails.

To use the caret character, you must place it before the pattern specified in the regular expression:

```
$ echo "The book store" | sed -n '/^book/p'
$
```

```
$ echo "Books are great" | sed -n '/^Book/p'
Books are great
$
```

The caret anchor character checks for the pattern at the beginning of each new line of data, as determined by the newline character:

```
$ cat data3
This is a test line.
this is another test line.
A line that tests this feature.
Yet more testing of this
$ sed -n '/^this/p' data3
this is another test line.
$
```

As long as the pattern appears at the start of a new line, the caret anchor catches it.

If you position the caret character in any place other than at the beginning of the pattern, it acts like a normal character and not as a special character:

```
$ echo "This ^ is a test" | sed -n '/s ^/p'
This ^ is a test
$
```

Because the caret character is listed last in the regular expression pattern, the sed editor uses it as a normal character to match text.

> **NOTE**
>
> If you need to specify a regular expression pattern using only the caret character, you don't need to escape it with a backslash. However, if you specify the caret character first, followed by additional text in the pattern, you need to use the escape character before the caret character.

Looking for the ending

The opposite of looking for a pattern at the start of a line is looking for it at the end of a line. The dollar sign ($) special character defines the end anchor. Add this special character after a text pattern to indicate that the line of data must end with the text pattern:

```
$ echo "This is a good book" | sed -n '/book$/p'
This is a good book
$ echo "This book is good" | sed -n '/book$/p'
$
```

The problem with an ending text pattern is that you must be careful what you're looking for:

```
$ echo "There are a lot of good books" | sed -n '/book$/p'
$
```

20

Making the word "book" plural at the end of the line means that it no longer matches the regular expression pattern, even though book is in the data stream. The text pattern must be the last thing on the line for the pattern to match.

Combining anchors

In some common situations, you can combine both the start and end anchor on the same line. In the first situation, suppose you want to look for a line of data containing only a specific text pattern:

```
$ cat data4
this is a test of using both anchors
I said this is a test
this is a test
I'm sure this is a test.
$ sed -n '/^this is a test$/p' data4
this is a test
$
```

The sed editor ignores the lines that include other text besides the specified text.

The second situation may seem a little odd at first but is extremely useful. By combining both anchors in a pattern with no text, you can filter blank lines from the data stream. Consider this example:

```
$ cat data5
This is one test line.

This is another test line.
$ sed '/^$/d' data5
This is one test line.
This is another test line.
$
```

The regular expression pattern that is defined looks for lines that have nothing between the start and end of the line. Because blank lines contain no text between the two newline characters, they match the regular expression pattern. The sed editor uses the d delete command to delete lines that match the regular expression pattern, thus removing all blank lines from the text. This is an effective way to remove blank lines from documents.

The dot character

The dot special character is used to match any single character except a newline character. The dot character must match a character, however; if there's no character in the place of the dot, then the pattern fails.

Let's look at a few examples of using the dot character in a regular expression pattern:

```
$ cat data6
This is a test of a line.
The cat is sleeping.
That is a very nice hat.
This test is at line four.
at ten o'clock we'll go home.
$ sed -n '/.at/p' data6
The cat is sleeping.
That is a very nice hat.
This test is at line four.
$
```

You should be able to figure out why the first line failed and why the second and third lines passed. The fourth line is a little tricky. Notice that we matched the at, but there's no character in front of it to match the dot character. Ah, but there is! In regular expressions, spaces count as characters, so the space in front of the at matches the pattern. The fifth line proves this, by putting the at in the front of the line, which fails to match the pattern.

Character classes

The dot special character is great for matching a character position against any character, but what if you want to limit what characters to match? This is called a *character class* in regular expressions.

You can define a class of characters that would match a position in a text pattern. If one of the characters from the character class is in the data stream, it matches the pattern.

To define a character class, you use square brackets. The brackets should contain any character you want to include in the class. You then use the entire class within a pattern just like any other wildcard character. This takes a little getting used to at first, but after you catch on, it can generate some pretty amazing results.

The following is an example of creating a character class:

```
$ sed -n '/[ch]at/p' data6
The cat is sleeping.
That is a very nice hat.
$
```

Using the same data file as in the dot special character example, we came up with a different result. This time we managed to filter out the line that just contained the word at. The only words that match this pattern are cat and hat. Also notice that the line that started with at didn't match as well. There must be a character in the character class that matches the appropriate position.

20

543

Character classes come in handy if you're not sure which case a character is in:

```
$ echo "Yes" | sed -n '/[Yy]es/p'
Yes
$ echo "yes" | sed -n '/[Yy]es/p'
yes
$
```

You can use more than one character class in a single expression:

```
$ echo "Yes" | sed -n '/[Yy][Ee][Ss]/p'
Yes
$ echo "yEs" | sed -n '/[Yy][Ee][Ss]/p'
yEs
$ echo "yeS" | sed -n '/[Yy][Ee][Ss]/p'
yeS
$
```

The regular expression used three character classes to cover both lower and upper cases for all three character positions.

Character classes don't have to contain just letters; you can use numbers in them as well:

```
$ cat data7
This line doesn't contain a number.
This line has 1 number on it.
This line a number 2 on it.
This line has a number 4 on it.
$ sed -n '/[0123]/p' data7
This line has 1 number on it.
This line a number 2 on it.
$
```

The regular expression pattern matches any lines that contain the numbers 0, 1, 2, or 3. Any other numbers are ignored, as are lines without numbers in them.

You can combine character classes to check for properly formatted numbers, such as phone numbers and ZIP codes. However, when you're trying to match a specific format, you must be careful. Here's an example of a ZIP code match gone wrong:

```
$ cat data8
60633
46201
223001
4353
22203
$ sed -n '
>/[0123456789][0123456789][0123456789][0123456789][0123456789]/p
>' data8
```

```
60633
46201
223001
22203
$
```

This might not have produced the result you were thinking of. It did a fine job of filtering out the number that was too short to be a ZIP code, because the last character class didn't have a character to match against. However, it still passed the six-digit number, even though we only defined five character classes.

Remember that the regular expression pattern can be found anywhere in the text of the data stream. You may always have additional characters besides the matching pattern characters. If you want to ensure that you match against only five numbers, you need to delineate them somehow, either with spaces, or as in this example, by showing that they're at the start and end of the line:

```
$ sed -n '
> /^[0123456789][0123456789][0123456789][0123456789][0123456789]$/p
> ' data8
60633
46201
22203
$
```

Now that's much better! Later in this chapter, we look at how to simplify this even further.

One extremely popular use for character classes is parsing words that might be misspelled, such as data entered from a user form. You can easily create regular expressions that can accept common misspellings in data:

```
$ cat data9
I need to have some maintenence done on my car.
I'll pay that in a seperate invoice.
After I pay for the maintenance my car will be as good as new.
$ sed -n '
/maint[ea]n[ae]nce/p
/sep[ea]r[ea]te/p
' data9
I need to have some maintenence done on my car.
I'll pay that in a seperate invoice.
After I pay for the maintenance my car will be as good as new.
$
```

The two sed print commands in this example utilize regular expression character classes to help catch the misspelled words, *maintenance* and *separate*, in the text. The same regular expression pattern also matches the properly spelled occurrence of "maintenance."

20

Negating character classes

In regular expression patterns, you can also reverse the effect of a character class. Instead of looking for a character contained in the class, you can look for any character that's not in the class. To do that, just place a caret character at the beginning of the character class range:

```
$ sed -n '/[^ch]at/p' data6
This test is at line four.
$
```

By negating the character class, the regular expression pattern matches any character that's neither a *c* nor an *h*, along with the text pattern. Because the space character fits this category, it passed the pattern match. However, even with the negation, the character class must still match a character, so the line with the at in the start of the line still doesn't match the pattern.

Using ranges

You may have noticed when I showed the ZIP code example earlier that it was somewhat awkward having to list all the possible digits in each character class. Fortunately, you can use a shortcut so you don't have to do that.

You can use a range of characters within a character class by using the dash symbol. Just specify the first character in the range, a dash, and then the last character in the range. The regular expression includes any character that's within the specified character range, according to the character set used by the Linux system (see Chapter 2).

Now you can simplify the ZIP code example by specifying a range of digits:

```
$ sed -n '/^[0-9][0-9][0-9][0-9][0-9]$/p' data8
60633
46201
45902
$
```

That saved lots of typing! Each character class matches any digit from 0 to 9. The pattern fails if a letter is present anywhere in the data:

```
$ echo "a8392" | sed -n '/^[0-9][0-9][0-9][0-9][0-9]$/p'
$
$ echo "1839a" | sed -n '/^[0-9][0-9][0-9][0-9][0-9]$/p'
$
$ echo "18a92" | sed -n '/^[0-9][0-9][0-9][0-9][0-9]$/p'
$
```

The same technique works with letters:

```
$ sed -n '/[c-h]at/p' data6
The cat is sleeping.
```

```
That is a very nice hat.
$
```

The new pattern [c-h]at matches words where the first letter is between the letter *c* and the letter *h*. In this case, the line with only the word at failed to match the pattern.

You can also specify multiple, non-continuous ranges in a single character class:

```
$ sed -n '/[a-ch-m]at/p' data6
The cat is sleeping.
That is a very nice hat.
$
```

The character class allows the ranges *a* through *c*, and *h* through *m* to appear before the at text. This range would reject any letters between *d* and *g*:

```
$ echo "I'm getting too fat." | sed -n '/[a-ch-m]at/p'
$
```

This pattern rejected the fat text, as it wasn't in the specified range.

Special character classes

In addition to defining your own character classes, the BRE contains special character classes you can use to match against specific types of characters. Table 20-1 describes the BRE special characters you can use.

TABLE 20-1 BRE Special Character Classes

Class	Description
[[:alpha:]]	Matches any alphabetical character, either upper or lower case
[[:alnum:]]	Matches any alphanumeric character 0–9, A–Z, or a–z
[[:blank:]]	Matches a space or Tab character
[[:digit:]]	Matches a numerical digit from 0 through 9
[[:lower:]]	Matches any lowercase alphabetical character a–z
[[:print:]]	Matches any printable character
[[:punct:]]	Matches a punctuation character
[[:space:]]	Matches any whitespace character: space, Tab, NL, FF, VT, CR
[[:upper:]]	Matches any uppercase alphabetical character A–Z

You use the special character classes just as you would a normal character class in your regular expression patterns:

```
$ echo "abc" | sed -n '/[[:digit:]]/p'
$
```

```
$ echo "abc" | sed -n '/[[:alpha:]]/p'
abc
$ echo "abc123" | sed -n '/[[:digit:]]/p'
abc123
$ echo "This is, a test" | sed -n '/[[:punct:]]/p'
This is, a test
$ echo "This is a test" | sed -n '/[[:punct:]]/p'
$
```

Using the special character classes is an easy way to define ranges. Instead of having to use a range [0–9], you can just use [[:digit:]].

The asterisk

Placing an asterisk after a character signifies that the character must appear zero or more times in the text to match the pattern:

```
$ echo "ik" | sed -n '/ie*k/p'
ik
$ echo "iek" | sed -n '/ie*k/p'
iek
$ echo "ieek" | sed -n '/ie*k/p'
ieek
$ echo "ieeek" | sed -n '/ie*k/p'
ieeek
$ echo "ieeeek" | sed -n '/ie*k/p'
ieeeek
$
```

This pattern symbol is commonly used for handling words that have a common misspelling or variations in language spellings. For example, if you need to write a script that may be used in either American or British English, you could write:

```
$ echo "I'm getting a color TV" | sed -n '/colou*r/p'
I'm getting a color TV
$ echo "I'm getting a colour TV" | sed -n '/colou*r/p'
I'm getting a colour TV
$
```

The u* in the pattern indicates that the letter *u* may or may not appear in the text to match the pattern. Similarly, if you know of a word that is commonly misspelled, you can accommodate it by using the asterisk:

```
$ echo "I ate a potatoe with my lunch." | sed -n '/potatoe*/p'
I ate a potatoe with my lunch.
$ echo "I ate a potato with my lunch." | sed -n '/potatoe*/p'
I ate a potato with my lunch.
$
```

Placing an asterisk next to the possible extra letter allows you to accept the misspelled word.

Another handy feature is combining the dot special character with the asterisk special character. This combination provides a pattern to match any number of any characters. It's often used between two text strings that may or may not appear next to each other in the data stream:

```
$ echo "this is a regular pattern expression" | sed -n '
> /regular.*expression/p'
this is a regular pattern expression
$
```

Using this pattern, you can easily search for multiple words that may appear anywhere in a line of text in the data stream.

The asterisk can also be applied to a character class. This allows you to specify a group or range of characters that can appear more than once in the text:

```
$ echo "bt" | sed -n '/b[ae]*t/p'
bt
$ echo "bat" | sed -n '/b[ae]*t/p'
bat
$ echo "bet" | sed -n '/b[ae]*t/p'
bet
$ echo "btt" | sed -n '/b[ae]*t/p'
btt
$
$ echo "baat" | sed -n '/b[ae]*t/p'
baat
$ echo "baaeeet" | sed -n '/b[ae]*t/p'
baaeeet
$ echo "baeeaeeat" | sed -n '/b[ae]*t/p'
baeeaeeat
$ echo "baakeeet" | sed -n '/b[ae]*t/p'
$
```

As long as the *a* and *e* characters appear in any combination between the *b* and *t* characters (including not appearing at all), the pattern matches. If any other character outside of the defined character class appears, the pattern match fails.

Extended Regular Expressions

The POSIX ERE patterns include a few additional symbols that are used by some Linux applications and utilities. The gawk program recognizes the ERE patterns, but the sed editor doesn't.

> **CAUTION**
>
> Remember that the regular expression engines in the `sed` editor and the `gawk` program are different. The `gawk` program can use most of the extended regular expression pattern symbols, and it can provide some additional filtering capabilities that the `sed` editor doesn't have. However, because of this, it is often slower in processing data streams.

This section describes the more commonly found ERE pattern symbols that you can use in your `gawk` program scripts.

The question mark

The question mark is similar to the asterisk, but with a slight twist. The question mark indicates that the preceding character can appear zero or one time, but that's all. It doesn't match repeating occurrences of the character:

```
$ echo "bt" | gawk '/be?t/{print $0}'
bt
$ echo "bet" | gawk '/be?t/{print $0}'
bet
$ echo "beet" | gawk '/be?t/{print $0}'
$
$ echo "beeet" | gawk '/be?t/{print $0}'
$
```

If the *e* character doesn't appear in the text, or as long as it appears only once in the text, the pattern matches.

As with the asterisk, you can use the question mark symbol along with a character class:

```
$ echo "bt" | gawk '/b[ae]?t/{print $0}'
bt
$ echo "bat" | gawk '/b[ae]?t/{print $0}'
bat
$ echo "bot" | gawk '/b[ae]?t/{print $0}'
$
$ echo "bet" | gawk '/b[ae]?t/{print $0}'
bet
$ echo "baet" | gawk '/b[ae]?t/{print $0}'
$
$ echo "beat" | gawk '/b[ae]?t/{print $0}'
$
$ echo "beet" | gawk '/b[ae]?t/{print $0}'
$
```

If zero or one character from the character class appears, the pattern match passes. However, if both characters appear, or if one of the characters appears twice, the pattern match fails.

The plus sign

The plus sign is another pattern symbol that's similar to the asterisk, but with a different twist than the question mark. The plus sign indicates that the preceding character can appear one or more times, but must be present at least once. The pattern doesn't match if the character is not present:

```
$ echo "beeet" | gawk '/be+t/{print $0}'
beeet
$ echo "beet" | gawk '/be+t/{print $0}'
beet
$ echo "bet" | gawk '/be+t/{print $0}'
bet
$ echo "bt" | gawk '/be+t/{print $0}'
$
```

If the *e* character is not present, the pattern match fails. The plus sign also works with character classes, the same way as the asterisk and question mark do:

```
$ echo "bt" | gawk '/b[ae]+t/{print $0}'
$
$ echo "bat" | gawk '/b[ae]+t/{print $0}'
bat
$ echo "bet" | gawk '/b[ae]+t/{print $0}'
bet
$ echo "beat" | gawk '/b[ae]+t/{print $0}'
beat
$ echo "beet" | gawk '/b[ae]+t/{print $0}'
beet
$ echo "beeat" | gawk '/b[ae]+t/{print $0}'
beeat
$
```

This time if either character defined in the character class appears, the text matches the specified pattern.

Using braces

Curly braces are available in ERE to allow you to specify a limit on a repeatable regular expression. This is often referred to as an *interval*. You can express the interval in two formats:

- m: The regular expression appears exactly *m* times.
- m, n: The regular expression appears at least *m* times, but no more than *n* times.

This feature allows you to fine-tune exactly how many times you allow a character (or character class) to appear in a pattern.

Here's an example of using a simple interval of one value:

```
$ echo "bt" | gawk --re-interval '/be{1}t/{print $0}'
$
$ echo "bet" | gawk --re-interval '/be{1}t/{print $0}'
bet
$ echo "beet" | gawk --re-interval '/be{1}t/{print $0}'
$
```

By specifying an interval of one, you restrict the number of times the character can be present for the string to match the pattern. If the character appears more times, the pattern match fails.

Often, specifying the lower and upper limit comes in handy:

```
$ echo "bt" | gawk --re-interval '/be{1,2}t/{print $0}'
$
$ echo "bet" | gawk --re-interval '/be{1,2}t/{print $0}'
bet
$ echo "beet" | gawk --re-interval '/be{1,2}t/{print $0}'
beet
$ echo "beeet" | gawk --re-interval '/be{1,2}t/{print $0}'
$
```

In this example, the *e* character can appear once or twice for the pattern match to pass; otherwise, the pattern match fails.

The interval pattern match also applies to character classes:

```
$ echo "bt" | gawk --re-interval '/b[ae]{1,2}t/{print $0}'
$
$ echo "bat" | gawk --re-interval '/b[ae]{1,2}t/{print $0}'
bat
$ echo "bet" | gawk --re-interval '/b[ae]{1,2}t/{print $0}'
bet
$ echo "beat" | gawk --re-interval '/b[ae]{1,2}t/{print $0}'
beat
$ echo "beet" | gawk --re-interval '/b[ae]{1,2}t/{print $0}'
beet
$ echo "beeat" | gawk --re-interval '/b[ae]{1,2}t/{print $0}'
$
$ echo "baeet" | gawk --re-interval '/b[ae]{1,2}t/{print $0}'
$
```

```
$ echo "baeaet" | gawk --re-interval '/b[ae]{1,2}t/{print $0}'
$
```

This regular expression pattern matches if there are exactly one or two instances of the letter *a* or *e* in the text pattern, but it fails if there are any more in any combination.

The pipe symbol

The pipe symbol allows to you to specify two or more patterns that the regular expression engine uses in a logical OR formula when examining the data stream. If any of the patterns match the data stream text, the text passes. If none of the patterns match, the data stream text fails.

Here's the format for using the pipe symbol:

```
expr1|expr2|...
```

Here's an example of this:

```
$ echo "The cat is asleep" | gawk '/cat|dog/{print $0}'
The cat is asleep
$ echo "The dog is asleep" | gawk '/cat|dog/{print $0}'
The dog is asleep
$ echo "The sheep is asleep" | gawk '/cat|dog/{print $0}'
$
```

This example looks for the regular expression cat or dog in the data stream. You can't place any spaces within the regular expressions and the pipe symbol, or they're added to the regular expression pattern.

The regular expressions on either side of the pipe symbol can use any regular expression pattern, including character classes, to define the text:

```
$ echo "He has a hat." | gawk '/[ch]at|dog/{print $0}'
He has a hat.
$
```

This example would match cat, hat, or dog in the data stream text.

Grouping expressions

Regular expression patterns can also be grouped by using parentheses. When you group a regular expression pattern, the group is treated like a standard character. You can apply a special character to the group just as you would to a regular character. For example:

```
$ echo "Sat" | gawk '/Sat(urday)?/{print $0}'
Sat
$ echo "Saturday" | gawk '/Sat(urday)?/{print $0}'
Saturday
$
```

20

The grouping of the "urday" ending along with the question mark allows the pattern to match either the full day name Saturday or the abbreviated name Sat.

It's common to use grouping along with the pipe symbol to create groups of possible pattern matches:

```
$ echo "cat" | gawk '/(c|b)a(b|t)/{print $0}'
cat
$ echo "cab" | gawk '/(c|b)a(b|t)/{print $0}'
cab
$ echo "bat" | gawk '/(c|b)a(b|t)/{print $0}'
bat
$ echo "bab" | gawk '/(c|b)a(b|t)/{print $0}'
bab
$ echo "tab" | gawk '/(c|b)a(b|t)/{print $0}'
$
$ echo "tac" | gawk '/(c|b)a(b|t)/{print $0}'
$
```

The pattern (c|b)a(b|t) matches any combination of the letters in the first group along with any combination of the letters in the second group.

Regular Expressions in Action

Now that you've seen the rules and a few simple demonstrations of using regular expression patterns, it's time to put that knowledge into action. The following sections demonstrate some common regular expression examples within shell scripts.

Counting directory files

To start things out, let's look at a shell script that counts the executable files that are present in the directories defined in your PATH environment variable. To do that, you need to parse out the PATH variable into separate directory names. Chapter 6 showed you how to display the PATH environment variable:

```
$ echo $PATH
/usr/local/sbin:/usr/local/bin:/usr/sbin:/usr/bin:/sbin:/bin:/usr/games:/usr/
local/games
$
```

Your PATH environment variable will differ, depending on where the applications are located on your Linux system. The key is to recognize that each directory in the PATH is separated by a colon. To get a listing of directories that you can use in a script, you must replace each colon with a space. You now recognize that the sed editor can do just that using a simple regular expression:

```
$ echo $PATH | sed 's/:/ /g'
/usr/local/sbin /usr/local/bin /usr/sbin /usr/bin /sbin /bin
/usr/games /usr/local/games
$
```

After you have the directories separated out, you can use them in a standard for statement (see Chapter 13) to iterate through each directory:

```
mypath=$(echo $PATH | sed 's/:/ /g')
for directory in $mypath
do
...
done
```

After you have each directory, you can use the ls command to list each file in each directory, and use another for statement to iterate through each file, incrementing a counter
for each file.

The final version of the script looks like this:

```
$ cat countfiles
#!/bin/bash
# count number of files in your PATH
mypath=$(echo $PATH | sed 's/:/ /g')
count=0
for directory in $mypath
do
    check=$(ls $directory)
    for item in $check
    do
        count=$[ $count + 1 ]
    done
    echo "$directory - $count"
    count=0
done
$ ./countfiles /usr/local/sbin - 0
/usr/local/bin - 2
/usr/sbin - 213
/usr/bin - 1427
/sbin - 186
/bin - 152
/usr/games - 5
/usr/local/games - 0
$
```

Now we're starting to see some of the power behind regular expressions!

20

Validating a phone number

The previous example showed how to incorporate the simple regular expression along with sed to replace characters in a data stream to process data. Often, regular expressions are used to validate data to ensure that data is in the correct format for a script.

A common data validation application checks phone numbers. Often, data entry forms request phone numbers, and often customers fail to enter a properly formatted phone number. People in the United States use several common ways to display a phone number:

```
(123)456-7890
(123) 456-7890
123-456-7890
123.456.7890
```

This leaves four possibilities for how customers can enter their phone number in a form. The regular expression must be robust enough to handle any of these situations.

When building a regular expression, it's best to start on the left side and build your pattern to match the possible characters you'll run into. In this example, there may or may not be a left parenthesis in the phone number. This can be matched by using the pattern:

```
^\(?
```

The caret is used to indicate the beginning of the data. Because the left parenthesis is a special character, you must escape it to use it as a normal character. The question mark indicates that the left parenthesis may or may not appear in the data to match.

Next is the three-digit area code. In the United States, area codes start with the number 2 (no area codes start with the digits 0 or 1), and can go to 9. To match the area code, you'd use the following pattern:

```
[2-9][0-9]{2}
```

This requires that the first character be a digit between 2 and 9, followed by any two digits. After the area code, the ending right parenthesis may or may not appear:

```
\)?
```

After the area code, there can be a space, no space, a dash, or a dot. You can group those using a character group along with the pipe symbol:

```
(| |-|\.)
```

The very first pipe symbol appears immediately after the left parenthesis to match the no space condition. You must use the escape character for the dot; otherwise, it is interpreted to match any character.

Next is the three-digit phone exchange number. Nothing special is required here:

```
[0-9]{3}
```

After the phone exchange number, you must match a space, a dash, or a dot (this time you don't have to worry about matching no space because there must be at least a space between the phone exchange number and the rest of the number):

```
( |-|\.)
```

Then to finish things off, you must match the four-digit local phone extension at the end of the string:

```
[0-9]{4}$
```

Putting the entire pattern together results in this:

```
^\(?[2-9][0-9]{2}\)?( |-|\.)[0-9]{3}( |-|\.)[0-9]{4}$
```

You can use this regular expression pattern in the gawk program to filter out bad phone numbers. Now you just need to create a simple script using the regular expression in a gawk program and filter your phone list through the script. Remember that when you use regular expression intervals in the gawk program, you must use the --re-interval command line option, or you won't get the correct results.

Here's the script:

```
$ cat isphone
#!/bin/bash
# script to filter out bad phone numbers
gawk --re-interval '/^\(?[2-9][0-9]{2}\)?( |-|\¬
[0-9]{3}( |-|\.)[0-9]{4}/{print $0}'
$
```

Although you can't tell from this listing, the gawk command is on a single line in the shell script. You can then redirect phone numbers to the script for processing:

```
$ echo "317-555-1234" | ./isphone
317-555-1234
$ echo "000-555-1234" | ./isphone
$ echo "312 555-1234" | ./isphone
312 555-1234
$
```

Or you can redirect an entire file of phone numbers to filter out the invalid ones:

```
$ cat phonelist
000-000-0000
123-456-7890
```

```
212-555-1234
(317)555-1234
(202) 555-9876
33523
1234567890
234.123.4567
$ cat phonelist | ./isphone
212-555-1234
(317)555-1234
(202) 555-9876
234.123.4567
$
```

Only the valid phone numbers that match the regular expression pattern appear.

Parsing an e-mail address

These days, e-mail has become a crucial form of communication. Trying to validate e-mail addresses has become quite a challenge for script builders because of the myriad ways to create an e-mail address. This is the basic form of an e-mail address:

username@hostname

The *username* value can use any alphanumeric character, along with several special characters:

- Dot
- Dash
- Plus sign
- Underscore

These characters can appear in any combination in a valid e-mail userid. The *hostname* portion of the e-mail address consists of one or more domain names and a server name. The server and domain names must also follow strict naming rules, allowing only alphanumeric characters, along with the special characters:

- Dot
- Underscore

The server and domain names are each separated by a dot, with the server name specified first, any subdomain names specified next, and finally, the top-level domain name without a trailing dot.

At one time, the top-level domains were fairly limited, and regular expression pattern builders attempted to add them all in patterns for validation. Unfortunately, as the Internet grew, so did the possible top-level domains. This technique is no longer a viable solution.

Let's start building the regular expression pattern from the left side. We know that there can be multiple valid characters in the username. This should be fairly easy:

```
^([a-zA-Z0-9_\-\.\+]+)@
```

This grouping specifies the allowable characters in the username and the plus sign to indicate that at least one character must be present. The next character obviously is the @ symbol — no surprises there.

The hostname pattern uses the same technique to match the server name and the subdomain names:

```
([a-zA-Z0-9_\-\.]+)
```

This pattern matches the text:

```
server
server.subdomain
server.subdomain.subdomain
```

There are special rules for the top-level domain. Top-level domains are only alphabetic characters, and they must be no fewer than two characters (used in country codes) and no more than five characters in length. The following is the regular expression pattern for the top-level domain:

```
\.([a-zA-Z]{2,5})$
```

Putting the entire pattern together results in the following:

```
^([a-zA-Z0-9_\-\.\+]+)@([a-zA-Z0-9_\-\.]+)\.([a-zA-Z]{2,5})$
```

This pattern filters out poorly formatted e-mail addresses from a data list. Now you can create your script to implement the regular expression:

```
$ echo "rich@here.now" | ./isemail
rich@here.now
$ echo "rich@here.now." | ./isemail
$
$ echo "rich@here.n" | ./isemail
$
$ echo "rich@here-now" | ./isemail
$
$ echo "rich.blum@here.now" | ./isemail
rich.blum@here.now
$ echo "rich_blum@here.now" | ./isemail
rich_blum@here.now
$ echo "rich/blum@here.now" | ./isemail
$
```

```
$ echo "rich#blum@here.now" | ./isemail
$
$ echo "rich*blum@here.now" | ./isemail
$
```

Summary

If you manipulate data files in shell scripts, you need to become familiar with regular expressions. Regular expressions are implemented in Linux utilities, programming languages, and applications using regular expression engines. A host of different regular expression engines is available in the Linux world. The two most popular are the POSIX Basic Regular Expression (BRE) engine and the POSIX Extended Regular Expression (ERE) engine. The sed editor conforms mainly to the BRE engine, while the gawk program utilizes most features found in the ERE engine.

A regular expression defines a pattern template that's used to filter text in a data stream. The pattern consists of a combination of standard text characters and special characters. The special characters are used by the regular expression engine to match a series of one or more characters, similarly to how wildcard characters work in other applications.

By combining characters and special characters, you can define a pattern to match almost any type of data. You can then use the sed editor or gawk program to filter specific data from a larger data stream, or for validating data received from data entry applications.

The next chapter digs deeper into using the sed editor to perform advanced text manipulation. Lots of advanced features are available in the sed editor that make it useful for handling large data streams and filtering out just what you need.

Advanced sed

C hapter 19 showed you how to use the basics of the sed editor to manipulate text in data streams. The basic sed editor commands are capable of handling most of your everyday text-editing requirements. This chapter looks at the more advanced features that the sed editor has to offer. These are features that you might not use as often. But when you need them, it's nice to know that they're available and how to use them.

Looking at Multiline Commands

When using the basic sed editor commands, you may have noticed a limitation. All the sed editor commands perform functions on a single line of data. As the sed editor reads a data stream, it divides the data into lines based on the presence of newline characters. The sed editor handles each data line one at a time, processing the defined script commands on the data line, and then moving on to the next line and repeating the processing.

Sometimes, you need to perform actions on data that spans more than one line. This is especially true if you're trying to find or replace a phrase.

For example, if you're looking for the phrase Linux System Administrators Group in your data, it's quite possible that the phrase's words can be split onto two lines. If you processed the text using a normal sed editor command, it would be impossible to detect the split phrase.

Fortunately, the designers behind the sed editor thought of that situation and devised a solution. The sed editor includes three special commands that you can use to process multiline text:

- N adds the next line in the data stream to create a multiline group for processing.
- D deletes a single line in a multiline group.
- P prints a single line in a multiline group.

The following sections examine these multiline commands more closely and demonstrate how you can use them in your scripts.

Navigating the next command

Before you can examine the multiline next command, you first need to look at how the single-line version of the next command works. After you know what that command does, it's much easier to understand how the multiline version of the next command operates.

Using the single-line next command

The lowercase n command tells the sed editor to move to the next line of text in the data stream, without going back to the beginning of the commands. Remember that normally the sed editor processes all the defined commands on a line before moving to the next line of text in the data stream. The single-line next command alters this flow.

This may sound somewhat complicated, and sometimes it is. In this example, you have a data file that contains five lines, two of which are empty. The goal is to remove the blank line after the header line but leave the blank line before the last line intact. If you write a sed script to just remove blank lines, you remove both blank lines:

```
$ cat data1.txt
This is the header line.

This is a data line.

This is the last line.
$
$ sed '/^$/d' data1.txt
This is the header line.
This is a data line.
This is the last line.
$
```

Because the line you want to remove is blank, you don't have any text you can search for to uniquely identify the line. The solution is to use the n command. In this next example, the script looks for a unique line that contains the word header. After the script identifies that line, the n command moves the sed editor to the next line of text, which is the empty line.

```
$ sed '/header/{n ; d}' data1.txt
This is the header line.
This is a data line.

This is the last line.
$
```

At that point, the sed editor continues processing the command list, which uses the d command to delete the empty line. When the sed editor reaches the end of the command script, it reads the next line of text from the data stream and starts processing commands from the top of the command script. The sed editor does not find another line with the word header; thus, no further lines are deleted.

Combining lines of text

Now that you've seen the single-line next command, you can look at the multiline version. The single-line next command moves the next line of text from the data stream into the processing space (called the *pattern space*) of the sed editor. The multiline version of the next command (which uses a capital N) adds the next line of text to the text already in the pattern space.

This has the effect of combining two lines of text from the data stream into the same pattern space. The lines of text are still separated by a newline character, but the sed editor can now treat both lines of text as one line.

Here's a demonstration of how the N command operates:

```
$ cat data2.txt
This is the header line.
This is the first data line.
This is the second data line.
This is the last line.
$
$ sed '/first/{ N ; s/\n/ / }' data2.txt
This is the header line.
This is the first data line. This is the second data line.
This is the last line.
$
```

The sed editor script searches for the line of text that contains the word "first" in it. When it finds the line, it uses the N command to combine the next line with that line. It then uses the substitution command (s) to replace the newline character with a space. The result is that the two lines in the text file appear as one line in the sed editor output.

This has a practical application if you're searching for a text phrase that may be split between two lines in the data file. Here's an example:

```
$ cat data3.txt
On Tuesday, the Linux System
Administrator's group meeting will be held.
All System Administrators should attend.
Thank you for your attendance.
$
$ sed 'N ; s/System Administrator/Desktop User/' data3.txt
On Tuesday, the Linux System
Administrator's group meeting will be held.
All Desktop Users should attend.
Thank you for your attendance.
$
```

The substitution command is looking for the specific two-word phrase System Administrator in the text file. In the single line where the phrase appears, everything is fine; the substitution command can replace the text. But in the situation where the phrase is split between two lines, the substitution command doesn't recognize the matching pattern.

The N command helps solve this problem:

```
$ sed 'N ; s/System.Administrator/Desktop User/' data3.txt
On Tuesday, the Linux Desktop User's group meeting will be held.
All Desktop Users should attend.
Thank you for your attendance.
$
```

By using the N command to combine the next line with the line where the first word is found, you can detect when a line split occurs in the phrase.

Notice that the substitution command uses a wildcard pattern (.) between the word System and the word Administrator to match both the space and the newline situation. However, when it matched the newline character, it removed it from the string, causing the two lines to merge into one line. This may not be exactly what you want.

To solve this problem, you can use two substitution commands in the sed editor script, one to match the multiline occurrence and one to match the single-line occurrence:

```
$ sed 'N
> s/System\nAdministrator/Desktop\nUser/
> s/System Administrator/Desktop User/
> ' data3.txt
On Tuesday, the Linux Desktop
```

```
User's group meeting will be held.
All Desktop Users should attend.
Thank you for your attendance.
$
```

The first substitution command specifically looks for the newline character between the two search words and includes it in the replacement string. This allows you to add the newline character in the same place in the new text.

There's still one subtle problem with this script, however. The script always reads the next line of text into the pattern space before executing the sed editor commands. When it reaches the last line of text, there isn't a next line of text to read, so the N command causes the sed editor to stop. If the matching text is on the last line in the data stream, the commands don't catch the matching data:

```
$ cat data4.txt
On Tuesday, the Linux System
Administrator's group meeting will be held.
All System Administrators should attend.
$
$ sed 'N
> s/System\nAdministrator/Desktop\nUser/
> s/System Administrator/Desktop User/
> ' data4.txt
On Tuesday, the Linux Desktop
User's group meeting will be held.
All System Administrators should attend.
$
```

Because the System Administrator text appears in the last line in the data stream, the N command misses it, as there isn't another line to read into the pattern space to combine. You can easily resolve this problem by moving your single-line commands before the N command and having only the multiline commands appear after the N command, like this:

```
$ sed '
> s/System Administrator/Desktop User/
> N
> s/System\nAdministrator/Desktop\nUser/
> ' data4.txt
On Tuesday, the Linux Desktop
User's group meeting will be held.
All Desktop Users should attend.
$
```

Now, the substitution command that looks for the phrase in a single line works just fine on the last line in the data stream, and the multiline substitution command covers the occurrence in the middle of the data stream.

Navigating the multiline delete command

Chapter 19 introduced the single-line delete command (d). The sed editor uses it to delete the current line in the pattern space. If you're working with the N command, however, you must be careful when using the single-line delete command:

```
$ sed 'N ; /System\nAdministrator/d' data4.txt
All System Administrators should attend.
$
```

The delete command looked for the words System and Administrator in separate lines and deleted both of the lines in the pattern space. This may or may not have been what you intended.

The sed editor provides the multiline delete command (D), which deletes only the first line in the pattern space. It removes all characters up to and including the newline character:

```
$ sed 'N ; /System\nAdministrator/D' data4.txt
Administrator's group meeting will be held.
All System Administrators should attend.
$
```

The second line of text, added to the pattern space by the N command, remains intact. This comes in handy if you need to remove a line of text that appears before a line that you find a data string in.

Here's an example of removing a blank line that appears before the first line in a data stream:

```
$ cat data5.txt

This is the header line.
This is a data line.

This is the last line.
$
$ sed '/^$/{N ; /header/D}' data5.txt
This is the header line.
This is a data line.

This is the last line.
$
```

This sed editor script looks for blank lines and then uses the N command to add the next line of text into the pattern space. If the new pattern space contents contain the word header, the D command removes the first line in the pattern space. Without the combination of the N and D commands, it would be impossible to remove the first blank line without removing all other blank lines.

Navigating the multiline print command

By now, you're probably catching on to the difference between the single-line and multiline versions of the commands. The multiline print command (P) follows along using the same technique. It prints only the first line in a multiline pattern space. This includes all characters up to the newline character in the pattern space. It is used in much the same way as the single-line p command to display text when you use the -n option to suppress output from the script.

```
$ sed -n 'N ; /System\nAdministrator/P' data3.txt
On Tuesday, the Linux System
$
```

When the multiline match occurs, the P command prints only the first line in the pattern space. The power of the multiline P command comes into play when you combine it with the N and D multiline commands.

The D command has a unique feature in that it forces the sed editor to return to the beginning of the script and repeat the commands on the same pattern space (it doesn't read a new line of text from the data stream). By including the N command in the command script, you can effectively single-step through the pattern space, matching multiple lines together.

Next, by using the P command, you can print the first line, and then using the D command, you can delete the first line and loop back to the beginning of the script. When you are back at the script's beginning, the N command reads in the next line of text and starts the process all over again. This loop continues until you reach the end of the data stream.

Holding Space

The *pattern space* is an active buffer area that holds the text examined by the sed editor while it processes commands. However, it isn't the only space available in the sed editor for storing text.

The sed editor utilizes another buffer area called the *hold space*. You can use the hold space to temporarily hold lines of text while working on other lines in the pattern space. The five commands associated with operating with the hold space are shown in Table 21-1.

TABLE 21-1 **The sed Editor Hold Space Commands**

Command	Description
h	Copies pattern space to hold space
H	Appends pattern space to hold space
g	Copies hold space to pattern space
G	Appends hold space to pattern space
x	Exchanges contents of pattern and hold spaces

These commands let you copy text from the pattern space to the hold space. This frees up the pattern space to load another string for processing.

Usually, after using the h or H commands to move a string to the hold space, eventually you want to use the g, G, or x commands to move the stored string back into the pattern space (otherwise, you wouldn't have cared about saving them in the first place).

With two buffer areas, trying to determine what line of text is in which buffer area can sometimes get confusing. Here's a short example that demonstrates how to use the h and g commands to move data back and forth between the sed editor buffer spaces:

```
$ cat data2.txt
This is the header line.
This is the first data line.
This is the second data line.
This is the last line.
$
$ sed -n '/first/ {h ; p ; n ; p ; g ; p }' data2.txt
This is the first data line.
This is the second data line.
This is the first data line.
$
```

Look at the preceding code example step by step:

1. The sed script uses a regular expression in the address to filter the line containing the word first.

2. When the line containing the word first appears, the initial command in { }, the h command, places the line in the hold space.

3. The next command, the p command, prints the contents of the pattern space, which is still the first data line.

4. The n command retrieves the next line in the data stream (This is the second data line) and places it in the pattern space.

5. The p command prints the contents of the pattern space, which is now the second data line.

6. The g command places the contents of the hold space
(This is the first data line) back into the pattern space, replacing the current text.

7. The p command prints the current contents of the pattern space, which is now back to the first data line.

By shuffling the text lines around using the hold space, you can force the first data line to appear after the second data line in the output. If you just drop the first p command, you can output the two lines in reverse order:

```
$ sed -n '/first/ {h ; n ; p ; g ; p }' data2.txt
This is the second data line.
This is the first data line.
$
```

This is the start of something useful. You can use this technique to create a sed script that reverses an entire file of text lines! To do that, however, you need to see the negating feature of the sed editor, which is what the next section is all about.

Negating a Command

Chapter 19 showed that the sed editor applies commands either to every text line in the data stream or to lines specifically indicated by either a single address or an address range. You can also configure a command to not apply to a specific address or address range in the data stream.

The exclamation mark command (!) is used to negate a command. This means in situations where the command would normally have been activated, it isn't. Here's an example demonstrating this feature:

```
$ sed -n '/header/!p' data2.txt
This is the first data line.
This is the second data line.
This is the last line.
$
```

The normal p command would have printed only the line in the data2 file that contained the word header. By adding the exclamation mark, the opposite happens — all lines in the file are printed except the one that contained the word header.

Using the exclamation mark comes in handy in several applications. Recall that earlier in the chapter, the "Navigating the next command" section showed a situation where a sed editor command wouldn't operate on the last line of text in the data stream because there wasn't a line after it. You can use the exclamation point to fix that problem:

```
$ sed 'N;
> s/System\nAdministrator/Desktop\nUser/
> s/System Administrator/Desktop User/
```

```
> ' data4.txt
On Tuesday, the Linux Desktop
User's group meeting will be held.
All System Administrators should attend.
$
$ sed '$!N;
> s/System\nAdministrator/Desktop\nUser/
> s/System Administrator/Desktop User/
> ' data4.txt
On Tuesday, the Linux Desktop
User's group meeting will be held.
All Desktop Users should attend.
$
```

This example shows the exclamation mark used with the N command, along with the dollar sign ($) special address. The dollar sign represents the last line of text in the data stream, so when the sed editor reaches the last line, it doesn't execute the N command. However, for all other lines, it does execute the command.

Using this technique, you can reverse the order of text lines in a data stream. To reverse the order of the lines as they appear in the text stream (display the last line first and the first line last), you need to do some fancy footwork using the hold space.

The pattern you need to work with goes like this:

1. Place a line in the pattern space.
2. Place the line from the pattern space to the hold space.
3. Put the next line of text in the pattern space.
4. Append the hold space to the pattern space.
5. Place everything in the pattern space into the hold space.
6. Repeat Steps 3 through 5 until you've put all the lines in reverse order in the hold space.
7. Retrieve the lines, and print them.

Figure 21-1 diagrams what this looks like in more detail.

When using this technique, you do not want to print lines as they are processed. This means using the -n command line option for sed. The next thing to determine is how to append the hold space text to the pattern space text. This is done by using the G command. The only problem is that you don't want to append the hold space to the first line of text processed. This is easily solved by using the exclamation mark command:

```
1!G
```

The next step is to place the new pattern space (the text line with the appended reverse lines) into the hold space. This is simple enough; just use the h command.

When you've got the entire data stream in the pattern space in reverse order, you just need to print the results. You know you have the entire data stream in the pattern space when you've reached the last line in the data stream. To print the results, just use the following command:

```
$p
```

FIGURE 21-1

Reversing the order of a text file using the hold space

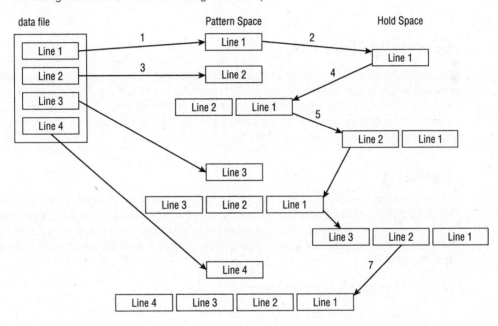

Those are the pieces you need to create your line-reversing sed editor script. Now try it out in a test run:

```
$ cat data2.txt
This is the header line.
This is the first data line.
This is the second data line.
This is the last line.
$
$ sed -n '{1!G ; h ; $p }' data2.txt
This is the last line.
This is the second data line.
This is the first data line.
This is the header line.
$
```

The sed editor script performed as expected. The output from the script reverses the original lines in the text file. This demonstrates the power of using the hold space in your sed scripts. It provides an easy way to manipulate the order of lines in the script output.

> **NOTE**
>
> In case you're wondering, a bash shell command can perform the function of reversing a text file. The tac command displays a text file in reverse order. You probably noticed the clever name of the command because it performs the reverse function of the cat command.

Changing the Flow

Normally, the sed editor processes commands starting at the top and proceeding toward the end of the script (the exception is the D command, which forces the sed editor to return to the top of the script without reading a new line of text). The sed editor provides a method for altering the flow of the command script, producing a result similar to that of a structured programming environment.

Branching

In the previous section, you saw how the exclamation mark command is used to negate the effect of a command on a line of text. The sed editor provides a way to negate an entire section of commands, based on an address, an address pattern, or an address range. This allows you to perform a group of commands only on a specific subset within the data stream.

Here's the format of the branch command:

```
[address]b [label]
```

The address parameter determines which line or lines of data trigger the branch command. The label parameter defines the location to branch to. If the label parameter is not present, the branch command proceeds to the end of the script.

```
$ cat data2.txt
This is the header line.
This is the first data line.
This is the second data line.
This is the last line.
$
$ sed '{2,3b ; s/This is/Is this/ ; s/line./test?/}' data2.txt
Is this the header test?
This is the first data line.
This is the second data line.
Is this the last test?
$
```

The branch command skips the two substitution commands for the second and third lines in the data stream.

Instead of going to the end of the script, you can define a label for the branch command to jump to. Labels start with a colon and can be up to seven characters in length:

```
:label2
```

To specify the label, just add it after the b command. Using labels allows you to skip commands that match the branch address but still process other commands in the script:

```
$ sed '{/first/b jump1 ; s/This is the/No jump on/
> :jump1
> s/This is the/Jump here on/}' data2.txt
No jump on header line
Jump here on first data line
No jump on second data line
No jump on last line
$
```

The branch command specifies that the program should jump to the script line labeled jump1 if the matching text "first" appears in the line. If the branch command pattern doesn't match, the sed editor continues processing commands in the script, including the command after the branch label. (Thus, all three substitution commands are processed on lines that don't match the branch pattern.)

If a line matches the branch pattern, the sed editor branches to the branch label line. Thus, only the last substitution command is executed.

The example shows branching to a label further down in the sed script. You can also branch to a label that appears earlier in the script, thus creating a looping effect:

```
$ echo "This, is, a, test, to, remove, commas." | sed -n '{
> :start
> s/,//1p
> b start
> }'
This is, a, test, to, remove, commas.
This is a, test, to, remove, commas.
This is a test, to, remove, commas.
This is a test to, remove, commas.
This is a test to remove, commas.
This is a test to remove commas.
^C
$
```

Each script iteration removes the first occurrence of a comma from the text string and prints the string. There's one catch to this script: It never ends. This situation creates an endless loop, searching for commas until you manually stop it by sending a signal with the Ctrl+C key combination.

To prevent this problem, you should specify an address pattern for the branch command to look for. If the pattern isn't present, the branching should stop:

```
$ echo "This, is, a, test, to, remove, commas." | sed -n '{
> :start
> s/,//1p
> /,/b start
> }'
This is, a, test, to, remove, commas.
This is a, test, to, remove, commas.
This is a test, to, remove, commas.
This is a test to, remove, commas.
This is a test to remove, commas.
This is a test to remove commas.
$
```

Now the branch command branches only if there's a comma in the line. After the last comma has been removed, the branch command doesn't execute, allowing the script to properly finish.

Testing

Similar to the branch command, the test command (t) is also used to modify the flow of the sed editor script. Instead of jumping to a label based on an address, the test command jumps to a label based on the outcome of a substitution command.

If the substitution command successfully matches and substitutes a pattern, the test command branches to the specified label. If the substitution command doesn't match the specified pattern, the test command doesn't branch.

The test command uses the same format as the branch command:

    [address]t [label]

Like the branch command, if you don't specify a label, sed branches to the end of the script if the test succeeds.

The test command provides a cheap way to perform a basic if-then statement on the text in the data stream. For example, if you don't need to make a substitution if another substitution was made, the test command can help:

```
$ sed '{
> s/first/matched/
> t
> s/This is the/No match on/
> }' data2.txt
No match on header line
```

```
This is the matched data line
No match on second data line
No match on last line
$
```

The first substitution command looks for the pattern text `first`. If it matches the pattern in the line, it replaces the text, and the `test` command jumps over the second substitution command. If the first substitution command doesn't match the pattern, the second substitution command is processed.

Using the `test` command, you can clean up the loop you tried using the `branch` command:

```
$ echo "This, is, a, test, to, remove, commas. " | sed -n '{
> :start
> s/,//1p
> t start
> }'
This is, a, test, to, remove, commas.
This is a, test, to, remove, commas.
This is a test, to, remove, commas.
This is a test to, remove, commas.
This is a test to remove, commas.
This is a test to remove commas.
$
```

When there are no more substitutions to make, the `test` command doesn't branch and continues with the rest of the script.

Replacing via a Pattern

You've seen how to use patterns in the sed commands to replace text in the data stream. However, when using wildcard characters it's not easy to know exactly what text will match the pattern.

For example, say that you want to place double quotation marks around a word you match in a line. That's simple enough if you're just looking for one word in the pattern to match:

```
$ echo "The cat sleeps in his hat." | sed 's/cat/"cat"/'
The "cat" sleeps in his hat.
$
```

But what if you use a wildcard character (.) in the pattern to match more than one word?

```
$ echo "The cat sleeps in his hat." | sed 's/.at/".at"/g'
The ".at" sleeps in his ".at".
$
```

The substitution string used the dot wildcard character to match any occurrence of a letter followed by "at". Unfortunately, the replacement string doesn't match the wildcard character value of the matching word.

Using the ampersand

The sed editor has a solution for you. The ampersand symbol (&) is used to represent the matching pattern in the substitution command. Whatever text matches the pattern defined, you can use the ampersand symbol to recall it in the replacement pattern. This lets you manipulate whatever word matches the pattern defined:

```
$ echo "The cat sleeps in his hat." | sed 's/.at/"&"/g'
The "cat" sleeps in his "hat".
$
```

When the pattern matches the word cat, "cat" appears in the substituted word. When it matches the word hat, "hat" appears in the substituted word.

Replacing individual words

The ampersand symbol retrieves the entire string that matches the pattern you specify in the substitution command. Sometimes, you'll only want to retrieve a subset of the string. You can do that, too, but it's a little tricky.

The sed editor uses parentheses to define a substring component within the substitution pattern. You can then reference each substring component using a special character in the replacement pattern. The replacement character consists of a backslash and a number. The number indicates the substring component's position. The sed editor assigns the first component the character \1, the second component the character \2, and so on.

> **CAUTION**
>
> When you use parentheses in the substitution command, you must use the escape character to identify them as grouping characters and not normal parentheses. This is the reverse of when you escape other special characters.

Look at an example of using this feature in a sed editor script:

```
$ echo "The System Administrator manual" | sed '
> s/\(System\) Administrator/\1 User/'
The System User manual
$
```

This substitution command uses one set of parentheses around the word System identifying it as a substring component. It then uses the \1 in the replacement pattern to recall the first identified component. This isn't too exciting, but it can really be useful when working with wildcard patterns.

If you need to replace a phrase with just a single word, that's a substring of the phrase, but that substring just happens to be using a wildcard character; using substring components is a lifesaver:

```
$ echo "That furry cat is pretty" | sed 's/furry \(.at\)/\1/'
That cat is pretty
$
$ echo "That furry hat is pretty" | sed 's/furry \(.at\)/\1/'
That hat is pretty
$
```

In this situation, you can't use the ampersand symbol, because it would replace the entire matching pattern. The substring component provides the answer, allowing you to select just which part of the pattern to use as the replacement pattern.

This feature can be especially helpful when you need to insert text between two or more substring components. Here's a script that uses substring components to insert a comma in long numbers:

```
$ echo "1234567" | sed '{
> :start
> s/\(.*[0-9]\)\([0-9]\{3\}\)/\1,\2/
> t start
> }'
1,234,567
$
```

The script divides the matching pattern into two components:

```
.*[0-9]
[0-9]{3}
```

This pattern looks for two substrings. The first substring is any number of characters, ending in a digit. The second substring is a series of three digits (see Chapter 20 for information about how to use braces in a regular expression). If this pattern is found in the text, the replacement text puts a comma between the two components, each identified by its component position. The script uses the test command to iterate through the number until all commas have been placed.

Placing sed Commands in Scripts

Now that you've seen the various parts of the sed editor, it's time to put them together and use them in your shell scripts. This section demonstrates some of the features that you should know about when using the sed editor in your bash shell scripts.

Using wrappers

You may have noticed that trying to implement a sed editor script can be cumbersome, especially if the script is long. Instead of having to retype the entire script each time you want to use it, you can place the sed editor command in a shell script *wrapper*. The wrapper acts as a go-between for the sed editor script and the command line.

Once inside the shell script, you can use normal shell variables and parameters with your sed editor scripts. Here's an example of using the command line parameter variable as the input to a sed script:

```
$ cat reverse.sh
#!/bin/bash
# Shell wrapper for sed editor script.
#                  to reverse text file lines.
#
sed -n '{ 1!G ; h ; $p }' $1
#
$
```

The shell script called reverse uses the sed editor script to reverse text lines in a data stream. It uses the $1 shell parameter to retrieve the first parameter from the command line, which should be the name of the file to reverse:

```
$ ./reverse.sh data2.txt
This is the last line.
This is the second data line.
This is the first data line.
This is the header line.
$
```

Now you can easily use the sed editor script on any file, without having to constantly retype the entire command line.

Redirecting sed output

By default, the sed editor outputs the results of the script to STDOUT. You can employ all the standard methods of redirecting the output of the sed editor in your shell scripts.

You can use dollar sign/parenthesis, $(), to redirect the output of your sed editor command to a variable for use later in the script. The following is an example of using the sed script to add commas to the result of a numeric computation:

```
$ cat fact.sh
#!/bin/bash
# Add commas to number in factorial answer
#
factorial=1
```

```
counter=1
number=$1
#
while [ $counter -le $number ]
do
    factorial=$[ $factorial * $counter ]
    counter=$[ $counter + 1 ]
done
#
result=$(echo $factorial | sed '{
:start
s/\(.*[0-9]\)\([0-9]\{3\}\)/\1,\2/
t start
}')
#
echo "The result is $result"
#
$
$ ./fact.sh 20
The result is 2,432,902,008,176,640,000
$
```

After you use the normal factorial calculation script, the result of that script is used as the input to the sed editor script, which adds commas. This value is then used in the echo statement to produce the result.

Creating sed Utilities

As you've seen in the short examples presented so far in this chapter, you can do lots of cool data-formatting things with the sed editor. This section shows a few handy well-known sed editor scripts for performing common data-handling functions.

Spacing with double lines

To start things off, look at a simple sed script to insert a blank line between lines in a text file:

```
$ sed 'G' data2.txt
This is the header line.

This is the first data line.

This is the second data line.

This is the last line.

$
```

That was pretty simple! The key to this trick is the default value of the hold space. Remember that the G command simply appends the contents of the hold space to the current pattern space contents. When you start the sed editor, the hold space contains an empty line. By appending that to an existing line, you create a blank line after the existing line.

You may have noticed that this script also adds a blank line to the last line in the data stream, producing a blank line at the end of the file. If you want to get rid of this, you can use the negate symbol and the last line symbol to ensure that the script doesn't add the blank line to the last line of the data stream:

```
$ sed '$!G' data2.txt
This is the header line.

This is the first data line.

This is the second data line.

This is the last line.
$
```

Now that looks a little better. As long as the line isn't the last line, the G command appends the contents of the hold space. When the sed editor gets to the last line, it skips the G command.

Spacing files that may have blanks

To take double spacing one step further, what if the text file already has a few blank lines, but you want to double space all the lines? If you use the previous script, you'll get some areas that have too many blank lines, because each existing blank line gets doubled:

```
$ cat data6.txt
This is line one.
This is line two.

This is line three.
This is line four.
$
$ sed '$!G' data6.txt
This is line one.

This is line two.


This is line three.

This is line four.
$
```

Now you have three blank lines where the original blank line was located. The solution to this problem is to first delete any blank lines from the data stream and then use the G command to insert new blank lines after all the lines. To delete existing blank lines, you just need to use the d command with a pattern that matches a blank line:

```
/^$/d
```

This pattern uses the start line tag (the caret) and the end line tag (the dollar sign). Adding this pattern to the script produces the desired results:

```
$ sed '/^$/d ; $!G' data6.txt
This is line one.

This is line two.

This is line three.

This is line four.
$
```

Perfect! It works just as expected.

Numbering lines in a file

Chapter 19 showed you how to use the equal sign to display the line numbers of lines in the data stream:

```
$ sed '=' data2.txt
1
This is the header line.
2
This is the first data line.
3
This is the second data line.
4
This is the last line.
$
```

This can be a little awkward to read, because the line number is on a line above the actual line in the data stream. A better solution is to place the line number on the same line as the text.

Now that you've seen how to combine lines using the N command, it shouldn't be too hard to utilize that information in the sed editor script. The trick to this utility, however, is that you can't combine the two commands in the same script.

After you have the output for the equal sign command, you can pipe the output to another sed editor script that uses the N command to combine the two lines. You also need to use the substitution command to replace the newline character with either a space or a tab character. Here's what the final solution looks like:

```
$ sed '=' data2.txt | sed 'N; s/\n/ /'
1 This is the header line.
2 This is the first data line.
3 This is the second data line.
4 This is the last line.
$
```

Now that looks much better. This is a great little utility to have around when working on programs where you need to see the line numbers used in error messages.

There are bash shell commands that can also add line numbers. However, they add some additional (and potentially unwanted spacing):

```
$ nl data2.txt
     1  This is the header line.
     2  This is the first data line.
     3  This is the second data line.
     4  This is the last line.
$
$ cat -n data2.txt
     1  This is the header line.
     2  This is the first data line.
     3  This is the second data line.
     4  This is the last line.
$
```

The sed editor script handles the output without any additional spacing.

Printing last lines

So far, you've seen how to use the p command to print all the lines in a data stream or just lines that match a specific pattern. What if you just need to work with the last few lines of a long listing, such as a log file?

The dollar sign represents the last line of a data stream, so it's easy to display just the last line:

```
$ sed -n '$p' data2.txt
This is the last line.
$
```

Now how can you use the dollar sign symbol to display a set number of lines at the end of the data stream? The answer is to create a *rolling window*.

A rolling window is a common way to examine blocks of text lines in the pattern space by combining them using the N command. The N command appends the next line of text to the text already in the pattern space. After you have a block of 10 text lines in the pattern space, you can check to see if you're at the end of the data stream using the dollar sign. If you're not at the end, continue adding more lines to the pattern space, while removing the original lines (remember the D command, which deletes the first line in the pattern space).

By looping through the N and D commands, you add new lines to the block of lines in the pattern space while removing old lines. The branch command is the perfect fit for the loop. To end the loop, just identify the last line and use the q command to quit.

Here's what the final sed editor script looks like:

```
$ cat data7.txt
This is line 1.
This is line 2.
This is line 3.
This is line 4.
This is line 5.
This is line 6.
This is line 7.
This is line 8.
This is line 9.
This is line 10.
This is line 11.
This is line 12.
This is line 13.
This is line 14.
This is line 15.
$
$ sed '{
> :start
> $q ; N ; 11,$D
> b start
> }' data7.txt
This is line 6.
This is line 7.
This is line 8.
This is line 9.
This is line 10.
This is line 11.
This is line 12.
This is line 13.
This is line 14.
This is line 15.
$
```

The script first checks whether the line is the last line in the data stream. If it is, the quit command stops the loop. The N command appends the next line to the current line in the pattern space. The 11,$D command deletes the first line in the pattern space if the current line is after line 10. This creates the sliding window effect in the pattern space. Thus, the sed program script displays only the last 10 lines of the data7.txt file.

Deleting lines

Another useful utility for the sed editor is to remove unwanted blank lines in a data stream. It's easy to remove all the blank lines from a data stream, but it takes a little ingenuity to selectively remove blank lines. This section shows you a couple of quick sed editor scripts that you can use to help remove unwanted blank lines from your data.

Deleting consecutive blank lines

It can be a nuisance when extra blank lines crop up in data files. Often you have a data file that contains blank lines, but sometimes a data line is missing and produces too many blank lines (as you saw in the double-spacing example earlier).

The easiest way to remove consecutive blank lines is to check the data stream using a range address. Chapter 19 showed you how to use ranges in addresses, including how to incorporate patterns in the address range. The sed editor executes the command for all lines that match within the specified address range.

The key to removing consecutive blank lines is to create an address range that includes a non-blank line and a blank line. If the sed editor comes across this range, it shouldn't delete the line. However, for lines that don't match that range (two or more blank lines in a row), it should delete the lines.

Here's the script to do this:

```
/./,/^$/!d
```

The range is /./ to /^$/. The start address in the range matches any line that contains at least one character. The end address in the range matches a blank line. Lines within this range aren't deleted.

Here's the script in action:

```
$ cat data8.txt
This is line one.


This is line two.

This is line three.



This is line four.
```

```
$
$ sed '/./,/^$/!d' data8.txt
This is line one.

This is line two.

This is line three.

This is line four.
$
```

No matter how many blank lines appear between lines of data in the file, the output places only one blank line between the lines.

Deleting leading blank lines

It is also a nuisance when data files contain multiple blank lines at the start of the file. Often when you are trying to import data from a text file into a database, the blank lines create null entries, throwing off any calculations using the data.

Removing blank lines from the top of a data stream is not a difficult task. Here's the script that accomplishes that function:

```
/./,$!d
```

The script uses an address range to determine what lines are deleted. The range starts with a line that contains a character and continues to the end of the data stream. Any line within this range is not deleted from the output. This means that any lines before the first line that contain a character are deleted.

Look at this simple script in action:

```
$ cat data9.txt


This is line one.

This is line two.
$
$ sed '/./,$!d' data9.txt
This is line one.

This is line two.
$
```

The test file contains two blank lines before the data lines. The script successfully removes both of the leading blank lines, while keeping the blank line within the data intact.

Deleting trailing blank lines

Unfortunately, deleting trailing blank lines is not as simple as deleting leading blank lines. Just like printing the end of a data stream, deleting blank lines at the end of a data stream requires a little ingenuity and looping.

Before we start the discussion, let's see what the script looks like:

```
sed '{
:start
/^\n*$/{$d; N; b start }
}'
```

This may look a little odd to you at first. Notice that there are braces within the normal script braces. This allows you to group commands together within the overall command script. The group of commands applies to the specified address pattern. The address pattern matches any line that contains only a newline character. When one is found, if it's the last line, the delete command deletes it. If it's not the last line, the N command appends the next line to it, and the branch command loops to the beginning to start over.

Here's the script in action:

```
$ cat data10.txt
This is the first line.
This is the second line.


$ sed '{
> :start
> /^\n*$/{$d ; N ; b start }
> }' data10.txt
This is the first line.
This is the second line.
$
```

The script successfully removed the blank lines from the end of the text file.

Removing HTML tags

These days, it's not uncommon to download text from a website to save or use as data in an application. Sometimes, however, when you download text from the website, you also get the HTML tags used to format the data. This can be a problem when all you want to see is the data.

A standard HTML web page contains several different types of HTML tags, identifying formatting features required to properly display the page information. Here's a sample of what an HTML file looks like:

```
$ cat data11.txt
<html>
<head>
<title>This is the page title</title>
</head>
<body>
<p>
This is the <b>first</b> line in the Web page.
This should provide some <i>useful</i>
information to use in our sed script.
</body>
</html>
$
```

HTML tags are identified by the less-than and greater-than symbols. Most HTML tags come in pairs. One tag starts the formatting process (for example, <b> for bolding), and another tag stops the formatting process (for example, </b> to turn off bolding).

Removing HTML tags creates a problem, however, if you're not careful. At first glance, you'd think that the way to remove HTML tags would be to just look for a text string that starts with a less-than symbol (<), ends with a greater-than symbol (>), and has data in between the symbols:

```
s/<.*>//g
```

Unfortunately, this command has some unintended consequences:

```
$ sed 's/<.*>//g' data11.txt




This is the  line in the Web page.
This should provide some
information to use in our sed script.


$
```

Notice that the title text is missing, along with the text that was bolded and italicized. The sed editor literally interpreted the script to mean any text between the less-than and greater-than sign, including other less-than and greater-than signs! Each time the text was enclosed in HTML tags (such as first), the sed script removed the entire text.

The solution to this problem is to have the sed editor ignore any embedded greater-than signs between the original tags. To do that, you can create a character class that negates the greater-than sign. This changes the script to:

```
s/<[^>]*>//g
```

This script now works properly, displaying the data you need to see from the web page HTML code:

```
$ sed 's/<[^>]*>//g' data11.txt


This is the page title



This is the first line in the Web page.
This should provide some useful
information to use in our sed script.


$
```

That's a little better. To clean things up some, you can add a delete command to get rid of those pesky blank lines:

```
$ sed 's/<[^>]*>//g ; /^$/d' data11.txt
This is the page title
This is the first line in the Web page.
This should provide some useful
information to use in our sed script.
$
```

Now that's much more compact; there's only the data you need to see.

Summary

The sed editor provides some advanced features that allow you to work with text patterns across multiple lines. This chapter showed you how to use the next command to retrieve the next line in a data stream and place it in the pattern space. Once in the pattern space, you can perform complex substitution commands to replace phrases that span more than one line of text.

## 21

The multiline `delete` command allows you to remove the first line when the pattern space contains two or more lines. This is a convenient way to iterate through multiple lines in the data stream. Similarly, the multiline `print` command allows you to print just the first line when the pattern space contains two or more lines of text. The combination of the multiline commands allows you to iterate through the data stream and create a multiline substitution system.

Next, we covered the hold space. The hold space allows you to set aside a line of text while processing more lines of text. You can recall the contents of the hold space at any time and either replace the text in the pattern space or append the contents of the hold space to the text in the pattern space. Using the hold space allows you to sort through data streams, reversing the order of text lines as they appear in the data.

Next we reviewed the various `sed` editor flow control commands. The `branch` command provides a way for you to alter the normal flow of `sed` editor commands in the script, creating loops or skipping commands under certain conditions. The `test` command provides an `if-then` type of statement for your `sed` editor command scripts. The `test` command branches only if a prior `substitution` command succeeds in replacing text in a line.

The chapter concluded with a discussion of how to use `sed` scripts in your shell scripts. A common technique for large `sed` scripts is to place the script in a shell wrapper. You can use command line parameter variables within the `sed` script to pass shell command line values. This creates an easy way to utilize your `sed` editor scripts directly from the command line, or even from other shell scripts.

The next chapter digs deeper into the `gawk` world. The `gawk` program supports many features of higher-level programming languages. You can create some pretty involved data manipulation and reporting programs just by using `gawk`. The chapter describes the various programming features and demonstrates how to use them to generate your own fancy reports from simple data.

Advanced gawk

C hapter 19 introduced the gawk program and demonstrated the basics of using it to produce formatted reports from raw data files. This chapter dives more deeply into customizing gawk to produce reports. The gawk program is a full-fledged programming language, providing features that allow you to write advanced programs to manipulate data. If you are jumping into the shell script world from another programming language, you should feel right at home with gawk. In this chapter, you'll see how to use the gawk programming language to write programs to handle just about any data-formatting task you'll run into.

Using Variables

One important feature of any programming language is the ability to store and recall values using variables. The gawk programming language supports two different types of variables:

- Built-in variables
- User-defined variables

Several built-in variables are available for you to use in gawk. The built-in variables contain information used in handling the data fields and records in the data file. You can also create your own variables in your gawk programs. The following sections walk you through how to use variables in your gawk programs.

Built-in variables

The gawk program uses built-in variables to reference specific features within the program data. This section describes the built-in variables available for you to use in your gawk programs and demonstrates how to use them.

The field and record separator variables

Chapter 19 demonstrated one type of built-in variable available in gawk: the *data field variables*. The data field variables allow you to reference individual data fields within a data record using a dollar sign and the numerical position of the data field in the record. Thus, to reference the first data field in the record, you use the $1 variable. To reference the second data field, you use the $2 variable, and so on.

Data fields are delineated by a field separator character. By default, the field separator character is a whitespace character, such as a space or a tab. Chapter 19 showed how to change the field separator character either on the command line by using the -F command line parameter or within the gawk program using the special FS built-in variable.

The FS built-in variable belongs to a group of built-in variables that control how gawk handles fields and records in both input data and output data. Table 22-1 lists the built-in variables contained in this group.

TABLE 22-1 The gawk Data Field and Record Variables

Variable	Description
FIELDWIDTHS	A space-separated list of numbers defining the exact width (in spaces) of each data field
FS	Input field separator character
RS	Input record separator character
OFS	Output field separator character
ORS	Output record separator character

The FS and OFS variables define how your gawk program handles data fields in the data stream. You've already seen how to use the FS variable to define what character separates data fields in a record. The OFS variable performs the same function but for the output by using the print command.

By default, gawk sets the OFS variable to a space, so when you use the command:

```
print $1,$2,$3
```

you see the output as:

```
field1 field2 field3
```

You can see this in the following example:

```
$ cat data1
data11,data12,data13,data14,data15
data21,data22,data23,data24,data25
data31,data32,data33,data34,data35
$ gawk 'BEGIN{FS=","} {print $1,$2,$3}' data1
data11 data12 data13
data21 data22 data23
data31 data32 data33
$
```

The print command automatically places the value of the OFS variable between each data field in the output. By setting the OFS variable, you can use any string to separate data fields in the output:

```
$ gawk 'BEGIN{FS=","; OFS="-"} {print $1,$2,$3}' data1
data11-data12-data13
data21-data22-data23
data31-data32-data33
$ gawk 'BEGIN{FS=","; OFS="--"} {print $1,$2,$3}' data1
data11--data12--data13
data21--data22--data23
data31--data32--data33
$ gawk 'BEGIN{FS=","; OFS="<-->"} {print $1,$2,$3}' data1
data11<-->data12<-->data13
data21<-->data22<-->data23
data31<-->data32<-->data33
$
```

The FIELDWIDTHS variable allows you to read records without using a field separator character. In some applications, instead of using a field separator character, data is placed in specific columns within the record. In these instances, you must set the FIELDWIDTHS variable to match the layout of the data in the records.

After you set the FIELDWIDTHS variable, gawk ignores the FS and calculates data fields based on the provided field width sizes. Here's an example using field widths instead of field separator characters:

```
$ cat data1b
1005.3247596.37
115-2.349194.00
05810.1298100.1
$ gawk 'BEGIN{FIELDWIDTHS="3 5 2 5"}{print $1,$2,$3,$4}' data1b
100 5.324 75 96.37
115 -2.34 91 94.00
058 10.12 98 100.1
$
```

The FIELDWIDTHS variable defines four data fields, and gawk parses the data record accordingly. The string of numbers in each record is split based on the defined field width values.

The RS and ORS variables define how your gawk program handles records in the data stream. By default, gawk sets the RS and ORS variables to the newline character. The default RS variable value indicates that each new line of text in the input data stream is a new record.

Sometimes, you run into situations where data fields are spread across multiple lines in the data stream. A classic example of this is data that includes an address and phone number, each on a separate line:

```
Riley Mullen
123 Main Street
Chicago, IL 60601
(312)555-1234
```

If you try to read this data using the default FS and RS variable values, gawk reads each line as a separate record and interprets each space in the record as a field separator. This isn't what you intended.

To solve this problem, you need to set the FS variable to the newline character. This indicates that each line in the data stream is a separate field and all the data on a line belongs to the data field. However, when you do that, you don't know where a new record starts.

To solve this problem, set the RS variable to an empty string, and leave a blank line between data records in the data stream. The gawk program interprets each blank line as a record separator.

The following is an example of using this technique:

```
$ cat data2
Riley Mullen
123 Main Street
Chicago, IL  60601
(312)555-1234

Frank Williams
456 Oak Street
Indianapolis, IN  46201
```

```
(317)555-9876

Haley Snell
4231 Elm Street
Detroit, MI 48201
(313)555-4938
$ gawk 'BEGIN{FS="\n"; RS=""} {print $1,$4}' data2
Riley Mullen (312)555-1234
Frank Williams (317)555-9876
Haley Snell (313)555-4938
$
```

Perfect! The gawk program interpreted each line in the file as a data field and the blank lines as record separators.

Data variables

Besides the field and record separator variables, gawk provides some other built-in variables to help you know what's going on with your data and extract information from the shell environment. Table 22-2 shows the other built-in variables in gawk.

TABLE 22-2   More gawk Built-In Variables

Variable	Description
ARGC	The number of command line parameters present
ARGIND	The index in ARGV of the current file being processed
ARGV	An array of command line parameters
CONVFMT	The conversion format for numbers (see the printf statement), with a default value of %.6 g
ENVIRON	An associative array of the current shell environment variables and their values
ERRNO	The system error if an error occurs when reading or closing input files
FILENAME	The filename of the data file used for input to the gawk program
FNR	The current record number in the data file
IGNORECASE	If set to a non-zero value, ignores the case of characters in strings used in the gawk command
NF	The total number of data fields in the data file
NR	The number of input records processed
OFMT	The output format for displaying numbers, with a default of %.6 g
RLENGTH	The length of the substring matched in the match function
RSTART	The start index of the substring matched in the match function

You should recognize a few of these variables from your shell script programming. The ARGC and ARGV variables allow you to retrieve the number of command line parameters and their values from the shell. This can be a little tricky, however, because gawk doesn't count the program script as part of the command line parameters:

```
$ gawk 'BEGIN{print ARGC,ARGV[1]}' data1
2 data1
$
```

The ARGC variable indicates that two parameters are on the command line. This includes the gawk command and the data1 parameter (remember that the program script doesn't count as a parameter). The ARGV array starts with an index of 0, which represents the command. The first array value is the first command line parameter after the gawk command.

> **NOTE**
>
> Note that unlike shell variables, when you reference a gawk variable in the script, you don't add a dollar sign before the variable name.

The ENVIRON variable may seem a little odd to you. It uses an *associative array* to retrieve shell environment variables. An associative array uses text for the array index values instead of numeric values.

The text in the array index is the shell environment variable. The value of the array is the value of the shell environment variable. The following is an example of this:

```
$ gawk '
> BEGIN{
> print ENVIRON["HOME"]
> print ENVIRON["PATH"]
> }'
/home/rich
/usr/local/bin:/bin:/usr/bin:/usr/X11R6/bin
$
```

The ENVIRON["HOME"] variable retrieves the HOME environment variable value from the shell. Likewise, the ENVIRON["PATH"] variable retrieves the PATH environment variable value. You can use this technique to retrieve any environment variable value from the shell to use in your gawk programs.

The FNR, NF, and NR variables come in handy when you're trying to keep track of data fields and records in your gawk program. Sometimes, you're in a situation where you don't know exactly how many data fields are in a record. The NF variable allows you to specify the last data field in the record without having to know its position:

```
$ gawk 'BEGIN{FS=":"; OFS=":"} {print $1,$NF}' /etc/passwd
rich:/bin/bash
testy:/bin/csh
mark:/bin/bash
```

```
dan:/bin/bash
mike:/bin/bash
test:/bin/bash
$
```

The NF variable contains the numerical value of the last data field in the data file. You can then use it as a data field variable by placing a dollar sign in front of it.

The FNR and NR variables are similar to each other, but slightly different. The FNR variable contains the number of records processed in the current data file. The NR variable contains the total number of records processed. Let's look at a couple of examples to see this difference:

```
$ gawk 'BEGIN{FS=","}{print $1,"FNR="FNR}' data1 data1
data11 FNR=1
data21 FNR=2
data31 FNR=3
data11 FNR=1
data21 FNR=2
data31 FNR=3
$
```

In this example, the gawk program command line defines two input files. (It specifies the same input file twice.) The script prints the first data field value and the current value of the FNR variable. Notice that the FNR value was reset to 1 when the gawk program processed the second data file.

Now, let's add the NR variable and see what that produces:

```
$ gawk '
> BEGIN {FS=","}
> {print $1,"FNR="FNR,"NR="NR}
> END{print "There were",NR,"records processed"}' data1 data1
data11 FNR=1 NR=1
data21 FNR=2 NR=2
data31 FNR=3 NR=3
data11 FNR=1 NR=4
data21 FNR=2 NR=5
data31 FNR=3 NR=6
There were 6 records processed
$
```

The FNR variable value was reset when gawk processed the second data file, but the NR variable maintained its count into the second data file. The bottom line is that if you're using only one data file for input, the FNR and NR values are the same. If you're using multiple data files for input, the FNR value is reset for each data file, and the NR value keeps count throughout all the data files.

> **NOTE**
>
> When using gawk, notice that the gawk script can often become larger than the rest of your shell script. In the examples in this chapter, for simplicity we just run the gawk scripts directly from the command line, using the multi-line feature of the shell. When you use gawk in a shell script, you should place different gawk commands on separate lines. This makes it much easier for you to read and follow, rather than trying to cram it all onto one line in the shell script. Also, if you find yourself using the same gawk scripts in different shell scripts, you can save the gawk script in a separate file and reference it using the −f parameter (see Chapter 19).

User-defined variables

Just like any other self-respecting programming language, gawk allows you to define your own variables for use within the program code. A gawk user-defined variable name can be any number of letters, digits, and underscores, but it can't begin with a digit. It is also important to remember that gawk variable names are case sensitive.

Assigning variables in scripts

Assigning values to variables in gawk programs is similar to doing so in a shell script, using an *assignment statement:*

```
$ gawk '
> BEGIN{
> testing="This is a test"
> print testing
> }'
This is a test
$
```

The output of the print statement is the current value of the testing variable. Like shell script variables, gawk variables can hold either numeric or text values:

```
$ gawk '
> BEGIN{
> testing="This is a test"
> print testing
> testing=45
> print testing
> }'
This is a test
45
$
```

In this example, the value of the testing variable is changed from a text value to a numeric value.

Assignment statements can also include mathematical algorithms to handle numeric values:

```
$ gawk 'BEGIN{x=4; x= x * 2 + 3; print x}'
11
$
```

As you can see from this example, the gawk programming language includes the standard mathematical operators for processing numerical values. These can include the remainder symbol (%) and the exponentiation symbol (using either ^ or **).

Assigning variables on the command line

You can also use the gawk command line to assign values to variables for the gawk program. This allows you to set values outside of the normal code, changing values on the fly. Here's an example of using a command line variable to display a specific data field in the file:

```
$ cat script1
BEGIN{FS=","}
{print $n}
$ gawk -f script1 n=2 data1
data12
data22
data32
$ gawk -f script1 n=3 data1
data13
data23
data33
$
```

This feature allows you to change the behavior of the script without necessitating that you change the actual script code. The first example displays the second data field in the file, while the second example displays the third data field, just by setting the value of the n variable in the command line.

There's one problem with using command line parameters to define variable values. When you set the variable, the value isn't available in the BEGIN section of the code:

```
$ cat script2
BEGIN{print "The starting value is",n; FS=","}
{print $n}
$ gawk -f script2 n=3 data1
The starting value is
data13
data23
data33
$
```

You can solve this using the -v command line parameter. This allows you to specify variables that are set before the BEGIN section of code. The -v command line parameter must be placed before the script code in the command line:

```
$ gawk -v n=3 -f script2 data1
The starting value is 3
data13
data23
data33
$
```

Now the n variable contains the value set in the command line during the BEGIN section of code.

Working with Arrays

Many programming languages provide arrays for storing multiple values in a single variable. The gawk programming language provides the array feature using *associative arrays*.

Associative arrays are different from numerical arrays in that the index value can be any text string. You don't have to use sequential numbers to identify data elements contained in the array. Instead, an associative array consists of a hodge-podge of strings referencing values. Each index string must be unique and uniquely identifies the data element that's assigned to it. If you're familiar with other programming languages, this is the same concept as hash maps or dictionaries.

The following sections walk you through using associative array variables in your gawk programs.

Defining array variables

You can define an array variable using a standard assignment statement. Here's the format of the array variable assignment:

```
var[index] = element
```

In this example, *var* is the variable name, *index* is the associative array index value, and *element* is the data element value. Here are some examples of array variables in gawk:

```
capital["Illinois"] = "Springfield"
capital["Indiana"] = "Indianapolis"
capital["Ohio"] = "Columbus"
```

When you reference an array variable, you must include the index value to retrieve the appropriate data element value:

```
$ gawk 'BEGIN{
> capital["Illinois"] = "Springfield"
```

```
> print capital["Illinois"]
> }'
Springfield
$
```

When you reference the array variable, the data element value appears. This also works with numeric data element values:

```
$ gawk 'BEGIN{
> var[1] = 34
> var[2] = 3
> total = var[1] + var[2]
> print total
> }'
37
$
```

As you can see from this example, you can use array variables just as you would any other variable in the gawk program.

Iterating through array variables

The problem with associative array variables is that you might not have any way of knowing what the index values are. Unlike numeric arrays, which use sequential numbers for index values, an associative array index can be anything.

If you need to iterate through an associate array in gawk, you can use a special format of the for statement:

```
for (var in array)
{
   statements
}
```

The for statement loops through the statements, each time assigning the variable *var* the next index value from the *array* associative array. It's important to remember that the variable is the value of the index and not the data element value. You can easily extract the data element value by using the variable as the array index:

```
$ gawk 'BEGIN{
> var["a"] = 1
> var["g"] = 2
> var["m"] = 3
> var["u"] = 4
> for (test in var)
> {
>    print "Index:",test," - Value:",var[test]
> }
> }'
```

```
Index: u   - Value: 4
Index: m   - Value: 3
Index: a   - Value: 1
Index: g   - Value: 2
$
```

Notice that the index values aren't returned in any particular order, but they each reference the appropriate data element value. This is somewhat important to know, because you can't count on the returned values being in the same order, just that the index and data values match.

Deleting array variables

Removing an array index from an associative array requires a special command:

```
delete array[index]
```

The delete command removes the associative index value and the associated data element value from the array:

```
$ gawk 'BEGIN{
> var["a"] = 1
> var["g"] = 2
> for (test in var)
> {
>    print "Index:",test," - Value:",var[test]
> }
> delete var["g"]
> print "---"
> for (test in var)
>    print "Index:",test," - Value:",var[test]
> }'
Index: a   - Value: 1
Index: g   - Value: 2
---
Index: a   - Value: 1
$
```

After you delete an index value from the associative array, you can't retrieve it.

Using Patterns

The gawk program supports several types of matching patterns to filter data records, in much the same way as the sed editor. Chapter 19 showed two special patterns in action. The BEGIN and END keywords are special patterns that execute statements before or after the data stream data has been read. Similarly, you can create other patterns to execute statements when matching data appears in the data stream.

This section demonstrates how to use matching patterns in your gawk scripts to limit what records a program script applies to.

Regular expressions

Chapter 20 showed how to use regular expressions as matching patterns. You can use either a Basic Regular Expression (BRE) or an Extended Regular Expression (ERE) to filter which lines in the data stream the program script applies to.

When using a regular expression, the regular expression must appear before the left brace of the program script that it controls:

```
$ gawk 'BEGIN{FS=","} /11/{print $1}' data1
data11
$
```

The regular expression /11/ matches records that contain the string 11 anywhere in the data fields. The gawk program matches the defined regular expression against all the data fields in the record, including the field separator character:

```
$ gawk 'BEGIN{FS=","} /,d/{print $1}' data1
data11
data21
data31
$
```

This example matches the comma used as the field separator in the regular expression. This is not always a good thing. It can lead to problems trying to match data specific to one data field that may also appear in another data field. If you need to match a regular expression to a specific data instance, you should use the matching operator.

The matching operator

The *matching operator* allows you to restrict a regular expression to a specific data field in the records. The matching operator is the tilde symbol (~). You specify the matching operator, along with the data field variable, and the regular expression to match:

```
$1 ~ /^data/
```

The $1 variable represents the first data field in the record. This expression filters records where the first data field starts with the text data. The following is an example of using the matching operator in a gawk program script:

```
$ gawk 'BEGIN{FS=","} $2 ~ /^data2/{print $0}' data1
data21,data22,data23,data24,data25
$
```

The matching operator compares the second data field with the regular expression /^data2/, which indicates the string starts with the text data2.

This is a powerful tool that is commonly used in gawk program scripts to search for specific data elements in a data file:

```
$ gawk -F: '$1 ~ /rich/{print $1,$NF}' /etc/passwd
rich /bin/bash
$
```

This example searches the first data field for the text rich. When it finds the pattern in a record, it prints the first and last data field values of the record.

You can also negate the regular expression match by using the ! symbol:

```
$1 !~ /expression/
```

If the regular expression isn't found in the record, the program script is applied to the record data:

```
$ gawk -F: '$1 !~ /rich/{print $1,$NF}' /etc/passwd
root /bin/bash
daemon /bin/sh
bin /bin/sh
sys /bin/sh
--- output truncated ---
$
```

In this example, the gawk program script prints the userid and shell for all the entries in the /etc/passwd file that don't match the userid rich!

Mathematical expressions

In addition to regular expressions, you can also use mathematical expressions in the matching pattern. This feature comes in handy when matching numerical values in data fields. For example, if you want to display all the system users who belong to the root users group (group number 0), you could use this script:

```
$ gawk -F: '$4 == 0{print $1}' /etc/passwd
root
sync
shutdown
halt
operator
$
```

The script checks for records where the fourth data field contains the value 0. On this Linux system, five user accounts belong to the root user group.

You can use any of the normal mathematical comparison expressions:

- x == y: Value *x* is equal to *y*.
- x <= y: Value *x* is less than or equal to *y*.
- x < y: Value *x* is less than *y*.
- x >= y: Value *x* is greater than or equal to *y*.
- x > y: Value *x* is greater than *y*.

You can also use expressions with text data, but you must be careful. Unlike regular expressions, expressions are an exact match. The data must match exactly with the pattern:

```
$ gawk -F, '$1 == "data"{print $1}' data1
$
$ gawk -F, '$1 == "data11"{print $1}' data1
data11
$
```

The first test doesn't match any records because the first data field value isn't data in any of the records. The second test matches one record with the value data11.

Structured Commands

The gawk programming language supports the usual cast of structured programming commands. This section describes each of these commands and demonstrates how to use them within a gawk programming environment.

The if statement

The gawk programming language supports the standard if-then-else format of the if statement. You must define a condition for the if statement to evaluate, enclosed in parentheses. If the condition evaluates to a TRUE condition, the statement immediately following the if statement is executed. If the condition evaluates to a FALSE condition, the statement is skipped. You can use this format:

```
if (condition)
   statement1
```

Or you can place it on one line, like this:

```
if (condition) statement1
```

Here's a simple example demonstrating this format:

```
$ cat data4
10
```

```
5
13
50
34
$ gawk '{if ($1 > 20) print $1}' data4
50
34
$
```

Not too complicated. If you need to execute multiple statements in the if statement, you must enclose them with braces:

```
$ gawk '{
> if ($1 > 20)
> {
>    x = $1 * 2
>    print x
> }
> }' data4
100
68
$
```

Be careful that you don't confuse the if statement braces with the braces used to start and stop the program script. The gawk program can detect missing braces and produces an error message if you mess up:

```
$ gawk '{
> if ($1 > 20)
> {
>    x = $1 * 2
>    print x
> }' data4
gawk: cmd. line:6: }
gawk: cmd. line:6:  ^ unexpected newline or end of string
$
```

The gawk if statement also supports the else clause, allowing you to execute one or more statements if the if statement condition fails. Here's an example of using the else clause:

```
$ gawk '{
> if ($1 > 20)
> {
>    x = $1 * 2
>    print x
> } else
> {
>    x = $1 / 2
>    print x
```

```
> }}' data4
5
2.5
6.5
100
68
$
```

You can use the else clause on a single line, but you must use a semicolon after the if statement section:

```
if (condition) statement1; else statement2
```

Here's the same example using the single line format:

```
$ gawk '{if ($1 > 20) print $1 * 2; else print $1 / 2}' data4
5
2.5
6.5
100
68
$
```

This format is more compact but can be harder to follow.

The while statement

The while statement provides a basic looping feature for gawk programs. Here's the format of the while statement:

```
while (condition)
{
   statements
}
```

The while loop allows you to iterate over a set of data, checking a condition that stops the iteration. This is useful if you have multiple data values in each record that you must use in calculations:

```
$ cat data5
130 120 135
160 113 140
145 170 215
$ gawk '{
> total = 0
> i = 1
> while (i < 4)
> {
```

```
>    total += $i
>    i++
> }
> avg = total / 3
> print "Average:",avg
> }' data5
Average: 128.333
Average: 137.667
Average: 176.667
$
```

The `while` statement iterates through the data fields in the record, adding each value to the total variable and incrementing the counter variable, `i`. When the counter value is equal to 4, the `while` condition becomes FALSE, and the loop terminates, dropping through to the next statement in the script. That statement calculates the average and prints the average. This process is repeated for each record in the data file.

The `gawk` programming language supports using the `break` and `continue` statements in `while` loops, allowing you to jump out of the middle of the loop:

```
$ gawk '{
> total = 0
> i = 1
> while (i < 4)
> {
>    total += $i
>    if (i == 2)
>       break
>    i++
> }
> avg = total / 2
> print "The average of the first two data elements is:",avg
> }' data5
The average of the first two data elements is: 125
The average of the first two data elements is: 136.5
The average of the first two data elements is: 157.5
$
```

The `break` statement is used to break out of the `while` loop if the value of the `i` variable is 2.

The do-while statement

The `do-while` statement is similar to the `while` statement but performs the statements before checking the condition statement. Here's the format for the `do-while` statement:

```
do
{
```

```
        statements
    } while (condition)
```

This format guarantees that the statements are executed at least one time before the condition is evaluated. This comes in handy when you need to perform statements before evaluating the condition:

```
$ gawk '{
> total = 0
> i = 1
> do
> {
>    total += $i
>    i++
> } while (total < 150)
> print total }' data5
250
160
315
$
```

The script reads the data fields from each record and totals them until the cumulative value reaches 150. If the first data field is over 150 (as seen in the second record), the script is guaranteed to read at least the first data field before evaluating the condition.

The for statement

The for statement is a common method used in many programming languages for looping. The gawk programming language supports the C-style of for loops:

```
for( variable assignment; condition; iteration process)
```

This helps simplify the loop by combining several functions in one statement:

```
$ gawk '{
> total = 0
> for (i = 1; i < 4; i++)
> {
>    total += $i
> }
> avg = total / 3
> print "Average:",avg
> }' data5
Average: 128.333
Average: 137.667
Average: 176.667
$
```

By defining the iteration counter in the for loop, you don't have to worry about incrementing it yourself as you did when using the while statement.

Formatted Printing

You may have noticed that the print statement doesn't exactly give you much control over how gawk displays your data. About all you can do is control the output field separator character (OFS). If you're creating detailed reports, often you need to place data in a specific format and location.

The solution is to use the formatted printing command, called printf. If you're familiar with C programming, the printf command in gawk performs the same way, allowing you to specify detailed instructions on how to display data.

Here's the format of the printf command:

```
printf "format string", var1, var2 . . .
```

The *format string* is the key to the formatted output. It specifies exactly how the formatted output should appear, using both text elements and *format specifiers*. A format specifier is a special code that indicates what type of variable is displayed and how to display it. The gawk program uses each format specifier as a placeholder for each variable listed in the command. The first format specifier matches the first variable listed, the second matches the second variable, and so on.

The format specifiers use the following format:

```
%[modifier] control-letter
```

In this example, *control-letter* is a one-character code that indicates what type of data value will be displayed, and *modifier* defines an optional formatting feature.

Table 22-3 lists the control letters that can be used in the format specifier.

TABLE 22-3 Format Specifier Control Letters

Control Letter	Description
c	Displays a number as an ASCII character
d	Displays an integer value
i	Displays an integer value (same as d)
e	Displays a number in scientific notation
f	Displays a floating-point value
g	Displays either scientific notation or floating point, whichever is shorter
o	Displays an octal value
s	Displays a text string

x	Displays a hexadecimal value
X	Displays a hexadecimal value, but using capital letters for A through F

Thus, if you need to display a string variable, you use the format specifier %s. If you need to display an integer variable, you use either %d or %i (%d is the C-style for decimals). If you want to display a large value using scientific notation, you use the %e format specifier:

```
$ gawk 'BEGIN{
> x = 10 * 100
> printf "The answer is: %e\n", x
> }'
The answer is: 1.000000e+03
$
```

In addition to the control letters, you can use three modifiers for even more control over your output:

- width: This is a numeric value that specifies the minimum width of the output field. If the output is shorter, printf pads the space with spaces, using right justification for the text. If the output is longer than the specified width, it over-rides the width value.

- prec: This is a numeric value that specifies the number of digits to the right of the decimal place in floating-point numbers, or the maximum number of characters displayed in a text string.

- - (minus sign): The minus sign indicates that left justification should be used instead of right justification when placing data in the formatted space.

When using the printf statement, you have complete control over how your output appears. For example, in the "Built-in variables" section, we used the print command to display data fields from our records:

```
$ gawk 'BEGIN{FS="\n"; RS=""} {print $1,$4}' data2
Riley Mullen (312)555-1234
Frank Williams (317)555-9876
Haley Snell (313)555-4938
$
```

You can use the printf command to help format the output so it looks better. First, let's just convert the print command to a printf command and see what that does:

```
$ gawk 'BEGIN{FS="\n"; RS=""} {printf "%s %s\n", $1, $4}' data2
Riley Mullen   (312)555-1234
Frank Williams   (317)555-9876
Haley Snell   (313)555-4938
$
```

That produces the same output as the print command. The printf command uses the %s format specifier as a placeholder for the two string values.

Notice that you have to manually add the newline character at the end of the printf command to force a new line. Without it, the printf command uses the same line on subsequent prints.

This is useful if you need to print multiple things on the same line, but using separate printf commands:

```
$ gawk 'BEGIN{FS=","} {printf "%s ", $1} END{printf "\n"}' data1
data11 data21 data31
$
```

Both printf outputs appear on the same line. To be able to terminate the line, the END section prints a single newline character.

Next, let's use a modifier to format the first string value:

```
$ gawk 'BEGIN{FS="\n"; RS=""} {printf "%16s   %s\n", $1, $4}' data2
    Riley Mullen   (312)555-1234
 Frank Williams   (317)555-9876
     Haley Snell   (313)555-4938
$
```

By adding the 16 modifier value, we force the output for the first string to use 16 spaces. By default, the printf command uses right justification to place the data in the format space. To make it left justified, just add a minus sign to the modifier:

```
$ gawk 'BEGIN{FS="\n"; RS=""} {printf "%-16s   %s\n", $1, $4}' data2
Riley Mullen       (312)555-1234
Frank Williams     (317)555-9876
Haley Snell        (313)555-4938
$
```

Now that looks pretty professional!

The printf command also comes in handy when dealing with floating-point values. By specifying a format for the variable, you can make the output look more uniform:

```
$ gawk '{
> total = 0
> for (i = 1; i < 4; i++)
> {
>    total += $i
> }
> avg = total / 3
> printf "Average: %5.1f\n",avg
> }' data5
```

```
Average: 128.3
Average: 137.7
Average: 176.7
$
```

By using the %5.1f format specifier, you can force the printf command to round the floating-point values to a single decimal place.

Built-In Functions

The gawk programming language provides quite a few built-in functions that perform common mathematical, string, and even time functions. You can utilize these functions in your gawk programs to help cut down on the coding requirements in your scripts. This section walks you through the different built-in functions available in gawk.

Mathematical functions

If you've done programming in any type of language, you're probably familiar with using built-in functions in your code to perform common mathematical functions. The gawk programming language doesn't disappoint those looking for advanced mathematical features.

Table 22-4 shows the mathematical built-in functions available in gawk.

TABLE 22-4   The gawk Mathematical Functions

Function	Description
atan2(x, y)	The arctangent of x / y, with x and y specified in radians
cos(x)	The cosine of x, with x specified in radians
exp(x)	The exponential of x
int(x)	The integer part of x, truncated toward 0
log(x)	The natural logarithm of x
rand()	A random floating point value larger than 0 and less than 1
sin(x)	The sine of x, with x specified in radians
sqrt(x)	The square root of x
srand(x)	Specifies a seed value for calculating random numbers

Although it does not have an extensive list of mathematical functions, gawk does provide some of the basic elements you need for standard mathematical processing. The int() function produces the integer portion of a value, but it doesn't round the value. It behaves much like a floor function found in other programming languages. It produces the nearest integer to a value between the value and 0.

This means that the int() function of the value 5.6 returns 5, while the int() function of the value -5.6 returns -5.

The rand() function is great for creating random numbers, but you need to use a trick to get meaningful values. The rand() function returns a random number, but only between the values 0 and 1 (not including 0 or 1). To get a larger number, you need to scale the returned value.

A common method for producing larger integer random numbers is to create an algorithm that uses the rand() function, along with the int() function:

```
x = int(10 * rand())
```

This returns a random integer value between (and including) 0 and 9. Just substitute the 10 in the equation with the upper limit value for your application, and you're ready to go.

Be careful when using some of the mathematical functions, because the gawk programming language does have a limited range of numeric values it can work with. If you go over that range, you get an error message:

```
$ gawk 'BEGIN{x=exp(100); print x}'
26881171418161356094253400435962903554686976
$ gawk 'BEGIN{x=exp(1000); print x}'
gawk: warning: exp argument 1000 is out of range
inf
$
```

The first example calculates the natural exponential function of 100, which is a very large number but within the range of the system. The second example attempts to calculate the natural exponential function of 1,000, which goes over the numerical range limit of the system and produces an error message.

Besides the standard mathematical functions, gawk also provides a few functions for bit-wise manipulating of data:

- and(v1, v2): Performs a bitwise AND of values v1 and v2
- compl(val): Performs the bitwise complement of val
- lshift(val, count): Shifts the value val count number of bits left
- or(v1, v2): Performs a bitwise OR of values v1 and v2
- rshift(val, count): Shifts the value val count number of bits right
- xor(v1, v2): Performs a bitwise XOR of values v1 and v2

The bit manipulation functions are useful when working with binary values in your data.

String functions

The gawk programming language also provides several functions you can use to manipulate string values, shown in Table 22-5.

TABLE 22-5 **The gawk String Functions**

Function	Description
asort(s [,d])	This function sorts an array s based on the data element values. The index values are replaced with sequential numbers indicating the new sort order. Alternatively, the new sorted array is stored in array d if specified.
asorti(s [,d])	This function sorts an array s based on the index values. The resulting array contains the index values as the data element values, with sequential number indexes indicating the sort order. Alternatively, the new sorted array is stored in array d if specified.
gensub(r, s, h [, t])	This function searches either the variable $0, or the target string t if supplied, for matches of the regular expression r. If h is a string beginning with either g or G, it replaces the matching text with s. If h is a number, it represents which occurrence of r to replace.
gsub(r, s [,t])	This function searches either the variable $0, or the target string t if supplied, for matches of the regular expression r. If found, it substitutes the string s globally.
index(s, t)	This function returns the index of the string t in string s, or 0 if not found.
length([s])	This function returns the length of string s, or if not specified, the length of $0.
match(s, r [,a])	This function returns the index of the string s where the regular expression r occurs. If array a is specified, it contains the portion of s that matches the regular expression.
split(s, a [,r])	This function splits s into array a using either the FS character, or the regular expression r if supplied. It returns the number of fields.
sprintf(format, variables)	This function returns a string similar to the output of printf using the format and variables supplied.
sub(r, s [,t])	This function searches either the variable $0, or the target string t, for matches of the regular expression r. If found, it substitutes the string s for the first occurrence.
substr(s, i [,n])	This function returns the nth character substring of s, starting at index i. If n is not supplied, the rest of s is used.
tolower(s)	This function converts all characters in s to lowercase.
toupper(s)	This function converts all characters in s to uppercase.

## 22

Some string functions are relatively self-explanatory:

```
$ gawk 'BEGIN{x = "testing"; print toupper(x); print length(x) }'
TESTING
7
$
```

However, some string functions can get pretty complicated. The asort and asorti functions are new gawk functions that allow you to sort an array variable based on either the data element values (asort) or the index values (asorti). Here's an example of using asort:

```
$ gawk 'BEGIN{
> var["a"] = 1
> var["g"] = 2
> var["m"] = 3
> var["u"] = 4
> asort(var, test)
> for (i in test)
>     print "Index:",i," - value:",test[i]
> }'
Index: 4  - value: 4
Index: 1  - value: 1
Index: 2  - value: 2
Index: 3  - value: 3
$
```

The new array, test, contains the newly sorted data elements of the original array, but the index values are now changed to numerical values, indicating the proper sort order.

The split function is a great way to push data fields into an array for further processing:

```
$ gawk 'BEGIN{ FS=","}{
> split($0, var)
> print var[1], var[5]
> }' data1
data11 data15
data21 data25
data31 data35
$
```

The new array uses sequential numbers for the array index, starting with index value 1 containing the first data field.

Time functions

The gawk programming language contains a few functions to help you deal with time values, shown in Table 22-6.

TABLE 22-6 The gawk Time Functions

Function	Description
mktime(*datespec*)	Converts a date specified in the format YYYY MM DD HH MM SS [DST] into a timestamp value
strftime(*format* [,*timestamp*])	Formats either the current time of day timestamp, or timestamp if provided, into a formatted day and date, using the date() shell function format
systime()	Returns the timestamp for the current time of day

The time functions are often used when working with log files that contain dates that you need to compare. By converting the text representation of a date to the epoch time (the number of seconds since midnight, January 1, 1970), you can easily compare dates.

The following is an example of using the time functions in a gawk program:

```
$ gawk 'BEGIN{
> date = systime()
> day = strftime("%A, %B %d, %Y", date)
> print day
> }'
Friday, December 26, 2014
$
```

This example uses the systime function to retrieve the current epoch timestamp from the system and then uses the strftime function to convert it into a human-readable format using the date shell command's date format characters.

User-Defined Functions

You're not limited to just using the built-in functions available in gawk. You can create your own functions for use in gawk programs. This section shows you how to define and use your own functions in gawk programs.

Defining a function

To define you own function, you must use the function keyword:

```
function name([variables])
{
    statements
}
```

The function name must uniquely identify your function. You can pass one or more variables into the function from the calling gawk program:

```
function printthird()
{
    print $3
}
```

This function prints the third data field in the record.

The function can also return a value using the return statement:

```
return value
```

The value can be a variable, or an equation that evaluates to a value:

```
function myrand(limit)
{
    return int(limit * rand())
}
```

You can assign the value returned from the function to a variable in the gawk program:

```
x = myrand(100)
```

The variable contains the value returned from the function.

Using your functions

When you define a function, it must appear by itself before you define any programming sections (including the BEGIN section). This may look a little odd at first, but it helps keep the function code separate from the rest of the gawk program:

```
$ gawk '
> function myprint()
> {
>     printf "%-16s - %s\n", $1, $4
> }
> BEGIN{FS="\n"; RS=""}
> {
>     myprint()
> }' data2
Riley Mullen      - (312)555-1234
Frank Williams    - (317)555-9876
Haley Snell       - (313)555-4938
$
```

The function defines the `myprint()` function, which formats the first and fourth data fields in the record for printing. The `gawk` program then uses the function to display the data from the data file.

After you define a function, you can use it as often as necessary in the program section of the code. This saves lots of work when using long algorithms.

Creating a function library

Obviously, having to rewrite your `gawk` functions every time you need them is not a pleasant experience. However, `gawk` provides a way for you to combine your functions into a single library file that you can use in all your `gawk` programming.

First, you need to create a file that contains all your `gawk` functions:

```
$ cat funclib
function myprint()
{
   printf "%-16s - %s\n", $1, $4
}
function myrand(limit)
{
   return int(limit * rand())
}
function printthird()
{
   print $3
}
$
```

The `funclib` file contains three function definitions. To use them, you need to use the `-f` command line parameter. Unfortunately, you can't combine the `-f` command line parameter with an inline `gawk` script, but you can use multiple `-f` parameters on the same command line.

Thus, to use your library, just create a file that contains your `gawk` program, and specify both the library file and your program file on the command line:

```
$ cat script4
BEGIN{ FS="\n"; RS="" }
{
    myprint()
}
$ gawk -f funclib -f script4 data2
Riley Mullen     - (312)555-1234
Frank Williams   - (317)555-9876
Haley Snell      - (313)555-4938
$
```

Now you just need to add the `funclib` file to your `gawk` command line whenever you need to use a function defined in the library.

Working through a Practical Example

The advanced `gawk` features come in handy if you have to handle data values in a data file, such as tabulating sales figures or calculating bowling scores. When you work with data files, the key is to first group related data records together and then perform any calculations required on the related data.

For example, let's work with a data file that contains the bowling scores from a game between two teams, each with two players:

```
$ cat scores.txt
Rich Blum,team1,100,115,95
Barbara Blum,team1,110,115,100
Christine Bresnahan,team2,120,115,118
Tim Bresnahan,team2,125,112,116
$
```

Each player has scores from three separate games in the data file, and each player is identified by a team name in the second column. Here's the shell script to sort the data for each team and calculate the totals and averages:

```
$ cat bowling.sh
#!/bin/bash

for team in $(gawk -F, '{print $2}' scores.txt | uniq)
do
    gawk -v team=$team 'BEGIN{FS=","; total=0}
    {
        if ($2==team)
        {
            total += $3 + $4 + $5;
        }
    }
    END {
        avg = total / 6;
        print "Total for", team, "is", total, ",the average is",avg
    }' scores.txt
done
$
```

The first `gawk` statement inside the `for` loop filters out the team names in the data file and then uses the `uniq` function to return one value for each separate team name. The `for` loop then iterates for each separate team name.

The `gawk` statement inside the `for` loop is what's doing the calculations. For each data record, it first determines if the team name matches the loop team. That's done by using the `-v` option in `gawk`, which allows us to pass a shell variable inside the `gawk` program. If the team name matches, the code keeps a running sum of the three scores in the data record, adding each data record's values, as long as that data record matches the team name.

At the end of each loop iteration, the `gawk` code displays the score totals, as well as the average of the scores. The output should look like this:

```
$ ./bowling.sh
Total for team1 is 635, the average is 105.833
Total for team2 is 706, the average is 117.667
$
```

Now you have a handy shell script to calculate the results of all your bowling tournaments; you just need to plug the data from each player into the data text file and run the script!

Summary

This chapter walked you through the more advanced features of the `gawk` programming language. Every programming language requires using variables, and `gawk` is no different. The `gawk` programming language includes some built-in variables that you can use to reference specific data field values and retrieve information about the number of data fields and records processed in the data file. You can also create your own variables for use in your scripts.

The `gawk` programming language also provides many of the standard structured commands you expect from a programming language. You can easily create fancy programs using `if-then` logic and `while`, `do-while`, and `for` loops. Each of these commands allows you to alter the flow of your `gawk` program script to iterate through data field values to create detailed data reports.

The `printf` command is a great tool to have if you need to customize your report output. It allows you to specify the exact format for displaying data from the `gawk` program script. You can easily create formatted reports, placing data elements in exactly the correct position.

Finally, this chapter discussed the many built-in functions available in the `gawk` programming language and showed you how to create your own functions. The `gawk` program contains many useful functions for handling mathematical features, such as standard square roots and logarithms, as well as trigonometric functions. There are also several string-related functions that make extracting substrings from larger strings a breeze.

You aren't limited to the built-in functions in the gawk program. If you're working on an application that uses lots of specialized algorithms, you can create your own functions to process the algorithms and use those functions in your own code. You can also set up a library file containing all the functions you use in your gawk programs, saving you time and effort in all your coding.

The next chapter switches gears a little. It examines a few other shell environments you may run into in your Linux shell-scripting endeavors. Although the bash shell is the most common shell used in Linux, it's not the only shell. It helps to know a little about some of the other shells available and how they differ from the bash shell.

CHAPTER

23

Working with Alternative Shells

Although the bash shell is the most widely used shell in Linux distributions, it isn't the only one. Now that you've seen the standard Linux bash shell and what you can do with it, it's time to examine a few other shells available in the Linux world. This chapter describes two other shells that you may run into in your Linux journey and how they differ from the bash shell.

What Is the dash Shell?

The Debian dash shell has had an interesting past. It's a direct descendant of the ash shell, a simple copy of the original Bourne shell available on Unix systems (see Chapter 1). Kenneth Almquist created a small-scale version of the Bourne shell for Unix systems and called it the Almquist shell, which was then shortened to *ash*. This original version of the ash shell was extremely small and fast but without many advanced features, such as command line editing or history features, making it difficult to use as an interactive shell.

The NetBSD Unix operating system adopted the ash shell and still uses it today as the default shell. The NetBSD developers customized the ash shell by adding several new features, making it closer to the Bourne shell. The new features include command line editing using both emacs and vi editor commands, as well as a history command to recall previously entered commands. This version of the ash shell is also used by the FreeBSD operating system as the default login shell.

The Debian Linux distribution created its own version of the ash shell (called Debian ash, or *dash*) for inclusion in its version of Linux. For the most part, dash copies the features of the NetBSD version of the ash shell, providing the advanced command line editing capabilities.

However, to add to the shell confusion, the dash shell is actually not the default shell in many Debian-based Linux distributions. Because of the popularity of the bash shell in Linux, most

Debian-based Linux distributions use the bash shell as the normal login shell and use the dash shell only as a quick-start shell for the installation script to install the distribution files.

The exception is the popular Ubuntu distribution. This often confuses shell script programmers and causes a great number of problems with running shell scripts in a Linux environment. The Ubuntu Linux distribution uses the bash shell as the default interactive shell, but uses the dash shell as the default /bin/sh shell. This "feature" really confuses shell script programmers.

As you saw in Chapter 11, every shell script must start with a line that declares the shell used for the script. In our bash shell scripts, we've been using this:

```
#!/bin/bash
```

This tells the shell to use the shell program located at /bin/bash to execute the script. In the Unix world, the default shell was always /bin/sh. Many shell script programmers familiar with the Unix environment copy this into their Linux shell scripts:

```
#!/bin/sh
```

On most Linux distributions, the /bin/sh file is a symbolic link (see Chapter 3) to the /bin/bash shell program. This allows you to easily port shell scripts designed for the Unix Bourne shell to the Linux environment without having to modify them.

Unfortunately, the Ubuntu Linux distribution links the /bin/sh file to the /bin/dash shell program. Because the dash shell contains only a subset of the commands available in the original Bourne shell, this can — and often does — cause some shell scripts to not work properly.

The next section walks you through the basics of the dash shell and how it differs from the bash shell. This is especially important to know if you write bash shell scripts that may need to be run in an Ubuntu environment.

The dash Shell Features

Although both the bash shell and the dash shell are modeled after the Bourne shell, they have some differences. This section walks you through the features found in the Debian dash shell to acquaint you with how the dash shell works before we dive into the shell scripting features.

The dash command line parameters

The dash shell uses command line parameters to control its behavior. Table 23-1 lists the command line parameters and describes what each one does.

TABLE 23-1   **The dash Command Line Parameters**

Parameter	Description
-a	Exports all variables assigned to the shell
-c	Reads commands from a specified command string
-e	If not interactive, exits immediately if any untested command fails
-f	Displays pathname wildcard characters
-n	If not interactive, reads commands but doesn't execute them
-u	Writes an error message to STDERR when attempting to expand a variable that is not set
-v	Writes input to STDERR as it is read
-x	Writes each command to STDERR as it is executed
-I	Ignores EOF characters from the input when in interactive mode
-i	Forces the shell to operate in interactive mode
-m	Turns on job control (enabled by default in interactive mode)
-s	Reads commands from STDIN (the default behavior if no file arguments are present)
-E	Enables the emacs command line editor
-V	Enables the vi command line editor

Debian added a few additional command line parameters to the original ash shell command line parameter list. The -E and -V command line parameters enable the special command line editing features of the dash shell.

The -E command line parameter allows you to use the emacs editor commands for editing command line text (see Chapter 10). You can use all the emacs commands for manipulating text on a single line using the Ctrl and Meta key combinations.

The -V command line parameter allows you to use the vi editor commands for editing command line text (again, see Chapter 10). This feature allows you to switch between normal mode and vi editor mode on the command line by using the Esc key. When you're in vi editor mode, you can use all the standard vi editor commands (such as x to delete a character, and i to insert text). After you finish editing the command line, you must press the Esc key again to exit vi editor mode.

The dash environment variables

The dash shell uses quite a few default environment variables uses to track information, and you can create your own environment variables as well. This section describes the environment variables and how dash handles them.

Default environment variables

The dash environment variables are very similar to the environment variables used in bash (see Chapter 6). This is not by accident. Remember that both the dash and bash shells are extensions of the Bourne shell, so they both incorporate many of its features. However, because of its goal of simplicity, the dash shell contains significantly fewer environment variables than the bash shell. You need to take this into consideration when creating shell scripts in a dash shell environment.

The dash shell uses the `set` command to display environment variables:

```
$set
COLORTERM=''
DESKTOP_SESSION='default'
DISPLAY=':0.0'
DM_CONTROL='/var/run/xdmctl'
GS_LIB='/home/atest/.fonts'
HOME='/home/atest'
IFS='
'
KDEROOTHOME='/root/.kde'
KDE_FULL_SESSION='true'
KDE_MULTIHEAD='false'
KONSOLE_DCOP='DCOPRef(konsole-5293,konsole)'
KONSOLE_DCOP_SESSION='DCOPRef(konsole-5293,session-1)'
LANG='en_US'
LANGUAGE='en'
LC_ALL='en_US'
LOGNAME='atest'
OPTIND='1'
PATH='/usr/local/sbin:/usr/local/bin:/usr/sbin:/usr/bin:/sbin:/bin'
PPID='5293'
PS1='$ '
PS2='> '
PS4='+ '
PWD='/home/atest'
SESSION_MANAGER='local/testbox:/tmp/.ICE-unix/5051'
SHELL='/bin/dash'
SHLVL='1'
TERM='xterm'
USER='atest'
XCURSOR_THEME='default'
_='ash'
$
```

Your default dash shell environment will most likely differ, because different Linux distributions assign different default environment variables at login.

Positional parameters

In addition to the default environment variables, the dash shell also assigns special variables to any parameters defined in the command line. Here are the positional parameter variables available for use in the dash shell:

- $0: The name of the shell
- $n: The nth position parameter
- $*: A single value with the contents of all the parameters, separated by the first character in the IFS environment variable, or a space if IFS isn't defined
- $@: Expands to multiple arguments consisting of all the command line parameters
- $#: The number of positional parameters
- $?: The exit status of the most recent command
- $-: The current option flags
- $$: The process ID (PID) of the current shell
- $!: The process ID (PID) of the most recent background command

All the dash positional parameters mimic the same positional parameters available in the bash shell. You can use each of the positional parameters in your shell scripts just as you would in the bash shell.

User-defined environment variables

The dash shell also allows you to set your own environment variables. As with bash, you can define a new environment variable on the command line by using the assignment statement:

```
$ testing=10 ; export testing
$ echo $testing
10
$
```

Without the `export` command, user-defined environment variables are visible only in the current shell or process.

> **CAUTION**
>
> There's one huge difference between dash variables and bash variables. The dash shell doesn't support variable arrays. This small feature causes all sorts of problems for advanced shell script writers.

The dash built-in commands

Just as with the bash shell, the dash shell contains a set of built-in commands that it recognizes. You can use these commands directly from the command line interface, or you can incorporate them in your shell scripts. Table 23-2 lists the dash shell built-in commands.

TABLE 23-2   The dash Shell Built-In Commands

Command	Description
alias	Creates an alias string to represent a text string
bg	Continues specified job in background mode
cd	Switches to the specified directory
echo	Displays a text string and environment variables
eval	Concatenates all arguments with a space
exec	Replaces the shell process with the specified command
exit	Terminates the shell process
export	Exports the specified environment variable for use in all child shells
fg	Continues specified job in foreground mode
getopts	Obtains options and arguments from a list of parameters
hash	Maintains and retrieves a hash table of recent commands and their locations
pwd	Displays the value of the current working directory
read	Reads a line from STDIN and assign the value to a variable
readonly	Reads a line from STDIN to a variable that can't be changed
printf	Displays text and variables using a formatted string
set	Lists or sets option flags and environment variables
shift	Shifts the positional parameters a specified number of times
test	Evaluates an expression and returns 0 if true or 1 if false
times	Displays the accumulated user and system times for the shell and all shell processes
trap	Parses and executes an action when the shell receives a specified signal
type	Interprets the specified name and displays the resolution (alias, built-in, command, keyword)
ulimit	Queries or sets limits on processes
umask	Sets the value of the default file and directory permissions
unalias	Removes the specified alias
unset	Removes the specified variable or option flag from the exported variables
wait	Waits for the specified job to complete and returns the exit status

You probably recognize all these built-in commands from the bash shell. The dash shell supports many of the same built-in commands as the bash shell. You'll notice that there are no commands for the command history file or for the directory stack. The dash shell doesn't support these features.

Scripting in dash

Unfortunately, the dash shell doesn't recognize all the scripting features of the bash shell. Shell scripts written for the bash environment often fail when run in the dash shell, causing all sorts of grief for shell script programmers. This section describes the differences you'll need to be aware of to get your shell scripts to run properly in a dash shell environment.

Creating dash scripts

You probably guessed by now that creating shell scripts for the dash shell is pretty similar to creating shell scripts for the bash shell. You should always specify which shell you want to use in your script to ensure that the script runs with the proper shell.

You do this on the first line of the shell:

```
#!/bin/dash
```

You can also specify a shell command line parameter on this line, as was documented earlier in "The dash command line parameters" section.

Things that don't work

Unfortunately, because the dash shell is only a subset of the Bourne shell features, some things in bash shell scripts don't work in the dash shell. These are often called *bashisms*. This section is a quick summary of bash shell features you may be used to using in your bash shell scripts that don't work if you're in a dash shell environment.

Using arithmetic

Chapter 11 showed three ways to express a mathematical operation in the bash shell script:

- **Using the** expr **command:** expr operation
- **Using square brackets:** $[operation]
- **Using double parentheses:** $((operation))

The dash shell supports the expr command and the double parentheses method but doesn't support the square bracket method. This can be a problem if you have lots of mathematical operations that use the square brackets.

The proper format for performing mathematical operations in dash shell scripts is to use the double parentheses method:

```
$ cat test5b
#!/bin/dash
# testing mathematical operations

value1=10
value2=15

value3=$(( $value1 * $value2 ))
echo "The answer is $value3"
$ ./test5b
The answer is 150
$
```

Now the shell can perform the calculation properly.

The test command

Although the dash shell supports the test command, you must be careful how you use it. The bash shell version of the test command is slightly different from the dash shell version.

The bash shell test command allows you to use the double equal sign (==) to test if two strings are equal. This is an add-on to accommodate programmers familiar with using this format in other programming languages.

However, the test command available in the dash shell doesn't recognize the == symbol for text comparisons. Instead, it only recognizes the = symbol. If you use the == symbol in your bash scripts, you need to change the text comparison symbol to just a single equal sign:

```
$ cat test7
#!/bin/dash
# testing the = comparison

test1=abcdef
test2=abcdef

if [ $test1 = $test2 ]
then
    echo "They're the same!"
else
    echo "They're different"
fi
$ ./test7
They're the same!
$
```

This little bashism is responsible for many hours of frustration for shell programmers!

The function Command

Chapter 17 showed you how to define your own functions in your shell scripts. The bash shell supports two methods for defining functions:

- Using the function() statement
- Using the function name only

The dash shell doesn't support the function statement. Instead, in the dash shell you must define a function using the function name with parentheses.

If you're writing shell scripts that may be used in the dash environment, always define functions using the function name and not the function() statement:

```
$ cat test10
#!/bin/dash
# testing functions

func1() {
    echo "This is an example of a function"
}

count=1
while [ $count -le 5 ]
do
    func1
    count=$(( $count + 1 ))
done
echo "This is the end of the loop"
func1
echo "This is the end of the script"
$ ./test10
This is an example of a function
This is an example of a function
This is an example of a function
This is an example of a function
This is an example of a function
This is the end of the loop
This is an example of a function
This is the end of the script
$
```

Now the dash shell recognizes the function defined in the script just fine and uses it within the script.

23

The zsh Shell

Another popular shell that you may run into is the Z shell (called zsh). The zsh shell is an open source Unix shell developed by Paul Falstad. It takes ideas from all the existing shells and adds many unique features to create a full-blown advanced shell designed for programmers.

The following are some of the features that make the zsh shell unique:

- Improved shell option handling
- Shell compatibility modes
- Loadable modules

Of all these features, a loadable module is the most advanced feature in shell design. As you've seen in the bash and dash shells, each shell contains a set of built-in commands that are available without the need for external utility programs. The benefit of built-in commands is execution speed. The shell doesn't have to load a utility program into memory before running it; the built-in commands are already in the shell memory, ready to go.

The zsh shell provides a core set of built-in commands, plus the capability to add more *command modules*. Each command module provides a set of additional built-in commands for specific circumstances, such as network support and advanced math functions. You can add only the modules you think you need for your specific situation.

This feature provides a great way to either limit the size of the zsh shell for situations that require a small shell size and few commands or expand the number of available built-in commands for situations that require faster execution speeds.

Parts of the zsh Shell

This section walks you through the basics of the zsh shell, showing the built-in commands that are available (or can be added by installing modules), as well as the command line parameters and environment variables used by the zsh shell.

Shell options

Most shells use command line parameters to define the behavior of the shell. The zsh shell uses a few command line parameters to define the operation of the shell, but mostly it uses *options* to customize the behavior of the shell. You can set shell options either on the command line or within the shell itself using the set command.

Table 23-3 lists the command line parameters available for the zsh shell.

TABLE 23-3   The zsh Shell Command Line Parameters

Parameter	Description
-c	Executes only the specified command and exits
-i	Starts as an interactive shell, providing a command line interface prompt
-s	Forces the shell to read commands from STDIN
-o	Specifies command line options

Although this may seem like a small set of command line parameters, the -o parameter is somewhat misleading. It allows you to set shell options that define features within the shell. By far, the zsh shell is the most customizable shell available. You can alter lots of features for your shell environment. The different options fit into several general categories:

- **Changing directories:** Options that control how the cd and dirs commands handle directory changes

- **Completion:** Options that control command completion features

- **Expansion and globbing:** Options that control file expansion in commands

- **History:** Options that control command history recall

- **Initialization:** Options that control how the shell handles variables and startup files when started

- **Input/output:** Options that control command handling

- **Job control:** Options that dictate how the shell handles and starts jobs

- **Prompting:** Options that define how the shell works with command line prompts

- **Scripts and functions:** Options that control how the shell processes shell scripts and defines shell functions

- **Shell emulation:** Options that allow you to set the behavior of the zsh shell to mimic the behavior of other shell types

- **Shell state:** Options that define what type of shell to start

- **zle:** Options for controlling the zsh line editor (zle) feature

- **Option aliases:** Special options that can be used as aliases for other option names

With this many different categories of shell options, you can imagine just how many actual options the zsh shell supports.

Built-in commands

The zsh shell is unique in that it allows you to expand the built-in commands available in the shell. This provides for a wealth of speedy utilities at your fingertips for a host of different applications.

23

This section describes the core built-in commands, along with the various modules available at the time of this writing.

Core built-in commands

The core of the zsh shell contains the basic built-in commands you're used to seeing in other shells. Table 23-4 describes the built-in commands available for you.

TABLE 23-4 The zsh Core Built-In Commands

Command	Description
alias	Defines an alternate name for a command and arguments
autoload	Preloads a shell function into memory for quicker access
bg	Executes a job in background mode
bindkey	Binds keyboard combinations to commands
builtin	Executes the specified built-in command instead of an executable file of the same name
bye	The same as exit
cd	Changes the current working directory
chdir	Changes the current working directory
command	Executes the specified command as an external file instead of a function or built-in command
declare	Sets the data type of a variable (same as typeset)
dirs	Displays the contents of the directory stack
disable	Temporarily disables the specified hash table elements
disown	Removes the specified job from the job table
echo	Displays variables and text
emulate	Sets zsh to emulate another shell, such as the Bourne, Korn, or C shells
enable	Enables the specified hash table elements
eval	Executes the specified command and arguments in the current shell process
exec	Executes the specified command and arguments replacing the current shell process
exit	Exits the shell with the specified exit status. If none specified, uses the exit status of the last command
export	Allows the specified environment variable names and values to be used in child shell processes
false	Returns an exit status of 1

`fc`	Selects a range of commands from the history list
`fg`	Executes the specified job in foreground mode
`float`	Sets the specified variable for use as a floating point variable
`functions`	Sets the specified name as a function
`getln`	Reads the next value in the buffer stack and places it in the specified variable
`getopts`	Retrieves the next valid option in the command line arguments and places it in the specified variable
`hash`	Directly modifies the contents of the command hash table
`history`	Lists the commands contained in the history file
`integer`	Sets the specified variable for use as an integer value
`jobs`	Lists information about the specified job or all jobs assigned to the shell process
`kill`	Sends a signal (Default `SIGTERM`) to the specified process or job
`let`	Evaluates a mathematical operation and assigns the result to a variable
`limit`	Sets or displays resource limits
`local`	Sets the data features for the specified variable
`log`	Displays all users currently logged in who are affected by the watch parameter
`logout`	Same as `exit`, but works only when the shell is a login shell
`popd`	Removes the next entry from the directory stack
`print`	Displays variables and text
`printf`	Displays variables and text using C-style format strings
`pushd`	Changes the current working directory and puts the previous directory in the directory stack
`pushln`	Places the specified arguments into the editing buffer stack
`pwd`	Displays the full pathname of the current working directory
`read`	Reads a line and assigns data fields to the specified variables using the `IFS` characters
`readonly`	Assigns a value to a variable that can't be changed
`rehash`	Rebuilds the command hash table
`set`	Sets options or positional parameters for the shell
`setopt`	Sets the options for a shell
`shift`	Reads and deletes the first positional parameter and shifts the remaining ones down one position

23

Continues

TABLE 23-4   *(continued)*

Command	Description
source	Finds the specified file and copies its contents into the current location
suspend	Suspends the execution of the shell until it receives a SIGCONT signal
test	Returns an exit status of 0 if the specified condition is TRUE
times	Displays the cumulative user and system times for the shell and processes that run in the shell
trap	Blocks the specified signals from being processed by the shell and executes the specified commands if the signals are received
true	Returns a zero exit status
ttyctl	Locks and unlocks the display
type	Displays how the specified command would be interpreted by the shell
typeset	Sets or displays attributes of variables
ulimit	Sets or displays resource limits of the shell or processes running in the shell
umask	Sets or displays the default permissions for creating files and directories
unalias	Removes the specified command alias
unfunction	Removes the specified defined function
unhash	Removes the specified command from the hash table
unlimit	Removes the specified resource limit
unset	Removes the specified variable attribute.
unsetopt	Removes the specified shell option
wait	Waits for the specified job or process to complete
whence	Displays how the specified command would be interpreted by the shell
where	Displays the pathname of the specified command if found by the shell
Which	Displays the pathname of the specified command using csh-style output
zcompile	Compiles the specified function or script for faster autoloading
zmodload	Performs operations on loadable zsh modules

The zsh shell is no slouch when it comes to providing built-in commands! You should recognize most of these commands from their bash counterparts. The most important features of the zsh shell built-in commands are modules.

Add-in modules

There's a long list of modules that provide additional built-in commands for the zsh shell, and the list continues to grow as resourceful programmers create new modules. Table 23-5 shows some of the more popular modules available.

TABLE 23-5 **The zsh Modules**

Module	Description
zsh/datetime	Additional date and time commands and variables
zsh/files	Commands for basic file handling
zsh/mapfile	Access to external files via associative arrays
zsh/mathfunc	Additional scientific functions
zsh/pcre	The extended regular expression library
zsh/net/socket	Unix domain socket support
zsh/stat	Access to the stat system call to provide system statistics
zsh/system	Interface for various low-level system features
zsh/net/tcp	Access to TCP sockets
zsh/zftp	A specialized FTP client command
zsh/zselect	Blocks and returns when file descriptors are ready
zsh/zutil	Various shell utilities

The zsh shell modules cover a wide range of topics, from providing simple command line editing features to advanced networking functions. The idea behind the zsh shell is to provide a basic minimum shell environment and let you add on the pieces you need to accomplish your programming job.

Viewing, adding, and removing modules

The zmodload command is the interface to the zsh modules. You use this command to view, add, and remove modules from the zsh shell session.

Using the zmodload command without any command line parameters displays the currently installed modules in your zsh shell:

```
% zmodload
zsh/zutil
zsh/complete
zsh/main
zsh/terminfo
zsh/zle
zsh/parameter
%
```

637

Different zsh shell implementations include different modules by default. To add a new module, just specify the module name on the `zmodload` command line:

```
% zmodload zsh/zftp
%
```

Nothing indicates that the module loaded. You can perform another `zmodload` command, and the new module should appear in the list of installed modules.

After you load a module, the commands associated with the module are available as built-in commands:

```
% zftp open myhost.com rich testing1
Welcome to the myhost FTP server.
% zftp cd test
% zftp dir
01-21-11 11:21PM      120823 test1
01-21-11 11:23PM      118432 test2
% zftp get test1 > test1.txt
% zftp close
%
```

The `zftp` command allows you to conduct a complete FTP session directly from your zsh shell command line! You can incorporate these commands into your zsh shell scripts to perform file transfers directly from your scripts.

To remove an installed module, use the `-u` parameter, along with the module name:

```
% zmodload -u zsh/zftp
% zftp
zsh: command not found: zftp
%
```

> **NOTE**
> It's a common practice to place `zmodload` commands in the `$HOME/.zshrc` startup file so your favorite functions load automatically when the zsh shell starts.

Scripting with zsh

The main purpose of the zsh shell was to provide an advanced programming environment for shell programmers. With that in mind, it's no surprise that the zsh shell offers many features that make shell scripting easier.

Mathematical operations

As you would expect, the zsh shell allows you to perform mathematical functions with ease. In the past, the Korn shell has led the way in supporting mathematical operations by providing support for floating-point numbers. The zsh shell has full support for floating-point numbers in all its mathematical operations!

Performing calculations

The zsh shell supports two methods for performing mathematical operations:

- The `let` command
- Double parentheses

When you use the `let` command, you should enclose the operation in double quotation marks to allow for spaces:

```
% let value1=" 4 * 5.1 / 3.2 "
% echo $value1
6.3750000000
%
```

Be careful, using floating point numbers may introduce a precision problem. To solve this, it's always a good idea to use the `printf` command and to specify the decimal precision needed to correctly display the answer:

```
% printf "%6.3f\n" $value1
6.375
%
```

Now that's much better!

The second method is to use the double parentheses. This method incorporates two techniques for defining the mathematical operation:

```
% value1=$(( 4 * 5.1 ))
% (( value2 = 4 * 5.1 ))
% printf "%6.3f\n" $value1 $value2
20.400
20.400
%
```

Notice that you can place the double parentheses either around just the operation (preceded by a dollar sign) or around the entire assignment statement. Both methods produce the same results.

If you don't use the `typeset` command to declare the data type of a variable beforehand, the zsh shell attempts to automatically assign the data type. This can be dangerous when working with both integer and floating-point numbers. Look at this example:

```
% value1=10
% value2=$(( $value1 / 3 ))
% echo $value2
3
%
```

Now, that's probably not the answer you want to come out from the calculation. When you specify numbers without decimal places, the zsh shell interprets them as integer values and performs integer calculations. To ensure that the result is a floating-point number, you must specify the numbers with decimal places:

```
% value1=10.
% value2=$(( $value1 / 3. ))
% echo $value2
3.3333333333333335
%
```

Now the result is in the floating-point format.

Mathematical functions

With the zsh shell, built-in mathematical functions are either feast or famine. The default zsh shell doesn't include any special mathematical function. However, if you install the zsh/mathfunc module, you have more math functions than you'll most likely ever need:

```
% value1=$(( sqrt(9) ))
zsh: unknown function: sqrt
% zmodload zsh/mathfunc
% value1=$(( sqrt(9) ))
% echo $value1
3.
%
```

That was simple! Now you have an entire math library of functions at your fingertips.

> **NOTE**
>
> Lots of mathematical functions are supported in zsh. For a complete listing of all the math functions that the zsh/mathfunc module provides, look at the manual page for zsh modules.

Structured commands

The zsh shell provides the usual set of structured commands for your shell scripts:

- if-then-else statements
- for loops (including the C-style)
- while loops

- until loops
- select statements
- case statements

The zsh shell uses the same syntax for each of these structured commands that you're used to from the bash shell. The zsh shell also includes a different structured command called repeat. The repeat command uses this format:

```
repeat param
do
    commands
done
```

The param parameter must be a number or a mathematical operation that evaluates to a number. The repeat command then performs the specified commands that number of times:

```
% cat test1
#!/bin/zsh
# using the repeat command

value1=$(( 10 / 2 ))
repeat $value1
do
    echo "This is a test"
done
$ ./test1
This is a test
This is a test
This is a test
This is a test
This is a test
%
```

This command allows you to repeat sections of code for a set number of times based on a calculation.

Functions

The zsh shell supports the creation of your own functions either using the function command or by defining the function name with parentheses:

```
% function functest1 {
> echo "This is the test1 function"
}
% functest2() {
> echo "This is the test2 function"
}
```

```
% functest1
This is the test1 function
% functest2
This is the test2 function
%
```

As with bash shell functions (see Chapter 17), you can define functions within your shell script and then either use global variables or pass parameters to your functions.

Summary

This chapter discussed two popular alternative Linux shells that you may run into. The dash shell was developed as part of the Debian Linux distribution and is mainly found in the Ubuntu Linux distribution. It's a smaller version of the Bourne shell, so it doesn't support as many features as the bash shell, which can cause problems for script writing.

The zsh shell is often found in programming environments, because it provides lots of cool features for shell script programmers. It uses loadable modules to load separate code libraries, which make using advanced functions as easy as running command line commands! There are loadable modules for lots of different functions, from complex mathematical algorithms to network applications such as FTP and HTTP.

The next section of this book dives into some specific scripting applications you might run into in the Linux environment. The next chapter shows how to write simple utilities to help with your day-to-day Linux administration functions. Those can greatly help simplify common tasks you perform on the system.

Part IV

Creating Practical Scripts

Writing Simple Script Utilities

N owhere is shell script programming more useful than writing script utilities for the Linux system administrator. The typical Linux system administrator has many various jobs to do daily, from monitoring disk space to backing up important files to managing user accounts. Shell script utilities can make these tasks much easier! This chapter demonstrates some of the capabilities you have writing script utilities in the bash shell.

Performing Archives

Whether you're responsible for a Linux system in a business environment or just using it at home, the loss of data can be catastrophic. To help prevent bad things from happening, it's always a good idea to perform regular backups (or archives).

However, what's a good idea and what's practical are often two separate things. Trying to arrange a backup schedule to store important files can be a challenge. This is another place where shell scripts often come to the rescue.

This section demonstrates two methods for using shell scripts to archive data on your Linux system.

Archiving data files

If you're using your Linux system to work on an important project, you can create a shell script that automatically takes snapshots of specific directories. Designating these directories in a configuration file allows you to change them when a particular project changes. This helps avoid a time-consuming restore process from your main archive files.

This section shows you how to create an automated shell script that can take snapshots of specified directories and keep an archive of your data's past versions.

Obtaining the required functions

The workhorse for archiving data in the Linux world is the `tar` command (see Chapter 4). The `tar` command is used to archive entire directories into a single file. Here's an example of creating an archive file of a working directory using the `tar` command:

```
$ tar -cf archive.tar /home/Christine/Project/*.*
tar: Removing leading '/' from member names
$
$ ls -l archive.tar
-rw-rw-r--. 1 Christine Christine 51200 Aug 27 10:51 archive.tar
$
```

The `tar` command responds with a warning message that it's removing the leading forward slash from the pathname to convert it from an absolute pathname to a relative pathname (see Chapter 3). This allows you to extract the `tar` archived files anywhere you want in your filesystem. You'll probably want to get rid of that message in your script. You can accomplish this by redirecting STDERR to the `/dev/null` file (see Chapter 15):

```
$ tar -cf archive.tar /home/Christine/Project/*.* 2>/dev/null
$
$ ls -l archive.tar
-rw-rw-r--. 1 Christine Christine 51200 Aug 27 10:53 archive.tar
$
```

Because a `tar` archive file can consume lots of disk space, it's a good idea to compress the file. You can do this by simply adding the `-z` option. This compresses the tar archive file into a gzipped `tar` file, which is called a *tarball*. Be sure to use the proper file extensions to denote that the file is a tarball. Either `.tar.gz` or `.tgz` is fine. Here's an example of creating a tarball of the project directory:

```
$ tar -zcf archive.tar.gz /home/Christine/Project/*.* 2>/dev/null
$
$ ls -l archive.tar.gz
-rw-rw-r--. 1 Christine Christine 3331 Aug 27 10:53 archive.tar.gz
$
```

Now you have the main component for your archive script completed.

Instead of modifying or creating a new archive script for each new directory or file you want to back up, you can use a configuration file. The configuration file should contain each directory or file you want to be included in the archive.

```
$ cat Files_To_Backup
/home/Christine/Project
/home/Christine/Downloads
/home/Does_not_exist
/home/Christine/Documents
$
```

> **NOTE**
> If you're using a Linux distribution that includes a graphical desktop, be careful about archiving your entire $HOME directory. Although this may be tempting, the $HOME directory contains lots of configuration and temporary files related to the graphical desktop. It creates a much larger archive file than you probably intended. Pick a subdirectory in which to store your working files, and use that subdirectory in your archive configuration file.

You can have the script read through the configuration file and add the names of each directory to the archive list. To do this, use the simple read command (see Chapter 14) to read each record from the file. But instead of using the cat command piped into a while loop (see Chapter 13), this script redirects standard input (STDIN) using the exec command (see Chapter 15). Here's how it looks:

```
exec < $CONFIG_FILE

read FILE_NAME
```

Notice that a variable is used for the archive configuration file, CONFIG_FILE. Each record is read in from the configuration file. As long as the read command finds a new configuration file record to read, it returns an exit value of 0 for success in the ? variable (see Chapter 11). You can use this as a test in a while loop in order to read all the records from the configuration file:

```
while [ $? -eq 0 ]
do
[...]
read FILE_NAME
done
```

When the read command hits the end of the configuration file, it returns a non-zero status. At that point, the while loop is exited.

In the while loop, two things need to happen. First, you must add the directory name to your archive list. Even more important is to check to see if that directory even exists! It would be very easy to remove a directory from the filesystem and forget to update the archive configuration file. You can check a directory's existence using a simple if statement (see Chapter 12). If the directory does exist, it is added to the list of directories to archive, FILE_LIST. Otherwise, a warning message is issued. Here is what this if statement looks like:

```
if [ -f $FILE_NAME -o -d $FILE_NAME ]
    then
            # If file exists, add its name to the list.
            FILE_LIST="$FILE_LIST $FILE_NAME"
    else
            # If file doesn't exist, issue warning
```

```
                    echo
                    echo "$FILE_NAME, does not exist."
                    echo "Obviously, I will not include it in this archive."
                    echo "It is listed on line $FILE_NO of the config file."
                    echo "Continuing to build archive list..."
                    echo
             fi
    #

             FILE_NO=$[$FILE_NO + 1]              # Increase Line/File number by one.
```

Because a record in our archive configuration file can be a filename or a directory, the if statement tests for the existence of both, using the -f and the -d options. The or option, -o, allows for either the file's or the directory's existence test to return a non-zero status for the entire if statement to be treated as true.

To provide a little extra help in tracking down non-existent directories and files, the variable FILE_NO is added. Thus, the script can tell you exactly what line number in the archive configuration file contains the incorrect or missing file or directory.

Creating a daily archive location

If you are just backing up a few files, it's fine to keep the archive in your personal directory. However, if several directories are being backed up, it is best to create a central repository archive directory:

```
$ sudo mkdir /archive
[sudo] password for Christine:
$
$ ls -ld /archive
drwxr-xr-x. 2 root root 4096 Aug 27 14:10 /archive
$
```

After you have your central repository archive directory created, you need to grant access to it for certain users. If you do not do this, trying to create files in this directory fails, as shown here:

```
$ mv Files_To_Backup /archive/
mv: cannot move 'Files_To_Backup' to
'/archive/Files_To_Backup': Permission denied
$
```

You could grant the users needing to create files in this directory permission via sudo or create a user group. In this case, a special user group is created, Archivers:

```
$ sudo groupadd Archivers
$
$ sudo chgrp Archivers /archive
$
$ ls -ld /archive
```

```
drwxr-xr-x. 2 root Archivers 4096 Aug 27 14:10 /archive
$
$ sudo usermod -aG Archivers Christine
[sudo] password for Christine:
$
$ sudo chmod 775 /archive
$
$ ls -ld /archive
drwxrwxr-x. 2 root Archivers 4096 Aug 27 14:10 /archive
$
```

After a user has been added to the Archivers group, the user must log out and log back in for the group membership to take effect. Now files can be created by this group's members without the use of super-user privileges:

```
$ mv Files_To_Backup /archive/
$
$ ls /archive
Files_To_Backup
$
```

Keep in mind that all Archivers group members can add and delete files from this directory. It may be best to add the sticky bit (see Chapter 7) to the directory, in order to keep group members from deleting each other's archive tarballs.

You should now have enough information to start building the script. The next section walks you through creating the daily archive script.

Creating a daily archive script

The Daily_Archive.sh script automatically creates an archive to a designated location, using the current date to uniquely identify the file. Here's the code for that portion of the script:

```
DATE=$(date +%y%m%d)
#
# Set Archive File Name
#
FILE=archive$DATE.tar.gz
#
# Set Configuration and Destination File
#
CONFIG_FILE=/archive/Files_To_Backup
DESTINATION=/archive/$FILE
#
```

The DESTINATION variable appends the full pathname for the archived file. The CONFIG_ FILE variable points to the archive configuration file containing the directories to be archived. These both can be easily changed to alternate directories and files if needed.

The `Daily_Archive.sh` script, all put together, now looks like this:

```
#!/bin/bash
#
# Daily_Archive - Archive designated files & directories
##########################################################
#
# Gather Current Date
#
DATE=$(date +%y%m%d)
#
# Set Archive File Name
#
FILE=archive$DATE.tar.gz
#
# Set Configuration and Destination File
#
CONFIG_FILE=/archive/Files_To_Backup
DESTINATION=/archive/$FILE
#
######### Main Script #########################
#
# Check Backup Config file exists
#
if [ -f $CONFIG_FILE ]    # Make sure the config file still exists.
then                # If it exists, do nothing but continue on.
    echo
else               # If it doesn't exist, issue error & exit script.
    echo
    echo "$CONFIG_FILE does not exist."
    echo "Backup not completed due to missing Configuration File"
    echo
    exit
fi
#
# Build the names of all the files to backup
#
FILE_NO=1              # Start on Line 1 of Config File.
exec < $CONFIG_FILE    # Redirect Std Input to name of Config File
#
```

```
read FILE_NAME              # Read 1st record
#
while [ $? -eq 0 ]          # Create list of files to backup.
do
        # Make sure the file or directory exists.
    if [ -f $FILE_NAME -o -d $FILE_NAME ]
    then
            # If file exists, add its name to the list.
            FILE_LIST="$FILE_LIST $FILE_NAME"
    else
            # If file doesn't exist, issue warning
            echo
            echo "$FILE_NAME, does not exist."
            echo "Obviously, I will not include it in this archive."
            echo "It is listed on line $FILE_NO of the config file."
            echo "Continuing to build archive list..."
            echo
    fi
#
    FILE_NO=$[$FILE_NO + 1]  # Increase Line/File number by one.
    read FILE_NAME           # Read next record.
done
#
######################################
#
# Backup the files and Compress Archive
#
echo "Starting archive..."
echo
#
tar -czf $DESTINATION $FILE_LIST 2> /dev/null
#
echo "Archive completed"
echo "Resulting archive file is: $DESTINATION"
echo
#
exit
```

Running the daily archive script

Before you attempt to test the script, remember that you need to change permissions on the script file (see Chapter 11). The file's owner must be given execute (x) privilege before the script can be run:

```
$ ls -l Daily_Archive.sh
-rw-rw-r--. 1 Christine Christine 1994 Aug 28 15:58 Daily_Archive.sh
$
$ chmod u+x Daily_Archive.sh
$
```

```
$ ls -l Daily_Archive.sh
-rwxrw-r--. 1 Christine Christine 1994 Aug 28 15:58 Daily_Archive.sh
$
```

Testing the `Daily_Archive.sh` script is straightforward:

```
$ ./Daily_Archive.sh


/home/Does_not_exist, does not exist.
Obviously, I will not include it in this archive.
It is listed on line 3 of the config file.
Continuing to build archive list...

Starting archive...

Archive completed
Resulting archive file is: /archive/archive140828.tar.gz

$ ls /archive
archive140828.tar.gz   Files_To_Backup
$
```

You can see that the script caught one directory that does not exist, /home/Does_not_
exist. It lets you know what line number in the configuration file this erroneous directory
is on and continues making a list and archiving the data. Your data is now safely archived
in a tarball file.

Creating an hourly archive script

If you are in a high-volume production environment where files are changing rapidly, a
daily archive might not be good enough. If you want to increase the archiving frequency to
hourly, you need to take another item into consideration.

When backing up files hourly and trying to use the date command to timestamp each
tarball, things can get pretty ugly pretty quickly. Sifting through a directory of tarballs
with filenames looking like this is tedious:

```
archive010211110233.tar.gz
```

Instead of placing all the archive files in the same folder, you can create a directory hierarchy for your archived files. Figure 24-1 demonstrates this principle.

FIGURE 24-1

Creating an archive directory hierarchy

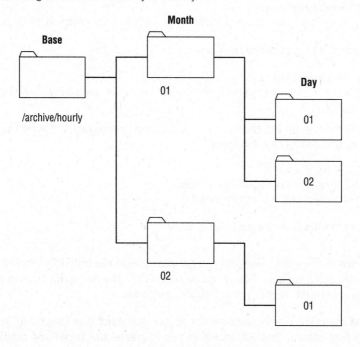

The archive directory contains directories for each month of the year, using the month number as the directory name. Each month's directory in turn contains folders for each day of the month (using the day's numerical value as the directory name). This allows you to just timestamp the individual tarballs and place them in the appropriate directory for the day and month.

First, the new directory /archive/hourly must be created, along with the appropriate permissions set upon it. Remember from early in this chapter that members of the Archivers group are granted permission to create archives in this directory area. Thus, the newly created directory must have its primary group and group permissions changed:

```
$ sudo mkdir /archive/hourly
[sudo] password for Christine:
$
```

```
$ sudo chgrp Archivers /archive/hourly
$
$ ls -ld /archive/hourly/
drwxr-xr-x. 2 root Archivers 4096 Sep  2 09:24 /archive/hourly/
$
$ sudo chmod 775 /archive/hourly
$
$ ls -ld /archive/hourly
drwxrwxr-x. 2 root Archivers 4096 Sep  2 09:24 /archive/hourly
$
```

After the new directory is set up, the Files_To_Backup configuration file for the hourly archives can be moved to the new directory:

```
$ cat Files_To_Backup
/usr/local/Production/Machine_Errors
/home/Development/Simulation_Logs
$
$ mv Files_To_Backup /archive/hourly/
$
```

Now, there is a new challenge to solve. The script must create the individual month and day directories automatically. If these directories already exist, and the script tries to create them, an error is generated. This is not a desirable outcome!

If you peruse the command line options for the mkdir command (see Chapter 3), you'll find the -p command line option. This option allows you to create directories and subdirectories in a single command; plus, the added benefit is that it doesn't produce an error message if the directory already exists. Perfect fit for what is needed in the script!

We're now ready to create the Hourly_Archive.sh script. Here is the top half of the script:

```
#!/bin/bash
#
# Hourly_Archive - Every hour create an archive
######################################################
#
# Set Configuration File
#
CONFIG_FILE=/archive/hourly/Files_To_Backup
#
# Set Base Archive Destination Location
#
BASEDEST=/archive/hourly
#
# Gather Current Day, Month & Time
#
```

```
DAY=$(date +%d)
MONTH=$(date +%m)
TIME=$(date +%k%M)
#
# Create Archive Destination Directory
#
mkdir -p $BASEDEST/$MONTH/$DAY
#
# Build Archive Destination File Name
#
DESTINATION=$BASEDEST/$MONTH/$DAY/archive$TIME.tar.gz
#
######### Main Script ###################
[...]
```

After the script reaches the "Main Script" portion of Hourly_Archive.sh, the script is an exact duplicate of the Daily_Archive.sh script. Lots of the work has already been done!

Hourly_Archive.sh retrieves the day and month values from the date command, along with the timestamp used to uniquely identify the archive file. It then uses that information to create the archive directory for the day (or to silently exit if it already exists). Finally, the script uses the tar command to create the archive and compress it into a tarball.

Running the hourly archive script

As with the Daily_Archive.sh script, it's a good idea to test the Hourly_Archive.sh script before putting it in the cron table. Before the script is run, the permissions must be modified. Also, the hour and minute is checked via the date command. Having the current hour and minute allows the final archive filename to be verified for correctness:

```
$ chmod u+x Hourly_Archive.sh
$
$ date +%k%M
1011
$
$ ./Hourly_Archive.sh

Starting archive...

Archive completed
Resulting archive file is: /archive/hourly/09/02/archive1011.tar.gz

$
$ ls /archive/hourly/09/02/
archive1011.tar.gz
$
```

The script worked fine the first time, creating the appropriate month and day directories, and then creating the properly named archive file. Notice that the archive file has the appropriate hour (10) and minute (11) in its name, `archive1011.tar.gz`.

> **NOTE**
>
> If you run the `Hourly_Archive.sh` script during the day, when the hour is in single digits, your archive
> file's name will only have three digits. For example, if you run the script at 1:15am, the archive file's name is
> `archive115.tar.gz`. If you prefer to always have four digits in the archive file name, modify the script line,
> `TIME=$(date +%k%M)`, to `TIME=$(date +%k0%M)`. By adding a zero (0) after the `%k`, any single digit hours
> are padded to two digits with a leading zero. Thus, `archive115.tar.gz` is instead named `archive0115`
> `.tar.gz`.

Just to test things out, the script was run a second time to see if it would have a problem with the existing directory, `/archive,hourly/09/02`:

```
$ date +%k%M
1017
$
$ ./Hourly_Archive.sh

Starting archive...

Archive completed
Resulting archive file is: /archive/hourly/09/02/archive1017.tar.gz

$ ls /archive/hourly/09/02/
archive1011.tar.gz  archive1017.tar.gz
$
```

No problems with the existing directory! The script again ran fine and created a second archive file. It's now ready for the `cron` table.

Managing User Accounts

Managing user accounts is much more than just adding, modifying, and deleting accounts. You must also consider security issues, the need to preserve work, and the accurate management of the accounts. This can be a time-consuming task. Here is another instance when writing script utilities is a real timesaver!

Obtaining the required functions

Deleting an account is the more complicated accounts management task. When deleting an account, at least four separate actions are required:

1. Obtain the correct user account name to delete.
2. Kill any processes currently running on the system that belongs to that account.
3. Determine all files on the system belonging to the account.
4. Remove the user account.

It's easy to miss a step. The shell script utility in this section helps you avoid making such mistakes.

Getting the correct account name

The first step in the account deletion process is the most important: obtaining the correct user account name to delete. Because this is an interactive script, you can use the read command (see Chapter 14) to obtain the account name. If the script user walks away and leaves the question hanging, you can use the -t option on the read command and timeout after giving the script user 60 seconds to answer the question:

```
echo "Please enter the username of the user "
echo -e "account you wish to delete from system: \c"
read -t 60 ANSWER
```

Because interruptions are part of life, it's best to give users three chances to answer the question. This is accomplished by using a while loop (Chapter 13) with the -z option, to test whether the ANSWER variable is empty. The ANSWER variable is empty when the script first enters the while loop on purpose. The question to fill the ANSWER variable is at the end of the loop:

```
while [ -z "$ANSWER" ]
do
[...]
echo "Please enter the username of the user "
echo -e "account you wish to delete from system: \c"
read -t 60 ANSWER
done
```

A way to communicate with the script user is needed when the first question timeout occurs, when there is one more chance to answer the question, and so on. The case statement (see Chapter 12) is the structured command that works perfectly here. Using the incremented `ASK_COUNT` variable, different messages can be set up to communicate to the script user. The code for this section looks like this:

```
case $ASK_COUNT in
2)
      echo
      echo "Please answer the question."
      echo
;;
3)
      echo
      echo "One last try...please answer the question."
      echo
;;
4)
      echo
      echo "Since you refuse to answer the question..."
      echo "exiting program."
      echo
      #
      exit
;;
esac
#
```

Now the script has all the structure it needs to ask the user what account to delete. There are several more questions in this script to ask the user and asking just that one question was lots of code! Therefore, let's turn this piece of code into a function (see Chapter 17) in order to use it in multiple locations in your `Delete_User.sh` script.

Creating a function to get the correct account name

The first thing you need to do is declare the function's name, `get_answer`. Next, clear out any previous answers to questions your script user gave using the `unset` command (see Chapter 6). The code to do these two items looks like this:

```
function get_answer {
#
unset ANSWER
```

The other original code item you need to change is the question to the script user. The script doesn't ask the same question each time, so two new variables are created, `LINE1` and `LINE2`, to handle question lines:

```
echo $LINE1
echo -e $LINE2" \c"
```

However, not every question has two lines to display. Some have only one line. An if statement (see Chapter 12) assists with this problem. The function tests if LINE2 is empty and only uses LINE1 if it is:

```
if [ -n "$LINE2" ]
then
      echo $LINE1
      echo -e $LINE2" \c"
else
      echo -e $LINE1" \c"
fi
```

Finally, the function needs to clean up after itself by clearing out the LINE1 and LINE2 variables. Thus, the function now looks like this:

```
function get_answer {
#
unset ANSWER
ASK_COUNT=0
#
while [ -z "$ANSWER" ]
do
      ASK_COUNT=$[ $ASK_COUNT + 1 ]
#
      case $ASK_COUNT in
      2)
            echo
[...]
      esac
#
      echo
      if [ -n "$LINE2" ]
      then                    #Print 2 lines
            echo $LINE1
            echo -e $LINE2" \c"
      else                    #Print 1 line
            echo -e $LINE1" \c"
      fi
#
      read -t 60 ANSWER
done
#
unset LINE1
unset LINE2
#
}  #End of get_answer function
```

To ask the script user what account to delete, a few variables must be set and the get_ answer function should be called. Using the new function makes the script code much simpler:

```
LINE1="Please enter the username of the user "
LINE2="account you wish to delete from system:"
get_answer
USER_ACCOUNT=$ANSWER
```

Verifying the entered account name

Because of potential typographical errors, the user account name that was entered should be verified. This is easy because the code is already in place to handle asking a question:

```
LINE1="Is $USER_ACCOUNT the user account "
LINE2="you wish to delete from the system? [y/n]"
get_answer
```

After the question is asked, the script must process the answer. The variable ANSWER again carries the script user's answer to the question. If the user answered "yes," the correct user account to delete has been entered and the script can continue. A case statement (see Chapter 12) processes the answer. The case statement must be coded so it checks for the multiple ways the answer "yes" can be entered.

```
case $ANSWER in
y|Y|YES|yes|Yes|yEs|yeS|YEs|yES )
#

;;
*)
        echo
        echo "Because the account, $USER_ACCOUNT, is not "
        echo "the one you wish to delete, we are leaving the script..."
        echo
        exit

;;
esac
```

Sometimes, this script needs to handle a yes/no answer from the user. Thus, again, it makes sense to create a function to handle this task. Only a few changes need to be made to the preceding code. The function's name must be declared and the variables EXIT_ LINE1 and EXIT_LINE2 added to the case statement. These changes, along with some variable cleanup at the end, result in the process_answer function:

```
function process_answer {
#
case $ANSWER in
y|Y|YES|yes|Yes|yEs|yeS|YEs|yES )
;;
*)
```

```
                echo
                echo $EXIT_LINE1
                echo $EXIT_LINE2
                echo
                exit
    ;;
    esac
    #
    unset EXIT_LINE1
    unset EXIT_LINE2
    #
} #End of process_answer function
```

A simple function call now processes the answer:

```
EXIT_LINE1="Because the account, $USER_ACCOUNT, is not "
EXIT_LINE2="the one you wish to delete, we are leaving the script..."
process_answer
```

Determining whether the account exists

The user has given us the name of the account to delete and has verified it. Now is a good time to double-check that the user account really exists on the system. Also, it is a good idea to show the full account record to the script user to check one more time that this is the account to delete. To accomplish these items, a variable, USER_ACCOUNT_RECORD, is set to the outcome of a grep (see Chapter 4) search for the account through the /etc/passwd file. The -w option allows an exact word match for this particular user account:

```
USER_ACCOUNT_RECORD=$(cat /etc/passwd | grep -w $USER_ACCOUNT)
```

If no user account record is found in /etc/passwd, the account has already been deleted or never existed in the first place. In either case, the script user must be notified of this situation and the script exited. The exit status of the grep command helps here. If the account record is not found, the ? variable is set to 1:

```
if [ $? -eq 1 ]
then
        echo
        echo "Account, $USER_ACCOUNT, not found. "
        echo "Leaving the script..."
        echo
        exit
fi
```

If the record was found, you still need to verify with the script user that this is the correct account. Here is where all the work to set up the functions really pays off! You just need to set the proper variables and call the functions:

```
echo "I found this record:"
echo $USER_ACCOUNT_RECORD
```

```
echo
#
LINE1="Is this the correct User Account? [y/n]"
get_answer
#
EXIT_LINE1="Because the account, $USER_ACCOUNT, is not"
EXIT_LINE2="the one you wish to delete, we are leaving the script..."
process_answer
```

Removing any account processes

So far, the script has obtained and verified the correct name of the user account to be deleted. In order to remove the user account from the system, the account cannot own any processes currently running. Thus, the next step is to find and kill off those processes. This is going to get a little complicated!

Finding the user processes is the easy part. Here the script can use the ps command (see Chapter 4) and the -u option to locate any running processes owned by the account. By redirecting the output to /dev/null, the user doesn't see any display. This is handy, because if there are no processes, the ps command only shows a header, which can be confusing to the script user:

```
ps -u $USER_ACCOUNT >/dev/null #Are user processes running?
```

The ps command's exit status and a case structure are used to determine the next step to take:

```
case $? in
1)    # No processes running for this User Account
      #
      echo "There are no processes for this account currently running."
      echo
;;
0)    # Processes running for this User Account.
      # Ask Script User if wants us to kill the processes.
      #
      echo "$USER_ACCOUNT has the following processes running: "
      echo
      ps -u $USER_ACCOUNT
      #
      LINE1="Would you like me to kill the process(es)? [y/n]"
      get_answer
      #
[...]
esac
```

If the ps command's exit status returns a 1, there are no processes running on the system that belong to the user account. However, if the exit status returns a 0, processes owned by this account are running on the system. In this case, the script needs to ask the script user if he would like to have these processes killed. This task can be accomplished by using the get_answer function.

You might think that the next action the script does is to call the process_answer function. Unfortunately, the next item is too complicated for process_answer. Another case statement must be embedded to process the script user's answer. The first part of the case statement looks very similar to the process_answer function:

```
case $ANSWER in
    y|Y|YES|yes|Yes|yEs|yeS|YEs|yES ) # If user answers "yes",
                                        #kill User Account processes.
[...]
;;
*)  # If user answers anything but "yes", do not kill.
    echo
    echo "Will not kill the process(es)"
    echo
;;
esac
```

As you can see, there is nothing interesting in the case statement itself. Where things get interesting is within the "yes" section of the case statement. Here, the user account processes need to be killed. To build the command necessary to kill off one or more processes, three commands are needed. The first command is the ps command again. It is needed to gather up the process IDs (PIDs) of the currently running user account processes. The necessary ps command is assigned to the variable, COMMAND_1:

```
COMMAND_1="ps -u $USER_ACCOUNT --no-heading"
```

The second command strips off just the PIDs. This simple gawk command (see Chapter 19) strips off the first field from the ps command's output, which happens to be the PIDs:

```
gawk '{print $1}'
```

The third command, xargs, has not yet been introduced in this book. The xargs command builds and executes commands from standard input, STDIN (see Chapter 15). It is a great command to use at the end of a pipe, building and executing commands from each STDIN item produced. The xargs command is actually killing off each process via its PID:

```
COMMAND_3="xargs -d \\n /usr/bin/sudo /bin/kill -9"
```

The xargs command is assigned to variable COMMAND_3. It uses the -d option to denote what is considered a delimiter. In other words, because the xargs command can accept multiple items as input, what separates one item from another item? In this case, \n (newline) is used to set the delimiter. Thus, when each PID is sent to xargs, it treats the PID as a separate item to be processed. Because the xargs command is being assigned to a variable, the backslash (\) in the \n must be escaped with an additional backslash (\).

24

Notice that xargs needs the full pathname of the commands it is using on each PID. Both the sudo and kill (see Chapter 4) commands are used to kill any of the user account's running processes. Notice also that the kill signal -9 is used.

All three commands are hooked together via a pipe. The ps command produces a list of the user's running processes, which include the PID of each process. The ps command passes its standard output (STDOUT) as STDIN to the gawk command. The gawk command, in turn, strips off only the PIDs from the ps command's STDOUT (see Chapter 15). The xargs command takes each PID the gawk command produces as STDIN. It creates and executes a kill command for each PID to kill all the user's running processes. The command pipe looks like this:

```
$COMMAND_1 | gawk '{print $1}' | $COMMAND_3
```

Thus, the complete case statement for killing off any of the user account's running processes is as follows:

```
case $ANSWER in
    y|Y|YES|yes|Yes|yEs|yeS|YES|yES ) # If user answers "yes",
                                      #kill User Account processes.
        echo
        echo "Killing off process(es)..."
        #
        # List user processes running code in variable, COMMAND_1
        COMMAND_1="ps -u $USER_ACCOUNT --no-heading"
        #
        # Create command to kill proccess in variable, COMMAND_3
        COMMAND_3="xargs -d \\n /usr/bin/sudo /bin/kill -9"
        #
        # Kill processes via piping commands together
        $COMMAND_1 | gawk '{print $1}' | $COMMAND_3
        #
        echo
        echo "Process(es) killed."
        ;;
```

By far, this is the most complicated piece of the script! However, now with any user account–owned processes killed, the script can move on to the next step: finding all the user account's files.

Finding account files

When a user account is deleted from the system, it is a good practice to archive all the files that belonged to that account. Along with that practice, it is also important to remove the files or assign their ownership to another account. If the account you delete has a User ID of 1003, and you don't remove or reassign those files, then the next account that is created with a User ID of 1003 owns those files! You can see the security disasters that can occur in this scenario.

The Delete_User.sh script doesn't do all that for you, but it creates a report that can be used in the Daily_Archive.sh script as an archive configuration file. And you can use the report to help you remove or reassign the files.

To find the user's files, you can use the find command. In this case, the find command searches the entire filesystem with the -u option, which pinpoints any user account–owned files. The command looks like the following:

```
find / -user $USER_ACCOUNT > $REPORT_FILE
```

That was pretty simple compared to dealing with the user account processes! It gets even easier in the next step of the Delete_User.sh script: actually removing the user account.

Removing the account

It's always a good idea to be a little paranoid about removing a user account from the system. Therefore, you should ask one more time if the script user really wants to remove the account.

```
LINE1="Remove $User_Account's account from system? [y/n]"
get_answer
#
EXIT_LINE1="Since you do not wish to remove the user account,"
EXIT_LINE2="$USER_ACCOUNT at this time, exiting the script..."
process_answer
```

Finally, we get to the main purpose of our script, actually removing the user account from the system. Here the userdel command (see Chapter 7) is used:

```
userdel $USER_ACCOUNT
```

Now that we have all the pieces, we are ready to put them together into a whole, useful script utility.

Creating the script

Recall that the Delete_User.sh script is highly interactive with the script's user. Therefore, it is important to include lots of verbiage to keep the script user informed about what is going on during the script's execution.

At the top of the script, the two functions get_answer and process_answer are declared. The script then goes to the four steps of removing the user: obtaining and confirming the user account name, finding and killing the user's processes, creating a report of all files owned by the user account, and actually removing the user account.

Here's the entire `Delete_User.sh` script:

```
#!/bin/bash
#
#Delete_User - Automates the 4 steps to remove an account
#
################################################################
# Define Functions
#
#####################################################
function get_answer {
#
unset ANSWER
ASK_COUNT=0
#
while [ -z "$ANSWER" ]    #While no answer is given, keep asking.
do
     ASK_COUNT=$[ $ASK_COUNT + 1 ]
#
     case $ASK_COUNT in    #If user gives no answer in time allotted
     2)
          echo
          echo "Please answer the question."
          echo
     ;;
     3)
          echo
          echo "One last try...please answer the question."
          echo
     ;;
     4)
          echo
          echo "Since you refuse to answer the question..."
          echo "exiting program."
          echo
          #
          exit
     ;;
     esac
#
```

```
        echo
#
    if [ -n "$LINE2" ]
    then                    #Print 2 lines
        echo $LINE1
        echo -e $LINE2" \c"
    else                     #Print 1 line
        echo -e $LINE1" \c"
    fi
#
#    Allow 60 seconds to answer before time-out
    read -t 60 ANSWER
done
# Do a little variable clean-up
unset LINE1
unset LINE2
#
}   #End of get_answer function
#
####################################################
function process_answer {
#
case $ANSWER in
y|Y|YES|yes|Yes|yEs|yeS|YEs|yES )
# If user answers "yes", do nothing.
;;
*)
# If user answers anything but "yes", exit script
        echo
        echo $EXIT_LINE1
        echo $EXIT_LINE2
        echo
        exit
;;
esac
#
# Do a little variable clean-up
#
unset EXIT_LINE1
unset EXIT_LINE2
#
} #End of process_answer function
#
##############################################
# End of Function Definitions
#
############# Main Script ###################
# Get name of User Account to check
#
```

```
echo "Step #1 - Determine User Account name to Delete "
echo
LINE1="Please enter the username of the user "
LINE2="account you wish to delete from system:"
get_answer
USER_ACCOUNT=$ANSWER
#
# Double check with script user that this is the correct User Account
#
LINE1="Is $USER_ACCOUNT the user account "
LINE2="you wish to delete from the system? [y/n]"
get_answer
#
# Call process_answer funtion:
#     if user answers anything but "yes", exit script
#
EXIT_LINE1="Because the account, $USER_ACCOUNT, is not "
EXIT_LINE2="the one you wish to delete, we are leaving the script..."
process_answer
#
################################################################
# Check that USER_ACCOUNT is really an account on the system
#
USER_ACCOUNT_RECORD=$(cat /etc/passwd | grep -w $USER_ACCOUNT)
#
if [ $? -eq 1 ]  # If the account is not found, exit script
then
      echo
      echo "Account, $USER_ACCOUNT, not found. "
      echo "Leaving the script..."
      echo
      exit
fi
#
echo
echo "I found this record:"
echo $USER_ACCOUNT_RECORD
#
LINE1="Is this the correct User Account? [y/n]"
get_answer
#
#
# Call process_answer function:
#   if user answers anything but "yes", exit script
#
EXIT_LINE1="Because the account, $USER_ACCOUNT, is not "
EXIT_LINE2="the one you wish to delete, we are leaving the script..."
process_answer
#
```

```
####################################################################
# Search for any running processes that belong to the User Account
#
echo
echo "Step #2 - Find process on system belonging to user account"
echo
#
ps -u $USER_ACCOUNT >/dev/null #Are user processes running?
#
case $? in
1)    # No processes running for this User Account
      #
      echo "There are no processes for this account currently running."
      echo
;;
0)    # Processes running for this User Account.
      # Ask Script User if wants us to kill the processes.
      #
      echo "$USER_ACCOUNT has the following processes running: "
      echo
      ps -u $USER_ACCOUNT
      #
      LINE1="Would you like me to kill the process(es)? [y/n]"
      get_answer
      #
      case $ANSWER in
      y|Y|YES|yes|Yes|yEs|yeS|YEs|yES )   # If user answers "yes",
                                          # kill User Account processes.
         #
         echo
         echo "Killing off process(es)..."
         #
         # List user processes running code in variable, COMMAND_1
         COMMAND_1="ps -u $USER_ACCOUNT --no-heading"
         #
         # Create command to kill proccess in variable, COMMAND_3
         COMMAND_3="xargs -d \\n /usr/bin/sudo /bin/kill -9"
         #
         # Kill processes via piping commands together
         $COMMAND_1 | gawk '{print $1}' | $COMMAND_3
         #
         echo
         echo "Process(es) killed."
      ;;
      *)    # If user answers anything but "yes", do not kill.
         echo
         echo "Will not kill the process(es)"
         echo
      ;;
```

```
        esac
;;
esac
##################################################################
# Create a report of all files owned by User Account
#
echo
echo "Step #3 - Find files on system belonging to user account"
echo
echo "Creating a report of all files owned by $USER_ACCOUNT."
echo
echo "It is recommended that you backup/archive these files,"
echo "and then do one of two things:"
echo "  1) Delete the files"
echo "  2) Change the files' ownership to a current user account."
echo
echo "Please wait. This may take a while..."
#
REPORT_DATE=$(date +%y%m%d)
REPORT_FILE=$USER_ACCOUNT"_Files_"$REPORT_DATE".rpt"
#
find / -user $USER_ACCOUNT > $REPORT_FILE 2>/dev/null
#
echo
echo "Report is complete."
echo "Name of report:      $REPORT_FILE"
echo "Location of report:  $(pwd)"
echo
####################################
#  Remove User Account
echo
echo "Step #4 - Remove user account"
echo
#
LINE1="Remove $USER_ACCOUNT's account from system? [y/n]"
get_answer
#
# Call process_answer function:
#      if user answers anything but "yes", exit script
#
EXIT_LINE1="Since you do not wish to remove the user account,"
EXIT_LINE2="$USER_ACCOUNT at this time, exiting the script..."
process_answer
#
userdel $USER_ACCOUNT           #delete user account
echo
echo "User account, $USER_ACCOUNT, has been removed"
echo
#
exit
```

That was lots of work! However, the Delete_User.sh script is a great timesaver and helps you avoid lots of nasty problems when deleting user accounts.

Running the script

Because it is intended to be an interactive script, the Delete_User.sh script should not be placed in the cron table. However, it is still important to ensure that it works as expected.

Before the script is tested, the appropriate permissions are set on the script's file:

```
$ chmod u+x Delete_User.sh
$
$ ls -l Delete_User.sh
-rwxr--r--. 1 Christine Christine 6413 Sep  2 14:20 Delete_User.sh
$
```

The script is tested by removing an account, Consultant, that was set up for a temporary consultant on this system:

```
$ sudo ./Delete_User.sh
[sudo] password for Christine:
Step #1 - Determine User Account name to Delete


Please enter the username of the user
account you wish to delete from system: Consultant

Is Consultant the user account
you wish to delete from the system? [y/n]
Please answer the question.

Is Consultant the user account
you wish to delete from the system? [y/n] y

I found this record:
Consultant:x:504:506::/home/Consultant:/bin/bash

Is this the correct User Account? [y/n] yes

Step #2 - Find process on system belonging to user account

Consultant has the following processes running:
```

24

```
    PID TTY          TIME CMD
   5443 pts/0    00:00:00 bash
   5444 pts/0    00:00:00 sleep

Would you like me to kill the process(es)? [y/n] Yes

Killing off process(es)...

Process(es) killed.

Step #3 - Find files on system belonging to user account

Creating a report of all files owned by Consultant.

It is recommended that you backup/archive these files,
and then do one of two things:
   1) Delete the files
   2) Change the files' ownership to a current user account.

Please wait. This may take a while...

Report is complete.
Name of report:      Consultant_Files_140902.rpt
Location of report:  /home/Christine

Step #4 - Remove user account

Remove Consultant's account from system? [y/n] y

User account, Consultant, has been removed

$
$ ls Consultant*.rpt
Consultant_Files_140902.rpt
$
$ cat Consultant_Files_140902.rpt
/home/Consultant
/home/Consultant/Project_393
/home/Consultant/Project_393/393_revisionQ.py
/home/Consultant/Project_393/393_Final.py
[...]
/home/Consultant/.bashrc
/var/spool/mail/Consultant
$
$ grep Consultant /etc/passwd
$
```

That worked great! Notice the script was run using `sudo`, because super-user privileges are needed for deleting accounts. Also notice that the `read` timeout was tested, by delaying answering the following question:

```
Is Consultant the user account
you wish to delete from the system? [y/n]
Please answer the question.
```

Note that several different versions of "yes" answers were used for the various questions to ensure that the `case` statement test was working correctly. And finally, notice that the `Consultant` user's files were found and put into a report file, and the account was deleted.

Now you have a script utility that assists you when you need to delete user accounts. Even better, you can modify it to meet your organization's needs!

Monitoring Disk Space

One of the biggest problems with multi-user Linux systems is the amount of available disk space. In some situations, such as in a file-sharing server, disk space can fill up almost immediately just because of one careless user.

> **TIP**
>
> If you have a production Linux system, you should not depend upon disk space reports to protect your server from its disk space filling up. Instead, consider setting disk quotas. If the `quota` package is installed, you can find out more information about managing disk quotas by typing `man -k quota` at the shell prompt. If the `quota` package is not currently installed on your system, use your favorite search engine instead to locate further information.

This shell script utility helps you determine the top ten disk space consumers for designated directories. It produces a date-stamped report that allows disk space consumption trends to be monitored.

Obtaining the required functions

The first tool you need to use is the `du` command (see Chapter 4). This command displays the disk usage for individual files and directories. The `-s` option lets you summarize totals at the directory level. This comes in handy when calculating the total disk space used by an individual user. Here's what it looks like to use the `du` command to summarize each user's $HOME directory for the /home directory contents:

```
$ sudo du -s /home/*
[sudo] password for Christine:
```

```
4204     /home/Christine
56       /home/Consultant
52       /home/Development
4        /home/NoSuchUser
96       /home/Samantha
36       /home/Timothy
1024     /home/user1
$
```

The -s option works well for users' $HOME directories, but what if we wanted to view disk consumption in a system directory such as /var/log?

```
$ sudo du -s /var/log/*
4        /var/log/anaconda.ifcfg.log
20       /var/log/anaconda.log
32       /var/log/anaconda.program.log
108      /var/log/anaconda.storage.log
40       /var/log/anaconda.syslog
56       /var/log/anaconda.xlog
116      /var/log/anaconda.yum.log
4392     /var/log/audit
4        /var/log/boot.log
[...]
$
```

The listing quickly becomes too detailed. The -S (capital S) option works better for our purposes here, providing a total for each directory and subdirectory individually. This allows you to pinpoint problem areas quickly:

```
$ sudo du -S /var/log/
4        /var/log/ppp
4        /var/log/sssd
3020     /var/log/sa
80       /var/log/prelink
4        /var/log/samba/old
4        /var/log/samba
4        /var/log/ntpstats
4        /var/log/cups
4392     /var/log/audit
420      /var/log/gdm
4        /var/log/httpd
152      /var/log/ConsoleKit
2976     /var/log/
$
```

Because we are interested in the directories consuming the biggest chunks of disk space, the sort command (see Chapter 4) is used on the listing produced by du:

```
$ sudo du -S /var/log/ | sort -rn
4392     /var/log/audit
```

```
3020    /var/log/sa
2976    /var/log/
420     /var/log/gdm
152     /var/log/ConsoleKit
80      /var/log/prelink
4       /var/log/sssd
4       /var/log/samba/old
4       /var/log/samba
4       /var/log/ppp
4       /var/log/ntpstats
4       /var/log/httpd
4       /var/log/cups
$
```

The -n option allows you to sort numerically. The -r option lists the largest numbers first (reverse order). This is perfect for finding the largest disk consumers.

The sed editor brings more clarity to this listing. To focus on the top ten disk space consumers, when line 11 is reached, sed is set to delete the rest of the listing. The next step is to add a line number for each line in the listing. Chapter 19 shows you how to accomplish this by adding an equal sign (=) to the sed command. To get those line numbers on the same line as the disk space text, combine the text lines using the N command, as was shown in Chapter 21. The sed commands needed look like this:

```
sed '{11,$D; =}' |
sed 'N; s/\n/ /' |
```

Now the output can be cleaned up using the gawk command (see Chapter 22). The output from the sed editor is piped into the gawk command and printed using the printf function.

```
gawk '{printf $1 ":" "\t" $2  "\t" $3 "\n"}'
```

After the line number, a colon (:) is added, and tab (\t) characters are put between the individual fields for each text line's output row. This produces a nicely formatted listing of the top ten disk space consumers.

```
$ sudo du -S /var/log/ |
> sort -rn |
> sed '{11,$D; =}' |
> sed 'N; s/\n/ /' |
> gawk '{printf $1 ":" "\t" $2 "\t" $3 "\n"}'
[sudo] password for Christine:
1:      4396    /var/log/audit
2:      3024    /var/log/sa
3:      2976    /var/log/
4:      420     /var/log/gdm
5:      152     /var/log/ConsoleKit
6:      80      /var/log/prelink
7:      4       /var/log/sssd
```

```
8:        4        /var/log/samba/old
9:        4        /var/log/samba
10:       4        /var/log/ppp
$
```

Now you're in business! The next step is to use this information to create the script.

Creating the script

To save time and effort, the script creates a report for multiple designated directories. A variable to accomplish this called CHECK_DIRECTORIES is used. For our purposes here, the variable is set to just two directories:

```
CHECK_DIRECTORIES=" /var/log /home"
```

The script contains a for loop to perform the du command on each directory listed in the variable. This technique is used (see Chapter 13) to read and process values in a list. Each time the for loop iterates through the list of values in the variable CHECK_DIRECTORIES, it assigns to the DIR_CHECK variable the next value in the list:

```
for DIR_CHECK in $CHECK_DIRECTORIES
do
[...]
  du -S $DIR_CHECK
[...]
done
```

To allow quick identification, a date stamp is added to the report's filename, using the date command. Using the exec command (see Chapter 15) the script redirects its output to the date stamped report file:

```
DATE=$(date '+%m%d%y')
exec > disk_space_$DATE.rpt
```

Now to produce a nicely formatted report, the script uses the echo command to put in a few report titles:

```
echo "Top Ten Disk Space Usage"
echo "for $CHECK_DIRECTORIES Directories"
```

So let's see what this script looks like all put together:

```
#!/bin/bash
#
# Big_Users - Find big disk space users in various directories
#############################################################
# Parameters for Script
#
CHECK_DIRECTORIES=" /var/log /home"  #Directories to check
#
```

```
############# Main Script ###############################
#
DATE=$(date '+%m%d%y')                #Date for report file
#
exec > disk_space_$DATE.rpt           #Make report file STDOUT
#
echo "Top Ten Disk Space Usage"       #Report header
echo "for $CHECK_DIRECTORIES Directories"
#
for DIR_CHECK in $CHECK_DIRECTORIES  #Loop to du directories
do
  echo ""
  echo "The $DIR_CHECK Directory:"    #Directory header
#
# Create a listing of top ten disk space users in this dir
  du -S $DIR_CHECK 2>/dev/null |
  sort -rn |
  sed '{11,$D; =}' |
  sed 'N; s/\n/ /' |
  gawk '{printf $1 ":" "\t" $2  "\t" $3 "\n"}'
#
done                                  #End of loop
#
exit
```

And there you have it. This simple shell script creates a date stamped report of the top ten disk space consumers for each directory you choose.

Running the script

Before having the Big_Users script run automatically, you want to test it a few times manually to ensure that it does what you think it should do. And as you know by now, before you test it, you must set the proper permissions. However, in this case, the bash command was used, so the chmod u+x command was not needed prior to running the script:

```
$ ls -l Big_Users.sh
-rw-r--r--. 1 Christine Christine 910 Sep  3 08:43 Big_Users.sh
$
$ sudo bash Big_Users.sh
  [sudo] password for Christine:
$
$ ls disk_space*.rpt
disk_space_090314.rpt
$
$ cat disk_space_090314.rpt
Top Ten Disk Space Usage
```

```
for  /var/log /home Directories

The /var/log Directory:
1:      4496     /var/log/audit
2:      3056     /var/log
3:      3032     /var/log/sa
4:      480      /var/log/gdm
5:      152      /var/log/ConsoleKit
6:      80       /var/log/prelink
7:      4        /var/log/sssd
8:      4        /var/log/samba/old
9:      4        /var/log/samba
10:     4        /var/log/ppp

The /home Directory:
1:      34084    /home/Christine/Documents/temp/reports/archive
2:      14372    /home/Christine/Documents/temp/reports
3:      4440     /home/Timothy/Project__42/log/universe
4:      4440     /home/Timothy/Project_254/Old_Data/revision.56
5:      4440     /home/Christine/Documents/temp/reports/report.txt
6:      3012     /home/Timothy/Project__42/log
7:      3012     /home/Timothy/Project_254/Old_Data/data2039432
8:      2968     /home/Timothy/Project__42/log/answer
9:      2968     /home/Timothy/Project_254/Old_Data/data2039432/answer
10:     2968     /home/Christine/Documents/temp/reports/answer
$
```

It worked! Now you can set up the shell script to execute automatically as needed. You do this using the cron table (see Chapter 16). It's a good idea to have it run early Monday morning. If you do this, you can have your coffee and review your weekly disk consumption report first thing Monday morning!

Summary

This chapter put some of the shell-scripting information presented in the book to good use for creating Linux utilities. When you're responsible for a Linux system, whether it's a large multi-user system or your own system, you need to watch lots of things. Instead of manually running commands, you can create shell script utilities to do the work for you.

The first section walked you through using shell scripts for archiving and backing up data files on the Linux system. The tar command is a popular command for archiving data. The chapter showed you how to use it in shell scripts to create archive files and how to manage the archive files in an archive directory.

The next section covered using a shell script for the four steps needed to delete user accounts. Creating functions for shell code that is repeated within a script makes the code easier to read and modify. This script combined many of the different structured commands, such as the `case` and `while` commands. The chapter demonstrated the difference in script structure for a script destined for the `cron` tables versus an interactive script.

The chapter ended with how to use the `du` command to determine disk space consumption. The `sed` and `gawk` commands were then used to retrieve specific information from the data. Passing the output from a command to `sed` and `gawk` to parse data is a common function in shell scripts, so it's a good idea to know how to do it.

Next, more advanced shell scripts are covered. These scripts cover database, web, and e-mail topics.

24

Producing Scripts for Database, Web, and E-Mail

So far we've covered many different features of shell scripts. However, there's still more! You can also utilize advanced applications outside your shell scripts to provide advanced features, such as accessing databases, retrieving data from the Internet, and e-mailing reports. This chapter shows how to use these three common features found in Linux systems all from within your shell scripts.

Using a MySQL Database

One of the problems with shell scripts is persistent data. You can store all the information you want in your shell script variables, but at the end of the script, the variables just go away. Sometimes, you'd like for your scripts to be able to store data that you can use later.

In the old days, to store and retrieve data from a shell script required creating a file, reading data from the file, parsing the data, and then saving the data back into the file. Searching for data in the file meant reading every record in the file to look for your data. Nowadays with databases being all the rage, it's a snap to interface your shell scripts with professional-quality open source databases. Currently, the most popular open source database used in the Linux world is MySQL. Its popularity has grown as a part of the Linux-Apache-MySQL-PHP (LAMP) server environment, which many Internet web servers use for hosting online stores, blogs, and applications.

This section describes how to use a MySQL database in your Linux environment to create database objects and how to use those objects in your shell scripts.

Using MySQL

Most Linux distributions include the MySQL server and client packages in their software repositories, making it a snap to install a full MySQL environment on your Linux system. Figure 25-1 demonstrates the Add Software feature in the Ubuntu Linux distribution.

FIGURE 25-1

Installing MySQL server on an Ubuntu Linux system

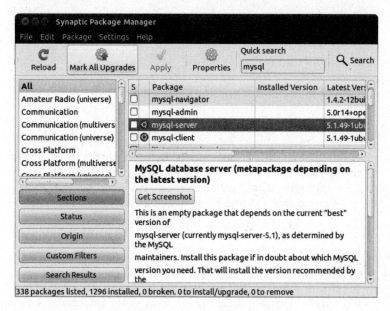

After searching for the mysql-server package, just select the mysql-server entry that appears, and the Package Manager downloads and installs the complete MySQL server (and client) software. It doesn't get any easier than that!

Once installed, the portal to the MySQL database is the mysql command line interface program. This section describes how to use the mysql client program to interact with your database.

Connecting to the server

The mysql client program allows you to connect to any MySQL database server anywhere on the network, using any user account and password. By default, if you enter the mysql program on a command line without any parameters, it attempts to connect to a MySQL server running on the same Linux system, using the Linux login username.

Most likely, this isn't how you want to connect to the database though. It's usually safer to create a special user account for the application to use, rather than using your standard user account in the MySQL server. That way, you can limit access to the application user, and if the application is compromised, you can easily delete and recreate it if necessary.

You use the -u command line parameter to specify the user name to log in as:

```
$ mysql -u root -p
Enter password:
Welcome to the MySQL monitor.  Commands end with ; or \g.
Your MySQL connection id is 42
Server version: 5.5.38-0ubuntu0.14.04.1 (Ubuntu)

Copyright (c) 2000, 2014, Oracle and/or its affiliates. All rights reserved.

Oracle is a registered trademark of Oracle Corporation and/or its
affiliates. Other names may be trademarks of their respective
owners.

Type 'help;' or '\h' for help. Type '\c' to clear the current input statement.

mysql>
```

The -p parameter tells the mysql program to prompt for a password to use with the user account to log in. Enter the password that you assigned to the root user account, either during the installation process, or using the mysqladmin utility. After you're logged in to the server, you can start entering commands.

The mysql commands

The mysql program uses two different types of commands:

- Special mysql commands
- Standard SQL statements

The mysql program uses its own set of commands that let you easily control the environment and retrieve information about the MySQL server. The mysql commands use either a full name (such as status) or a shortcut (such as \s).

You can use either the full command or the shortcut command directly from the mysql command prompt:

```
mysql> \s
--------------
mysql  Ver 14.14 Distrib 5.5.38, for debian-linux-gnu (i686) using readline 6.3

Connection id:          43
```

25

```
Current database:
Current user:            root@localhost
SSL:                     Not in use
Current pager:           stdout
Using outfile:           ''
Using delimiter:         ;
Server version:          5.5.38-0ubuntu0.14.04.1 (Ubuntu)
Protocol version:        10
Connection:              Localhost via UNIX socket
Server characterset:     latin1
Db      characterset:    latin1
Client characterset:     utf8
Conn.  characterset:     utf8
UNIX socket:             /var/run/mysqld/mysqld.sock
Uptime:                  2 min 24 sec

Threads: 1 Questions: 575 Slow queries: 0 Opens: 421 Flush tables: 1
     Open tables: 41  Queries per second avg: 3.993
--------------

mysql>
```

The `mysql` program implements all the standard Structured Query Language (SQL) commands supported by the MySQL server. One uncommon SQL command that the `mysql` program implements is the SHOW command. Using this command, you can extract information about the MySQL server, such as the databases and tables created:

```
mysql> SHOW DATABASES;
+--------------------+
| Database           |
+--------------------+
| information_schema |
| mysql              |
+--------------------+
2 rows in set (0.04 sec)

mysql> USE mysql;
Database changed
mysql> SHOW TABLES;
+---------------------------+
| Tables_in_mysql           |
+---------------------------+
| columns_priv              |
| db                        |
| func                      |
| help_category             |
| help_keyword              |
| help_relation             |
| help_topic                |
```

```
| host                       |
| proc                       |
| procs_priv                 |
| tables_priv                |
| time_zone                  |
| time_zone_leap_second      |
| time_zone_name             |
| time_zone_transition       |
| time_zone_transition_type  |
| user                       |
+----------------------------+
17 rows in set (0.00 sec)
mysql>
```

In this example, we used the SHOW SQL command to display the databases currently configured on the MySQL server and the USE SQL command to connect to a single database. Your
mysql session can be connected to only one database at a time.

You'll notice that we added a semicolon after each command. The semicolon indicates the
end of a command to the mysql program. If you don't use a semicolon, it prompts for more
data:

```
mysql> SHOW
    -> DATABASES;
+--------------------+
| Database           |
+--------------------+
| information_schema |
| mysql              |
+--------------------+
2 rows in set (0.00 sec)

mysql>
```

This feature can come in handy when you're working with long commands. You can enter
part of the command on a line, press the Enter key, and continue on the next line. This can
continue for as many lines as you like until you use the semicolon to indicate the end of
the command.

> **NOTE**
>
> Throughout this chapter, we use uppercase letters for SQL commands. This has become a common way to write SQL
> commands, but the mysql program allows you to specify SQL commands using either uppercase or lowercase.

Creating a database

The MySQL server organizes data into *databases*. A database usually holds the data for
a single application, separating it from other applications that use the database server.

25

Creating a separate database for each shell script application helps eliminate confusion and data mix-ups.

Here's the SQL statement required to create a new database:

```
CREATE DATABASE name;
```

That's pretty simple. Of course, you must have the proper privileges to create new databases on the MySQL server. The easiest way to do that is to log in as the root user account:

```
$ mysql -u root -p
Enter password:
Welcome to the MySQL monitor.  Commands end with ; or \g.
Your MySQL connection id is 42
Server version: 5.5.38-0ubuntu0.14.04.1 (Ubuntu)

Copyright (c) 2000, 2014, Oracle and/or its affiliates. All rights reserved.

Oracle is a registered trademark of Oracle Corporation and/or its
affiliates. Other names may be trademarks of their respective
owners.

Type 'help;' or '\h' for help. Type '\c' to clear the current input statement.

mysql> CREATE DATABASE mytest;
Query OK, 1 row affected (0.02 sec)

mysql>
```

You can see whether the new database was created by using the SHOW command:

```
mysql> SHOW DATABASES;
+--------------------+
| Database           |
+--------------------+
| information_schema |
| mysql              |
| mytest             |
+--------------------+
3 rows in set (0.01 sec)

mysql>
```

Yes, it was successfully created. Now you can create a user account to access the new database.

Creating a user account

So far, you've seen how to connect to the MySQL server using the `root` administrator account. This account has total control over all the MySQL server objects (much like how the `root` Linux account has complete control over the Linux system).

It's extremely dangerous to use the `root` MySQL account for normal applications. If there were a breach of security and someone figured out the password for the root user account, all sorts of bad things could happen to your system (and data).

To prevent that, it's wise to create a separate user account in MySQL that has privileges only for the database used in the application. You do this with the GRANT SQL statement:

```
mysql> GRANT SELECT,INSERT,DELETE,UPDATE ON test.* TO test IDENTIFIED
by 'test';
Query OK, 0 rows affected (0.35 sec)

mysql>
```

That's quite a long command. Let's walk through the pieces and see what it's doing.

The first section defines the privileges the user account has on the database(s). This statement allows the user account to query the database data (the select privilege), insert new data records, delete existing data records, and update existing data records.

The `test.*` entry defines the database and tables to which the privileges apply. This is specified in the following format:

```
database.table
```

As you can see from this example, you're allowed to use wildcard characters when specifying the database and tables. This format applies the specified privileges to all the tables contained in the database named test.

Finally, you specify the user account(s) to which the privileges apply. The neat thing about the `grant` command is that if the user account doesn't exist, it creates it. The `identified` by portion allows you to set a default password for the new user account.

You can test the new user account directly from the `mysql` program:

```
$ mysql mytest -u test -p
Enter password:
Welcome to the MySQL monitor.  Commands end with ; or \g.
Your MySQL connection id is 42
```

25

```
Server version: 5.5.38-0ubuntu0.14.04.1 (Ubuntu)

Copyright (c) 2000, 2014, Oracle and/or its affiliates. All rights reserved.

Oracle is a registered trademark of Oracle Corporation and/or its
affiliates. Other names may be trademarks of their respective
owners.

Type 'help;' or '\h' for help. Type '\c' to clear the current input statement.

mysql>
```

The first parameter specifies the default database to use (mytest), and as you've already seen, the -u parameter defines the user account to log in as, along with the -p to prompt for the password. After entering the password assigned to the test user account, you're connected to the server.

Now that you have a database and a user account, you're ready to create some tables for the data.

Creating a table

The MySQL server is considered a *relational* database. In a relational database, data is organized by *data fields, records,* and *tables.* A data field is a single piece of information, such as an employee's last name or a salary. A record is a collection of related data fields, such as the employee ID number, last name, first name, address, and salary. Each record indicates one set of the data fields.

The table contains all the records that hold the related data. Thus, you'll have a table called Employees that holds the records for each employee.

To create a new table in the database, you need to use the CREATE TABLE SQL command:

```
$ mysql mytest -u root -p
Enter password:
mysql> CREATE TABLE employees (
   -> empid int not null,
   -> lastname varchar(30),
   -> firstname varchar(30),
   -> salary float,
   -> primary key (empid));
Query OK, 0 rows affected (0.14 sec)

mysql>
```

First, notice that to create the new table, we needed to log in to MySQL using the root user account because the test user doesn't have privileges to create a new table. Next, notice that we specified the mytest database on the mysql program command line. If we hadn't done that, we would need to use the USE SQL command to connect to the test database.

CAUTION

It's extremely important to make sure you're in the right database before creating the new table. Also, make sure you're logged in using the administrative user account (`root` for MySQL) to create the tables.

Each data field in the table is defined using a data type. The MySQL database supports lots of different data types. Table 25-1 shows some of the more popular data types you may need.

TABLE 25-1 MySQL Data Types

Data Type	Description
char	A fixed-length string value
varchar	A variable-length string value
int	An integer value
float	A floating-point value
boolean	A Boolean true/false value
date	A date value in YYYY-MM-DD format
time	A time value in HH:mm:ss format
timestamp	A date and time value together
text	A long string value
BLOB	A large binary value, such as an image or video clip

The `empid` data field also specifies a *data constraint*. A data constraint restricts what type of data you can enter to create a valid record. The `not null` data constraint indicates that every record must have an `empid` value specified.

Finally, the `primary key` defines a data field that uniquely identifies each individual record. This means that each data record must have a unique `empid` value in the table.

After creating the new table, you can use the appropriate command to ensure that it's created. In `mysql`, it's the `show tables` command:

```
mysql> show tables;
+----------------+
| Tables_in_test |
+----------------+
| employees      |
+----------------+
1 row in set (0.00 sec)

mysql>
```

25

With the table created, you're now ready to start saving some data. The next section covers how to do that.

Inserting and deleting data

Not surprisingly, you use the INSERT SQL command to insert new data records into the table. Each INSERT command must specify the data field values for the MySQL server to accept the record.

Here's the format of the INSERT SQL command:

```
INSERT INTO table VALUES (...)
```

The values are in a comma-separated list of the data values for each data field:

```
$ mysql mytest -u test -p
Enter password:

mysql> INSERT INTO employees VALUES (1, 'Blum', 'Rich', 25000.00);
Query OK, 1 row affected (0.35 sec)
```

The example uses the –u command line prompt to log in as the test user account that was created in MySQL.

The INSERT command pushes the data values you specify into the data fields in the table. If you attempt to add another record that duplicates the empid data field value, you get an error message:

```
mysql> INSERT INTO employees VALUES (1, 'Blum', 'Barbara', 45000.00);
ERROR 1062 (23000): Duplicate entry '1' for key 1
```

However, if you change the empid value to a unique value, everything should be okay:

```
mysql> INSERT INTO employees VALUES (2, 'Blum', 'Barbara', 45000.00);
Query OK, 1 row affected (0.00 sec)
```

You should now have two data records in your table.

If you need to remove data from your table, you use the DELETE SQL command. However, you need to be very careful with it.

Here's the basic DELETE command format:

```
DELETE FROM table;
```

where table specifies the table to delete records from. There's just one small problem with this command: It removes all the records in the table.

To just specify a single record or a group of records to delete, you must use the WHERE clause. The WHERE clause allows you to create a filter that identifies which records to remove. You use the WHERE clause like this:

```
DELETE FROM employees WHERE empid = 2;
```

This restricts the deletion process to all the records that have an empid value of 2. When you execute this command, the mysql program returns a message indicating how many records matched the filter:

```
mysql> DELETE FROM employees WHERE empid = 2;
Query OK, 1 row affected (0.29 sec)
```

As expected, only one record matched the filter and was removed.

Querying data

After you have all your data in your database, it's time to start running reports to extract information.

The workhorse for all your querying is the SQL SELECT command. The SELECT command is extremely versatile, but with versatility comes complexity.

Here's the basic format of a SELECT statement:

```
SELECT datafields FROM table
```

The *datafields* parameter is a comma-separated list of the data field names you want the query to return. If you want to receive all the data field values, you can use an asterisk as a wildcard character.

You must also specify the specific table you want the query to search. To get meaningful results, you must match your query data fields with the proper table.

By default, the SELECT command returns all the data records in the specified table:

```
mysql> SELECT * FROM employees;
+-------+----------+------------+--------+
| empid | lastname | firstname  | salary |
+-------+----------+------------+--------+
|     1 | Blum     | Rich       |  25000 |
|     2 | Blum     | Barbara    |  45000 |
|     3 | Blum     | Katie Jane |  34500 |
|     4 | Blum     | Jessica    |  52340 |
+-------+----------+------------+--------+
4 rows in set (0.00 sec)

mysql>
```

25

You can use one or more modifiers to define how the database server returns the data requested by the query. Here's a list of commonly used modifiers:

- WHERE: Displays a subset of records that meet a specific condition
- ORDER BY: Displays records in a specified order
- LIMIT: Displays only a subset of records

The WHERE clause is the most common SELECT command modifier. It allows you to specify conditions to filter data from the result set. Here's an example of using the WHERE clause:

```
mysql> SELECT * FROM employees WHERE salary > 40000;
+--------+----------+-----------+--------+
| empid  | lastname | firstname | salary |
+--------+----------+-----------+--------+
|      2 | Blum     | Barbara   |  45000 |
|      4 | Blum     | Jessica   |  52340 |
+--------+----------+-----------+--------+
2 rows in set (0.01 sec)

mysql>
```

Now you can see the power of adding database access to your shell scripts! You can easily control your data management needs just with a few SQL commands and the mysql program. The next section describes how you can incorporate these features into your shell scripts.

Using the database in your scripts

Now that you have a working database going, it's finally time to turn our attention back to the shell scripting world. This section describes what you need to do to interact with your databases using shell scripts.

Logging into the server

If you've created a special user account in MySQL for your shell scripts, you need to use it to log in with the mysql command. There are a couple ways to do that. One method is to include the password on the command line using the -p parameter:

```
mysql mytest -u test -p test
```

This, however, is not a good idea. Anyone who has access to your script will know the user account and password for your database.

To solve this problem, you can use a special configuration file used by the mysql program. The mysql program uses the $HOME/.my.cnf file to read special startup commands and settings. One of those settings is the default password for mysql sessions started by the user account.

To set the default password in this file, just create the following:

```
$ cat .my.cnf
[client]
password = test
$ chmod 400 .my.cnf
$
```

The chmod command is used to restrict the .my.cnf file so only you can view it. You can test this now from the command line:

```
$ mysql mytest -u test
Reading table information for completion of table and column names
You can turn off this feature to get a quicker startup with -A

Welcome to the MySQL monitor.  Commands end with ; or \g.
Your MySQL connection id is 44
Server version: 5.5.38-0ubuntu0.14.04.1 (Ubuntu)

Copyright (c) 2000, 2014, Oracle and/or its affiliates. All rights reserved.

Oracle is a registered trademark of Oracle Corporation and/or its
affiliates. Other names may be trademarks of their respective
owners.

Type 'help;' or '\h' for help. Type '\c' to clear the current input statement.

mysql>
```

Perfect! Now you don't have to include the password on the command line in your shell scripts.

Sending commands to the server

After establishing the connection to the server, you'll want to send commands to interact with your database. There are two methods to do this:

- Send a single command and exit.
- Send multiple commands.

To send a single command, you must include the command as part of the mysql command line. For the mysql command, you do this using the -e parameter:

```
$ cat mtest1
#!/bin/bash
# send a command to the MySQL server

MYSQL=$(which mysql)

$MYSQL mytest -u test -e 'select * from employees'
```

25

```
$ ./mtest1
+-------+----------+------------+---------+
| empid | lastname | firstname  | salary  |
+-------+----------+------------+---------+
|     1 | Blum     | Rich       | 25000   |
|     2 | Blum     | Barbara    | 45000   |
|     3 | Blum     | Katie Jane | 34500   |
|     4 | Blum     | Jessica    | 52340   |
+-------+----------+------------+---------+
$
```

The database servers return the results from the SQL commands to the shell scripts, which display them in STDOUT.

If you need to send more than one SQL command, you can use file redirection (see Chapter 15). To redirect lines in the shell script, you must define an *end of file* string. The end of file string indicates the beginning and end of the redirected data.

This is an example of defining an end of file string, with data in it:

```
$ cat mtest2
#!/bin/bash
# sending multiple commands to MySQL

MYSQL=$(which mysql)
$MYSQL mytest -u test <<EOF
show tables;
select * from employees where salary > 40000;
EOF
$ ./mtest2
Tables_in_test
employees
empid    lastname    firstname    salary
2        Blum        Barbara      45000
4        Blum        Jessica      52340
$
```

The shell redirects everything with the EOF delimiters to the mysql command, which executes the lines as if you typed them yourself at the prompt. Using this method, you can send as many commands to the MySQL server as you need. You'll notice, however, that there's no separation between the output from each command. In the next section, "Formatting data," you'll see how to fix this problem.

> **NOTE**
> You should also notice that the `mysql` program changed the default output style when you used the redirected input method. Instead of creating the ASCII symbol boxes around the data, the `mysql` program detected that the input was redirected, so it returned just the raw data. This comes in handy when you need to extract the individual data elements.

Of course, you're not limited to just retrieving data from the tables. You can use any type of SQL command in your script, such as an INSERT statement:

```
$ cat mtest3
#!/bin/bash
# send data to the table in the MySQL database

MYSQL=$(which mysql)

if [ $# -ne 4 ]
then
  echo "Usage: mtest3 empid lastname firstname salary"
else
  statement="INSERT INTO employees VALUES ($1, '$2', '$3', $4)"
  $MYSQL mytest -u test << EOF
  $statement
EOF
  if [ $? -eq 0 ]
  then
     echo Data successfully added
  else
     echo Problem adding data
  fi
fi
$ ./mtest3
Usage: mtest3 empid lastname firstname salary
$ ./mtest3 5 Blum Jasper 100000
Data added successfully
$
$ ./mtest3 5 Blum Jasper 100000
ERROR 1062 (23000) at line 1: Duplicate entry '5' for key 1
Problem adding data
$
```

This example demonstrates a few things about using this technique. When you specify the end of file string, it must be the only thing on the line, and the line must start with the string. If we had indented the EOF text to match the rest of the if-then indentation, it wouldn't work.

Inside the INSERT statement, notice that there are single quotes around the text values and double quotes around the entire INSERT statement. It's important not to mix up the quotes used for the string values with the quotes used to define the script variable text.

Also, notice how we used the special $? variable to test the exit status of the mysql program. This helps you determine whether the command failed.

Just sending output from the commands to STDOUT is not the easiest way to manage and manipulate the data. The next section shows you some tricks you can use to help your scripts capture data retrieved from the database.

Formatting data

The standard output from the mysql command doesn't lend itself to data retrieval. If you need to actually do something with the data you retrieve, you need to do some fancy data manipulation. This section describes some of the tricks you can use to help extract data from your database reports.

The first step in trying to capture database data is to redirect the output from the mysql and psql commands in an environment variable. This allows you to use the output information in other commands. Here's an example:

```
$ cat mtest4
#!/bin/bash
# redirecting SQL output to a variable

MYSQL=$(which mysql)

dbs=$($MYSQL mytest -u test -Bse 'show databases')
for db in $dbs
do
 echo $db
done
$ ./mtest4
information_schema
test
$
```

This example uses two additional parameters on the mysql program command line. The -B parameter specifies for the mysql program to work in batch mode, and in combination with the -s (silent) parameter, the column headings and formatting symbols are suppressed.

By redirecting the output of the mysql command to a variable, this example is able to step through the individual values of each returned record.

The mysql program also supports an additional popular format, called Extensible Markup Language (XML). This language uses HTML-like tags to identify data names and values.

For the mysql program, you do this using the -X command line parameter:

```
$ mysql mytest -u test -X -e 'select * from employees where empid = 1'
<?xml version="1.0"?>

<resultset statement="select * from employees">
<row>
    <field name="empid">1</field>
    <field name="lastname">Blum</field>
    <field name="firstname">Rich</field>
    <field name="salary">25000</field>
</row>
</resultset>
$
```

Using XML, you can easily identify individual rows of data, along with the individual data values in each record. You can then use standard Linux string handling functions to extract the data you need!

Using the Web

Often when you think of shell script programming, the last thing you think of is the Internet. The command line world often seems foreign to the fancy, graphical world of the Internet. There are, however, several different utilities you can easily use in your shell scripts to gain access to data content on the web, as well as on other network devices.

Almost as old as the Internet itself, the Lynx program was created in 1992 by students at the University of Kansas as a text-based browser. Because it's text-based, the Lynx program allows you to browse websites directly from a terminal session, replacing the fancy graphics on web pages with HTML text tags. This allows you to surf the Internet from just about any type of Linux terminal. A sample Lynx screen is shown in Figure 25-2.

25

FIGURE 25-2

Viewing a web page using Lynx

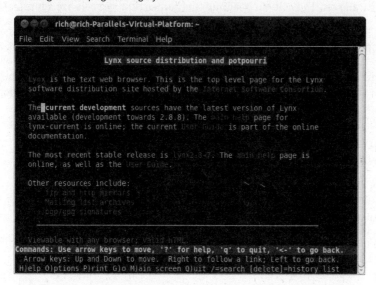

Lynx uses the standard keyboard keys to navigate around the web page. Links appear as highlighted text within the web page. Using the right-arrow key allows you to follow a link to the next web page.

You may be wondering how you can use a graphical text program in your shell scripts. The Lynx program also provides a feature that allows you to dump the text contents of a web page to STDOUT. This feature is great for mining for data contained within a web page. This section describes how to use the Lynx program within your shell scripts to extract data from websites.

Installing Lynx

Even though the Lynx program is somewhat old, it's still in active development. At the time of this writing, the latest version of Lynx is version 2.8.8, released in June 2010, with a new release in development. Because of its popularity among shell script programmers, many Linux distributions install the Lynx program in their default installations.

If you're using an installation that doesn't provide the Lynx program, check your distribution's installation packages. Most likely you'll find it there for easy installation.

If your distribution doesn't include the Lynx package, or if you just want the latest version, you can download the source code from the lynx.isc.org website and compile it yourself (assuming that you've got the C development libraries installed on your Linux system). See Chapter 9 for information on how to compile and install source code distribution packages.

> **NOTE**
> The Lynx program uses the curses text-graphics library in Linux. Most distributions have this installed by default. If your distribution doesn't, consult your particular distribution's instructions on installing the curses library before trying to compile Lynx.

The next section describes how to use the `lynx` command from the command line.

The lynx command line

The `lynx` command line command is extremely versatile in what information it can retrieve from the remote website. When you view a web page in your browser, you're only seeing part of the information that's transferred to your browser. Web pages consist of three types of data elements:

- HTTP headers
- Cookies
- HTML content

HTTP headers provide information about the type of data sent in the connection, the server sending the data, and the type of security used in the connection. If you're sending special types of data, such as video or audio clips, the server identifies that in the HTTP headers. The Lynx program allows you to view all the HTTP headers sent within a web page session.

If you've done any type of web browsing, no doubt you're familiar with web page *cookies*. Websites use cookies to store data about your website visit for future use. Each individual site can store information, but it can only access the information it sets. The `lynx` command provides options for you to view cookies sent by web servers, as well as reject or accept specific cookies sent from servers.

The Lynx program allows you to view the actual HTML content of the web page in three different formats:

- In a text-graphics display on the terminal session using the curses graphical library
- As a text file, dumping the raw data from the web page
- As a text file, dumping the raw HTML source code from the web page

For shell scripts, viewing the raw data or HTML source code is a gold mine. After you capture the data retrieved from a website, you can easily extract individual pieces of information.

25

As you can see, the Lynx program is extremely versatile in what it can do. However, with versatility comes complexity, especially when it comes to command line parameters. The Lynx program is one of the more complex programs you'll run into in the Linux world.

Here's the basic format of the `lynx` command:

```
lynx options URL
```

where *URL* is the HTTP or HTTPS destination you want to connect to, and *options* are one or more options that modify the behavior of Lynx as it interacts with the remote website. There are options for just about any type of web interaction required by Lynx. Use the man command to view all the options available for Lynx.

Many of the command line parameters define behaviors that control Lynx when you're using it in full-screen mode, allowing you to customize the behavior of Lynx as you're traversing web pages.

There are often groups of command line parameters that you find useful in your normal browsing environment. Instead of having to enter these parameters on the command line every time you use Lynx, Lynx provides a general configuration file that defines the base behavior when you use Lynx. This configuration file is discussed in the next section.

The Lynx configuration file

The `lynx` command reads a configuration file for many of its parameter settings. By default, this file is located at `/usr/local/lib/lynx.cfg`, although you'll find that many Linux distributions change this to the `/etc` directory (`/etc/lynx.cfg`) (the Ubuntu distribution places the `lynx.cfg file` in the `/etc/lynx-cur` folder).

The `lynx.cfg` configuration file groups related parameters into sections to make finding parameters easier. Here's the format of an entry in the configuration file:

```
PARAMETER:value
```

where *PARAMETER* is the full name of the parameter (often, but not always in uppercase letters) and *value* is the value associated with the parameter.

Perusing this file, you'll find many parameters that are similar to the command line parameters, such as the ACCEPT_ALL_COOKIES parameter, which is equivalent to setting the -accept_all_cookies command line parameter.

There are also a few configuration parameters that are similar in function but different in name. The FORCE_SSL_COOKIES_SECURE configuration file parameter setting can be overridden by the -force_secure command line parameter.

However, you'll also find quite a few configuration parameters that don't match with command line parameters. These values can be set only from the configuration file.

The most common configuration parameters that you can't set on the command line are for the *proxy servers*. Some networks (especially corporate networks) use a proxy server as a middleman between the client's browser and the destination website server. Instead of sending HTTP requests directly to the remote web server, client browsers must send their requests to the proxy server. The proxy server in turn sends the requests to the remote web server, retrieves the results, and forwards them back to the client browser.

This may seem like a waste of time, but it's a vital function in protecting clients from dangers on the Internet. A proxy server can filter inappropriate content and malicious coding, or even detect sites used for Internet data phishing schemes (rogue servers pretending to be someone else in order to capture customer data). Proxy servers can also help reduce Internet bandwidth usage, because they cache commonly viewed web pages and return them to clients instead of having to download the original page again.

These are the configuration parameters used to define proxy servers:

```
http_proxy:http://some.server.dom:port/
https_proxy:http://some.server.dom:port/
ftp_proxy:http://some.server.dom:port/
gopher_proxy:http://some.server.dom:port/
news_proxy:http://some.server.dom:port/
newspost_proxy:http://some.server.dom:port/
newsreply_proxy:http://some.server.dom:port/
snews_proxy:http://some.server.dom:port/
snewspost_proxy:http://some.server.dom:port/
snewsreply_proxy:http://some.server.dom:port/
nntp_proxy:http://some.server.dom:port/
wais_proxy:http://some.server.dom:port/
finger_proxy:http://some.server.dom:port/
cso_proxy:http://some.server.dom:port/
no_proxy:host.domain.dom
```

You can define a different proxy server for any network protocol supported by Lynx. The NO_PROXY parameter is a comma-separated list of websites that you prefer to have direct access to without using the proxy server. These are often internal websites that don't require filtering.

Capturing data from Lynx

When you use Lynx in a shell script, most likely you're trying to obtain a specific piece (or pieces) of information from a web page. The technique to accomplish this is called *screen scraping*. In screen scraping, you're trying to programmatically find data in a specific location on a graphical screen so you can capture it and use it in your shell script.

The easiest way to perform screen scraping with lynx is to use the -dump option. This option doesn't bother trying to display the web page on the terminal screen. Instead, it displays the web page text data directly to STDOUT:

25

```
$ lynx -dump http://localhost/RecipeCenter/
The Recipe Center
        "Just like mom used to make"
Welcome
    [1]Home
    [2]Login to post
    [3]Register for free login
    _____

    [4]Post a new recipe
```

Each link is identified by a tag number, and Lynx displays a listing of all the tag references after the web page data.

After you have all the text data from the web page, you probably know what tools we're going to get out of the toolbox to start work on extracting data. That's right, our old friends the sed and gawk programs (see Chapter 19).

First, let's find some interesting data to collect. The Yahoo! weather web page is a great source for finding the current weather conditions anywhere in the world. Each location uses a separate URL to display weather information for that city (you can find the specific URL for your city by going to the site in a normal browser and entering your city's information). Here's the lynx command for finding the weather in Chicago, Illinois:

```
lynx -dump http://weather.yahoo.com/united-states/illinois/chicago-2379574/
```

This command dumps lots and lots of data from the web page. The first step is to find the precise information you want. To do that, redirect the output from the lynx command to a file, and then search the file for your data. After doing that with the preceding command, we found this text in the output file:

```
Current conditions as of 1:54 pm EDT
Mostly Cloudy

    Feels Like:
            32 °F

    Barometer:
            30.13 in and rising

    Humidity:
            50%

    Visibility:
            10 mi

    Dewpoint:
            15 °F

    Wind:
            W 10 mph
```

That's all the information about the current weather you really need. There's just one small problem with this output. You'll notice that the numbers are on a line below the heading. Trying to just extract individual numbers will be difficult. Chapter 19 discusses how to deal with a problem just like this.

The key to solving this is to write a sed script that can search for the data heading first. When you find it, you can then go to the correct line to extract the data. We're fortunate in this example in that all the data we need are on lines by themselves. We should be able to solve this with just the sed script. If there had also been other text on the same line, we'd need to get out the gawk tool to filter out just the data we needed.

First, you need to create a sed script that looks for the location text and then skips to the next line to get the text that describes the current weather condition and prints it. Here's what that looks like for the Chicago weather page:

```
$ cat sedcond
/IL, United States/{
n
p
}
$
```

The address specifies to look for the line with the desired text. If the sed command finds it, the n command skips to the next line, and the p command prints the contents of the line, which is the text describing the current weather conditions of the city.

Next, you'll need a sed script that can search for the Feels Like text and then go to the next line to print the temperature:

```
$ cat sedtemp
/Feels Like/{
p
}
$
```

Perfect. Now, you can use these two sed scripts in a shell script that first captures the lynx output of the web page to a temporary file, and then applies the two sed scripts to the web page data to extract only the data you're looking for. Here's an example of how to do that:

```
$ cat weather
#!/bin/bash
# extract the current weather for Chicago, IL

URL="http://weather.yahoo.com/united-states/illinois/chicago-2379574/"
LYNX=$(which lynx)
TMPFILE=$(mktemp tmpXXXXXX)
$LYNX -dump $URL > $TMPFILE
```

25

```
conditions=$(cat $TMPFILE | sed -n -f sedcond)
temp=$(cat $TMPFILE | sed -n -f sedtemp | awk '{print $4}')
rm -f $TMPFILE
echo "Current conditions: $conditions"
echo The current temp outside is: $temp
$ ./weather
Current conditions: Mostly Cloudy
The current temp outside is: 32 °F
$
```

The weather script connects to the Yahoo! weather web page for the desired city, saves the web page to a temporary file, extracts the appropriate text, removes the temporary file, and then displays the weather information. The beauty of this is that after you've extracted the data from a website, you can do whatever you want with it, such as create a table of temperatures. You can then create a `cron` job (see Chapter 16) that runs every day to track daily temperatures.

> **CAUTION**
>
> The Internet is a dynamic place. Don't be surprised if you spend hours working out the precise location of data on a web page, only to find that it's moved a couple of weeks later, breaking your scripts. In fact, it's quite possible that this example won't work by the time you read this book. The important thing is to know the process for extracting data from web pages. You can then apply that principle to any situation.

Using E-Mail

With the popularity of e-mail, these days just about everyone has an e-mail address. Because of that, people often expect to receive data via e-mail instead of seeing files or printouts. That's no different in the shell scripting world. If you generate any type of report from your shell script, most likely at some point you'll be asked to e-mail the results to someone.

The main tool you have available for sending e-mail messages from your shell scripts is the Mailx program. Not only can you use it interactively to read and send messages, but you can also use the command line parameters to specify how to send a message.

> **NOTE**
>
> Some Linux distributions require that you also install a mail server package (such as sendmail or Postfix) before you can install the mailutils package that includes the Mailx program.

Here's the format for the Mailx program's command line for sending messages:

```
mail [-eIinv] [-a header] [-b addr] [-c addr] [-s subj] to-addr
```

The `mail` command uses the command line parameters shown in Table 25-2.

TABLE 25-2   The Mailx Command Line Parameters

Parameter	Description
-a	Specifies additional SMTP header lines
-b	Adds a BCC: recipient to the message
-c	Adds a CC: recipient to the message
-e	Doesn't send the message if it's empty
-i	Ignores TTY interrupt signals
-I	Forces Mailx to run in interactive mode
-n	Doesn't read the /etc/mail.rc startup file
-s	Specifies a Subject line
-v	Displays details of the delivery on the terminal

As you can see from Table 25-2, you can pretty much create an entire e-mail message just from the command line parameters. You just need to add the message body.

To do that, you need to redirect text to the `mail` command. Here's a simple example of how to create and send an e-mail message directly from the command line:

```
$ echo "This is a test message" | mailx -s "Test message" rich
```

The Mailx program sends the text from the `echo` command as the message body. This provides an easy way for you to send messages from your shell scripts. Here's a quick example:

```
$ cat factmail
#!/bin/bash
# mailing the answer to a factorial

MAIL=$(which mailx)

factorial=1
counter=1

read -p "Enter the number: " value
while [ $counter -le $value ]
do
    factorial=$[$factorial * $counter]
    counter=$[$counter + 1]
```

```
done

echo The factorial of $value is $factorial | $MAIL -s "Factorial
answer" $USER
echo "The result has been mailed to you."
```

This script does not assume that the Mailx program is located in the standard location. It uses the which command to determine just where the mail program is.

After calculating the result of the factorial function, the shell script uses the mail command to send the message to the user-defined $USER environment variable, which should be the person executing the script.

```
$ ./factmail
Enter the number: 5
The result has been mailed to you.
$
```

You just need to check your mail to see if the answer arrived:

```
$ mail
"/var/mail/rich": 1 message 1 new
>N   1 Rich Blum         Mon Sep  1 10:32  13/586    Factorial answer
?
Return-Path: <rich@rich-Parallels-Virtual-Platform>
X-Original-To: rich@rich-Parallels-Virtual-Platform
Delivered-To: rich@rich-Parallels-Virtual-Platform
Received: by rich-Parallels-Virtual-Platform (Postfix, from userid 1000)
        id B4A2A260081; Mon,  1 Sep 2014 10:32:24 -0500 (EST)
Subject: Factorial answer
To: <rich@rich-Parallels-Virtual-Platform>
X-Mailer: mail (GNU Mailutils 2.1)
Message-Id: <20101209153224.B4A2A260081@rich-Parallels-Virtual-Platform>
Date: Mon,  1 Sep 2014 10:32:24 -0500 (EST)
From: rich@rich-Parallels-Virtual-Platform (Rich Blum)

The factorial of 5 is 120
?
```

It's not always convenient to send just one line of text in the message body. Often, you'll need to send an entire output as the e-mail message. In those situations, you can always redirect text to a temporary file and use the cat command to redirect the output to the mail program.

Here's an example of sending a larger amount of data in an e-mail message:

```
$ cat diskmail
#!/bin/bash
```

```
# sending the current disk statistics in an e-mail message

date=$(date +%m/%d/%Y)
MAIL=$(which mailx)
TEMP=$(mktemp tmp.XXXXXX)

df -k > $TEMP
cat $TEMP | $MAIL -s "Disk stats for $date" $1
rm -f $TEMP
```

The diskmail program gets the current date using the date command (along with some special formatting), finds the location of the Mailx program, and creates a temporary file. After all that, it uses the df command to display the current disk space statistics (see Chapter 4), redirecting the output to the temporary file.

It then redirects the temporary file to the mail command, using the first command line parameter for the destination address and the current date in the Subject header. When you run the script, you don't see anything appear on the command line output:

```
$ ./diskmail rich
```

But if you check your mail, you should see the sent message:

```
$ mail
"/var/mail/rich": 1 message 1 new
>N   1 Rich Blum          Mon Sep  1 10:35  19/1020  Disk stats for 09/01/2014
?
Return-Path: <rich@rich-Parallels-Virtual-Platform>
X-Original-To: rich@rich-Parallels-Virtual-Platform
Delivered-To: rich@rich-Parallels-Virtual-Platform
Received: by rich-Parallels-Virtual-Platform (Postfix, from userid 1000)
        id 3671B260081; Mon,  1 Sep 2014 10:35:39 -0500 (EST)
Subject: Disk stats for 09/01/2014
To: <rich@rich-Parallels-Virtual-Platform>
X-Mailer: mail (GNU Mailutils 2.1)
Message-Id: <20101209153539.3671B260081@rich-Parallels-Virtual-Platform>
Date: Mon,  1 Sep 2014 10:35:39 -0500 (EST)
From: rich@rich-Parallels-Virtual-Platform (Rich Blum)

Filesystem            1K-blocks      Used  Available Use% Mounted on
/dev/sda1              63315876   2595552   57504044   5% /
none                    507052       228     506824   1% /dev
none                    512648       192     512456   1% /dev/shm
none                    512648       100     512548   1% /var/run
none                    512648         0     512648   0% /var/lock
none                4294967296         0 4294967296   0% /media/psf
?
```

Now you just need to schedule the script to run every day using the cron feature, and you can get disk space reports automatically e-mailed to your inbox! System administration doesn't get much easier than that!

Summary

This chapter walked through how to use some advanced features within your shell scripts. First, we discussed how to use the MySQL server to store persistent data for your applications. Just create a database and unique user account in MySQL for your application, and grant the user account privileges to only that database. You can then create tables to store the data that your application uses. The shell script uses the `mysql` command line tool to interface with the MySQL server, submit SELECT queries, and retrieve the results to display. Next we discussed how to use the `lynx` text-based browser to extract data from websites on the Internet. The `lynx` tool can dump all the text from a web page, and you can use standard shell programming skills to store that data and search it for the content you're looking for. Finally, we walked through how to use the standard Mailx program to send reports using the Linux e-mail server installed on your Linux system. The Mailx program allows you to easily send output from commands to any e-mail address.

In the next chapter we finish up by looking at some more shell script examples that show you just what you can do with your shell scripting knowledge.

Creating Fun Little Shell Scripts

The primary reason for learning to write bash shell scripts is to be able to create your own Linux system utilities. Understanding how to write useful and practical script utilities is important. However, sometimes it helps to do something fun to learn a concept or skill. The scripts in this chapter are not necessarily practical, but they can be lots of fun! And they help solidify script-writing concepts.

Sending a Message

Messages can be sent in many ways in an office or a home environment — text message, e-mail, and even making a phone call. One method, not commonly used any more, is sending a message directly to a fellow system user's terminal. Because this technique is largely unknown, it can be fun to communicate with someone with this method.

This shell script utility helps you to quickly and easily send a message to someone who is logged onto your Linux system. It is a rather simple script, but it can be loads of fun!

Understanding the required functions

For this simple script, only a few functions are required. Several of the commands are common and have been covered in the book. However, a few of the commands have only been touched on, and you may not be familiar with the primary command needed. This section looks at the commands needed to put together this simple, but interesting script.

Determining who is on the system

The first utility needed is the `who` command. The `who` utility allows you to see all the users currently logged into the system:

```
$ who
christine tty2          2015-09-10 11:43
timothy   tty3          2015-09-10 11:46
[...]
$
```

In this partial listing, all the information needed for sending messages is shown. By default, the `who` command gives you the short version of information available. The same information is provided, when `who -s` is issued:

- User name
- User's terminal
- Time the user logged into the system

To send a message, you only need the first two items. Both the user name and the user's current terminal are necessary.

Allowing messages

Users can disallow anyone to send them messages via the `mesg` utility. Therefore, before you start attempting to send messages, it's a good idea to check whether messages are allowed. For yourself, you can simply enter the `mesg` command as follows:

```
$ mesg
is n
$
```

The `is n` result shows that messaging is turned off. If the result showed `is y`, messages would be allowed.

> **TIP**
>
> Some distributions, such as Ubuntu, come with messaging turned off by default. Other distributions, such as CentOS, come with messaging turned on by default. Thus, you need to check your status and other user's message status before attempting to send a message.

To check everyone else's message status, you can use the `who` command again. Keep in mind that this checks the message status only for those who are currently logged into the system. You use the `-T` option to check their message status:

```
$ who -T
christine - tty2        2015-09-10 12:56
```

```
timothy    - tty3        2015-09-10 11:46
[...]
$
```

The dash (-) after each user name indicates that messaging is turned off for those users. If it is turned on, you see a plus (+) sign.

To allow messages to be sent to you, if it is turned off, you need to use the message command with the y option:

```
$ whoami
christine
$
$ mesg y
$
$ mesg
is y
$
```

Messaging is turned on by the user christine, when the command mesg y is issued. The user's individual message status is checked, by issuing the mesg command. Sure enough, the command shows is y, which indicates messages are allowed to this user.

Using the who command, other users can see how the user christine has changed her message status. The message status is now set to a plus sign, which indicates the user is allowing messages to be sent to her.

```
$ who -T
christine + tty2        2015-09-10 12:56
timothy    - tty3        2015-09-10 11:46
[...]
$
```

For two-way communication, you need to allow messaging and one or more users also need to allow messaging. In this example, the user timothy has also turned on his messaging:

```
$ who -T
christine + tty2        2015-09-10 12:56
timothy    + tty3        2015-09-10 11:46
[...]
$
```

Now that messaging is allowed between you and at least one other user, you can try out the command to send messages. However, the who command is also still needed, because it provides the necessary information in order to send a message.

Sending a message to another user

The primary tool for this script is the write command. As long as messaging is allowed, the write command allows you to send a message to another logged-in user using his username and current terminal.

In this example, a message is sent from user christine to user timothy logged on the tty3 terminal. From christine's terminal, the session looks as follows:

```
$ who
christine tty2          2015-09-10 13:54
timothy    tty3         2015-09-10 11:46
[...]
$
$ write timothy tty3
Hello Tim!
$
```

After the message is initiated by the write command, a blank line is shown for you to begin inputting the message text. It may be as many lines as you desire. When the Enter key is pressed, a new line is available for more message text. After you are finished entering message text, the whole message is sent by pressing the Ctrl+D key combination.

The receiver of the message sees something like the following:

```
Message from christine@server01 on tty2 at 14:11 ...
Hello Tim!
EOF
```

The receiver can see which user on which terminal sent the message. A time stamp is also included. Notice the EOF shown at the message's bottom. It indicates End Of File, which lets the message recipient know that the entire message is being displayed.

Now you can send messages! The next step is to use these commands to create the script.

Creating the script

Using a script to send messages helps overcome a few potential problems. First, if you have lots of users on the system, trying to find the one user you want to send a message to can be a pain! You must also determine whether that particular user has messaging turned on.

In addition, a script speeds things up allowing you to quickly send a message to a particular user in one easy step.

Checking if user is logged on

The first issue is to let the script know to which user you want to send a message. This is easily done by sending a parameter (Chapter 14) along with the script's execution. For the script to determine whether that particular user is logged on the system, the who command is employed as shown in this bit of script code:

```
# Determine if user is logged on:
#
logged_on=$(who | grep -i -m 1 $1 | gawk '{print $1}')
#
```

In the preceding code, the results of the who command are piped into the grep command (Chapter 4). The grep command uses the -i option to ignore case, which allows the username to be entered using uppercase or lowercase letters. The -m 1 option is included on the grep command, in case the user is logged into the system multiple times. The grep command produces either nothing, if the user is not logged on, or the username's first login information. This output is passed to the gawk command (Chapter 19). The gawk command returns only the first item, either nothing or the username. This final output from the gawk command is stored in the variable logged_on.

> **TIP**
>
> Some Linux distributions, such as Ubuntu, may not have the gawk command installed by default. To install it, type `sudo apt-get install gawk`. Also, you can find more information about installing software packages in Chapter 9.

When the variable, logged_on, contains either nothing (if the user is not logged on) or the username, it can be tested and acted upon:

```
#
if [ -z $logged_on ]
then
    echo "$1 is not logged on."
    echo "Exiting script..."
    exit
fi
#
```

Employing the use of an if statement and a test command (Chapter 12), the logged_on variable is tested to determine if it is a zero-length variable. If it is a zero-length variable, the script user is informed via echo commands that the user is not currently logged onto the system, and the script is exited via the exit command. If the user is logged onto the system, the logged_on variable contains the user's username, and the script continues.

In the following example, a username, Charlie, is passed as a parameter to the shell script. This user is not currently logged onto the system:

```
$ ./mu.sh Charlie
Charlie is not logged on.
Exiting script...
$
```

The code worked perfectly! Now instead of you digging through the who command results to determine whether a user is logged onto the system, the message script does that for you.

Checking if user accepts messages

The next important item is to determine whether a logged on user accepts messages. This script portion operates very closely to the script section for determining whether a user is logged on:

```
# Determine if user allows messaging:
#
allowed=$(who -T | grep -i -m 1 $1 | gawk '{print $2}')
#
if [ $allowed != "+" ]
then
    echo "$1 does not allowing messaging."
    echo "Exiting script..."
    exit
fi
#
```

Notice that this time, the who -T command and option are used. This displays a + next to the username, if messaging is allowed. Otherwise, it displays a - next to the username, if messaging is not allowed. The results from the who command are then piped into grep and gawk to pull out only the messaging indicator. The messaging indicator is stored in the allowed variable. Finally, an if statement is employed to test for a messaging indicator not set to +. If the indicator is not set to +, the script user is informed and the script is exited. However, if the messaging indicator shows messaging is allowed, the script continues.

To test out this script's section, a user who is logged into the system with messaging disabled is tested. The user Samantha currently has messaging disabled:

```
$ ./mu.sh Samantha
Samantha does not allowing messaging.
Exiting script...
$
```

The test worked as expected. This script portion eliminates any need to manually check for messaging being enabled or disabled.

Checking if message was included

The message to be sent is also included as a script parameter. Therefore, another needed check is whether a message was included as a parameter to the mu.sh shell script. To test for the message parameter, an if statement, similar to those used earlier, must be included in the script's code:

```
# Determine if a message was included:
#
if [ -z $2 ]
then
    echo "No message parameter included."
    echo "Exiting script..."
    exit
fi
#
```

To test out this script portion, a message was not included for a user who is both logged into the system and allows messaging:

```
$ ./mu.sh Timothy
No message parameter included.
Exiting script...
$
```

This is exactly what is needed! Now that the script has performed these preliminary checks, the primary task of sending a message can be undertaken.

Transmitting a simple message

Before a message is sent, the user's current terminal must be identified and stored in a variable. The who, grep, and gawk commands are employed again:

```
# Send message to user:
#
uterminal=$(who | grep -i -m 1 $1 | gawk '{print $2}')
#
```

To transmit the message, both the echo and the write commands are used:

```
#
echo $2 | write $logged_on $uterminal
#
```

Because write is an interactive utility, it must have the message piped into it for the script to work properly. The echo command is used to send the message, $2, to STDOUT, which in turn is piped into the write command. The logged_on variable holds the user-name, and the uterminal variable holds the user's current terminal.

Now, you can test sending a simple message to a designated user via the script:

```
$ ./mu.sh Timothy test
$
```

The user Timothy receives the following message on his terminal:

```
Message from christine@server01 on tty2 at 10:23 ...
test
EOF
```

Success! You can now send simple one word messages to other users on your system via your script.

Transmitting a long message

Often, you want to send more than just a single word to another system user. Let's try a longer message using the current script:

```
$ ./mu.sh Timothy Boss is coming. Look busy.
$
```

The user Timothy receives the following message on his terminal:

```
Message from christine@server01 on tty2 at 10:24 ...
Boss
EOF
```

It didn't work. Only the first word of the message, Boss, was sent. This is due to the script using parameters (Chapter 14). Recall that the bash shell considers a space to differentiate between parameters. Thus, because there are spaces in the message, each word is treated as a different parameter. The script must be modified to fix this problem.

The shift command (Chapter 14) and a while loop (Chapter 13) help with this long message issue:

```
# Determine if there is more to the message:
#
shift
#
while [ -n "$1" ]
do
    whole_message=$whole_message' '$1
    shift
done
#
```

Recall that the shift command allows you to process the various provided script parameters without knowing the total number of parameters. The shift command simply moves the next parameter in line down to parameter $1. First, a primary shift must be issued before the while loop, because the message starts in parameter $2, instead of parameter $1.

After the while loop is initiated, it continues grabbing each message word, tacking the word onto the whole_message variable. The loop then shifts to the next parameter. After the final parameter is processed, the while loop exits and the whole_message variable contains the entire message to send.

One additional script modification is needed to fix this problem. Instead of just sending parameter $2 to the write utility, the script is modified to send the variable, whole_message:

```
# Send message to user:
#
uterminal=$(who | grep -i -m 1 $1 | gawk '{print $2}')
#
echo $whole_message | write $logged_on $uterminal
#
```

Now, again try to send that warning message about the boss coming his way to Timothy:

```
$ ./mu.sh Timothy Boss is coming
Usage: grep [OPTION]... PATTERN [FILE]...
Try 'grep --help' for more information.
$
```

Oops! That didn't work either. This is because when shift was used in the script, the $1 parameter contents were removed. Thus, when the script attempts to use $1 in the grep command, it generates an error. To fix this problem a variable, muser, is used to capture the $1 parameter's value:

```
# Save the username parameter
#
muser=$1
#
```

Now muser stores the username. The $1 parameter in the script's various grep and echo commands can be replaced by the muser variable:

```
# Determine if user is logged on:
#
logged_on=$(who | grep -i -m 1 $muser | gawk '{print $1}')
[...]
    echo "$muser is not logged on."
[...]
# Determine if user allows messaging:
#
```

```
    allowed=$(who -T | grep -i -m 1 $muser | gawk '{print $2}')
    [...]
       echo "$muser does not allowing messaging."
    [...]
    # Send message to user:
    #
    uterminal=$(who | grep -i -m 1 $muser | gawk '{print $2}')
    [...]
```

To test out the script changes, a multi-word message is sent again. In addition, some emphasis is added to the message by tacking on exclamation points:

```
$ ./mu.sh Timothy The boss is coming! Look busy!
$
```

The user Timothy receives the following message on his terminal:

```
Message from christine@server01 on tty2 at 10:30 ...
The boss is coming! Look busy!
EOF
```

It worked! You can now employ the script to quickly send messages to other users on the system. Here's the final message script with all the needed checks and changes:

```
#!/bin/bash
#
#mu.sh - Send a Message to a particular user
###############################################
#
# Save the username parameter
#
muser=$1
#
# Determine if user is logged on:
#
logged_on=$(who | grep -i -m 1 $muser | gawk '{print $1}')
#
if [ -z $logged_on ]
then
    echo "$muser is not logged on."
    echo "Exiting script..."
    exit
fi
#
# Determine if user allows messaging:
#
allowed=$(who -T | grep -i -m 1 $muser | gawk '{print $2}')
#
```

```
if [ $allowed != "+" ]
then
    echo "$muser does not allowing messaging."
    echo "Exiting script..."
    exit
fi
#
# Determine if a message was included:
#
if [ -z $2 ]
then
    echo "No message parameter included."
    echo "Exiting script..."
    exit
fi
#
# Determine if there is more to the message:
#
shift
#
while [ -n "$1" ]
do
    whole_message=$whole_message' '$1
    shift
done
#
# Send message to user:
#
uterminal=$(who | grep -i -m 1 $muser | gawk '{print $2}')
#
echo $whole_message | write $logged_on $uterminal
#
exit
```

Because you have made it to the last chapter in this book, you should be ready for a script-writing challenge. Here are some suggested improvements for the message script that you can attempt on your own:

- Instead of passing the username and message as parameters, use options (see Chapter 14).

- If a user is logged into multiple terminals, allow a message to be sent to those multiple terminals. (Hint: Use multiple write commands.)

- If the message to be sent is for a user who is currently only logged into the GUI, produce a message for the script user and exit the script. (Remember the write command can only write to virtual console terminals.)

- Allow a long message stored in a file to be sent to a terminal. (Hint: Use the cat command output piped into the write utility, instead of the echo command.)

Not only does reading through the script help solidify the script-writing concepts you are learning, but so does modifying the script. Come up with your own creative modification. Have a little fun! It helps you learn.

Obtaining a Quote

Inspirational quotes have long been used in the business environment. You may have a few on your office wall right now. This fun little and interesting script helps you obtain a daily inspirational quote to use as you please.

This section takes you through how to create this script. Included is a new rich utility that has not been covered in the book yet. The script also uses some utilities that have been covered, such as sed and gawk.

Understanding the required functions

Several great websites allow you to obtain daily inspiration quotes. Just open your favorite search engine, and you can find many sites. After you find a site for your daily quote, you need a utility to download that quote. For this script, the wget utility is just what's needed.

Learning about the wget utility

The wget utility is a flexible tool that allows web pages to be downloaded to your local Linux system. From these pages, you can glean your daily inspirational quote.

> **NOTE**
> The wget command is an extremely rich utility. In this chapter, only a small portion of its power is used. Find out more about wget via the man pages.

To download a web page via wget, you just need the wget command and the website's address:

```
$ wget www.quotationspage.com/qotd.html
--2015-09-23 09:14:28--  http://www.quotationspage.com/qotd.html
Resolving www.quotationspage.com... 67.228.101.64
Connecting to www.quotationspage.com|67.228.101.64|:80. connected
HTTP request sent, awaiting response... 200 OK
Length: unspecified [text/html]
```

```
Saving to: "qotd.html"

    [ <=>                                    ] 13,806  --.-K/s   in 0.1s

2015-09-23 09:14:28 (118 KB/s) - "qotd.html" saved [13806]

$
```

The website's information is stored in a file named after the web page. In this case, it's qotd.html. And as you might have guessed by now, the file is full of HTML code:

```
$ cat qotd.html

<!DOCTYPE HTML PUBLIC "-//W3C//DTD HTML 4.0 Transitional//EN">

<html xmlns:fb="http://ogp.me/ns/fb#">
<head>
        <title>Quotes of the Day - The Quotations Page</title>
[...]
```

Only a partial HTML code listing is shown here. For the script, the sed and gawk utilities help strip out the desired inspirational quote. But before tackling the script, you need a little more control over the wget utility's input and output.

You can use a variable to hold the web address (URL). Simply pass the variable to wget as a parameter. Just don't forget to use the $ along with the variable name:

```
$ url=www.quotationspage.com/qotd.html
$
$ wget $url
--2015-09-23 09:24:21--  http://www.quotationspage.com/qotd.html
Resolving www.quotationspage.com... 67.228.101.64
Connecting to www.quotationspage.com|67.228.101.64|:80 connected.
HTTP request sent, awaiting response... 200 OK
Length: unspecified [text/html]
Saving to: "qotd.html.3"

    [ <=>                                    ] 13,806      --.-K/s   in 0.1s

2015-09-23 09:24:21 (98.6 KB/s) - "qotd.html.3" saved [13806]

$
```

The daily inspiration quote script is eventually to be run daily via cron (Chapter 16) or some other script automation utility. Thus, having the wget command's session output display to STDOUT is undesirable. To store the session output to a log file, use the option -o. This allows session output to be viewed at a later time:

```
$ url=www.quotationspage.com/qotd.html
$
```

```
$ wget -o quote.log $url
$
$ cat quote.log
--2015-09-23 09:41:46--  http://www.quotationspage.com/qotd.html
Resolving www.quotationspage.com... 67.228.101.64
Connecting to www.quotationspage.com|67.228.101.64|:80 connected.
HTTP request sent, awaiting response... 200 OK
Length: unspecified [text/html]
Saving to: "qotd.html.1"

   OK .......... ...                                        81.7K=0.2s

2015-09-23 09:41:46 (81.7 KB/s) - "qotd.html.1" saved [13806]

$
```

The wget utility now stores its session output into the log file as it retrieves web page information. If desired, you can view the logged session output by using the cat command, as shown in the preceding code.

> **NOTE**
>
> For various reasons, you may decide that you do not want wget to produce a log file or display session output. In this case, just use the -q option, and the wget command quietly performs its directed duties.

To control where the web page information is stored, use the -O option on the wget command. Thus, instead of having the web address as the storage file name, you can use the filename of your choice:

```
$ url=www.quotationspage.com/qotd.html
$
$ wget -o quote.log -O Daily_Quote.html $url
$
$ cat Daily_Quote.html

<!DOCTYPE HTML PUBLIC "-//W3C//DTD HTML 4.0 Transitional//EN">

<html xmlns:fb="http://ogp.me/ns/fb#">
<head>
[...]
$
```

Using the -O option allows the web page data to be stored in the designated file, Daily_ Quote.html. Now that the wget utility's output is controlled, the next required function, checking the web address's validity, can be explored.

Testing a web address

Web addresses change. Sometimes, it seems this happens daily. Therefore, it is important to test the address validity within the script. The wget utility gives the ability to conduct such a test with the --spider option:

```
$ url=www.quotationspage.com/qotd.html
$
$ wget --spider $url
Spider mode enabled. Check if remote file exists.
--2015-09-23 12:45:41--  http://www.quotationspage.com/qotd.html
Resolving www.quotationspage.com... 67.228.101.64
Connecting to www.quotationspage.com|67.228.101.64|:80 connected.
HTTP request sent, awaiting response... 200 OK
Length: unspecified [text/html]
Remote file exists and could contain further links,
but recursion is disabled -- not retrieving.

$
```

This output indicates that the URL is valid, but it's too much to read through. You can cut down on the output by adding the -nv option, which stands for non-verbose:

```
$ wget -nv --spider $url
2015-09-23 12:49:13
URL: http://www.quotationspage.com/qotd.html 200 OK
$
```

The -nv option allows just the web address's status to be displayed, making the output much easier to read. Contrary to what you may think, the OK at the non-verbose line's end does not indicate that the web address is valid. The indication is that the web address came back as it was sent. This concept is a little unclear, until you see an invalid web address.

To see an invalid web address indicator, the URL variable is changed to an incorrect web address. The wget command is reissued using this bad address:

```
$ url=www.quotationspage.com/BAD_URL.html
$
$ wget -nv --spider $url
2015-09-23 12:54:33
URL: http://www.quotationspage.com/error404.html 200 OK
$
```

Notice that the output still has an OK at its end. However, the web address ends in error404.html. This indicates the web address is invalid.

With the necessary `wget` command to grab the inspirational quote's web page information, and the ability to test the web page's address, it is time to start building the script. Your daily inspirational quote awaits retrieval.

Creating the script

To test the script as it is built, a parameter containing the website's URL is passed to the script. Within the script, the variable `quote_url` contains the passed parameter's value:

```
#
quote_url=$1
#
```

Checking the passed URL

It is always a good idea to have checks in place within your script. The first check is to ensure that the daily inspirational quote script website's URL is still valid.

As you would expect, the script checks the web address validity with `wget` and the `--spider` option. However, the resulting indicator must be saved so the indicator can be checked later with an `if` statement test. Thus, the resulting indicator must be saved to a variable. This is a little tricky with the `wget` command.

To save the indicator output, the standard `$()` syntax is used around the command. But in addition, `STDERR` and `STDOUT` redirection is needed. This is accomplished by tacking on `2>&1` to the end of the `wget` command:

```
#
check_url=$(wget -nv --spider $quote_url 2>&1)
#
```

Now the indicator status message is saved within the `check_url` variable. To carve out the error indicator, `error404`, from the `check_url` string, parameter expansion and the `echo` command can be used:

```
#
bad_url=$(echo ${check_url/*error404*/error404})
#
```

In this example, *string parameter expansion* allows the string stored in `check_url` to be searched. Think of string parameter expansion as a quick and easy `sed` alternative. Using wildcards around the search word, `*error404*` allows the entire string to be searched. If the search is successful, the `echo` command sends the string `error404` to be stored into the `bad_url` variable. If the search is not successful, the `bad_url` variable contains the `check_url` variable's contents.

Now an `if` statement (Chapter 12) is employed to check the bad_url variable's string. If the string error404 is found, a message is displayed and the script exits:

```
#
if [ "$bad_url" = "error404" ]
then
    echo "Bad web address"
    echo "$quote_url invalid"
    echo "Exiting script..."
    exit
fi
#
```

An easier and shorter method can be used. This method removes the need for string parameter expansion and the bad_url variable altogether. A double bracket `if` statement allows a search to be conducted of the check_url variable:

```
if [[ $check_url == *error404* ]]
then
    echo "Bad web address"
    echo "$quote_url invalid"
    echo "Exiting script..."
    exit
fi
```

The test statement within the `if` structure searches the check_url variable's string. If the string error404 is found anywhere within the variable string, a message is displayed and the script exits. If the indicator string does not contain the error message, the script continues. This statement saves time and effort. No need for any string parameter expansion or even the bad_url variable.

Now that the check is in place, the script can be tested with an invalid web address. The url variable is set to an incorrect URL and passed to the get_quote.sh script:

```
$ url=www.quotationspage.com/BAD_URL.html
$
$ ./get_quote.sh $url
Bad web address
www.quotationspage.com/BAD_URL.html invalid
Exiting script...
$
```

That works great. Just to make sure that all is well, now a valid web address is tested:

```
$ url=www.quotationspage.com/qotd.html
$
```

```
$ ./get_quote.sh $url
$
```

No error message received. The script works perfectly so far! This is the only check needed, so the next item to be added to the script is obtaining the web page's data.

Obtaining web page information

Grabbing the inspiration daily quote's web page data is simple. The wget command shown earlier in the chapter is used in the script. The only needed change is to store the log file and the HTML file, which contains the web page information, in the /tmp directory:

```
#
wget -o /tmp/quote.log -O /tmp/quote.html $quote_url
#
```

Before moving on to the rest of the script, this code section should be tested using a valid web address:

```
$ url=www.quotationspage.com/qotd.html
$
$ ./get_quote.sh $url
$
$ ls /tmp/quote.*
/tmp/quote.log   /tmp/quote.html
$
$ cat /tmp/quote.html

<!DOCTYPE HTML PUBLIC "-//W3C//DTD HTML 4.0 Transitional//EN">

<html xmlns:fb="http://ogp.me/ns/fb#">
<head>
[...]
</body>
</html>
$
```

The script still works well! The log file, /tmp/quote.log, and the html file, /tmp/quote .html, were properly created.

> **TIP**
>
> If you do not want cookies to be involved when obtaining website information, you can add the --no-cookies option to the wget command. By default, storing cookies is turned off.

The next task is to dig the daily inspirational quote out of the HTML code within the downloaded web page HTML file. This task requires both the sed and the gawk utilities.

Parsing out the desired information

In order to pull out the actual inspirational quote, some processing must take place. This part of the script uses sed and gawk to parse out the desired information.

The script first needs to remove all the HTML tags from the downloaded web page's information stored in the /tmp/quote.html file. The sed utility can provide this capability:

```
#
sed 's/<[^>]*//g' /tmp/quote.html
#
```

The preceding code should look very familiar. It was covered in Chapter 21 in the "Removing HTML tags" section.

After the HTML tags are removed, the output looks like the following:

```
$ url=www.quotationspage.com/qotd.html
$
$ ./get_quote.sh $url
[...]
        >Quotes of the Day - The Quotations Page>
>
[...]
>>Selected from Michael Moncur's Collection of Quotations
 - September 23, 2015>>
>>>Horse sense is the thing a horse has which keeps
[...]
>
$
```

This snipped listing shows that there is still too much unnecessary data in this file. Therefore, some additional parsing must be done. Fortunately, the quote text needed is situated right next to the current date. Therefore, the script can use the current date as a search term!

The grep command, the $() format, and the date command can help here. The output from the sed command is piped into the grep command. The grep command uses the current date formatted to match the date used on the quotation's web page. After the date text line is found, two additional text lines are pulled with the -A2 parameter:

```
#
sed 's/<[^>]*//g' /tmp/quote.html |
grep "$(date +%B' '%-d,' '%Y)" -A2
#
```

Now the script's output looks similar to the following:

```
$ ./get_quote.sh $url
>>Selected from Michael Moncur's Collection of Quotations
   - September 23, 2015>>
>>>Horse sense is the thing a horse has which keeps it from
  betting on people.> >>>>>>>>>>>>>>>W. C. Fields> (1880 -
  1946)>   >>>
>>Newspapermen learn to call a murderer 'an alleged murderer'
  and the King of England 'the alleged King of England' to
avoid libel suits.> >>>>>>>>>>>>>>>Stephen Leacock> (1869
   - 1944)>   >>> - More quotations on: [>Journalism>] >
$
```

TIP

If your Linux system's date is set differently than the quote of the day page's date, you get a blank line instead of a quote. The preceding grep command assumes your system date is the same as the web page's date.

Although the output is greatly reduced, there is still too much clutter in the text. The extra > symbols can easily be removed with the sed utility. In the script, the output from the grep command is piped into the sed utility, which strips off the > symbols:

```
#
sed 's/<[^>]*//g' /tmp/quote.html |
grep "$(date +%B' '%-d,' '%Y)" -A2 |
sed 's/>//g'
#
```

With the new script line, the output is now a little clearer:

```
$ ./get_quote.sh $url
Selected from Michael Moncur's Collection of Quotations
   - September 23, 2015
Horse sense is the thing a horse has which keeps it from
  betting on people. W. C. Fields (1880 - 1946)  
Newspapermen learn to call a murderer 'an alleged murderer'
  and the King of England 'the alleged King of England' to
avoid libel suits. Stephen Leacock (1869 - 1944)     -
More quotations on: [Journalism]
$
```

Now we're getting somewhere! However, we can still remove a little more clutter from the quotation.

You may have noticed that two quotations are listed in the output instead of one. This happens occasionally with this particular website. Some days, it may be one quote, and other days, it may be two. Therefore, the script needs a way to pull out only the first quote.

The sed utility can help again with this problem. Using the sed utility's next and delete commands (Chapter 21), the string   is located. After it's found, sed moves to the next line of the data and deletes it:

```
#
sed 's/<[^>]*//g' /tmp/quote.html |
grep "$(date +%B' '%-d,' '%Y)" -A2 |
sed 's/>//g' |
sed '/ /{n ; d}'
#
```

Now the script can be tested to see if the new sed addition fixes the multiple quotation problem:

```
$ ./get_quote.sh $url
Selected from Michael Moncur's Collection of Quotations
 - September 23, 2015
Horse sense is the thing a horse has which keeps it from
betting on people. W. C. Fields (1880 - 1946)  
$
```

The extra quotation is removed! One item remains for the quotation cleanup. At the quotation's end, the string   is still hanging around. The script could use another sed command to remove this pesky item, but just for variety, the gawk command is used:

```
#
sed 's/<[^>]*//g' /tmp/quote.html |
grep "$(date +%B' '%-d,' '%Y)" -A2 |
sed 's/>//g' |
sed '/ /{n ; d}' |
gawk 'BEGIN{FS=" "} {print $1}'
#
```

In the preceding code, the input field separator variable, FS, is used with the gawk command (Chapter 22). The string   is set as a field separator, which causes gawk to drop it from the output:

```
$ ./get_quote.sh $url
Selected from Michael Moncur's Collection of Quotations
 - September 23, 2015
Horse sense is the thing a horse has which keeps it from
betting on people. W. C. Fields (1880 - 1946)
$
```

One last needed script action is to save this quotation text to a file. Here the `tee` command (Chapter 15) helps. Now the entire quote extraction process looks as follows:

```
#
sed 's/<[^>]*//g' /tmp/quote.html |
grep "$(date +%B' '%-d,' '%Y)" -A2 |
sed 's/>//g' |
sed '/ /{n ; d}' |
gawk 'BEGIN{FS=" "} {print $1}' |
tee /tmp/daily_quote.txt  > /dev/null
#
```

The extracted quote is saved to /tmp/daily_quote.txt, and any output produced by the gawk command is redirected to /dev/null (see Chapter 15). To make the script a little more self-directed, the URL is hard-coded into the script:

```
#
quote_url=www.quotationspage.com/qotd.html
#
```

Now these two new changes to the daily inspirational quote script can be tested:

```
$ ./get_quote.sh
$
$ cat /tmp/daily_quote.txt
Selected from Michael Moncur's Collection of Quotations
  - September 23, 2015
Horse sense is the thing a horse has which keeps it from
betting on people. W. C. Fields (1880 - 1946)
$
```

That works perfectly! The daily inspiration quote was extracted from the website's data and stored in a text file. You may have noticed by now that this quotation is less a traditional inspirational quote and more a humorous quote. Just know that some people find humor inspirational!

For your review, here's the final daily inspirational quote script with all the needed checks and changes:

```
#!/bin/bash
#
# Get a Daily Inspirational Quote
###################################
#
# Script Variables ####
#
quote_url=www.quotationspage.com/qotd.html
#
# Check url validity ###
#
```

```
check_url=$(wget -nv --spider $quote_url 2>&1)
#
if [[ $check_url == *error404* ]]
then
    echo "Bad web address"
    echo "$quote_url invalid"
    echo "Exiting script..."
    exit
fi
#
# Download Web Site's Information
#
wget -o /tmp/quote.log -O /tmp/quote.html $quote_url
#
# Extract the Desired Data
#
sed 's/<[^>]*//g' /tmp/quote.html |
grep "$(date +%B' '%-d,' '%Y)" -A2 |
sed 's/>//g' |
sed '/ /{n ; d}' |
gawk 'BEGIN{FS=" "} {print $1}' |
tee /tmp/daily_quote.txt  > /dev/null
#
exit
```

This script is an excellent opportunity to try out some of your newly learned script writing and command line skills. The following are a few suggested changes for the daily inspirational quote script that you can attempt on your own:

- Change the website to your favorite quotation or sayings website, and make the necessary changes to the quote extraction commands.

- Try different sed and gawk commands for extracting the daily quotation.

- Set up the script to run daily on an automated basis via cron (see Chapter 16).

- Add a command to display the quote text file at certain times, such as when you first log in for the day.

Reading your daily quotes can inspire you. They may just inspire you to get out of that next business meeting. The next chapter section helps you write a script that does just that.

Generating an Excuse

You've been there. That endless staff meeting that is full of unimportant information. You would really rather be working on that fascinating bash shell script project back at your desk. Here's a little fun script you can use to get out of the next staff meeting.

Short Message Service (SMS) allows text messages to be sent between cell phones. However, you can also use SMS to send text messages directly from e-mail or the command line. The script in this section allows you to construct a text message to be sent at a specified time directly to your phone. Receiving a "critical" message from your Linux system is the perfect excuse for leaving a staff meeting early.

Understanding the required functions

You can send an SMS message from the command line in several ways. One way is via your system's e-mail using your phone carrier's SMS service. Another way is using the curl utility.

Learning about curl

Similar to wget, the curl utility allows you to transfer data from a particular web server. Unlike wget, it also allows you to transfer data to a web server. Transferring data to a particular web server is exactly what is needed here.

> **TIP**
>
> Some Linux distributions, such as Ubuntu, may not have the curl command installed by default. To install it, type `sudo apt-get install curl`. Also, you can find more information about installing software packages in Chapter 9.

Besides the curl utility, you need a website that provides free SMS message transfer. The one used here for this script is http://textbelt.com/text. This website allows you to send up to 75 text messages per day for free. You need it only for one text message, so it should be no problem.

> **TIP**
>
> If your company already uses an SMS provider, such as http://sendhub.com or http://eztexting.com, you can use those sites in your script instead. Be aware that the syntax needs to change depending upon those SMS provider's requirements.

To use curl and http://textbelt.com/text to send yourself a text message, you need to use the following syntax:

```
$ curl http://textbelt.com/text \
-d number=YourPhoneNumber \
-d "message=Your Text Message"
```

The -d option tells curl to send specified data to the website. In this case, the website needs particular data sent in order to send a text message. This data includes

YourPhoneNumber, which is your cell phone number starting with the area code. And it also includes *Your Text Message*, which is the text message you desire to send.

NOTE

The `curl` utility can handle much more than simply transferring data to and from a web server. It can handle many other network protocols, such as FTP, without any human intervention as well. Look at the man pages for `curl` to discover its rich power.

When the message is sent, the website provides a success message, `"success": true`, if no problems occurred:

```
$ curl http://textbelt.com/text \
> -d number=3173334444 \
> -d "message=Test from curl"
{
  "success": true
}$
$
```

Or it provides a fail message, `"success": false`, if data, such as the phone number, is incorrect:

```
$ curl http://textbelt.com/text \
-d number=317AAABBBB \
-d "message=Test from curl"
{
  "success": false,
  "message": "Invalid phone number."
}$
$
```

NOTE

If your cell phone carrier is not in the United States of America, it is likely that `http://textbelt.com/text` will not work for you. You can try `http://textbelt.com/Canada` if your cell phone carrier is in Canada. If your cell phone carrier is located elsewhere, try `http://textbell.com/intl` instead. For additional help, see `http://textbelt.com`.

The success/fail messages are very helpful, but they are unwanted for the script. To remove these messages, simply redirect `STDOUT` to `/dev/null` (see Chapter 15). Unfortunately, now `curl` supplies undesired output:

```
$ curl http://textbelt.com/text \
> -d number=3173334444 \
> -d "message=Test from curl" > /dev/null
```

```
      % Total    % Received % Xferd  Average Speed...
                                     Dload  Upload...
        0    21    0    21    0    45    27    58 ...
   $
```

The preceding snipped listing shows various statistics, which may be helpful when debugging your `curl` command. However, for the script, this information must be suppressed. Fortunately, the `curl` command has a `-s` option, which makes it silent:

```
$ curl -s http://textbelt.com/text \
> -d number=3173334444 \
> -d "message=Test from curl" > /dev/null
```

That is much better. The `curl` command is ready to be put into a script. However, before looking at the script, one more topic needs to be addressed: sending text messages via e-mail.

Choosing to use e-mail

If you choose not to use the text message relay service provided by `http://textbelt.com/text` or if for some reason it doesn't work for you, you can always substitute sending a text message via e-mail. This section briefly covers how to accomplish this substitution.

> **CAUTION**
>
> If your cell phone carrier is not in the United States of America, it is likely that this web service will not work for you. Also, your cell phone carrier may block SMS messages from this site. In this case, you must attempt to use e-mail instead.

Whether or not e-mail works as a substitute depends upon your cell phone carrier. If your cell phone carrier has an SMS gateway, you are in luck. Contact your cell phone carrier and find out the name of the gateway. Often, it is something similar to `txt.att.net` or `vtext.com`.

> **TIP**
>
> You can often find out your cell phone carrier's SMS gateway on your own via the Internet. One great site listing various SMS gateways, along with usage tips, is `http://martinfitzpatrick.name/list-of-email-to-sms-gateways/`. If you cannot find your carrier there, use your favorite search engine to locate it.

The basic syntax for sending a text message via e-mail is as follows:

```
mail -s "your text message" your_phone_number@your_sms_gateway
```

> **NOTE**
>
> If the `mail` command does not work on your Linux system, you need to install the `mailutils` package. See Chapter 9 for a review of installing software packages.

Unfortunately, after you enter the syntax, you must type your message and press Ctrl+D to send the text message. This is similar to sending a regular e-mail (see Chapter 24). Using this method doesn't work well in a script. Instead, you can store your e-mail message in a file and use it to send a text message. The basic idea for this method is as follows:

```
$ echo "This is a test" > message.txt
$ mail -s "Test from email" \
3173334444@vtext.com < message.txt
```

Now the e-mail syntax is more compatible with a script. However, be aware that many problems may exist with this approach. First, you must have a mail server running on your system (see Chapter 24). Secondly, your phone service provider may block SMS messages coming from your system via e-mail. This is often true, if you are attempting this method from your home.

> **TIP**
>
> If your phone service provider blocks SMS messages coming from your system, you can use a cloud-based e-mail provider as an SMS relay. Use your favorite Internet browser and search for the words `SMS relay` `your_favorite_cloud_email` and see what sites come up.

Although sending a text message via e-mail is a potential alternative, it can be fraught with problems. If you can, it is much easier to use a free SMS relay website and the `curl` utility. The script in the next section uses `curl` to send a text message to the phone of your choice.

Creating the script

After you have the required functions, creating the script to send a text message is fairly simple. You just need a few variables and the `curl` command.

You need three variables for the script. Setting up these particular data items as variables makes it easier if any of this information changes. The variables are shown here:

```
#
phone="3173334444"
SMSrelay_url=http://textbelt.com/text
```

```
text_message="System Code Red"
#
```

The only other needed item is the `curl` utility. Thus, here is the entire send a text message script:

```
#!/bin/bash
#
# Send a Text Message
###############################
#
# Script Variables ####
#
phone="3173334444"
SMSrelay_url=http://textbelt.com/text
text_message="System Code Red"
#
# Send text ##########
#
curl -s $SMSrelay_url -d \
number=$phone \
-d "message=$text_message" > /dev/null
#
exit
```

If you see this script as simple and easy, you are right! Even more important, that means you have learned a great deal about shell script writing. Even easy scripts need to be tested, so be sure to test this script using your cell phone number in the phone variable before continuing.

> **TIP**
>
> While you are testing your script, be aware that this website, http://textbelt.com/text, does not allow you to send more than three text messages to the same phone number in less than three minutes.

To have a text message sent to you at a desired time, you must employ the `at` command. If you need a reminder, the `at` command was covered in Chapter 16.

First, you can test the use of the `at` command with your new script. Have the `at` utility execute the script by using the -f option along with the script's file name, send_text .sh, in this case. Have the script run immediately using the Now option:

```
$ at -f send_text.sh Now
job 22 at 2015-09-24 10:22
$
```

The script runs instantly. However, it may be a minute or two before you receive the text message on your phone.

To have the script run at another time, you simply use other `at` command options (see Chapter 16). In the following example, the script is run 25 minutes from the current time.

```
$ at -f send_text.sh Now + 25 minutes
job 23 at 2015-09-24 10:48
$
```

Note in the example, the `at` command provides an informational message when the script is submitted. The date and time listed in that message is when the script will execute.

What fun! Now you have a script utility that will be of assistance when you need an excuse to get out of that staff meeting. Better yet, you could modify the script to send yourself truly serious system messages that need to be addressed.

Summary

This chapter showed how to put some of the shell-scripting information presented in the book to use for fun little shell scripts. Each script reinforced material covered in the chapters along with a few new commands and ideas.

The chapter demonstrated how to send a message to another user on the Linux system. The script checked to see whether the user was logged on to the system and whether the user allowed messaging. After those checks were made, the passed message was sent using the `write` command. Included were some suggestions for modifying this script, which improve your shell-scripting abilities.

The next section walked you through obtaining website information using the `wget` utility. The created script pulled a quote from the web. After retrieval, the script used several utilities to pull out the actual quote text. These now familiar commands included `sed`, `grep`, `gawk`, and the `tee` command. For this script, suggestions were made for how the script could be modified. These are well worth pursuing to solidify and improve your new skills.

The chapter ended with a very fun and simple script for sending yourself a text message. We explored the `curl` utility, along with SMS concepts. Although this is a fun script, it can be modified and used for more serious purposes.

Thanks for joining us on this journey through the Linux command line and shell scripting. We hope you've enjoyed the journey and have learned how to get around on the command line and how to create shell scripts to save time. But don't stop your command line education here. There's always something new being developed in the open source world, whether it's a new command line utility or a full-blown shell. Stay in touch with the Linux community and follow along with the new advances and features.

Quick Guide to bash Commands

IN THIS APPENDIX

Viewing the bash built-in commands

Reviewing GNU additional shell commands

Looking at bash environment variables

As you've seen throughout this book, the bash shell contains lots of features and thus has lots of commands available. This appendix provides a concise guide to allow you to quickly look up a feature or command that you can use from the bash command line or from a bash shell script.

Reviewing Built-In Commands

The bash shell includes many popular commands built into the shell. This provides for faster processing times when using these commands. Table A-1 shows the built-in commands available directly from the bash shell.

TABLE A-1   **bash Built-In Commands**

Command	Description
:	Expands listed arguments and redirects as specified
.	Reads and executes commands from a designated file in the current shell
alias	Defines an alias for the specified command
bg	Resumes a job in background mode
bind	Binds a keyboard sequence to a readline function or macro
break	Exits from a for, while, select, or until loop
builtin	Executes the specified shell built-in command
caller	Returns the context of any active subroutine call
cd	Changes the current directory to the specified directory

Continues

TABLE A-1 *(continued)*

Command	Description
command	Executes the specified command without the normal shell lookup
compgen	Generates possible completion matches for the specified word
complete	Displays how the specified words would be completed
compopt	Changes options for how the specified words would be completed
continue	Resumes the next iteration of a for, while, select, or until loop
declare	Declares a variable or variable type
dirs	Displays a list of currently remembered directories
disown	Removes the specified jobs from the jobs table for the process
echo	Displays the specified string to STDOUT
enable	Enables or disables the specified built-in shell command
eval	Concatenates the specified arguments into a single command, and executes the command
exec	Replaces the shell process with the specified command
exit	Forces the shell to exit with the specified exit status
export	Sets the specified variables to be available for child shell processes
fc	Selects a list of commands from the history list
fg	Resumes a job in foreground mode
getopts	Parses the specified positional parameters
hash	Finds and remembers the full pathname of the specified command
help	Displays a help file
history	Displays the command history
jobs	Lists the active jobs
kill	Sends a system signal to the specified process ID (PID)
let	Evaluates each argument in a mathematical expression
local	Creates a limited-scope variable in a function
logout	Exits a login shell
mapfile	Reads STDIN lines and puts them into an indexed array
popd	Removes entries from the directory stack
printf	Displays text using formatted strings
pushd	Adds a directory to the directory stack

pwd	Displays the pathname of the current working directory
read	Reads one line of data from STDIN, and assigns it to a variable
readarray	Reads STDIN lines, and puts them into an indexed array
readonly	Reads one line of data from STDIN, and assigns it to a variable that can't be changed
return	Forces a function to exit with a value that can be retrieved by the calling script
set	Sets and displays environment variable values and shell attributes
shift	Rotates positional parameters down one position
shopt	Toggles the values of variables controlling optional shell behavior
source	Reads and executes commands from a designated file in the current shell
suspend	Suspends the execution of the shell until a SIGCONT signal is received
test	Returns an exit status of 0 or 1 based on the specified condition
times	Displays the accumulated user and system shell times.
trap	Executes the specified command if the specified system signal is received
type	Displays how the specified word would be interpreted if used as a command
typeset	Declares a variable or variable type
ulimit	Sets a limit on the specified resource for system users
umask	Sets default permissions for newly created files and directories
unalias	Removes the specified alias
unset	Removes the specified environment variable or shell attribute
wait	Waits for the specified process to complete, and returns the exit status

The built-in commands provide higher performance than external commands, but the more built-in commands that are added to a shell, the more memory it consumes with commands that you may never use. The bash shell also contains external commands that provide extended functionality for the shell. These are discussed in the following section.

Looking at Common bash Commands

In addition to the built-in commands, the bash shell utilizes external commands to allow you to maneuver around the filesystem and manipulate files and directories. Table A-2 shows the common external commands you'll want to use when working in the bash shell.

TABLE A-2 **The bash Shell External Commands**

Command	Description
bzip2	Compresses using the Burrows-Wheeler block sorting text compression algorithm and Huffman coding
cat	Lists the contents of the specified file
chage	Changes the password expiration date for the specified system user account
chfn	Changes the specified user account's comment information
chgrp	Changes the default group of the specified file or directory
chmod	Changes system security permissions for the specified file or directory
chown	Changes the default owner of the specified file or directory
chpasswd	Reads a file of login name and password pairs and updates the passwords
chsh	Changes the specified user account's default shell
clear	Removes text from a terminal emulator or virtual console terminal
compress	Original Unix file compression utility
coproc	Spawns a subshell in background mode and executes the designated command
cp	Copies the specified files to an alternate location
crontab	Initiates the editor for the user's crontable file, if allowed
cut	Removes a designated portion of each specified file's lines
date	Displays the date in various formats
df	Displays current disk space statistics for all mounted devices
du	Displays disk usage statistics for the specified file path
emacs	Invokes the emacs text editor
file	Views the file type of the specified file
find	Performs a recursive search for files
free	Checks available and used memory on the system
gawk	Streams editing using programming language commands
grep	Searches a file for the specified text string
gedit	Invokes the GNOME Desktop editor
getopt	Parses command options including long options
groups	Displays group membership of the designated user
groupadd	Creates a new system group
groupmod	Modifies an existing system group
gzip	The GNU Project's compression using Lempel-Ziv compression

head	Displays the first portion of the specified file's contents
help	Displays the help pages for bash built-in commands
killall	Sends a system signal to a running process based on process name
kwrite	Invokes the KWrite text editor
less	Advanced viewing of file contents
link	Creates a link to a file using an alias name
ln	Creates a symbolic or hard link to a designated file
ls	Lists directory contents
makewhatis	Creates the whatis database allowing man page keyword searches
man	Displays the man pages for the designated command or topic
mkdir	Creates the specified directory under the current directory
more	Lists the contents of the specified file, pausing after each screen of data
mount	Displays or mounts disk devices into the virtual filesystem
mv	Renames a file
nano	Invokes the nano text editor
nice	Runs a command using a different priority level on the system
passwd	Changes the password for a system user account
ps	Displays information about the running processes on the system
pwd	Displays the current directory
renice	Changes the priority of a running application on the system
rm	Deletes the specified file
rmdir	Deletes the specified directory
sed	Streams line editing using editor commands
sleep	Pauses bash shell operation for a specified amount of time
sort	Organizes data in a data file based on the specified order
stat	Views the file statistics of the specified file
sudo	Runs an application as the root user account
tail	Displays the last portion of the specified file's contents
tar	Archives data and directories into a single file
top	Displays the active processes, showing vital system statistics
touch	Creates a new empty file or updates the timestamp on an existing file
umount	Removes a mounted disk device from the virtual filesystem
uptime	Displays information on how long the system has been running
useradd	Creates a new system user account

Continues

TABLE A-2 *(continued)*

Command	Description
userdel	Removes an existing system user account.
usermod	Modifies an existing system user account
vi	Invokes the vim text editor
vmstat	Produces a detailed report on memory and CPU usage on the system
whereis	Displays a designated command's files, including binary, source code, and man pages
which	Finds the location of an executable file
who	Displays users currently logged into system
whoami	Displays the current user's username
xargs	Takes items from STDIN, builds commands, and executes the commands
zip	Unix version of the Windows PKZIP program

You can accomplish just about any task you need to on the command line using these commands.

Assessing Environment Variables

The bash shell also utilizes many environment variables. Although environment variables aren't commands, they often affect how shell commands operate, so it's important to know the shell environment variables. Table A-3 shows the default environment variables available in the bash shell.

TABLE A-3   bash Shell Default Environment Variables

Variable	Description
*	Contains all the command line parameters as a single text value
@	Contains all the command line parameters as separate text values
#	The number of command line parameters
?	The exit status of the most recently used foreground process
-	The current command line option flags
$	The process ID (PID) of the current shell

!	The PID of the most recently executed background process
0	The name of the command from the command line
_	The absolute pathname of the shell
BASH	The full filename used to invoke the shell
BASHOPTS	Enabled shell options in a colon-separated list
BASHPID	The current bash shell's process ID
BASH_ALIASES	An array containing the currently used aliases.
BASH_ARGC	The number of parameters in the current subroutine
BASH_ARGV	An array containing all the command line parameters specified
BASH_CMDS	An array containing the internal hash table of commands
BASH_COMMAND	The name of the command currently being executed
BASH_ENV	When set, each bash script attempts to execute a startup file defined by this variable before running.
BASH_EXECUTION_STRING	The command used in the -c command line option
BASH_LINENO	An array containing the line numbers of each command in the script
BASH_REMATCH	An array containing text elements that match a specified regular expression
BASH_SOURCE	An array containing source file names for the declared functions in the shell
BASH_SUBSHELL	The number of subshells spawned by the current shell
BASH_VERSINFO	A variable array that contains the individual major and minor version numbers of the current instance of the bash shell
BASH_VERSION	The version number of the current instance of the bash shell
BASH_XTRACEFD	When set to a valid file descriptor integer, trace output is generated and separated from diagnostic and error messages. The file descriptor must have set -x enabled.
COLUMNS	Contains the terminal width of the terminal used for the current instance of the bash shell
COMP_CWORD	An index into the variable COMP_WORDS, which contains the current cursor position

Continues

TABLE A-3   *(continued)*

Command	Description
COMP_KEY	The completion invocation character keyboard key
COMP_LINE	The current command line
COMP_POINT	The index of the current cursor position relative to the beginning of the current command
COMP_TYPE	The completion type integer value
COM_WORDBREAKS	A set of characters used as word separators when performing word completion
COMP_WORDS	A variable array that contains the individual words on the current command line
COMPREPLY	A variable array that contains the possible completion codes generated by a shell function
COPROC	A variable array that holds file descriptors for an unnamed coprocess' I/O
DIRSTACK	A variable array that contains the current contents of the directory stack
EMACS	When set, the shell assumes it's running in an emacs shell buffer and disables line editing.
ENV	When the shell is invoked in POSIX mode, each bash script attempts to execute a startup file defined by this variable before running.
EUID	The numeric effective user ID of the current user
FCEDIT	The default editor used by the fc command
FIGNORE	A colon-separated list of suffixes to ignore when performing file name completion
FUNCNAME	The name of the currently executing shell function
FUNCNEST	The maximum level for nesting functions
GLOBIGNORE	A colon-separated list of patterns defining the set of filenames to be ignored by file name expansion
GROUPS	A variable array containing the list of groups of which the current user is a member
histchars	Up to three characters that control history expansion

HISTCMD	The history number of the current command
HISTCONTROL	Controls what commands are entered in the shell history list
HISTFILE	The name of the file to save the shell history list (.bash_history by default)
HISTFILESIZE	The maximum number of lines to save in the history file
HISTIGNORE	A colon-separated list of patterns used to decide which commands are ignored for the history file
HISTSIZE	The maximum number of commands stored in the history file
HISTTIMEFORMAT	When set, determines the format string for the history file entries' time stamps
HOSTFILE	Contains the name of the file that should be read when the shell needs to complete a hostname
HOSTNAME	The name of the current host
HOSTTYPE	A string describing the machine the bash shell is running on
IGNOREEOF	The number of consecutive EOF characters the shell must receive before exiting. If this value doesn't exist, the default is 1.
INPUTRC	The name of the readline initialization file (The default is .inputrc.)
LANG	The locale category for the shell
LC_ALL	Overrides the LANG variable, defining a locale category
LC_COLLATE	Sets the collation order used when sorting string values
LC_CTYPE	Determines the interpretation of characters used in file name expansion and pattern matching
LC_MESSAGES	Determines the locale setting used when interpreting double-quoted strings preceded by a dollar sign
LC_NUMERIC	Determines the locale setting used when formatting numbers
LINENO	The line number in a script currently executing
LINES	Defines the number of lines available on the terminal
MACHTYPE	A string defining the system type in *cpu-company-system* format

Continues

TABLE A-3 *(continued)*

Command	Description
MAILCHECK	How often (in seconds) the shell should check for new mail (default is 60)
MAPFILE	Array variable containing the mapfile command's read text; used only when no variable name is given
OLDPWD	The previous working directory used in the shell
OPTERR	If set to 1, the bash shell displays errors generated by the getopts command.
OSTYPE	A string defining the operating system the shell is running on
PIPESTATUS	A variable array containing a list of exit status values from the processes in the foreground process
POSIXLY_CORRECT	If set, bash starts in POSIX mode.
PPID	The process ID (PID) of the bash shell's parent process
PROMPT_COMMAND	If set, the command to execute before displaying the primary prompt
PS1	The primary command line prompt string
PS2	The secondary command line prompt string
PS3	The prompt to use for the select command
PS4	The prompt displayed before the command line is echoed if the bash -x parameter is used.
PWD	The current working directory
RANDOM	Returns a random number between 0 and 32767. Assigning a value to this variable seeds the random number generator.
READLINE_LINE	The readline line buffer contents
READLINE_POINT	The current readline line buffer's insertion point position
REPLY	The default variable for the read command
SECONDS	The number of seconds since the shell was started. Assigning a value resets the timer to the value.
SHELL	The shell's full pathname
SHELLOPTS	A colon-separated list of enabled bash shell options
SHLVL	Indicates the shell level, incremented by 1 each time a new bash shell is started

TIMEFORMAT	A format specifying how the shell displays time values
TMOUT	The value of how long (in seconds) the select and read commands should wait for input. The default of 0 indicates to wait indefinitely.
TMPDIR	When set to a directory name, the shell uses the directory as a location for temporary shell files.
UID	The numeric real user ID of the current user

A

You display the environment variables using the set built-in command. The default shell environment variables set at boot time can and often do vary between different Linux distributions.

Quick Guide to sed and gawk

IN THIS APPENDIX

The basics for using sed

What you need to know about gawk

I f you do any type of data handling in your shell scripts, most likely you'll need to use either the sed program or the gawk program (and sometimes both). This appendix provides a quick reference for sed and gawk commands that come in handy when working with data in your shell scripts.

The sed Editor

The sed editor can manipulate data in a data stream based on commands you either enter into the command line or store in a command text file. It reads one line of data at a time from the input and matches that data with the supplied editor commands, changes data in the stream as specified in the commands, and then outputs the new data to STDOUT.

Starting the sed editor

Here's the format for using the sed command:

```
sed options script file
```

The *options* parameters allow you to customize the behavior of the sed command and include the options shown in Table B-1.

TABLE B-1 **The sed Command Options**

Option	Description
-e *script*	Adds commands specified in *script* to the commands run while processing the input
-f *file*	Adds the commands specified in the file *file* to the commands run while processing the input
-n	Doesn't produce output for each command, but waits for the print command

The *script* parameter specifies a single command to apply against the stream data. If more than one command is required, you must use either the -e option to specify them in the command line or the -f option to specify them in a separate file.

sed commands

The sed editor script contains commands that sed processes for each line of data in the input stream. This section describes some of the more common sed commands you'll want to use.

Substitution

The s command substitutes text in the input stream. Here's the format of the s command:

    s/pattern/replacement/flags

pattern is the text to replace, and *replacement* is the new text that sed inserts in its place.

The *flags* parameter controls how the substitution takes place. Four types of substitution flags are available:

- A number indicates the pattern occurrence that should be replaced.
- g indicates that all occurrences of the text should be replaced.
- p indicates that the contents of the original line should be printed.
- w *file* indicates that the results of the substitution should be written to a file.

In the first type of substitution, you can specify which occurrence of the matching pattern the sed editor should replace. For example, you use the number 2 to replace only the second occurrence of the pattern.

Addressing

By default, the commands you use in the sed editor apply to all lines of the text data. If you want to apply a command to only a specific line, or a group of lines, you must use *line addressing*.

There are two forms of line addressing in the sed editor:

- A numeric range of lines
- A text pattern that filters out a line

Both forms use the same format for specifying the address:

    [address] command

When using numeric line addressing, you reference lines by their line position in the text stream. The sed editor assigns the first line in the text stream as line number 1 and continues sequentially for each new line.

```
$ sed '2,3s/dog/cat/' data1
```

The other method of restricting which lines a command applies to is a bit more complicated. The sed editor allows you to specify a text pattern that it uses to filter lines for the command. Here's the format for this:

```
/pattern/command
```

You must encapsulate the *pattern* you specify in forward slashes. The sed editor applies the command only to lines that contain the text pattern that you specify.

```
$ sed '/rich/s/bash/csh/' /etc/passwd
```

This filter finds the line that contains the text rich and replaces the text bash with csh.

You can also group more than one command together for a specific address:

```
address {
    command1
    command2
    command3 }
```

The sed editor applies each of the commands you specify only to lines that match the address specified. The sed editor processes each command listed on the address line(s):

```
$ sed '2{
> s/fox/elephant/
> s/dog/cat/
> }' data1
```

The sed editor applies each of the substitutions to the second line in the data file.

Deleting lines

The delete command, d, pretty much does what it says. It deletes any text lines that match the addressing scheme supplied. Be careful with the delete command, because if you forget to include an addressing scheme, all the lines are deleted from the stream:

```
$ sed 'd' data1
```

The delete command is obviously most useful when used in conjunction with a specified address. This allows you to delete specific lines of text from the data stream, either by line number:

```
$ sed '3d' data6
```

or by a specific range of lines:

```
$ sed '2,3d' data6
```

The pattern-matching feature of the sed editor also applies to the delete command:

```
$ sed '/number 1/d' data6
```

Only lines matching the specified text are deleted from the stream.

Inserting and appending text

As you would expect, like any other editor, the sed editor allows you to insert and append text lines to the data stream. The difference between the two actions can be confusing:

- The insert command (i) adds a new line before the specified line.
- The append command (a) adds a new line after the specified line.

The format of these two commands can be confusing: You can't use these commands on a single command line. You must specify the line to insert or append on a separate line by itself. Here's the format for doing this:

```
sed '[address]command\
new line'
```

The text in *new line* appears in the sed editor output in the place you specify. Remember that when you use the insert command, the text appears before the data stream text:

```
$ echo "testing" | sed 'i\
> This is a test'
This is a test
testing
$
```

And when you use the append command, the text appears after the data stream text:

```
$ echo "testing" | sed 'a\
> This is a test'
testing
This is a test
$
```

This allows you to insert text at the end of the normal text.

Changing lines

The change command allows you to change the contents of an entire line of text in the data stream. It works the same as the insert and append commands, in that you must specify the new line separately from the rest of the sed command:

```
$ sed '3c\
> This is a changed line of text.' data6
```

The backslash character is used to indicate the new line of data in the script.

Transform command

The transform command (y) is the only sed editor command that operates on a single character. The transform command uses this format:

```
[address]y/inchars/outchars/
```

The transform command performs a one-to-one mapping of the *inchars* and the *outchars* values. The first character in *inchars* is converted to the first character in *outchars*. The second character in *inchars* is converted to the second character in *outchars*. This mapping continues throughout the length of the specified characters. If the *inchars* and *outchars* are not the same length, the sed editor produces an error message.

Printing lines

Similar to the p flag in the substitution command, the p command prints a line in the sed editor output. The most common use for the print command is for printing lines that contain matching text from a text pattern:

```
$ sed -n '/number 3/p' data6
This is line number 3.
$
```

The print command allows you to filter only specific lines of data from the input stream.

Writing to a file

The w command is used to write lines to a file. Here's the format for the w command:

```
[address]w filename
```

The *filename* can be specified as either a relative or absolute pathname, but in either case, the person running the sed editor must have write permissions for the file. The *address* can be any type of addressing method used in sed, such as a single line number, a text pattern, or a range of line numbers or text patterns.

Here's an example that prints only the first two lines of a data stream to a text file:

```
$ sed '1,2w test' data6
```

The output file test contains only the first two lines from the input stream.

Reading from a file

You've already seen how to insert and append text into a data stream from the sed command line. The read command (r) allows you to insert data contained in a separate file.

Here's the format of the read command:

```
[address]r filename
```

The `filename` parameter specifies either an absolute or relative pathname for the file that contains the data. You can't use a range of addresses for the read command. You can specify only a single line number or text pattern address. The `sed` editor inserts the text from the file after the address.

```
$ sed '3r data' data2
```

The `sed` editor inserts the complete text from the data file into the data2 file, starting at line 3 of the data2 file.

The gawk Program

The `gawk` program is the GNU version of the original `awk` program in Unix. The `awk` program takes stream editing one step further than the `sed` editor by providing a programming language instead of just editor commands. This section describes the basics of the `gawk` program as a quick reference to its abilities.

The gawk command format

The basic format of the `gawk` program is as follows:

```
gawk options program file
```

Table B-2 shows the options available with the `gawk` program.

TABLE B-2 **The gawk Options**

Option	Description
-F fs	Specifies a file separator for delineating data fields in a line
-f file	Specifies a file name to read the program from
-v var=value	Defines a variable and default value used in the gawk program
-mf N	Specifies the maximum number of fields to process in the data file
-mr N	Specifies the maximum record size in the data file
-W keyword	Specifies the compatibility mode or warning level for gawk. Use the help option to list all the available keywords.

The command line options provide an easy way to customize features in the `gawk` program.

Using gawk

You can use gawk either directly from the command line or from within your shell scripts. This section demonstrates how to use the gawk program and how to enter scripts for gawk to process.

Reading the program script from the command line

A gawk program script is defined by an opening and closing brace. You must place script commands between the two braces. Because the gawk command line assumes that the script is a single text string, you must also enclose your script in single quotation marks. Here's an example of a simple gawk program script specified on the command line:

```
$ gawk '{print $1}'
```

This script displays the first data field in every line of the input stream.

Using multiple commands in the program script

A programming language wouldn't be very useful if you could execute only one command. The gawk programming language allows you to combine commands into a normal program. To use multiple commands in the program script specified on the command line, just place a semicolon between commands:

```
$ echo "My name is Rich" | gawk '{$4="Dave"; print $0}'
My name is Dave
$
```

The script performs two commands: It replaces the fourth data field with a different value, and then it displays the entire data line in the stream.

Reading the program from a file

As with the sed editor, the gawk editor allows you to store your programs in a file and refer to them in the command line:

```
$ cat script2
{ print $5 "'s userid is " $1 }
$ gawk -F: -f script2 /etc/passwd
```

The gawk program processes all the commands specified in the file on the input stream data.

Running scripts before processing data

The gawk program also allows you to specify when the program script is run. By default, gawk reads a line of text from the input and then executes the program script on the data in the line of text. Sometimes, you may need to run a script before processing data, such as to create a header section for a report. To do that, you use the BEGIN keyword. This forces gawk to execute the program script specified after the BEGIN keyword before reading the data:

```
$ gawk 'BEGIN {print "This is a test report"}'
This is a test report
$
```

You can place any type of gawk command in the BEGIN section, such as commands that assign default values to variables.

Running scripts after processing data

Similar to the BEGIN keyword, the END keyword allows you to specify a program script that gawk executes after reading the data:

```
$ gawk 'BEGIN {print "Hello World!"} {print $0} END {print
      "byebye"}' data1
Hello World!
This is a test
This is a test
This is another test.
This is another test.
byebye
$
```

The gawk program executes the code in the BEGIN section first, then processes any data in the input stream, and then executes the code in the END section.

The gawk variables

The gawk program is more than just an editor; it's a complete programming environment. As such, lots of commands and features are associated with gawk. This section shows the main features you need to know for programming with gawk.

Built-in variables

The gawk program uses built-in variables to reference specific features within the program data. This section describes the gawk built-in variables available for you to use in your gawk programs and demonstrates how to use them.

The gawk program defines data as records and data fields. A *record* is a line of data (delineated by the newline characters by default), and a *data field* is a separate data element within the line (delineated by a white space character, such as a space or tab, by default).

The gawk program uses data field variables to reference data elements within each record. Table B-3 describes these variables.

TABLE B-3   The gawk Data Field and Record Variables

Variable	Description
$0	The entire data record
$1	The first data field in the record
$2	The second data field in the record
$n	The nth data field in the record
FIELDWIDTHS	A space-separated list of numbers defining the exact width (in spaces) of each data field
FS	Input field separator character
RS	Input record separator character
OFS	Output field separator character
ORS	Output record separator character

In addition to the field and record separator variables, gawk provides some other built-in variables to help you know what's going on with your data and extract information from the shell environment. Table B-4 shows the other built-in variables in gawk.

TABLE B-4   More gawk Built-In Variables

Variable	Description
ARGC	The number of command line parameters present
ARGIND	The index in ARGV of the current file being processed
ARGV	An array of command line parameters
CONVFMT	The conversion format for numbers (see the printf statement), with a default value of %.6 g
ENVIRON	An associative array of the current shell environment variables and their values
ERRNO	The system error if an error occurs reading or closing input files
FILENAME	The filename of the data file used for input to the gawk program
FNR	The current record number in the data file
IGNORECASE	If set to a non-zero value, gawk all string functions (including regular expressions); ignore the case of characters.
NF	The total number of data fields in the data file
NR	The number of input records processed

Continues

TABLE B-4   *(continued)*

Variable	Description
OFMT	The output format for displaying numbers, with a default of %.6 g
RLENGTH	The length of the substring matched in the match function
RSTART	The start index of the substring matched in the match function

You can use the built-in variables anywhere in the gawk program script, including the BEGIN and END sections.

Assigning variables in scripts

Assigning values to variables in gawk programs is similar to how you assign values to variables in a shell script — using an *assignment statement:*

```
$ gawk '
> BEGIN{
> testing="This is a test"
> print testing
> }'
This is a test
$
```

After you assign a value to a variable, you can use that variable anywhere in your gawk script.

Assigning variables in the command line

You can also use the gawk command line to assign values to variables for the gawk program. This allows you to set values outside of the normal code, changing values on the fly. Here's an example of using a command line variable to display a specific data field in the file:

```
$ cat script1
BEGIN{FS=","}
{print $n}
$ gawk -f script1 n=2 data1
$ gawk -f script1 n=3 data1
```

This feature is a great way to process data from your shell scripts in the gawk script.

The gawk program features

Some features of the gawk program make it handy for manipulating data, allowing you to create gawk scripts that can parse just about any type of text file, including log files.

Regular expressions

You can use either a Basic Regular Expression (BRE) or an Extended Regular Expression (ERE) to filter the lines in the data stream to which the program script applies.

When using a regular expression, the regular expression must appear before the left brace of the program script that it controls:

```
$ gawk 'BEGIN{FS=","} /test/{print $1}' data1
This is a test
$
```

The matching operator

The *matching operator* allows you to restrict a regular expression to a specific data field in the records. The matching operator is the tilde character (~). You specify the matching operator, along with the data field variable, and the regular expression to match:

```
$1 ~ /^data/
```

This expression filters records where the first data field starts with the text data.

Mathematical expressions

In addition to regular expressions, you can also use mathematical expressions in the matching pattern. This feature comes in handy when matching numerical values in data fields. For example, if you want to display all the system users who belong to the root users group (group number 0), you could use this script:

```
$ gawk -F: '$4 == 0{print $1}' /etc/passwd
```

This script displays the first data field value for all lines that contain the value 0 in the fourth data field.

Structured commands

The gawk program supports the structured commands discussed in this section.

The if-then-else statement:

```
if (condition) statement1; else statement2
```

The while statement:

```
while (condition)
{
    statements
}
```

The do-while statement:

```
do {
    statements
} while (condition)
```

The for statement:

```
for(variable assignment; condition; iteration process)
```

This provides a wealth of programming opportunities for the gawk script programmer. You can write gawk programs that rival the functions of just about any higher-level language program.

Index

Symbols

Index

C

Index

P

Package Management System
(PMS), 211–212
  aptitude, 212–220
    installing software
      packages, 215–217
    main window, 213
    managing packages,
      212–215
    repositories, 219–220
    uninstalling software,
      218–219
    updating software, 217–218
  urpm, 221
    broken dependencies, 227
    installing software, 224
    listing installed software,
      221
    package details, 222
    repositories, 228
    uninstalling software, 225
    updating software, 225
  yum, 221–228
    broken dependencies,
      225–227
    installing software,
      223–224
    listing installed packages,
      221–223
    repositories, 227–228
    uninstalling software, 225
    updating software, 224–225
  zypper, 221
    broken dependencies, 227
    installing software, 224
    listing installed software,
      221
    package details, 222
    repositories, 228
    uninstalling software, 225
    updating software, 225
pager, 50
pages, 6
PAM. *See* Pluggable
  Authentication Modules
parameters. *See also* command
  line parameters
  dash shell
    command line, 624–625

command-line, 624–625
  positional, 627
list, 482
ls, 59–62, 69, 70
mysql, 693–694
passing arrays as, 462
passing to function, 456–459
positional, 366, 627
ps, 86–92, 116, 117
  BSD-style, 89–91
  GNU long, 91–92
  Unix-style, 86–89
rm, 73, 76
testing, 370
useradd
  change default values, 167
  command line, 166–167
  -D, 165, 167
parent directories, 74
parent process ID (PPID), 116
parent shell, child relationships,
  115–125
parity entry, 202
partitions
  changing type, 203–204
  creating, 193–196
  extended, 195
  primary, 195
partprobe, 196
passwd, 169–170
passwords
  aging, 171–172
  changing, 169–170
  group, 173
  MySQL, 692–693
  reading, 391
  storage of, 163
PATH environment variable, 148–
  150, 165, 271, 359
pattern matching
  double bracket command,
    326–327
  filtering file listings, 63–64
  gawk, 602–605
    matching operator, 603–
      604
    mathematical expressions,
      604–605
    regular expressions, 603,
      761

grep, 107–108
  sed, 520, 526
pattern space, 563, 567, 570–571
/pattern/command, 753
pausing processes, 421–422
PCLinuxOS, 19
  LiveCD, 20
permanent redirection, 401–402
permissions, 651
  access triplets, 176–177
  file, 175–179
    changing, 179–181
    codes, 177–179
    comparisons by, 319–321
    default, 177–179
    Octal mode, 178
    symbols, 176–177
  group, 172
phone numbers, validating,
  556–558
physical volumes (PV), 200
  defining, 203–205
PID. *See* process ID
pipe character, 106, 553
pipes, 121
  loop output, 358–359
  reading from files, 391
  scripting, 281–284
  tee command, 414–415
PKZIP, 109
Pluggable Authentication Modules
  (PAM), 151
plus sign, 551
PMS. *See* Package Management
  System
positional parameters, 366, 627
POSIX Basic Regular Expression
  engine (BRE), 537
POSIX Extended Regular
  Expression engine
  (ERE), 537
Postfix, 704
PPID. *See* parent process ID
present working directory, 56–57
primary key, 689
primary partition, 195
print command, 593
printenv, 136, 138, 156
printf command, 610–613,
  639, 675

774